MW00342831

SAS® Certification Prep Guide
Advanced Programming for SAS®9
Fourth Edition

SAS® Documentation

The correct bibliographic citation for this manual is as follows: SAS Institute Inc. 2014. *SAS® Certification Prep Guide: Advanced Programming for SAS®9, Fourth Edition.* Cary, NC: SAS Institute Inc.

SAS® Certification Prep Guide: Advanced Programming for SAS®9, Fourth Edition

SAS provides a complete selection of books and electronic products to help customers use SAS® software to its fullest potential. For more information about our offerings, visit **sas.com/store/books** or call 1-800-727-0025.

Contents

PART 2   SAS Macro Language   285

PART 3 Advanced SAS Programming Techniques 445

PART 4   Optimizing SAS Programs   649

PART 5   Quiz Answer Keys   795

About This Book

Audience

The *SAS Certification Prep Guide: Advanced Programming for SAS® 9, Fourth Edition* is for new or experienced SAS programmers who want to prepare for the SAS Advanced Programming for SAS 9 exam.

Requirements and Details

Purpose and Content

This guide helps prepare you to take the SAS Advanced Programming for SAS 9 exam. New or experienced SAS users will find this guide to be an invaluable resource that covers the objectives tested on the exam.

Major topics include SQL processing with SAS and the SAS macro language, advanced SAS programming techniques, and optimizing SAS programs. You will also become familiar with the enhancements and new functionality that are available in SAS®9.

The book includes quizzes that test your understanding of material in each chapter. Quiz solutions are included at the end of the book.

To find updates to this guide, visit the SAS Training and Books website at http://support.sas.com/publishing/cert.

Note: Exam objectives are subject to change. See the current exam objectives at http://support.sas.com/certify.

Prerequisites

Candidates must earn the SAS Certified Base Programmer for SAS 9 credential before taking the SAS Advanced Programming for SAS 9 exam. The *SAS Certification Prep Guide: Base Programming for SAS® 9* covers the objectives tested on the SAS Base Programming for SAS 9 exam, including importing and exporting raw data files; creating and modifying SAS data sets; and identifying and correcting data, syntax, and programming logic errors.

To see if you have the necessary prerequisite Base SAS programming knowledge, visit http://support.sas.com/basepractice.

How to Create Practice Data

SAS Windowing Environment

To set up practice data in SAS, select **Help** ⇨ **Learning SAS Programming** from the main SAS menu. When the SAS Online Training Sample Data window appears, click **OK** to create sample data.

SAS Studio and SAS University Edition

If you are using SAS Studio or SAS University Edition, you might not have Write access to the Sasuser directory where the sample data is stored.

To determine whether the Sasuser folder is Read only, submit the following code:

```
proc options option=rsasuser;
run;
```

If the result from the PROC OPTIONS code is NORSASUSER, the Sasuser folder is writable, and you can take the following steps to set up practice data in SAS Studio:

1. Copy the sample data program into a new Code window in SAS Studio. You can access the sample data at http://support.sas.com/publishing/cert/sampdata.txt.

2. Click **Run**.

If the result from the PROC OPTIONS code is RSASUSER, the Sasuser folder is Read only, and you must redirect the Sasuser folder by using the LIBNAME statement. To set up practice data:

1. In the **Folders** pane, select **My Folders**. Then, right-click and select **New** ⇨ **Folder**.

2. In the **Name** box, type a folder name. In our examples, we use the name `certprep`. Click **Save**.

3. Redirect your SASUSER library to the new folder as follows:

   If you are using SAS University Edition, submit a LIBNAME statement by copying the following code into the **Code** tab:

   ```
   libname sasuser "/folders/myfolders/certprep";
   ```

   Note: You must use the filename of the new directory. In our examples, we use the name `certprep`. If you use another filename, substitute the name that you created for `certprep`.

   If you are using SAS Studio, do the following:

   a. Right-click the new folder that you created and select **Properties**.

   b. Copy the path in the **Location** field.

   c. Enter the following code, replacing *location field* with the path that you copied from the **Location** field.

      ```
      libname sasuser "location field";
      ```

   d. Click **Run**.

   e. Save the program as libname_cert.sas. You must resubmit this LIBNAME statement program every time you work with the sample data.

    f. Copy the sample data program into a new Code window in SAS Studio. You can access the sample data at http://support.sas.com/publishing/cert/sampdata.txt.

    g. Click **Run**.

Now that you have the sample data stored in a permanent directory, reissue the LIBNAME statement whenever you want to use the data.

SAS Enterprise Guide

To download the sample data:

1. Start SAS Enterprise Guide.

2. In the Welcome to SAS Enterprise window, select **New Project**.

3. Select **File** ⇨ **New** ⇨ **Program**.

4. Depending on your network configuration, you might not have Write access to the Sasuser directory where the sample data is stored. To determine the status of the Sasuser directory, submit the following code:

   ```
   proc options option=rsasuser;
   run;
   ```

5. If the result from the PROC OPTIONS code is RSASUSER, you must redirect the Sasuser folder by creating a new folder. From your server area, open the Files folder, right-click on a drive or folder, and select **New Folder**. Enter the new folder name.

   Note: If the result from the PROC OPTIONS code is NORSASUSER, the Sasuser folder is writable, and you do not have to redirect the Sasuser folder. Therefore, you can skip this step and the next one.

6. Submit the following code in a Code window:

   ```
   libname sasuser "/folders/myfolders/certprep";
   ```

   Note: You must use the filename of the new folder. In our examples, we use the name **certprep**. If you use another filename, substitute the folder name that you created for **certprep**.

7. Copy the sample data program into the Program window and then run the program. You can access the sample data at http://support.sas.com/publishing/cert/sampdata.txt.

8. Because you will not need to use these shortcuts, you can delete the **Program** item and all the shortcuts from the project. This action will not delete the data that you created. To delete the item from the project, right-click **Program** and select **Delete**.

9. In the Confirmation window, click **Yes**.

Exams

The SAS Certification Practice Exam: Advanced Programming for SAS 9 helps you prepare for the SAS Advanced Programming for SAS 9 exam. This practice exam tests the same knowledge and skills as the official certification exam. You can access this exam under the SAS Certification category at https://support.sas.com/edu/schedules.html?id=449. There is a fee for this practice exam.

To register for the official SAS Advanced Programming for SAS 9 exam, visit the SAS Global Certification website at http://support.sas.com/certify.

Additional Resources

The following resources can help you as you learn SAS programming.

From SAS Software	
Help	For SAS®9, select **Help ⇨ SAS Help and Documentation**
	SAS Enterprise Guide, select **Help ⇨ SAS Enterprise Guide Help**
Documentation	For SAS®9, select **Help ⇨ SAS Help and Documentation**
	SAS Studio, select

On the Web	
Bookstore	http://support.sas.com/publishing/
Training	http://support.sas.com/training/
Documentation (including SAS Enterprise Guide)	http://support.sas.com/documentation/
Certification	http://support.sas.com/certify/
SAS Global Academic Program	http://support.sas.com/learn/ap
SAS OnDemand	http://support.sas.com/ondemand/
Knowledge Base	http://support.sas.com/resources/
Support	http://support.sas.com/techsup/
Learning Center	http://support.sas.com/learn/
Community	http://support.sas.com/community/

Syntax Conventions

The following example shows the general form of SAS code as shown in the book.

PROC SQL;

  SELECT *column-1<...column-n>*

    FROM *table-1|view-1<...table-n|view-n>*

    <WHERE *expression*>

    <GROUP BY *column-1<, ... column-n>>*

    <ORDER BY *column-1<,... column-n>>*;

PROC SQL
  invokes the SQL procedure.

SELECT
  specifies the column(s) to be selected.

FROM
  specifies the table(s) to be queried.

WHERE
  subsets the data based on a condition.

GROUP BY
  classifies the data into groups based on the specified column(s).

ORDER BY
  sorts the rows that the query returns by the value(s) of the specified column(s).

Here are details.

SELECT, FROM, WHERE, GROUP BY, and ORDER BY
  are in uppercase because they must be spelled as shown.

column-1, *table-1*, *view-1*, and *expression*
  are in italics because each represents a value that you supply.

<...column-n>
  is enclosed in angle brackets because it is optional syntax.

table-1 and *view-1*
  are separated by a vertical bar (|) to indicate that they are mutually exclusive.

This book covers the basic syntax that you need to know to prepare for the certification exam. For complete syntax, see the appropriate SAS reference guide.

Part 1

SQL Processing with SAS

Chapter 1

Performing Queries Using PROC SQL

Overview

Introduction

Sometimes you need quick answers to questions about your data. You might want to query (retrieve data from) a single SAS data set or a combination of data sets to do the following:

- examine relationships between data values

- view a subset of your data

- compute values quickly.

The SQL procedure (PROC SQL) provides an easy, flexible way to query and combine your data. This chapter shows you how to create a basic query using one or more tables (data sets). You learn how to create a new table from your query.

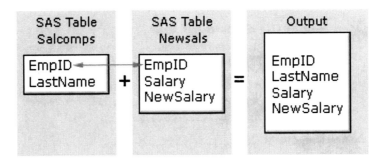

PROC SQL Basics

Overview

PROC SQL is the SAS implementation of Structured Query Language (SQL), which is a standardized language that is widely used to retrieve and update data in tables and in views that are based on those tables.

The following chart shows terms used in data processing, SAS, and SQL that are synonymous. The SQL terms are used in this chapter. A SAS data set (or SAS data file) can be a table or a view.

Data Processing	SAS	SQL
file	SAS data file	table
record	observation	row
field	variable	column

PROC SQL can often be used as an alternative to other SAS procedures or the DATA step. You can use PROC SQL to do the following:

- retrieve data from and manipulate SAS tables

- add or modify data values in a table

- add, modify, or drop columns in a table

- create tables and views

- join multiple tables (whether they contain columns with the same name)

- generate reports.

Like other SAS procedures, PROC SQL also enables you to combine data from two or more different types of data sources and present them as a single table. For example, you can combine data from two different types of external databases, or you can combine data from an external database and a SAS data set.

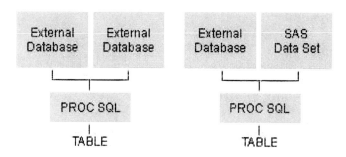

How PROC SQL Is Unique

PROC SQL differs from most other SAS procedures in several ways:

- Unlike other PROC statements, many statements in PROC SQL include clauses. For example, the following PROC SQL step contains two statements: the PROC SQL statement and the SELECT statement. The SELECT statement contains several clauses: SELECT, FROM, WHERE, and ORDER BY.

```
proc sql;
   select empid,jobcode,salary,
          salary*.06 as bonus
      from sasuser.payrollmaster
      where salary<32000
      order by jobcode;
```

- The PROC SQL step does not require a RUN statement. PROC SQL executes each query automatically. If you use a RUN statement with a PROC SQL step, SAS ignores the RUN statement, executes the statements as usual, and generates the note shown below in the SAS log.

Table 1.1 *SAS Log*

```
1884 proc sql;
1885    select empid,jobcode,salary,
1886          salary*.06 as bonus
1887      from sasuser.payrollmaster
1888      where salary<32000
1889      order by jobcode;
1890 run;
NOTE: PROC SQL statements are executed immediately;
      The RUN statement has no effect.
```

- Unlike many other SAS procedures, PROC SQL continues to run after you submit a step. To end the procedure, you must submit another PROC step, a DATA step, or a QUIT statement, as shown:

```
proc sql;
   select empid,jobcode,salary,
         salary*.06 as bonus
      from sasuser.payrollmaster
      where salary<32000
      order by jobcode;
quit;
```

When you submit a PROC SQL step without ending it, the status bar displays the message:

```
PROC SQL running
```

Note: As a precaution, SAS Enterprise Guide automatically adds a QUIT statement to your code when you submit it to SAS. However, you should get in the habit of adding the QUIT statement to your code.

Writing a PROC SQL Step

Overview

Before creating a query, you must first reference the library in which your table is stored. Then you write a PROC SQL step to query your table.

General form, basic PROC SQL step to perform a query:

PROC SQL;

    SELECT *column-1<,...column-n>*

        FROM *table-1|view-1<,...table-n|view-n>*

        <WHERE expression>

        <GROUP BY column-1<, ... column-n>>

        <ORDER BY column-1<,... column-n>>;

Here is an explanation of the syntax:

PROC SQL
    invokes the SQL procedure

SELECT
    specifies the column(s) to be selected

FROM
    specifies the table(s) to be queried

WHERE
    subsets the data based on one or more conditions

GROUP BY
    classifies the data into groups based on the specified column(s)

ORDER BY
    sorts the rows that the query returns by the value(s) of the specified column(s).

CAUTION:

    Unlike other SAS procedures the order of clauses with a SELECT statement in PROC SQL is important. Clauses must appear in the order shown above.

Note: A query can also include a HAVING clause, which is introduced at the end of this chapter. To learn more about the HAVING clause, see Chapter 2, "Performing Advanced Queries Using PROC SQL," on page 26.

The SELECT Statement

The SELECT statement, which follows the PROC SQL statement, retrieves and displays data. It consists of clauses that begin with a keyword, and is followed by one or more components. The SELECT statement in the following sample code contains four clauses: the required clauses SELECT and FROM, and the optional clauses WHERE and ORDER BY. The end of the statement is indicated by a semicolon.

```
proc sql;
 |-select empid,jobcode,salary,
 |       salary*.06 as bonus
 |----from sasuser.payrollmaster
 |----where salary<32000
 |----order by jobcode;
```

Note: A PROC SQL step that contains one or more SELECT statements is referred to as a PROC SQL query. The SELECT statement is only one of several statements that can be used with PROC SQL.

The following PROC SQL query creates the output report that is shown:

```
proc sql;
   select empid,jobcode,salary,
          salary*.06 as bonus
     from sasuser.payrollmaster
     where salary<32000
     order by jobcode;
```

EmpID	JobCode	Salary	bonus
1970	FA1	$31,661	1899.66
1422	FA1	$31,436	1886.16
1113	FA1	$31,314	1878.84
1132	FA1	$31,378	1882.68
1094	FA1	$31,175	1870.5
1789	SCP	$25,656	1539.36
1564	SCP	$26,366	1581.96
1354	SCP	$25,669	1540.14
1101	SCP	$26,212	1572.72
1658	SCP	$25,120	1507.2
1405	SCP	$25,278	1516.68
1104	SCP	$25,124	1507.44

A PROC SQL query produces a result set that can be output as a report, a table, or a PROC SQL view.

Type of Output	PROC SQL Statement
report	SELECT
table	CREATE TABLE
PROC SQL view	CREATE VIEW

Note: The CREATE TABLE statement is introduced later in this chapter. You can learn about creating tables in Chapter 5, "Creating and Managing Tables Using PROC SQL," on page 167. You can learn more about PROC SQL views in Chapter 7, "Creating and Managing Views Using PROC SQL," on page 248.

You learn more about the SELECT statement in the following sections.

Selecting Columns

Overview

To specify which column(s) to display in a query, you write a SELECT clause, the first clause in the SELECT statement. After the keyword SELECT, list one or more column names and separate the column names with commas. In the SELECT clause, you can both specify existing columns (columns that are already stored in a table) and create new columns.

The following SELECT clause specifies the columns EmpID, JobCode, Salary, and **bonus**. The columns EmpID, JobCode, and Salary are existing columns. The column named **bonus** is a new column.

```
proc sql;
   select empid,jobcode,salary,
          salary*.06 as bonus
      from sasuser.payrollmaster
      where salary<32000
      order by jobcode;
```

Creating New Columns

You can create new columns that contain either text or a calculation. New columns appear in output, along with any existing columns that are selected. Keep in mind that new columns exist only for the duration of the query, unless a table or a view is created.

To create a new column, include any valid SAS expression in the SELECT clause list of columns. You can assign a column alias, a name, to a new column by using the keyword AS followed by the name that you would like to use.

Note: A column alias must follow the rules for SAS names.

In the sample PROC SQL query, shown below, an expression is used to calculate the new column: the values of Salary are multiplied by .06. The keyword AS is used to assign the column alias **bonus** to the new column.

```
proc sql;
   select empid,jobcode,salary,
          salary*.06 as bonus
      from sasuser.payrollmaster
      where salary<32000
      order by jobcode;
```

A column alias is useful because it enables you to reference the column elsewhere in the query.

Note: You can learn more about referencing a calculated column from other clauses in Chapter 2, "Performing Advanced Queries Using PROC SQL," on page 26.

Also, the column alias appears as a column heading in the output.

The following output shows how the calculated column **bonus** is displayed. Notice that the column alias **bonus** appears in lowercase, exactly as it is specified in the SELECT clause.

EmpID	JobCode	Salary	bonus
1970	FA1	$31,661	1899.66
1422	FA1	$31,436	1886.16
1113	FA1	$31,314	1878.84
1132	FA1	$31,378	1882.68
1094	FA1	$31,175	1870.5
1789	SCP	$25,656	1539.36
1564	SCP	$26,366	1581.96
1354	SCP	$25,669	1540.14
1101	SCP	$26,212	1572.72
1658	SCP	$25,120	1507.2
1405	SCP	$25,278	1516.68
1104	SCP	$25,124	1507.44

In the SELECT clause, you can specify a label for an existing column or a new column. If both a label alias and a column alias are specified for a new column, the label is displayed as the column heading in the output[1]. If only a column alias is specified, it is important that you specify the column alias exactly as you want it to appear in the output.

Note: You can learn about creating new columns that contain text and about specifying labels for columns in Chapter 2, "Performing Advanced Queries Using PROC SQL," on page 26.

Specifying the Table

After writing the SELECT clause, you specify the table to be queried in the FROM clause. Enter the keyword FROM, followed by the name of the table, as shown:

```
proc sql;
    select empid,jobcode,salary,
           salary*.06 as bonus
        from sasuser.payrollmaster
        where salary<32000
        order by jobcode;
```

The PROC SQL step above queries the permanent SAS table Payrollmaster, which is stored in a SAS library to which the libref Sasuser has been assigned.

---

[1] Displaying labels for a column is further determined by the LABEL|NOLABEL system option. If this option is set to NOLABEL, then the label not displayed as the column heading in the output. This option can be set by your site administrator.

Specifying Subsetting Criteria

To subset data based on a condition, use a WHERE clause in the SELECT statement. As in the WHERE statement and the WHERE command used in other SAS procedures, the expression in the WHERE clause can be any valid SQL expression. In the WHERE clause, you can specify any column(s) from the underlying table(s). The columns specified in the WHERE clause do not have to be specified in the SELECT clause.

In the following PROC SQL query, the WHERE clause selects rows in which the value of the column Salary is less than 32,000. The output is also shown.

```
proc sql;
    select empid,jobcode,salary,
           salary*.06 as bonus
       from sasuser.payrollmaster
       where salary<32000
       order by jobcode;
```

EmpID	JobCode	Salary	bonus
1970	FA1	$31,661	1899.66
1422	FA1	$31,436	1886.16
1113	FA1	$31,314	1878.84
1132	FA1	$31,378	1882.68
1094	FA1	$31,175	1870.5
1789	SCP	$25,656	1539.36
1564	SCP	$26,366	1581.96
1354	SCP	$25,669	1540.14
1101	SCP	$26,212	1572.72
1658	SCP	$25,120	1507.2
1405	SCP	$25,278	1516.68
1104	SCP	$25,124	1507.44

Ordering Rows

Overview

The order of rows in the output of a PROC SQL query cannot be guaranteed, unless you specify a sort order. To sort rows by the values of specific columns, you can use the ORDER BY clause in the SELECT statement. Specify the keywords ORDER BY, followed by one or more column names separated by commas.

In the following PROC SQL query, the ORDER BY clause sorts rows by values of the column JobCode:

```
proc sql;
```

```
select empid,jobcode,salary,
       salary*.06 as bonus
  from sasuser.payrollmaster
  where salary<32000
  order by jobcode;
```

Note: In this example, the ORDER BY clause is the last clause in the SELECT statement, so the ORDER BY clause ends with a semicolon.

In the output of the sample query, shown below, the rows are sorted by the values of JobCode. By default, the ORDER BY clause sorts rows in ascending order.

EmpID	JobCode	Salary	bonus
1970	FA1	$31,661	1899.66
1422	FA1	$31,436	1886.16
1113	FA1	$31,314	1878.84
1132	FA1	$31,378	1882.68
1094	FA1	$31,175	1870.5
1789	SCP	$25,656	1539.36
1564	SCP	$26,366	1581.96
1354	SCP	$25,669	1540.14
1101	SCP	$26,212	1572.72
1658	SCP	$25,120	1507.2
1405	SCP	$25,278	1516.68
1104	SCP	$25,124	1507.44

To sort rows in descending order, specify the keyword DESC following the column name. For example, the preceding ORDER BY clause could be modified as follows:

```
order by jobcode desc;
```

In the ORDER BY clause, you can alternatively reference a column by the column's position in the SELECT clause list rather than by name. Use an integer to indicate the column's position. The ORDER BY clause in the preceding PROC SQL query has been modified, below, to specify the column JobCode by the column's position in the SELECT clause list (*2*) rather than by name:

```
proc sql;
   select empid,jobcode,salary,
          salary*.06 as bonus
     from sasuser.payrollmaster
     where salary<32000
     order by 2;
```

Ordering by Multiple Columns

To sort rows by the values of two or more columns, list multiple column names (or numbers) in the ORDER BY clause, and use commas to separate the column names (or numbers). In the following PROC SQL query, the ORDER BY clause sorts by the values of two columns, JobCode and EmpID:

```
proc sql;
   select empid,jobcode,salary,
          salary*.06 as bonus
      from sasuser.payrollmaster
      where salary<32000
      order by jobcode,empid;
```

The rows are sorted first by JobCode and then by EmpID, as shown in the following output.

EmpID	JobCode	Salary	bonus
1094	FA1	$31,175	1870.5
1113	FA1	$31,314	1878.84
1132	FA1	$31,378	1882.68
1422	FA1	$31,436	1886.16
1970	FA1	$31,661	1899.66
1101	SCP	$26,212	1572.72
1104	SCP	$25,124	1507.44
1354	SCP	$25,669	1540.14
1405	SCP	$25,278	1516.68
1564	SCP	$26,366	1581.96
1658	SCP	$25,120	1507.2
1789	SCP	$25,656	1539.36

Note: You can mix the two types of column references, names and numbers, in the ORDER BY clause. For example, the preceding ORDER BY clause could be rewritten as follows:

```
order by 2,empid;
```

You can also reference column aliases in the ORDER BY clause. Here is an example:

```
order by 2, empid, bonus;
```

Querying Multiple Tables

Overview

This topic deals with the more complex task of extracting data from two or more tables.

Previously, you learned how to write a PROC SQL step to query a single table. Suppose you now want to examine data that is stored in two tables. PROC SQL enables you to combine tables horizontally, in other words, to combine rows of data.

In SQL terminology, combining tables horizontally is called joining tables. Joins do not alter the original tables.

Suppose you want to create a report that displays the following information for employees of a company: employee identification number, last name, original salary, and new salary. There is no single table that contains all of these columns, so you must join the two tables Sasuser.Salcomps and Sasuser.Newsals. In your query, you want to select four columns, two from the first table and two from the second table. You also need to ensure that the rows that you join belong to the same employee. To check this, you want to match employee identification numbers for rows that you merge and to select only the rows that match.

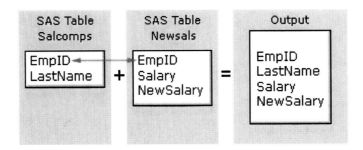

This type of join is known as an inner join. An inner join returns a result set for all of the rows in a table that have one or more matching rows in another table.

Note: For more information about PROC SQL joins, see Chapter 3, "Combining Tables Horizontally Using PROC SQL," on page 82.

You can write a PROC SQL step to combine tables. To join two tables for a query, you can use a PROC SQL step such as the one below. This step uses the SELECT statement to join data from the tables Salcomps and Newsals. Both of these tables are stored in a SAS library to which the libref Sasuser has been assigned.

```
proc sql;
   select salcomps.empid,lastname,
          newsals.salary,newsalary
      from sasuser.salcomps,sasuser.newsals
      where salcomps.empid=newsals.empid
      order by lastname;
```

We examine each clause of this PROC SQL step.

Specifying Columns That Appear in Multiple Tables

When you join two or more tables, list the columns that you want to select from both tables in the SELECT clause. Separate all column names with commas.

If the tables that you are querying contain same-named columns and you want to list one of these columns in the SELECT clause, you must specify a table name as a prefix for that column. Specifying a table-name prefix with a column that only exists in one table is syntactically acceptable.

Note: Prefixing a table name to a column name is called qualifying the column name.

The following PROC SQL step joins the two tables *Sasuser.Salcomps* and Sasuser.Newsals, both of which contain columns named EmpID. To tell PROC SQL where to read the column EmpID, the SELECT clause specifies the table name Salcomps as a prefix for Empid. The Newsals prefix for Salary is not required, but it is correct syntax and it identifies the source table for this column.

```
proc sql;
   select salcomps.empid,lastname,
          newsals.salary,newsalary
      from sasuser.salcomps,sasuser.newsals
 where salcomps.empid=newsals.empid
order by lastname;
```

Specifying Multiple Table Names

When you join multiple tables in a PROC SQL query, you specify each table name in the FROM clause, as shown below:

```
proc sql;
   select salcomps.empid,lastname,
          newsals.salary,newsalary
      from sasuser.salcomps,sasuser.newsals
      where salcomps.empid=newsals.empid
      order by lastname;
```

As in the SELECT clause, you separate names in the FROM clause (in this case, table names) with commas.

Specifying a Join Condition

As in a query on a single table, the WHERE clause in the SELECT statement selects rows from two or more tables, based on a condition. When you join multiple tables, ensure that the WHERE clause specifies columns with data whose values match. If none of the values match, then zero rows are returned. Also, the columns in the join condition must be of the same type. The SQL procedure does not attempt to convert data types.

In the following example, the WHERE clause selects only rows in which the value for EmpID in Sasuser.Salcomps matches the value for EmpID in Sasuser.Newsals. Qualified column names must be used in the WHERE clause to specify each of the two EmpID columns.

```
proc sql;
   select salcomps.empid,lastname,
          newsals.salary,newsalary
      from sasuser.salcomps,sasuser.newsals
      where salcomps.empid=newsals.empid
      order by lastname;
```

The output is shown, in part, below.

EmpID	LastName	Employee Salary	New Salary
E00042	ANDERSON	$32,000	$38,023.96
E00006	ANDERSON	$31,000	$33,753.70
E00008	BADINE	$85,000	$93,811.78
E00021	BAKER JR.	$43,000	$43,386.40
E00002	BOWER	$27,000	$31,153.98
E00027	BOWMAN	$31,000	$35,579.22
E00030	BREWER	$38,000	$41,055.05
E00025	BROCKLEBANK	$23,000	$25,673.57
E00015	BROWN	$41,000	$45,394.20
E00041	BRUTON	$45,000	$53,399.58
E00049	CHASE JR.	$29,000	$32,892.87
E00024	COCKERHAM	$21,000	$21,213.88
E00032	COUCH	$24,000	$28,775.81
E00018	CROSS	$33,000	$35,947.80

Note: In the table Sasuser.Newsals, the Salary column has the label Employee Salary, as shown in this output.

CAUTION:
If you join tables that do not contain one or more columns with tables that do not have matching data values, several unexpected results might occur. Either you might produce a large amount of data or you might produce all possible row combinations.

Ordering Rows

As in PROC SQL steps that query just one table, the ORDER BY clause specifies which column(s) should be used to sort rows in the output. In the following query, the rows are sorted by LastName:

```
proc sql;
   select salcomps.empid,lastname,
          newsals.salary,newsalary
      from sasuser.salcomps,sasuser.newsals
      where salcomps.empid=newsals.empid
      order by lastname;
```

EmpID	LastName	Employee Salary	New Salary
E00042	ANDERSON	$32,000	$38,023.96
E00006	ANDERSON	$31,000	$33,753.70
E00008	BADINE	$85,000	$93,811.78
E00021	BAKER JR.	$43,000	$43,386.40
E00002	BOWER	$27,000	$31,153.98
E00027	BOWMAN	$31,000	$35,579.22
E00030	BREWER	$38,000	$41,055.05
E00025	BROCKLEBANK	$23,000	$25,873.57
E00015	BROWN	$41,000	$45,394.20

Summarizing Groups of Data

We can use PROC SQL steps to create detail reports. But you might also want to summarize data in groups. To group data for summarizing, you can use the GROUP BY clause. The GROUP BY clause is used in queries that include one or more summary functions. Summary functions produce a statistical summary for each group that is defined in the GROUP BY clause.

Example

The following example demonstrates the GROUP BY clause and summary functions.

Suppose you want to determine the total number of miles traveled by frequent-flyer program members in each of three membership classes (Gold, Silver, and Bronze). Frequent-flyer program information is stored in the table Sasuser.Frequentflyers. To summarize your data, you can submit the following PROC SQL step:

```
proc sql;
   select membertype,
          sum(milestraveled) as TotalMiles
      from sasuser.frequentflyers
      group by membertype;
```

In this case, the SUM function totals the values of the MilesTraveled column to create the TotalMiles column. The GROUP BY clause groups the data by the values of MemberType.

As in the ORDER BY clause, in the GROUP BY clause that you specify the keywords GROUP BY, followed by one or more column names separated by commas.

The results show total miles by membership class (MemberType).

MemberType	TotalMiles
BRONZE	3229225
GOLD	2903569
SILVER	4345169

Note: If you specify a GROUP BY clause in a query that does not contain a summary function, your clause is changed to an ORDER BY clause, and a message to that effect is written to the SAS log.

Summary Functions

To summarize data, you can use the following summary functions with PROC SQL. Notice that some functions have more than one name to accommodate both SAS and SQL conventions. Where multiple names are listed, the first name is the SQL name.

AVG,MEAN	mean or average of values
COUNT, FREQ, N	number of nonmissing values
CSS	corrected sum of squares
CV	coefficient of variation (percent)
MAX	largest value
MIN	smallest value
NMISS	number of missing values
PRT	probability of a greater absolute value of student's t
RANGE	range of values
STD	standard deviation
STDERR	standard error of the mean
SUM	sum of values
T	student's t value for testing the hypothesis that the population mean is zero
USS	uncorrected sum of squares
VAR	variance

Creating Output Tables

Overview

To create a new table from the results of a query, use a CREATE TABLE statement that includes the keyword AS and the clauses that are used in a PROC SQL query: SELECT, FROM, and any optional clauses, such as ORDER BY. The CREATE TABLE statement stores your query results in a table instead of displaying the results as a report.

General form, basic PROC SQL step for creating a table from a query result:

PROC SQL;

    CREATE TABLE *table-name* **AS**

    SELECT *column-1<,...column-n>*

        FROM *table-1|view-1<,...table-n|view-n>*

        <WHERE expression>

        <GROUP BY column-1<,... column-n>>

        <ORDER BY column-1<,... column-n>>;

Here is an explanation of the syntax:

table-name
    specifies the name of the table to be created.

Note: A query can also include a HAVING clause, which is introduced at the end of this chapter. To learn more about the HAVING clause, see Chapter 2, "Performing Advanced Queries Using PROC SQL," on page 26.

Note: The CREATE TABLE statement does not generate output. To view the contents of the table, use a SELECT statement as described in "The SELECT Statement" on page 7.

Example

Suppose that after determining the total miles traveled for each frequent-flyer membership class in the Sasuser.Frequentflyers table, you want to store this information in the temporary table Work.Miles. To do so, you can submit the following PROC SQL step:

```
proc sql;
   create table work.miles as
      select membertype,
             sum(milestraveled) as TotalMiles
      from sasuser.frequentflyers
      group by membertype;
```

Because the CREATE TABLE statement is used, this query does not create a report. The SAS log verifies that the table was created and indicates how many rows and columns the table contains.

Table 1.2 *SAS Log*

```
NOTE: Table WORK.MILES created, with three rows and two columns.
```

TIP In this example, you are instructed to save the data to a temporary table that is deleted at the end of the SAS session. To save the table permanently in the Sasuser library, use the libref Sasuser instead of the libref Work in the CREATE TABLE clause.

Additional Features

To further refine a PROC SQL query that contains a GROUP BY clause, you can use a HAVING clause. A HAVING clause works with the GROUP BY clause to restrict the groups that are displayed in the output, based on one or more specified conditions.

For example, the following PROC SQL query groups the output rows by JobCode. The HAVING clause uses the summary function AVG to specify that only the groups that have an average salary that is greater than 40,000 is displayed in the output.

```
proc sql;
   select jobcode,avg(salary) as Avg
      from sasuser.payrollmaster
      group by jobcode
      having Avg>40000
      order by jobcode;
```

Note: You can learn more about the use of the HAVING clause in Chapter 2, "Performing Advanced Queries Using PROC SQL," on page 26.

Summary

Text Summary

PROC SQL Basics

PROC SQL uses statements that are written in Structured Query Language (SQL), which is a standardized language that is widely used to retrieve and update data in tables and in views that are based on those tables. When you want to examine relationships between data values, subset your data, or compute values, the SQL procedure provides an easy, flexible way to analyze your data.

PROC SQL differs from most other SAS procedures in several ways:

- Many statements in PROC SQL, such as the SELECT statement, include clauses.

- The PROC SQL step does not require a RUN statement.

- PROC SQL continues to run after you submit a step. To end the procedure, you must submit another PROC step, a DATA step, or a QUIT statement.

Writing a PROC SQL Step

Before creating a query, you must assign a libref to the SAS library in which the table to be used is stored. Then you submit a PROC SQL step. You use the PROC SQL statement to invoke the SQL procedure.

Selecting Columns

To specify which column(s) to display in a query, you write a SELECT clause as the first clause in the SELECT statement. In the SELECT clause, you can specify existing columns and create new columns that contain either text or a calculation.

Specifying Tables

You specify the tables to be queried in the FROM clause.

Specifying Subsetting Criteria

To subset data based on a condition, write a WHERE clause that contains an expression.

Ordering Rows

The order of rows in the output of a PROC SQL query cannot be guaranteed, unless you specify a sort order. To sort rows by the values of specific columns, use the ORDER BY clause.

Querying Multiple Tables

You can use a PROC SQL step to query data that is stored in two or more tables. In SQL terminology, this is called joining tables. Follow these steps to join multiple tables:

1. Specify column names from one or both tables in the SELECT clause and, if you are selecting a column that has the same name in multiple tables, prefix the table name to that column name.

2. Specify each table name in the FROM clause.

3. Use the WHERE clause to select rows from two or more tables, based on a condition.

4. Use the ORDER BY clause to sort rows that are retrieved from two or more tables by the values of the selected column(s).

Summarizing Groups of Data

You can use a GROUP BY clause in your PROC SQL step to summarize data in groups. The GROUP BY clause is used in queries that include one or more summary functions. Summary functions produce a statistical summary for each group that is defined in the GROUP BY clause.

Creating Output Tables

To create a new table from the results of your query, you can use the CREATE TABLE statement in your PROC SQL step. This statement enables you to store your results in a table instead of displaying the query results as a report.

Additional Features

To further refine a PROC SQL query that contains a GROUP BY clause, you can use a HAVING clause. A HAVING clause works with the GROUP BY clause to restrict the groups that are displayed in the output, based on one or more specified conditions.

Sample Programs

Querying a Table

```
proc sql;
   select empid,jobcode,salary,
          salary*.06 as bonus
      from sasuser.payrollmaster
      where salary<32000
      order by jobcode;
quit;
```

Summarizing Groups of Data

```
proc sql;
   select membertype,
          sum(milestraveled) as TotalMiles
      from sasuser.frequentflyers
      group by membertype;
quit;
```

Creating a Table from the Results of a Query on Two Tables

```
proc sql;
   create table work.miles as
      select salcomps.empid,lastname,
             newsals.salary,newsalary
      from sasuser.salcomps,sasuser.newsals
      where salcomps.empid=newsals.empid
      order by 2;
quit;
```

Points to Remember

- Do not use a RUN statement with the SQL procedure.

- Do not end a clause with a semicolon unless it is the last clause in the statement.

- When you join multiple tables, be sure to specify columns that have matching data values in the WHERE clause.

- To end the SQL procedure, you can submit another PROC step, a DATA step, or a QUIT statement.

Quiz

Select the best answer for each question. After completing the quiz, check your answers using the answer key in the appendix.

1. Which of the clauses in the PROC SQL program below is written incorrectly?

```
proc sql;
   select style sqfeet bedrooms
      from choice.houses
```

```
    where sqfeet ge 800;
```

a. SELECT

b. FROM

c. WHERE

d. both a and c

2. How many statements does the program below contain?

```
proc sql;
    select grapes,oranges,
            grapes + oranges as sumsales
        from sales.produce
        order by sumsales;
```

a. two

b. three

c. four

d. five

3. Complete the following PROC SQL query to select the columns Address and SqFeet from the table List.Size and to select Price from the table List.Price. (Only the Address column appears in both tables.)

```
proc sql;

    _____

        where size.address = price.address;
        from list.size,list.price;
```

a. select address,sqfeet,price

b. select size.address,sqfeet,price

c. select price.address,sqfeet,price

d. either b or c

4. Which of the clauses below correctly sorts rows by the values of the columns Price and SqFeet?

a. order price, sqfeet

b. order by price,sqfeet

c. sort by price sqfeet

d. sort price sqfeet

5. Which clause below specifies that the two tables Produce and Hardware be queried? Both tables are located in a library to which the libref Sales has been assigned.

a. select sales.produce sales.hardware

b. from sales.produce sales.hardware

c. from sales.produce,sales.hardware

d. where sales.produce, sales.hardware

6. Complete the SELECT clause below to create a new column named Profit by subtracting the values of the column Cost from those of the column Price.

```
select fruit,cost,price,

    _____
```

a. `Profit=price-cost`

b. `price-cost as Profit`

c. `profit=price-cost`

d. `Profit as price-cost`

7. What happens if you use a GROUP BY clause in a PROC SQL step without a summary function?

a. The step does not execute.

b. The first numeric column is summed by default.

c. The GROUP BY clause is changed to an ORDER BY clause.

d. The step executes but does not group or sort data.

8. If you specify a CREATE TABLE statement in your PROC SQL step,

a. the results of the query are displayed, and a new table is created.

b. a new table is created, but it does not contain any summarization that was specified in the PROC SQL step.

c. a new table is created, but no report is displayed.

d. results are grouped by the value of the summarized column.

9. Which statement is true regarding the use of the PROC SQL step to query data that is stored in two or more tables?

a. When you join multiple tables, the tables must contain a common column.

b. You must specify the table from which you want each column to be read.

c. The tables that are being joined must be from the same type of data source.

d. If two tables that are being joined contain a same-named column, then you must specify the table from which you want the column to be read.

10. Which clause in the following program is incorrect?

```
proc sql;
   select sex,mean(weight) as avgweight
      from company.employees company.health
      where employees.id=health.id
      group by sex;
```

a. SELECT

b. FROM

c. WHERE

d. GROUP BY

Chapter 2
Performing Advanced Queries Using PROC SQL

Overview

Introduction

The SELECT statement is the primary tool of PROC SQL. Using the SELECT statement, you can identify, manipulate, and retrieve columns of data from one or more tables and views.

You should already know how to create basic PROC SQL queries by using the SELECT statement and most of its subordinate clauses. To build on your existing skills, this chapter presents a variety of useful query techniques, such as the use of subqueries to subset data.

The PROC SQL query shown below illustrates some of the new query techniques:

```
proc sql outobs=20;
title 'Job Groups with Average Salary';
title2 '> Company Average';
   select jobcode,
          avg(salary) as AvgSalary format=dollar11.2,
          count(*) as Count
      from sasuser.payrollmaster
      group by jobcode
      having avg(salary) >
         (select avg(salary)
            from sasuser.payrollmaster)
      order by avgsalary desc;
```

Job Groups with Average Salary > Company Average		
JobCode	AvgSalary	Count
PT3	$154,706.50	2
PT2	$122,253.40	10
PT1	$95,071.13	8
NA2	$73,336.00	3
ME3	$59,374.86	7
NA1	$58,845.00	5
TA3	$55,551.42	12

Viewing SELECT Statement Syntax

The SELECT statement and its subordinate clauses are the building blocks for constructing all PROC SQL queries.

General form, SELECT statement:

SELECT *column-1<, ... column-n>*

    FROM *table-1 | view-1<, ... table-n | view-n>*

    <WHERE expression>

    <GROUP BY column-1<, ... column-n>>

    <HAVING expression>

    <ORDER BY column-1<, ... column-n>>;

Here is an explanation of the syntax:

SELECT
    specifies the column(s) that appear in the output

FROM
    specifies the table(s) or view(s) to be queried

WHERE
    uses an expression to subset or restrict the data based on one or more condition(s)

GROUP BY
    classifies the data into groups based on the specified column(s)

HAVING
    uses an expression to subset or restrict groups of data based on group condition(s)

ORDER BY
    sorts the rows that the query returns by the value(s) of the specified column(s).

Note: The clauses in a PROC SQL SELECT statement must be specified in the order shown.

You should be familiar with all of the SELECT statement clauses except for the HAVING clause. The use of the HAVING clause is presented later in this chapter.

Now, we look at some ways that you can limit and subset the number of columns that are displayed in query output.

Displaying All Columns

You already know how to select specific columns for output by listing them in the SELECT statement. However, for some tasks, you find it useful to display *all* columns of a table concurrently. For example, before you create a complex query, you might want to see the contents of the table that you are working with.

Using SELECT *

To display all columns in the order in which they are stored in a table, use an asterisk (*) in the SELECT clause. All rows are displayed, by default, unless you limit or subset them.

The following SELECT step displays all columns and rows in the table Sasuser.Staffchanges, which lists all employees in a company who have had changes in their employment status.

```
proc sql;
   select *
      from sasuser.staffchanges;
```

As shown in the output, the table contains six columns and six rows.

EmpID	LastName	FirstName	City	State	PhoneNumber
1639	CARTER	KAREN	STAMFORD	CT	203/781-8839
1065	CHAPMAN	NEIL	NEW YORK	NY	718/384-5618
1561	SANDERS	RAYMOND	NEW YORK	NY	212/588-6615
1221	WALTERS	DIANE	NEW YORK	NY	718/384-1918
1447	BRIDESTON	AMY	NEW YORK	NY	718/384-1213
1998	POWELL	JIM	NEW YORK	NY	718/384-8642

Using the FEEDBACK Option

When you specify SELECT *, you can also use the FEEDBACK option in the PROC SQL statement, which writes the expanded list of columns to the SAS log. For example, the PROC SQL query shown below contains the FEEDBACK option:

```
proc sql feedback;
   select *
      from sasuser.staffchanges;
```

This query produces the following feedback in the SAS log.

Table 2.1 *SAS Log*

```
202 proc sql feedback;
203 select *
204 from sasuser.staffchanges;
NOTE: Statement transforms to:

      select STAFFCHANGES.EmpID,
STAFFCHANGES.LastName, STAFFCHANGES.FirstName,
STAFFCHANGES.City, STAFFCHANGES.State,
STAFFCHANGES.PhoneNumber
         from SASUSER.STAFFCHANGES
```

The FEEDBACK option is a debugging tool that lets you see exactly what is being submitted to the SQL processor. The resulting message in the SAS log not only expands asterisks (*) into column lists, but it also resolves macro variables and places parentheses around expressions to show their order of evaluation.

Limiting the Number of Rows Displayed

Overview

When you create PROC SQL queries, you sometimes find it useful to limit the number of rows that PROC SQL displays in the output. To indicate the maximum number of rows to be displayed, you can use the OUTOBS= option in the PROC SQL statement.

General form, PROC SQL statement with OUTOBS= option:

PROC SQL OUTOBS= *n*;

Here is an explanation of the syntax:

n

specifies the number of rows.

Note: The OUTOBS= option restricts the rows that are displayed, but not the rows that are read. To restrict the number of rows that PROC SQL takes as input from any single source, use the INOBS= option. For more information about the INOBS= option, see Chapter 8, "Managing Processing Using PROC SQL," on page 264.

Example

Suppose you want to quickly review the types of values that are stored in a table, without printing out all the rows. The following PROC SQL query selects data from the table Sasuser.Flightschedule, which contains more than 200 rows. To print only the first 10 rows of output, you add the OUTOBS= option to the PROC SQL statement.

```
proc sql outobs=10;
   select flightnumber, date
      from sasuser.flightschedule;
```

FlightNumber	Date
132	01MAR2000
132	01MAR2000
132	01MAR2000
132	01MAR2000
132	01MAR2000
132	01MAR2000
182	01MAR2000
182	01MAR2000
182	01MAR2000
182	01MAR2000

When you limit the number of rows that are displayed, a message similar to the following appears in the SAS log.

Table 2.2 *SAS Log*

```
WARNING: Statement terminated early due to OUTOBS=10 option.
```

Note: The OUTOBS= and INOBS= options affect tables that are created by using the CREATE TABLE statement and your report output.

Note: In many of the examples in this chapter, OUTOBS= is used to limit the number of rows that are displayed in output.

Eliminating Duplicate Rows from Output

In some situations, you might want to display only the unique values or combinations of values in the column(s) listed in the SELECT clause. You can eliminate duplicate rows from your query results by using the keyword DISTINCT in the SELECT clause. The DISTINCT keyword applies to all columns, and only those columns, that are listed in the SELECT clause. We see how this works in the following example.

Example

Suppose you want to display a list of the unique flight numbers and destinations of all international flights that are flown during the month.

The following SELECT statement in PROC SQL selects the columns FlightNumber and Destination in the table Sasuser.Internationalflights:

```
proc sql outobs=12;
   select flightnumber, destination
      from sasuser.internationalflights;
```

Here is the output.

FlightNumber	Destination
182	YYZ
219	LHR
387	CPH
622	FRA
821	LHR
132	YYZ
271	CDG
182	YYZ
219	LHR
387	CPH
622	FRA
821	LHR

As you can see, there are several duplicate pairs of values for FlightNumber and Destination in the first 12 rows alone. For example, flight number 182 to YYZ appears in rows 1 and 8. The entire table contains many more rows with duplicate values for each flight number and destination because each flight has a regular schedule.

To remove rows that contain duplicate values, add the keyword DISTINCT to the SELECT statement, following the keyword SELECT, as shown in the following example:

```
proc sql;
   select distinct flightnumber, destination
      from sasuser.internationalflights
      order by 1;
```

With duplicate values removed, the output contains many fewer rows, so the OUTOBS= option has been removed from the PROC SQL statement. Also, to sort the output by FlightNumber (column 1 in the SELECT clause list), the ORDER BY clause has been added.

Here is the output from the modified program.

FlightNumber	Destination
132	YYZ
182	YYZ
219	LHR
271	CDG
387	CPH
622	FRA
821	LHR

There are no duplicate rows in the output. There are seven unique FlightNumber-Destination value pairs in this table.

Subsetting Rows By Using Conditional Operators

Overview

In the WHERE clause of a PROC SQL query, you can specify any valid SAS expression to subset or restrict the data that is displayed in output. The expression might contain any of various types of operators, such as the following.

Type of Operator	Example
comparison	where membertype='GOLD'
logical	where visits<=3 or status='new'
concatenation	where name=trim(last) ||', '||first

Note: For a complete list of operators that can be used in SAS expressions, see the SAS documentation.

Using Operators in PROC SQL

Comparison, logical, and concatenation operators are used in PROC SQL as they are used in other SAS procedures. For example, the following WHERE clause contains

- the logical operator AND, which joins multiple conditions

- two comparison operators: an equal sign (=) and a greater than symbol (>).

```
proc sql;
   select ffid, name, state, pointsused
      from sasuser.frequentflyers
      where membertype='GOLD' and pointsused>0
      order by pointsused;
```

In PROC SQL queries, you can also use the following conditional operators. All of these operators except for ANY, ALL, and EXISTS, can also be used in other SAS procedures.

Conditional Operator	Tests for ...	Example
BETWEEN-AND	values that occur within an inclusive range	`where salary between 70000` `                   and 80000`
CONTAINS or ?	values that contain a specified string	`where name contains 'ER'` `where name ? 'ER'`
IN	values that match one of a list of values	`where code in ('PT' , 'NA', 'FA')`
IS MISSING or IS NULL	missing values	`where dateofbirth is missing` `where dateofbirth is null`
LIKE (with %, _)	values that match a specified pattern	`where address like '% P%PLACE'`
=*	values that *sound like* a specified value	`where lastname=* 'Smith'`

ANY	values that meet a specified condition with respect to *any one* of the values returned by a subquery	`where dateofbirth < any`
		`    (select dateofbirth`
		`        from sasuser.payrollmaster`
		`        where jobcode='FA3')`

ALL	values that meet a specified condition with respect to *all* the values returned by a subquery	`where dateofbirth < all`
		`    (select dateofbirth`
		`        from sasuser.payrollmaster`
		`        where jobcode='FA3')`

EXISTS	the existence of values returned by a subquery	`where exists`
		`    (select *`
		`        from sasuser.flightschedule`
		`        where fa.empid=`
		`            flightschedule.empid)`

TIP To create a negative condition, you can precede any of these conditional operators, except for ANY and ALL, with the NOT operator.

Most of these conditional operators, and their uses, are covered in the next several sections. ANY, ALL, and EXISTS are discussed later in the chapter.

Using the BETWEEN-AND Operator to Select within a Range of Values

To select rows based on a range of numeric or character values, you use the BETWEEN-AND operator in the WHERE clause. The BETWEEN-AND operator is inclusive, so the values that you specify as limits for the range of values are included in the query results, in addition to any values that occur between the limits.

General form, BETWEEN-AND operator:

BETWEEN *value-1* **AND** *value-2*

Here is an explanation of the syntax:

value-1
   is the value at the one end of the range

value-2
   is the value at the other end of the range.

Note: When specifying the limits for the range of values, it is not necessary to specify the smaller value first.

Here are several examples of WHERE clauses that contain the BETWEEN-AND operator. The last example shows the use of the NOT operator with the BETWEEN-AND operator.

Example	Returns rows in which...

`where date between '01mar2000'd`
`         and '07mar2000'd`
 	
In this example, the values are specified as date constants.
	the value of Date is **01mar2000**, **07mar2000**, or any date value in between

`where salary between 70000` `          and 80000`	the value of Salary is 70000, 80000, or any numeric value in between
`where salary not between 70000` `              and 80000`	the value of Salary is not between or equal to 70000 and 80000

Using the CONTAINS or Question Mark (?) Operator to Select a String

The CONTAINS or question mark (?) operator is usually used to select rows for which a character column includes a particular string. These operators are interchangeable.

General form, CONTAINS operator:

sql-expression **CONTAINS** *sql-expression*

sql-expression **?** *sql-expression*

Here is an explanation of the syntax:

sql-expression
    is a character column, string (character constant), or expression. A string is a sequence of characters to be matched that must be enclosed in quotation marks.

Note: PROC SQL retrieves a row for output no matter where the string (or second sql-expression) occurs within the column's (or first sql-expression's) values. Matching is case sensitive when making comparisons.

Note: The CONTAINS or question mark (?) operator is not part of the ANSI standard; it is a SAS enhancement.

Example

The following PROC SQL query uses CONTAINS to select rows in which the Name column contains the string ER. As the output shows, all rows that contain ER anywhere within the Name column are displayed.

```
proc sql outobs=10;
    select name
        from sasuser.frequentflyers
        where name contains 'ER';
```

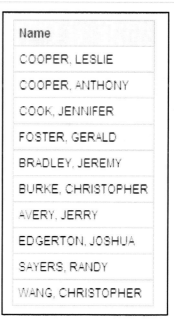

Name
COOPER, LESLIE
COOPER, ANTHONY
COOK, JENNIFER
FOSTER, GERALD
BRADLEY, JEREMY
BURKE, CHRISTOPHER
AVERY, JERRY
EDGERTON, JOSHUA
SAYERS, RANDY
WANG, CHRISTOPHER

Using the IN Operator to Select Values from a List

To select only the rows that match one of the values in a list of fixed values, either numeric or character, use the IN operator.

General form, IN operator:

column **IN** (*constant-1<,...constant-n>*)

Here is an explanation of the syntax:

column
 specifies the selected column name

constant-1 and *constant-n*
 represent a list that contains one or more specific values. The list of values must be enclosed in parentheses and separated by either commas or spaces. Values can be either numeric or character. Character values must be enclosed in quotation marks.

Here are examples of WHERE clauses that contain the IN operator.

Example	Returns rows in which...
`where jobcategory in ('PT','NA','FA')`	the value of JobCategory is **PT**, **NA**, or **FA**
`where dayofweek in (2,4,6)`	the value of DayOfWeek is **2**, **4**, or **6**
`where chesspiece not in` `('pawn','king','queen')`	the value of chesspiece is **rook**, **knight**, or `bishop`

Using the IS MISSING or IS NULL Operator to Select Missing Values

To select rows that contain missing values, both character and numeric, use the IS MISSING or IS NULL operator. These operators are interchangeable.

General form, IS MISSING or IS NULL operator:

column **IS MISSING**

column **IS NULL**

Here is an explanation of the syntax:

column
 specifies the selected column name.

Note: The IS MISSING operator is not part of the ANSI standard for SQL. It is a SAS enhancement.

Example

Suppose you want to find out whether the table Sasuser. Marchflights has any missing values in the column Boarded. You can use the following PROC SQL query to retrieve rows from the table that have missing values:

```
proc sql;
   select boarded, transferred,
          nonrevenue, deplaned
      from sasuser.marchflights
      where boarded is missing;
```

The output shows that two rows in the table have missing values for Boarded.

Boarded	Transferred	NonRevenue	Deplaned
.	9	0	210
.	16	5	79

TIP Alternatively, you can specify missing values without using the IS MISSING or IS NULL operator, as shown in the following examples:

```
where boarded = .
where flight = ' '
```

However, the advantage of using the IS MISSING or IS NULL operator is that you do not have to specify the data type (character or numeric) of the column.

Using the LIKE Operator to Select a Pattern

To select rows that have values that match as specific pattern of characters rather than a fixed character string, use the LIKE operator. For example, using the LIKE operator, you can select all rows in which the LastName value starts with H. (If you wanted to select all rows in which the last name contains the string HAR, you would use the CONTAINS operator.)

General form, LIKE operator:

column **LIKE** *'pattern'*

Here is an explanation of the syntax:

column
specifies the column name

pattern
specifies the pattern to be matched and contains one or both of the special characters underscore (_) and percent sign (%). The entire pattern must be enclosed in quotation marks and matching is case sensitive.

When you use the LIKE operator in a query, PROC SQL uses pattern matching to compare each value in the specified column with the pattern that you specify using the LIKE operator in the WHERE clause. The query output displays all rows in which there is a match.

You specify a pattern using one or both of the special characters shown below.

Special Character	Represents
underscore (_)	any single character
percent sign (%)	any sequence of zero or more characters

Note: The underscore (_) and percent sign (%) are sometimes referred to as wildcard characters.

Specifying a Pattern

To specify a pattern, combine one or both of the special characters with any other characters that you want to match. The special characters can appear before, after, or on both sides of other characters.

Consider how the special characters can be combined to specify a pattern. Suppose you are working with a table column that contains the following list of names:

- Diana
- Diane
- Dianna
- Dianthus
- Dyan

Here are several patterns that you can use to select one or more of the names from the list. Each pattern uses one or both of the special characters.

LIKE Pattern	Name(s) Selected
LIKE 'D_an'	Dyan
LIKE 'D_an_'	Diana, Diane
LIKE 'D_an__'	Dianna
LIKE 'D_an%'	all names from the list

Example

The following PROC SQL query uses the LIKE operator to find all frequent-flyer club members whose street name begins with P and ends with the word PLACE. The following PROC SQL step performs this query:

```
proc sql;
   select ffid, name, address
      from sasuser.frequentflyers
      where address like '% P%PLACE';
```

The pattern '% P%PLACE' specifies the following sequence:

- any number of characters (%)
- a space
- the letter P
- any number of characters (%)
- the word PLACE.

Here are the results of this query.

FFID	Name	Address
WD8375	COOPER, ANTHONY	12 PIEDPIPER PLACE
WD6271	MORGAN, GEORGE	39 PEPPER PLACE
WD6184	STARR, WILLIAM	12 PINEY PLACE
WD2118	JOHNSON, ANTHONY	78 PIPER PLACE
WD3827	KING, WILLIAM	14 PICTURE PLACE
WD8789	HOWARD, LEONARD	45 PECAN PLACE
WD6169	WILDER, NEIL	78 PUMPKIN PLACE
WD8667	YOUNG, DEBORAH	53 PINE PLACE
WD5687	EDWARDS, JENNIFER	3 PEGBOARD PLACE

Using the Sounds-Like (=) Operator to Select a Spelling Variation*

To select rows that contain a value that sounds like another value that you specify, use the sounds-like operator (=*) in the WHERE clause.

General form, sounds-like (=*) operator:

sql-expression = sql-expression*

Here is an explanation of the syntax:

sql-expression
>   is a character column, string (character constant), or expression. A string is a sequence of characters to be matched that must be enclosed in quotation marks.

The sounds-like (=*) operator uses the SOUNDEX algorithm to compare each value of a column (or other sql-expression) with the word or words (or other sql-expression) that you specify. Any rows that contain a spelling variation of the value that you specified are selected for output.

For example, here is a WHERE clause that contains the sounds-like operator:

```
where lastname =* 'Smith';
```

The sounds-like operator does not always select all possible values. For example, suppose you use the preceding WHERE clause to select rows from the following list of names that sound like Smith:

- Schmitt

- Smith

- Smithson

- Smitt

- Smythe

Two of the names in this list are not selected: Schmitt and Smithson.

Note: The SOUNDEX algorithm is English-biased and is less useful for languages other than English. For more information about the SOUNDEX algorithm, see the SAS documentation.

Subsetting Rows By Using Calculated Values

Understanding How PROC SQL Processes Calculated Columns

You should already know how to define a new column by using the SELECT clause and performing a calculation. For example, the following PROC SQL query creates the new column Total by adding the values of three existing columns: Boarded, Transferred, and Nonrevenue:

```
proc sql outobs=10;
   select flightnumber, date, destination,
          boarded + transferred + nonrevenue
          as Total
      from sasuser.marchflights
```

You can also use a calculated column in the WHERE clause to subset rows. However, because of how SQL queries are processed, you cannot just specify the column alias in the WHERE clause. To see what happens, we take the preceding PROC SQL query and add a WHERE clause in the SELECT statement to reference the calculated column Total, as shown below:

```
proc sql outobs=10;
   select flightnumber, date, destination,
          boarded + transferred + nonrevenue
          as Total
      from sasuser.marchflights
      where total < 100;
```

When this query is executed, the following error message is displayed in the SAS log.

Table 2.3 *SAS Log*

```
519  proc sql outobs=10;
520     select flightnumber, date, destination,
521            boarded + transferred + nonrevenue
522            as Total
523        from sasuser.marchflights
524        where total < 100;
ERROR: The following columns were not found in the contributing tables: total.
```

This error message is generated because, in SQL queries, the WHERE clause is processed before the SELECT clause. The SQL processor looks in the table for each column named in the WHERE clause. The table Sasuser.Marchflights does not contain a column named Total, so SAS generates an error message.

Using the Keyword CALCULATED

When you use a column alias in the WHERE clause to refer to a calculated value, you must use the keyword CALCULATED along with the alias. The CALCULATED keyword informs PROC SQL that the value is calculated within the query. Now, the PROC SQL query looks like this:

```
proc sql outobs=10;
   select flightnumber, date, destination,
          boarded + transferred + nonrevenue
          as Total
       from sasuser.marchflights
       where calculated total < 100;
```

This query executes successfully and produces the following output.

FlightNumber	Date	Destination	Total
982	01MAR2000	DFW	70
416	01MAR2000	WAS	93
829	01MAR2000	WAS	96
416	02MAR2000	WAS	90
302	02MAR2000	WAS	93
132	03MAR2000	YYZ	88
921	03MAR2000	DFW	85
290	05MAR2000	WAS	55
523	05MAR2000	ORD	59
416	05MAR2000	WAS	31

Note: As an alternative to using the keyword CALCULATED, repeat the calculation in the WHERE clause. However, this method is inefficient because PROC SQL has to perform the calculation twice. In the preceding query, the alternate WHERE statement would be:

```
where boarded + transferred + nonrevenue <100;
```

You can also use the CALCULATED keyword in other parts of a query. In the following example, the SELECT clause calculates the new column Total and then calculates a second new column based on Total. To create the second calculated column, you have to specify the keyword CALCULATED in the SELECT clause.

```
proc sql outobs=10;
   select flightnumber, date, destination,
          boarded + transferred + nonrevenue
          as Total,
          calculated total/2 as Half
       from sasuser.marchflights;
```

This query produces the following output.

FlightNumber	Date	Destination	Total	Half
182	01MAR2000	YYZ	123	61.5
114	01MAR2000	LAX	196	98
202	01MAR2000	ORD	167	83.5
219	01MAR2000	LHR	222	111
439	01MAR2000	LAX	185	92.5
387	01MAR2000	CPH	163	81.5
290	01MAR2000	WAS	119	59.5
523	01MAR2000	ORD	200	100
982	01MAR2000	DFW	70	35
622	01MAR2000	FRA	227	113.5

Note: The CALCULATED keyword is a SAS enhancement and is not specified in the ANSI Standard for SQL.

Enhancing Query Output

Overview

When you are using PROC SQL, you might find that the data in a table is not formatted as you would like it to appear. Fortunately, with PROC SQL you can use enhancements, such as the following, to improve the appearance of your query output:

- column labels and formats
- titles and footnotes
- columns that contain a character constant.

You know how to use the first two enhancements with other SAS procedures. You can also enhance PROC SQL query output by working with the following query:

```
proc sql outobs=15;
   select empid, jobcode, salary,
          salary * .10 as Bonus
      from sasuser.payrollmaster
      where salary>75000
      order by salary desc;
```

This query limits output to 15 observations. The SELECT clause selects three existing columns from the table Sasuser.Payrollmaster, and calculates a fourth (Bonus). The WHERE clause retrieves only rows in which salary is greater than 75,000. The ORDER BY clause sorts by the Salary column and uses the keyword DESC to sort in descending order.

Here is the output from this query.

EmpID	JobCode	Salary	Bonus
1118	PT3	$155,931	15593.1
1777	PT3	$153,482	15348.2
1404	PT2	$127,926	12792.6
1107	PT2	$125,968	12596.8
1928	PT2	$125,801	12580.1
1106	PT2	$125,485	12548.5
1333	PT2	$124,048	12404.8
1890	PT2	$120,254	12025.4
1410	PT2	$118,559	11855.9
1442	PT2	$118,350	11835
1830	PT2	$118,259	11825.9
1478	PT2	$117,884	11788.4
1556	PT1	$99,889	9988.9
1439	PT1	$99,030	9903
1428	PT1	$96,274	9627.4

Note: The Salary column has the format DOLLAR9. specified in the table.

Look closely at this output and you see that improvements can be made. You learn how to enhance this output in the following ways:

- replace original column names with new labels

- specify a format for the Bonus column, so that all values are displayed with the same number of decimal places

- display a title at the top of the output

- add a column using a character constant.

Specifying Column Formats and Labels

By default, PROC SQL formats output using column attributes that are already saved in the table or, if none are saved, the default attributes. To control the formatting of columns in output, you can specify column modifiers, such as LABEL= and FORMAT=, after any column name specified in the SELECT clause. When you define a new column in the SELECT clause, you can assign a label rather than an alias, if you prefer.

Column Modifier	Specifies...	Example
LABEL=	the label to be displayed for the column	`select hiredate` `        label='Date of Hire'`

Column Modifier	Specifies...	Example
FORMAT=	the format used to display column data	`select hiredate format=date9.`

Note: LABEL= and FORMAT= are not part of the ANSI standard. These column modifiers are SAS enhancements.

TIP To force PROC SQL to ignore permanent labels in a table, specify the NOLABEL system option.

Your first task is to specify column labels for the first two columns. Below, the LABEL= option has been added after both EmpID and JobCode, and the text of each label is enclosed in quotation marks. For easier reading, each of the four columns in the SELECT clause is now listed on its own line.

```
proc sql outobs=15;
   select empid label='Employee ID',
          jobcode label='Job Code',
          salary,
          salary * .10 as Bonus
      from sasuser.payrollmaster
      where salary>75000
      order by salary desc;
```

Next, you add a format for the Bonus column. Because the Bonus values are dollar amounts, you use the format Dollar12.2. The FORMAT= modifier has been added to the SELECT clause, below, immediately following the column alias Bonus:

```
proc sql outobs=15;
   select empid label='Employee ID',
          jobcode label='Job Code',
          salary,
          salary * .10 as Bonus
          format=dollar12.2
      from sasuser.payrollmaster
      where salary>75000
      order by salary desc;
```

Now that column formats and labels have been specified, you can add a title to this PROC SQL query.

Specifying Titles and Footnotes

You should already know how to specify and cancel titles and footnotes with other SAS procedures. When you specify titles and footnotes with a PROC SQL query, you must place the TITLE and FOOTNOTE statements in either of the following locations:

- before the PROC SQL statement

- between the PROC SQL statement and the SELECT statement.

In the following PROC SQL query, two title lines have been added between the PROC SQL statement and the SELECT statement:

```
proc sql outobs=15;
title 'Current Bonus Information';
title2 'Employees with Salaries > $75,000';
```

```
select empid label='Employee ID',
       jobcode label='Job Code',
       salary,
       salary * .10 as Bonus
       format=dollar12.2
   from sasuser.payrollmaster
   where salary>75000
   order by salary desc;
```

Now that these changes have been made, you can look at the enhanced query output.

Current Bonus Information Employees with Salaries > $75,000			
Employee ID	Job Code	Salary	Bonus
1118	PT3	$155,931	$15,593.10
1777	PT3	$153,482	$15,348.20
1404	PT2	$127,926	$12,792.60
1107	PT2	$125,968	$12,596.80
1928	PT2	$125,801	$12,580.10
1106	PT2	$125,485	$12,548.50
1333	PT2	$124,048	$12,404.80
1890	PT2	$120,254	$12,025.40
1410	PT2	$118,559	$11,855.90
1442	PT2	$118,350	$11,835.00
1830	PT2	$118,259	$11,825.90
1478	PT2	$117,884	$11,788.40
1556	PT1	$99,889	$9,988.90
1439	PT1	$99,030	$9,903.00
1428	PT1	$96,274	$9,627.40

The first two columns have new labels, the Bonus values are consistently formatted, and two title lines are displayed at the top of the output.

Adding a Character Constant to Output

Another way of enhancing PROC SQL query output is to define a column that contains a character constant. To do this, you include a text string in quotation marks in the SELECT clause.

> *TIP*   You can define a column that contains a numeric constant in a similar way, by listing a numeric value (without quotation marks) in the SELECT clause.

You can look at the preceding PROC SQL query output again and determine where you can add a text string.

Current Bonus Information Employees with Salaries > $75,000			
Employee ID	Job Code	Salary	Bonus
1118	PT3	$155,931	$15,593.10
1777	PT3	$153,482	$15,348.20
1404	PT2	$127,926	$12,792.60
1107	PT2	$125,968	$12,596.80
1928	PT2	$125,801	$12,580.10
1106	PT2	$125,485	$12,548.50
1333	PT2	$124,048	$12,404.80
1890	PT2	$120,254	$12,025.40
1410	PT2	$118,559	$11,855.90
1442	PT2	$118,350	$11,835.00
1830	PT2	$118,259	$11,825.90
1478	PT2	$117,884	$11,788.40
1556	PT1	$99,889	$9,988.90
1439	PT1	$99,030	$9,903.00
1428	PT1	$96,274	$9,627.40

You can remove the column label Bonus and display the text bonus is: in a new column to the left of the Bonus column. This is how you want the columns and rows to appear in the query output.

Current Bonus Information Employees with Salaries > $75,000				
Employee ID	Job Code	Salary		
1118	PT3	$155,931	bonus is:	$15,593.10
1777	PT3	$153,482	bonus is:	$15,348.20
1404	PT2	$127,926	bonus is:	$12,792.60
1107	PT2	$125,968	bonus is:	$12,596.80
1928	PT2	$125,801	bonus is:	$12,580.10
1106	PT2	$125,485	bonus is:	$12,548.50
1333	PT2	$124,048	bonus is:	$12,404.80
1890	PT2	$120,254	bonus is:	$12,025.40
1410	PT2	$118,559	bonus is:	$11,855.90
1442	PT2	$118,350	bonus is:	$11,835.00
1830	PT2	$118,259	bonus is:	$11,825.90
1478	PT2	$117,884	bonus is:	$11,788.40
1556	PT1	$99,889	bonus is:	$9,988.90
1439	PT1	$99,030	bonus is:	$9,903.00
1428	PT1	$96,274	bonus is:	$9,627.40

To specify a new column that contains a character constant, you include the text string in quotation marks in the SELECT clause list. Your modified PROC SQL query is shown below:

```
proc sql outobs=15;
title 'Current Bonus Information';
title2 'Employees with Salaries > $75,000';
   select empid label='Employee ID',
          jobcode label='Job Code',
          salary,
          'bonus is:',
          salary * .10 format=dollar12.2
      from sasuser.payrollmaster
      where salary>75000
      order by salary desc;
```

In the SELECT clause list, the text string **bonus is**: has been added between Salary and Bonus.

Note that the code **as Bonus** has been removed from the last line of the SELECT clause. Now that the character constant has been added, the column alias Bonus is no longer needed.

Summarizing and Grouping Data

Overview

Instead of just listing individual rows, you can use a summary function (also called an aggregate function) to produce a statistical summary of data in a table. For example, in the SELECT clause in the following query, the AVG function calculates the average (or mean) miles traveled by frequent-flyer club members. The GROUP BY clause tells PROC SQL to calculate and display the average for each membership group (MemberType).

```
proc sql;
    select membertype,
           avg(milestraveled)
           as AvgMilesTraveled
    from sasuser.frequentflyers
    group by membertype;
```

MemberType	AvgMilesTraveled
BRONZE	52938.11
GOLD	48392.82
SILVER	51119.64

You should already be familiar with the list of summary functions that can be used in a PROC SQL query.

PROC SQL calculates summary functions and outputs results in different ways depending on a combination of factors. Four key factors are

- whether the summary function specifies one or multiple columns as arguments

- whether the query contains a GROUP BY clause

- if the summary function is specified in a SELECT clause, whether there are additional columns listed that are outside of a summary function

- whether the WHERE clause, if there is one, contains only columns that are specified in the SELECT clause.

To ensure that your PROC SQL queries produce the intended output, it is important to understand how the factors listed above affect the processing of summary functions. Consider an overview of all the factors, followed by a detailed example that illustrates each factor.

Number of Arguments and Summary Function Processing

Summary functions specify one or more arguments in parentheses. In the examples shown in this chapter, the arguments are always columns in the table being queried.

Note: The ANSI-standard summary functions, such as AVG and COUNT, can be used only with a single argument. The SAS summary functions, such as MEAN and N, can be used with either single or multiple arguments.

The following chart shows how the number of columns specified as arguments affects how PROC SQL calculates a summary function.

If a summary function...	Then the calculation is...	Example
specifies one column as argument	performed down the column	```proc sql; select avg(salary)as AvgSalary from sasuser.payrollmaster;```
specifies multiple columns as arguments	performed across columns for each row	```proc sql outobs=10; select sum(boarded,transferred,nonrevenue) as Total from sasuser.marchflights;```

Groups and Summary Function Processing

Summary functions perform calculations on groups of data. When PROC SQL processes a summary function, it looks for a GROUP BY clause:

If a GROUP BY clause...	Then PROC SQL...	Example
is not present in the query	applies the function to the entire table	```proc sql outobs=10; select jobcode, avg(salary) as AvgSalary from sasuser.payrollmaster;```
is present in the query	applies the function to each group specified in the GROUP BY clause	```proc sql outobs=10; select jobcode, avg(salary) as AvgSalary from sasuser.payrollmaster group by jobcode;``` If a query contains a GROUP BY clause, all columns in the SELECT clause that do not contain a summary function should be listed in the GROUP BY clause or unexpected results might be returned.

SELECT Clause Columns and Summary Function Processing

A SELECT clause that contains a summary function can also list additional columns that are not specified in the summary function. The presence of these additional columns in the SELECT clause list causes PROC SQL to display the output differently.

If a SELECT clause...	Then PROC SQL...	Example
contains summary function(s) and no columns outside of summary functions	calculates a single value by using the summary function for the entire table or, if groups are specified in the GROUP BY clause, for each group combines or rolls up the information into a single row of output for the entire table or, if groups are specified, for each group	```proc sql; select avg(salary) as AvgSalary from sasuser.payrollmaster;```
contains summary function(s) and additional columns outside of summary functions	calculates a single value for the entire table or, if groups are specified, for each group, and displays all rows of output with the single or grouped value(s) repeated	```proc sql; select jobcode, gender, avg(salary) as AvgSalary from sasuser.payrollmaster group by jobcode,gender;```

Note: WHERE clause columns also affect summary function processing. If there is a WHERE clause that references only columns that are specified in the SELECT clause, PROC SQL combines information into a single row of output. However, this condition is not covered in this chapter. For more information, see the SAS documentation for the SQL procedure.

In the next few sections, look more closely at the query examples shown above to see how the first three factors impact summary function processing.

Compare two PROC SQL queries that contain a summary function: one with a single argument and the other with multiple arguments. To keep things simple, these queries do not contain a GROUP BY clause.

Using a Summary Function with a Single Argument (Column)

Below is a PROC SQL query that displays the average salary of all employees listed in the table Sasuser.Payrollmaster:

```
proc sql;
   select avg(salary) as AvgSalary
      from sasuser.payrollmaster;
```

The SELECT statement contains the summary function AVG with Salary as its argument. Because there is only one column as an argument, the function calculates the statistic down the Salary column to display a single value: the average salary for all employees. The output is shown here.

AvgSalary
54079.62

Using a Summary Function with Multiple Arguments (Columns)

Consider a PROC SQL query that contains a summary function with multiple columns as arguments. This query calculates the total number of passengers for each flight in March by adding the number of boarded, transferred, and nonrevenue passengers:

```
proc sql outobs=10;
   select sum(boarded,transferred,nonrevenue)
          as Total
      from sasuser.marchflights;
```

The SELECT clause contains the summary function SUM with three columns as arguments. Because the function contains multiple arguments, the statistic is calculated across the three columns for each row to produce the following output.

Total
123
196
167
222
185
163
119
200
70
227

Note: Without the OUTOBS= option, all rows in the table would be displayed in the output.

Consider how a PROC SQL query with a summary function is affected by including a GROUP BY clause and including columns outside of a summary function.

Using a Summary Function without a GROUP BY Clause

Once again, here is the PROC SQL query that displays the average salary of all employees listed in the table Sasuser.Payrollmaster. This query contains a summary function but, since the goal is to display the average across all employees, there is no GROUP BY clause.

```
proc sql outobs=20;
   select avg(salary) as AvgSalary
      from sasuser.payrollmaster;
```

Note that the SELECT clause lists only one column: a new column that is defined by a summary function calculation. There are no columns listed outside of the summary function.

Here is the query output.

Using a Summary Function with Columns outside of the Function

Suppose you calculate an average for each job group and group the results by job code. Your first step is to add an existing column (JobCode) to the SELECT clause list. The modified query is shown here:

```
proc sql outobs=20;
   select jobcode, avg(salary) as AvgSalary
      from sasuser.payrollmaster;
```

Consider what the query output looks like now that the SELECT statement contains a column (JobCode) that is not a summary function argument.

JobCode	AvgSalary
TA2	54079.62
ME2	54079.62
ME1	54079.62
FA3	54079.62
TA3	54079.62
ME3	54079.62
SCP	54079.62
PT2	54079.62
TA2	54079.62
TA3	54079.62
ME1	54079.62
PT1	54079.62
SCP	54079.62
PT1	54079.62
ME2	54079.62
ME2	54079.62
BCK	54079.62
FA2	54079.62
SCP	54079.62
PT2	54079.62

Note: Remember that this PROC SQL query uses the OUTOBS= option to limit the output to 20 rows. Without this limitation, the output of this query would display all 148 rows in the table.

As this result shows, adding a column to the SELECT clause that is not within a summary function causes PROC SQL to output all rows instead of a single value. To generate this output, PROC SQL

- calculated the average salary down the column as a single value (54079.62)

- displayed all rows in the output, because JobCode is not specified in a summary function.

Therefore, the single value for AvgSalary is repeated for each row.

Note: When this query is submitted, the SAS log displays a message indicating that data remerging has occurred. Data remerging is explained later in this chapter.

This result is interesting, but you have not yet reached your goal: grouping the data by JobCode. The next step is to add the GROUP BY clause.

Using a Summary Function with a GROUP BY Clause

Below is the PROC SQL query from the previous page, to which has been added a GROUP BY clause that specifies the column JobCode. (In the SELECT clause, JobCode is specified but is not used as a summary function argument.) Other changes to the query include removing the OUTOBS= option (it is unnecessary) and specifying a format for the AvgSalary column.

```
proc sql;
   select jobcode,
          avg(salary) as AvgSalary format=dollar11.2
      from sasuser.payrollmaster
      group by jobcode;
```

Consider how the addition of the GROUP BY clause affects the output.

JobCode	AvgSalary
BCK	$36,111.89
FA1	$32,255.18
FA2	$39,181.50
FA3	$46,107.57
ME1	$39,900.50
ME2	$49,807.64
ME3	$59,374.86
NA1	$58,845.00
NA2	$73,336.00
PT1	$95,071.13
PT2	$122,253.40
PT3	$154,706.50
SCP	$25,632.14
TA1	$38,809.89
TA2	$47,004.90
TA3	$55,551.42

Success! The summary function has been calculated for each JobCode group, and the results are grouped by JobCode.

Counting Values By Using the COUNT Summary Function

Sometimes you want to count the number of rows in an entire table or in groups of rows. In PROC SQL, you can use the COUNT summary function to count the number of rows that have nonmissing values. There are three main ways to use the COUNT function.

Using this form of COUNT...	Returns...	Example
COUNT(*)	the total number of rows in a group or in a table	`select count(*) as Count`
COUNT(*column*)	the total number of rows in a group or in a table for which there is a nonmissing value in the selected column	`select count(jobcode) as Count`
COUNT(DISTINCT column)	the total number of unique values in a column	`select count(distinct jobcode) as Count`

CAUTION:

The COUNT summary function counts only the nonmissing values; missing values are ignored. Many other summary functions also ignore missing values. For example, the AVG function returns the average of the nonmissing values only. When you use a summary function with data that contains missing values, the results might not provide the information that you expect. It is a good idea to familiarize yourself with the data before you use summary functions in queries.

TIP   To count the number of missing values, use the NMISS function. For more information about the NMISS function, see the SAS documentation.

Consider the three ways of using the COUNT function.

Counting All Rows

Suppose you want to know how many employees are listed in the table Sasuser. Payrollmaster. This table contains a separate row for each employee, so counting the number of rows in the table gives you the number of employees. The following PROC SQL query accomplishes this task:

```
proc sql;
   select count(*) as Count
      from sasuser.payrollmaster;
```

Count
148

Note: The COUNT summary function is the only function that enables you to use an asterisk (*) as an argument.

You can also use COUNT(*) to count rows within groups of data. To do this, you specify the groups in the GROUP BY clause. Consider a more complex PROC SQL query that uses COUNT(*) with grouping. This time, the goal is to find the total number of employees within each job category, using the same table that is used above.

```
proc sql;
   select substr(jobcode,1,2)
          label='Job Category',
          count(*) as Count
      from sasuser.payrollmaster
      group by 1;
```

This query defines two new columns in the SELECT clause. The first column that is labeled **JobCategory**, is created by using the SAS function SUBSTR to extract the two-character job category from the existing JobCode field. The second column, Count, is created by using the COUNT function. The GROUP BY clause specifies that the results are to be grouped by the first defined column (referenced by 1 because the column was not assigned a name).

Job Category	Count
BC	9
FA	34
ME	29
NA	8
PT	20
SC	7
TA	41

CAUTION:
When a column contains missing values, PROC SQL treats the missing values as a single group. This can sometimes produce unexpected results.

Counting All Non-Missing Values in a Column

Suppose you want to count all of the nonmissing values in a specific column instead of in the entire table. To do this, you specify the name of the column as an argument of the COUNT function. For example, the following PROC SQL query counts all nonmissing values in the column JobCode:

```
proc sql;
   select count(JobCode) as Count
      from sasuser.payrollmaster;
```

Count
148

Because the table has no missing data, you get the same output with this query as you would by using COUNT(*). JobCode has a nonmissing value for each row in the table. However, if the JobCode column contained missing values, this query would produce a lower value of Count than the previous query. For example, if JobCode contained three missing values, the value of Count would be 145.

Counting All Unique Values in a Column

To count all unique values in a column, add the keyword DISTINCT before the name of the column that is used as an argument. For example, here is the previous query modified to count only the unique values:

```
proc sql;
    select count(distinct jobcode) as Count
        from sasuser.payrollmaster;
```

This query counts 16 unique values for JobCode.

To display the unique JobCode values, you can apply the method of eliminating duplicates, which was discussed earlier. The following query lists only the unique values for JobCode.

```
proc sql;
    select distinct jobcode
        from sasuser.payrollmaster;
```

There are 16 job codes, so the output contains 16 rows.

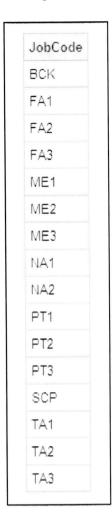

Selecting Groups By Using the HAVING Clause

You have seen how to use the GROUP BY clause to group data. For example, the following query calculates the average salary within each job-code group, and displays the average for each job code:

```
proc sql;
   select jobcode,
          avg(salary) as AvgSalary
          format=dollar11.2
      from sasuser.payrollmaster
      group by jobcode;
```

There are 16 job codes in the table, so the output displays 16 rows.

JobCode	AvgSalary
BCK	$36,111.89
FA1	$32,255.18
FA2	$39,181.50
FA3	$46,107.57
ME1	$39,900.50
ME2	$49,807.64
ME3	$59,374.86
NA1	$58,845.00
NA2	$73,336.00
PT1	$95,071.13
PT2	$122,253.40
PT3	$154,706.50
SCP	$25,632.14
TA1	$38,809.89
TA2	$47,004.90
TA3	$55,551.42

Now, suppose you want to select only a subset of groups for your query output. You can use a HAVING clause, following a GROUP BY clause, to select (or filter) the groups to be displayed. The way a HAVING clause affects groups is similar to how a WHERE clause affects individual rows. As in a WHERE clause, the HAVING clause contains an expression that is used to subset the data. Any valid SAS expression can be used. When you use a HAVING clause, PROC SQL displays only the groups that satisfy the HAVING expression.

Note: You can use summary functions in a HAVING clause but not in a WHERE clause, because a HAVING clause is used with groups, but a WHERE clause can be used only with individual rows.

Modify the query shown above so that it selects only the JobCode groups with an average salary of more than $56,000. The HAVING clause has been added at the end of the query.

```
proc sql;
   select jobcode,
          avg(salary) as AvgSalary
          format=dollar11.2
      from sasuser.payrollmaster
      group by jobcode
      having avg(salary) > 56000;
```

TIP   Alternatively, because the average salary is already calculated in the SELECT clause, the HAVING clause could specify the column alias AvgSalary:

```
having AvgSalary > 56000
```

Note that you do not have to specify the keyword CALCULATED in a HAVING clause; you would have to specify it in a WHERE clause.

The query output is shown below. This output is smaller than the previous output, because only a subset of the job-code groups is displayed.

JobCode	AvgSalary
ME3	$59,374.86
NA1	$58,845.00
NA2	$73,336.00
PT1	$95,071.13
PT2	$122,263.40
PT3	$154,706.50

If you omit the GROUP BY clause in a query that contains a HAVING clause, then the HAVING clause and summary functions (if any are specified) treat the entire table as one group. Without a GROUP BY clause, the HAVING clause in the example shown above calculates the average salary for the table as a whole (all jobs in the company), not for each group (each job code). The output contains either all the rows in the table (if the average salary for the entire table is greater than $56,000) or none of the rows in the table (if the average salary for the entire table is less than $56,000).

Understanding Data Remerging

Sometimes, when you use a summary function in a SELECT clause or a HAVING clause, PROC SQL must remerge data (make two passes through the table). Remerging requires additional processing time and is often unavoidable. However, there are some situations in which you might be able to modify your query to avoid remerging. Understanding how and when remerging occurs increases your ability to write efficient queries.

Consider a PROC SQL query that requires remerging. This query calculates each navigator's salary as a percentage of all navigators' salaries:

```
proc sql;
   select empid, salary,
          (salary/sum(salary)) as Percent
          format=percent8.2
      from sasuser.payrollmaster
      where jobcode contains 'NA';
```

When you submit this query, the SAS log displays the following message.

Table 2.4 SAS Log

NOTE: The query requires remerging summary statistics back
with the original data.

Remerging occurs whenever any of the following conditions exist:

• The values returned by a summary function are used in a calculation.

- The SELECT clause specifies a column that contains a summary function and other column(s) that are not listed in a GROUP BY clause.

- The HAVING clause specifies one or more columns or column expressions that are not included in a subquery or a GROUP BY clause.

During remerging, PROC SQL makes two passes through the table:

1. PROC SQL calculates and returns the value of summary functions. PROC SQL also groups data according to the GROUP BY clause.

2. PROC SQL retrieves any additional columns and rows that it needs to display in the output, and uses the result from the summary function to calculate any arithmetic expressions in which the summary function participates.

Example

Consider how PROC SQL remerges data when it processes the following query:

```
proc sql;
   select empid, salary,
          (salary/sum(salary)) as Percent
          format=percent8.2
      from sasuser.payrollmaster
      where jobcode contains 'NA';
```

In the first pass, for each row in which the jobcode contains '**NA**', PROC SQL calculates and returns the value of the SUM function (specified in the SELECT clause).

In the second pass, PROC SQL retrieves the additional columns and rows that it needs to display in output (EmpID, Salary) and the rows in which JobCode contains '**NA**'. PROC SQL also uses the result from the SUM function to calculate the arithmetic expression (salary/sum(salary)).

CAUTION:

Some implementations of SQL do not support remerging and would consider the preceding example to be in error.

TIP   You can obtain the same results by using a subquery. Subqueries are discussed later in this chapter.

Subsetting Data By Using Subqueries

Introducing Subqueries

The WHERE and HAVING clauses both subset data based on an expression. In the query examples shown earlier in this chapter, the WHERE and HAVING clauses contained standard SAS expressions. For example, the expression in the following WHERE clause uses the BETWEEN-AND conditional operator and specifies the Salary column as an operand:

```
where salary between 70000 and 80000
```

PROC SQL also offers another type of expression that can be used for subsetting in WHERE and HAVING clauses: a query expression or subquery. A subquery is a query that is nested in, and is part of, another query. A PROC SQL query might contain subqueries at one or more levels.

Note: Subqueries are also known as nested queries, inner queries, and sub-selects.

The following PROC SQL query contains a subquery in the HAVING clause that returns all jobcodes where the average salary for that jobcode is greater than the company average salary.

```
proc sql;
   select jobcode,
          avg(salary) as AvgSalary
          format=dollar11.2
      from sasuser.payrollmaster
      group by jobcode
      having avg(salary) >
         (select avg(salary)
            from sasuser.payrollmaster);
```

TIP   It is recommended that you enclose a subquery (inner query) in parentheses, as shown here.

A subquery selects one or more rows from a table, and then returns single or multiple values to be used by the outer query. The subquery shown above is a single-value subquery; it returns a single value, the average salary from the table Sasuser.Payrollmaster, to the outer query. A subquery can return values for multiple rows but only for a single column.

The table that a subquery references can be either the same as or different from the table referenced by the outer query. In the PROC SQL query shown above, the subquery selects data from the same table as the outer query.

Types of Subqueries

There are two types of subqueries.

Type of Subquery	Description
noncorrelated	a self-contained subquery that executes independently of the outer query
correlated	a dependent subquery that requires one or more values to be passed to it by the outer query before the subquery can return a value to the outer query

Both noncorrelated and correlated subqueries can return either single or multiple values to the outer query.

The next few sections provide a more in-depth look at noncorrelated and correlated subqueries, and how they are processed.

Subsetting Data By Using Noncorrelated Subqueries

A noncorrelated subquery is a self-contained subquery that executes independently of the outer query.

Using Single-Value Noncorrelated Subqueries

The simplest type of subquery is a noncorrelated subquery that returns a single value.

The following PROC SQL query is the same query that is used in the previous section. This query displays job codes for which the group's average salary exceeds the company's average salary. The HAVING clause contains a noncorrelated subquery.

```
proc sql;
   select jobcode,
          avg(salary) as AvgSalary
          format=dollar11.2
      from sasuser.payrollmaster
      group by jobcode
      having avg(salary) >
         (select avg(salary)
            from sasuser.payrollmaster);
```

PROC SQL always evaluates a noncorrelated subquery before the outer query. If a query contains noncorrelated subqueries at more than one level, PROC SQL evaluates the innermost subquery first and works outward, evaluating the outermost query last.

In the query shown above, the inner query and outer query are processed as follows:

1. To complete the expression in the HAVING clause, the subquery calculates the average salary for the entire company (all rows in the table), using the AVG summary function with Salary as an argument.

2. The subquery returns the value of the average salary to the outer query.

3. The outer query calculates the average salary (in the SELECT clause) for each JobCode group (as defined in the GROUP BY clause), and selects only the groups whose average salary is greater than the company's average salary.

The query output is shown here.

JobCode	AvgSalary
ME3	$59,374.86
NA1	$58,845.00
NA2	$73,336.00
PT1	$95,071.13
PT2	$122,253.40
PT3	$164,706.50
TA3	$55,551.42

This noncorrelated subquery returns only a single value, the average salary for the whole company, to the outer query. Both the subquery query and the outer query use the same table as a source.

Using Multiple-Value Noncorrelated Subqueries

Some subqueries are multiple-value subqueries: they return more than one value (row) to the outer query. If your noncorrelated subquery might return a value for more than one row, be sure to use one of the following operators in the WHERE or HAVING clause that can handle multiple values:

- the conditional operator IN

- a comparison operator that is modified by ANY or ALL

- the conditional operator EXISTS.

CAUTION:

If you create a noncorrelated subquery that returns multiple values, but the WHERE or HAVING clause in the outer query contains an operator other than one of the operators that are specified above, the query fails. An error message is displayed in the SAS log, which indicates that the subquery evaluated to more than one row. For example, if you use the equal (=) operator with a noncorrelated subquery that returns multiple values, the query fails. The equal operator can handle only a single value.

Consider a query that contains both the conditional operator IN and a noncorrelated subquery that returns multiple values. (The operators ANY, ALL, and EXISTS are presented later in this chapter.)

Example

Suppose you want to send birthday cards to employees who have birthdays coming up. You decide to create a PROC SQL query that lists the names and addresses of all employees who have birthdays in February. This query, unlike the one shown on the previous page, selects data from two different tables:

- employee names and addresses in the table Sasuser.Staffmaster

- employee birthdates in the table Sasuser.Payrollmaster.

In both tables, the employees are identified by their employee identification number (EmpID).

In the following PROC SQL query, the WHERE clause contains the conditional operator IN followed by a noncorrelated subquery:

```
proc sql;
   select empid, lastname, firstname,
          city, state
      from sasuser.staffmaster
      where empid in
         (select empid
             from sasuser.payrollmaster
             where month(dateofbirth)=2);
```

This query is processed as follows:

1. To complete the expression in the WHERE clause of the outer query, the subquery selects the employees whose date of birth is February. Note that the MONTH function is used in the subquery.

2. The subquery then returns the EmpID values of the selected employees to the outer query.

3. The outer query displays data (from the columns identified in the SELECT clause) for the employees identified by the subquery.

The output, shown below, lists the six employees who have February birthdays.

EmpID	LastName	FirstName	City	State
1403	BOWDEN	EARL	BRIDGEPORT	CT
1404	CARTER	DONALD	NEW YORK	NY
1834	LONG	RUSSELL	NEW YORK	NY
1103	MCDANIEL	RONDA	NEW YORK	NY
1420	ROUSE	JEREMY	PATERSON	NJ
1390	SMART	JONATHAN	NEW YORK	NY

Although an inner join would have generated the same results, it is better to use a subquery in this example since no columns from the sasuser.payrollmaster table were in the output.

Using Comparisons with Subqueries

Sometimes it is helpful to compare a value with a set of values returned by a subquery. When a subquery might return multiple values, you must use one of the conditional operators ANY or ALL to modify a comparison operator in the WHERE or HAVING clause immediately before the subquery. For example, the following WHERE clause contains the less than (<) comparison operator and the conditional operator ANY:

```
where dateofbirth < any
   <subquery...>
```

CAUTION:

> If you create a noncorrelated subquery that returns multiple values, and if the WHERE or HAVING clause in the outer query contains a comparison operator that is not modified by ANY or ALL, the query fails.

When the outer query contains a comparison operator that is modified by ANY or ALL, the outer query compares each value that it retrieves against the value(s) returned by the subquery. All values for which the comparison is true are then included in the query output. If ANY is specified, then the comparison is true if it is true for any one of the values that are returned by the subquery. If ALL is specified, then the comparison is true only if it is true for all values that are returned by the subquery.

Note: The operators ANY and ALL can be used with correlated subqueries, but they are usually used only with noncorrelated subqueries.

Consider how the operators ANY or ALL are used.

Using the ANY Operator

An outer query that specifies the ANY operator selects values that pass the comparison test with any of the values that are returned by the subquery.

For example, suppose you have an outer query containing the following WHERE clause:

```
where dateofbirth < any
   <subquery...>
```

This WHERE clause specifies that DateofBirth (the operand) should be less than any (the comparison operator) of the values returned by the subquery.

The following chart shows the effect of using ANY with these common comparison operators: greater than (>), less than (<) and equal to (=).

Comparison Operator with ANY	Outer Query Selects...	Example
> ANY	values that are greater than any value returned by the subquery	If the subquery returns the values 20, 30, 40, then the outer query selects all values that are > 20 (the lowest value that was returned by the subquery).
< ANY	values that are less than any value returned by the subquery	If the subquery returns the values 20, 30, 40, then the outer query selects all values that are < 40 (the highest value that was returned by the subquery).
= ANY	values that are equal to any value returned by the subquery	If the subquery returns the values 20, 30, 40, the outer query selects all values that are = 20 or = 30 or = 40.

TIP   Instead of using the ANY operator with a subquery, there are some SAS functions that you can use to achieve the same result with greater efficiency. Instead of > ANY, use the MIN function in the subquery. Instead of < ANY, use the MAX function in the subquery.

Example

Suppose you want to identify any flight attendants at level 1 or level 2 who are older than any of the flight attendants at level 3. Job type and level are identified in JobCode;

each flight attendant has the job code FA1, FA2, or FA3. The following PROC SQL query accomplishes this task by using a subquery and the ANY operator:

```
proc sql;
   select empid, jobcode, dateofbirth
      from sasuser.payrollmaster
      where jobcode in ('FA1','FA2')
           and dateofbirth < any
               (select dateofbirth
                   from sasuser.payrollmaster
                   where jobcode='FA3');
```

Here is what happens when this query is processed:

1. The subquery returns the birthdates of all level-3 flight attendants.

2. The outer query selects only those level-1 and level-2 flight attendants whose birthdate is less than any of the dates returned by the subquery.

Note that both the outer query and subquery use the same table.

Note: Internally, SAS represents a date value as the number of days from January 1, 1960, to the given date. For example, the SAS date for 17 October 1991 is 11612. Representing dates as the number of days from a reference date makes it easy for the computer to store them and perform calendar calculations. These numbers are not meaningful to users, however, so several formats are available for displaying dates and datetime values in most of the commonly used notations.

Below are the query results.

EmpID	JobCode	DateOfBirth
1574	FA2	01MAY1958
1475	FA2	19DEC1959
1124	FA1	13JUL1956
1422	FA1	08JUN1962
1368	FA2	15JUN1959
1411	FA2	31MAY1959
1477	FA2	25MAR1962
1970	FA1	29SEP1962
1413	FA2	20SEP1963
1434	FA2	14JUL1960
1390	FA2	23FEB1963
1135	FA2	24SEP1958
1415	FA2	12MAR1956
1122	FA2	04MAY1961

> TIP   Using the ANY operator to solve this problem results in a large number of calculations, which increases processing time. For this example, it would be more efficient to use the MAX function in the subquery. The alternative WHERE clause follows:

```
where jobcode in ('FA1','FA2')
    and dateofbirth <
        (select max(dateofbirth)
            from [...]
```

For more information about the MAX function, see the SAS documentation.

Using the ALL Operator

An outer query that specifies the ALL operator selects values that pass the comparison test with all of the values that are returned by the subquery.

The following chart shows the effect of using ALL with these common comparison operators: greater than (>) and less than (<).

Comparison Operator with ALL	Sample Values Returned by Subquery	Signifies...
> *ALL*	(20, 30, 40)	> 40 (greater than the highest number in the list)
< ALL	(20, 30, 40)	< 20 (less than the lowest number in the list)

Example

Substitute ALL for ANY in the previous query example. The following query identifies level-1 and level-2 flight attendants who are older than all of the level-3 flight attendants:

```
proc sql;
    select empid, jobcode, dateofbirth
        from sasuser.payrollmaster
        where jobcode in ('FA1','FA2')
            and dateofbirth < all
                (select dateofbirth
                    from sasuser.payrollmaster
                    where jobcode='FA3');
```

Here is what happens when this query is processed:

1. The subquery returns the birthdates of all level-3 flight attendants.

2. The outer query selects only those level-1 and level-2 flight attendants whose birthdate is less than all of the dates returned by the subquery.

The query results, below, show that only two level-1 or level-2 flight attendants are older than all of the level-3 flight attendants.

EmpID	JobCode	DateOfBirth
1124	FA1	13JUL1956
1415	FA2	12MAR1956

TIP For this example, it would be more efficient to solve this problem using the MIN function in the subquery instead of the ALL operator. The alternative WHERE clause follows:

```
where jobcode in ('FA1','FA2')
      and dateofbirth <
        (select min(dateofbirth)
            from [...]
```

For more information about the MIN function, see the SAS documentation.

Subsetting Data By Using Correlated Subqueries

Overview

Correlated subqueries cannot be evaluated independently, but depend on the values passed to them by the outer query for their results. Correlated subqueries are evaluated for each row in the outer query and therefore tend to require more processing time than noncorrelated subqueries.

Note: Usually, a PROC SQL join is a more efficient alternative to a correlated subquery. You should already be familiar with basic PROC SQL joins.

Example

Consider an example of a PROC SQL query that contains a correlated subquery. The following query displays the names of all navigators who are also managers. The WHERE clause in the subquery lists the column Staffmaster.EmpID. The outer query must pass this column to the correlated subquery.

```
proc sql;
   select lastname, firstname
      from sasuser.staffmaster
      where 'NA'=
            (select jobcategory
                from sasuser.supervisors
                where staffmaster.empid =
                      supervisors.empid);
```

Note: When a column appears in more than one table, the column name is preceded by the table name or alias to avoid ambiguity. In this example, EmpID appears in both tables, so the appropriate table name is specified in front of each reference to that column.

The output from this query is shown below. There are three navigators who are also managers.

LastName	FirstName
FERNANDEZ	KATRINA
NEWKIRK	WILLIAM
RIVERS	SIMON

Using the EXISTS and NOT EXISTS Conditional Operators

In the WHERE clause or in the HAVING clause of an outer query, you can use the EXISTS or NOT EXISTS conditional operator to test for the existence or non-existence of a set of values returned by a subquery.

Condition	Is true if...
EXISTS	the subquery returns at least one row
NOT EXISTS	the subquery returns no data

Note: The operators EXISTS and NOT EXISTS can be used with both correlated and noncorrelated subqueries.

Example: Correlated Subquery with NOT EXISTS

Consider a sample PROC SQL query that includes the NOT EXISTS conditional operator. Suppose you are working with the following tables:

- Sasuser.Flightattendants contains the names and employee ID numbers of all flight attendants.

- Sasuser.Flightschedule contains one row for each crew member assigned to a flight for each date.

As shown in the diagram below, the intersection of these two tables contains data for all flight attendants who have been scheduled to work.

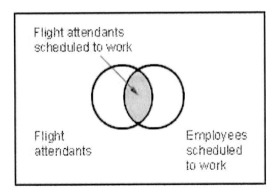

Now suppose you want to list by name the flight attendants who are not scheduled. That is, you want to identify the data in the area highlighted below.

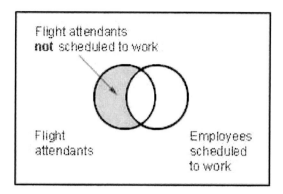

The following PROC SQL query accomplishes this task by using a correlated subquery and the NOT EXISTS operator:

```
proc sql;
   select lastname, firstname
      from sasuser.flightattendants
      where not exists
         (select *
            from sasuser.flightschedule
                        where flightattendants.empid=
                              flightschedule.empid);
```

The output is shown below.

LastName	FirstName
PATTERSON	RENEE
VEGA	FRANKLIN

Validating Query Syntax

Overview

When you are building a PROC SQL query, you might find it more efficient to check your query without actually executing it. To verify the syntax and the existence of columns and tables that are referenced in the query without executing the query, use either of the following:

- the NOEXEC option in the PROC SQL statement
- the VALIDATE keyword before a SELECT statement.

Consider how you specify the NOEXEC option and the VALIDATE keyword, and examine the minor differences between them.

Using the NOEXEC Option

The NOEXEC option is specified in the following PROC SQL statement:

```
proc sql noexec;
```

```
select empid, jobcode, salary
   from sasuser.payrollmaster
   where jobcode contains 'NA'
   order by salary;
```

If the query is valid and all referenced columns and tables exist, the SAS log displays the following message.

Table 2.5 *SAS Log*

NOTE: Statement not executed due to NOEXEC option.

Or, if there are any errors in the query, SAS displays the standard error messages in the log.

When you invoke the NOEXEC option, SAS checks the syntax of all queries in that PROC SQL step for accuracy but does not execute them.

Using the VALIDATE Keyword

You specify the VALIDATE keyword just before a SELECT statement; it is not used with any other PROC SQL statement.

We will modify the preceding PROC SQL query by using the VALIDATE keyword instead of the NOEXEC option:

```
proc sql;
   validate
   select empid, jobcode, salary
      from sasuser.payrollmaster
      where jobcode contains 'NA'
      order by salary;
```

Note: Note that the VALIDATE keyword is not followed by a semicolon.

If the query is valid, the SAS log displays the following message.

Table 2.6 *SAS Log*

NOTE: PROC SQL statement has valid syntax.

If there are errors in the query, SAS displays the standard error messages in the log.

The main difference between the VALIDATE keyword and the NOEXEC option is that the VALIDATE keyword only affects the SELECT statement that immediately follows it, whereas the NOEXEC option applies to all queries in the PROC SQL step. If you are working with a PROC SQL query that contains multiple SELECT statements, the VALIDATE keyword must be specified before each SELECT statement that you want to check.

Additional Features

In addition to the SELECT statement, PROC SQL supports the following statements.

Statement	Use to ...
ALTER TABLE *expression*;	add, drop, and modify columns in a table
CREATE *expression*;	build new tables, views, or indexes
DELETE *expression*;	eliminate unwanted rows from a table or view
DESCRIBE *expression*;	display table and view attributes
DROP *expression*;	eliminate entire tables, views, or indexes
INSERT *expression*	add rows of data to tables or views
RESET *<option(s)>*;	add to or change PROC SQL options without re-invoking the procedure
UPDATE *expression*;	modify data values in existing rows of a table or view

Summary

Text Summary

Viewing SELECT Statement Syntax
The SELECT statement and its subordinate clauses are the building blocks that you use to construct all PROC SQL queries.

Displaying All Columns
To display all columns in the order in which they are stored in the table, use an asterisk (*) in the SELECT clause. To write the expanded list of columns to the SAS log, use the FEEDBACK option in the PROC SQL statement.

Limiting the Number of Rows Displayed
To limit the number of rows that PROC SQL displays as output, use the OUTOBS=*n* option in the PROC SQL statement.

Eliminating Duplicate Rows from Output
To eliminate duplicate rows from your query results, use the keyword DISTINCT in the SELECT clause.

Subsetting Rows By Using Conditional Operators
In a PROC SQL query, use the WHERE clause with any valid SAS expression to subset data. The SAS expression can contain one or more operators, including the following conditional operators:

- the BETWEEN-AND operator selects within an inclusive range of values

- the CONTAINS or ? operator selects a character string

- the IN operator selects from a list of fixed values

- the IS MISSING or IS NULL operator selects missing values

- the LIKE operator selects a pattern

- the sounds-like (=*) operator selects a spelling variation

Subsetting Rows By Using Calculated Values
It is important to understand how PROC SQL processes calculated columns. When you use a column alias in the WHERE clause to refer to a calculated value, you must use the keyword CALCULATED with the alias.

Enhancing Query Output
You can enhance PROC SQL query output by using SAS enhancements such as column formats and labels, titles and footnotes, and character constraints.

Summarizing and Grouping Data
PROC SQL calculates summary functions and outputs results differently, depending on a combination of factors:

- whether the summary function specifies one or more multiple columns as arguments

- whether the query contains a GROUP BY clause

- if the summary function is specified in a SELECT clause, whether there are additional columns listed that are outside the summary function

- whether the WHERE clause, if there is one, contains only columns that are specified in the SELECT clause.

To count nonmissing values, use the COUNT summary function.

To select the groups to be displayed, use a HAVING clause following a GROUP BY clause.

When you use a summary function in a SELECT clause or a HAVING clause, in some situations, PROC SQL must remerge data. When PROC SQL remerges data, it makes two passes through the data, and this requires additional processing time.

Subsetting Data By Using Subqueries
In the WHERE clause or the HAVING clause of a PROC SQL query, you can use a subquery to subset data. A subquery is a query that is nested in, and is part of, another query. Subqueries can return values from a single row or multiple rows to the outer query but can return values only from a single column.

Subsetting Data By Using Noncorrelated Subqueries
Noncorrelated subqueries execute independently of the outer query. You can use noncorrelated subqueries that return a single value or multiple values. To further qualify a comparison specified in a WHERE clause or a HAVING clause, you can use the conditional operators ANY and ALL immediately before a noncorrelated (or correlated) subquery.

Subsetting Data By Using Correlated Subqueries
Correlated subqueries cannot be evaluated independently because their results are dependent on the values returned by the outer query. In the WHERE clause or the HAVING clause of an outer query, you can use the EXISTS and NOT EXISTS

conditional operators to test for the existence or non-existence of a set of values returned by the subquery.

Validating Query Syntax

To check the validity of the query syntax without actually executing the query, use the NOEXEC option or the VALIDATE keyword.

Additional Features

PROC SQL supports many statements in addition to the SELECT statement.

Sample Programs

Displaying All Columns in Output and an Expanded Column List in the SAS Log

```
proc sql feedback;
   select *
      from sasuser.staffchanges;
quit;
```

Eliminating Duplicate Rows from Output

```
proc sql;
   select distinct flightnumber, destination
      from sasuser.internationalflights
      order by 1;
quit;
```

Subsetting Rows By Using Calculated Values

```
proc sql outobs=10;
   validate
   select flightnumber,
          date label="Flight Date", destination,
          boarded + transferred + nonrevenue
          as Total
      from sasuser.marchflights
      where calculated total between 100 and 150;
quit;
```

Subsetting Data By Using a Noncorrelated Subquery

```
proc sql noexec;
   select jobcode,
          avg(salary) as AvgSalary
          format=dollar11.2
      from sasuser.payrollmaster
      group by jobcode
      having avg(salary) >
         (select avg(salary)
             from sasuser.payrollmaster);
quit;
```

Subsetting Data By Using a Correlated Subquery

```
proc sql;
```

```
title 'Frequent Flyers Who Are Not Employees';
   select count(*) as Count
      from sasuser.frequentflyers
      where not exists
         (select *
            from sasuser.staffmaster
            where name=
                  trim(lastname)||', '||firstname);
quit;
```

Points to Remember

- When you use summary functions, look for missing values. If a table contains missing values, your results might not be what you expect. Many summary functions ignore missing values when performing calculations, and PROC SQL treats missing values in a column as a single group.

- When you create complex queries, it is helpful to use the NOEXEC option or the VALIDATE statement to validate your query without executing it.

Quiz

Select the best answer for each question. After completing the quiz, check your answers using the answer key in the appendix.

1. Which PROC SQL query removes duplicate values of MemberType from the query output, so that only the unique values are listed?

   a. ```
      proc sql nodup;
         select membertype
            from sasuser.frequentflyers;
      ```

   b. ```
      proc sql;
         select distinct(membertype)
               as MemberType
            from sasuser.frequentflyers;
      ```

   c. ```
      proc sql;
         select unique membertype
            from sasuser.frequentflyers
            group by membertype;
      ```

   d. ```
      proc sql;
         select distinct membertype
            from sasuser.frequentflyers;
      ```

2. Which of the following causes PROC SQL to list rows that have no data in the Address column?

   a. WHERE address is missing

   b. WHERE address not exists

   c. WHERE address is null

   d. both a and c

3. You are creating a PROC SQL query that lists all employees who have spent (or overspent) their allotted 120 hours of vacation for the current year. The hours that each employee used are stored in the existing column Spent. Your query defines a new column, Balance, to calculate each employee's balance of vacation hours.

   Which query produces the report that you want?

   a.
   ```
   proc sql;
       select name, spent,
               120-spent as calculated Balance
           from Company.Absences
           where balance <= 0;
   ```

   b.
   ```
   proc sql;
       select name, spent,
               120-spent as Balance
           from Company.Absences
           where calculated balance <= 0;
   ```

   c.
   ```
   proc sql;
       select name, spent,
               120-spent as Balance
           from Company.Absences
           where balance <= 0;
   ```

   d.
   ```
   proc sql;
       select name, spent,
               120-spent as calculated Balance
           from Company.Absences
           where calculated balance <= 0;
   ```

4. Consider this PROC SQL query:

   ```
   proc sql;
       select flightnumber,
               count(*) as Flights,
               avg(boarded)
               label="Average Boarded"
               format=3.
           from sasuser.internationalflights
           group by flightnumber
           having avg(boarded) > 150;
   ```

   The table Sasuser.Internationalflights contains 201 rows, 7 unique values of FlightNumber, 115 unique values of Boarded, and 4 different flight numbers that have an average value of Boarded that is greater than 150. How many rows of output is generated by the query?

   a. 150

   b. 7

   c. 4

   d. 1

5. You are writing a PROC SQL query that displays the names of all library cardholders who work as volunteers for the library, and the number of books that each volunteer currently has checked out. You use one or both of the following tables:

   - Library.Circulation lists the name and contact information for all library cardholders, and the number of books that each cardholder currently has checked out.

- Library.Volunteers lists the name and contact information for all library volunteers.

Assume that the values of Name are unique in both tables.

Which of the following PROC SQL queries produces your report?

a.
```
proc sql;
    select name, checkedout
       from library.circulation
       where * in
           (select *
               from library.volunteers);
```

b.
```
proc sql;
    select name, checkedout
       from library.circulation
       where name in
           (select name
               from library.volunteers);
```

c.
```
proc sql;
    select name
       from library.volunteers
       where name, checkedout in
           (select name, checkedout
               from library.circulation);
```

d.
```
proc sql;
    select name, checkedout
       from library.circulation
       where name in
           (select name
               from library.volunteers;);
```

6. By definition, a noncorrelated subquery is a nested query that

   a. returns a single value to the outer query.

   b. contains at least one summary function.

   c. executes independently of the outer query.

   d. requires only a single value to be passed to it by the outer query.

7. Which statement about the following PROC SQL query is false?

```
proc sql;
    validate
    select name label='Country',
           rate label='Literacy Rate'
       from world.literacy
       where 'Asia' =
           (select continent
               from world.continents
               where literacy.name =
                   continents.country)
       order by 2;
```

   a. The query syntax is not valid.

   b. The outer query must pass values to the subquery before the subquery can return values to the outer query.

   c. PROC SQL cannot execute this query when it is submitted.

   d. After the query is submitted, the SAS log indicates whether the query has valid syntax.

8. Consider the following PROC SQL query:

```
proc sql;
    select lastname, firstname,
           total, since
      from charity.donors
      where not exists
         (select lastname
            from charity.current
            where donors.lastname =
                current.lastname);
```

The query references two tables:

- Charity.Donors lists name and contact information for all donors who have made contributions since the charity was founded. The table also contains these two columns: Total, which shows the total dollars given by each donor, and **Since**, which stores the first year in which each donor gave money.

- Charity.Current lists the names of all donors who have made contributions in the current year, and the total dollars each has given this year (YearTotal).

Assume that the values of LastName are unique in both tables.

The output of this query displays

   a. all donors whose rows do not contain any missing values.

   b. all donors who made a contribution in the current year.

   c. all donors who did not make a contribution in the current year.

   d. all donors whose current year's donation in Charity.Current has not yet been added to Total in Charity.Donors.

9. Which statement about data remerging is true?

   a. When PROC SQL remerges data, it combines data from two tables.

   b. By using data remerging, PROC SQL can avoid making two passes through the data.

   c. When PROC SQL remerges data, it displays a related message in the SAS log.

   d. PROC SQL does not attempt to remerge data unless a subquery is used.

10. A public library has several categories of books. Each book in the library is assigned to only one category. The table Library.Inventory contains one row for each book in the library. The Checkouts column indicates the number of times that each book has been checked out.

You want to display only the categories that have an average circulation (number of checkouts) that is less than 2500. Does the following PROC SQL query produce the results that you want?

```
proc sql;
title 'Categories with Average Circulation';
title2 'Less Than 2500';
    select category,
           avg(checkouts) as AvgCheckouts
      from library.inventory
```

```
having avg(checkouts) < 2500
order by 1;
```

a. No. This query does not run because a HAVING clause cannot contain a summary function.

b. No. This query does not run because the HAVING clause must include the CALCULATED keyword before the summary function.

c. No. Because there is no GROUP BY clause, the HAVING clause treats the entire table as one group.

d. Yes.

Chapter 3

Combining Tables Horizontally Using PROC SQL

Overview

Introduction

When you need to select data from multiple tables and combine the tables horizontally (side by side), PROC SQL can be an efficient alternative to other SAS procedures or the DATA step. You can use a PROC SQL join to combine tables horizontally:

```
proc sql;
   select *
      from a, b
      where a.x=b.x;
```

A PROC SQL join is a query that specifies multiple tables and/or views to be combined and, typically, specifies the conditions on which rows are matched and returned in the result set.

You should already be familiar with the basics of using PROC SQL to join tables. In this chapter, you take a more in-depth look at joining tables.

Understanding Joins

Joins combine tables horizontally (side by side) by combining rows. The tables being joined are not required to have the same number of rows or columns.

Note: You can use a join to combine views as well as tables. Most of the following references to tables are also applicable to views; any exceptions are noted. In-line views are introduced later in this chapter. For more information about PROC SQL views, see Chapter 7, "Creating and Managing Views Using PROC SQL," on page 248.

When you use a PROC SQL query to join tables, you must decide how you want the rows from the various tables to be combined. There are two main types of joins, as shown below.

Type of Join	Output
Inner join	Only the rows that match across all table(s)

Type of Join	Output
Outer join	Rows that match across tables (as in the inner join) plus nonmatching rows from one or more tables

When any type of join is processed, PROC SQL starts by generating a Cartesian product, which contains all possible combinations of rows from all tables. consider how a Cartesian product is generated.

Generating a Cartesian Product

The most basic type of join combines data from two tables that are specified in the FROM clause of a SELECT statement. When you specify multiple tables in the FROM clause but do not include a WHERE statement to subset data, PROC SQL returns the Cartesian product of the tables. In a Cartesian product, each row in the first table is combined with every row in the second table. Below is an example of this type of query, which joins the tables One and Two.

```
proc sql;
   select *
      from one, two;
```

One

X	A
1	a
2	b
4	d

Two

X	B
2	x
3	y
5	v

X	A	X	B
1	a	2	x
1	a	3	y
1	a	5	v
2	b	2	x
2	b	3	y
2	b	5	v
4	d	2	x
4	d	3	y
4	d	5	v

The output shown above displays all possible combinations of each row in table One with all rows in table Two. Note that each table has a column named X, and both of these columns appear in the output. A Cartesian product includes all columns from the source tables. Columns that have common names are not overlaid.

In most cases, generating all possible combinations of rows from multiple tables does not yield useful results, so a Cartesian product is rarely the query outcome that you want. For example, in the Cartesian product of two tables that contain employee information, each row of output might contain information about two different employees. Usually, you want your join to return only a subset of rows from the tables.

The size of a Cartesian product can also be problematic. The number of rows in a Cartesian product is equal to the product of the number of rows in the contributing tables.

The tables One and Two, used in the preceding example, contain three rows each, as shown below.

One			Two	
X	A		X	B
1	a		2	x
2	b		3	y
4	d		6	v

The number of rows in the Cartesian product of tables One and Two is calculated as follows:

```
3 x 3 = 9 rows
```

Joining small tables such as One and Two results in a relatively small Cartesian product. However, the Cartesian product of large tables can be huge and can require a large amount of system resources for processing.

For example, joining two tables of 1,000 rows each results in output of the following size:

```
1,000 x 1,000 = 1,000,000 rows
```

When you run a query that involves a Cartesian product that cannot be optimized, PROC SQL writes the following warning message to the SAS log.

Table 3.1 *SAS Log*

```
NOTE: The execution of this query involves performing one or
more Cartesian product joins that cannot be optimized.
```

Although you often do not choose to create a query that returns a Cartesian product, it is important to understand how a Cartesian product is built. In all types of joins, PROC SQL generates a Cartesian product first, and then eliminates rows that do not meet any subsetting criteria that you have specified.

Note: In many cases, PROC SQL can optimize the processing of a join, thereby minimizing the resources that are required to generate a Cartesian product.

Using Inner Joins

Introducing Inner Join Syntax

An inner join combines and displays only the rows from the first table that match rows from the second table, based on the matching criteria (also known as join conditions) that are specified in the WHERE clause. A join condition is an expression that specifies the column(s) on which the tables are to be joined.

The following diagram illustrates an inner join of two tables. The shaded area of overlap represents the matching rows (the subset of rows) that the inner join returns as output.

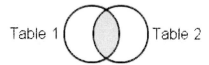

Note: An inner join is sometimes called a conventional join.

Inner join syntax builds on the syntax of the simplest type of join that was shown earlier. In an inner join, a WHERE clause is added to restrict the rows of the Cartesian product that is displayed in output.

General form, SELECT statement for inner join:

SELECT *column-1<,...column-n>*

    FROM *table-1 | view-1, table-2 | view-2<,...table-n | view-n>*

    WHERE *join-condition(s)*

        <AND other subsetting condition(s)>

    <other clauses>;

Here is an explanation of the syntax:

join-condition(s)
    refers to one or more expressions that specify the column or columns on which the tables are to be joined.

other subsetting condition(s)
    refers to optional expressions that are used to subset rows in the query results.

<other clauses>
    refers to optional PROC SQL clauses.

Note: The maximum number of tables that you can combine in a single inner join depends on your version of SAS. For more information see the SAS documentation. If the join involves views (either in-line views or PROC SQL views), it is the number of tables that underlie the views, not the number of views themselves, that counts toward the limit. In-line views are covered later in this chapter and PROC SQL views are discussed in Chapter 7, "Creating and Managing Views Using PROC SQL," on page 248.

Example

When a WHERE clause is added to the PROC SQL query shown earlier, only a subset of rows is included in output. The modified query, tables, and output are shown below:

```
proc sql;
   select *
      from one, two
      where one.x = two.x;
```

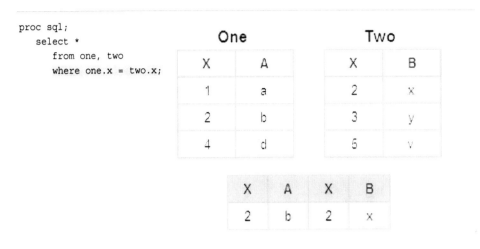

Because of the WHERE clause, this inner join does not display all rows from the Cartesian product (all possible combinations of rows from both tables) but only a subset of rows. The WHERE clause expression (join condition) specifies that the result set should include only rows whose values of column X in the table One are equal to values in column X of the table Two. Only one row from One and one row from Two have matching values of X. Those two rows are combined into one row of output.

Note: PROC SQL does not perform a join unless the columns that are compared in the join condition (in this example, One.X, and Two.X) have the same data type. However, the two columns are not required to have the same name. For example, the join condition shown in the following WHERE statement is valid if ID and EmpID have the same data type:

```
where table1.id = table2.empid
```

Note: The join condition that is specified in the WHERE clause often contains the equal (=) operator, but the expression might contain one or more other operators instead. An inner join that matches rows based on the equal (=) operator, in which the value of a column or expression in one table must be equivalent to the value of a column or expression in another table, is called an equijoin.

Consider how PROC SQL processes this inner join.

Understanding How Joins Are Processed

Understanding how PROC SQL processes inner and outer joins helps you understand which output is generated by each type of join. Conceptually, PROC SQL follows these steps to process a join:

- builds a Cartesian product of rows from the indicated tables

- evaluates each row in the Cartesian product, based on the join conditions specified in the WHERE clause (along with any other subsetting conditions), and removes any rows that do not meet the specified conditions

- if summary functions are specified, summarizes the applicable rows

- returns the rows that are to be displayed in output.

Note: The PROC SQL query optimizer follows a more complex process than the conceptual approach described here, by breaking the Cartesian product into smaller pieces. For each query, the optimizer selects the most efficient processing method for the specific situation.

By default, PROC SQL joins do not overlay columns with the same name. Instead, the output displays all columns that have the same name. To avoid having columns with the same name in the output from an inner or outer join, you can eliminate or rename the duplicate columns.

TIP You can also use the COALESCE function with an inner or outer join to overlay columns with the same name. The COALESCE function is discussed, along with outer joins, later in this chapter.

Eliminating Duplicate Columns

Consider the sample PROC SQL query that uses an inner join to combine the tables One and Two:

```
proc sql;
    select *
       from one, two
       where one.x = two.x;
```

One

X	A
1	a
2	b
4	d

Two

X	B
2	x
3	y
5	v

X	A	X	B
2	b	2	x

The two tables have a column with an identical name (X). Because the SELECT clause in the query shown above contains an asterisk, the output displays all columns from both tables.

To eliminate a duplicate column, you can specify just one of the duplicate columns in the SELECT statement. The SELECT statement in the preceding PROC SQL query can be modified as follows:

```
proc sql;
   select one.x, a, b
      from one, two
      where one.x = two.x
```

Here, the SELECT clause specifies that only the column X from table One is included in output. The output, which now displays only one column X, is shown below.

Note: In an inner equijoin, like the one shown here, it does not matter which of the same-named columns is listed in the SELECT statement. The SELECT statement in this example could have specified Two.X instead of One.X.

Another way to eliminate the duplicate X column in the preceding example is shown below:

```
proc sql;
   select one.*, b
      from one, two
      where one.x = two.x;
```

By using the asterisk (*) to select all columns from table One, and only B from table Two, this query generates the same output as the preceding version.

Renaming a Column By Using a Column Alias

If you are working with several tables that have a column with a common name but slightly different data, you might want both columns to appear in output. To avoid the confusion of displaying two different columns with the same name, you can rename one of the duplicate columns by specifying a column alias in the SELECT statement. For example, you could modify the SELECT statement of the sample query as follows:

```
proc sql;
   select one.x as ID, two.x, a, b
      from one, two
      where one.x = two.x;
```

The output of the modified query is shown here.

Now that the column One.X has been renamed to ID, the output clearly indicates that ID and X are two different columns.

Joining Tables That Have Rows with Matching Values

Consider what happens when you join two tables in which multiple rows have duplicate values of the column on which the tables are being joined. Each of the tables Three and Four has multiple rows that contain the value 2 for column X. The following PROC SQL inner join matches rows from the two tables based on the common column X:

```
proc sql;
    select *
        from three, four
        where three.x=four.x;
```

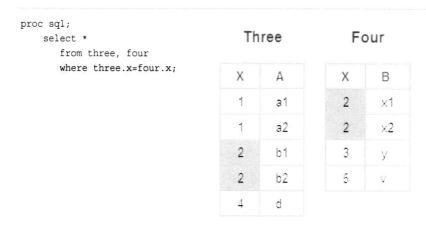

The output shows how this inner join handles the duplicate values of X.

X	A	X	B
2	b1	2	x1
2	b1	2	x2
2	b2	2	x1
2	b2	2	x2

All possible combinations of the duplicate rows are displayed. There are no matches on any other values of X, so no other rows are displayed in output.

Note: A DATA step match-merge would output only two rows, because it processes data sequentially from top to bottom. Later in this chapter, there is a comparison of PROC SQL joins and DATA step match-merges.

Specifying a Table Alias

To enable PROC SQL to distinguish between same-named columns from different tables, you use qualified column names. To create a qualified column name, you prefix the column name with its table name. For example, the following PROC SQL inner join contains several qualified column names (shown highlighted):

```
proc sql;
title 'Employee Names and Job Codes';
    select staffmaster.empid, lastname, firstname, jobcode
        from sasuser.staffmaster, sasuser.payrollmaster
        where staffmaster.empid=payrollmaster.empid;
```

It can be difficult to read PROC SQL code that contains lengthy qualified column names. In addition, entering long table names can be time-consuming. Fortunately, you can use a temporary, alternate name for any or all tables in any PROC SQL query. This temporary name, which is called a table alias, is specified after the table name in the FROM clause. The keyword AS is often used, although its use is optional.

The following modified PROC SQL query specifies table aliases in the FROM clause, and then uses the table aliases to qualify column names in the SELECT and WHERE clauses:

```
proc sql;
title 'Employee Names and Job Codes';
   select s.empid, lastname, firstname, jobcode
      from sasuser.staffmaster as s,
            sasuser.payrollmaster as p
      where s.empid=p.empid;
```

In this query, the optional keyword AS is used to define the table aliases in the FROM clause. The FROM clause would be equally valid with AS omitted, as shown below:

```
from sasuser.staffmaster s,
      sasuser.payrollmaster p
```

Note: While using table aliases help you work more efficiently, the use of table aliases does not cause SAS to execute the query more quickly.

Table aliases are usually optional. However, there are two situations that require their use, as shown below.

Table aliases are required when...	Example
a table is joined to itself (called a self-join or reflexive join)	`from airline.staffmaster as s1,` `            airline.staffmaster as s2`

you need to reference columns from same-named tables in different libraries	`from airline.flightdelays as af,`
	`            work.flightdelays as wf`
	`where af.delay > wf.delay`

So far, you have seen relatively simple examples of inner joins. However, as in any other PROC SQL query, inner joins can include more advanced components, such as

- titles and footers
- functions and expressions in the SELECT clause
- multiple conditions in the WHERE clause
- an ORDER BY clause for sorting
- summary functions with grouping.

Here are a few examples of more complex inner joins.

Example: Complex PROC SQL Inner Join

Suppose you want to display the names (first initial and last name), job codes, and ages of all company employees who live in New York. You also want the results to be sorted by job code and age.

The data that you need is stored in the two tables listed below.

Table	Relevant Columns
Sasuser.Staffmaster	EmpID, LastName, FirstName, State

Table	Relevant Columns
Sasuser.Payrollmaster	EmpID, JobCode, DateOfBirth

Of the three columns that you want to display, JobCode is the only column that already exists in the tables. The other two columns need to be created from existing columns.

The PROC SQL query shown here uses an inner join to generate the output that you want:

```
proc sql outobs=15;
title 'New York Employees';
   select substr(firstname,1,1) || '. ' || lastname
          as Name,
          jobcode,
          int((today() - dateofbirth)/365.25)
          as Age
      from sasuser.payrollmaster as p,
           sasuser.staffmaster as s
      where p.empid =
            s.empid
            and state='NY'
      order by 2, 3;
```

New York Employees

Name	JobCode	Age
R. LONG	BCK	41
T. BURNETTE	BCK	45
J. MARKS	BCK	46
N. JONES	BCK	46
R. VANDEUSEN	BCK	52
J. PEARSON	BCK	53
L. GORDON	BCK	53
C. PEARCE	FA1	40
D. WOOD	FA1	41
C. RICHARDS	FA1	43
L. JONES	FA1	45
R. MCDANIEL	FA1	45
A. PARKER	FA1	48
D. FIELDS	FA1	54
R. PATTERSON	FA2	43

The SELECT clause, shown below, specifies the new column Name, the existing column JobCode, and the new column Age:

```
select substr(firstname,1,1) || '. ' || lastname
       as Name,
       jobcode,
       int((today() - dateofbirth)/365.25)
       as Age
```

To create the two new columns, the SELECT clause uses functions and expressions as follows:

- To create Name, the SUBSTR function extracts the first initial from FirstName. Then the concatenation operator combines the first initial with a period, a space, and then the contents of the LastName column. Finally, the keyword AS names the new column.

- To calculate Age, the INT function returns the integer portion of the result of the calculation. In the expression that is used as an argument of the INT function, the employee's birthdate (DateOfBirth) is subtracted from today's date (returned by the TODAY function), and the difference is divided by the number of days in a year (365.25).

The WHERE clause contains two expressions linked by the logical operator AND:

```
where p.empid =
      s.empid
      and state='NY'
```

This query only outputs rows that have matching values of EmpID and rows in which the value of State is **NY**. You do not need to prefix the column name State with a table name, because State occurs in only one of the tables.

Example: PROC SQL Inner Join with Summary Functions

You can also summarize and group data in a PROC SQL join. To illustrate, modify the previous PROC SQL inner join so that the output displays the following summarized columns for New York employees in each job code: number of employees and average age. The modified query is shown below:

```
proc sql outobs=15;
title 'Avg Age of New York Employees';
   select jobcode,
          count(p.empid) as Employees,
          avg(int((today() - dateofbirth)/365.25))
          format=4.1 as AvgAge
      from sasuser.payrollmaster as p,
           sasuser.staffmaster as s
      where p.empid =
            s.empid
            and state='NY'
      group by jobcode
      order by jobcode;
```

To create two new columns, the SELECT clause uses summary functions as follows:

- To create Employees, the COUNT function is used with p.EmpID (Payrollmaster.EmpID) as its argument.

- To create AvgAge, the AVG function is used with an expression as its argument. As described in the previous example, the expression uses the INT function to calculate each employee's age.

The output of this modified query is shown below.

Avg Age of New York Employees		
JobCode	Employees	AvgAge
BCK	7	48.0
FA1	7	46.1
FA2	9	48.7
FA3	4	50.8
ME1	5	44.0
ME2	9	52.1
ME3	2	52.0
NA1	1	42.0
NA2	1	52.0
PT1	5	43.8
PT2	5	58.0
PT3	2	66.0
SCP	6	48.5
TA1	5	47.6
TA2	12	47.1

Using Outer Joins

Introducing Types of Outer Joins

An outer join combines and displays all rows that match across tables, based on the specified matching criteria (also known as join conditions), plus some or all of the rows that do not match. You can think of an outer join as an augmentation of an inner join: an outer join returns all rows generated by an inner join, plus additional (nonmatching) rows.

Type of Outer Join	Output
Left	All matching rows plus nonmatching rows from the first table specified in the FROM clause (the left table)
Right	All matching rows plus nonmatching rows from the second table specified in the FROM clause (the right table)
Full	All matching rows plus nonmatching rows in both tables

The syntax of an outer join is shown below.

General form, SELECT statement for outer join:

SELECT *column-1<,...column-n>*

> **FROM** *table-1 | view-1*

>> **LEFT JOIN | RIGHT JOIN | FULL JOIN**

>> *table-2 | view-2*

>> **ON** *join-condition(s)*

> *<other clauses>*;

Here is an explanation of the syntax:

LEFT JOIN, RIGHT JOIN, FULL JOIN
   are keywords that specify the type of outer join.

ON
   specifies *join-condition(s)*, which are expression(s) that specify the column or columns on which the tables are to be joined.

<other clauses>
   refers to optional PROC SQL clauses.

Note: To further subset the rows in the query output, you can follow the ON clause with a WHERE clause. The WHERE clause subsets the individual detail rows before the outer join is performed. The ON clause then specifies how the remaining rows are to be selected for output.

Note: You can perform an outer join on only two tables or views at a time. Views are covered later in this chapter.

Consider how each type of outer join works.

Using a Left Outer Join

A left outer join retrieves all rows that match across tables, based on the specified matching criteria (join conditions), plus nonmatching rows from the left table (the first table specified in the FROM clause).

Suppose you are using the following PROC SQL left join to combine the two tables One and Two. The join condition is stated in the expression following the ON keyword. The two tables and the three rows of output are shown below:

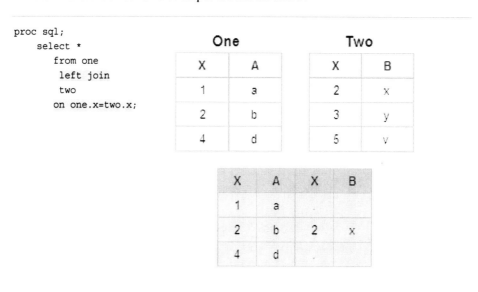

```
proc sql;
    select *
        from one
            left join
        two
        on one.x=two.x;
```

In each row of output, the first two columns correspond to table One (the left table) and the last two columns correspond to table Two (the right table).

Because this is a left join, all rows (both matching and nonmatching) from table One (the left table) are included in the output (the first two columns). Rows from table Two (the right table) are displayed in the output (the last two columns) only if they match a row from table One.

In this example, the second row of output is the only row in which the row from table One matched a row from table Two, based on the matching criteria (join conditions) specified in the ON clause. In the first and third rows of output, the row from table One had no matching row in table Two.

Note: In all three types of outer joins (left, right, and full), the columns in the result (combined) row that are from the unmatched row are set to missing values.

To eliminate one of the duplicate columns (in this case, X) in any outer join, as shown earlier with an inner join, you can modify the SELECT clause to list the specific columns that is displayed. Here, the SELECT clause from the preceding query has been modified to remove the duplicate X column:

```
proc sql;
    select one.x, a, b
        from one
        left join
        two
        on one.x=two.x;
```

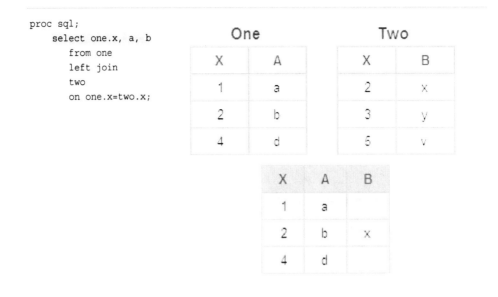

Using a Right Outer Join

A right outer join retrieves all rows that match across tables, based on the specified matching criteria (join conditions), plus nonmatching rows from the right table (the second table specified in the FROM clause).

Consider what happens when you use a right join to combine the two tables used in the previous example. The following PROC SQL query uses a right join to combine rows from One and Two, based on the join conditions specified in the ON clause:

```
proc sql;
    select *
        from one
        right join
        two
        on one.x=two.x;
```

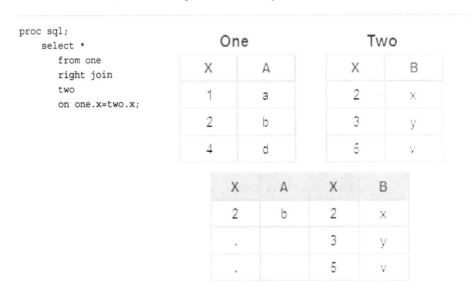

In each row of output, the first two columns correspond to table One (the left table) and the last two columns correspond to table Two (the right table).

Because this is a right join, all rows (both matching and nonmatching) from table Two (the right table) are included in the output (the last two columns). Rows from table One (the left table) are displayed in the output (the first two columns) only if they match a row from table Two.

In this example, there is only one row in table One that matches a value of X in table Two, and these two matching rows combine to form the first row of output. In the remaining rows of output, there is no match and the columns corresponding to table One are set to missing values.

Using a Full Outer Join

A full outer join retrieves both matching rows and nonmatching rows from both tables.

Combine the same two tables again, this time using a full join. The PROC SQL query, the tables, and the output are shown below:

```
proc sql;
    select *
        from one
        full join
        two
        on one.x=two.x;
```

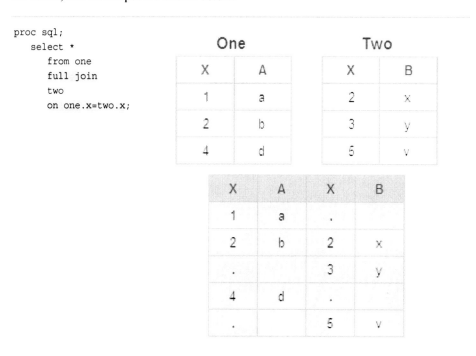

Because this is a full join, all rows (both matching and nonmatching) from both tables are included in the output. There is only one match between table One and table Two, so only one row of output displays values in all columns. All remaining rows of output contain only values from table One or table Two. The remaining columns are set to missing values.

Example: Outer Join

Now that you have seen how the three types of outer joins work, consider a realistic situation requiring the use of an outer join.

Suppose you want to list all of an airline's flights that were scheduled for March, along with corresponding delay information (if it exists). Each flight is identified by both a flight date and a flight number. Your output should display the following data: flight date, flight number, destination, and length of delay in minutes.

The data that you need is stored in the two tables shown below. The applicable columns from each table are identified.

Table	Relevant Columns
Sasuser.Marchflights	`Date, FlightNumber, Destination`
Sasuser.Flightdelays	`Date, FlightNumber, Destination, Delay`

Your output should include the columns that are listed above and all of the following rows:

- rows that have matching values of Date and FlightNumber across the two tables
- rows from Sasuser.Marchflights that have no matching row in Sasuser.Flightdelays.

To generate the output that you want, the following PROC SQL query uses a left outer join. Sasuser.Marchflights is specified as the left (first) table.

```
proc sql outobs=20;
title 'All March Flights';
   select m.date,
          m.flightnumber
                 label='Flight Number',
          m.destination
          label='Left',
          f.destination
          label='Right',
          delay
          label='Delay in Minutes'
      from sasuser.marchflights as m
          left join
          sasuser.flightdelays as f
      on m.date=f.date
         and m.flightnumber=
             f.flightnumber
      order by delay;
```

Notice the following:

- The SELECT clause eliminates the duplicate Date and FlightNumber columns by specifying their source as Sasuser.Marchflights. However, the SELECT clause list specifies the Destination columns from both tables and assigns a table alias to each to distinguish between them.
- The ON clause contains two join conditions, which match the tables on the two columns Date and FlightNumber.

The query output is shown below.

All March Flights

Date	Flight Number	Left	Right	Delay in Minutes
14MAR2000	271	CDG		
16MAR2000	622	FRA		
	132	YYZ		
22MAR2000	183	WAS		
11MAR2000	290	WAS		
27MAR2000	982	DFW		
29MAR2000	829	WAS		
11MAR2000	202	ORD		
08MAR2000	182	YYZ		
17MAR2000	182	YYZ		
03MAR2000	416	WAS		
25MAR2000	872	LAX		
09MAR2000	821	LHR	LHR	-10
25MAR2000	829	WAS	WAS	-10
02MAR2000	387	CPH	CPH	-10
10MAR2000	523	ORD	ORD	-10
07MAR2000	523	ORD	ORD	-10
18MAR2000	219	LHR	LHR	-10
14MAR2000	829	WAS	WAS	-10
27MAR2000	182	YYZ	YYZ	-9

The first 12 rows of output display rows from Sasuser.Marchflights (the left table) that have no matching rows in Sasuser.Flightdelays. Therefore, in these 12 rows, the last 2 columns are set to missing values.

Note: The same results could be generated by using a right outer join. Sasuser.Marchflights is specified as the right (second) table.

Creating an Inner Join with Outer Join-Style Syntax

If you want to use a consistent syntax for all joins, you can write an inner join using the same style of syntax that is used for an outer join.

General form, SELECT statement for inner join (alternate syntax):

SELECT *column-1<,...column-n>*

    FROM *table-1 | view-1*

        INNER JOIN

        table-2 | view-2

        ON *join-condition(s)*

    <other clauses>;

Here is an explanation of the syntax:

INNER JOIN
  is a keyword.

ON
  specifies *join-condition(s)*, which are expression(s) that specify the column or columns on which the tables are to be joined.

<other clauses>
  refers to optional PROC SQL clauses.

Note: An inner join that uses this syntax can be performed on only two tables or views at a time. When an inner join uses the syntax that was presented earlier, up to 256 tables or views can be combined at once. In-line views are covered later in this chapter.

Comparing SQL Joins and DATA Step Match-Merges

Overview

You should be familiar with the use of the DATA step to merge data sets. DATA step match-merges and PROC SQL joins can produce the same results. However, there are important differences between these two techniques. For example, a join does not require that you sort the data first; a DATA step match-merge requires that the data be sorted.

Compare the use of SQL joins and DATA step match-merges in the following situations:

- when all of the values of the selected variable (column) match

- when only some of the values of the selected variable (column) match.

When All of the Values Match

When all of the values of the BY variable match, you can use a PROC SQL inner join to produce the same results as a DATA step match-merge.

Suppose you want to combine the tables One and Two, as shown below.

One		Two	
X	A	X	B
1	a	1	x
2	b	2	y
3	c	3	z

These two tables have the column X in common, and all values of X in each row match across the two tables. Both tables are already sorted by X.

The following DATA step match-merge (followed by a PROC PRINT step) and the PROC SQL inner join produce identical reports.

DATA Step Match-Merge	PROC SQL Inner Join
``` data merged; merge one two; by x; run; proc print data=merged noobs; title 'Table Merged'; run; ```	``` proc sql; title 'Table Merged'; select one.x, a, b from one, two where one.x = two.x order by x; ```

One		Two	
X	A	X	B
1	a	1	x
2	b	2	y
3	c	3	z

X	A	B
1	a	x
2	b	y
3	c	z

Note: The DATA step match-merge creates a data set whereas the PROC SQL inner join, as shown here, creates only a report as output. To make these two programs completely identical, the PROC SQL inner join could be rewritten to create a table.

For detailed information about creating tables with PROC SQL, see Chapter 5, "Creating and Managing Tables Using PROC SQL," on page 167.

Note: If the order of rows in the output does not matter, the ORDER BY clause can be removed from the PROC SQL join. Without the ORDER BY clause, this join is more efficient, because PROC SQL does not need to make a second pass through the data.

When Only Some of the Values Match

When only some of the values of the BY variable match, you can use a PROC SQL full outer join to produce the same result as a DATA step match-merge. Unlike the DATA step match-merge, however, a PROC SQL outer join does not overlay the two common columns by default. To overlay common columns, you must use the COALESCE function in the PROC SQL full outer join.

Note: The COALESCE function can also be used with inner join operators.

Consider what happens when you use a PROC SQL full outer join without the COALESCE function. Suppose you want to combine the tables Three and Four. These two tables have the column X in common, but most of the values of X do not match across tables. Both tables are already sorted by X. The following DATA step match-merge (followed by a PROC PRINT step) and the PROC SQL outer join combine these tables, but do not generate the same output. The COALESCE function can also be used with inner join operators.

DATA Step Match-Merge	PROC SQL Full Outer Join
| ```
data merged;
   merge three four;
   by x;
run;

proc print data=merged noobs;
   title 'Table Merged';
run;
``` | ```
proc sql;
title 'Table Merged';
   select three.x, a, b
         from three
         full join
         four
         on three.x = four.x
         order by x;
``` |

Three

X	A
1	a
2	b
4	d

Four

X	B
2	x
3	y
5	v

DATA Step Match-Merge
Output

Table Merged

X	A	B
1	a	
2	b	x
3		y
4	d	
5		v

PROC SQL Full Outer Join
Output

Table Merged

X	A	B
.		y
.		v
1	a	
2	b	x
4	d	

The DATA step match-merge automatically overlays the common column, X. The PROC SQL outer join selects the value of X from just one of the tables, table Three, so that no X values from table Four are included in the PROC SQL output. However, the PROC SQL outer join cannot overlay the columns by default. The values that vary across the two merged tables are in bold above.

Consider how the COALESCE function is used in the PROC SQL outer join to overlay the common columns.

When Only Some of the Values Match: Using the COALESCE Function

When you add the COALESCE function to the SELECT clause of the PROC SQL outer join, the PROC SQL outer join can produce the same result as a DATA step match-merge.

General form, COALESCE function in a basic SELECT clause:

SELECT COALESCE *(column-1<,...column-n>)*

Here is an explanation of the syntax:

column-1 through *column-n*
    are the names of two or more columns to be overlaid. The COALESCE function requires that all arguments have the same data type.

The COALESCE function overlays the specified columns by

- checking the value of each column in the order in which the columns are listed

- returning the first value that is a SAS nonmissing value.

Note: If all returned values are missing, COALESCE returns a missing value.

When the COALESCE function is added to the preceding PROC SQL full outer join, the DATA step match-merge (with PROC PRINT step) and the PROC SQL full outer join will combine rows in the same way. The two programs, the tables, and the output are shown below.

DATA Step Match-Merge	PROC SQL Full Outer Join

```
data merged;
   merge three four;
   by x;
run;
proc print data=merged noobs;
   title 'Table Merged';
run;
```

```
proc sql;
 title 'Table Merged';
    select coalesce(three.x, four.x)
      as X, a, b
      from three
      full join
      four
      on three.x = four.x;
```

Three

X	A
1	a
2	b
4	d

Four

X	B
2	x
3	y
5	v

Table Merged

X	A	B
1	a	
2	b	x
3		y
4	d	
5		v

Understanding the Advantages of PROC SQL Joins

DATA step match-merges and PROC SQL joins both have advantages and disadvantages. Here are some of the main advantages of PROC SQL joins.

Advantage	Example
| PROC SQL joins do not require sorted or indexed tables. | ```
proc sql;
    select table1.x, a, b
        from table1
            full join
            table2
            on table1.x = table2.x;
```<br><br>where table-1 is sorted by column X and table-2 is not |
| PROC SQL joins do not require that the columns in join expressions have the same name. | ```
proc sql;
    select table1.x, lastname,
            status
        from table1, table2
        where table1.id =
                table2.custnum;
``` |
| PROC SQL joins can use comparison operators other than the equal sign (=). | ```
proc sql;
    select a.itemnumber, cost,
            price
        from table1 as a,
            table2 as b
        where a.itemnumber = b.itemnumber
                and a.cost>b.price;
``` |

Note: Join performance can be substantially improved when the tables are indexed on the column(s) on which the tables are being joined. You can learn more about indexing in Chapter 6, "Creating and Managing Indexes Using PROC SQL," on page 226.

Using In-Line Views

Introducing In-Line Views

Sometimes, you might want to specify an in-line view rather than a table as the source of data for a PROC SQL query. An in-line view is a nested query that is specified in the outer query's FROM clause. (You should already be familiar with a subquery, which is a nested query that is specified in a WHERE clause.) An in-line view selects data from one or more tables in order to produce a temporary (or virtual) table that the outer query then uses to select data for output.

For example, the following FROM clause specifies an in-line view:

```
from (select flightnumber, date,
            boarded/passengercapacity*100
            as pctfull
            format=4.1 label='Percent Full'
        from sasuser.marchflights)
```

This in-line view selects two existing columns (FlightNumber and Date) and defines the new column PctFull based on the table Sasuser.Marchflights.
```

Unlike a table, an in-line view exists only during query execution. Because it is temporary, an in-line view can be referenced only in the query in which it is defined. In addition, an in-line view can be assigned an alias but it cannot be assigned a permanent name.

Note: In a FROM clause, you can also specify a PROC SQL view, which is a query that has been created (using the CREATE statement) and stored. You can learn more about creating PROC SQL views in Chapter 7, "Creating and Managing Views Using PROC SQL," on page 248.

Note: Unlike other queries, an in-line view cannot contain an ORDER BY clause.

There are two potential advantages to using an in-line view instead of a table in a PROC SQL query:

- The complexity of the code is usually reduced, so that the code is easier to write, and understand.

- In some cases, PROC SQL might be able to process the code more efficiently.

Referencing an In-Line View with Other Views or Tables

The preceding FROM clause is from a simple PROC SQL query that references just one data source: the in-line view. However, a PROC SQL query can join multiple tables and in-line views. For example, the FROM clause shown below specifies both a table (Sasuser.Flightschedule) and an in-line view.

```
from sasuser.flightschedule,
     (select flightnumber, date,
             boarded/passengercapacity*100
             as pctfull
             format=4.1 label='Percent Full'
       from sasuser.marchflights)
```

Referencing Multiple Tables in an In-Line View

You can specify more than one table in the FROM clause of an in-line view, as shown in the following example:

```
from (select marchflights.flightnumber,
             marchflights.date,
             boarded/passengercapacity*100
             as pctfull
             format=4.1 label='Percent Full',
             delay
       from sasuser.marchflights,
            sasuser.flightdelays
       where marchflights.flightnumber=
             flightdelays.flightnumber
             and marchflights.date=
             flightdelays.date)
```

In other words, you can base an in-line view on a join.

Note: Remember that each table that is referenced in an in-line view counts toward the 256-table limit for an inner join.

Assigning an Alias to an In-Line View

You can assign an alias to an in-line view just as you can to a table. In the following example, the alias **f** has been added in the first FROM clause to reference the table Sasuser.Flightschedule and the alias **m** is associated with the results from the in-line view. After the main FROM clause, a WHERE clause that uses both of the aliases has been added.

```
from sasuser.flightschedule as f,
     (select flightnumber, date
             boarded/passengercapacity*100
             as pctfull
             format=4.1 label='Percent Full'
         from sasuser.marchflights) as m
where m.flightnumber=f.flightnumber
      and m.date=f.date
```

Example: Query That Contains an In-Line View

Suppose you want to identify the air travel destinations that experienced the worst delays in March. You would like your output to show all of the following data:

- destination

- average delay

- maximum delay

- probability of delay.

Your PROC SQL query uses an in-line view to calculate all of the new columns except for the last one:

```
proc sql;
title "Flight Destinations and Delays";
   select destination,
          average format=3.0 label='Average Delay',
          max format=3.0 label='Maximum Delay',
          late/(late+early) as prob format=5.2
          label='Probability of Delay'
      from (select destination,
                   avg(delay) as average,
                   max(delay) as max,
                   sum(delay > 0) as late,
                   sum(delay <= 0) as early
               from sasuser.flightdelays
               group by destination)
      order by average;
```

Consider each clause of the outer query, starting with the FROM clause, because PROC SQL evaluates the FROM clause before the SELECT clause.

The FROM clause specifies an in-line view rather than a table. The in-line view (nested query) specifies the following columns that are in the table Sasuser.Flightdelays or are based on a column in that table:

- the existing column Destination

- the new column Average

- the new column Max

- the new column Late

- the new column Early.

The columns Average, Max, Late, and Early are all calculated by using summary functions.

In the calculation for the columns Late and Early, a Boolean expression is used as the argument for the summary function. A Boolean function resolves either to 1 (true) or 0 (false). For example, Late is calculated by taking the sum of the Boolean expression `delay > 0`. For every value of Delay that is greater than 0, the Boolean expression resolves to 1; values that are equal to or less than 0 resolve to 0. The SUM function adds all values of Delay to indicate the number of delays that occurred for each destination.

The in-line view concludes with the clause `group by destination`, specifying that the in-line view data should be grouped, and summarized by the values of Destination.

If you submitted this in-line view (nested query) as a separate query, it would generate the following output.

Destination	average	max	late	early
CDG	9.192308	39	21	5
CPH	5.740741	26	16	11
DFW	2.721311	20	38	23
FRA	5.961538	34	14	12
LAX	4.666667	27	82	41
LHR	5.551724	30	39	19
ORD	3.032609	19	51	41
WAS	0.635762	15	76	75
YYZ	2.016667	14	36	24

Consider the outer query's SELECT and ORDER BY clauses:

```
proc sql;
title "Flight Destinations and Delays";
   select destination,
          average format=3.0 label='Average Delay',
          max format=3.0 label='Maximum Delay',
          late/(late+early) as prob format=5.2
          label='Probability of Delay'
      from (select destination,
                   avg(delay) as average,
                   max(delay) as max,
                   sum(delay > 0) as late,
                   sum(delay <= 0) as early
                   from sasuser.flightdelays
                   group by destination)
      order by average;
```

The outer query's SELECT clause specifies columns as follows:

- Destination is an existing column in the table.

- Average and Max are calculated in the in-line view, and are assigned labels and formats in this SELECT clause.

- Prob (with the label "Probability of Delay") is calculated in this SELECT clause by using two columns that were calculated in the in-line view: Late and Early. The outer query's SELECT clause can refer to the calculated columns Late and Early without using the keyword CALCULATED because PROC SQL evaluates the in-line view (the outer query's FROM clause) first.

The outer query's last clause is an ORDER BY clause. The output is sorted by the values of Average.

This PROC SQL query generates the following output.

Flight Destinations and Delays			
Destination	Average Delay	Maximum Delay	Probability of Delay
WAS	1	15	0.50
YYZ	2	14	0.60
DFW	3	20	0.62
ORD	3	19	0.55
LAX	5	27	0.67
LHR	6	30	0.67
CPH	6	26	0.59
FRA	6	34	0.54
CDG	9	39	0.81

Later in this chapter, a PROC SQL query that combines multiple tables and uses an in-line view is explained.

Joining Multiple Tables and Views

So far, this chapter has presented PROC SQL queries that combine only two tables horizontally. However, there might be situations in which you have to create complex queries to combine more than two tables. Here is an example of a complex query that combines four different tables.

Example: Complex Query That Combines Four Tables

Suppose you want to list the names of supervisors for the crew on the flight to Copenhagen on March 4, 2000. To solve this problem, you need to use the following four tables.

Table	Relevant Columns
Sasuser.Flightschedule identifies the crew who flew to Copenhagen on March 4, 2000	EmpID, Date, Destination
Sasuser.Staffmaster identifies the names and states of residence for the employees	EmpID, FirstName, LastName, State
Sasuser.Payrollmaster identifies the job categories for the employees	EmpID, JobCode
Sasuser.Supervisors identifies the employees who are supervisors	EmpID, State, JobCategory

Note: Supervisors live in the same state as the employees that they supervise. There is one supervisor for each state and job category.

This problem can be handled in a number of different ways. Examine and compare three different techniques:

- Technique 1: using PROC SQL subqueries, joins, and in-line views

- Technique 2: using a multi-way join that combines four different tables and a reflexive join (joining a table with itself)

- Technique 3: using traditional SAS programming (a series of PROC SORT and DATA steps, followed by a PROC PRINT step)

Example: Technique 1 (PROC SQL Subqueries, Joins, and In-Line Views)

Overview

Task	List the names of supervisors for the crew on the flight to Copenhagen on March 4, 2000.
Data	Sasuser.Flightschedule (EmpID, Date, Destination)
	Sasuser.Staffmaster (EmpID, FirstName, LastName, State)
	Sasuser.Payrollmaster (EmpID, JobCode)
	Sasuser.Supervisors (EmpID, State, JobCategory)

Note: Supervisors live in the same state as the employees that they supervise. There is one supervisor for each state and job category.

Completing the stated task requires a complex query that includes several subqueries, joins, and an in-line view. To make the task more manageable, build the complex query piece-by-piece in four steps:

1. Identify the crew for the Copenhagen flight.

2. Find the states and job categories of the crew members that were returned by the first query.

3. Find the employee numbers of the crew supervisors, based on the states and job categories that were returned by the second query.

4. Find the names of the supervisors, based on the employee numbers that were returned by the third query.

Note that at each of the four steps, a new piece of the final query is added. The final query is included in the four separate pieces.

Query 1: Identify the Crew for the Copenhagen (CPH) Flight

This query lists the employee ID numbers of all six crew members on the Copenhagen flight:

```
proc sql;
   select empid
      from sasuser.flightschedule
      where date='04mar2000'd
            and destination='CPH';
```

EmpID
1556
1830
1124
1135
1437
1839

Query 2: Find the States and Job Categories of the Crew Members

Query 1 becomes a subquery and returns the employee ID numbers of the six Copenhagen crew members to the outer query, Query 2. (Query 2 is shaded.) Query 2 uses an inner join to combine two tables. Query 2 selects the job category (by using the SUBSTR function to extract the job category from JobCode) and state for each of the six crew members.

```
proc sql;
   select substr(JobCode,1,2) as JobCategory,
          state
      from sasuser.staffmaster as s,
           sasuser.payrollmaster as p
      where s.empid=p.empid and s.empid in
         (select empid
             from sasuser.flightschedule
             where date='04mar2000'd
                   and destination='CPH');
```

JobCategory	State
FA	CT
FA	NY
NA	NY
PT	NY
PT	CT
FA	NY

Query 3: Find the Employee Numbers of the Crew Supervisors

Query 2 becomes an in-line view within Query 3, and the alias c has been assigned to the in-line view. Query 2 returns to Query 3 the job category and state for each crew member. Query 3 selects the employee ID numbers for supervisors whose job category and state match the job category and state of a crew member.

Note: Sasuser.Supervisors specifies the label Supervisor ID for the EmpID column, and this label appears in the output.

	Supervisor Id
	1431
	1983
	1352
	1118
	1106
	1983

```
proc sql;
   select empid
      from sasuser.supervisors as m,
         (select substr(jobcode,1,2) as JobCategory,
               state
            from sasuser.staffmaster as s,
               sasuser.payrollmaster as p
            where s.empid=p.empid and s.empid in
               (select empid
                  from sasuser.flightschedule
                  where date='04mar2000'd
                     and destination='CPH')) as c
      where m.jobcategory=c.jobcategory
         and m.state=c.state;
```

Note that two rows contain the same value of EmpID: 1983. This duplication indicates that two different crew members have the same manager. In all, there are five supervisors for the six crew members of the Copenhagen flight.

Query 4: Find the Names of the Supervisors

Query 3 becomes a subquery within Query 4. Query 3 returns to Query 4 the employee numbers (supervisor IDs) for the supervisors of the Copenhagen crew. Query 4 selects the names of the supervisors.

FirstName	LastName
SHARON	DEAN
ROGER	DENNIS
JASPER	MARSHBURN
SIMON	RIVERS
DEBORAH	YOUNG

```
proc sql;
   select firstname, lastname
      from sasuser.staffmaster
      where empid in
         (select empid
            from sasuser.supervisors as m,
               (select substr(jobcode,1,2)
                     as JobCategory,
                     state
                  from sasuser.staffmaster as s,
                     sasuser.payrollmaster as p
                  where s.empid=p.empid
                     and s.empid in
                     (select empid
                        from sasuser.flightschedule
                        where date='04mar2000'd
                           and destination='CPH'))
                        as c
            where m.jobcategory=c.jobcategory
               and m.state=c.state);
```

Note that the output has five rows, one for each supervisor. The duplicate name of a supervisor has been eliminated.

Technique 1 produces a PROC SQL query that includes

* four SELECT statements

- four tables, each read separately.

This program is not optimized and, in addition, includes complex code that is likely to take a long time to write.

Example: Technique 2 (PROC SQL Multi-way Join with Reflexive Join)

Task	List the names of supervisors for the crew on the flight to Copenhagen on March 4, 2000.
Data	Sasuser.Flightschedule (EmpID, Date, Destination)
	Sasuser.Staffmaster (EmpID, FirstName, LastName, State)
	Sasuser.Payrollmaster (EmpID, JobCode)
	Sasuser.Supervisors (EmpID, State, JobCategory)

Note: Supervisors live in the same state as the employees that they supervise. There is one supervisor for each state and job category.

You can also solve this problem by using a multi-way join with a reflexive join (joining a table to itself). The code is shown below:

```
proc sql;
    select distinct e.firstname, e.lastname
        from sasuser.flightschedule as a,
             sasuser.staffmaster as b,
             sasuser.payrollmaster as c,
             sasuser.supervisors as d,
             sasuser.staffmaster as e
        where a.date='04mar2000'd and
              a.destination='CPH' and
              a.empid=b.empid and
              a.empid=c.empid and
              d.jobcategory=substr(c.jobcode,1,2)
              and d.state=b.state
              and d.empid=e.empid;
```

FirstName	LastName
DEBORAH	YOUNG
JASPER	MARSHBURN
ROGER	DENNIS
SHARON	DEAN
SIMON	RIVERS

Technique 2, which uses a multi-way join, provides a more efficient solution to the problem than Technique 1. In a multi-way join, PROC SQL joins two tables at a time and performs the joins in the most efficient order (the order minimizes the size of the Cartesian product). This multi-way join code is more difficult to build step-by-step than the code in Technique 1.

Note that Sasuser.Staffmaster is read two separate times in this query: this is the reflexive join. As you can see in the FROM clause, Sasuser.Staffmaster is assigned a different table alias each time it is read: first **b**, then **e**. The table is read the first time (alias **b**) to look up the states of the Copenhagen crew members, the second time (alias **e**) to look up the names of the supervisors.

Example: Technique 3 (Traditional SAS Programming)

Task	List the names of supervisors for the crew on the flight to Copenhagen on March 4, 2000.
Data	Sasuser.Flightschedule (EmpID, Date, Destination)
	Sasuser.Staffmaster (EmpID, FirstName, LastName, State)
	Sasuser.Payrollmaster (EmpID, JobCode)
	Sasuser.Supervisors (EmpID, State, JobCategory)

Note: Supervisors live in the same state as the employees that they supervise. There is one supervisor for each state and job category.

For comparison, look at the traditional SAS programming that can be used to solve this problem. The code is shown below, followed by the output.

```
/* Find the crew for the flight. */

proc sort data=sasuser.flightschedule (drop=flightnumber)
        out=crew (keep=empid);
   where destination='CPH' and date='04MAR2000'd;
   by empid;
run;


/* Find the State and job code for the crew. */

proc sort data=sasuser.payrollmaster
              (keep=empid jobcode)
        out=payroll;
   by empid;
run;

proc sort data=sasuser.staffmaster
              (keep=empid state firstname lastname)
        out=staff;
   by empid;
run;

data st_cat (keep=state jobcategory);
   merge crew (in=c)
         staff
         payroll;
   by empid;
   if c;
   jobcategory=substr(jobcode,1,2);
run;


/* Find the supervisor IDs. */

proc sort
    data=st_cat;
        by jobcategory state;
run;
```

```
proc sort data=sasuser.supervisors
          out=superv;
   by jobcategory state;
run;

data super (keep=empid);
   merge st_cat(in=s)
         superv;
   by jobcategory state;
   if s;
run;

/* Find the names of the supervisors. */

proc sort data=super;
   by empid;
run;

data names(drop=empid);
   merge super (in=super)
         staff (keep=empid firstname lastname);
   by empid;
   if super;
run;

proc print data=names noobs uniform;
run;
```

LastName	FirstName
MARSHBURN	JASPER
DENNIS	ROGER
RIVERS	SIMON
YOUNG	DEBORAH
DEAN	SHARON
DEAN	SHARON

This output is not identical to the output of the PROC SQL approaches (Techniques 1 and 2). The SQL queries eliminated the duplicate names that are seen here. When you use Technique 3, you can eliminate duplicates by adding the NODUPKEY option to the last PROC SORT statement, as shown below:

```
proc sort data=super nodupkey;
```

Based on a mainframe benchmark in batch mode, the SQL queries use less CPU time, but more I/O operations, than this non-SQL program.

Summary

Text Summary

Understanding Joins

A PROC SQL join is a query that combines tables horizontally (side by side) by combining rows. The two main types of joins are inner joins and outer joins.

Generating a Cartesian Product

When you specify multiple tables in the FROM clause but do not include a WHERE statement to subset data, PROC SQL returns the Cartesian product of the tables. In a Cartesian product, each row in the first table is combined with every row in the second table. In all types of joins, PROC SQL generates a Cartesian product first, and then eliminates rows that do not meet any subsetting criteria that you have specified.

Using Inner Joins

An inner join combines and displays the rows from the first table that match rows from the second table, based on the matching criteria (also known as join conditions) that are specified in the WHERE clause. When the tables that are being joined contain a column with a common name, you might want to eliminate the duplicate column from results or specify a column alias to rename one of the duplicate columns. To refer to tables in an inner join, or in any PROC SQL step, you can specify a temporary name called a table alias.

Using Outer Joins

An outer join combines and displays all rows that match across tables, based on the specified matching criteria (also known as join conditions), plus some or all of the rows that do not match. There are three types of outer joins:

- A left outer join retrieves all rows that match across tables, based on the specified matching criteria (join conditions), plus nonmatching rows from the left table (the first table specified in the FROM clause).

- A right outer join retrieves all rows that match across tables, based on the specified matching criteria (join conditions), plus nonmatching rows from the right table (the second table specified in the FROM clause).

- A full outer join retrieves both matching rows and nonmatching rows from both tables.

Creating an Inner Join with Outer Join-Style Syntax

If you want to use a consistent syntax for all joins, you can write an inner join using the same style of syntax as used for an outer join.

Comparing SQL Joins and DATA Step Match-Merges

DATA step match-merges and PROC SQL joins can produce the same results, although there are important differences between these two techniques.

- When all the values of the BY variable (column) match and there are no duplicate BY variables, you can use a PROC SQL inner join.

- When only some of the values of the BY variable match, you can use a PROC SQL full outer join. To overlay common columns, you must use the COALESCE function with the PROC SQL join.

Using In-Line Views

An in-line view is a subquery that appears in a FROM clause. An in-line view selects data from one or more tables to produce a temporary (or virtual) table that the outer query uses to select data for output. You can reference an in-line view with other views or tables, reference multiple tables in an in-line view, and assign an alias to an in-line view.

Joining Multiple Tables and Views

When you perform a complex query that combines more than two tables or views, you might need to choose between several techniques.

Sample Programs

Combining Tables By Using an Inner Join

```
proc sql outobs=15;
title 'New York Employees';
   select substr(firstname,1,1) || '. ' || lastname
          as Name,
          jobcode,
          int((today() - dateofbirth)/365.25)
          as Age
       from sasuser.payrollmaster as p,
            sasuser.staffmaster as s
       where p.empid =
             s.empid
             and state='NY'
       order by 2, 3;
quit;
```

Combining Tables By Using a Left Outer Join

```
proc sql outobs=20;
title 'All March Flights';
   select m.date,
          m.flightnumber
             label='Flight Number',
          m.destination
          label='Left',
          f.destination
          label='Right',
          delay
          label='Delay in Minutes'
       from sasuser.marchflights as m
            left join
            sasuser.flightdelays as f
       on m.date=f.date
          and m.flightnumber=
                f.flightnumber
       order by delay;
   quit;
```

Overlaying Common Columns in a Full Outer Join

```
proc sql;
   select coalesce(p.empid, s.empid)
          as ID, firstname, lastname, gender
      from sasuser.payrollmaster as p
               full join
          sasuser.staffmaster as s
      on p.empid = s.empid
      order by id;
quit;
```

Joining Tables By Using a Subquery and an In-Line View

```
proc sql;
   select empid
      from sasuser.supervisors as m,
         (select substr(jobcode,1,2) as JobCategory,
                 state
            from sasuser.staffmaster as s,
                 sasuser.payrollmaster as p
            where s.empid=p.empid and s.empid in
               (select empid
                   from sasuser.flightschedule
                   where date='04mar2000'd
                        and destination='CPH')) as c
      where  m.jobcategory=c.jobcategory
             and m.state=c.state;
quit;
```

Points to Remember

- In most cases, generating all possible combinations of rows from multiple tables does not yield useful results, so a Cartesian product is rarely the query outcome that you want.

- The maximum number of tables that you can combine in a single inner join depends on your version of SAS. If the join involves views, it is the number of tables that underlie the views, not the number of views, that counts toward the limit. An outer join can be performed on only two tables or views at a time.

Quiz

Select the best answer for each question. After completing the quiz, check your answers using the answer key in the appendix.

1. A Cartesian product is returned when

    a. join conditions are not specified in a PROC SQL join.

    b. join conditions are not specified in a PROC SQL set operation.

    c. more than two tables are specified in a PROC SQL join.

    d. the keyword ALL is used with the OUTER UNION operator.

2. Given the PROC SQL query and tables shown below, which output is generated?

```
proc sql;
   select *
      from store1,
      store2
      where store1.wk=
            store2.wk;
```

Store1			Store2	
Wk	**Sales**		**Wk**	**Sales**
1	$515.07		1	$1368.99
2	$772.29		2	$1506.23
3	$888.88		3	$1200.57
4	$1000.01		4	$1784.11
			5	$43.00

a.

Wk	Sales	Wk	Sales
1	$515.07	1	$1368.99
2	$772.29	2	$1506.23
3	$888.88	3	$1200.57
4	$1000.01	4	$1784.11
.	.	5	$43.00

b.

Wk	Sales	Wk	Sales
1	$515.07	1	$1368.99
2	$772.29	2	$1506.23
3	$888.88	3	$1200.57
4	$1000.01	4	$1784.11

c.

Wk	Sales
1	$515.07
2	$772.29
3	$888.88
4	$1000.01

d.

Wk	Sales
1	$515.07
2	$772.29
3	$888.88
4	$1000.01
1	$1368.99
2	$1506.23
3	$1200.57
4	$1784.11

3. Given the PROC SQL query and tables shown below, which output is generated?

```
proc sql;
    select s.*, bonus
        from bonus as b
        right join
        salary as s
        on b.id=
            s.id;
```

Bonus

ID	Bonus
123	5000
456	7000
744	3500

Salary

ID	Salary
123	70000
456	80000
978	55000

a.

Id	Salary	Bonus
123	70000	5000
456	80000	7000
978	55000	3500

b.

Id	Salary	Bonus
123	70000	5000
456	80000	7000
744	.	3500

c.

Id	Salary	Bonus
123	70000	5000
456	80000	7000
744	55000	3500

d.

Id	Salary	Bonus
123	70000	5000
456	80000	7000
978	55000	.

4. Which PROC SQL query produces the same output as the query shown here?

```
proc sql;
    select a.*,
            duration
        from groupa as a,
            groupb as b
        where a.obs=b.obs;
```

Note: Assume that the table Groupa contains the columns Obs and Med. Groupb contains the columns Obs and Duration.

a.
```
proc sql;
    select a.obs label='Obs',
            med
            b.obs label='Obs',
            duration
        from groupa as a, groupb as b
        where a.obs=b.obs;
```

b.
```
proc sql;
    select coalesce(a.obs, b.obs)
            label='Obs', med, duration
        from groupa as a
        full join
        groupb as b
        on a.obs=b.obs;
```

c.
```
proc sql;
    select a.*, duration
        from groupa as a
        left join
        groupb as b
        where a.obs=b.obs;
```

d.
```
proc sql;
    select a.*, duration
        from groupa as a
        inner join
        groupb as b
        on a.obs=b.obs;
```

5. Which output is generated by the following PROC SQL query?

```
proc sql;
    select *
        from table1
        left join
        table2
            on table1.g3=
                table2.g3;
```

Table1			Table2	
G3	**Z**		**G3**	**R**
89	FL		46	BC
46	UI		85	FL
47	BA		99	BA

a.

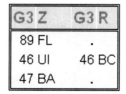

G3	Z	G3	R
89	FL		.
46	UI	46	BC
47	BA		.

b.

G3	Z	G3	R
46	FL	46	BC
.		85	FL
.		99	BA

c.

d.

6. In order for PROC SQL to perform an inner join,

   a. the tables being joined must contain the same number of columns.

   b. the tables must be sorted before they are joined.

   c. the columns that are specified in a join condition in the WHERE clause must have the same data type.

   d. the columns that are specified in a join condition in the WHERE clause must have the same name.

7. Which statement about in-line views is false?

   a. Once defined, an in-line view can be referenced in any PROC SQL query in the current SAS session.

   b. An in-line view can be assigned a table alias but not a permanent name.

   c. In-line views can be combined with tables in PROC SQL joins.

   d. This PROC SQL query contains an in-line view that uses valid syntax:

```
proc sql;
   select name, numvisits
      from (select name, sum(checkin)
            as numvisits
               from facility as f, members as m
               where area='POOL' and
                     f.id=m.id
               group by name)
      where numvisits<=10
      order by 1;
```

8. Which PROC SQL query generates the same output as the DATA step match-merge and PRINT step shown below?

```
data merged;
   merge table1 table2;
   by g3;
run;

proc print data=merged
      noobs;
   title 'Merged';
run;
```

a. `proc sql;`

```
          title 'Merged';
             select a.g3, z, r
                from table1 as a
                full join
                table2 as b
                on a.g3 = b.g3
                order by 1;
```

b. ```
   proc sql;
       title 'Merged';
          select a.g3, z, r
             from table1 as a
             table2 as b
             on a.g3 = b.g3
             order by 1;
   ```

c. ```
   proc sql;
       title 'Merged';
          select coalesce(a.g3, b.g3)
                label='G3', z, r
             from table1 as a
             full join
             table2 as b
             on a.g3 = b.g3
             order by 1;
   ```

d. ```
   proc sql;
       title 'Merged';
          select g3, z, r
             from table1 as a
             full join
             table2 as b
             on a.g3 = b.g3
             order by 1;
   ```

9. A PROC SQL inner join can combine

   a. a maximum of 2 tables or in-line views, but multiple joins can be chained together.

   b. a maximum of 256 tables or 2 in-line views.

   c. a maximum of 256 tables, which includes any tables referenced by an in-line view.

   d. a maximum of 2 tables and 32 columns.

10. Which statement about the use of table aliases is false?

   a. Table aliases must be used when referencing identical table names from different libraries.

   b. Table aliases can be referenced by using the keyword AS.

   c. Table aliases (or full table names) must be used when referencing a column name that is the same in two or more tables.

   d. Table aliases must be used when using summary functions.
   ```

Chapter 4

Combining Tables Vertically Using PROC SQL

Overview

Introduction

Suppose you are generating a report based on data from a health clinic. You want to display the results of individual patient stress tests taken in 1998 (which are stored in Table A), followed by the results from stress tests taken in 1999 (which are stored in Table B). Instead of combining the table rows horizontally, as you would in a PROC SQL join, you want to combine the table rows vertically (one on top of the other).

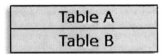

When you need to select data from multiple tables and combine the tables vertically, PROC SQL can be an efficient alternative to using other SAS procedures or the DATA step. In a PROC SQL set operation, you use one of four set operators (EXCEPT, INTERSECT, UNION, and OUTER UNION) to combine tables (and views) vertically by combining the results of two queries:

```
proc sql;
   select *
      from a
   set-operator
   select *
      from b;
```

Each set operator combines the query results in a different way.

In this chapter, you learn how to use the various set operators, with or without the optional keywords ALL and CORR (CORRESPONDING), to combine the results of multiple queries.

Note: In this chapter, the references to tables are also applicable to views, unless otherwise noted.

Understanding Set Operations

Overview

A set operation contains

- two queries (each beginning with a SELECT clause)

- a set operator

- one or both of the keywords ALL and CORR (CORRESPONDING).

General form of an SQL query using a set operator:

SELECT *column-1<, ... column-n>*

    FROM *table-1 | view-1<, ... table-n | view-n>*

    <optional query clauses>

set-operator <ALL> <CORR>

SELECT *column-1<, ... column-n>*

    FROM *table-1 | view-1<, ... table-n | view-n>*

    <optional query clauses>;

Here is an explanation of the syntax:

SELECT
    specifies the column(s) that will appear in the result.

FROM
    specifies the table(s) or view(s) to be queried.

optional query clauses
    are used to refine the query further and include the clauses WHERE, GROUP BY, HAVING, and ORDER BY.

- the set-operator is one of the following: EXCEPT | INTERSECT | UNION | OUTER UNION.

- the optional keywords ALL and CORR (CORRESPONDING) further modify the set operation.

The query or set operation contains one semicolon, which is placed after the last SELECT statement.

Example

In the following PROC SQL step, the SELECT statement contains one set operation. The set operation uses the set operator UNION to combine the result of a query on the table Sasuser.Stress98 with the result of a query on the table Sasuser.Stress99.

```
proc sql;
   select *
      from sasuser.stress98
   union
   select *
      from sasuser.stress99;
```

You learn the details about using each set operator later in this chapter.

Processing a Single Set Operation

PROC SQL evaluates a SELECT statement with one set operation as follows:

1. Each query is evaluated to produce an intermediate (internal) result table.

2. Each intermediate result table then becomes an operand linked with a set operator to form an expression (for example, Table1 UNION Table2).

3. PROC SQL evaluates the entire expression to produce a single output result set.

Using Multiple Set Operators

A single SELECT statement can contain more than one set operation. Each additional set operation includes a set operator and a group of query clauses, as shown in the following example:

```
proc sql;
   select *
      from table1
   set-operator
   select *
      from table2
   set-operator
   select *
      from table3;
```

This SELECT statement uses two set operators to link together three queries.

Regardless of the number of set operations in a SELECT statement, the statement contains only one semicolon, which is placed after the last query.

Example

The following PROC SQL step contains two set operators (both are OUTER UNION) that combine three queries:

```
proc sql;
   select *
      from sasuser.mechanicslevel1
   outer union
   select *
      from sasuser.mechanicslevel2
   outer union
   select *
      from sasuser.mechanicslevel3;
```

Processing Multiple Set Operations

When PROC SQL evaluates a SELECT statement that contains multiple set operations, an additional processing step (step 3 below) is required:

1. Each query is evaluated to produce an intermediate (internal) result table.

2. Each intermediate result table then becomes an operand linked with a set operator to form an expression (for example, Table1 UNION Table2).

3. If the set operation contains more than two queries, then the result from the first two queries (enclosed in parentheses in the following examples) becomes an operand for the next set operator and operand. For example:

   • with two set operators: (Table1 UNION Table2) EXCEPT Table3

   • with three set operators: ((Table1 UNION Table2) EXCEPT Table3) INTERSECT Table4.

4. PROC SQL evaluates the entire expression to produce a single output result set.

Note: When processing set operators, PROC SQL follows a default order of precedence, unless this order is overridden by parentheses in the expression(s). By default, INTERSECT is evaluated first. OUTER UNION, UNION, and EXCEPT all have the same level of precedence.

Introducing Set Operators

Each of the four set operators EXCEPT, INTERSECT, UNION, and OUTER UNION selects rows and handles columns in a different way, as described below.

Note: In the following chart, Table 1 is the table that is referenced in the first query and Table 2 is the table that is referenced in the second query.

Set Operator	Treatment of Rows	Treatment of Columns	Example
EXCEPT	Selects unique rows from the first table that are not found in the second table.	Overlays columns based on their position in the SELECT clause without regard to the individual column names.	```proc sql; select * from table1 except select * from table2;```
INTERSECT	Selects unique rows that are common to both tables.	Overlays columns based on their position in the SELECT clause without regard to the individual column names.	```proc sql; select * from table1 intersect select * from table2;```
UNION	Selects unique rows from both tables.	Overlays columns based on their position in the SELECT clause without regard to the individual column names.	```proc sql; select * from table1 union select * from table2;```

Set Operator	Treatment of Rows	Treatment of Columns	Example
OUTER UNION	Selects all rows from both tables. The OUTER UNION operator concatenates the results of the queries. Table 1 ◯ ◯ Table 2	Does not overlay columns.	```proc sql; select * from table1 outer union select * from table2;```

Note: A set operator that selects only unique rows displays one occurrence of a given row in output.

Processing Unique versus Duplicate Rows

When processing a set operation that displays only unique rows (a set operation that contains the set operator EXCEPT, INTERSECT, or UNION), PROC SQL makes two passes through the data, by default:

1. PROC SQL eliminates duplicate (nonunique) rows in the tables.

2. PROC SQL selects the rows that meet the criteria and, where requested, overlays columns.

For set operations that display both unique and duplicate rows, only one pass through the data (step 2 above) is required.

Combining and Overlaying Columns

You can use a set operation to combine tables that have different numbers of columns and rows or that have columns in a different order.

Three of the four set operators (EXCEPT, INTERSECT, and UNION) combine columns by overlaying them. (The set operator OUTER UNION does not overlay columns.)

By default, the set operators EXCEPT, INTERSECT, and UNION overlay columns based on the relative position of the columns in the SELECT clause. Column names are ignored. You control how PROC SQL maps columns in one table to columns in another table by specifying the columns in the appropriate order in the SELECT clause. The first column specified in the first query's SELECT clause and the first column specified in the second query's SELECT clause are overlaid, and so on.

When columns are overlaid, PROC SQL uses the column name from the first table (the table referenced in the first query). If there is no column name in the first table, the column name from the second table is used. When the SELECT clause contains an asterisk (*) instead of a list of column names, the set operation combines the tables (and, if applicable, overlays columns) based on the positions of the columns in the tables.

For example, the following set operation uses the set operator EXCEPT, so columns are overlaid. The SELECT clause in each query uses an asterisk (*), so the columns are overlaid based on their positions in the tables. The first column in table One (X) is overlaid on the first column in table Two (X), and so on.

```
proc sql;
    select *
        from one
    except
    select *
        from two;
```

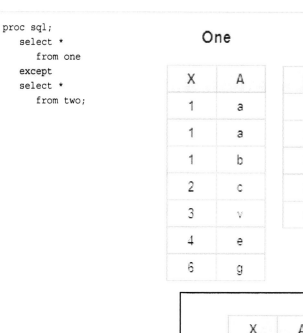

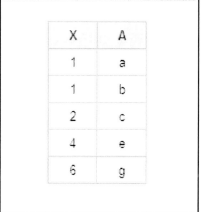

In order to be overlaid, columns in the same relative position in the two SELECT clauses must have the same data type. If they do not, PROC SQL generates a warning message in the SAS log and stops executing. For example, in the tables shown above, if the column One.X had a different data type than column Two.X, the SAS log would display the following error message.

Table 4.1 *SAS Log*

```
ERROR: Column 1 from the first contributor of EXCEPT
is not the same type as its counterpart from the second.
```

Next, we use the keywords ALL and CORR to modify the default action of the set operators.

Modifying Results By Using Keywords

To modify the behavior of set operators, you can use either or both of the keywords ALL and CORR immediately following the set operator:

```
proc sql;
    select *
```

```
   from table1
set-operator <all> <corr>
select *
   from table2;
```

The use of each keyword is described below.

Keyword	Action	Used When...
ALL	Makes only one pass through the data and does not remove duplicate rows.	You do not care if there are duplicates. Duplicates are not possible. ALL cannot be used with OUTER UNION.
CORR (or CORRESPONDING)	Compares and overlays columns by name instead of by position: • When used with EXCEPT, INTERSECT, and UNION, removes any columns that do not have the same name in both tables. • When used with OUTER UNION, overlays same-named columns and displays columns that have nonmatching names without overlaying. If an alias is assigned to a column in the SELECT clause, CORR use the alias instead of the permanent column name.	Two tables have some or all columns in common, but the columns are not in the same order.

In the remainder of this chapter, you learn more about the use of each set operator, with and without the keywords ALL and CORR.

Using the EXCEPT Set Operator

Overview

The set operator EXCEPT does both of the following:

- selects unique rows from the first table (the table specified in the first query) that are not found in the second table (the table specified in the second query)

- overlays columns.

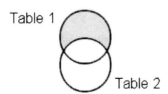

Table 1

Table 2

Consider how EXCEPT works when used alone and with the keywords ALL and CORR.

Using the EXCEPT Operator Alone

Suppose you want to display the unique rows in table One that are not found in table Two. The PROC SQL set operation that includes the EXCEPT operator, the tables One and Two, and the output of the set operation are shown below:

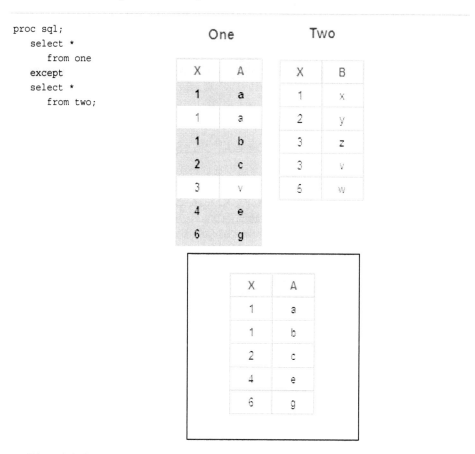

```
proc sql;
   select *
      from one
   except
   select *
      from two;
```

The set operator EXCEPT overlays columns by their position. In this output, the following columns are overlaid:

- the first columns, One.X, and Two.X, both of which are numeric

- the second columns, One.A, and Two.B, both of which are character.

The column names from table One are used, so the second column of output is named A rather than B.

Consider how PROC SQL selects rows from table One to display in output.

In the first pass, PROC SQL eliminates any duplicate rows from the tables. As shown below, there is one duplicate row: in table One, the second row is a duplicate of the first row. All remaining rows in table One are still candidates in PROC SQL's selection process.

```
proc sql;
   select *
      from one
   except
   select *
      from two;
```

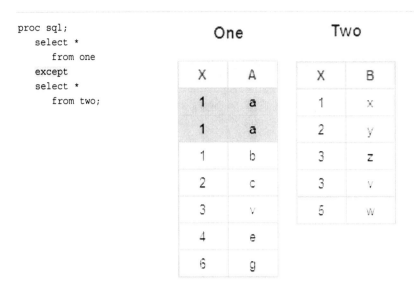

In the second pass, PROC SQL identifies any rows in table One for which there is a matching row in table Two and eliminates them. There is one matching row in the two tables, as shown below, which is eliminated.

```
proc sql;
   select *
      from one
   except
   select *
      from two;
```

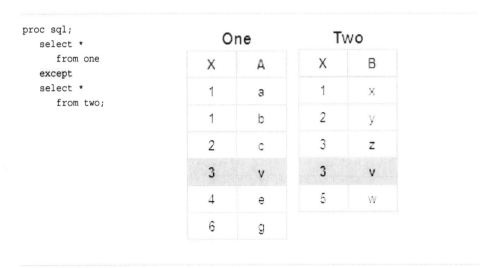

The five remaining rows in table One, the unique rows, are displayed in the output.

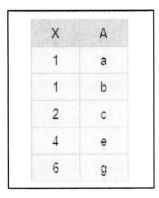

Using the Keyword ALL with the EXCEPT Operator

To select all rows in the first table (both unique and duplicate) that do not have a matching row in the second table, add the keyword ALL after the EXCEPT set operator. The modified PROC SQL set operation, the tables One and Two, and the output are shown below:

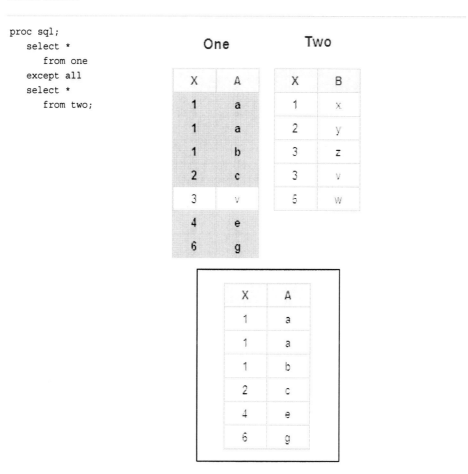

```
proc sql;
    select *
        from one
    except all
    select *
        from two;
```

The output now contains six rows. PROC SQL has again eliminated the one row in table One (the fifth row) that has a matching row in table Two (the fourth row). Remember that when the keyword ALL is used with the EXCEPT operator, PROC SQL does not make an extra pass through the data to remove duplicate rows within table One. Therefore, the second row in table One, which is a duplicate of the first row, is now included in the output.

Using the Keyword CORR with the EXCEPT Operator

To display both of the following, add the keyword CORR after the set operator.

- only columns that have the same name
- all unique rows in the first table that do not appear in the second table.

The modified PROC SQL set operation, the tables One and Two, and the output are shown below:

```
proc sql;
   select *
      from one
   except corr
   select *
      from two;
```

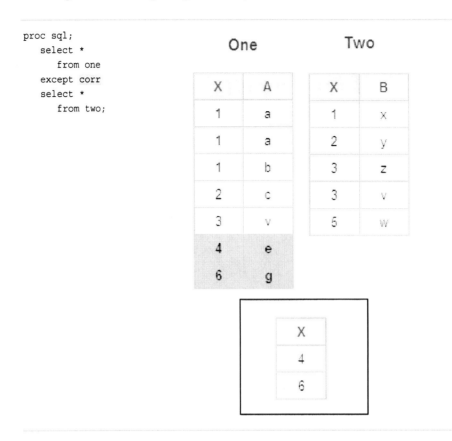

X is the only column that has the same name in both tables, so X is the only column that PROC SQL examines and displays in the output.

In the first pass, PROC SQL eliminates the second and third rows of table One from the output because they are not unique within the table; they contain values of X that duplicate the value of X in the first row of table One. In the second pass, PROC SQL eliminates the first, fourth, and fifth rows of table One because each contains a value of X that matches a value of X in a row of table Two. The output displays the two remaining rows in table One, the rows that are unique in table One and that do not have a row in table Two that has a matching value of X.

Using the Keywords ALL and CORR with the EXCEPT Operator

If the keywords ALL and CORR are used together, the EXCEPT operator displays all unique and duplicate rows in the first table that do not appear in the second table, and overlays and display only columns that have the same name. The modified PROC SQL set operation, the tables One and Two, and the output are shown below:

```
proc sql;
   select *
      from one
   except all corr
   select *
      from two;
```

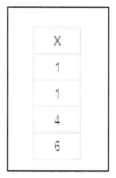

Once again, PROC SQL looks at and displays only the column that has the same name in the two tables: X. Because the ALL keyword is used, PROC SQL does not eliminate any duplicate rows in table One. Therefore, the second and third rows in table One, which are duplicates of the first row in table One, appear in the output. PROC SQL does eliminate the first, fourth, and fifth rows in table One from the output because for each one of these three rows there is a corresponding row in table Two that has a matching value of X.

As this example shows, when the ALL keyword is used with the EXCEPT operator, a row in table One cannot be eliminated from the output unless it has a separate matching row in table Two. Table One contains three rows in which the value of X is 1, but table Two contains only one row in which the value of X is 1. That one row in table Two causes the first of the three rows in table One that have a matching value of X to be eliminated from the output. However, table Two does not have two additional rows in which the value of X is 1, so the other two rows in table One are not eliminated, and do appear in the output.

Example: EXCEPT Operator

The EXCEPT operator can be used to solve a realistic business problem. Suppose you want to display the names of all new employees of a company. There is no table that contains information for only the new employees, so you use data from the following two tables.

Table	Relevant Columns
Sasuser.Staffchanges lists information for all new employees and existing employees who have had a change in salary or job code	FirstName, LastName
Sasuser.Staffmaster lists information for all existing employees	FirstName, LastName

The relationship between these two tables is shown in the diagram below:

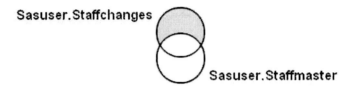

The intersection of these two tables includes information for all existing employees who have had changes in job code or salary. The shaded portion, the portion of Sasuser.Staffchanges that does not overlap with Sasuser.Staffmaster, includes information for the people that you want: new employees.

To separate the new employees from the existing employees in Sasuser.Staffchanges, you create a set operation that displays all rows from the first table (Sasuser.Staffchanges) that do not exist in the second table (Sasuser.Staffmaster). The following PROC SQL step solves the problem:

```
proc sql;
   select firstname, lastname
      from sasuser.staffchanges
   except all
   select firstname, lastname
      from sasuser.staffmaster;
```

This PROC SQL set operation includes the operator EXCEPT and the keyword ALL. Although you do not want the output to contain duplicate rows, you already know that there are no duplicates in these two tables. Therefore, ALL is specified to prevent PROC SQL from making an extra pass through the data, which speeds up the processing of this query.

PROC SQL compares only the columns that are specified in the SELECT clauses, and these columns are compared in the order in which they are specified. The output displays the first and last names of the two new employees.

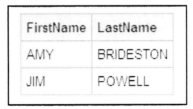

Note: In a set operation that uses the EXCEPT operator, the order in which the tables are listed in the SELECT statement makes a difference. If the tables in this example were listed in the opposite order, the output would display all existing employees who have had no changes in salary or job code.

Example: EXCEPT Operator in an In-Line View

This example is a variation of the preceding set operation. Suppose you want to display the number of existing employees who have had no changes in salary or job code. Once again, the query uses the following tables and columns.

Table	Relevant Columns
Sasuser.Staffchanges lists information for all new employees and existing employees who have had a change in salary or job code	FirstName, LastName
Sasuser.Staffmaster lists information for all existing employees	FirstName, LastName

The following PROC SQL query solves this problem:

```
proc sql;
   select count(*) label='No. of Persons'
      from (select EmpID
              from sasuser.staffmaster
           except all
           select EmpID
              from sasuser.staffchanges);
```

This PROC SQL query uses

- the COUNT function with an asterisk (*) as an argument to count the number of employee IDs returned from the set operation
- the set operator EXCEPT within an in-line view.

The in-line view returns a virtual table that contains employees who have had no changes in salary or job code. This virtual table is then passed to the COUNT(*) summary function, which counts the number of rows in the virtual table. The output shows that there are 144 existing employees who have had no changes in salary or job code.

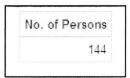

No. of Persons
144

Using the INTERSECT Set Operator

Overview

The set operator INTERSECT does both of the following:

- selects unique rows that are common to both tables
- overlays columns.

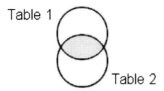

The following example demonstrates how INTERSECT works when used alone and with the keywords ALL and CORR.

Using the INTERSECT Operator Alone

The INTERSECT operator compares and overlays columns in the same way as the EXCEPT operator, by column position instead of column name. However, INTERSECT selects rows differently and is displayed in output the unique rows that are common to both tables. The following PROC SQL set operation uses the INTERSECT operator to combine the tables One and Two, which were introduced previously:

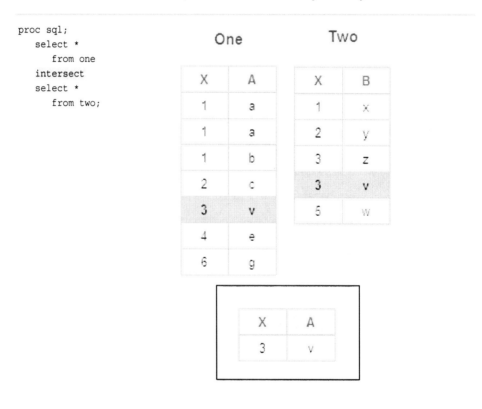

Tables One and Two have only one unique row in common and this row is displayed in the output. (This is the same row that was eliminated in the earlier example that contained the EXCEPT operator.)

Using the Keyword ALL with the INTERSECT Operator

Adding the keyword ALL to the preceding PROC SQL query prevents PROC SQL from making an extra pass through the data. If there were any rows common to tables One and Two that were duplicates of other common rows, they would also be included in output. However, as you have seen, there is only one common row in these tables. The modified PROC SQL query, the tables One and Two, and the output are shown below:

```
proc sql;
   select *
      from one
   intersect all
   select *
      from two;
```

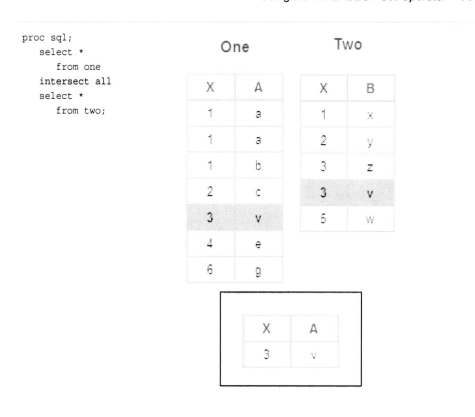

As before, there is just one row of output.

Using the Keyword CORR with the INTERSECT Operator

To display the unique rows that are common to the two tables based on the column name instead of the column position, add the CORR keyword to the PROC SQL set operation. The modified query, the tables One and Two, and the output are shown below:

```
proc sql;
    select *
        from one
    intersect corr
    select *
        from two;
```

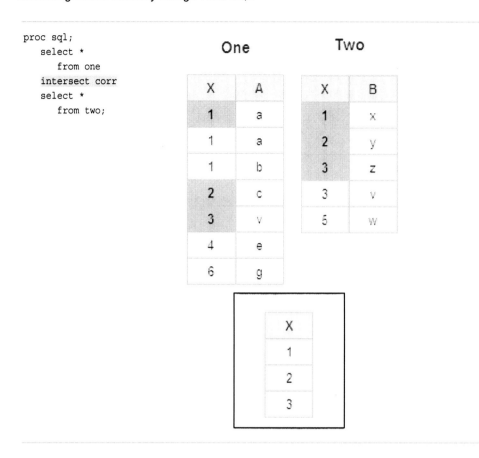

X is the only column name that is common to both tables, so X is the only column that PROC SQL examines and displays in the output. In the first pass, PROC SQL eliminates the rows that are duplicated within each table: the second and third rows in table One contain the same value for X as the first row, and the fourth row in table Two contains the same value for X as the third row. In the second pass, PROC SQL eliminates any rows that are not common across tables: the fourth and fifth rows in table One and the fifth row in table Two do not have a matching value of X in the other table. The output displays the three rows with unique values of X that are also common to both tables.

Using the Keywords ALL and CORR with the INTERSECT Operator

If the keywords ALL and CORR are used together, the INTERSECT operator displays all unique and nonunique (duplicate) rows that are common to the two tables, based on columns that have the same name. The modified query, the tables One and Two, and the output are shown below:

```
proc sql;
   select *
      from one
   intersect all corr
   select *
      from two;
```

One

X	A
1	a
1	a
1	b
2	c
3	v
4	e
6	g

Two

X	B
1	x
2	y
3	z
3	v
5	w

X
1
2
3

PROC SQL examines and displays only the column with the same name, X. There are three common rows across the two tables, which are highlighted above, and these are the three rows that are displayed in the output.

Note that each of the tables contains at least one other row that duplicates a value of X in one of the common rows. For example, in the second and third rows in table One, the value of X is 1, as in one of the common rows. However, in order to be considered a common row and to be included in the output, every duplicate row in one table must have a separate duplicate row in the other table. In this example, there are no rows that have duplicate values and that are also common across tables. Therefore, in this example, the set operation with the keywords ALL and CORR generates the same output as with the keyword CORR alone.

Example: INTERSECT Operator

Now that you have seen how the INTERSECT set operator works with very small tables, we can use INTERSECT in a realistic business problem. Suppose you want to display the names of the existing employees who have changed their salary or job code. (This query is the opposite of the query that you solved with the EXCEPT operator.)

Once again, you use the following tables.

Table	Relevant Columns
Sasuser.Staffchanges lists information for all new employees and existing employees who have had a change in salary or job code	FirstName, LastName

Table	Relevant Columns
Sasuser.Staffmaster lists information for all existing employees	FirstName, LastName

The relationship between these two tables is shown in the diagram below:

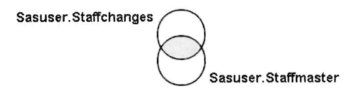

As shown in the earlier example with EXCEPT, the intersection of these two tables includes information for all existing employees who have had changes in job code or salary. It is the intersection of these two tables, shaded above, that you want to display.

To display the unique rows that are common to both tables, you use a PROC SQL set operation that contains INTERSECT. It is known that these tables contain no duplicates, so ALL is used to speed up query processing. The PROC SQL set operation is shown below:

```
proc sql;
   select firstname, lastname
      from sasuser.staffchanges
   intersect all
   select firstname, lastname
      from sasuser.staffmaster;
```

Note: In this PROC SQL step, which contains just one INTERSECT set operator, the order in which you list the tables in the SELECT statement does not make a difference. However, in a more complex PROC SQL step that contains multiple stacked INTERSECT set operators, it is important to think through the table order carefully, depending on when you want the non-matches to be eliminated. The output shows that there are four existing employees who have changed their salary or job code.

FirstName	LastName
DIANE	WALTERS
KAREN	CARTER
NEIL	CHAPMAN
RAYMOND	SANDERS

Using the UNION Set Operator

Overview

The set operator UNION does both of the following:

- selects unique rows from both tables
- overlays columns.

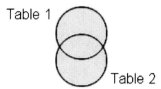

The following example demonstrates how UNION works when used alone and with the keywords ALL and CORR.

Using the UNION Operator Alone

To display all rows from the tables One and Two that are unique in the combined set of rows from both tables, use a PROC SQL set operation that includes the UNION operator:

```
proc sql;
    select *
        from one
    union
    select *
        from two;
```

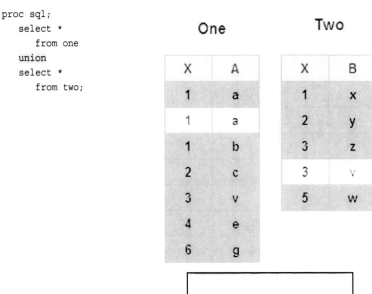

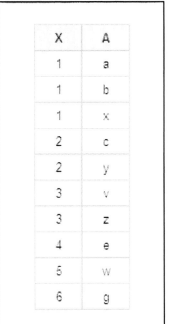

With the UNION operator, PROC SQL first concatenates and sorts the rows from the two tables, and eliminates any duplicate rows. In this example, two rows are eliminated: the second row in table One is a duplicate of the first row, and the fourth row in table Two matches the fifth row in table One. All remaining rows, the unique rows, are included in the output. The columns are overlaid by position.

Using the Keyword ALL with the UNION Operator

When the keyword ALL is added to the UNION operator, the output displays all rows from both tables, both unique and duplicate. The modified PROC SQL set operation, the tables One and Two, and the new output are shown below:

```
proc sql;
    select *
        from one
    union all
    select *
        from two;
```

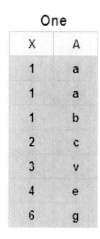

When the ALL keyword is used, PROC SQL does not remove duplicates or sort the rows. The output now includes the two duplicate rows that were eliminated in the previous example: the second row in table One and the fourth row in table Two. Note that the rows are in a different order in this output than they were in the output from the previous set operation.

Using the Keyword CORR with the UNION Operator

To display all rows from the tables One and Two that are unique in the combined set of rows from both tables, based on columns that have the same name rather than the same position, add the keyword CORR after the set operator. The modified query, the tables One and Two, and the output are shown below:

```
proc sql;
   select *
      from one
   union corr
   select *
      from two;
```

One

X	A
1	a
1	a
1	b
2	c
3	v
4	e
6	g

Two

X	B
1	x
2	y
3	z
3	v
5	w

X
1
2
3
4
5
6

X is the only column name that is common to both tables, so X is the only column that PROC SQL examines and displays in the output. In the combined set of rows from the two tables, there are duplicates of the values 1, 2, and 3, and these duplicate rows are eliminated from the output. The output displays the six unique values of X.

Using the Keywords ALL and CORR with the UNION Operator

If the keywords ALL and CORR are used together, the UNION operator displays all rows in the two tables both unique and duplicate, based on the columns that have the same name. In this example, the output displays all 12 values for X, the one column that has the same name in both tables.

```
proc sql;
   select *
      from one
   union all corr
   select *
      from two;
```

Example: UNION Operator

The UNION operator can be used to solve a realistic business problem. Suppose you are generating a report based on data from a health clinic. You want to display the results of individual patient stress tests taken in 1998, followed by the results from stress tests taken in 1999. To do this, you use the UNION operator to combine the tables Sasuser.Stress98 and Sasuser.Stress99. These two tables are similar in structure:

- both tables contain nine columns that have the same names

- each row contains data for an individual patient.

You are not sure whether the tables contain duplicate records, but you do not want duplicates in your output. Because the tables have the same column structure, you can overlay the columns by position, and the CORR keyword is not necessary. The PROC SQL set operation and output are shown below (the rows are ordered by IDs.):

```
proc sql;
  select *
    from sasuser.stress98
  union
  select *
    from sasuser.stress99;
```

ID	Name	RestHR	MaxHR	RecHR	TimeMin	TimeSec	Tolerance	Year
2458	Murray, W	72	185	128	12	38	D	1993
2462	Almers, C	68	171	133	10	5	I	1998
2501	Bonaventure,	78	177	139	11	13	I	1999
2523	Johnson, R	69	162	114	9	42	S	1998
2539	LaMance, K	75	183	141	11	46	D	1993
2544	Jones, M	79	137	138	12	26	N	1999
2552	Peterson, P	69	153	139	15	41	D	1999
2555	King, E	70	137	122	13	13	I	1998
2563	Pitts, D	71	159	118	10	22	S	1998
2568	Eberhardt, S	72	182	122	16	49	N	1999
2571	Nunnelly, A	65	181	141	15	2	I	1999
2572	Oberon, M	74	177	138	12	11	D	1993
2574	Peterson, V	80	154	137	14	9	D	1998
2575	Quigley, M	74	152	113	11	26	I	1993
2578	Cameron, L	75	156	108	14	27	I	1999
2579	Underwood, K	72	185	127	13	19	S	1999
2584	Takahashi, Y	75	183	135	16	7	D	1998
2586	Derber, B	68	173	119	17	35	N	1993
2588	Ivan, H	70	132	125	15	41	N	1999
2589	Wilcox, E	78	169	133	14	57	I	1993
2595	Warren, C	77	172	136	12	10	S	1999

TIP If you can determine that these tables have no duplicate records, you could add the keyword ALL to speed up processing by avoiding an extra pass through the data.

Example: UNION Operator and Summary Functions

We can demonstrate another realistic business problem, to see how summary functions can be used with a set operator (in this case, UNION). Suppose you want to display the following summarized data for members of a frequent-flyer program: total points earned, total points used, and total miles traveled. All three values can be calculated from columns in the table Sasuser.Frequentflyers by using summary functions.

You might wonder why set operations are needed when only one table is involved. If you wanted to display the three summarized values horizontally, in three separate columns, you could solve the problem without a set operation, using the following simple SELECT statement:

```
proc sql;
  select sum(pointsearned) format=comma12.
         label='Total Points Earned',
         sum(pointsused) format=comma12.
         label='Total Points Used',
         sum(milestraveled) format=comma12.
         label='Total Miles Traveled'
    from sasuser.frequentflyers;
```

Total Points Earned	Total Points Used	Total Miles Traveled
10,583,463	4,429,670	10,477,963

Assume, however, that you want the three values to be displayed vertically in a single column. To generate this output, you create three different queries on the same table, and then use two UNION set operators to combine the three query results:

```
proc sql;
title 'Points and Miles Traveled';
title2 'by Frequent Flyers';
   select 'Total Points Traveled:',
          sum(MilesTraveled) format=comma12.
     from sasuser.frequentflyers
   union
   select 'Total Points Earned:',
          sum(PointsEarned) format=comma12.
     from sasuser.frequentflyers
   union
   select 'Total Points Used:',
          sum(PointsUsed) format=comma12.
     from sasuser.frequentflyers;
```

Each SELECT clause defines two columns: a character constant as a label and the summarized value. The output is shown below.

Points and Miles Traveled by Frequent Flyers	
Total Points Earned:	10,583,463
Total Points Traveled:	10,477,963
Total Points Used:	4,429,670

Note: The preceding program reads the same table three times, so it is not the most efficient way to solve this problem.

Using the OUTER UNION Set Operator

Overview

The set operator OUTER UNION concatenates the results of the queries by the following:

- selecting all rows (both unique and nonunique) from both tables

- not overlaying columns.

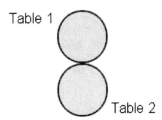

Table 1

Table 2

We can demonstrate how OUTER UNION works when used alone and with the keyword CORR. The ALL keyword is not used with OUTER UNION because this operator's default action is to include all rows in output.

Using the OUTER UNION Operator Alone

Suppose you want to display all rows from both of the tables One and Two, without overlaying columns. The PROC SQL set operation that includes the OUTER UNION operator, the two tables, and the output are shown below:

```
proc sql;
   select *
      from one
   outer union
   select *
      from two;
```

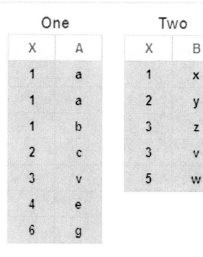

X	A	X	B
1	a		
1	a		
1	b		
2	c		
3	v		
4	e		
6	g		
		1	x
		2	y
		3	z
		3	v
		5	w

In the output, the columns are not overlaid. Instead, all four columns from both tables are displayed. Each row of output contains missing values in the two columns that correspond to the other table.

Using the Keyword CORR with the OUTER UNION Operator

The output from the preceding set operation contains two columns with the same name. To overlay the columns with a common name, add the CORR keyword to the set operation:

```
proc sql;
   select *
      from one
   outer union corr
   select *
      from two;
```

One	
X	A
1	a
1	a
1	b
2	c
3	v
4	e
6	g

Two	
X	B
1	x
2	y
3	z
3	v
5	w

X	A	B
1	a	
1	a	
1	b	
2	c	
3	v	
4	e	
6	g	
1		x
2		y
3		z
3		v
5		w

The output from the modified set operation contains only three columns, because the two columns named X are overlaid.

Example: OUTER UNION Operator

There are many business situations that require two or more tables to be concatenated. For example, suppose you want to display the employee numbers, job codes, and salaries of all mechanics working for an airline. The mechanic job has three levels and there is a separate table containing data for the mechanics at each level: Sasuser.Mechanicslevel1, Sasuser.Mechanicslevel2, and Sasuser.Mechanicslevel3. These tables all contain the same three columns.

The following PROC SQL step uses two OUTER UNION operators to concatenate the tables, and the CORR keyword to overlay the columns that have common names:

```
proc sql;
   select *
      from sasuser.mechanicslevel1
   outer union corr
   select *
      from sasuser.mechanicslevel2
   outer union corr
   select *
      from sasuser.mechanicslevel3;
```

EmpID	JobCode	Salary
1400	ME1	$41,677
1403	ME1	$39,301
1120	ME1	$40,067
1121	ME1	$40,757
1412	ME1	$38,919
1200	ME1	$38,942
1995	ME1	$40,334
1418	ME1	$39,207
1653	ME2	$49,151
1782	ME2	$49,483
1244	ME2	$51,695
1065	ME2	$49,126
1129	ME2	$48,901
1406	ME2	$49,259
1356	ME2	$51,617
1292	ME2	$51,367
1440	ME2	$50,060
1900	ME2	$49,147
1423	ME2	$50,082
1432	ME2	$49,458
1050	ME2	$49,234
1105	ME2	$48,727
1499	ME3	$60,235
1409	ME3	$58,171
1379	ME3	$59,170
1521	ME3	$58,136
1385	ME3	$61,460
1420	ME3	$60,299
1882	ME3	$58,153

Comparing Outer Unions and Other SAS Techniques

A PROC SQL set operation that uses the OUTER UNION operator is just one SAS technique that you can use to concatenate tables, as shown in the following programs. Program 1 is the PROC SQL set operation that was shown earlier in this chapter. Program 2 uses a different SAS technique to concatenate the hypothetical tables One and Two.

Program 1: PROC SQL OUTER UNION Set Operation with CORR

```
proc sql;
   create table three as
      select * from one
      outer union corr
      select * from two;
quit;
```

Program 2: DATA Step, SET Statement, and PROC PRINT Step

```
data three;
   set one two;
run;
proc print data=three noobs;
run;
```

These two programs create the same table as output, as shown below.

One | Two

X	A
1	a
1	a
1	b
2	c
3	v
4	e
6	g

X	B
1	x
2	y
3	z
3	v
5	w

X	A	B
1	a	
1	a	
1	b	
2	c	
3	v	
4	e	
6	g	
1		x
2		y
3		z
3		v
5		w

When tables have a same-named column, the PROC SQL outer union does not produce the same output unless the keyword CORR is also used. CORR causes the same-named columns (in this example, the two columns named X) to be overlaid; without CORR, the OUTER UNION operator includes both of the same-named columns in the result set. The DATA step program generates only one column X.

The two concatenation techniques shown above also vary in efficiency. A PROC SQL set operation generally requires more computer resources but might be more convenient and flexible than the DATA step equivalent.

Summary

Text Summary

Understanding Set Operations
A set operation combines tables or views vertically (one on top of the other) by combining the results of two queries. A set operation is a SELECT statement that contains

- two queries (each beginning with a SELECT clause)

- one of the set operators EXCEPT, INTERSECT, UNION, and OUTER UNION

- one or both of the keywords ALL and CORR (CORRESPONDING) as modifiers.

A single SELECT statement can contain multiple set operations.

When processing a set operation that displays only unique rows (a set operation that contains the set operator EXCEPT, INTERSECT, or UNION), PROC SQL makes two passes through the data, by default. For set operations that display both unique and duplicate rows, only one pass through the data is required.

For the set operators EXCEPT, INTERSECT, and UNION, columns are overlaid based on the relative position of the columns in the SELECT clause rather than by column name. In order to be overlaid, columns in the same relative position in the two SELECT clauses must have the same data type.

One or both keywords can be used to modify the default action of a set operator.

Using the EXCEPT Set Operator

The set operator EXCEPT selects unique rows from the first table (the table specified in the first query) that are not found in the second table (the table specified in the second query) and overlays columns. This set operation can be modified by using either or both of the keywords ALL and CORR.

Using the INTERSECT Set Operator

The set operator INTERSECT selects unique rows that are common to both tables and overlays columns. This set operation can be modified by using either or both of the keywords ALL and CORR.

Using the UNION Set Operator

The set operator UNION selects unique rows from both tables and overlays columns. This set operation can be modified by using either or both of the keywords ALL and CORR.

Using the OUTER UNION Set Operator

The set operator OUTER UNION concatenates the results of two queries by selecting all rows (both unique and nonunique) from both tables and not overlaying columns. This set operation can be modified by using the keyword CORR.

Comparing Outer Unions and Other SAS Techniques

A PROC SQL set operation that uses the OUTER UNION set operator is not the only way to concatenate tables in SAS. Other SAS techniques can be used, such as a program that consists of a DATA step, a SET statement, and a PROC PRINT step.

Sample Program

```
proc sql;
   select firstname, lastname
      from sasuser.staffchanges
   intersect all
   select firstname, lastname
      from sasuser.staffmaster;
quit;
```

Points to Remember

- Regardless of the number of set operations in a SELECT statement, the statement contains only one semicolon, which is placed after the last query.

- In order to be overlaid, columns must have the same data type.

Quiz

Select the best answer for each question. After completing the quiz, check your answers using the answer key in the appendix.

1. Which statement is false with respect to a set operation that uses the EXCEPT, UNION, or INTERSECT set operator without a keyword?

   a. Column names in the result set are determined by the first table.

   b. To be overlaid, columns must be of the same data type.

   c. To be overlaid, columns must have the same name.

   d. By default, only unique rows are displayed in the result set.

2. The keyword ALL cannot be used with which of the following set operators?

   a. EXCEPT

   b. INTERSECT

   c. UNION

   d. OUTER UNION

3. Which PROC SQL step combines the tables Summer and Winter to produce the output displayed below?

Summer		
Month	**Temp**	**Precip**
7	78	.05
8	85	.04
9	83	.15

Winter		
Mo	**Temp**	**Precip**
1	29	.15
2	32	.17
3	38	.20
2	32	.17

Month	Temp	Precip
1	29	.15
2	32	.17
3	38	.20
7	78	.05
8	85	.04
9	83	.15

a.
```
proc sql;
    select *
       from summer
    intersect all
    select *
       from winter;
```

b.
```
proc sql;
    select *
       from summer
```

```
       outer union
       select *
          from winter;
```

c.
```
   proc sql;
       select *
          from summer
       union corr
       select *
          from winter;
```

d.
```
   proc sql;
       select *
          from summer
       union
       select *
          from winter;
```

4. Which PROC SQL step combines tables but does not overlay any columns?

   a.
   ```
   proc sql;
       select *
          from groupa
       outer union
       select *
          from groupb;
   ```

   b.
   ```
   proc sql;
       select *
          from groupa as a
       outer union corr
       select *
          from groupb as b;
   ```

   c.
   ```
   proc sql;
       select coalesce(a.obs, b.obs)
             label='Obs', med, duration
          from groupa as a
          full join
          groupb as b
          on a.obs=b.obs;
   ```

   d.
   ```
   proc sql;
       select *
          from groupa as a
       intersect
       select *
          from groupb as b;
   ```

5. Which statement is false regarding the keyword CORRESPONDING?

   a. It cannot be used with the keyword ALL.

   b. It overlays columns by name, not by position.

   c. When used in EXCEPT, INTERSECT, and UNION set operations, it removes any columns not found in both tables.

   d. When used in OUTER UNION set operations, it causes same-named columns to be overlaid.

6. Which PROC SQL step generates the following output from the tables Dogs and Pets?

Dogs

Name	Price
FIFI	$101
GEORGE	$75
SPARKY	$136
TRUFFLE	$250

Pets

Name	Price	Arr
ANA	$25	09JAN2002
FIFI	$101	14MAR2002
GAO	$57	08DEC2001
GAO	$57	08DEC2001
SPARKY	$136	16SEP2002
TRUFFLE	$250	20DEC2002
ZEUS	$500	08JUN2002

Name	Price
ANA	$25
GAO	$57
ZEUS	$500

a.
```
proc sql;
     select name, price
        from pets
     except all
     select *
        from dogs;
```

b.
```
proc sql;
     select name, price
        from pets
     except
     select *
        from dogs;
```

c.
```
proc sql;
     select name, price
        from pets
     except corr all
     select *
        from dogs;
```

d.
```
proc sql;
     select *
        from dogs
     except corr
     select name, price
        from pets;
```

7. The PROG1 and PROG2 tables list students who took the PROG1 and PROG2 courses, respectively. Which PROC SQL step gives you the names of the students who took only the PROG1 class?

PROG1

FName	LName
Pete	Henry
Mary	Johnson
Alex	Kinsley
Dori	O'Neil

PROG2

FName	LName
Clara	Addams
Pete	Henry
Dori	O'Neil
Cindy	Phillips
Mandi	Young

PROG1 Only

FName	LName
Alex	Kinsley
Mary	Johnson

a.
```
proc sql;
    select fname, lname
        from prog1
    intersect
    select fname, lname
        from prog2;
```

b.
```
proc sql;
    select fname, lname
        from prog1
    except all
    select fname, lname
        from prog2;
```

c.
```
proc sql;
    select *
        from prog2
    intersect corr
    select *
        from prog1;
```

d.
```
proc sql;
    select *
        from prog2
    union
    select *
        from prog1;
```

8. Which PROC SQL step returns the names of all the students who took PROG1, PROG2, or both classes?

PROG1			PROG2			PROG1, PROG2, or Both	
FName	**LName**		**FName**	**LName**		**FName**	**LName**
Pete	Henry		Clara	Addams		Alex	Kinsley
Mary	Johnson		Pete	Henry		Cindy	Phillips
Alex	Kinsley		Dori	O'Neil		Clara	Addams
Dori	O'Neil		Cindy	Phillips		Dori	O'Neil
			Mandi	Young		Mandi	Young
						Mary	Johnson
						Pete	Henry

a.
```
proc sql;
    select fname, lname
        from prog1
    intersect
    select fname, lname
        from prog2;
```

b.
```
proc sql;
    select fname, lname
        from prog1
    outer union corr
    select fname, lname
        from prog2;
```

c.
```
proc sql;
    select fname, lname
        from prog1
```

```
        union
        select fname, lname
            from prog2;
```

d.
```
proc sql;
    select fname, lname
        from prog1
    except corr
    select fname, lname
        from prog2;
```

9. Which PROC SQL step returns the names of all the students who took both the PROG1 and PROG2 classes?

PROG1		PROG2		PROG1 & PROG2	
FName	**LName**	**FName**	**LName**	**FName**	**LName**
Pete	Henry	Clara	Addams	Dori	O'Neil
Mary	Johnson	Pete	Henry	Pete	Henry
Alex	Kinsley	Dori	O'Neil		
Dori	O'Neil	Cindy	Phillips		
		Mandi	Young		

a.
```
proc sql;
    select fname, lname
        from prog1
    union
    select fname, lname
        from prog2;
```

b.
```
proc sql;
    select fname, lname
        from prog1
    except corr
    select fname, lname
        from prog2;
```

c.
```
proc sql;
    select fname, lname
        from prog1
    intersect all
    select fname, lname
        from prog2;
```

d.
```
proc sql;
    select fname, lname
        from prog1
    union corr
    select fname, lname
        from prog2;
```

10. Which PROC SQL step generates the same results as the following DATA step?

```
data allstudents;
    set prog1 prog2;
    by lname;
run;
proc print noobs;
run;
```

PROG1	
FName	**LName**
Pete	Henry
Mary	Johnson
Alex	Kinsley
Dori	O'Neil

PROG2	
FName	**LName**
Clara	Addams
Pete	Henry
Dori	O'Neil
Cindy	Phillips
Mandi	Young

a. ```
proc sql;
    select fname, lname
        from prog1
    outer union corr
    select fname, lname
        from prog2
    order by lname;
```

b. ```
proc sql;
    select fname, lname
        from prog1
    union
    select fname, lname
        from prog2
    order by lname;
```

c. ```
proc sql;
    select fname, lname
        from prog2
    outer union
    select fname, lname
        from prog1
    order by lname;
```

d. ```
proc sql;
    select fname, lname
        from prog2
    union corr
    select fname, lname
        from prog1
    order by lname;
```

Chapter 5
Creating and Managing Tables Using PROC SQL

Overview

Introduction

By using PROC SQL, you can create, modify, and drop (delete) tables quickly and efficiently. Many PROC SQL statements are quite versatile, enabling you to perform the same action in several ways. For example, there are three methods of creating a table by using the CREATE TABLE statement:

- creating an empty table (a table without rows) by defining columns

- creating an empty table that has the same columns and attributes as another table

- creating a table from a query result.

The following PROC SQL step uses the CREATE TABLE statement to create an empty table by defining columns, and uses the DESCRIBE TABLE statement to display information about the table's structure in the SAS log:

```
proc sql;
   create table work.discount
         (Destination char(3),
          BeginDate num Format=date9.,
          EndDate num format=date9.,
          Discount num);
   describe table work.discount;
```

Table 5.1 *SAS Log*

```
1    proc sql;
2       create table work.discount
3             (Destination char(3),
4                 BeginDate num Format=date9.,
5                 EndDate num format=date9.,
6                 Discount num);
NOTE: Table WORK.DISCOUNT created, with 0 rows and 4 columns.
7          describe table work.discount;
NOTE: SQL table WORK.DISCOUNT was created like:

create table WORK.DISCOUNT( bufsize=4096 )
            (
            Destination char(3),
            BeginDate num format=DATE9.,
            EndDate num format=DATE9.,
            Discount num
            );
```

Understanding Methods of Creating Tables

You can use PROC SQL to create a table in three ways. The CREATE TABLE statement is used for all three methods, although the syntax of the statement varies for each method.

Method of Creating a Table	Example

create an empty table by defining columns	```proc sql;
	    create table work.discount
	        (Destination char(3),
	        BeginDate num Format=date9.,
	        EndDate num format=date9.,
	        Discount num);```

create an empty table that is like (has the same columns and attributes as) an existing table	```proc sql;
	    create table work.flightdelays2
	        like sasuser.flightdelays;```

create a populated table (a table with both columns and rows of data) from a query result	```proc sql;
	    create table work.ticketagents as
	        select lastname, firstname,
	            jobcode, salary
	        from sasuser.payrollmaster,
	            sasuser.staffmaster
	        where payrollmaster.empid
	            = staffmaster.empid
	        and jobcode contains 'TA';```

The CREATE TABLE statement generates only a table as output, not a report. The SAS log displays a message that indicates that the table has been created, and the number of rows and columns that it contains.

Table 5.2 SAS Log

```
NOTE: Table WORK.FLIGHTDELAYS2 created, with 0 rows and 8 columns.
```

Note: You can display additional information about a table's structure in the SAS log by using the DESCRIBE TABLE statement in PROC SQL. The DESCRIBE TABLE statement is discussed later in this chapter.

Creating an Empty Table By Defining Columns

Overview

Sometimes you want to create a new table that is unlike any existing table. In this case, you need to define all of the table's columns and attributes. To accomplish this, use the

CREATE TABLE statement that includes column specifications for the columns that you want to include. This statement creates a table without rows (an empty table).

Note: In addition, integrity constraints can be specified in the CREATE TABLE statement. Integrity constraints are discussed later in this chapter.

General form, basic CREATE TABLE statement with column specifications:

CREATE TABLE *table-name*

(*column-specification-1*<,

...*column-specification-n*>);

Here is an explanation of the syntax:

table-name
specifies the name of the table to be created.

column-specification
specifies a column to be included in the table, and consists of

column-definition <*column-constraint-1*<, ...*column-constraint-n*>>

<MESSAGE=*'message-string'*<MSGTYPE=*message-type*>>

Here is an explanation of the syntax:

column-definition consists of the following:
column-name data-type<(*column-width*)><*column-modifier-1*<... *column-modifier-n*>>

column-name
specifies the name of the column. The column name is stored in the table in the same case that is used in *column-name*.

data-type
is enclosed in parentheses and specifies one of the following: CHARACTER (or CHAR) | VARCHAR | INTEGER (or INT) | SMALLINT | DECIMAL (or DEC) | NUMERIC (or NUM) | FLOAT | REAL | DOUBLE PRECISION | DATE.

column-width
which is enclosed in parentheses, is an integer that specifies the width of the column. (PROC SQL processes this value only for the CHARACTER and VARCHAR data types.)

column-modifier
is one of the following: INFORMAT= | FORMAT= | LABEL= . More than one column-modifier might be specified.

column-constraint
specifies an integrity constraint.

MESSAGE= and MSGTYPE=
specify an error message that is related to an integrity constraint. (Integrity constraints, the column-constraint, MESSAGE=, and MSGTYPE= are not elaborated here, but are discussed in detail later in this chapter.)

Note: The entire set of column-specifications must be enclosed in parentheses. Multiple column-specifications must be separated by commas. Elements within a column-specification must be separated by spaces.

Example

Suppose you want to create the temporary table Work.Discount, which contains data about discounts that are offered by an airline. There is no existing table that contains the four columns (and column attributes) that you would like to include: Destination,

BeginDate, EndDate, and Discount. You use the following PROC SQL step to create the table, based on column definitions that you specify:

```
proc sql;
   create table work.discount
          (Destination char(3),
          BeginDate num Format=date9.,
          EndDate num format=date9.,
          Discount num);
```

The SAS log confirms that the table has been created.

Table 5.3 *SAS Log*

```
NOTE: Table WORK.DISCOUNT created, with 0 rows and 4 columns.
```

> **TIP** In this example and all other examples in this chapter, you are instructed to save your data to a temporary table (in the library Work) that is deleted at the end of the SAS session. To save the table permanently in a different library, use the appropriate libref instead of the libref Work in the CREATE TABLE clause.

In the next few sections, you learn more about specifying data types and column modifiers in a column specification.

Note: You learn to insert rows of data in a table later in this chapter.

Specifying Data Types

When you create a table by defining columns, you must specify a data type for each column, following the column name:

*column-name **data-type** <(column-width)> <column-modifier-1<...column-modifier-n>>*

For example, the following PROC SQL step (shown also in the previous section) defines four columns: one-character column (Destination) and three numeric columns (BeginDate, EndDate, and Discount):

```
proc sql;
   create table work.discount
          (Destination char(3),
          BeginDate num format=date9.,
          EndDate num format=date9.,
          Discount num);
```

SAS tables use two data types: numeric and character. However, PROC SQL supports additional data types (many, but not all, of the data types that SQL-based databases support). Therefore, in the CREATE TABLE statement, you can specify any of 10 different data types. When the table is created, PROC SQL converts the supported data types that are not SAS data types to either numeric or character format.

Table 5.4 *Character Data Types Supported by PROC SQL*

Specified Data Type	SAS Data Type
CHARACTER (or CHAR)	CHARACTER
VARCHAR	CHARACTER

Table 5.5 *Numeric Data Types Supported by PROC SQL*

Specified Data Type	Description	SAS Data Type
NUMERIC (or NUM)	floating-point	NUMERIC
DECIMAL (or DEC)	floating-point	NUMERIC
FLOAT	floating-point	NUMERIC
REAL	floating-point	NUMERIC
DOUBLE PRECISION	floating-point	NUMERIC
INTEGER (or INT)	integer	NUMERIC
SMALLINT	integer	NUMERIC
DATE	date	NUMERIC with a DATE.7 informat and format

The following PROC SQL step is very similar to the previous example. The only difference is that this step specifies three supported data types other than CHAR and NUM: VARCHAR, DATE, and FLOAT.

```
proc sql;
   create table work.discount2
         (Destination varchar(3),
         BeginDate date,
         EndDate date,
         Discount float);
```

PROC SQL converts these data types to either character or numeric, as indicated in the charts above. Therefore, the table Work.Discount2 (created by this PROC SQL step) and Work.Discount (created by the previous PROC SQL step) contains identical columns.

By supporting data types other than SAS data types, PROC SQL can save you time. In many cases, you can copy native code from an implementation of SQL that is external to SAS without having to modify the data types.

Specifying Column Widths

In SAS, the default column width for both character and numeric columns is 8 bytes. However, character and numeric data values are stored differently:

- Character data is stored one character per byte.

- Numeric data is stored as floating point numbers in real binary representation, which allows for 16- or 17-digit precision within 8 bytes.

PROC SQL enables you to specify a column width for character columns but not for numeric columns.

Note: PROC SQL allows the WIDTH and NDEC (decimal places) arguments to be included in the column specification for the DECIMAL, NUMERIC, and FLOAT data types. However, PROC SQL ignores this specification and uses the SAS defaults.

In a column specification, the column width follows the data type and is specified as an integer enclosed in parentheses:

column-name data-type <(column-width)> <column-modifier-1<...column-modifier-n>>

In the following PROC SQL step, the first column specification indicates a column width of 3 for the character column Destination:

```
proc sql;
   create table work.discount
         (Destination char(3),
          BeginDate num format=date9.,
          EndDate num format=date9.,
          Discount num);
```

Because the last three columns are numeric, no width is specified and these columns have the default column width of 8 bytes.

Specifying Column Modifiers

In the CREATE TABLE statement, a column specification might include one or more of the following SAS column modifiers: INFORMAT=, FORMAT=, and LABEL=. Column modifiers, if used, are specified at the end of the column specification.

column-name data-type <(column-width)> <...column-modifier-1 <...column-modifier-n>>

Note: A fourth SAS column modifier, LENGTH=, is not allowed in a CREATE TABLE clause. It can be used in a SELECT clause.

Example

The following PROC SQL step creates the table Work.Departments by specifying 4 columns. The column modifiers LABEL= and FORMAT= are used to specify additional column attributes.

```
proc sql;
   create table work.departments
         (Dept varchar(20) label='Department',
          Code integer label='Dept Code',
          Manager varchar(20),
          AuditDate num format=date9.);
```

The SAS log verifies that the table was created.

Table 5.6 *SAS Log*

```
NOTE: Table WORK.DEPARTMENTS created, with 0 rows and 4 columns.
```

Displaying the Structure of a Table

Overview

Sometimes you want to look at the structure (the columns and column attributes) of a table that you created or of a table that was created by someone else. When you create a table, the CREATE TABLE statement writes a message to the SAS log, which indicates the number of rows and columns in the table that was created. However, that message does not contain information about column attributes.

If you are working with an existing table that contains rows of data, you can use a PROC SQL query to generate a report that shows all of the columns in a table. However, the report does not list the column attributes, and a PROC SQL query does not generate output for an empty table.

To display a list of columns and column attributes for one or more tables in the SAS log, regardless of whether the tables contain rows of data, you can use the DESCRIBE TABLE statement in PROC SQL.

General form, DESCRIBE TABLE statement:

DESCRIBE TABLE *table-name-1*<, ... *table-name-n*>;

Here is an explanation of the syntax:

table-name
  specifies the table to be described as one of the following:

  • a one-level name

  • a two-level *libref.table* name

  • a physical pathname that is enclosed in single quotation marks.

The DESCRIBE TABLE statement writes a CREATE TABLE statement that includes column definitions to the SAS log for the specified table, regardless of how the table was originally created. For example, if the DESCRIBE TABLE statement specifies a table that was created with the DATA step, a CREATE TABLE statement is still displayed.

Note: The DESCRIBE TABLE statement also displays information about any indexes that are defined on a table. You can learn more about using the DESCRIBE TABLE statement to display information about indexes in Chapter 6, "Creating and Managing Indexes Using PROC SQL," on page 226.

TIP As an alternative to the DESCRIBE TABLE statement, you can use other SAS procedures, like PROC CONTENTS, to list a table's columns and column attributes. PROC CONTENTS generates a report instead of writing a message to the SAS log, as the DESCRIBE TABLE statement does.

Example

Earlier in this chapter, the empty table Work.Discount was created by using the CREATE TABLE statement and column specifications shown below:

```
proc sql;
   create table work.discount
```

```
(Destination char(3),
BeginDate num format=date9.,
EndDate num format=date9.,
Discount num);
```

The following DESCRIBE TABLE statement writes a CREATE TABLE statement to the SAS log for the table *Work.Discount*:

```
proc sql;
   describe table work.discount;
```

Note: For more information about the BUFSIZE= option, see "Using the BUFSIZE= Option" on page 661.

Table 5.7 *SAS Log*

```
NOTE: SQL table WORK.DISCOUNT was created like:

create table WORK.DISCOUNT( bufsize=4096 )
          (
          Destination char(3),
          BeginDate num format=DATE9.,
          EndDate num format=DATE9.,
          Discount num
          )
```

Creating an Empty Table That Is like Another Table

Overview

Sometimes you want to create a new table that has the same columns and attributes as an existing table, but has no rows. To create an empty table that is like another table, use a CREATE TABLE statement with a *LIKE clause*.

General form, CREATE TABLE statement with a LIKE clause:

CREATE TABLE *table-name*

      LIKE *table-1*;

Here is an explanation of the syntax:

table-name
    specifies the name of the table to be created.

table-1
    specifies the table whose columns and attributes are copied to the new table.

Example

Suppose you want to create a new table, Work.Flightdelays2, that contains data about flight delays. You would like the new table to contain the same columns and attributes as the existing table Sasuser.Flightdelays, but you do not want to include any of the existing data. The following PROC SQL step uses a CREATE TABLE statement and a LIKE clause to create Work.Flightdelays2:

```
proc sql;
   create table work.flightdelays2
      like sasuser.flightdelays;
```

The following DESCRIBE TABLE statement displays the structure of the empty table Work.Flightdelays2:

```
proc sql;
   describe table work.flightdelays2;
```

Table 5.8 *SAS Log*

```
NOTE: SQL table WORK.FLIGHTDELAYS2 was created like:

create table WORK.FLIGHTDELAYS2( bufsize=8192 )
  (
  Date num format=DATE9. informat=DATE9.,
  FlightNumber char(3),
  Origin char(3),
  Destination char(3),
  DelayCategory char(15),
  DestinationType char(15),
  DayOfWeek num,
  Delay num
  );
```

Work.Flightdelays2 contains eight columns, as listed.

Specifying a Subset of Columns from a Table

If you want to create an empty table that contains only a specified subset of columns from an existing table, use the SAS data set options DROP= or KEEP=.

General form, DROP=, and KEEP= data set options:

(DROP | KEEP =*column-1< ...column-n>***)**

Here is an explanation of the syntax:

column
> specifies the name of a column to be dropped or kept. Multiple column names must be separated by spaces. The entire option must be enclosed in parentheses.

In the CREATE TABLE statement, the DROP= or KEEP= option can be inserted in either of the following locations:

- between the name of the table that is being created and the LIKE clause (as shown in the following example)

- after the name of the source table, at the end of the LIKE clause.

Example

The following PROC SQL step creates the new table Work.Flightdelays3 that contains a subset of columns from the table Sasuser.Flightdelays. The DROP= option is used to specify that all columns except DelayCategory and DestinationType are included in the new table.

```
proc sql;
   create table work.flightdelays3
          (drop=delaycategory destinationtype)
      like sasuser.flightdelays;
```

For comparison, the results of running the DESCRIBE TABLE statement for the original table and the new table are shown below.

Table 5.9 *SAS Log*

```
NOTE: SQL table WORK.FLIGHTDELAYS was created like:

create table SASUSER.FLIGHTDELAYS( bufsize=8192 )
  (
  Date num format=DATE9. informat=DATE9.,
  FlightNumber char(3),
  Origin char(3),
  Destination char(3),
  DelayCategory char(15),
  DestinationType char(15),
  DayOfWeek num,
  Delay num
  );
```

Table 5.10 *SAS Log*

```
NOTE: SQL table WORK.FLIGHTDELAYS was created like:

create table WORK.FLIGHTDELAYS3( bufsize=4096 )
  (
  Date num format=DATE9. informat=DATE9.,
  FlightNumber char(3),
  Origin char(3),
  Destination char(3),
  DayOfWeek num,
  Delay num
  );
```

As these messages show, Sasuser.Flightdelays contains the columns DelayCategory and DestinationType. Work.Flightdelays3 does not contain the columns.

Note: In PROC SQL, you can apply most of the SAS data set options, such as DROP= and KEEP=, to tables anytime that you specify a table. You can use a more limited set of SAS data set options with PROC SQL views. However, because the DROP= and KEEP= options are SAS options and not part of the ANSI standard for SQL, you can use the DROP= and KEEP= options only with the SAS implementation of SQL.

Creating a Table from a Query Result

Overview

Sometimes you want to create a new table that contains both columns and rows that are derived from an existing table or set of tables. In this situation, you can submit one PROC SQL step that does both of the following:

- creates a new table

- populates the table with data from the result of a PROC SQL query.

To create a table from a query result, use a CREATE TABLE statement that includes the keyword AS and the clauses that are used in a query: SELECT, FROM, and any optional clauses, such as ORDER BY.

General form, CREATE TABLE statement with query clauses:

CREATE TABLE *table-name* **AS**

    SELECT *column-1<, ... column-n>*

        FROM *table-1 | view-1<, ... table-n | view-n>*

        <optional query clauses>;

Here is an explanation of the syntax:

table-name
    specifies the name of the table to be created.

SELECT
    specifies the column(s) that appear in the table.

FROM
    specifies the table(s) or view(s) to be queried.

optional query clauses
    are used to refine the query further and include WHERE, GROUP BY, HAVING, and ORDER BY.

You should be familiar with the use of the CREATE TABLE statement to create a table from a query result. Here is a review of this method.

When a table is created from a query result,

- the new table is populated with data that is derived from one or more tables or views that are referenced in the query's FROM clause

- the new table contains the columns that are specified in the query's SELECT clause

- the new table's columns have the same column attributes (type, length, informat, and format) as those of the selected source columns.

Note: When you are creating a table, if you do not specify a column alias for a calculated column, SAS assigns a column name, such as _TEMA001.

When query clauses are used within a CREATE TABLE statement, that query's automatic report generation is shut off. Only the new table is generated as output.

Example

Suppose you want to create a new, temporary table that contains data for ticket agents who are employed by an airline. The data that you need is a subset of the data contained in two existing tables, Sasuser.Payrollmaster and Sasuser.Staffmaster. The following PROC SQL step creates the new table Work.Ticketagents from the result of a query on the two existing tables. The WHERE clause joins the table by matching EMPID and selects the subset of rows for employees whose JobCode contains TA.

```
proc sql;
   create table work.ticketagents as
      select lastname, firstname,
             jobcode, salary
         from sasuser.payrollmaster,
              sasuser.staffmaster
         where payrollmaster.empid
             = staffmaster.empid
             and jobcode contains 'TA';
```

Note: Because this query lists two tables in the FROM clause and subsets rows based on a WHERE clause, the query is actually a PROC SQL inner join.

The new table Work.Ticketagents is not empty; it contains rows of data. Therefore, you can submit a SELECT statement to display Work.Ticketagents as a report:

```
select *
   from work.ticketagents;
```

The first four rows of Work.Ticketagents are shown below.

LastName	FirstName	JobCode	Salary
ADAMS	GERALD	TA2	$48,126
AVERY	JERRY	TA3	$54,351
BLALOCK	RALPH	TA2	$45,661
BOSTIC	MARIE	TA3	$54,299

The SAS log also displays a message, indicating that the table has been created.

Table 5.11 *SAS Log*

```
NOTE: Table WORK.TICKETAGENTS created, with 41 rows and 4 columns.
```

Copying a Table

To copy a table quickly, you can use the CREATE TABLE statement with a query that returns an entire table instead of a subset of columns and rows. The CREATE TABLE statement should contain only the following clauses:

- a SELECT clause that specifies that all columns from the source table should be selected

- a FROM clause that specifies the source table.

Note: Remember that the order of rows in a PROC SQL query result cannot be guaranteed, unless you use an ORDER BY clause. Therefore, a CREATE TABLE statement without an ORDER BY clause can create a table that contains the same rows as the original table, but the rows might be in a different order.

Example

The following PROC SQL step creates the new table Work.Supervisors2, which is an exact duplicate of the source table Sasuser.Supervisors:

```
proc sql;
   create table work.supervisors2 as
      select *
         from sasuser.supervisors;
```

The first four rows of the two tables are shown below.

Figure 5.1 *Source Table: Sasuser.Supervisors*

Supervisor Id	State	Job Category
1677	CT	BC
1834	NY	BC
1431	CT	FA
1433	NJ	FA

Figure 5.2 *New Table: Work.Supervisors2*

Supervisor Id	State	Job Category
1677	CT	BC
1834	NY	BC
1431	CT	FA
1433	NJ	FA

Inserting Rows of Data into a Table

Overview

After you have created an empty table, you will want to insert rows of data. You might also want to insert additional rows of data into tables that already contain data. You can use the INSERT statement in three different ways to insert rows of data into existing tables, either empty or populated.

Note: You can also use the INSERT statement to insert rows of data in a single table that underlies a PROC SQL view. To learn more about PROC SQL views, see Chapter 7, "Creating and Managing Views Using PROC SQL," on page 248.

Method of Inserting Row	Example

insert values by column name by using the SET clause	```proc sql;```
	 ``` insert into work.discount```
	 ``` set destination='LHR',```
	 ``` begindate='01MAR2000'd,```
	 ``` enddate='05MAR2000'd,```
	 ``` discount=.33```
	 ``` set destination='CPH',```
	 ``` begindate='03MAR2000'd,```
	 ``` enddate='10MAR2000'd,```
	 ``` discount=.15;```

insert lists of values by using the VALUES clause	```proc sql;```
	 ``` insert into work.discount (destination,```
	 ``` begindate,enddate,discount)```
	 ``` values ('LHR','01MAR2000'd,```
	 ``` '05MAR2000'd,.33)```
	 ``` values ('CPH','03MAR2000'd,```
	 ``` '10MAR2000'd,.15);```

insert rows that are copied from another table by using a query result	```proc sql;```
	 ``` insert into payrollchanges2```
	 ``` select empid,salary,dateofhire```
	 ``` from sasuser.payrollmaster```
	 ``` where empid in ('1919','1350','1401');```

In each method, the INSERT statement inserts new rows of data into the table. To indicate that the rows have been inserted, the SAS log displays a message similar to the following.

Table 5.12 *SAS Log*

```
NOTE: 1 row was inserted into WORK.DISCOUNT.
```

Here is information about how to use each of these methods to insert rows of data into a table.

Inserting Rows By Using the SET Clause

Sometimes you need to add rows of data to a table, but the data is not currently contained in any table. In this situation, you can use either the SET clause or the VALUES clause in the INSERT statement to specify the data to be added.

The SET clause in the INSERT statement enables you to specify new data to be added to a table. The SET clause specifies column names and values in pairs. PROC SQL reads each column name-value pair and assigns the value to the specified column. A separate SET clause is used for each row to be added to the table.

The syntax of the INSERT statement that contains the SET clause is shown below.

General form, INSERT statement containing the SET clause:

INSERT INTO *table-name <(target-column-1<, ... target-column-n)>*

> **SET** *column-1=value-1<, ... column-n=value-n>*

> *<... SET column-1=value-1<, ... column-n=value-n>>*;

Here is an explanation of the syntax:

table-name
> specifies the name of the table to which rows are inserted.

target-column
> specifies the name of a column into which data is inserted.

each *SET* clause
> specifies one or more values to be inserted in one or more specified columns in a row. Multiple SET clauses are not separated by commas.

column
> specifies the name of a column into which data is inserted.

value
> specifies a data value to be inserted into the specified column. Character values must be enclosed in quotation marks.

multiple *column=value* pairs in a SET clause
> are separated by commas.

Note: It is optional to include a list of target column names after the table name in the INSERT TABLE statement that includes a SET clause. The list can include the names of all or only a subset of columns in the table. If you specify an optional list of target column names, then you can specify values only for columns that are in the list. You can list target columns in any order, regardless of their position in the table. Any columns that are in the table but not listed are given missing values in the inserted rows.

Note: Although it is recommended that the SET clause list column-value pairs in order (as they appear in the table column list or the optional column list), it is not required.

Example

Consider the table Work.Discount, which was presented in the last topic. Work.Discount stores airline discounts for certain flight destinations and time periods in March. By submitting a DESCRIBE TABLE statement, you can see this table's columns and column attributes.

Table 5.13 *SAS Log*

```
NOTE: SQL table WORK.DISCOUNT was created like:

create table WORK.DISCOUNT( bufsize=4096 )
  (
  Destination char(3),
  BeginDate num format=DATE9.,
  EndDate num format=DATE9.,
  Discount num
  );
```

The following PROC SQL step does both of the following:

- adds two rows of new data to Work.Discount by using an INSERT statement that contains two SET clauses, one for each row

- generates a report that displays Work.Discount, with its two new rows, by using a SELECT statement.

In this situation, you do not need to include an optional list of column names.

```
proc sql;
    insert into work.discount
        set destination='LHR',
            begindate='01MAR2000'd,
            enddate='05MAR2000'd,
            discount=.33
        set destination='CPH',
            begindate='03MAR2000'd,
            enddate='10MAR2000'd,
            discount=.15;
    select *
      from discount;
```

Destination	BeginDate	EndDate	Discount
LHR	01MAR2000	05MAR2000	0.33
CPH	03MAR2000	10MAR2000	0.15

Inserting Rows By Using the VALUES Clause

The INSERT statement uses the VALUES clause to insert a list of values into a table. Unlike the SET clause, the VALUES clause does not specify a column name for each value, so the values must be listed in the correct order. Values must be specified in the order in which the columns appear in the table or, if an optional column list is specified, in the order in which the columns appear in that list. A separate VALUES clause is used for each row to be added to the table.

General form, INSERT statement containing the VALUES clause:

INSERT INTO *table-name* <*(target-column-1*<, *... target-column-n)*>

       VALUES (*value-1*<, *... value-n)*>

       <*... VALUES* (*value-1*<, *... value-n*>)>;

Here is an explanation of the syntax:

table-name
    specifies the name of the table to which rows are inserted.

target-column
    specifies the name of a column into which data is inserted.

each *VALUES* clause
    lists the values to be inserted in some or all columns in one row, which is enclosed in parentheses. Multiple VALUES clauses are not separated by commas.

value
    specifies a data value to be added. Character values must be enclosed in quotation marks. Multiple values must be separated by commas. Values must be listed in positional order, either as they appear in the table or, if the optional column list is specified, as they appear in the column list.

Note: It is optional to include a list of target column names after the table name in the INSERT TABLE statement that includes a VALUES clause. The list can include the names of all or only a subset of columns in the table. If an optional list of target column names is specified, then only those columns are given values by the statement. Target columns can be listed in any order, regardless of their position in the table. Any columns that are in the table but not listed are given missing values in the inserted rows.

You can use the VALUES clause to insert a value for all or only some of the columns in the table.

If you want to ...	Then ...	Example
| insert a value for all columns in the table | You can omit the optional list of column names in the INSERT statement.<br><br>PROC SQL<br><br>• reads values in the order in which they are specified in the VALUES clause<br><br>• inserts the values into columns in the order in which the columns appear in the table. | ```
insert into work.newtable
    values ('WI','FLUTE',6)
    values ('ST','VIOLIN',3);
``` |
```

If you want to ...	Then ...	Example
insert a value for only some of the columns in the table	You must include a list of column names in the INSERT statement. PROC SQL • reads values in the order in which they are specified in the VALUES clause • inserts the values into columns in the order in which the columns are specified in the column list.	```insert into work.newtable (item,qty) values ('FLUTE',6) values ('VIOLIN',3);```

You must list a value for every column into which PROC SQL inserts values (as specified in either the table list or the optional list of column names). To specify that a value is missing, use a space enclosed in single quotation marks for character values and a period for numeric values. For example, the following VALUES clause specifies values to be inserted in three columns; the first two values are missing:

```
values (' ', ., 45)
```

In this example, the first value specified is a missing value for a character column, and the second value is a missing value for a numeric column.

Example

Suppose you want to insert two more rows into the table Work.Discount, which stores airline discounts for certain flight destinations and time periods in March. In the previous section, you inserted two rows into Work.Discount by using the SET clause, so the table now looks like the following table.

Destination	BeginDate	EndDate	Discount
LHR	01MAR2000	05MAR2000	0.33
CPH	03MAR2000	10MAR2000	0.15

Add two more rows, by using the VALUES clause. The following PROC SQL step adds two rows of new data to Work.Discount and generates a report that displays the updated table:

```
proc sql;
   insert into work.discount (destination,
        begindate,enddate,discount)
      values ('ORD','05MAR2000'd,'15MAR2000'd,.25)
      values ('YYZ','06MAR2000'd,'20MAR2000'd,.10);
   select *
      from work.discount;
```

Destination	BeginDate	EndDate	Discount
LHR	01MAR2000	05MAR2000	0.33
CPH	03MAR2000	10MAR2000	0.15
ORD	05MAR2000	15MAR2000	0.25
YYZ	06MAR2000	20MAR2000	0.1

The two rows that were just inserted by using the VALUES clause are the third and fourth rows above.

You might have noticed that the INSERT statement in this example includes an optional list of column names. In this example, data is being inserted into all columns of the table, and the values are listed in the order in which the columns appear in the table, so it is not strictly necessary to use a column list. However, including the list of column names makes it easier to read the code and understand what the code is doing.

Inserting Rows from a Query Result

The fastest way to insert rows of data into a table is to use a query to select existing rows from one or more tables (or views) and to insert the rows into another table. You can insert rows from a query result into either an empty table or a table that already contains rows of data. When you add rows of data to a table that already contains rows, the new rows are added at the end of the table.

To insert rows from a query result, use an INSERT statement that includes the clauses that are used in a query: SELECT, FROM, and any optional clauses, such as ORDER BY. Values from the query result are inserted into columns in the order in which the columns appear in the table or, if an optional column list is specified, in the order in which the columns appear in that list.

General form, INSERT statement containing query clauses:

INSERT INTO *table-name* <*(target-column-1*<, *... target-column-n)*>

    SELECT *column-1*<, *... column-n*>

        FROM *table-1* | *view-1*<, *... table-n* | *view-n*>

        <*optional query clauses*>;

Here is an explanation of the syntax:

table-name
    specifies the name of the table to which rows are inserted.

target-column
    specifies the name of a column into which data is inserted.

SELECT
    specifies the column(s) that is inserted.

FROM
    specifies the table(s) or view(s) to be queried.

optional query clauses
    are used to refine the query further. These include the WHERE, GROUP BY, and HAVING, clauses.

Note: It is optional to include a list of target column names after the table name in the INSERT TABLE statement that includes query clauses. The list can include the names of all or only a subset of columns in the table. If an optional list of target column names is specified, then only those columns are given values by the statement. Target columns might be listed in any order, regardless of their position in the table. Any columns that are in the table but not listed are given missing values in the inserted rows.

Example

A mechanic at a company has been promoted from level 2 to level 3, and you need to add this employee to Sasuser.Mechanicslevel3, a table that lists all level-3 mechanics. Create a temporary copy of Sasuser.Mechanicslevel3 called Work.Mechanicslevel3_New, and display the new table in a report:

```
proc sql;
    create table work.mechanicslevel3_new
        select *
            from sasuser.mechanicslevel3;
```

EmpID	JobCode	Salary
1499	ME3	$60.235
1409	ME3	$58.171
1379	ME3	$59.170
1521	ME3	$58.136
1385	ME3	$61.460
1420	ME3	$60.299
1882	ME3	$58.153

Next, you insert a row into Work.Mechanicslevel3_New for the new level-3 employee, whose EmpID is **1653**. This employee is currently listed in Sasuser.Mechanicslevel2, so your INSERT statement queries the table Sasuser.Mechanicslevel2. Your PROC SQL step ends with a SELECT statement that outputs the revised table Work.Mechanicslevel3_New to a report.

```
proc sql;
    insert into work.mechanicslevel3_new
        select empid, jobcode, salary
            from sasuser.mechanicslevel2
            where empid='1653';
        select *
            from work.mechanicslevel3_new;
```

EmpID	JobCode	Salary
1499	ME3	$60.235
1409	ME3	$58.171
1379	ME3	$59.170
1521	ME3	$58.136
1385	ME3	$61.460
1420	ME3	$60.299
1882	ME3	$58.153
1653	ME2	$49.151

The row that you have inserted into Work.Mechanicslevel3_New is row 8 above. As you can see, the values for JobCode and Salary for the new employee have to be changed. Updating existing values in a table is covered later in this chapter.

Note: Although the new row is shown here at the bottom of the table, the order of rows in a PROC SQL query cannot be guaranteed if an ORDER BY clause is not used.

Creating a Table That Has Integrity Constraints

Overview

Integrity constraints are rules that you can specify in order to restrict the data values that can be stored for a column in a table. SAS enforces integrity constraints when values associated with a column are added, updated, or deleted. Integrity constraints help you preserve the validity and consistency of your data.

You can create integrity constraints by using either PROC SQL or PROC DATASETS. PROC DATASETS can assign constraints only to an existing table. PROC SQL can assign constraints either as it creates a new table or as it modifies an existing table. This chapter discusses the use of PROC SQL to Create integrity constraints while creating a table.

Note: To learn more about the use of PROC DATASETS to Create integrity constraints, see Chapter 18, "Modifying SAS Data Sets and Tracking Changes," on page 608. For additional information about integrity constraints, see the SAS documentation.

Note: To add integrity constraints to an existing table using PROC SQL, use the ALTER TABLE statement.

When you place integrity constraints on a table, you specify the type of constraint that you want to create. Each constraint has a different action.

Constraint Type	Action
CHECK	Ensures that a specific set or range of values are the only values in a column. It can also check the validity of a value in one column based on a value in another column within the same row.
NOT NULL	Guarantees that a column has nonmissing values in each row.
UNIQUE	Enforces uniqueness for the values of a column.
PRIMARY KEY	Uniquely defines a row within a table, which can be a single column or a set of columns. A table can have only one PRIMARY KEY. The PRIMARY KEY includes the attributes of the constraints NOT NULL and UNIQUE.
FOREIGN KEY	Links one or more rows in a table to a specific row in another table by matching a column or set of columns (a FOREIGN KEY) in one table with the PRIMARY KEY in another table. This parent/child relationship limits modifications made to both PRIMARY KEY and FOREIGN KEY constraints. The only acceptable values for a FOREIGN KEY are values of the PRIMARY KEY or missing values.

Note: When you add an integrity constraint to a table that contains data, SAS checks all data values to determine whether they satisfy the constraint before the constraint is added.

You can use integrity constraints in two ways, general and referential. General constraints enable you to restrict the data values accepted for a column in a single table. Referential constraints enable you to link the data values of a column in one table to the data values of columns in another table.

General Integrity Constraints

General integrity constraints enable you to restrict the values of columns within a single table. The following four integrity constraints can be used as general integrity constraints:

- CHECK
- NOT NULL
- UNIQUE
- PRIMARY KEY.

Note: A PRIMARY KEY constraint is a general integrity constraint if it does not have any FOREIGN KEY constraints referencing it. A PRIMARY KEY used as a general constraint is a shortcut for assigning the constraints NOT NULL and UNIQUE.

Referential Integrity Constraints

A referential integrity constraint is created when a PRIMARY KEY integrity constraint in one table is referenced by a FOREIGN KEY integrity constraint in another table. There are two steps that must be followed to create a referential integrity constraint:

1. Define a PRIMARY KEY constraint on the first table.

2. Define a FOREIGN KEY constraint on other tables.

Note: Integrity constraints

- follow ANSI standards
- cannot be defined for views
- cannot be defined for historical versions of generation data sets.

To create a table that has integrity constraints, use a CREATE TABLE statement that specifies both columns and constraints. There are two ways to specify integrity constraints in the CREATE TABLE statement:

- in a column specification
- as a separate constraint specification.

You can use either or both of these methods in the same CREATE TABLE statement.

Creating a Constraint in a Column Specification

Earlier in this chapter, you learned how to create a table by using a CREATE TABLE statement that contains column specifications:

CREATE TABLE *table-name*

        (*column-specification-1<,*

        ...column-specification-n>);

You also learned that a column specification consists of these elements:

column-definition <column-constraint-1<, ... column-constraint-n>>
  <MESSAGE='message-string' <MSGTYPE=message-type>>

The column specifications used in earlier examples contained only the column definition. Now we learn how to create an integrity constraint with a column, by specifying the optional column constraint in the column specification:

General form, column-constraint in a column-specification:

column-definition <column-constraint-1<, ... column-constraint-n>>

<MESSAGE='message-string' <MSGTYPE=message-type>>

Here is an explanation of the syntax:

column-constraint
  is one of the following:

  CHECK (*expression*)
    specifies that all rows in the table (which is specified in the CREATE TABLE statement) satisfy the *expression*, which can be any valid where-expression.

  DISTINCT
    specifies that the values of the column must be unique within the table. This constraint is identical to UNIQUE.

  NOT NULL
    specifies that the column does not contain a null or missing value, including special missing values.

  PRIMARY KEY
    specifies that the column is a PRIMARY KEY column, that is, a column that does not contain missing values and whose values are unique.

  REFERENCES *table-name* <ON DELETE *referential-action*> <ON UPDATE *referential-action*>
    specifies that the column is a FOREIGN KEY, that is, a column whose values are linked to the values of the PRIMARY KEY column in another table (the *table-name* that is specified for REFERENCES). The *referential-actions* are performed when the values of a PRIMARY KEY column that is referenced by the FOREIGN KEY are updated or deleted. The *referential-action* specifies the type of action to be performed on all matching FOREIGN KEY values and is one of the following:

  CASCADE
    allows PRIMARY KEY data values to be updated, and updates matching values in the FOREIGN KEY to the same values.

> *Note:* This referential action is currently supported for updates only.

  RESTRICT
    occurs only if there are matching FOREIGN KEY values. This referential action is the default.

  SET NULL
    sets all matching FOREIGN KEY values to NULL.

  UNIQUE
    specifies that the values of the column must be unique within the table. This constraint is identical to DISTINCT.

Note: The optional MSGTYPE= and MESSAGE= elements are discussed later in this chapter.

Just like a column, an integrity constraint must have a unique name within the table. If you create an integrity constraint by specifying a column constraint in a column specification, then SAS automatically assigns a name to the constraint. The form of the constraint name depends on the type of constraint, as shown below:

Constraint Type	Default Name
CHECK	_CKxxxx_
FOREIGN KEY	_FKxxxx_
NOT NULL	_NMxxxx_
PRIMARY KEY	_PKxxxx_
UNIQUE	_UNxxxx_

Note: xxxx is a counter that begins at 0001.

Here is an example of a PROC SQL step that creates integrity constraints by specifying one or more column constraints in a column specification.

Example

Suppose you need to create the table Work.Employees to store the identification number, name, gender, and hire date for all employees. In addition, you want to ensure the following:

- the ID column contains only values that are nonmissing and unique
- the Gender column contains only the values **M** and **F**.

The following PROC SQL step creates the table Work.Employees, that contains four columns and integrity constraints for two of those columns:

```
proc sql;
   create table work.employees
      (ID char (5) primary key,
      Name char(10),
      Gender char(1) not null check(gender in ('M','F')),
      HDate date label='Hire Date');
```

In the column specification for ID, the PRIMARY KEY column constraint ensures that the ID column contains only values that are nonmissing and unique.

The column specification for Gender defines two integrity constraints:

- The NOT NULL column constraint ensures that the values of Gender are nonmissing values.
- The CHECK column constraint ensures that the values of Gender satisfy the expression **gender in ('M','F')**.

Here is another method of creating integrity constraints: specifying a constraint specification in the CREATE TABLE statement.

Creating a Constraint By Using a Constraint Specification

Sometimes you might prefer to Create integrity constraints outside of column specifications, by specifying individual constraint specifications in the CREATE TABLE statement:

CREATE TABLE *table-name*

>(*column-specification-1*<,
>
>...*column-specification-n*><,
>
>*constraint-specification-1*><,
>
>...*constraint-specification-n*>**);**

The first specification in the CREATE TABLE statement must be a column specification. However, following the initial column specification in the statement, you can include multiple additional column specifications, constraint specifications, or both. All specifications after the first column specification can be listed in any order. The entire list of column specifications and constraint specifications follows the same guidelines that were presented earlier for column specifications:

- The entire set of column specifications and constraint specifications must be enclosed in parentheses.

- Multiple column specifications and constraint specifications must be separated by commas.

There are several important differences between specifying an integrity constraint within a column specification and specifying an integrity constraint by using a separate constraint specification. Using a constraint specification offers the following advantages:

- You can specify a name for the constraint. In fact, you must specify a name, because SAS does not automatically assign one.

- For certain constraint types, you can define a constraint for multiple columns in a single specification.

The syntax of a constraint specification is shown below.

CONSTRAINT *constraint-name constraint* <MESSAGE=*'message-string'* <MSGTYPE=*message-type*>>

constraint-name
> specifies a name for the constraint that is being specified. The name must be a valid SAS name.

> ***CAUTION:***
> > PRIMARY, FOREIGN, MESSAGE, UNIQUE, DISTINCT, CHECK, and NOT cannot be used as values for *constraint-name*.

constraint
> is one of the following:

> CHECK (*expression*)
> > specifies that all rows in *table-name* (which is specified in the CREATE TABLE statement) satisfy the expression, which can be any valid where-expression.

> DISTINCT (*column-1*<, ... *column-n*>)
> > specifies that the values of each column must be unique within the table. This constraint is identical to UNIQUE.

FOREIGN KEY (*column-1<, ... column-n>*)
REFERENCES *table-name*
<ON DELETE *referential-action*>
<ON UPDATE *referential-action*>

> specifies a FOREIGN KEY, that is, a set of columns whose values are linked to the values of the PRIMARY KEY column in another table (the table name that is specified for REFERENCES). The *referential-actions* are performed when the values of a PRIMARY KEY column that is referenced by the FOREIGN KEY are updated or deleted. The *referential-action* specifies the type of action to be performed on all matching FOREIGN KEY values, and is one of the following:

> - CASCADE
>
>   allows PRIMARY KEY data values to be updated, and updates matching values in the FOREIGN KEY to the same values.
>
>   *Note:* This referential action is currently supported for updates only.
>
> - RESTRICT
>
>   occurs only if there are matching FOREIGN KEY values. This referential action is the default.
>
> - SET NULL
>
>   sets all matching FOREIGN KEY values to NULL.

NOT NULL (*column*)

> specifies that the column does not contain a null or missing value, including special missing values.

PRIMARY KEY (*column-1<, ... column-n>*)

> specifies one or more columns as PRIMARY KEY columns, that is, columns that do not contain missing values and whose values are unique.

UNIQUE (*column-1<, ... column-n>*)

> specifies that the values of each column must be unique within the table. This constraint is identical to DISTINCT.

MESSAGE=

> specifies a *message-string* that specifies the text of an error message that is written to the SAS log when the integrity constraint is not met. The maximum length of message-string is 250 characters.

MSGTYPE=

> specifies the *message-type*, which specifies how the error message is displayed in the SAS log when an integrity constraint is not met. The message-type is one of the following:

> | | |
> |---|---|
> | NEWLINE | the text that is specified for MESSAGE= is displayed in addition to the default error message for that integrity constraint. |
> | USER | only the text that is specified for MESSAGE= is displayed. |

Note: Elements within a constraint-specification must be separated by spaces.

You might have noticed another difference between the two methods of creating an integrity constraint. When you use a column specification to create a FOREIGN KEY integrity constraint, you use the keyword FOREIGN KEY in addition to the keyword REFERENCES.

Here is an example of a PROC SQL step that uses column specifications to Create integrity constraints on a column.

Example

In an example earlier in this chapter, the table Work.Discount was created to hold data about discounts that are offered by an airline. Suppose you now want to ensure that the table

- holds only discounts that are less than or equal to .5

- does not allow missing values for Destination.

Create a new version of the table Work.Discount, called Work.Discount3, that includes two integrity constraints. One integrity constraint limits the values that can be entered in the Discount column and the other prevents missing values from being entered in the Destination column. The following PROC SQL step creates Work.Discount3 by specifying four columns and two integrity constraints:

```
proc sql;
   create table work.discount3
          (Destination char(3),
           BeginDate num Format=date9.,
           EndDate num format=date9.,
           Discount num,
           constraint ok_discount check (discount le .5),
           constraint notnull_dest not null(destination));
```

The CHECK integrity constraint named OK_Discount uses the WHERE expression `discount le .5` to limit the values that can be added to the Discount column.

The NOT NULL integrity constraint named NotNull_Dest prevents missing values from being entered in Destination.

Handling Errors in Row Insertions

Overview

When you add rows to a table that has integrity constraints, PROC SQL evaluates the new data to ensure that it meets the conditions that are determined by the integrity constraints. If the new (or modified) data complies with the integrity constraints, the rows are added. However, if you add data that does not comply with the integrity constraints, the rows are not added. To find out whether rows of data have been successfully added, you need to check the SAS log.

Note: PROC SQL also evaluates changes that are made to existing data by using the UPDATE and DELETE statements. These statements are discussed later in this chapter.

Example

In a previous section of this chapter, the following PROC SQL step was used to create the table Work.Discount3 with two integrity constraints, one on the column Discount and the other on the column Destination:

```
proc sql;
   create table work.discount3
```

```
(Destination char(3),
BeginDate num Format=date9.,
EndDate num format=date9.,
Discount num,
constraint ok_discount check (discount le .5),
constraint notnull_dest not null(destination));
```

This table does not yet contain any rows, so add some data. The following INSERT statement uses the VALUES clause to add two rows of data to the table:

```
proc sql;
    insert into work.discount3
            values('CDG','03MAR2000'd,'10MAR2000'd,.15)
            values('LHR','10MAR2000'd,'12MAR2000'd,.55);
```

When this PROC SQL step is submitted, the following messages are displayed in the SAS log.

Table 5.14   *SAS Log*

```
ERROR: Add/Update failed for data set WORK.DISCOUNT3
because data value(s) do not comply with integrity constraint
ok_discount.
NOTE: This insert failed while attempting to add data from
VALUES clause 2 to the data set.
NOTE: Deleting the successful inserts before error noted above
to restore table to a consistent state.
```

The three parts of this message explain what the problem is:

- The error message indicates that this attempt to add rows failed. One or more of the data values for Discount does not comply with the integrity constraint OK_Discount, which specifies that values in the column Discount must be less than or equal to .5.

- The first note indicates that there is a problem with the second VALUES clause. This clause specifies a value of .55 for the column Discount, which does not comply.

    CAUTION:
    Even if multiple VALUES clauses specify non-compliant data values, the SAS log lists only the first VALUES clause that violates the constraint.

- The second note indicates that SAS is "deleting the successful inserts" before the error. Even though all the other specified data is valid, none of the data has been added to the table.

We need to consider why SAS prevented any of the data from being added to the table.

Using the UNDO_POLICY= Option to Control UNDO Processing

When you use the INSERT or UPDATE statement to add or modify data in a table, you can control how PROC SQL handles updated data if any errors occur during the insertion or update process. You can use the UNDO_POLICY= option in the PROC SQL statement to specify whether PROC SQL accepts or unaccepts the changes that you submitted up to the point of the error.

You can specify one of the following values for the UNDO_POLICY= option.

UNDO_POLICY=Setting	Description
REQUIRED	PROC SQL performs UNDO processing for INSERT and UPDATE statements. If the UNDO operation cannot be done reliably, PROC SQL does not execute the statement and issues an ERROR message. This is the PROC SQL default.
NONE	PROC SQL skips records that cannot be inserted or updated, and writes a warning message to the SAS log similar to that written by PROC APPEND. Any data that meets the integrity constraints is added or updated.
OPTIONAL	PROC SQL performs UNDO processing if it can be done reliably. If the UNDO cannot be done reliably, then no UNDO processing is attempted. This action is a combination of REQUIRED and NONE. If UNDO can be done reliably, then it is done, and PROC SQL proceeds as if UNDO_POLICY=REQUIRED is in effect. Otherwise, it proceeds as if UNDO_POLICY=NONE was specified.

CAUTION:
In the following two situations, you cannot reliably attempt the UNDO operation:

A SAS data set that is accessed through a SAS/SHARE server and opened with CNTLLEV=RECORD can allow other users to update newly inserted records. An error during the insert deletes the record that the other user updated.

Changes made through a SAS/ACCESS view might not be able to reverse changes made by the INSERT or UPDATE statement without reversing other changes at the same time.

Note: The ANSI standard for SQL includes a ROLLBACK statement that is used for UNDO processing. The ROLLBACK statement is not currently supported in PROC SQL.

Note: When you use the UNDO_POLICY= option, the value that you set remains in effect for the entire PROC SQL statement or until a RESET statement is used to change the option. To learn more about the RESET statement, see Chapter 8, "Managing Processing Using PROC SQL," on page 264.

Example

In the last example, the INSERT step was used to insert two rows of data into the table Work.Discount3, which has two integrity constraints. Because the UNDO_POLICY= option was not specified in the code, PROC SQL used the default policy, which is UNDO_POLICY=REQUIRED. When PROC SQL encountered a value in the INSERT statement that violated an integrity constraint, none of the new values specified in the INSERT statement were added to the table.

Consider what happens when we submit the same INSERT statement and specify the option UNDO_POLICY=NONE.

The following PROC SQL step creates the table Work.Discount4, which has four columns and two integrity constraints, and inserts the same two rows of data that were inserted in the earlier example. In this case, however, the option UNDO_POLICY=NONE is specified.

```
proc sql undo_policy=none;
   create table work.discount4
          (Destination char(3),
          BeginDate num Format=date9.,
          EndDate num format=date9.,
          Discount num,
          constraint ok_discount check (discount le .5),
          constraint notnull_dest not null(destination));
   insert into work.discount4
          values('CDG','03MAR2000'd,'10MAR2000'd,.15)
          values('LHR','10MAR2000'd,'12MAR2000'd,.55);
```

As you know, one of the data values for the column Discount violates the specified constraint. When this step is submitted, the SAS log displays the following messages.

Table 5.15 *SAS Log*

```
WARNING: The SQL option UNDO_POLICY=REQUIRED is not in effect.
If an error is detected when processing this INSERT statement,
that error will not cause the entire statement to fail.
ERROR: Add/Update failed for data set WORK.DISCOUNT4 because
data value(s) do not comply with integrity constraint ok_discount.
NOTE: This insert failed while attempting to add data from VALUES
clause 2 to the data set.

NOTE: 2 rows were inserted into WORK.DISCOUNT4 -- of these 1 row
was rejected as an ERROR, leaving 1 row that was inserted
successfully.
```

The four parts of this message explain what the problem is and how PROC SQL will handle UNDO processing:

• The warning tells you that you have specified a setting for the UNDO_POLICY= option that is different from the default (REQUIRED). The warning also explains that, as a result, if an error is detected, the error does not cause the entire INSERT statement to fail.

• The error message was also displayed in the earlier example, when the default setting of UNDO_POLICY= was in effect. This message states that the INSERT statement failed and explains why.

• The first note was also displayed in the earlier example, when the default setting of UNDO_POLICY= was in effect. This note identifies the first VALUES clause that contains non-compliant data.

• The second note tells you that one row (the first row of the two rows that you specified) was inserted successfully into the table.

Displaying Integrity Constraints for a Table

Overview

Sometimes you want to add data to a table but you are not sure what integrity constraints, if any, the table has. To display only the integrity constraints for a specified table, use a DESCRIBE TABLE CONSTRAINTS statement. (The DESCRIBE TABLE statement, which is discussed earlier in this chapter, lists both a CREATE TABLE statement and the table's integrity constraints in the SAS log.)

Note: Some versions of SAS display information about integrity constraints in output as well as in the SAS log.

General form, DESCRIBE TABLE CONSTRAINTS statement:

DESCRIBE TABLE CONSTRAINTS *table-name-1<, ... table-name-n>*;

Here is an explanation of the syntax:

table-name
> specifies the table to be described as one of the following:

> - a one-level name

> - a two-level *libref.table* name

> - a physical pathname that is enclosed in single quotation marks.

Example

To display only the table constraints for the table Work.Discount4 that was created earlier, you submit the following PROC SQL step:

```
proc sql;
    describe table constraints work.discount4;
```

Table 5.16 *SAS Log*

```
NOTE: SQL table WORK.DISCOUNT4 ( bufsize=4096 ) has the
following integrity constraint(s):

-----Alphabetic List of Integrity Constraints-----

      Integrity                      Where
    * Constraint   Type      Variables   Clause
    ---------------------------------------------
    1   notnull_dest Not Null Destination
    2   ok_discount Check Discount<=0.5
```

-----Alphabetic List of Integrity Constraints-----				
#	Integrity Constraint	Type	Variables	Where Clause
1	notnull_dest	Not Null	Destination	
2	ok_discount	Check		Discount<=0.5

As shown, Work.Discount4 has two integrity constraints: NotNull_Dest and OK_Discount.

Updating Values in Existing Table Rows

Overview

To modify data values in some or all of the existing rows in a table, you use the UPDATE statement in PROC SQL. In the UPDATE statement, for each column whose rows you want to modify, you specify an expression that indicates how the values should be modified. For example, the following expression indicates that the values for the column Units should be multiplied by 4:

```
units=units*4
```

You can use the UPDATE statement in two main ways.

Method of Updating Table	Example
update all (or a subset of) rows in a column with the same expression	```proc sql; update work.payrollmaster_new set salary=salary*1.05 where jobcode like '__1';```
update different rows in a column with different expressions	```proc sql; update work.payrollmaster_new set salary=salary* case when substr(jobcode,3,1)='1' then 1.05 when substr(jobcode,3,1)='2' then 1.10 when substr(jobcode,3,1)='3' then 1.15 else 1.08 end;```

Note: The UPDATE statement does not insert new rows into the table. To insert rows, you must use the INSERT statement.

Note: You can also use the UPDATE statement to update existing values in a table that underlies a PROC SQL view. For details, see Chapter 7, "Creating and Managing Views Using PROC SQL," on page 248.

We consider each of these methods for updating existing rows in a table.

Updating Rows By Using the Same Expression

To update all (or a subset of) rows in a column with the same expression, use an UPDATE statement that contains a SET clause and a possible WHERE clause.

General form, basic UPDATE statement for updating table rows:

UPDATE *table-name*

    SET *column-1=expression<, ... column-n=expression>>*

    <WHERE expression>;

Here is an explanation of the syntax:

table-name
    specifies the name of the table in which values are updated.

SET
    specifies one or more pairs of *column* names to be updated, and *expression*s that indicate how each column is to be updated.

WHERE
    is used to specify an *expression* that subsets the rows to be updated.

CAUTION:
    If you want to update only a subset of rows in the table, you must specify a WHERE clause or all rows of the table that are updated.

Example

Suppose a company is considering giving all level-1 employees a 5% raise. Employee salaries are stored in the table Sasuser.Payrollmaster. You do not want to update the original table, so you create a temporary copy of Sasuser.Payrollmaster, called Work.Payrollmaster_New. The following PROC SQL step creates Work.Payrollmaster_New based on a query result and generates an output report of the new table:

```
proc sql;
   create table work.payrollmaster_new as
      select *
         from sasuser.payrollmaster;
   select *
      from work.payrollmaster_new;
```

The first 10 rows of Work.Payrollmaster_New, the table in which you update salaries, are shown below.

DateOfBirth	DateOfHire	EmpID	Gender	JobCode	Salary
16SEP1958	07JUN1985	1919	M	TA2	$48,126
19OCT1962	12AUG1988	1653	F	ME2	$49,151
08NOV1965	19OCT1988	1400	M	ME1	$41,677
04SEP1963	01AUG1988	1350	F	FA3	$46,040
16DEC1948	21NOV1983	1401	M	TA3	$54,351
29APR1952	11JUN1978	1499	M	ME3	$60,235
09JUN1960	04OCT1988	1101	M	SCP	$26,212
03APR1959	14FEB1979	1333	M	PT2	$124,048
20JAN1961	05DEC1988	1402	M	TA2	$45,661
26DEC1966	09OCT1987	1479	F	TA3	$54,299

Next, you write a PROC SQL step that updates the specified rows. The UPDATE statement contains both of the following:

- a SET clause that specifies the expression to be used in updating Salary

- a WHERE clause that specifies a subset of rows (level-1 employees) to be updated.

```
proc sql;
   update work.payrollmaster_new
      set salary=salary*1.05
      where jobcode like '__1';
```

Finally, you can use a SELECT statement to display the updated table as a report. The first 10 rows of Work.Payrollmaster_New, with updates, are shown below.

DateOfBirth	DateOfHire	EmpID	Gender	JobCode	Salary
16SEP1958	07JUN1985	1919	M	TA2	$48,126
19OCT1962	12AUG1988	1653	F	ME2	$49,151
08NOV1965	19OCT1988	1400	M	ME1	$43,761
04SEP1963	01AUG1988	1350	F	FA3	$46,040
16DEC1948	21NOV1983	1401	M	TA3	$54,351
29APR1952	11JUN1978	1499	M	ME3	$60,235
09JUN1960	04OCT1988	1101	M	SCP	$26,212
03APR1959	14FEB1979	1333	M	PT2	$124,048
20JAN1961	05DEC1988	1402	M	TA2	$45,661
26DEC1966	09OCT1987	1479	F	TA3	$54,299

The third row lists data for a level-1 employee, and that person's salary has been updated.

If you wanted to increase all of the salaries, you would simply remove the WHERE clause from the UPDATE statement:

```
proc sql;
   update work.payrollmaster_new
      set salary=salary*1.05;
```

Updating Rows By Using Different Expressions

Sometimes you want to use different expressions to modify values for different subsets of rows within a column.

For example, instead of only raising the salary of level-1 employees by 5%, you might also want to raise the salaries of level-2 employees by 10%, and so on, using a different percentage increase for each group of employees.

There are two possible ways to use different expressions to update different subsets of rows.

Method of Updating Table	Example
use multiple UPDATE statements subset of rows A single UPDATE statement can contain only a single WHERE clause, so multiple UPDATE statements are needed to specify expressions for multiple subsets of rows.	```proc sql; update work.payrollmaster_new set salary=salary*1.05 where substr(jobcode,3,1)='1'; update work.payrollmaster_new set salary=salary*1.10 where substr(jobcode,3,1)='2'; update work.payrollmaster_new set salary=salary*1.15 where substr(jobcode,3,1)='3';```
use a single UPDATE statement that contains a CASE expression	```proc sql; update work.payrollmaster_new set salary=salary* case when substr(jobcode,3,1)='1' then 1.05 when substr(jobcode,3,1)='2' then 1.10 when substr(jobcode,3,1)='3' then 1.15 else 1.08 end;```

The first method, which requires the use of multiple UPDATE statements, is cumbersome because the SET statement and expression must be repeated in each UPDATE statement. In this example, the first method is inefficient because the table Work.Payrollmaster_New must be read three times.

The second method, which uses conditional processing (the CASE expression), is recommended. We now consider the second method.

To update different subsets of rows in a table in different ways, you can incorporate conditional processing by using the CASE expression in the SET clause of an UPDATE statement. The CASE expression selects result values that satisfy specified conditions.

General form, CASE expression:

CASE *<case-operand>*

> **WHEN** *when-condition* **THEN** *result-expression*
>
> *<...WHEN when-condition THEN result-expression>*
>
> *<ELSE result-expression>*

END;

Here is an explanation of the syntax:

CASE
> performs conditional processing.

case-operand
> is an optional expression that resolves to a table column whose values are compared to all the *when-conditions*.

WHEN
> specifies a *when-condition*, a shortened expression that assumes *case-operand* as one of its operands, and that resolves to true or false.

THEN
> specifies a *result-expression*, an expression that resolves to a value.

ELSE
> specifies a *result-expression*, which provides an alternate action if none of the *when-conditions* is executed.

END
> indicates the end of the CASE expression.

CAUTION:
> Although the ELSE clause is optional, its use is strongly recommended. If you omit the ELSE clause, each row that is not described in one of the WHEN clauses receives a missing value for the column that you are updating.

Note: You can also use the CASE expression in the INSERT and SELECT statements.

Example

In the following UPDATE statement, the CASE expression contains three WHEN-THEN clauses that specify three different subsets of rows in the table Work.Insure_New:

- homeowners that are insured by Acme

- homeowners that are insured by Reliable

- homeowners that are insured by Homelife.

```
update work.insure_new
   set pctinsured=pctinsured*
      case
         when company='ACME'
              then 1.10
         when company='RELIABLE'
              then 1.15
         when company='HOMELIFE'
```

```
                    then 1.25
            else 1
        end;
```

PROC SQL updates each specified subset of rows differently, according to the corresponding WHEN-THEN (or ELSE) clause.

How PROC SQL Updates Rows Based on a CASE Expression

When you specify a CASE expression, PROC SQL updates each row as follows:

1. In the CASE expression, PROC SQL finds the WHEN-THEN clause that contains a condition that the row matches.

2. The CASE expression then returns the result from the matching WHEN-THEN clause to the SET clause. The returned value completes the expression in the SET clause.

3. The SET clause uses the completed expression to update the value of the specified column in the current row.

The use of the CASE expression is efficient because of how PROC SQL processes the WHEN-THEN clauses. The WHEN-THEN clauses in the CASE expression are evaluated sequentially. When a matching case is found, the THEN expression is evaluated and set, and the remaining WHEN cases are not considered.

How the Case Operand Works

In the next few sections, you learn about the use of the CASE expression in the UPDATE statement, without and with the optional case operand:

CASE *<case-operand>*

Updating Rows By Using the CASE Expression without a Case Operand

Here is an example of an UPDATE statement that uses the CASE expression for conditional processing. This example shows the form of the CASE expression that does not include the optional case operand.

Example

Suppose a company is considering giving raises to all of its employees, with a different percentage for each employee level:

- level-1 employees get a 5% raise

- level-2 employees get a 10% raise

- level-3 employees get a 15% raise.

First, you create the temporary table Work.Payrollmaster3, which is a copy of Sasuser.Payrollmaster, the table containing the employee salary data. The first 10 rows of Work.Payrollmaster3 are shown below.

DateOfBirth	DateOfHire	EmpID	Gender	JobCode	Salary
16SEP1958	07JUN1985	1919	M	TA2	$48,126
19OCT1962	12AUG1988	1653	F	ME2	$49,151
08NOV1965	19OCT1988	1400	M	ME1	$41,677
04SEP1963	01AUG1988	1350	F	FA3	$46,040
16DEC1948	21NOV1983	1401	M	TA3	$54,351
29APR1952	11JUN1978	1499	M	ME3	$60,235
09JUN1960	04OCT1988	1101	M	SCP	$26,212
03APR1959	14FEB1979	1333	M	PT2	$124,048
20JAN1961	05DEC1988	1402	M	TA2	$45,661
26DEC1966	09OCT1987	1479	F	TA3	$54,299

Next, you create a PROC SQL step that updates rows by using an UPDATE statement that contains a SET clause and a CASE expression:

```
proc sql;
   update work.payrollmaster3
      set salary=salary*
         case
            when substr(jobcode,3,1)='1'
                 then 1.05
            when substr(jobcode,3,1)='2'
                 then 1.10
            when substr(jobcode,3,1)='3'
                 then 1.15
            else 1.08
         end;
```

In this example, the CASE expression contains three WHEN clauses, one for each subset of rows (level-1, level-2, and level-3 employees), followed by an ELSE clause to handle any rows that do not meet the expected conditions.

The first 10 rows of Work.Payrollmaster3, after the rows have been updated, are shown below.

DateOfBirth	DateOfHire	EmpID	Gender	JobCode	Salary
16SEP1958	07JUN1985	1919	M	TA2	$52,939
19OCT1962	12AUG1988	1653	F	ME2	$54,066
08NOV1965	19OCT1988	1400	M	ME1	$43,761
04SEP1963	01AUG1988	1350	F	FA3	$52,946
16DEC1948	21NOV1983	1401	M	TA3	$62,504
29APR1952	11JUN1978	1499	M	ME3	$69,270
09JUN1960	04OCT1988	1101	M	SCP	$28,309
03APR1959	14FEB1979	1333	M	PT2	$136,453
20JAN1961	05DEC1988	1402	M	TA2	$50,227
26DEC1966	09OCT1987	1479	F	TA3	$62,444

By comparing the values of Salary in the original and updated versions of Work.Payrollmaster3 (as shown above), you can see how the values changed according to the job level indicated in the JobCode.

Updating Rows By Using the CASE Expression with a Case Operand

If the expression in the SET clause uses an equals (=) comparison operator, you might use the optional case operand in the CASE expression. Consider PROC SQL step that was shown in the preceding example, and see how the CASE expression in the UPDATE statement can be rewritten by using the alternate syntax.

Example

In the following PROC SQL step, which was shown earlier, the CASE expression contains three WHEN-THEN clauses. These clauses contain similar expressions, each of which specifies the same SUBSTR function:

```
proc sql;
   update work.payrollmaster_new2
      set salary=salary*
         case
            when substr(jobcode,3,1)='1'
                  then 1.05
            when substr(jobcode,3,1)='2'
                  then 1.10
            when substr(jobcode,3,1)='3'
                  then 1.15
            else 1.08
         end;
```

Because the expression in this SET clause uses an equals (=) operator, you can restructure the CASE expression for more efficient processing. In the alternate syntax, the repeated SUBSTR function is removed from each WHEN-THEN clause and is placed after the keyword CASE, as an operand:

```
proc sql;
   update work.payrollmaster_new2
      set salary=salary*
         case substr(jobcode,3,1)
            when '1'
                  then 1.05
            when '2'
                  then 1.10
            when '3'
                  then 1.15
            else 1.08
         end;
```

Using the alternate syntax, the SUBSTR function is evaluated only once, so this PROC SQL step is more efficient than the original version.

Note: You might use the case operand syntax only if the SET clause expression uses the equals (=) comparison operator.

Using the CASE Expression in the SELECT Statement

You can use the CASE expression in three different PROC SQL statements: UPDATE, INSERT, and SELECT. In the SELECT statement, you can use the CASE expression within a new column definition to specify different values for different subsets of rows.

Example

Suppose you want to generate an output report that displays employee names, job codes, and job levels. Your PROC SQL query selects LastName and FirstName from Sasuser.Staffmaster, and JobCode from Sasuser.Payrollmaster. The SELECT statement must define JobLevel as a new column, because it does not exist as a separate column in either table.

You want to assign the values of JobLevel, based on the number at the end of each jobcode. (The number at the end of each JobCode value is expected to be **1**, **2**, or **3**.) To create JobLevel, you can use the case operand form of the CASE expression to specify the three possible conditions (plus an ELSE condition, just in case).

The PROC SQL query is shown below:

```
proc sql outobs=10;
    select lastname, firstname, jobcode,
        case substr(jobcode,3,1)
            when '1'
                then 'junior'
            when '2'
                then 'intermediate'
            when '3'
                then 'senior'
            else 'none'
        end as JobLevel
    from sasuser.payrollmaster,
        sasuser.staffmaster
    where staffmaster.empid=
        payrollmaster.empid;
```

LastName	FirstName	JobCode	JobLevel
ADAMS	GERALD	TA2	intermediate
ALEXANDER	SUSAN	ME2	intermediate
APPLE	TROY	ME1	junior
ARTHUR	BARBARA	FA3	senior
AVERY	JERRY	TA3	senior
BAREFOOT	JOSEPH	ME3	senior
BAUCOM	WALTER	SCP	none
BLAIR	JUSTIN	PT2	intermediate
BLALOCK	RALPH	TA2	intermediate
BOSTIC	MARIE	TA3	senior

The SELECT clause uses the CASE expression to assign a value of **junior**, **intermediate**, **senior**, or **none** to each row in the new JobLevel column.

Deleting Rows in a Table

Overview

To delete some or all of the rows in a table, use the DELETE statement. When the statement is successfully executed, the SAS log shows a message that indicates the number of rows that have been deleted.

General form, DELETE statement for deleting rows in a table:

DELETE FROM *table-name*

       <WHERE *expression*>;

Here is an explanation of the syntax:

table-name
    specifies the name of the table in which rows will be deleted.

WHERE
    is used to specify an *expression* that subsets the rows to be deleted.

CAUTION:
    If you want to delete only a subset of rows in the table, you must specify a WHERE clause or all rows in the table will be deleted.

Note: You can also use the DELETE statement to delete rows in a table that underlies a PROC SQL view. For more information about referencing a PROC SQL view in a DELETE statement, see Chapter 7, "Creating and Managing Views Using PROC SQL," on page 248.

Example

Suppose you want to delete the records for all frequent-flyer program members who have used up all of their frequent flyer miles or have spent more miles than they had in their accounts.

First, you create the temporary table Work.Frequentflyers2 by copying a subset of columns from the existing table Sasuser.Frequentflyers:

```
proc sql;
   create table work.frequentflyers2 as
      select ffid, milestraveled,
             pointsearned, pointsused
         from sasuser.frequentflyers;
```

The first 10 rows of Work.Frequentflyers2 are shown below.

FFID	MilesTraveled	PointsEarned	PointsUsed
WD7152	30833	31333	0
WD8472	25570	26070	0
WD1576	56144	58644	27000
WD3947	40922	45922	23000
WD9347	4839	9839	0
WD8375	30007	30507	25000
WD7208	48943	49443	30000
WD6061	60142	60642	40000
WD0646	87044	89544	25000
WD9829	1901	4401	0

Next, you write a PROC SQL step that deletes the specified rows:

```
proc sql;
   delete from work.frequentflyers2
      where pointsearned-pointsused <= 0;
```

A message in the SAS log tells you how many rows were deleted.

Table 5.17 *SAS Log*

```
NOTE: 13 rows were deleted from WORK.FREQUENTFLYERS2
```

TIP   To delete all of the rows in the table, remove the WHERE clause from the DELETE statement.

Altering Columns in a Table

Overview

You have seen how to delete rows in a table using the DELETE statement. To add, drop (delete), or modify columns in a table, use the ALTER TABLE statement.

General form, ALTER TABLE statement:

ALTER TABLE *table-name*

        <ADD *column-definition-1<, ... column-definition-n>>*

        <DROP *column-name-1<, ... column-name-n>>*

        <MODIFY *column-definition-1<, ... column-definition-n>>*;

Here is an explanation of the syntax:

table-name
> specifies the name of the table in which columns will be added, dropped, or modified.

<ADD, DROP, MODIFY>
> at least one of the following clauses must be specified:

> ADD
> > specifies one or more *column-definition*s for columns to be added.

> DROP
> > specifies one or more *column-name*s for columns to be dropped (deleted).

> MODIFY
> > specifies one or more *column-definition*s for columns to be modified, where *column-definition* specifies a column to be added or modified, and is formatted as follows:

> > *column-name data-type <(column-width)> <column-modifier-1*
> >   *<...column-modifier-n>>*

In all three clauses, multiple *column-definition*s or *column-name*s must be separated by commas.

Note: You cannot use the ALTER TABLE statement with views.

Note: The ALTER TABLE statement also supports similar clauses that add, drop, and modify integrity constraints in an existing table. These clauses are not discussed in this chapter. To find out more about adding, dropping, and modifying integrity constraints, see the SAS documentation for the SQL procedure.

Consider each type of modification that can be made to a column by using the ALTER TABLE statement.

Adding Columns to a Table

To add columns to a table, use the ADD clause in the ALTER TABLE statement. The ADD clause specifies one or more column definitions. The syntax of a column definition is the same as in the CREATE TABLE statement:

column-name data-type <(column-width)> <column-modifier-1< ...column-modifier-n>>

However, in the ALTER statement, the entire group of column definitions is not enclosed in parentheses.

Example

Suppose you are working with the temporary table Work.Payrollmaster4, which is an exact copy of the existing table Sasuser.Payrollmaster. The first 10 rows of Work.Payrollmaster4 are shown below.

DateOfBirth	DateOfHire	EmpID	Gender	JobCode	Salary
16SEP1958	07JUN1985	1919	M	TA2	$48,126
19OCT1962	12AUG1988	1653	F	ME2	$49,151
08NOV1965	19OCT1988	1400	M	ME1	$41,677
04SEP1963	01AUG1988	1350	F	FA3	$46,040
16DEC1948	21NOV1983	1401	M	TA3	$54,351
29APR1952	11JUN1978	1499	M	ME3	$60,235
09JUN1960	04OCT1988	1101	M	SCP	$26,212
03APR1959	14FEB1979	1333	M	PT2	$124,048
20JAN1961	05DEC1988	1402	M	TA2	$45,661
26DEC1966	09OCT1987	1479	F	TA3	$54,299

The following PROC SQL step uses the ADD clause in the ALTER TABLE statement to add the columns Bonus and Level to Work.Payrollmaster4:

```
proc sql;
   alter table work.payrollmaster4
      add Bonus num format=comma10.2,
         Level char(3);
```

The first 10 rows of Work.Payrollmaster4, with the two new columns, are shown below.

DateOfBirth	DateOfHire	EmpID	Gender	JobCode	Salary	Bonus	Level
16SEP1958	07JUN1985	1919	M	TA2	$48,126		
19OCT1962	12AUG1988	1653	F	ME2	$49,151		
08NOV1965	19OCT1988	1400	M	ME1	$41,677		
04SEP1963	01AUG1988	1350	F	FA3	$46,040		
16DEC1948	21NOV1983	1401	M	TA3	$54,351		
29APR1952	11JUN1978	1499	M	ME3	$60,235		
09JUN1960	04OCT1988	1101	M	SCP	$26,212		
03APR1959	14FEB1979	1333	M	PT2	$124,048		
20JAN1961	05DEC1988	1402	M	TA2	$45,661		
26DEC1966	09OCT1987	1479	F	TA3	$54,299		

Use the UPDATE statement to populate the new columns.

Dropping Columns from a Table

To drop (delete) existing columns from a table, use the DROP clause in the ALTER TABLE statement. The DROP clause specifies one or more column names, and multiple column names are separated by commas.

Example

Suppose you want to drop the existing columns Bonus and Level from the temporary table Work.Payrollmaster4. (These two columns were added to the table in the example in the previous section.) The first 10 rows of Work.Payrollmaster4 are shown below.

DateOfBirth	DateOfHire	EmpID	Gender	JobCode	Salary	Bonus	Level
16SEP1958	07JUN1985	1919	M	TA2	$48,126		
19OCT1962	12AUG1988	1653	F	ME2	$49,151		
08NOV1965	19OCT1988	1400	M	ME1	$41,677		
04SEP1963	01AUG1988	1350	F	FA3	$46,040		
16DEC1948	21NOV1983	1401	M	TA3	$54,351		
29APR1952	11JUN1978	1499	M	ME3	$60,235		
09JUN1960	04OCT1988	1101	M	SCP	$26,212		
03APR1959	14FEB1979	1333	M	PT2	$124,048		
20JAN1961	05DEC1988	1402	M	TA2	$45,661		
26DEC1966	09OCT1987	1479	F	TA3	$54,299		

The following PROC SQL step uses the DROP clause in the ALTER TABLE statement to drop the columns Bonus and Level from Work.Payrollmaster4:

```
proc sql;
   alter table work.payrollmaster4
      drop bonus, level;
```

The first 10 rows of Work.Payrollmaster4, without Bonus and Level, are shown below.

DateOfBirth	DateOfHire	EmpID	Gender	JobCode	Salary
16SEP1958	07JUN1985	1919	M	TA2	$48,126
19OCT1962	12AUG1988	1653	F	ME2	$49,151
08NOV1965	19OCT1988	1400	M	ME1	$41,677
04SEP1963	01AUG1988	1350	F	FA3	$46,040
16DEC1948	21NOV1983	1401	M	TA3	$54,351
29APR1952	11JUN1978	1499	M	ME3	$60,235
09JUN1960	04OCT1988	1101	M	SCP	$26,212
03APR1959	14FEB1979	1333	M	PT2	$124,048
20JAN1961	05DEC1988	1402	M	TA2	$45,661
26DEC1966	09OCT1987	1479	F	TA3	$54,299

Modifying Columns in a Table

To modify the attributes of one or more existing columns in a table, use the MODIFY clause in the ALTER TABLE statement. You can use the MODIFY clause to change a column's

- length (column width) — for a character column only
- informat
- format
- label.

Note: You cannot use the MODIFY clause to do the following:

- change a character column to numeric or vice versa. To change a column's data type, drop the column and then add it (and its data) again, or use the DATA step.
- change a column's name. You cannot change this attribute by using the ALTER TABLE statement. Instead, you can use the SAS data set option RENAME= or the DATASETS procedure with the RENAME statement. You can find out more about the DATASETS procedure with the RENAME statement in Chapter 13, "Creating Indexes," on page 448.

Like the ADD clause, the MODIFY clause specifies one or more column definitions, each of which consists of the following:

column-name <data-type (column-width)> <column-modifier-1 < ...column-modifier-n>>

In each column definition, you specify the required element (the column name), followed by any of the optional attributes that you want to modify.

Note: When you use a column definition to add a new column by using the ADD clause in the ALTER TABLE statement, or to specify a new column in the CREATE TABLE statement, *data-type* is a required element. However, when you are using a column definition in the MODIFY clause in the ALTER TABLE statement, as shown in the following example, *data-type* is never required for numeric columns and is optional for character columns. You must specify *data-type* (*column-width*) only if you want to modify the column width of a character column.

Note: When modifying the width of a character variable, it is possible to truncate the variable's value if the length specification is too small.

```
alter table work.payrollmaster
modify jobcode char(2);
select * from payrollmaster;
```

Example

Suppose you want to modify the attributes of the existing column Salary in the temporary table Work.Payrollmaster4. The first 10 rows of Work.Payrollmaster4 (as it existed at the end of the previous example) are shown below.

DateOfBirth	DateOfHire	EmpID	Gender	JobCode	Salary
16SEP1958	07JUN1985	1919	M	TA2	$48,126
19OCT1962	12AUG1988	1653	F	ME2	$49,151
08NOV1965	19OCT1988	1400	M	ME1	$41,677
04SEP1963	01AUG1988	1350	F	FA3	$46,040
16DEC1948	21NOV1983	1401	M	TA3	$54,351
29APR1952	11JUN1978	1499	M	ME3	$60,235
09JUN1960	04OCT1988	1101	M	SCP	$26,212
03APR1959	14FEB1979	1333	M	PT2	$124,048
20JAN1961	05DEC1988	1402	M	TA2	$45,661
26DEC1966	09OCT1987	1479	F	TA3	$54,299

The column Salary is a numeric field that currently has the format DOLLAR9. The following PROC SQL step modifies the format and adds a label for Salary:

```
proc sql;
    alter table work.payrollmaster4
        modify salary format=dollar11.2 label="Salary Amt";
```

The first 10 rows of Work.Payrollmaster4, with the new column attributes for Salary, are shown below.

DateOfBirth	DateOfHire	EmpID	Gender	JobCode	Salary Amt
16SEP1958	07JUN1985	1919	M	TA2	$48,126.00
19OCT1962	12AUG1988	1653	F	ME2	$49,151.00
08NOV1965	19OCT1988	1400	M	ME1	$41,677.00
04SEP1963	01AUG1988	1350	F	FA3	$46,040.00
16DEC1948	21NOV1983	1401	M	TA3	$54,351.00
29APR1952	11JUN1978	1499	M	ME3	$60,235.00
09JUN1960	04OCT1988	1101	M	SCP	$26,212.00
03APR1959	14FEB1979	1333	M	PT2	$124,048.00
20JAN1961	05DEC1988	1402	M	TA2	$45,661.00
26DEC1966	09OCT1987	1479	F	TA3	$54,299.00

Adding, Dropping, and Modifying Columns in a Single Statement

In the last few examples, the ALTER TABLE statement has made only one alteration to columns in a table, by using just one clause. However, you can include multiple clauses in a single ALTER TABLE statement to add, drop, and modify columns all at once.

Example

Suppose you want to use a single ALTER TABLE statement to make *all* of the following alterations to the table Work.Payrollmaster4:

- add the new column Age, by using the ADD clause

- change the format of the DateOfHire column (which is currently DATE9.) to MMDDYY10., by using the MODIFY clause

- drop the DateOfBirth and Gender columns, by using the DROP clause.

The first 10 rows of Work.Payrollmaster4, as it was at the end of the last example, are shown below.

DateOfBirth	DateOfHire	EmpID	Gender	JobCode	Salary Amt
16SEP1958	07JUN1985	1919	M	TA2	$48,126.00
19OCT1962	12AUG1988	1653	F	ME2	$49,151.00
08NOV1965	19OCT1988	1400	M	ME1	$41,677.00
04SEP1963	01AUG1988	1350	F	FA3	$46,040.00
16DEC1948	21NOV1983	1401	M	TA3	$54,351.00
29APR1952	11JUN1978	1499	M	ME3	$60,235.00
09JUN1960	04OCT1988	1101	M	SCP	$26,212.00
03APR1959	14FEB1979	1333	M	PT2	$124,048.00
20JAN1961	05DEC1988	1402	M	TA2	$45,661.00
26DEC1966	09OCT1987	1479	F	TA3	$54,299.00

The following PROC SQL step uses multiple clauses in the ALTER TABLE statement to make all three of the alterations listed above:

```
proc sql;
    alter table work.payrollmaster4
        add Age num
        modify dateofhire date format=mmddyy10.
        drop dateofbirth, gender;
```

The first 10 rows of Work.Payrollmaster4, with the three alterations, are shown below.

DateOfHire	EmpID	JobCode	Salary Amt	Age
06/07/1985	1919	TA2	$48,126.00	.
08/12/1988	1653	ME2	$49,151.00	.
10/19/1988	1400	ME1	$41,677.00	.
08/01/1988	1350	FA3	$46,040.00	.
11/21/1983	1401	TA3	$54,351.00	.
06/11/1978	1499	ME3	$60,235.00	.
10/04/1988	1101	SCP	$26,212.00	.
02/14/1979	1333	PT2	$124,048.00	.
12/05/1988	1402	TA2	$45,661.00	.
10/09/1987	1479	TA3	$54,299.00	.

Use the UPDATE statement to populate the new columns.

Dropping Tables

Overview

To drop (delete) one or more entire tables, use the DROP TABLE statement.

General form, DROP TABLE statement:

DROP TABLE *table-name-1* <, ... *table-name-n*>;

Here is an explanation of the syntax:

table-name
    specifies the name of a table to be dropped, and can be one of the following:

- a one-level name

- a two-level libref.table name

- a physical pathname that is enclosed in single quotation marks.

Example

In the last few examples, you made several alterations to the temporary table Work.Payrollmaster4. Now you decide that you do not need this table anymore. The following PROC SQL step uses the DROP TABLE statement to drop Work.Payrollmaster4:

```
proc sql;
    drop table work.payrollmaster4;
```

The SAS log displays a message indicating that the table has been dropped:

Table 5.18 *SAS Log*

```
NOTE: Table WORK.PAYROLLMASTER4 has been dropped.
```

Summary

Text Summary

Understanding Methods of Creating Tables
You can use the CREATE TABLE statement to create a table in three different ways:

- create a table with no rows (an empty table) by defining columns

- create an empty table that is like another table

- create a table that contains rows, based on a query result.

Creating an Empty Table By Defining Columns

You can create a table with no rows by using a CREATE TABLE statement that contains column specifications. A column specification includes the following elements: column name (required), data type (required), column width (optional), one or more column modifiers (optional), and a column constraint (optional).

Displaying the Structure of a Table

To display, in the SAS log, a list of a table's columns and their attributes and other information about a table, use the DESCRIBE TABLE statement.

Creating an Empty Table That Is like Another Table

To create a table with no rows that has the same structure as an existing table, use a CREATE TABLE statement that contains the keyword LIKE. To specify a subset of columns to be copied from the existing table, use the SAS data set options DROP= or KEEP= in your CREATE TABLE statement.

Creating a Table from a Query Result

To create a new table that contains both columns and rows that are derived from an existing table or set of tables, use a CREATE TABLE statement that includes the keyword AS and the clauses that are used in a query. This method enables you to copy an existing table quickly.

Inserting Rows of Data into a Table

The INSERT statement can be used in three ways to insert rows of data in existing tables, either empty or populated. You can insert rows by using

- the SET clause to specify column names and values in pairs

- the VALUES clause to specify a list of values

- the clauses that are used in a query to return rows from an existing table.

Creating a Table That Has Integrity Constraints

Integrity constraints are rules that you can specify in order to restrict the data values that can be stored for a column in a table. To create a table that has integrity constraints, use a CREATE TABLE statement. Integrity constraints can be defined in two different ways in the CREATE TABLE statement:

- by specifying a column constraint in a column specification

- by using a constraint specification.

Handling Errors in Row Insertions

When you add rows to a table that has integrity constraints, PROC SQL evaluates the new data to ensure that it meets the conditions that are determined by the integrity constraints. When you use the INSERT or UPDATE statement to add or modify data in a table, you can use the UNDO_POLICY= option in the PROC SQL statement to specify whether PROC SQL will make or undo the changes that you submitted up to the point of the error.

Displaying Integrity Constraints for a Table

To display the integrity constraints for a specified table in the SAS log, use the DESCRIBE TABLE CONSTRAINTS statement.

Updating Values in Existing Table Rows

To modify data values in some or all of the existing rows in a table, use the UPDATE statement with the following:

- a SET clause and possibly a WHERE clause that specifies a single expression to update rows. To update rows with multiple expressions, use multiple UPDATE statements.

- a CASE expression that specifies multiple expressions to update rows. The CASE expression can be specified without an optional case operand or, if the expression in the SET clause uses an equals (=) comparison operator, with a case operand.

The CASE expression can also be used in the SELECT statement in a new column definition to specify different values for different subsets of rows.

Deleting Rows in a Table

To delete some or all of the rows in a table, use the DELETE statement.

Altering Columns in a Table

To alter columns in a table, use the ALTER TABLE statement that contains one or more of the following clauses:

- the ADD clause, to add one or more columns to a table

- the DROP clause, to drop (delete) one or more columns in a table

- the MODIFY clause, to modify the attributes of columns in a table.

Dropping Tables

To drop (delete) one or more entire tables, use the DROP TABLE statement.

Sample Programs

Creating an Empty Table By Defining Columns

```
proc sql;
    create table work.discount
            (Destination char(3),
            BeginDate num Format=date9.,
            EndDate num format=date9.,
            Discount num);
quit;
```

Creating an Empty Table That Is like Another Table

```
proc sql;
    create table work.flightdelays2
            (drop=delaycategory destinationtype)
        like sasuser.flightdelays;
quit;
```

Creating a Table from a Query Result

```
proc sql;
    create table work.ticketagents as
        select lastname, firstname,
                jobcode, salary
            from sasuser.payrollmaster,
```

```
              sasuser.staffmaster
        where payrollmaster.empid
            = staffmaster.empid
            and jobcode contains 'TA';
    quit;
```

Displaying the Structure of a Table

```
proc sql;
    describe table work.discount;
quit;
```

Inserting Rows into a Table By Specifying Column Names and Values

```
proc sql;
    insert into work.discount
        set destination='LHR',
            begindate='01MAR2000'd,
            enddate='05MAR2000'd,
            discount=.33
        set destination='CPH',
            begindate='03MAR2000'd,
            enddate='10MAR2000'd,
            discount=.15;
quit;
```

Inserting Rows into a Table By Specifying Lists of Values

```
proc sql;
    insert into work.discount (destination,
        begindate,enddate, discount)
      values ('LHR','01MAR2000'd,
            '05MAR2000'd,.33)
      values ('CPH','03MAR2000'd,
            '10MAR2000'd,.15);
quit;
```

Inserting Rows into a Table from a Query Result

```
proc sql;
    insert into work.payrollchanges2
      select empid, salary, dateofhire
        from sasuser.payrollmaster
          where empid in ('1919','1350','1401');
quit;
```

Creating a Table That Has Integrity Constraints

```
proc sql;
    create table work.employees
            (Name char(10),
            Gender char(1),
            HDate date label='Hire Date' not null,
            constraint prim_key primary key(name),
            constraint gender check(gender in ('M' 'F')));
quit;
```

Displaying Integrity Constraints for a Table

```
proc sql;
    describe table constraints work.discount4;
quit;
```

Updating Rows in a Table Based on an Expression

```
proc sql;
    update work.payrollmaster_new
        set salary=salary*1.05
        where jobcode like '__1';
quit;
```

Updating Rows in a Table By Using a CASE Expression

```
proc sql;
    update work.payrollmaster_new
        set salary=salary*
            case
                when substr(jobcode,3,1)='1'
                    then 1.05
                when substr(jobcode,3,1)='2'
                    then 1.10
                when substr(jobcode,3,1)='3'
                    then 1.15
                else 1.08
            end;
quit;
```

Updating Rows in a Table By Using a CASE Expression (Alternate Syntax)

```
proc sql outobs=10;
    select lastname, firstname, jobcode,
            case substr(jobcode,3,1)
                when '1'
                    then 'junior'
                when '2'
                    then 'intermediate'
                when '3'
                    then 'senior'
                else 'none'
            end as JobLevel
        from sasuser.payrollmaster,
            sasuser.staffmaster
        where staffmaster.empid=
            payrollmaster.empid;
quit;
```

Deleting Rows in a Table

```
proc sql;
    delete from work.frequentflyers2
        where pointsearned-pointsused<=0;
quit;
```

Adding, Modifying, and Dropping Columns in a Table

```
proc sql;
    alter table work.payrollmaster4
        add Age num
        modify dateofhire date format=mmddyy10.
        drop dateofbirth, gender;
quit;
```

Dropping a Table

```
proc sql;
    drop table work.payrollmaster4;
quit;
```

Points to Remember

- The CREATE TABLE statement generates only a table as output, not a report.

- The UPDATE statement does not insert new rows into a table. To insert rows, you must use the INSERT statement.

Quiz

Select the best answer for each question. After completing the quiz, check your answers using the answer key in the appendix.

1. Which of the following PROC SQL steps creates a new table by copying only the column structure (but not the rows) of an existing table?

   a. ```
      proc sql;
          create table work.newpayroll as
              select *
                  from sasuser.payrollmaster;
      ```

   b. ```
      proc sql;
          create table work.newpayroll
              like sasuser.payrollmaster;
      ```

   c. ```
      proc sql;
          create table work.newpayroll
              copy sasuser.payrollmaster;
      ```

   d. ```
      proc sql;
          create table work.newpayroll
              describe sasuser.payrollmaster;
      ```

2. Which of the following PROC SQL steps creates a table that contains rows for the level-1 flight attendants only?

   a. ```
      proc sql;
          create table work.newpayroll as
              select *
                  from sasuser.payrollmaster
                  where jobcode='FA1';
      ```

   b. ```
      proc sql;
          create work.newpayroll as
```

```
        select *
            from sasuser.payrollmaster
            where jobcode='FA1';
```

c.
```
proc sql;
    create table work.newpayroll
        copy sasuser.payrollmaster
            where jobcode='FA1';
```

d.
```
proc sql;
    create table work.newpayroll as
            sasuser.payrollmaster
        where jobcode='FA1';
```

3. Which of the following statements is true regarding the UNDO_POLICY=REQUIRED option?

    a. It must be used with the REQUIRED integrity constraint.

    b. It ignores the specified integrity constraints if any of the rows that you want to insert or update do not meet the constraint criteria.

    c. It restores your table to its original state if any of the rows that you try to insert or update do not meet the specified integrity constraint criteria.

    d. It allows rows that meet the specified integrity constraint criteria to be inserted or updated, but rejects rows that do not meet the integrity constraint criteria.

4. Which of the following is not a type of integrity constraint?

    a. CHECK

    b. NULL

    c. UNIQUE

    d. PRIMARY KEY

5. Which of the following PROC SQL steps deletes rows for all frequent-flyer program members who traveled less than 10,000 miles?

    a.
    ```
    proc sql;
        delete rows
            from work.frequentflyers
            where milestraveled < 10000;
    ```

    b.
    ```
    proc sql;
        drop rows
            from work.frequentflyers
            where milestraveled < 10000;
    ```

    c.
    ```
    proc sql;
        drop table
            from work.frequentflyers
            where milestraveled < 10000;
    ```

    d.
    ```
    proc sql;
        delete
            from work.frequentflyers
            where milestraveled < 10000;
    ```

6. Which of the following PROC SQL steps gives bonuses (in points) to frequent-flyer program members as follows:

    •   a 50% bonus for members who traveled less than 10,000 miles

- a 100% bonus for members who traveled 10,000 miles or more?

a.
```
proc sql;
    update work.frequentflyers
    set pointsearned=pointsearned*
      case if milestraveled < 10000
              then 1.5
           if milestraveled >= 10000
              then 2
           else 1
      end;
```

b.
```
proc sql;
    update work.frequentflyers
    set pointsearned=pointsearned*
      case when milestraveled < 10000
              then 1.5
           when milestraveled >= 10000
              then 2
           else 1
      end;
```

c.
```
proc sql;
    update work.frequentflyers
    set pointsearned=pointsearned*
      case if milestraveled < 10000
              then pointsearned*1.5
           if milestraveled >= 10000
              then pointsearned*2
           else 1
      end;
```

d.
```
proc sql;
    update work.frequentflyers
    set pointsearned=pointsearned*
      case if milestraveled < 10000
              then pointsearned*1.5
           if milestraveled >= 10000
              then pointsearned*2
           else pointsearned*1
      end;
```

7. Which of the following statements is used to add new rows to a table?

   a. INSERT

   b. LOAD

   c. VALUES

   d. CREATE TABLE

8. Which of the following statements regarding the ALTER TABLE statement is false?

   a. It enables you to update column attributes.

   b. It enables you to add new columns in your table.

   c. It enables you to drop columns in your table.

   d. It enables you to change a character column to a numeric column.

9. Which of the following displays the structure of a table in the SAS log?

a. ```
proc sql;
   describe as
      select *
         from sasuser.payrollmaster;
```

b. ```
proc sql;
   describe contents sasuser.payrollmaster;
```

c. ```
proc sql;
   describe table sasuser.payrollmaster;
```

d. ```
proc sql;
   describe * from sasuser.payrollmaster;
```

10. Which of the following creates an empty table that contains the two columns FullName and Age?

a. ```
proc sql;
   create table work.names
          (FullName char(25), Age num);
```

b. ```
proc sql;
   create table work.names as
          (FullName char(25), Age num);
```

c. ```
proc sql;
   create work.names
          (FullName char(25), Age num);
```

d. ```
proc sql;
   create table work.names
      set (FullName char(25), Age num);
```

Chapter 6

Creating and Managing Indexes Using PROC SQL

Overview

Introduction

When processing a query that contains a subsetting WHERE clause or that joins multiple tables, PROC SQL must locate specific rows in the referenced table(s). Creating an index for a table enables PROC SQL, in certain circumstances, to locate specific rows more quickly and efficiently. An index is an auxiliary file that stores the physical location of values for one or more specified columns (key columns) in a table. In an index, each unique value of the key column(s) is paired with a location identifier for the row that contains that value. In the same way that you use a book's subject index to find a page that discusses a particular subject, PROC SQL uses the system of directions in an index to access specific rows in the table directly, by index value. You can create more than one index for a single table. All indexes for a SAS table are stored in one index file.

Note: You cannot create an index on a view.

The following PROC SQL step uses the CREATE INDEX statement to create an index for a table, and uses the DESCRIBE TABLE statement to display information about the index, along with other information about the table, in the SAS log:

```
proc sql;
    create unique index empid
        on work.payrollmaster(empid);
    describe table work.payrollmaster;
```

Note: For more information about the BUFSIZE= option, see "Using the BUFSIZE= Option" on page 661.

Table 6.1 *SAS Log*

```
create table WORK.PAYROLLMASTER( bufsize=4096 )
  (
   DateOfBirth num format=DATE9. informat=DATE9.,
   DateOfHire num format=DATE9. informat=DATE9.,
   EmpID char(4),
   Gender char(1),
   JobCode char(3),
   Salary num format=DOLLAR9.
  );
create unique index EmpID on WORK.PAYROLLMASTER(EmpID);
```

In this chapter, you learn to create and manage various types of indexes with PROC SQL.

Understanding Indexes

Accessing Rows in a Table

When you submit a query on a table that does not have an index, PROC SQL accesses rows sequentially, in the order in which they are stored in the table. For example, suppose you are working with a table that contains information about employees. You have written a PROC SQL query to select the rows in which the value of Name (the first column) is **Smith**. To access the rows that you want, PROC SQL begins with the first row and reads through all rows in the table, selecting the rows that satisfy the condition that is expressed in the WHERE clause.

SAS Table

Anderson	09JAN2000	X	34
Baker	14OCT2001	X	54
Davis	30MAR2000	Y	49
Edwards	28JUN2002	X	52
Smith	15JAN2000	Y	62
Yates	04AUG2002	X	59

When you execute a program that retrieves a small subset of rows from a large table, it can be time-consuming for PROC SQL to read the rows sequentially. In some situations, using an index on a table allows PROC SQL to access a subset of rows more efficiently.

An index stores unique values for a specified column or columns in ascending value order, and includes information about the location of those values in the table. That is, an index includes value/identifier pairs that enable you to access a row directly, by value. For example, suppose you have created an index on your table that is based on the column Name. Using the index, PROC SQL accesses the row(s) that you want directly, without having to read all the other rows.

SAS Table

Anderson	09JAN2000	X	34
Baker	14OCT2001	X	54
Davis	30MAR2000	Y	49
Edwards	28JUN2002	X	52
Smith	15JAN2000	Y	62
Yates	04AUG2002	X	59

Simple and Composite Indexes

You can create two types of indexes:

- simple

- composite.

A simple index is based on one column that you specify. The indexed column can be either character or numeric. When you create a simple index by using PROC SQL, you must specify the name of the indexed column as the name of the index.

A composite index is based on two or more columns that you specify. The indexed columns can be character, numeric, or a combination of both. In the index, the values of the key columns are concatenated to form a single value.

For example, if you build a composite index on the key columns LastName and FirstName, a value for the index consists of the value for LastName followed by the value for FirstName. Often, a WHERE clause might use only the first column (the primary key) of a composite index, which means that the program reads only the first part of each concatenated value.

When you create a composite index, you must specify a unique name for the index that is not the name of any existing column or index in the table. In the example described above, the composite index cannot be named Lastname or Firstname.

Unique Indexes

If you want to require that values for the key column(s) are unique for each row, you can create either a simple index or a composite index as a unique index. Once a unique index is defined on one or more columns in a table, SAS rejects any change to the table that would cause more than one row to have the same value(s) for the specified column or composite group of columns.

Example

Suppose you are working with the table Sasuser.Payrollmaster. The first eight rows of this table are shown below.

DateOfBirth	DateOfHire	EmpID	Gender	JobCode	Salary
16SEP1958	07JUN1985	1919	M	TA2	$48,126
19OCT1962	12AUG1988	1653	F	ME2	$49,151
08NOV1965	19OCT1988	1400	M	ME1	$41,677
04SEP1963	01AUG1988	1350	F	FA3	$46,040
19DEC1948	21NOV1983	1401	M	TA3	$54,351
29APR1952	11JUN1978	1499	M	ME3	$60,235
09JUN1960	04OCT1988	1101	M	SCP	$26,212
03APR1959	14FEB1979	1333	M	PT2	$124,048

If you know that the column JobCode is often specified in a WHERE clause expression, you might want to create a simple index on the column JobCode. You must specify the name of the key column, JobCode, as the index name.

Now suppose you are planning to write many queries that specify both EmpID and DateOfHire in a WHERE clause expression. In this case, you might want to create a composite index on these two columns. Because employee identification numbers should be unique, it is appropriate to create this index as a unique index. Therefore, you should specify a name for your index that is not the same as the name of any existing column or index in the table. For example, you could name this index Whenhired.

Deciding Whether to Create an Index

Overview

An index can reduce the time required to locate a set of rows, especially for a large data file. However, there are costs associated with creating, storing, and maintaining the index. When deciding whether to create an index, you must weigh any benefits in performance improvement against the costs of increased resource usage.

Note: This chapter discusses the benefits and costs that are associated with using indexes specifically with PROC SQL. To learn about the costs and benefits of using indexes with other SAS procedures, see the SAS documentation.

PROC SQL Queries That Can Be Optimized by an Index

To use indexes effectively with PROC SQL, it is important to know the classes of queries that can be processed more efficiently by using an index. The classes of queries that can be optimized are specified below.

Query performance is optimized when the key column occurs in ...	Example
| a WHERE clause expression that contains<br><br>• a comparison operator<br>• the TRIM or SUBSTR function<br>• the CONTAINS operator<br>• the LIKE operator. | ```
proc sql;
    select empid, jobcode, salary
        from sasuser.payrollmaster
        where jobcode='FA3'
        order by empid;
```<br><br>Key Column(s): JobCode |
| a subquery returning values to the IN operator. | ```
proc sql;
    select empid, lastname, firstname,
            city, state
        from sasuser.staffmaster
        where empid in
            (select empid
                from sasuser.payrollmaster
                where salary>40000);
```<br><br>Key Column(s): EmpID |
| a correlated subquery, in which the column being compared with the correlated reference is indexed | ```
proc sql;
    select lastname, firstname
        from sasuser.staffmaster
        where 'NA'=
            (select jobcategory
                from sasuser.supervisors
                where staffmaster.empid =
                        supervisors.empid);
```<br><br>Key Column(s): Supervisors.EmpID |
```

Query performance is optimized when the key column occurs in ...	Example

a join in which
 	
• the join expression contains the equals (=) operator (an equijoin)
 	
• all the columns in the join expression are indexed in one of the tables being joined.
	``
	proc sql;
	    select *
	        from sasuser.payrollmaster as p,
	             sasuser.staffmaster as s
	        where p.empid =
	              s.empid
	        order by jobcode;
	``
	
	Key Column(s): Payrollmaster.EmpID or Staffmaster.EmpID

Benefits of Using an Index

For PROC SQL, there are three main benefits to using an index to access data directly (instead of reading the data sequentially):

• A small subset of data (<15% of rows) can be accessed more quickly. (As the size of the subset increases, the advantage of using an index decreases.)

• Equijoins can be performed without internal sorts.

• Uniqueness can be enforced by creating a unique index.

Example: Using an Index to Access a Small Subset of Data

Suppose you are writing a query that references the table Work.Payrollmaster. (Work.Payrollmaster is a duplicate of the table Sasuser.Payrollmaster.) Work.Payrollmaster stores payroll information for employees, and a simple index is defined on the column JobCode. Your query's WHERE clause expression references the key column:

```
proc sql;
    select empid, jobcode, salary
        from work.payrollmaster
        where jobcode='FA3'
        order by empid;
```

If the value of JobCode for most of the rows in the table is **FA3**, then the use of an index does not significantly improve the efficiency of the following query. In fact, performance might be degraded.

However, if only 10% of the rows have a value of **FA3**, then PROC SQL can process the query more efficiently by using the index.

Note: In this chapter, if you want to submit any sample code that references a temporary table (a table that is stored in the Work library), you first need to create the temporary table by copying the table in the Sasuser library that has the same name.

Understanding the Costs of Using an Index

When you are deciding whether to create an index, you should consider the associated increase in resource usage, which includes the following:

- Additional CPU time is necessary to create an index, to maintain the index when the table is modified, and to use an index to read a row from a table.

- Using an index to read rows from a table might require additional I/O (input/output) requests when compared to reading the table sequentially.

- Using an index requires additional memory for buffers into which the index pages and code are loaded for processing.

- Additional disk space is required to store the index file, which can show up as a separate file (in the Windows and UNIX operating environments, for example) or can appear to be part of the data file (in the z/OS operating environment).

Guidelines for Creating Indexes

To use indexes effectively, follow these guidelines for creating indexes:

- Keep the number of indexes to a minimum to reduce disk storage and update costs.

- Do not create an index for small tables. Sequential access is faster on small tables.

- Do not create an index based on columns that have a very small number of distinct values, low cardinality (for example, a Gender column that contains only the two values **Male** and **Female**).

- Use indexes for queries that retrieve a relatively small subset of rows — that is, less than 15%.

- Do not create more than one index that is based on the same column as the primary key.

TIP   Many factors affect the processing of SAS programs. The most accurate way to find out whether to create an index for a particular table or column is to perform benchmarking tests.

Creating an Index

Overview

To create an index on one or more columns of a table, use the CREATE INDEX statement.

General form, CREATE INDEX statement:

CREATE <UNIQUE> INDEX *index-name*

 ON *table-name* (*column-name-1*<, *...column-name-n*>);

Here is an explanation of the syntax:

UNIQUE
 is a keyword that specifies that all values of the column(s) specified in the statement must be unique.

index-name
 specifies the name of the index to be created. If you are creating an index on one column only, then *index-name* must be the same as *column-name-1*. If you are creating an index on more than one column, then *index-name* cannot be the same as the name of any existing column or index in the table.

table-name
 specifies the name of the table on which the index is created.

column-name
 specifies a column to be indexed. Columns can be specified in any order. However, column order is important for data retrieval. The first-named column is the primary key, the second-named column is the secondary key, and so on.

TIP When creating a composite index, specify the columns in the same order as you would specify them in an ORDER BY clause.

TIP You can achieve improved index performance if you create the index on a pre-sorted table.

SAS maintains indexes for all changes to the table, whether the changes originate from PROC SQL or some other source, as long as the entire table is not re-created. If you alter a column's definition or update its values, then SAS updates the indexes also. However, if a key column in a table is dropped (deleted), then the index on that column is also dropped.

Creating Multiple Indexes

You cannot create multiple simple indexes that are based on the same column or multiple composite indexes that are based on the same set of columns. Although it is possible to create both a simple index and a composite index on the same column, it is usually not advantageous to do this. If a simple index is defined on a column and that column is also the primary key in a composite index, PROC SQL uses the composite index in processing a query that references that column.

You can create multiple indexes on the same table, but you must use a separate CREATE INDEX statement for each index that you want to create.

Example: Creating a Simple Index

The following PROC SQL step uses the CREATE INDEX statement to create a simple, unique index that is based on the column EmpID in the temporary table Work.Payrollmaster. (Work.Payrollmaster is a duplicate of the table Sasuser.Payrollmaster.)

```
proc sql;
   create unique index EmpID
      on work.payrollmaster(empid);
```

The specified index name (EmpID) must be the same as the name of the key column.

When this step is submitted, the SAS log displays the following message.

Table 6.2 *SAS Log*

```
NOTE: Simple index EmpID has been defined.
```

Example: Creating a Composite, Unique Index

The following PROC SQL step uses the CREATE INDEX statement to create the composite, unique index daily on the columns FlightNumber and Date:

```
proc sql;
   create unique index daily
      on work.marchflights(flightnumber,date);
```

When this step is submitted, the SAS log displays the following message.

Table 6.3 *SAS Log*

```
NOTE: Composite index daily has been defined.
```

Note: The note in the SAS log displays the index name exactly as you specified it. In this example, the index name daily was specified in lowercase. In the previous example, the index name EmpID was specified in mixed case. However, the use of uppercase and lowercase for index names is not significant because SAS recognizes index names regardless of how they are formatted in code.

If the set of key columns FlightNumber and Date had duplicate values, the index would not be created. Instead, the SAS log would display a message like the following.

Table 6.4 *SAS Log*

```
ERROR: Duplicate values not allowed on index daily for file MARCHFLIGHTS.
```

Displaying Index Specifications

Overview

Sometimes you want to know whether an existing table has any indexes. To display a CREATE INDEX statement in the SAS log for each index that is defined for one or more specified tables, you can use the DESCRIBE TABLE statement. (The DESCRIBE TABLE statement also writes a CREATE TABLE statement to the SAS log for each specified table.)

General form, DESCRIBE TABLE statement:

DESCRIBE TABLE *table-name-1<, ... table-name-n>*;

Here is an explanation of the syntax:

table-name
> specifies the table to be described as one of the following:
>
> - a one-level name
>
> - a two-level *libref.table* name
>
> - a physical pathname that is enclosed in single quotation marks.

If a specified table has no indexes, a CREATE INDEX statement does not appear.

Example

Earlier in this chapter, the following code was used to create a unique composite index named daily on the columns FlightNumber and Date in the temporary table Marchflights.

```
proc sql;
   create unique index daily
      on work.marchflights(flightnumber,date);
```

The following DESCRIBE TABLE statement writes a CREATE INDEX statement to the SAS log (after the CREATE TABLE statement) for the table Marchflights:

```
proc sql;
   describe table marchflights;
```

Table 6.5 *SAS Log*

```
NOTE: SQL table WORK.MARCHFLIGHTS was created like:

create table WORK.MARCHFLIGHTS( bufsize=8192 )
   (
   Date num format=DATE9. informat=DATE9.,
   DepartureTime num format=TIME5. informat=TIME5.,
   FlightNumber char(3),
   Origin char(3),
   Destination char(3),
   Distance num,
   Mail num,
   Freight num,
   Boarded num,
   Transferred num,
   NonRevenue num,
   Deplaned num,
   PassengerCapacity num
   );
create unique index daily on WORK.MARCHFLIGHTS(FlightNumber,Date);
```

If the table Marchflights had no index defined, no CREATE INDEX statement would appear in the SAS log.

Alternatives to the DESCRIBE TABLE Statement

The DESCRIBE TABLE statement is only one of several methods that can be used to list information about indexes that are defined on a table. One alternative is to query the special table Dictionary.Indexes, which contains information about indexes that are defined for all tables that are known to the current SAS session. (Dictionary.Indexes is one of many read-only dictionary tables that are created at PROC SQL initialization. These tables contain information about SAS libraries, SAS macros, and external files that are in use or available in the current SAS session.)

You can also use other SAS procedures, such as PROC CONTENTS and PROC DATASETS, to generate a report that contains information about indexes.

Note: To learn more about the use of dictionary tables, see Chapter 8, "Managing Processing Using PROC SQL," on page 264. To learn more about using PROC CONTENTS and PROC DATASETS, see Chapter 13, "Creating Indexes," on page 448.

Managing Index Usage

Overview

To manage indexes effectively, it is important to know

- how SAS decides whether to use an index and which index to use
- how to determine whether SAS is using an index
- how to control whether SAS uses an index, or which index it uses.

Understanding How SAS Decides Whether to Use an Index

By default, each time you submit a query (or other SAS program) that contains a WHERE expression, SAS decides whether to use an index, or to read all the observations in the data file sequentially. To make this decision, SAS does the following:

1. Identifies an available index or indexes.

2. Estimates the number of rows that would be qualified. If multiple indexes are available, SAS selects the index that it estimates returns the smallest subset of rows.

3. Compares resource usage to decide whether it is more efficient to satisfy the WHERE expression by using the index or by reading all the observations sequentially.

Next, consider how you can find out whether SAS is using an index.

Determining Whether SAS Is Using an Index

After you create an index, it is important to monitor whether the index is being used. If an index is not being used, the costs of maintaining the index might be greater than the benefits, and you should consider dropping (deleting) the index.

By default, when a PROC SQL query or any other program is submitted in SAS, only notes, warnings, and error messages are written to the SAS log. To display additional messages, such as information about indexes that have been defined and that have been used in processing the program, specify the SAS system option MSGLEVEL=I. You specify the MSGLEVEL= option in the OPTIONS statement, before the PROC SQL statement.

General form, MSGLEVEL= option:

OPTIONS MSGLEVEL=N | I;

Here is an explanation of the syntax:

N

    displays notes, warnings, and error messages only. This is the default.

I

    displays additional notes pertaining to index usage, merge processing, and sort utilities along with standard notes, warnings, and error messages.

Usually, the option MSGLEVEL= is set to I for debugging and testing, and set to N for production jobs.

Example: Query That Uses an Index

Suppose you are writing a PROC SQL query that references the temporary table Marchflights. Earlier in this chapter, a unique composite index named daily was created on the columns FlightNumber and Date in Marchflights. The WHERE expression in your query specifies the key column FlightNumber. To determine whether PROC SQL uses the index daily when your query is processed, you specify MSGLEVEL=I before the query:

```
options msglevel=i;
proc sql;
   select *
      from marchflights
      where flightnumber='182';
```

The message in the SAS log shows that the index was used in processing.

Table 6.6 *SAS Log*

```
INFO: Index daily selected for WHERE clause optimization.
```

Example: Query That Does Not Use an Index

Suppose you submit a different query that also references the key column FlightNumber:

```
proc sql;
   select *
      from marchflights
      where flightnumber in ('182','202');
```

In this example, the SAS log shows that the query does not use the index.

Table 6.7 *SAS Log*

```
INFO: Index daily not used. Sorting into index order may help.
INFO: Index daily not used. Increasing bufno to 8 may help.
```

Note: For more information about the BUFSIZE= option, see "Using the BUFSIZE= Option" on page 661.

Note: SAS Version 8 displays informational messages that indicate when an index *is* used, but does not display messages that indicate when an index is not used.

TIP Because the OPTIONS statement is global, the settings remain in effect until you modify them or until you end your SAS session. Therefore, you do not need to specify MSGLEVEL=I in this second query or any subsequent queries until you want to change the setting or until your SAS session ends.

Controlling Index Usage

In general, it is recommended that you allow SAS to decide whether to use an index, or which index to use, in processing a PROC SQL query (or other SAS program). However, in some situations, such as testing, you might find it useful to control the use of indexes by SAS.

To control index usage, use the IDXWHERE= and IDXNAME= SAS data set options to override the default settings. You can use either of these options, but you cannot use both options at the same time. As with other SAS data set options, you specify the IDXWHERE= or IDXNAME= option in parentheses after the table name in the FROM clause of a PROC SQL query.

Using IDXWHERE= to Direct SAS to Use or Not to Use an Index

The IDXWHERE= option enables you to override the decision that SAS makes about whether to use an index.

General form, IDXWHERE= option:

IDXWHERE=YES | NO;

Here is an explanation of the syntax:

YES
   tells SAS to choose the best index to optimize a WHERE expression, and to disregard the possibility that a sequential search of the table might be more resource-efficient.

NO
   tells SAS to ignore all indexes and satisfy the conditions of a WHERE expression with a sequential search of the table.

Note: Use the IDXWHERE=NO option when you know an available index does not optimize WHERE clause processing.

Example

In an earlier example, you used the option MSGLEVEL=I to verify that PROC SQL *does* use an index to process the following query:

```
options msglevel=i;
proc sql;
   select *
      from marchflights
      where flightnumber='182';
```

To force SAS to ignore the index and to process the rows of the table sequentially, specify IDXWHERE=NO in the query:

```
proc sql;
   select *
      from marchflights (idxwhere=no)
      where flightnumber='182';
```

A message in the SAS log indicates that SAS was forced to process the data sequentially.

Table 6.8 *SAS Log*

```
INFO: Data set option (IDXWHERE=NO) forced a sequential pass of the data
rather than use of an index for where-clause processing.
```

Using IDXNAME= to Direct SAS to Use a Specified Index

The IDXNAME= option directs SAS to use an index that you specify, even if SAS would have selected not to use an index or to use a different index.

General form, IDXNAME= option:

IDXNAME=*index-name*;

Here is an explanation of the syntax:

index-name
   specifies the name of the index that should be used for processing.

SAS uses the specified index if the following conditions are true:

• The specified index must exist.

• The specified index must be suitable by having at least its first or only column match a condition in the WHERE expression.

Note: Use the IDXNAME= option when you know the better index so that SAS does not have to do the evaluation.

Example

In an earlier example, a composite index named daily was defined on the columns FlightNumber and Date in the temporary table Marchflights. Suppose you create a second index, a simple index, on the column Date (the secondary key in the composite index) by using the following PROC SQL step:

```
proc sql;
   create index Date
      on work.marchflights(Date);
```

Next, you submit the following query:

```
proc sql;
   select *
      from marchflights
      where date='01MAR2000'd;
```

The WHERE clause in this query references the key column Date. By default, SAS decides whether to use an index and, if an index is used, which index to use. The SAS log indicates that, with both a simple index and a composite index defined on Date, PROC SQL used the simple index Date to process the query.

Table 6.9   *SAS Log*

```
INFO: Index Date selected for WHERE clause optimization.
```

Note: This example assumes that the option MSGLEVEL=I, which was specified in the previous example, is still in effect.

You decide that you want to force PROC SQL to use the index daily instead of Date, so you add IDXNAME= to your query:

```
proc sql;
   select *
      from marchflights (idxname=daily)
      where flightnumber='182';
```

After this query is submitted, a message in the SAS log indicates that PROC SQL used the index daily:

Table 6.10   *SAS Log*

```
INFO: Index daily selected for WHERE clause optimization.
```

Dropping Indexes

Overview

To drop (delete) one or more indexes, use the DROP INDEX statement.

General form, DROP INDEX statement:

DROP INDEX *index-name-1 <, ...index-name-2>*

      FROM *table-name*;

Here is an explanation of the syntax:

index-name
    specifies an index that exists.

table-name
    specifies a table that contains the specified index(es). The *table-name* can be one of the
    following:

- a one-level name

- a two-level libref.table name

- a physical pathname that is enclosed in single quotation marks.

Example: Dropping a Composite Index

The following PROC SQL step uses the DROP INDEX statement to drop the composite,
unique index daily from the temporary table Marchflights. (This index was created in an
example earlier in this chapter.)

```
proc sql;
   drop index daily
      from work.marchflights;
```

When this step is submitted, the SAS log displays a message indicating that the index
has been dropped.

Table 6.11 *SAS Log*

```
NOTE: Index daily has been dropped.
```

Summary

Text Summary

Understanding Indexes
An index is an auxiliary file that is defined on one or more of a table's columns, which
are called key columns. The index stores the unique column values and a system of
directions that enable access to rows in that table by index value. When an index is used
to process a PROC SQL query, PROC SQL accesses directly (without having to read all
the prior rows) instead of sequentially.

You can create two types of indexes:

- simple index (an index on one column)

- composite index (an index on two or more columns).

You can define either type of index as a unique index, which requires that values for the key column(s) be unique for each row.

Deciding Whether to Create an Index

When deciding whether to create an index, you must weigh any benefits in performance improvement against the costs of increased resource usage. Certain classes of PROC SQL queries can be optimized by using an index. To optimize the performance of your PROC SQL queries, you can follow some basic guidelines for creating indexes.

Creating an Index

To create an index on one or more columns of a table, use the CREATE INDEX statement. To specify a unique index, you add the keyword UNIQUE.

Displaying Index Specifications

To display a CREATE INDEX statement in the SAS log for each index that is defined for one or more specified tables, use the DESCRIBE TABLE statement.

Managing Index Usage

To manage indexes effectively, it is important to know how SAS decides whether to use an index and which index to use.

To find out whether an index is being used, specify the SAS option MSGLEVEL=I in an OPTIONS statement before the PROC SQL statement. This option enables SAS to write informational messages about index usage (and other additional information) to the SAS log. The default setting MSGLEVEL=N displays notes, warnings, and error messages only.

To force SAS to use the best available index, to use a specific index, or not to use an index at all, include either the SAS data set option IDXWHERE= or IDXNAME= in your PROC SQL query.

Dropping Indexes

To drop (delete) one or more indexes, use the DROP INDEX statement.

Sample Programs

Creating a Simple, Unique Index, and a Composite Index

```
proc sql;
   create unique index EmpID
      on work.payrollmaster(empid);
   create index daily
      on work.marchflights(flightnumber,date);
quit;
```

Displaying Index Specifications

```
proc sql;
   describe table marchflights;
quit;
```

Determining Whether SAS Is Using an Index

```
options msglevel=i;
proc sql;
```

```
        select *
           from marchflights
           where flightnumber='182';
    quit;
```

Directing SAS to Ignore All Indexes

```
proc sql;
    select *
        from marchflights (idxwhere=no)
        where flightnumber='182';
quit;
```

Directing SAS to Use a Specified Index

```
proc sql;
    select *
        from marchflights (idxname=daily)
        where flightnumber='182';
quit;
```

Dropping an Index

```
proc sql;
    drop index daily
        from work.marchflights;
quit;
```

Points to Remember

- An index cannot be created on a view.

- Keep the number of indexes to a minimum to reduce disk storage and update costs.

- Do not create an index for small tables; sequential access is faster on small tables.

- Do not create an index based on columns that have a very small number of distinct values, low cardinality (for example, a Gender column that contains only the two values **Male** and **Female**).

- Use indexes for queries that retrieve a relatively small subset of rows — that is, less than 15%.

- Do not create more than one index that is based on the same column as the primary key.

Quiz

Select the best answer for each question. After completing the quiz, check your answers using the answer key in the appendix.

1. Which of the following creates an index on the column EmpID for the table Sasuser.Staffmaster?

   a. ```
      proc sql;
          create simple index(empid)
              on sasuser.staffmaster;
      ```
      ```

```
b. proc sql;
      create empid index
         on sasuser.staffmaster(empid);
```

```
c. proc sql;
      create simple index
         on empid from sasuser.staffmaster;
```

```
d. proc sql;
      create index empid
         on sasuser.staffmaster(empid);
```

2. Which keyword must you add to your index definition in the CREATE INDEX statement to ensure that no duplicate values of the key column can exist?

   a. KEY

   b. UNIQUE

   c. NODUPS

   d. NODUPKEY

3. Which of the following creates a composite index for the table Sasuser.Flightdelays? (Sasuser.Flightdelays contains the following columns: Date, FlightNumber, Origin, Destination, DelayCategory, DestinationType, DayOfWeek, and Delay.)

```
a. proc sql;
      create index destination
         on sasuser.flightdelays(flightnumber,
                                 destination);
```

```
b. proc sql;
      create composite index places
         on sasuser.flightdelays (flightnumber,
                                  destination);
```

```
c. proc sql;
      create index on flightnumber,destination
         from sasuser.flightdelays (places);
```

```
d. proc sql;
      create index places
         on sasuser.flightdelays (flightnumber,
                                  destination);
```

4. Which of the following writes a message to the SAS log that shows whether PROC SQL has used an index?

```
a. options msglevel=i;
   proc sql;
      select *
         from sasuser.internationalflights
         where date between '01mar2000'd
            and '07mar2000'd;
```

```
b. options index=yes;
   proc sql;
      select *
         from sasuser.internationalflights
         where date between '01mar2000'd
            and '07mar2000'd;
```

```
c. proc sql;
```

```
          select * (idxwhere=yes)
             from sasuser.internationalflights
             where date between '01mar2000'd
                   and '07mar2000'd;
```

d. ```
   proc sql;
       select * (msglevel=i)
          from sasuser.internationalflights
          where date between '01mar2000'd
                and '07mar2000'd;
   ```

5. Which of the following drops (deletes) an index from a table?

   a. ```
      proc sql;
          drop composite index flights
             from sasuser.marchflights;
      ```

   b. ```
      proc sql;
          delete index flights
             on sasuser.staffmaster(flightnumber, date);
      ```

   c. ```
      proc sql;
          drop index flights
             from sasuser.marchflights;
      ```

   d. ```
      proc sql;
          delete index
             on sasuser.marchflights(flightnumber,
                                     flightdate);
      ```

6. Which of the following statements shows you all the indexes that are defined for a table?

   a. DESCRIBE INDEX

   b. DESCRIBE TABLE

   c. SELECT

   d. IDXNAME

7. What is the purpose of specifying the data set option IDXWHERE=YES?

   a. It forces SAS to use the best available index to process the WHERE expression.

   b. It creates an index from the expression in the WHERE clause.

   c. It writes messages about index usage to the SAS log.

   d. It stops SAS from using any index.

8. Which of the following is false regarding the use of an index?

   a. Equijoins can be performed without internal sorts.

   b. Indexes provide fast access to a small subset of data.

   c. Indexes can be created for numeric columns only.

   d. Indexes can enforce uniqueness.

9. Using an index is not likely to optimize a PROC SQL query in which of the following situations?

   a. The query contains an IN subquery that references the key column.
      ```

   b. The key column is specified in a WHERE clause expression that contains a comparison operator, the TRIM or SUBSTR function, the CONTAINS operator, or the LIKE operator.

   c. The query is an equijoin, and all the columns in the join expression are indexed in one of the tables being joined.

   d. The key column is specified only in a SELECT clause.

10. Which of the following is false regarding the IDXNAME= data set option?

   a. The specified index must exist.

   b. The specified index must be suitable by having at least its first or only column match a condition in the WHERE expression.

   c. The option enables you to create and name an index on the table.

   d. The option directs SAS to use an index that you specify.

Chapter 7
Creating and Managing Views Using PROC SQL

Overview

Introduction

A PROC SQL view is a stored query expression that reads data values from its underlying files, which can include SAS data files, DATA step views, other PROC SQL views, or DBMS data.

You can refer to views in queries as if they were tables. The view derives its data from the tables or views that are listed in its FROM clause. The data that is accessed by a view is a subset or superset of the data that is in its underlying table(s) or view(s).

```
proc sql;
    create view sasuser.raisev as
        select empid, jobcode,
                salary format=dollar12.2,
                salary/12 as MonthlySalary
                format=dollar12.2
            from payrollmaster;
    select *
        from sasuser.raisev
        where jobcode in ('PT2','PT3');
```

EmpID	JobCode	Salary	Monthly Salary
1333	PT2	$124,048.00	$10,337.33
1404	PT2	$127,926.00	$10,660.50
1118	PT3	$155,931.00	$12,994.25
1410	PT2	$118,559.00	$9,879.92
1777	PT3	$153,482.00	$12,790.17
1106	PT2	$125,485.00	$10,457.08
1442	PT2	$118,350.00	$9,862.50
1478	PT2	$117,884.00	$9,823.67
1890	PT2	$120,254.00	$10,021.17
1107	PT2	$125,968.00	$10,497.33
1830	PT2	$118,259.00	$9,854.92
1928	PT2	$125,801.00	$10,483.42

PROC SQL views

- can be used in SAS programs in place of an actual SAS data file

- can be joined with tables or other views

- can be derived from one or more tables, PROC SQL views, or DATA step views

- can access data from a SAS data set, a DATA step view, a PROC SQL view, or a relational database table

- extract underlying data, which enables you to access the most current data.

Creating and Using PROC SQL Views

PROC SQL Views

A PROC SQL view is a stored query that is executed when you use the view in a SAS procedure or DATA step. A view contains only the descriptor and other information required to retrieve the data values from other SAS files (SAS data files, DATA step views, or other PROC SQL views) or external files (DBMS data files). The view contains only the logic for accessing the data, not the data itself.

Because PROC SQL views are not separate copies of data, they are referred to as virtual tables. They do not exist as independent entities like real tables. However, views use the same naming conventions as tables and can be used in SAS programs in place of an actual SAS table. Like tables, views are considered to be SAS data sets.

Views are useful because they do the following:

- often save space (a view is usually quite small compared with the data that it accesses)

- prevent users from continually submitting queries to omit unwanted columns or rows

- ensure that input data sets are always current, because data is derived from tables at execution time

- shield sensitive or confidential columns from users while enabling the same users to view other columns in the same table

- hide complex joins or queries from users.

Creating PROC SQL Views

You use the CREATE VIEW statement to create a view.

General form, CREATE VIEW statement:

CREATE VIEW *proc-sql-view* **AS**

    SELECT *column-1<, ... column-n>*

        FROM *table-1 | view-1<, ... table-n | view-n>*

        <optional query clauses>;

Here is an explanation of the syntax:

- *proc-sql-view* specifies the name of the PROC SQL view that you are creating.

- SELECT specifies the column(s) that appear in the table.

- FROM specifies the table(s) or view(s) to be queried.

- *optional query clauses* are used to refine the query further and include the WHERE, GROUP BY, HAVING, and ORDER BY clauses.

A PROC SQL view derives its data from the tables or views that are listed in the FROM clause. The data that is accessed by a view is a subset or superset of the data that is in its underlying table(s) or view(s). When a view is referenced by a SAS procedure or in a DATA step, it is executed and, conceptually, an internal table is built. PROC SQL processes this internal table as if it were any other table.

Example

The following PROC SQL step creates a view that contains information for flight attendants. The view always returns the employee's age as of the current date.

The view Sasuser.Faview creates a virtual table from the accompanying SELECT statement. Although the underlying tables, Sasuser.Payrollmaster and Sasuser.Staffmaster, can change, the instructions that comprise the view stay constant. The libref specified in the FROM clause is optional. It is assumed that the contributing tables are stored in the same library as the view itself, unless otherwise specified.

```
proc sql;
   create view sasuser.faview as
      select lastname, firstname, gender,
             int((today()-dateofbirth)/365.25) as Age,
             substr(jobcode,3,1) as Level,
             salary
         from sasuser.payrollmaster,
             sasuser.staffmaster
         where jobcode contains 'FA' and
             staffmaster.empid=
             payrollmaster.empid;
```

When this PROC SQL step is submitted, SAS does not actually execute the SELECT statement that follows the AS keyword, but partially compiles and stores the SELECT statement in a data file with a member type of VIEW. A message in the SAS log confirms that the view has been defined.

Table 7.1 *SAS Log*

```
1     proc sql;
2           create view sasuser.faview as
3             select lastname, firstname, gender,
4                    int((today()-dateofbirth)/365.25)
5                    as Age,
6                    substr(jobcode,3,1) as Level,
7                    salary
8                 from sasuser.payrollmaster,
9                     sasuser.staffmaster
10                where jobcode contains 'FA' and
11                    staffmaster.empid=
12                    payrollmaster.empid;
NOTE: SQL view SASUSER.FAVIEW has been defined.
```

T I P   It is helpful to give a PROC SQL view a name that easily identifies it as a view, for example, Faview or Fav.

Note: In the Windows and UNIX operating environments, the default extension for PROC SQL views (and DATA step views) is .sas7bvew.

Using PROC SQL Views

You can use a view in a subsequent PROC SQL step, or later in the same step, just as you would use an actual SAS table. In the following example, the PROC SQL view Sasuser.Faview is used in a query. Because the query stored in the view calculates the age of each flight attendant based on the current date, the resulting output from this PROC SQL step shows each flight attendant's age as of the current date. If Sasuser.Faview were a static table, instead of a view, the age shown for each flight attendant would never change.

```
proc sql;
   select *
      from sasuser.faview;
```

Partial output is shown below.

LastName	FirstName	Gender	Age	Level	Salary
ARTHUR	BARBARA	F	47	3	$46,040
CAHILL	MARSHALL	M	52	2	$40,001
CARTER	DOROTHY	F	52	3	$46,346
COOPER	ANTHONY	M	53	3	$45,104
DEAN	SHARON	F	51	3	$46,787
DUNLAP	DONNA	F	44	2	$40,443
EATON	ALICIA	F	51	2	$38,902
FIELDS	DIANA	F	54	1	$32,448
FLETCHER	MARIE	F	48	1	$31,436
GOMEZ	ALAN	M	42	1	$31,175

TIP   You can use PROC SQL views in other SAS procedures and DATA steps. In the following example, PROC TABULATE calculates the flight attendants' mean age by level, using the view Sasuser.Faview:

```
proc tabulate data=sasuser.faview;
   class level;
   var age;
   table level*age*mean;
run;
```

Level		
1	2	3
Age	Age	Age
Mean	Mean	Mean
44.27	48.31	49.86

Note: The values for the variable Age vary, because the calculation is dependent on the date on which the code is executed.

Note: For information about the TABULATE procedure, see the SAS documentation.

Displaying the Definition for a PROC SQL View

Overview

You can use a DESCRIBE VIEW statement to display a definition of a view in the SAS log.

General form, DESCRIBE VIEW statement:

DESCRIBE VIEW *proc-sql-view-1<,...proc-sql-view-n>*;

Here is an explanation of the syntax:

proc-sql-view
    specifies a PROC SQL view and can be one of the following:

- a one-level name

- a two-level libref.view name

- a physical pathname that is enclosed in single quotation marks.

TIP If you use a PROC SQL view in a DESCRIBE VIEW statement that is based on or derived from another view, then you might want to use the FEEDBACK option in the PROC SQL statement. This option is displayed in the SAS log how the underlying view is defined and expands any expressions that are used in this view definition.

Example

The following PROC SQL step writes the view definition for Sasuser.Faview to the SAS log:

```
proc sql;
    describe view sasuser.faview;
```

Table 7.2 *SAS Log*

```
NOTE: SQL view SASUSER.FAVIEW is defined as:
      select lastname, firstname, gender,
             INT((TODAY()-dateofbirth)/365.25) as Age,
      SUBSTR(jobcode, 3, 1) as Level, salary
      from SASUSER.PAYROLLMASTER, SASUSER.STAFFMASTER
      where jobcode contains 'FA' and
             (staffmaster.empid=payrollmaster.empid);
```

Managing PROC SQL Views

Guidelines for Using PROC SQL Views

When you are working with PROC SQL views, it is best to follow these guidelines:

- Avoid using an ORDER BY clause in a view definition, which causes the data to be sorted every time the view is executed. Users of the view might differ in how or whether they want the data to be sorted, so it is more efficient to specify an ORDER BY clause in a query that references the view.

- If the same data is used many times in one program or in multiple programs, it is more efficient to create a table rather than a view because the data must be accessed at each view reference. (This table can be a temporary table in the Work library.)

- Avoid creating views that are based on tables whose structure might change. A view is no longer valid when it references a nonexistent column.

- If a view resides in the same SAS library as the contributing table(s), it is best to specify a one-level name in the FROM clause.

Omitting the Libref

The default libref for the table or tables in the FROM clause is the libref of the library that contains the view. Using a one-level name in the FROM clause prevents you from having to change the view if you assign a different libref to the SAS library that contains the view and its contributing table or tables.

The following PROC SQL step creates the view Sasuser.Payrollv. The FROM clause specifies a two-level name for the contributing table, Sasuser.Payrollmaster. However, it is not necessary to specify the libref Sasuser because the contributing table is assumed to be stored in the same library as the view.

```
proc sql;
   create view sasuser.payrollv as
      select *
         from sasuser.payrollmaster;
```

When the one-level name Payrollmaster is used in the FROM clause, Sasuser.Payrollmaster is being specified, though it appears that Work.Payrollmaster is being specified.

```
proc sql;
   create view sasuser.payrollv as
      select *
         from payrollmaster;
```

CAUTION:
If you are creating a view that is stored in a different library than the table(s) referenced in the FROM clause, you must specify a two-level name for the table(s).

Using an Embedded LIBNAME Statement

As an alternative to omitting the libref in the FROM clause, you can embed a LIBNAME statement in a USING clause to store a SAS libref in a view. Embedding a LIBNAME statement is a more flexible approach because

- it can be used regardless of whether the view table and the underlying table reside in the same library

- it avoids the confusion that might arise if a libref is omitted from a table name in the FROM clause.

An embedded LIBNAME statement can be used only with a PROC SQL view. A libref created with an embedded LIBNAME statement does not conflict with an identically named libref in the SAS session.

General form, USING clause:

USING *libname-clause-1<,... libname-clause-n>*;

Here is an explanation of the syntax:

libname-clause
    is one of the following:

- a valid LIBNAME statement
- a valid SAS/ACCESS LIBNAME statement.

CAUTION:
    The USING clause must be the last clause in the CREATE VIEW statement.

Example

In the following example, while the view Sasuser.Payrollv is executing in the PROC PRINT step, the libref Airline is dynamically assigned in the USING clause.

```
proc sql;
   create view sasuser.payrollv as
      select*
         from airline.payrollmaster
         using libname airline 'SAS-library-one';
quit;
proc print data=sasuser.payrollv;
run;
```

If an earlier assignment of the libref AIRLINE exists, the EMBEDDED LIBNAME statement overrides the assignment for the duration of the view's execution. After the view executes, the original libref assignment is reestablished and the embedded assignment is cleared.

Creating a View to Enhance Table Security

One advantage of PROC SQL views is that they can bring data together from separate sources. This enables views to be used to shield sensitive or confidential columns from some users while enabling the same users to view other columns in the same table.

CAUTION:
    Although PROC SQL views can be used to enhance table security, it is strongly recommended that you use the security features that are available in your operating environment to maintain table security.

Example

The following PROC SQL step creates the view Manager.Infoview. The view accesses data about flight attendants that is stored in three SAS libraries: Fa1, Fa2, and Fa3. The Fa1, Fa2, and Fa3 libraries can be assigned access privileges at the operating system level to prevent

- Level 1 flight attendants from reading the data stored in the Fa2 and Fa3 libraries
- Level 2 flight attendants from reading the data stored in the Fa1 and Fa3 libraries
- Level 3 flight attendants from reading the data stored in the Fa1 and Fa2 libraries.

Access privileges can also be assigned to permit managers (who are authorized to access all SAS libraries) to view all of the information.

```
proc sql;
   create view manager.infoview as
      select *
         from fa1.info
      outer union corr
      select *
         from fa2.info
      outer union corr
      select *
         from fa3.info;
```

Updating PROC SQL Views

Overview

You can update the data underlying a PROC SQL view using the INSERT, DELETE, and UPDATE statements under the following conditions:

- You can update only a single table through a view. The table cannot be joined or linked to another table, nor can it contain a subquery.

- You can update a column using the column's alias, but you cannot update a derived column (a column that is produced by an expression).

- You can update a view that contains a WHERE clause. The WHERE clause can be specified in the UPDATE clause or in the view. You cannot update a view that contains any other clause such as an ORDER BY or a HAVING clause.

- You cannot update a summary view (a view that contains a GROUP BY clause).

Updating a view does not change the stored instructions for the view. Only the data in the underlying table(s) is updated.

Example

The following PROC SQL step creates the view Sasuser.Raisev, which includes the columns Salary and MonthlySalary. A subsequent query that references the view shows the columns.

```
proc sql;
   create view sasuser.raisev as
      select empid, jobcode,
             salary format=dollar12.,
             salary/12 as MonthlySalary
             format=dollar12.
          from payrollmaster;

proc sql;
   select *
      from sasuser.raisev
      where jobcode in ('PT2','PT3');
```

EmpID	JobCode	Salary	Monthly Salary
1333	PT2	$124,048	$10,337
1404	PT2	$127,926	$10,661
1118	PT3	$155,931	$12,994
1410	PT2	$118,559	$9,880
1777	PT3	$153,482	$12,790
1106	PT2	$125,485	$10,457
1442	PT2	$118,350	$9,863
1478	PT2	$117,884	$9,824
1890	PT2	$120,254	$10,021
1107	PT2	$125,968	$10,497
1830	PT2	$118,259	$9,855
1928	PT2	$125,801	$10,483

Suppose you want to update the view to show a salary increase for employees whose job code is **PT3**. You can use an UPDATE statement to change the column Salary and a WHERE clause in the UPDATE clause to identify the rows where the value of JobCode equals **PT3**. Though MonthlySalary is a derived column and cannot be changed using an UPDATE statement, it is updated because it is derived from Salary.

When the PROC SQL step is submitted, a note appears in the SAS log that indicates how many rows were updated:

```
proc sql;
   update sasuser.raisev
      set salary=salary * 1.20
      where jobcode='PT3';
```

Table 7.3 *SAS Log*

```
116    proc sql;
117        update sasuser.raisev
118            set salary=salary * 1.20
119            where jobcode='PT3';
NOTE: 2 rows were updated in SASUSER.RAISEV.
```

Note: Remember that the rows were updated in the table that underlies the view Sasuser.Raisev.

When you resubmit the query, the updated values for Salary and MonthlySalary appear in the rows where JobCode equals **PT3**:

```
proc sql;
   select *
      from sasuser.raisev
      where jobcode in ('PT2','PT3');
```

EmpID	JobCode	Salary	Monthly Salary
1333	PT2	$124,048	$10,337
1404	PT2	$127,926	$10,661
1118	PT3	$187,117	$15,593
1410	PT2	$118,559	$9,880
1777	PT3	$184,178	$15,348
1106	PT2	$125,486	$10,457
1442	PT2	$118,350	$9,863
1478	PT2	$117,884	$9,824
1890	PT2	$120,254	$10,021
1107	PT2	$125,968	$10,497
1830	PT2	$118,259	$9,855
1928	PT2	$125,801	$10,483

Dropping PROC SQL Views

Overview

To drop (delete) a view, use the DROP VIEW statement.

General form, DROP VIEW statement:

DROP VIEW *view-name-1* <*,...view-name-n*>;

Here is an explanation of the syntax:

view-name
   specifies a SAS data view of any type (PROC SQL view or DATA step view) and can be one of the following:

   • a one-level name

   • a two-level *libref.view* name

   • a physical pathname that is enclosed in single quotation marks.

Example

The following PROC SQL step drops the view Sasuser.Raisev. After the step is submitted, a message appears in the SAS log to confirm that the view has been dropped.

```
proc sql;
   drop view sasuser.raisev;
```

Table 7.4 SAS Log

```
21   proc sql;
22      drop view sasuser.raisev;
NOTE: View SASUSER.RAISEV has been dropped.
```

Summary

Text Summary

Using PROC SQL Views

A PROC SQL view is a stored query that is executed when you use the view in a SAS procedure or DATA step. A view contains only the descriptor and other information required to retrieve the data values from other SAS files (SAS data files, DATA step views, or other PROC SQL views) or external files (DBMS data files). When executed, a PROC SQL view's output can be a subset or superset of one or more underlying files. A view contains no data, but describes or defines data that is stored elsewhere.

PROC SQL views

- can be used in SAS programs in place of an actual SAS data file

- can be joined with tables or other views

- can be derived from one or more tables, PROC SQL views, DATA step views, or SAS/ACCESS views.

- extract underlying data, which enables you to access the most current data.

Because PROC SQL views are not separate copies of data, they are referred to as virtual tables. They do not exist as independent entities like real tables. However, views use the same naming conventions as tables and can be used in SAS programs in place of an actual SAS table. Like tables, views are considered to be SAS data sets.

Creating SQL Views

You use the CREATE VIEW statement to create a view. A PROC SQL view derives its data from the tables or views that are listed in the FROM clause. The data that is accessed by a view is a subset or superset of the data that is in its underlying tables(s) or view(s). When a view is referenced by a SAS procedure or in a DATA step, it is executed and, conceptually, an internal table is built. PROC SQL processes this internal table as if it were any other table. A view can be used in a subsequent PROC SQL step just as you would use an actual SAS table.

Displaying the Definition for a PROC SQL View

You can use a DESCRIBE VIEW statement to display a definition of a view in the SAS log.

Managing PROC SQL Views

The default libref for the table or tables in the FROM clause is the libref of the library that contains the view. Using a one-level name prevents you from having to change the view if you assign a different libref to the SAS library that contains the view and its contributing table or tables.

As a more flexible alternative to omitting the libref in the FROM clause, you can embed a LIBNAME statement in a USING clause if you want to store a SAS libref in a view. Embedding a LIBNAME statement in a USING clause does not conflict with an identically named libref in the SAS session.

One advantage of PROC SQL views is that they can bring data together from separate sources. This enables views to be used to shield sensitive or confidential columns from some users while enabling the same users to view other columns in the same table. Although PROC SQL views can be used to enhance table security, it is strongly recommended that you use the security features that are available in your operating environment to maintain table security.

Updating PROC SQL Views

You can update the data underlying a PROC SQL view using the INSERT, DELETE, and UPDATE statements under the following conditions:

- You can update only a single table through a view. The table cannot be joined or linked to another table, nor can it contain a subquery.

- You can update a column using the column's alias, but you cannot update a derived column (a column that is produced by an expression).

- You can update a view that contains a WHERE clause. The WHERE clause can be in the UPDATE clause or in the view. You cannot update a view that contains any other clause such as an ORDER BY or a HAVING clause.

- You cannot update a summary view (a view that contains a GROUP BY clause).

Dropping PROC SQL Views

To drop (delete) a view, use the DROP VIEW statement.

Sample Programs

Creating a PROC SQL View

```
proc sql;
   create view sasuser.raisev as
      select empid, jobcode,
              salary format=dollar12.2,
              salary/12 as MonthlySalary
              format=dollar12.
           from payrollmaster
           using libname airline 'c:\data\ia';
quit;
```

Displaying the Definition for a PROC SQL View

```
proc sql;
   describe view sasuser.raisev;
quit;
```

Using a PROC SQL View in a Query

```
proc sql;
   select *
```

```
            from sasuser.raisev
            where jobcode in ('PT2','PT3');
     quit;
```

Updating a PROC SQL View

```
proc sql;
   update sasuser.raisev
       set salary=salary * 1.20
       where jobcode='PT3';
quit;
```

Dropping a PROC SQL View

```
proc sql;
   drop view sasuser.raisev;
quit;
```

Points to Remember

- Avoid using an ORDER BY clause in a view definition, which causes the data to be sorted every time the view is executed. Users of the view might differ in how or whether they want the data to be sorted, so it is more efficient to specify an ORDER BY clause in a query that references the view.

- If the same data is used many times in one program or in multiple programs, it is more efficient to create a table rather than a view because the data must be accessed at each view reference. (This table can be a temporary table in the Work library.)

- Avoid creating views that are based on tables whose structure might change. A view is no longer valid when it references a nonexistent column.

- If a view resides in the same SAS library as the contributing table(s), it is best to specify a one-level name in the FROM clause.

Quiz

Select the best answer for each question. After completing the quiz, check your answers using the answer key in the appendix.

1. Which of the following statements is false regarding a PROC SQL view?

   a. A view cannot be used in a join.

   b. A view accesses the most current underlying data.

   c. A view follows the same naming conventions as a table.

   d. A view can be used in SAS programs in place of an actual SAS data file.

2. Which of the following statements describes an advantage of using a PROC SQL view?

   a. Views often save space, because a view is usually quite small compared with the data that it accesses.

   b. Views prevent users from continually submitting queries to omit unwanted columns or rows.

    c. Views hide complex joins or queries from users.

    d. all of the above

3. Which PROC SQL step creates a view that queries the table Sasuser.Payrollmaster?

    a.
```
proc sql;
    insert into sasuser.newview
        select * from sasuser.payrollmaster;
```

    b.
```
proc sql;
    create sasuser.newview as
        select * from sasuser.payrollmaster;
```

    c.
```
proc sql;
    create view sasuser.newview as
        select * from sasuser.payrollmaster;
```

    d.
```
proc sql;
    select * from sasuser.payrollmaster
        into view sasuser.newview;
```

4. Which of the following PROC SQL steps enables you to see a description of the view definition?

    a.
```
proc sql;
    select * from sasuser.payrollmasterv;
```

    b.
```
proc sql;
    describe view sasuser.payrollmasterv;
```

    c.
```
proc sql;
    list sasuser.payrollmasterv;
```

    d.
```
proc sql;
    contents view=sasuser.payrollmasterv;
```

5. Which PROC SQL step correctly references the view Data.Empview?

    a.
```
proc sql;
    select *
        from data.empview;
```

    b.
```
proc sql;
    select *
        from view data.empview;
```

    c.
```
proc sql;
    select view *
        from data.empview;
```

    d.
```
proc sql;
    select *
        from data
        where view='empview';
```

6. Which of the following PROC SQL steps correctly embeds a LIBNAME statement with a view definition?

    a.
```
proc sql;
    insert into sasuser.newview
        select * from airline.supervisors
            libname airline 'c:\mysql';
```

    b.
```
proc sql;
```

```
        create view sasuser.newview as
           from airline.supervisors
              embed libname airline 'c:\mysql';
```

c. ```
   proc sql;
      using airline 'c:\mysql';
         insert into sasuser.newview
            select * from airline.supervisors;
   ```

d. ```
   proc sql;
      create view sasuser.newview as
         select * from airline.supervisors
            using libname airline 'c:\mysql';
   ```

7. PROC SQL views can access data from:

   a. a SAS data file.

   b. another PROC SQL view.

   c. a relational database table.

   d. all of the above

8. When you are working with PROC SQL views, it is best to:

   a. avoid using an ORDER BY clause in a view.

   b. avoid creating views that are based on tables whose structure might change.

   c. specify a one-level name in the FROM clause if the view resides in the same SAS library as the contributing table(s).

   d. all of the above

9. You can update the data underlying PROC SQL view using the INSERT, DELETE, and UPDATE statements under which of the following conditions:

   a. The view is joined or linked to another table.

   b. The view contains a subquery.

   c. The view contains a WHERE clause.

   d. all of the above

10. Which of the following programs drops (deletes) a view?

    a. ```
       proc sql;
          delete sasuser.newview;
       ```

    b. ```
       proc sql;
          drop view sasuser.newview;
       ```

    c. ```
       proc sql;
          erase view sasuser.newview;
       ```

    d. ```
       proc sql;
          remove newview from sasuser;
       ```

Chapter 8
Managing Processing Using PROC SQL

Overview

Introduction

The SQL procedure offers a variety of options that control processing. Some options control execution. For example, you can limit the number of rows read or written during a query. Other options control output. For example, you can control the appearance of long character columns, double-space output, or (as shown below) number your rows. Options are also available for testing and evaluating performance.

Row	FlightNumber	Destination
1	182	YYZ
2	219	LHR
3	387	CPH
4	622	FRA
5	821	LHR
6	132	YYZ
7	271	CDG
8	182	YYZ
9	219	LHR
10	387	CPH

Metadata is a description or definition of data or information. SAS session metadata is stored in Dictionary tables, which are special, read-only SAS tables that contain information about SAS libraries, SAS data sets, SAS macros, and external files that are available in the current SAS session. Dictionary tables also contain the settings for SAS system options and SAS titles and footnotes that are currently in effect. You can use the SQL procedure to access the metadata stored in Dictionary tables. For example, you can query a Dictionary table to find out which tables in a SAS library contain a specified column.

Specifying SQL Options

Remember that PROC SQL options are specified in the PROC SQL statement.

General form, PROC SQL statement:

PROC SQL *<option(s)>*;

Here is an explanation of the syntax:

option(s)
    names the option(s) to be used.

CAUTION:
    After you specify an option, it remains in effect until you change it or you re-invoke
    PROC SQL.

The following tables list the options for controlling processing that are covered in this
chapter. A complete description and an example of each option appears in the following
sections.

Table 8.1 *Options to Control Execution*

To do this...	Use this option...
Restrict the number of input rows	INOBS=
Restrict the number of output rows	OUTOBS=

Table 8.2 *Options to Control Output*

To do this...	Use this option...
Double-space the output	DOUBLE | NODOUBLE
Flow characters within a column	FLOW | NOFLOW | FLOW=*n* | FLOW=*n m*

Table 8.3 *Options for Testing and Evaluating Performance*

To do this...	Use this option...
Specify whether PROC SQL writes timing information for each statement to the SAS log	STIMER | NOSTIMER

Note: For a complete list of options, see the SAS documentation for the SQL procedure.

Controlling Execution

Restricting Row Processing

When you are developing queries against large tables, you can reduce the amount of
time that it takes for the queries to run by reducing the number of rows that PROC SQL

processes. Subsetting the tables with WHERE clauses is one way to do this. Using the INOBS= and OUTOBS= options in PROC SQL is another way.

You already know that you can use the OUTOBS= option to restrict the number of rows that PROC SQL displays or writes to a table. However, the OUTOBS= option does not restrict the rows that are read. The INOBS= option restricts the number of rows that PROC SQL takes as input from any single source. The INOBS= option is similar to the SAS system option OBS= and is useful for debugging queries on large tables.

Note: For more information about the OUTOBS= option, see Chapter 2, "Performing Advanced Queries Using PROC SQL," on page 26.

Example

In the following PROC SQL set operation, INOBS=5 is specified. As indicated in the log, only five rows from each source table, Sasuser.Mechanicslevel1 and Sasuser.Mechanicslevel2, are used. The resulting table contains 10 rows.

```
proc sql inobs=5;
   select *
      from sasuser.mechanicslevel1
   outer union corr
   select *
      from sasuser.mechanicslevel2;
```

Table 8.4 *SAS Log*

```
183    proc sql inobs=5;
184      select *
185         from sasuser.mechanicslevel1
186      outer union corr
187      select *
188         from sasuser.mechanicslevel2;

WARNING: Only 5 records were read from SASUSER.MECHANICSLEVEL1
         due to INOBS= option.
WARNING: Only 5 records were read from SASUSER.MECHANICSLEVEL2
         due to INOBS= option.
```

EmpID	JobCode	Salary
1400	ME1	$41,677
1403	ME1	$39,301
1120	ME1	$40,067
1121	ME1	$40,757
1412	ME1	$38,919
1653	ME2	$49,151
1782	ME2	$49,483
1244	ME2	$51,695
1065	ME2	$49,126
1129	ME2	$48,901

TIP You can use the PROMPT | NOPROMPT option with the INOBS= and OUTOBS= options so that you are prompted to stop or continue processing when the limits set by these options are reached.

Note: For more information about PROC SQL set operations, see Chapter 4, "Combining Tables Vertically Using PROC SQL," on page 126.

CAUTION:

In a simple query, there might be no apparent differences between using INOBS= or OUTOBS=. Other times, it is important to choose the correct option. For example, using the average function on a column with the PROC SQL option INOBS=10 returns an average of only the 10 values read for that column.

Controlling Output

Including a Column of Row Numbers

The NUMBER | NONUMBER option specifies whether the output from a query should include a column named ROW, which displays row numbers. NONUMBER is the default. The option is similar to the NOOBS option in the PRINT procedure.

Example

The following PROC SQL step specifies the NUMBER option. Output from the step includes a column named Row, which contains row numbers.

```
proc sql inobs=10 number;
   select flightnumber, destination
      from sasuser.internationalflights;
```

Row	FlightNumber	Destination
1	182	YYZ
2	219	LHR
3	387	CPH
4	622	FRA
5	821	LHR
6	132	YYZ
7	271	CDG
8	182	YYZ
9	219	LHR
10	387	CPH

Double-Spacing Output

In some cases, double-spacing your output can make it easier to read. The
DOUBLE | NODOUBLE option specifies whether PROC SQL output is double-spaced.
The default is NODOUBLE.

Note: The DOUBLE | NODOUBLE option does not affect the appearance of the
HTML, PDF, or RTF output. To see the effect of this option, select the text in SAS
Enterprise Guide.

Example

The following PROC SQL step specifies the DOUBLE option. The listing output from
this step is double spaced. The HTML output from this step remains single-spaced.

```
proc sql inobs=10 double;
   select flightnumber, destination
      from sasuser.internationalflights;
```

Figure 8.1 *Listing Output*

```
                          The SAS System


             FlightNumber           Destination

             182                     YYZ

             219                     LHR

             387                     CPH

             622                     FRA

             821                     LHR

             132                     YYZ

             271                     CDG

             182                     YYZ

             219                     LHR

             387                     CPH
```

Figure 8.2 *HTML Output*

Row	FlightNumber	Destination
1	182	YYZ
2	219	LHR
3	387	CPH
4	622	FRA
5	821	LHR
6	132	YYZ
7	271	CDG
8	182	YYZ
9	219	LHR
10	387	CPH

Flowing Characters within a Column

The FLOW | NOFLOW | FLOW=n | FLOW=n m option controls the appearance of wide character columns in listing output. The FLOW option causes text to be flowed in its column instead of wrapping the entire row. Specifying *n* sets the width of the flowed column. Specifying *n* and *m* floats the width of the column between limits to achieve a balanced layout.

Note: The FLOW | NOFLOW | FLOW=*n* | FLOW=*nm* option does not affect the appearance of HTML, PDF, or RTF output. To see the effect of this option, select the text output in SAS Enterprise Guide.

Example

The following PROC SQL step does not specify the FLOW option. Notice that in the output the name and values for the column ZipCode appear under the name and values for the column FFID due to the wide character columns.

```
proc sql inobs=5;
   select ffid, membertype, name, address, city,
          state, zipcode
      from sasuser.frequentflyers
      order by pointsused;
```

Figure 8.3   *Output from PROC SQL Step without FLOW Option*

Specifying `flow=10 15` causes the text within each character column to float between 10 and 15 spaces, which prevents the ZipCode column from wrapping underneath the FFID column.

```
proc sql inobs=5 flow=10 15;
   select ffid, membertype, name, address, city,
          state, zipcode
      from sasuser.frequentflyers
      order by pointsused;
```

Figure 8.4   *Output from PROC SQL Step with FLOW Option*

Testing and Evaluating Performance

Writing Timing Information for Each Statement

The PROC SQL option STIMER | NOSTIMER specifies whether PROC SQL writes timing information for each statement to the SAS log, instead of writing a cumulative value for the entire procedure. NOSTIMER is the default.

In order to use the STIMER option in PROC SQL, the SAS system option STIMER (the default) must also be in effect. Some host operating environments require that you specify the SAS system option STIMER when you invoke SAS. The STIMER system option controls the printing of performance statistics in the SAS log. If you use the system option alone, the results will contain timing information for the entire procedure, not on a statement-by-statement basis.

You can use the OPTIONS procedure to list the current settings of SAS system options. To find out if the SAS system STIMER option is enabled on your operating environment, submit the following program:

```
proc options option=stimer value;
run;
```

Table 8.5 *SAS Log*

```
Option Value Information For SAS Option STIMER
    Option Value: STIMER
    Option Scope: SAS Session
    How option value set: Shipped Default
```

Note: PROC OPTIONS produces additional information that is specific to the operating environment under which you are running SAS. For more information about this and for descriptions of host-specific options, see the SAS documentation for your operating environment.

Example

Both of the queries in the following PROC SQL step list the name, address, city, state, and ZIP code of customers listed in the Sasuser.FrequentFlyers table. However, the second query lists only this information for customers who have earned more than 7000 points and used less than 3000 points.

When the PROC SQL statement is submitted without the STIMER option, timing information for both queries is written to the SAS log as a cumulative value for the entire procedure.

```
proc sql;
   select name, address, city, state, zipcode
      from sasuser.frequentflyers;
   select name, address, city, state, zipcode
      from sasuser.frequentflyers
      where pointsearned gt 7000 and pointsused lt 3000;
quit;
```

Note: Timing information for a PROC SQL step is not written to the SAS log until a QUIT statement is submitted or another PROC or DATA step is started.

Table 8.6 *SAS Log*

```
28   proc sql;
29   select name, address, city, state, zipcode
        from sasuser.frequentflyers;
30   select name, address, city, state, zipcode
        from sasuser.frequentflyers
31     where pointsearned gt 7000 and pointsused lt 3000;
32   quit;
NOTE: PROCEDURE SQL used (Total process time):
      real time 0.34 seconds
      cpu time 0.30 seconds
```

When the PROC SQL statement is submitted with the STIMER option, timing information is written to the SAS log for each SELECT statement.

```
proc sql stimer;
   select name, address, city, state, zipcode
      from sasuser.frequentflyers;
   select name, address, city, state, zipcode
      from sasuser.frequentflyers
      where pointsearned gt 7000 and pointsused lt 3000;
quit;
```

Table 8.7 *SAS Log*

```
33   proc sql stimer;
NOTE: SQL Statement used (Total process time):
      real time            0.00 seconds
      cpu time             0.00 seconds

34 select name, address, city, state, zipcode
      from sasuser.frequentflyers;
NOTE: SQL Statement used (Total process time):
      real time 0.22 seconds
      cpu time 0.17 seconds

35 select name, address, city, state, zipcode
      from sasuser.frequentflyers
36   where pointsearned gt 7000 and pointsused lt 3000;
NOTE: SQL Statement used (Total process time):
      real time 0.25 seconds
      cpu time 0.08 seconds

37 quit;
NOTE: PROCEDURE SQL used (Total process time):
      real time 0.29 seconds
      cpu time 0.03 seconds
```

Note: When the STIMER option is used in PROC SQL, the exact wording of the Notes that are written to the SAS log might vary for different versions of SAS.

Note: The STIMER option in PROC SQL is useful when an operation can be accomplished in more than one way and you are benchmarking each technique.

Although factors such as code readability and maintenance come into consideration, you might also want to know which PROC SQL step runs the fastest.

Resetting Options

Overview

After you specify an option, it remains in effect until you change it, or you re-invoke PROC SQL. You can use the RESET statement to add, drop, or change PROC SQL options without re-invoking the SQL procedure.

General form, RESET statement:

RESET *<option(s)>*;

Here is an explanation of the syntax:

option(s)
    lists the options in any order.

Options are additive. For example, you can specify the NOPRINT option in a PROC SQL statement, submit a query, and submit the RESET statement with the NUMBER option, without affecting the NOPRINT option.

Example

Suppose you want to submit two PROC SQL queries in a single PROC SQL step. You want

- both queries to display only the first five rows of output
- the second query to display row numbers in the output.

In the following PROC SQL step, the PROC SQL statement specifies the OUTOBS= option to restrict the number of rows that is displayed in the output. After the first SELECT statement, the RESET statement adds the NUMBER option to display row numbers in the result set.

```
proc sql outobs=5;
   select flightnumber, destination
      from sasuser.internationalflights;
reset number;
   select flightnumber, destination
      from sasuser.internationalflights
      where boarded gt 200;
```

The output, which contains two result sets, is shown below. The result set from the first SELECT statement reflects only by the OUTOBS= option. The result set from the second SELECT statement reflects both the OUTOBS= option and the NUMBER option that is specified in the RESET statement.

FlightNumber	Destination
182	YYZ
219	LHR
387	CPH
622	FRA
821	LHR

Row	FlightNumber	Destination
1	622	FRA
2	821	LHR
3	821	LHR
4	219	LHR
5	219	LHR

Now suppose you want to modify the PROC SQL step so that the result set from only the first SELECT statement is restricted to five rows of output. In the modified PROC SQL step, the OUTOBS= option is added to the RESET statement to change (reset) the OUTOBS= option that is specified in the PROC SQL statement. The modified step follows:

```
proc sql outobs=5;
   select flightnumber, destination
      from sasuser.internationalflights;
reset outobs= number;
   select flightnumber, destination
      from sasuser.internationalflights
      where boarded gt 200;
```

In the output, the result set from the second SELECT statement now contains all the rows that are generated by the query.

FlightNumber	Destination
182	YYZ
219	LHR
387	CPH
622	FRA
821	LHR

Row	FlightNumber	Destination
1	622	FRA
2	821	LHR
3	821	LHR
4	219	LHR
5	219	LHR
6	622	FRA
7	821	LHR
8	219	LHR
9	821	LHR
10	219	LHR
11	622	FRA
12	219	LHR
13	821	LHR
14	219	LHR
15	219	LHR
16	821	LHR
17	219	LHR
18	622	FRA
19	622	FRA
20	219	LHR
21	821	LHR
22	622	FRA
23	821	LHR

Using Dictionary Tables

Overview

Dictionary tables are commonly used to monitor and manage SAS sessions because the data is easier to manipulate than the output from procedures such as PROC DATASETS.

Dictionary tables are special, read-only SAS tables that contain information about SAS libraries, SAS macros, and external files that are in use or available in the current SAS session. Dictionary tables also contain the settings for SAS system options and SAS titles and footnotes that are currently in effect. For example, the Dictionary.Columns table contains information (such as name, type, length, and format) about all columns in all tables that are known to the current SAS session.

Dictionary tables are

- created each time they are referenced in a SAS program

- updated automatically

- limited to Read-Only access.

Accessing a Dictionary table causes SAS to determine the current state of the SAS session and return the information that you want. Dictionary tables can be accessed by running a PROC SQL query against the table, using the Dictionary libref. Though SAS librefs are usually limited to eight characters, Dictionary is an automatically assigned, reserved word. You can also access a Dictionary table by referring to the PROC SQL view of the table that is stored in the Sashelp library.

The following table describes some of the Dictionary tables that are available and lists the corresponding Sashelp views. For a complete list of Dictionary tables, see the SAS documentation for the SQL procedure.

Dictionary table	Sashelp view	Contains
Catalogs	Vcatalg	information about catalog entries
Columns	Vcolumn	detailed information about variables and their attributes
Extfiles	Vextfl	currently assigned filerefs
Indexes	Vindex	information about indexes defined for data files
Macros	Vmacro	information about both user and system defined macro variables
Members	VmemberVsaccesVs catlgVslibVstableVst abvwVsview	general information about data library members
Options	Voption	current settings of SAS system options

Dictionary table	Sashelp view	Contains
Tables	Vtable	detailed information about data sets
Titles	Vtitle	text assigned to titles and footnotes
Views	Vview	general information about data views

Exploring and Using Dictionary Tables

You can query Dictionary tables the same way you query any other table, including subsetting with a WHERE clause, ordering the results, creating tables, and creating PROC SQL views. Because Dictionary tables are read-only objects, you cannot insert rows or columns, alter column attributes, or add integrity constraints to them.

To see how each Dictionary table is defined, submit a DESCRIBE TABLE statement. The DESCRIBE TABLE statement writes a CREATE TABLE statement to the SAS log for the table specified in the DESCRIBE TABLE statement. After you know how a table is defined, you can use its column names in a subsetting WHERE clause in order to retrieve specific information.

Example

The Dictionary.Tables table contains detailed information about tables. The following DESCRIBE TABLE statement displays information about the Dictionary.Tables table in the log window. The information includes the names of the columns stored in the table.

```
proc sql;
   describe table dictionary.tables;
```

Table 8.8 *SAS Log*

```
create table DICTIONARY.TABLES
  (
  libname char(8) label='Library Name',
  memname char(32) label='Member Name',
  memtype char(8) label='Member Type',
  memlabel char(256) label='Dataset Label',
  typemem char(8) label='Dataset Type',
  crdate num format=DATETIME informat=DATETIME label='Date Created',
...);
```

To display information about the files in a specific library, specify the column names in a SELECT statement and the Dictionary table name in the FROM clause.

For example, the following PROC SQL step displays the columns

- Memname (name)

- Nobs (number of observations)

- Nvar (number of variables)

- Crdate (creation date) of the tables in the *Sasuser* library.

The Dictionary column names are specified in the SELECT statement and the Dictionary table name, Dictionary.Tables, is specified in the FROM clause. The library name, Sasuser, is specified in the WHERE clause.

CAUTION:

Note that you must specify the library name in the WHERE clause in uppercase letters (because that is how it is stored within SAS) and enclose it in quotation marks.

```
proc sql;
   select memname format=$20., nobs, nvar, crdate
      from dictionary.tables
      where libname='SASUSER';
```

Partial output is shown below.

Member Name	Number of Physical Observations	Number of Variables	Date Created
ACITIES	50	4	05APR11:13:25:24
ADMIT	21	9	05APR11:13:25:17
ADMITJUNE	21	9	05APR11:13:25:17
AIRPORTS	50	4	05APR11:13:25:24
ALL	.	12	05APR11:13:25:25
ALLEMPS	50	5	05APR11:13:25:24
CAP2000	50	8	05APR11:13:25:24
CAP2001	50	8	05APR11:13:25:24
CAPACITY	50	7	05APR11:13:25:24
CAPINFO	50	7	05APR11:13:25:24

Note: The **nobs** value for ALL is missing because it is a view, not a table.

Note: Your output might differ from that shown above, depending on the contents of your Sasuser library.

You can also use Dictionary tables to determine more specific information such as which tables in a SAS library contain a specific column.

Example

The Dictionary.Columns table contains detailed information about variables and their attributes. As in Dictionary.Tables, the Dictionary.Columns table contains a column that is titled Memname, which lists the name of each table within a library.

```
proc sql;
   describe table dictionary.columns;
```

Table 8.9 *SAS Log*

```
create table DICTIONARY.COLUMNS
  (
  libname char(8) label='Library Name',
  memname char(32) label='Member Name',
  memtype char(8) label='Member Type',
  name char(32) label='Column Name',
  type char(4) label='Column Type',
  length num label='Column Length',
...);
```

The following PROC SQL step lists all the tables in the Sasuser library that contain a column named EmpID. The dictionary column name, Memname, is specified in the SELECT statement. The Dictionary table, Dictionary.Columns, is specified in the FROM clause. The library name, Sasuser, and the column name, EmpID, are specified in the WHERE clause.

```
proc sql;
   select memname
      from dictionary.columns
      where libname='SASUSER'
            and name='EmpID';
```

Partial output is shown below.

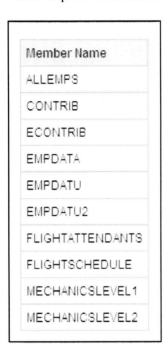

Member Name
ALLEMPS
CONTRIB
ECONTRIB
EMPDATA
EMPDATU
EMPDATU2
FLIGHTATTENDANTS
FLIGHTSCHEDULE
MECHANICSLEVEL1
MECHANICSLEVEL2

Remember that you can also access a Dictionary table by referring to the PROC SQL view of the table that is stored in the Sashelp library. In the following PROC PRINT step, the Sashelp view Vcolumn is specified in the DATA= option. The results of the PROC PRINT step are identical to the preceding output.

```
proc print data=sashelp.vcolumn;
   var memname;
   where libname='SASUSER' and name='EmpID';
run;
```

CAUTION:
Note that column names in the WHERE clause must be specified in the same case that is used in the Dictionary table and must be enclosed in quotation marks.

Note: You can use Sashelp views in any SAS procedure or DATA step. However, Dictionary tables can be read only by using the SQL procedure.

Additional Features

Restricting the Number of Loops

The LOOPS= option restricts the number of iterations of the inner loop in PROC SQL. By setting a limit, you can prevent queries from consuming excessive resources.

For example, joining three large tables without meeting the join-matching conditions could create a huge internal table that would be inefficient to process. Use the LOOPS= option to prevent this from happening.

You can use the PROMPT | NOPROMPT option to modify the effect of the LOOPS= option so that you are prompted to stop or continue processing when the limit set by the LOOPS= option is reached.

Note: You can use the number of iterations that are reported in the SQLOOPS macro variable (after each PROC SQL statement is executed) to gauge an appropriate value for the LOOPS= option. For more information about the SQLOOPS macro variable, see the SAS documentation for the SQL procedure.

Stopping Execution in PROC SQL after an Error

You already know that you can use the EXEC | NOEXEC option to specify whether a statement should be executed after its syntax is checked for accuracy. If the EXEC option is in effect, SAS checks the PROC SQL syntax for accuracy and, if no error is found, executes the SQL statement.

The ERRORSTOP | NOERRORSTOP option specifies whether PROC SQL stops executing if it encounters an error. This option is useful only when the EXEC option is in effect. The default is ERRORSTOP in batch or in a noninteractive session and NOERRORSTOP in an interactive SAS session.

ERRORSTOP instructs PROC SQL to stop executing the statements but to continue checking the syntax after it has encountered an error. ERRORSTOP has an effect only when SAS is running in batch or in noninteractive execution mode.

NOERRORSTOP instructs PROC SQL to execute the statements and to continue checking the syntax after an error occurs. NOERRORSTOP is useful if you want a batch job to continue executing SQL procedure statements after an error is encountered.

Summary

Text Summary

Specifying SQL Options

The SQL procedure offers a variety of options that affect processing. Some options control execution. For example, you can limit the number of rows read or written during a query or limit the number of internal loops PROC SQL performs. Other options control output. For example, you can flow character columns, number your rows, or double-space output. Options are also available for testing and evaluating performance. Options are specified in the PROC SQL statement.

Restricting Row Processing

The OUTOBS= option restricts the number of rows that PROC SQL displays or writes to a table. The INOBS= option restricts the number of rows that PROC SQL takes as input from any single source. The INOBS= option is similar to the SAS system option OBS= and is useful for debugging queries on large tables.

Controlling Output

The NUMBER | NONUMBER option specifies whether the SELECT statement should include a column named ROW, which is the row number of the data as it is retrieved. NONUMBER is the default. The option is similar to the NOOBS option in the PRINT procedure.

In some cases, double-spacing your output can make it easier to read. The DOUBLE | NODOUBLE option specifies whether PROC SQL output is double-spaced in the listing output. The default is NODOUBLE.

The FLOW | NOFLOW | FLOW=n| FLOW=n m option controls the appearance of wide character columns in the listing output. The FLOW option causes text to be flowed in its column instead of wrapping the entire row. Specifying n sets the width of the flowed column. Specifying n and m floats the width of the column between limits to achieve a balanced layout.

Testing and Evaluating Performance

The STIMER | NOSTIMER option specifies whether PROC SQL writes timing information for each statement to the SAS log, in addition to writing a cumulative value for the entire procedure. NOSTIMER is the default. In order to use the STIMER option in PROC SQL, the SAS system option STIMER (the default) must also be in effect.

Resetting Options

After you specify an option, it remains in effect until you change it or you re-invoke PROC SQL. You can use the RESET statement to add, drop, or change PROC SQL options without re-invoking the SQL procedure.

Using Dictionary Tables

SAS session metadata is stored in Dictionary tables, which are special, read-only SAS tables that contain information about SAS libraries, SAS macros, and external files that are available in the current SAS session. A Dictionary table also contains the settings for SAS system options and SAS titles and footnotes that are currently in effect.

Accessing a Dictionary table causes PROC SQL to determine the current state of the SAS session and return the information that you want. Dictionary tables can be accessed by running a PROC SQL query against the table, using the Dictionary libref. You can also access a Dictionary table by referring to the PROC SQL view of the table that is stored in the Sashelp library.

To see how each Dictionary table is defined, submit a DESCRIBE TABLE statement. After you know how a table is defined, you can use its column names in a subsetting WHERE clause in order to retrieve specific information. To display information about the files in a specific library, specify the column names in a SELECT statement and the dictionary table name in the FROM clause. You can also use Dictionary tables to determine more specific information such as which tables in a SAS library contain a specific column.

Additional Features

The LOOPS= option restricts the number of iterations of the inner loop in PROC SQL. By setting a limit, you can prevent queries from consuming excessive resources.

The ERRORSTOP | NOERRORSTOP option specifies whether PROC SQL stops executing if it encounters an error.

Sample Programs

Querying a Table Using PROC SQL Options

```
proc sql outobs=5;
   select flightnumber, destination
      from sasuser.internationalflights;
reset number;
   select flightnumber, destination
      from sasuser.internationalflights
      where boarded gt 200;
quit;
```

Describing and Querying a Dictionary Table

```
proc sql;
   describe table dictionary.columns;
   select memname
      from dictionary.columns
      where libname='SASUSER'
            and name='EmpID';
quit;
```

Points to Remember

- After you specify an option, it remains in effect until you change it or you re-invoke PROC SQL.

- The DOUBLE | NODOUBLE and the FLOW | NOFLOW | FLOW=*n*| FLOW=*n m* options do not affect the appearance of HTML, PDF, or RTF output that is created with the Output Delivery System.

- If you query a Dictionary table about the files in a specific library, the library name used in the WHERE clause must be specified in uppercase letters because that is how it is stored in SAS. Column names used in the WHERE clause must be specified in the same case as they appear in the Dictionary table.

Quiz

Select the best answer for each question. After completing the quiz, check your answers using the answer key in the appendix.

1. PROC SQL options are specified in

   a. the PROC SQL statement.

   b. an OPTIONS statement.

   c. a SELECT statement.

    d. the OPTIONS procedure.

2. Which of the following SQL options restricts the number of rows that PROC SQL takes as input from any single source?

    a. OUTOBS=

    b. INOBS=

    c. OBS=

    d. none of the above

3. Which PROC SQL step creates the output shown below?

EmpID	JobCode	LastName	FirstName
1124	FA1	FIELDS	DIANA
1422	FA1	FLETCHER	MARIE
1094	FA1	GOMEZ	ALAN
1113	FA1	JONES	LESLIE
1103	FA1	MCDANIEL	RONDA
1970	FA1	PARKER	ANNE
1132	FA1	PEARCE	CAROL
1116	FA1	RICHARDS	CASEY
1414	FA1	SANDERSON	NATHAN
1425	FA1	UNDERWOOD	JENNY
1130	FA1	WOOD	DEBORAH

Row	EmpID	JobCode	LastName	FirstName
1	1574	FA2	CAHILL	MARSHALL
2	1125	FA2	DUNLAP	DONNA
3	1475	FA2	EATON	ALICIA
4	1368	FA2	JEPSEN	RONALD
5	1411	FA2	JOHNSON	JACKSON
6	1441	FA2	LAWRENCE	KATHY
7	1477	FA2	MEYERS	PRESTON
8	1424	FA2	PATTERSON	RENEE
9	1413	FA2	PETERS	RANDALL
10	1555	FA2	RODRIGUEZ	JULIA

    a.
```
proc sql nonumber outobs=10;
    select *
      from sasuser.flightattendants
      where jobcode='FA1';
    select *
      from sasuser.flightattendants
      where jobcode='FA2';
```

    b.
```
proc sql number;
    select *
      from sasuser.flightattendants
      where jobcode='FA1';
```

```
      reset nonumber outobs=10;
         select *
            from sasuser.flightattendants
            where jobcode='FA2';
```

c. ```
   proc sql nonumber;
      select *
         from sasuser.flightattendants
         where jobcode='FA1';
   reset number outobs=10;
      select *
         from sasuser.flightattendants
         where jobcode='FA2';
   ```

d. ```
   proc sql;
      select *
         from sasuser.flightattendants
         where jobcode='FA1';
   reset outobs=10;
      select *
         from sasuser.flightattendants
         where jobcode='FA2';
   ```

4. Which of the following options does not affect the appearance of HTML, PDF, or RTF output?

   a. NUMBER | NONUMBER

   b. DOUBLE | NODOUBLE

   c. FLOW | NOFLOW | FLOW=n | FLOW=n m

   d. b and c

5. Which of the following statements is true regarding the STIMER option in PROC SQL?

   a. The STIMER option in PROC SQL writes timing information for each statement to the SAS log.

   b. The STIMER option in PROC SQL writes only cumulative timing information for the entire procedure to the SAS log.

   c. When using the STIMER option in PROC SQL, the SAS system option STIMER must also be in effect.

   d. a and c

6. A Dictionary table contains which of the following?

   a. information about SAS libraries.

   b. information about SAS data sets.

   c. information about SAS macros.

   d. all of the above

7. Dictionary tables are

   a. created each time they are referenced in a SAS program.

   b. updated automatically.

   c. limited to Read-Only access.

   d. all of the above

8. Dictionary tables can be accessed

    a. by running a PROC SQL query against the table, using the Dictionary libref.

    b. by referring to the PROC SQL view of the table that is stored in the Sashelp library.

    c. by referring to the PROC SQL view of the table that is stored in the Sasuser library.

    d. a and b

9. Which of the following PROC SQL steps displays information about the Dictionary table Dictionary.Titles?

    a.
```
proc sql;
    describe dictionary.titles;
```

    b.
```
proc sql;
    describe table dictionary.titles;
```

    c. `proc sql describe table dictionary.titles;`

    d. `proc sql describe dictionary titles;`

10. Which of the following PROC SQL steps displays the name (Memname), modification date (Modate), number of variables (Nvar), and the number of observations (Nobs) for each table in the Sasuser library?

    a.
```
proc sql;
    select memname, modate, nvar, nobs
        from dictionary.tables
        where libname='SASUSER';
```

    b.
```
proc sql;
    select memname, modate, nvar, nobs
        from dictionary.tables
        where libname='Sasuser';
```

    c.
```
proc sql;
    select memname, modate, nvar, nobs
        from 'SASUSER'
        where table=dictionary.tables;
```

    d.
```
proc sql;
    select SASUSER
        from dictionary.tables
        where cols= 'memname, modate, nvar, nobs';
```

Part 2

SAS Macro Language

Chapter 9
Introducing Macro Variables

Overview

Introduction

SAS macro variables enable you to substitute text in your SAS programs. Macro variables can supply a variety of information, including

- operating system information

- SAS session information

- text strings.

When you reference a macro variable in a SAS program, SAS replaces the reference with the text value that has been assigned to that macro variable. By substituting text into programs, SAS macro variables make your programs more reusable and dynamic.

The following sample code shows how a macro variable might be used to substitute a year value throughout a program, enabling you to quickly and easily change the value of **year** throughout the program:

```
%let year=2002;
proc print data=sasuser.schedule;
    where year(begin_date)=&year;
    title "Scheduled Classes for &year";
run;
proc means data=sasuser.all sum;
    where year(begin_date)=&year;
```

```
      class location;
      var fee;
      title1 "Total Fees for &year Classes";
      title2 "by Training Center";
   run;
```

Basic Concepts

Overview

In the SAS programs that you write, you might find that you need to reference the same variable, data set, or text string multiple times.

```
title "Total Sales for 2002";
data perm.sales2002;
   set perm.sales;
   if year(enddate)=2002;
run;
proc print data=perm.sales2002;
run;
```

Then, you might need to change the references in your program in order to reference a different variable, data set, or text string. Especially if your programs are lengthy, scanning for specific references and updating them manually can take a lot of time, and it is easy to overlook a reference that needs to be updated.

```
title "Total Sales for 2001";
data perm.sales2001;
   set perm.sales;
   if year(enddate)=2002;
run;
proc print data=perm.sales2001;
run;
```

If you use a macro variable in your program, these updates are quick and easy because you need to make the change in only one place.

```
%let year=2002;
title "Total Sales for &year";
data perm.sales&year;
   set perm.sales;
   if year(enddate)=&year;
run;
proc print data=perm.sales&year;
run;
```

The value of the macro variable is inserted into your program, so you can make one change and have the change appear throughout the program.

Macro Variables

Macro variables are part of the SAS macro facility, which is a tool for extending and customizing SAS and for reducing the amount of program code that you must enter in order to perform common tasks. The macro facility has its own language, which enables you to package small or large amounts of text into units that have names. From then on, you can work with the names rather than with the text itself.

There are two types of macro variables:

- automatic macro variables, which are provided by SAS

- user-defined macro variables, whose values you create and define.

Whether automatic or user-defined, a macro variable is independent of a SAS data set and contains one text string value that remains constant until you change it. The value of a macro variable is substituted into your program wherever the macro variable is referenced.

The value of a macro variable is stored in a symbol table. The values of automatic macro variables are always stored in the global symbol table, meaning that these values are always available in your SAS session. The values of user-defined macro variables are often stored in the global symbol table as well.

```
%let city=Dallas;
%let date=05JAN2000;
%let amount=975;
```

Global Symbol Table		
SYSTIME	09:31	— *automatic variables*
SYSVER	9.2	
CITY	*Dallas*	— *user-defined variables*
DATE	*05JAN2000*	
AMOUNT	*975*	

Macro variables can be defined and referenced anywhere in a SAS program except within the data lines of a DATALINES statement. You learn more about how to define and reference macro variables throughout this chapter.

Referencing Macro Variables

In order to substitute the value of a macro variable in your program, you must reference the macro variable. A macro variable reference is created by preceding the macro variable name with an ampersand (&). The reference causes the macro processor to search for the named variable in the symbol table and to return the value of the variable if the variable exists. If you need to reference a macro variable within quotation marks, such as in a title, you must use double quotation marks. The macro processor does not resolve macro variable references that appear within single quotation marks.

Note: You learn more about the macro processor later in this chapter.

Global Symbol Table	
CITY	*Dallas*
DATE	*05JAN2000*
AMOUNT	*975*

Example: Referencing a Macro Variable

To reference the macro variable `amount` from the global symbol table that is represented above, you place `&amount` in your program, as follows:

```
data new;
   set perm.mast;
   where fee>&amount;
run;
proc print;
run;
```

Code After Substitution

```
data new;
   set perm.mast;
   where fee>975;
run;
proc print;
run;
```

Note: You will see representations of code after substitution throughout this chapter. In a SAS session, you do not see this code. These representations are meant to show you what happens to your code behind the scenes, after macro processing.

Example: Referencing a Macro Variable in a Title

To reference the macro variable `city` in a title, you must use double quotation marks to enclose the title text in the TITLE statement, as follows:

```
title "Students from &city";
```

When the macro processor cannot resolve a macro variable reference, a message is printed in the SAS log. For example, referencing a nonexistent macro variable results in a warning message. Referencing an invalid macro variable name results in an error message.

Table 9.1 *SAS Log*

```
34 title "Students from &cityst";
WARNING: Apparent symbolic reference CITYST not resolved.
35
36 title "Students from "the_city_in_which_the_student_is_located";
ERROR: Symbolic variable name THE_CITY_IN_WHICH_THE_STUDENT_I must
       be 32 or fewer characters long.
```

Using Automatic Macro Variables

Overview

SAS creates and defines several automatic macro variables for you. Automatic macro variables contain information about your computing environment, such as the date and time of the session, and the version of SAS that you are running. These automatic macro variables

* are created when SAS is invoked

- are global (always available)
- are usually assigned values by SAS
- can be assigned values by the user in some cases.

Some automatic macro variables have fixed values that are set when SAS is invoked.

Name	Value
SYSDATE	the date of the SAS invocation (DATE7.)
SYSDATE9	the date of the SAS invocation (DATE9.)
SYSDAY	the day of the week of the SAS invocation
SYSTIME	the time of the SAS invocation
SYSENV	FORE (interactive execution) or BACK (noninteractive or batch execution)
SYSSCP	an abbreviation for the operating system that is being used, such as WIN or LINUX
SYSVER	the release of SAS that is being used
SYSJOBID	an identifier for the current SAS session or for the current batch job (the user ID or job name for mainframe systems, the process ID (PID) for other systems)

Some automatic macro variables have values that automatically change based on submitted SAS statements.

Name	Value
SYSLAST	the name of the most recently created SAS data set, in the form LIBREF.NAME. This value is always stored in all capital letters. If no data set has been created, the value is _NULL_
	Note: Throughout this book, the keyword _NULL_ is often used in place of the data set name in sample programs. Using _NULL_ suppresses the creation of an output data set. Using _NULL_ when benchmarking enables you to determine what resources are used to read a SAS data set.
SYSPARM	text that is specified when SAS is invoked
SYSERR	contains a return code status that is set by the DATA step and some SAS procedures to indicate whether the step or procedure executed successfully

Example

You can substitute system information such as the time, day, and date on which your SAS session was invoked and the version of SAS that you are running in footnotes for a report.

```
footnote1 "Created &systime &sysday, &sysdate9";
footnote2 "on the &sysscp system using Release &sysver";
title "REVENUES FOR DALLAS TRAINING CENTER";
proc tabulate data=sasuser.all(keep=location course_title fee);
    where upcase(location)="DALLAS";
        class course_title;
        var fee;
        table course_title=" " all="TOTALS",
              fee=" "*(n*f=3. sum*f=dollar10.)
              / rts=30 box="COURSE";
run;
```

COURSE	N	Sum
Artificial Intelligence	25	$10,000
Basic Telecommunications	18	$14,310
Computer Aided Design	19	$30,400
Database Design	23	$8,625
Local Area Networks	24	$15,600
Structured Query Language	24	$27,600
TOTALS	133	$106,535

Created 08:37 **1** Wednesday **2** , 20APR2011 **3**
on the WIN **4** system using Release 9.3 **5**

1. time of day (SYSTIME)

2. day of the week (SYSDAY)

3. date (day, month, and year) (SYSDATE9)

4. operating environment (SYSSCP)

5. release of SAS (SYSVER)

Using User-Defined Macro Variables

The %LET Statement

You have seen that SAS provides a variety of automatic macro variables for you. You can also create your own macro variables.

The simplest way to define your own macro variables is to use a %LET statement. The %LET statement enables you to define a macro variable and to assign a value to it.

General form, %LET statement:

%LET *variable=value*;

Here is an explanation of the syntax:

variable
　is any name that follows the SAS naming convention.

value
　can be any string from 0 to 65,534 characters.

variable or *value*
　if either contains a reference to another macro variable (such as **&macvar**), the reference is
　evaluated before the assignment is made.

Note: If *variable* already exists, *value* replaces the current value.

Example

To create a macro variable named **time** and assign a value of **afternoon** to it, you would submit the following %LET statement:

```
%let time=afternoon;
```

When you use the %LET statement to define macro variables, you should keep in mind the following rules:

- All values are stored as character strings.

- Mathematical expressions are not evaluated.

- The case of the value is preserved.

- Quotation marks that enclose literals are stored as part of the value.

- Leading and trailing blanks are removed from the value before the assignment is made.

%LET Statement Examples

When you define a macro variable, remember that its value is always a character string. This table provides examples of macro variable assignment statements to illustrate the rules that are listed in the previous section.

%LET Statement	Variable Name	Variable Value	Length
`%let name= Ed Norton ;`	name	*Ed Norton*	9
`%let name2=' Ed Norton ';`	name2	*' Ed Norton '*	13
`%let title="Joan's Report";`	title	*"Joan's Report"*	15
`%let start=;`	start		0

%LET Statement	Variable Name	Variable Value	Length
%let total=0;	total	*0*	1
%let sum=4+3;	sum	*4+3*	3
%let total=&total+&sum	total	*0+4+3*	5
%let x=varlist;	x	*varlist*	7
%let &x=name age height;	varlist	*name age height*	15

In the following example, the value DALLAS is assigned to the macro variable `site`. The macro variable `site` is then used to control program output.

```
%let site=DALLAS;
title "REVENUES FOR &site TRAINING CENTER";
proc tabulate data=sasuser.all(keep=location
                        course_title fee);
    where upcase(location)="&site";
    class course_title;
    var fee;
    table course_title=' ' all='TOTALS',
        fee=' '*(n*f=3. sum*f=dollar10.)
        / rts=30 box='COURSE';
run;
```

REVENUES FOR DALLAS TRAINING CENTER

COURSE	N	Sum
Artificial Intelligence	25	$10,000
Basic Telecommunications	18	$14,310
Computer Aided Design	19	$30,400
Database Design	23	$8,625
Local Area Networks	24	$15,600
Structured Query Language	24	$27,600
TOTALS	133	$106,535

Processing Macro Variables

SAS Processing

You have seen how to create and reference macro variables. In order to work with macro variables in the programs that you write, you need to understand how macro variables are processed and stored. First, it is important that you understand how SAS processing works.

A SAS program can be any combination of the following:

- DATA steps and PROC steps

- global statements

- SAS Component Language (SCL) code

- Structured Query Language (SQL) code

- SAS macro language code.

When you submit a program, it goes to an area of memory called the input stack. This is true for all code that you submit, such as a DATA step, SCL code, or SQL code.

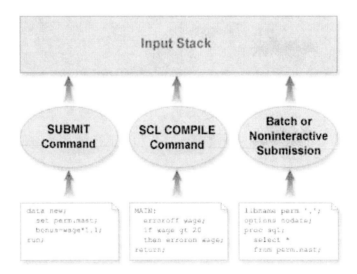

Once SAS code is in the input stack, SAS

- reads the text in the input stack (left-to-right, top-to-bottom)

- routes text to the appropriate compiler upon demand

- suspends this activity when a step boundary such as a RUN statement is reached

- executes the compiled code if there are no compilation errors

- repeats this process for any subsequent steps.

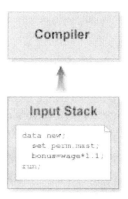

Tokenization

Between the input stack and the compiler, SAS programs are tokenized into smaller pieces. A component of SAS known as the word scanner divides program text into fundamental units called tokens.

- Tokens are passed on demand to the compiler.

- The compiler requests tokens until it receives a semicolon.

- The compiler performs a syntax check on the statement.

SAS stops sending statements to the compiler when it reaches a step boundary. Examples of step boundaries include a RUN statement (**run;**) or the beginning of a new DATA or PROC step. Once the entire step has been compiled, it is executed.

The word scanner recognizes four types of tokens:

- A literal token is a string of characters that are treated as a unit. The string is enclosed in either single or double quotation marks.

  Examples: **"Any text" 'Any text'**

- A number token is a string of numerals that can include a period or E notation (real numbers). Date constants, time constants, datetime constants, and hexadecimal constants are also number tokens.

  Examples: `23 109 '01jan2002'd 5e8 42.7`

- A name token is a string of characters that begins with a letter or underscore and that continues with underscores, letters, or digits. A period can sometimes be part of a name.

  Examples: `infile _n_ item3 univariate dollar10.2`

- A special token is any character or group of characters that has a reserved meaning to the compiler.

  Examples: `* / + - ** ; $ ( ) . & %`

A token ends when the word scanner detects

- the beginning of another token

- a blank after a token.

The maximum length of any token is 32,767 characters.

Examples

- `var x1-x10    z   ;`

  This example contains six tokens: `var x1 - x10 z ;`

- `title 'Report for May';`

  This example contains three tokens: `title 'Report for May' ;`

Macro Triggers

Macro variable references and %LET statements are part of the macro language. The macro facility includes a macro processor that is responsible for handling all macro language elements. Certain token sequences, known as macro triggers, alert the word scanner that the subsequent code should be sent to the macro processor.

The word scanner recognizes the following token sequences as macro triggers:

- % followed immediately by a name token (such as %let)

- & followed immediately by a name token (such as &amt).

When a macro trigger is detected, the word scanner passes it to the macro processor for evaluation. The macro processor

- examines these tokens

- requests additional tokens as necessary

- performs the action indicated.

For macro variables, the processor does one of the following:

- creates a macro variable in the symbol table and assigns a value to the variable

- changes the value of an existing macro variable in the symbol table

- looks up an existing macro variable in the symbol table and returns the variable's value to the input stack in place of the original reference.

The word scanner then resumes processing tokens from the input stack.

Note: The word scanner does not recognize macro triggers that are enclosed in single quotation marks. Remember that if you need to reference a macro variable within a literal token, such as the title text in a TITLE statement, you must enclose the text string in double quotation marks or the macro variable reference is not resolved.

Displaying Macro Variable Values in the SAS Log

The SYMBOLGEN Option

When you submit a macro variable reference, the macro processor resolves the reference and passes the value directly back to the input stack. Therefore, you do not see the value that the compiler receives. In order to debug your programs, it might be useful for you to see the value that replaces your macro variable reference. You can use the SYMBOLGEN system option to monitor the value that is substituted for a macro variable reference.

General form, OPTIONS statement with SYMBOLGEN option:

OPTIONS NOSYMBOLGEN | SYMBOLGEN;

Here is an explanation of the syntax:

NOSYMBOLGEN
 specifies that log messages about macro variable references are not displayed. This is the default.

SYMBOLGEN
 specifies that log messages about macro variable references are displayed.

This system option displays the results of resolving macro variable references in the SAS log. That is, when the SYMBOLGEN option is turned on, SAS writes a message to the log for each macro variable that is referenced in your program. The message states the macro variable name and the resolved value.

Note: Remember that since SYMBOLGEN is a system option, its setting remains in effect until you modify it or until you end your SAS session.

Example

Suppose you have previously assigned values to the macro variables **amount**, **city**, and **company**, and you submit the following code:

```
data new;
   set sasuser.all;
   where fee>&amount;
   where also city_state contains "&city";
   where also student_company contains '&company';
run;
```

Here is a sample SAS log that shows the messages that are generated by the SYMBOLGEN option for this code. The WHERE ALSO conditions augment the initial WHERE condition using the AND operator. In this example, the where processing is done for the following condition: (fee>&amount) AND (city_state contains "&city") AND (student_company contains '&company').

Table 9.2   *SAS Log*

```
110 where fee>&amount;
SYMBOLGEN: Macro variable AMOUNT resolves to 975
111 where city_state contains "&city";
SYMBOLGEN: Macro variable CITY resolves to Dallas
112 where student_company contains '&company';
```

Notice that no message is displayed for the final macro variable reference (`'&company'`). Because this macro variable reference is enclosed in single quotation marks rather than in double quotation marks, the word scanner does not call the macro facility to resolve it.

The %PUT Statement

Another way of verifying the values of macro variables is to write your own messages to the SAS log. The %PUT statement writes text to the SAS log.

General form, basic %PUT statement:

%PUT *text*;

Here is an explanation of the syntax:

text
    is any text string.

The %PUT statement

- writes only to the SAS log

- always writes to a new log line, starting in column one

- writes a blank line if text is not specified

- does not require quotation marks around text

- resolves macro triggers in text before text is written

- removes leading and trailing blanks from text unless a macro quoting function is used

- wraps lines when the length of text is greater than the current line size setting

- can be used either inside or outside a macro definition.

Example

Suppose you want to verify the value of the macro variable `city`. Since the %PUT statement resolves macro references in text before writing text to the SAS log, you can use it to show the stored value of `city`.

```
%put The value of the macro variable CITY is: &city;
```

Table 9.3 *SAS Log*

```
120 %put The value of the macro variable CITY is: &city;
The value of the macro variable CITY is: Dallas
```

You can also simply submit the statement **&put &city;** without any additional text. This statement writes the resolved value of the macro variable **city** to the SAS log. However, it does not write any additional text to the log. You might find that it is a good idea to add explanatory text to your %PUT statements in order to maintain clarity in the SAS log. The %PUT statement has several optional arguments that you can add.

Argument	Result in SAS Log
ALL	Lists the values of all macro variables
AUTOMATIC	Lists the values of all automatic macro variables
LOCAL	Lists user-generated local macro variables
USER	Lists the values of all user-defined macro variables

Table 9.4 *SAS Log*

```
121 %let year=2002;
122 %let city=New York;
123 %let region=South;
124 %put _all_;
GLOBAL YEAR 2002
GLOBAL REGION South
GLOBAL CITY New York
AUTOMATIC AFDSID 0
AUTOMATIC AFDSNAME
AUTOMATIC AFLIB
AUTOMATIC AFSTR1
AUTOMATIC AFSTR2
AUTOMATIC FSPBDV
AUTOMATIC SYSBUFFR
AUTOMATIC SYSCC 0
AUTOMATIC SYSCHARWIDTH 1
AUTOMATIC SYSCMD
AUTOMATIC SYSDATE 29MAY02
```

Notice that when you use optional arguments such as _ALL_, each macro variable name is also written to the SAS log, along with a label of either AUTOMATIC or GLOBAL.

Using Macro Functions to Mask Special Characters

Macro Quoting Functions

The SAS programming language uses matched pairs of either double or single quotation marks to distinguish character constants from names. The quotation marks are not stored as part of the token that they define. For example, in the following program, **var** is stored as a four-byte variable that has the value **text**. If **text** were not enclosed in quotation marks, it would be treated as a variable name. **var2** is stored as a seven-byte variable that has the value **example**.

```
data one;
   var='text';
   text='example';
   var2=text;
run;
```

Similarly, the title text in the following example is **Joan's Report**. Although the TITLE statement contains a matched pair of double quotation marks, the title itself does not include these outer quotation marks. However, the outer quotation marks cause the unmatched single quotation mark within the text to be interpreted as an apostrophe that is part of the title text.

```
proc print;
   title "Joan's Report";
run;
```

Example

Earlier you learned that macro variable values are character strings, and you saw examples of macro variables whose values included special characters. Now, suppose you want to store one or more SAS statements in a macro variable. For example, suppose you want to create a macro variable named **prog** with **data new; x=1; run;** stored as its value.

```
options symbolgen;
%let prog=data new; x=1; run;;
&prog
proc print;
run;
```

Here is part of the SAS log that results from the above program.

Table 9.5 *SAS Log*

```
25 options symbolgen;
26
27 %let prog=data new; x=1; run;
27 %let prog=data new; x=1; run;
                          -
                         180
ERROR 180-322: Statement is not valid or it is used out of proper order.
SYMBOLGEN: Macro variable PROG resolves to data new
28      &prog
29      proc print;
30      run;
NOTE: The data set WORK.NEW has 1 observations and 0 variables.
NOTE: The data set WORK.PROC has 1 observations and 0 variables.
NOTE: The data set WORK.PRINT has 1 observations and 0 variables.
NOTE: DATA statement used (Total process time):
      real time           0.25 seconds
      cpu time            0.07 seconds
```

Notice that according to the SYMBOLGEN statement in the log, the macro variable
`prog` has been assigned a value of `data new`. SAS interpreted the first semicolon as
the end of the macro assignment statement. In this case, we want the semicolon to be
part of the macro variable value, but SAS has no way of knowing that. In this situation,
you need to mask text that you want to assign to a macro variable. That is, you need to
hide the normal meaning of the semicolon from the macro processor. You can use a
macro quoting function to do this.

The %STR Function

The %STR function is used to mask (or write quotation marks around) tokens during
compilation so that the macro processor does not interpret them as macro-level syntax.
That is, the %STR function hides the normal meaning of a semicolon and other special
tokens and mnemonic equivalents of comparison or logical operators so that they appear
as constant text. Special tokens and mnemonic equivalents include

```
; + - * / , < > = blank ^ ~ # |
LT EQ GT AND OR NOT LE GE NE IN
```

The %STR function also

- enables macro triggers to work normally

- preserves leading and trailing blanks in its argument.

General form, %STR function:

%STR (*argument*)

Here is an explanation of the syntax:

argument
    is any combination of text and macro triggers.

Applying this to our previous example, there are a number of ways that text can be
quoted. Remember that we wanted to create a macro variable named `prog` that has
`data new; x=1; run;` as its value.

Method One
> You could quote all text. `%let prog=%str(data new; x=1; run;);`

Method Two
> You could quote only the semicolons. `%let prog=data new%str(;)`
> `x=1%str(;)run%str(;);`

Method Three
> You could create an additional macro variable, assign a quoted value to it, and reference it in the assignment statement for the **prog** macro variable. `%let s=`
> `%str(;); %let prog=data new&s x=1&s run&s;`

Each of these methods accomplishes the same thing: they all assign the value `data=new; x=1; run;` to the macro variable **prog**.

The %STR function can also be used to quote tokens that typically occur in pairs:

`' " ) (`

Example

Suppose you want to assign text that contains an apostrophe (') to a macro variable. Without any quoting, this leads to errors.

```
options symbolgen;
%let text=Joan's Report;
proc print data=sasuser.courses;
   where days > 3;
title "&text";
run;
```

Table 9.6 *SAS Log*

```
75 %let text=Joan's Report;
                 ---------
                 32
WARNING 32-169: The quoted string currently being processed has
                become more than 262 characters long. You may
                have unbalanced quotation marks.
```

The word scanner interprets the apostrophe as the beginning of a literal that is defined by a pair of single quotation marks. You can use the %STR function to avoid this error. In the last section you saw several methods of using the %STR function to mask the normal meaning of a semicolon. However, none of the methods shown correctly mask the apostrophe in our current example.

When you quote tokens that typically appear in pairs, such as quotation marks or parentheses, you must take one additional step. To perform this quoting, you precede the token that you want to quote with a percent sign (%) within the %STR function argument.

```
%let text=%str(Joan%'s Report);
%let text=Joan%str(%')s Report;
```

The value of **text** is **Joan's Report** in both cases.

The %NRSTR Function

Sometimes you might want to hide the normal meaning of an ampersand or a percent sign. The %NRSTR function performs the same quoting function as %STR, except it also masks macro triggers (& and %). The NR in the name %NRSTR stands for No Resolution. %NRSTR has the same syntax as %STR.

Example

Suppose you want to create a macro variable named **period** and to assign a value of **May&Jun** to it. If you attempt to use the %STR function in the assignment statement, SAS interprets the ampersand as a macro trigger and generate a warning message. You need to use the %NRSTR function instead.

```
%let Period=%str(May&Jun);
%put Period resolves to: &period;
%let Period=%nrstr(May&Jun);
%put Period resolves to: &period;
```

The following portion of a SAS log shows the results of both the %STR function and the %NRSTR function for this example.

Table 9.7 *SAS Log*

```
1    %let Period=%str(May&Jun);
WARNING: Apparent symbolic reference JUN not resolved.
2    %put Period resolves to &period:
WARNING: Apparent symbolic reference JUN not resolved.
Period resolves to: May&Jun
3
4    %let Period=%nrstr(May&Jun);
5    %put Period resolves to &period;
Period resolves to: May&Jun
```

The %BQUOTE Function

Like the %STR function, the %BQUOTE function is used to mask (or write quotation marks around) special characters and mnemonic operators. The %STR function performs during compilation, and the %BQUOTE function performs during execution. That is, the %BQUOTE function masks a character string or resolved value of a text expression during execution of a macro or macro language statement so that special characters and mnemonic operators are not interpreted as anything other than plain text. Special tokens and mnemonic equivalents include

```
'  "  ( ) + - * / < > = ¬ ^ ~ ; , # blank
AND  OR  NOT  EQ  NE  LE  LT  GE  GT  IN
```

The %BQUOTE function also

- does not require that quotation marks be marked
- enables macro triggers to work normally
- preserves leading and trailing blanks in its argument.

General form, %BQUOTE function:

%BQUOTE (*argument*)

Here is an explanation of the syntax:

argument
   is any combination of text and macro triggers.

Example

Remember the example where you want to assign text that contains an apostrophe (') to a macro variable. You used the %STR function to mask the apostrophe.

```
%let text=%str(Joan%'s Report);
%let text=Joan%str(%')s Report;
```

You can accomplish this task using the %BQUOTE function. The %BQUOTE function does not require that unmatched quotation marks be marked, so the title that contains an apostrophe requires no special syntax.

```
%let text=%bquote(Joan's Report);
```

Using Macro Functions to Manipulate Character Strings

Macro Character Functions

Often when working with macro variables, you need to manipulate character strings. You can do this by using macro character functions. With macro character functions, you can do the following:

- change lowercase letters to uppercase

- produce a substring of a character string

- extract a word from a character string

- determine the length of a character string, and more.

Macro character functions have the same basic syntax as the corresponding DATA step functions, and they yield similar results. It is important to remember that although they might be similar, macro character functions are distinct from DATA step functions. As part of the macro language, macro functions enable you to communicate with the macro processor in order to manipulate text strings that you insert into your SAS programs. The next few sections explore several macro character functions in greater detail.

The %UPCASE Function

The %UPCASE function enables you to change the value of a macro variable from lowercase to uppercase before substituting that value in a SAS program. Since most comparison operators in the SAS language are case sensitive, it is often necessary to change values to uppercase.

General form, %UPCASE function:

%UPCASE (*argument*)

Here is an explanation of the syntax:

argument
    is a character string.

Example

The Sasuser.All data set contains student information and registration information for computer training courses. Suppose you want to create a summary of the uncollected course fees:

```
%let paidval=n;
proc means data=sasuser.all sum maxdec=0;
   where paid="&paidval";
   var fee;
   class course_title;
title "Uncollected Fees for Each Course";
run;
```

Table 9.8 *SAS Log*

```
163  %let paidval=n;
164  proc means data=sasuser.all sum maxdec=0;
165      where paid="&paidval";
166      var fee;
167      class course_title;
168  title "Uncollected Fees for Each Course";
169  run;


NOTE: No observations were selected from data set SASUSER.ALL.
```

Because the value of the macro variable **paidval** was specified in lowercase, the WHERE expression finds no matching observations. All the values of the data set variable **Paid** are stored in uppercase.

Now we can use the %UPCASE function in the WHERE statement:

```
%let paidval=n;
proc means data=sasuser.all sum maxdec=0;
   where paid="%upcase(&paidval)";
   var fee;
   class course_title;
title "Uncollected Fees for Each Course";
run;
```

You can see that this time the WHERE expression does find matching observations.

```
Uncollected Fees for Each Course

       The MEANS Procedure


    Analysis Variable : Fee Course Fee

  Description                 N Obs   Sum

  Artificial Intelligence        24   9600

  Basic Telecommunications       14  11130

  Computer Aided Design          13  20800

  Database Design                17   6375

  Local Area Networks            19  12350

  Structured Query Language      20  23000
```

The %QUPCASE Function

If the argument contains a special character, a mnemonic operator, or a macro trigger, you need to use the %QUPCASE function. %QUPCASE has the same syntax as the %UPCASE function, and it works the same as %UPCASE except that it also masks mnemonic operators and special characters (including macro triggers) in the function result.

Example

These statements show the results produced by %UPCASE and %QUPCASE:

```
%let a=begin;
%let b=%nrstr(&a);

%put UPCASE produces: %upcase(&b);
%put QUPCASE produces: %qupcase(&b);
```

In the first %PUT statement, the macro reference &b resolves to &a, which is converted to &A because of the %UPCASE function. Since the resolved value contains a macro trigger, it is treated as a macro variable reference and &A resolves to the value **begin**. The second %PUT statement uses the %QUPCASE function, which masks the ampersand in the resolved value of the macro variable **b** so that this value is not treated as another macro variable reference. Executing these statements produces the following messages in the SAS log.

Table 9.9 *SAS Log*

```
6     %let a=begin;
7     %let b=%nrstr(&a);
8
9     %put UPCASE produces: %upcase(&b);
UPCASE produces: begin
10    %put QUPCASE produces: %qupcase(&b);
QUPCASE produces: &A
```

The %SUBSTR Function

The %SUBSTR function enables you to extract part of a character string from the value of a macro variable.

General form, %SUBSTR function:

%SUBSTR (*argument, position<,n>*)

Here is an explanation of the syntax:

argument
  is a character string or a text expression from which a substring is returned.

position
  is an integer or an expression (text, logical, or mathematical) that yields an integer, which specifies the position of the first character in the substring.

n
  is an optional integer or an expression (text, logical, or mathematical) that yields an integer that specifies the number of characters in the substring.

Note: If the length of *n* is greater than the number of characters following position in argument, %SUBSTR issues a warning message and returns a substring that contains the characters from position to the end of the string. If *n* is not specified, %SUBSTR also returns a substring that contains the characters from position to the end of the string.

For example, assume that the macro variable `date` has the value `05JAN2002`.

- The code `%substr(&date,3)` returns the value `JAN2002`.

- The code `%substr(&date,3,3)` returns the value `JAN`.

- The code `%substr(&date,3,9)` returns the value `JAN2002` and produces a warning message.

The values of `position` and *n* can also be the result of a mathematical expression that yields an integer. For example, `%substr(&var,%length(&var)-1)` returns the last two characters of the value of the macro variable `var`.

Note: The %LENGTH function accepts an argument that is either a character string or a text expression. If the argument is a character string, %LENGTH returns the length of the string. If the argument is a text expression, %LENGTH returns the length of the resolved value. If the argument has a null value, %LENGTH returns 0.

Example

Suppose you want to print a report on all courses that have been taught since the start of the current month. You can use the %SUBSTR function and the SYSDATE9 macro variable to determine the month and year. To start, we need to create an updated class schedule based on the data in sasuser.schedule, which is too old for this example:

```
* Update the class schedule based on previous ;
data update_schedule;
  set sasuser.schedule;
  begin_date + 3652;
run;
```

Next, we select observations from the updated schedule that are within the current month:

```
* Print a list of courses that started this month;
proc print data=update_schedule;
    where begin_date between
        "01%substr(&sysdate9,3)"d and
        "&sysdate9"d;
    title "All Courses Held So Far This Month";
    title2 "(as of &sysdate9)";
run;
```

All Courses Held So Far This Month (as of 20APR2011)					
Obs	Course_Number	Course_Code	Location	Begin_Date	Teacher
6	6	C006	Boston	02APR2011	Berthan, Ms. Judy

The %QSUBSTR Function

If the argument contains a special character, a mnemonic operator, or a macro trigger, you need to use the %QSUBSTR function. %QSUBSTR has the same syntax as the %SUBSTR function, and it works the same as %SUBSTR except that it also masks mnemonic operators and special characters (including macro triggers) in the function result.

Example

These statements show the results produced by %SUBSTR and %QSUBSTR:

```
%let a=one;
%let b=two;
%let c=%nrstr(&a &b);

%put C: &c;
%put With SUBSTR: %substr(&c,1,2);
%put With QSUBSTR: %qsubstr(&c,1,2);
```

Executing these statements produces the following messages in the SAS log. As you can see, the first %PUT statement shows that &c resolves to the value &a &b. In the second %PUT statement, the %SUBSTR function extracts the value &a from the resolved value of the macro variable reference &c, and resolves &a to one. The third %PUT statement shows that the %QSUBSTR function prevents the value &a from being resolved further.

Table 9.10 *SAS Log*

```
11    %let a=one;
12    %let b=two;
13    %let c=%nrstr(&a &b);
14
15    %put C: &c;
C: &a &b
16    %put With SUBSTR: %substr(&c,1,2);
With SUBSTR: one
17    %put With QSUBSTR: %qsubstr(&c,1,2);
With QSUBSTR: &a
```

The %INDEX Function

The %INDEX function enables you to determine the position of the first character of a string within another string.

General form, %INDEX function:

%INDEX (*source,string*)

Here is an explanation of the syntax:

source and *string*
   both are character strings or text expressions that can include

   * constant text

   * macro variable references

   * macro functions

   * macro calls.

The %INDEX function

* searches *source* for the first occurrence of *string*

* returns a number representing the position in *source* of the first character of *string* when there is an exact pattern match

* returns 0 when there is no pattern match.

Example

The following statements find the first character V in a string:

```
%let a=a very long value;
%let b=%index(&a,v);
%put The character v appears at position &b.;
```

Executing these statements writes the following line to the SAS log.

Table 9.11 *SAS Log*

```
The character v appears at position 3.
```

The %SCAN Function

The %SCAN function enables you to extract words from the value of a macro variable.

General form, %SCAN function:

%SCAN (*argument, n<,delimiters>*)

Here is an explanation of the syntax:

argument
consists of constant text, macro variable references, macro functions, or macro calls.

n
is an integer or a text expression that yields an integer, which specifies the position of the word to return. If *n* is greater than the number of words in *argument*, the functions return a null string.

delimiters
specifies an optional list of one or more characters that separate "words" or text expressions that yield one or more characters.

CAUTION:
If *argument* contains a comma, you must enclose *argument* in a quoting function. Similarly, in order to use a single blank or a single comma as the only delimiter, you must enclose the character in the %STR function.

The delimiters that %SCAN recognizes vary between ASCII and EBCDIC systems. If you omit delimiters, SAS treats the following characters as default delimiters:

- ASCII systems: `blank . < ( + & ! $ * ) ; ^ - / , % |`
- EBCDIC systems: `blank . < ( + | & ! $ * ) ; ¬ - / , % | ¢`

If the delimiter list includes any of the default delimiters for your system, the remaining default delimiters are treated as text.

Example

You can use PROC DATASETS along with the %SCAN function and the SYSLAST macro variable to investigate the structure of the most recently created data set:

```
data work.thisyear;
   set sasuser.schedule;
    where year(begin_date) =
          year("&sysdate9"d);
run;

%let libref=%scan(&syslast,1,.);
%let dsname=%scan(&syslast,2,.);
proc datasets lib=&libref nolist;
```

```
title "Contents of the Data Set &syslast";
   contents data=&dsname;
run;
quit;
```

<table>
<tr><td colspan="4" align="center">Contents of the Data Set WORK.THISYEAR</td></tr>
<tr><td colspan="4" align="center">The DATASETS Procedure</td></tr>
<tr><td>Data Set Name</td><td>WORK.THISYEAR</td><td>Observations</td><td>0</td></tr>
<tr><td>Member Type</td><td>DATA</td><td>Variables</td><td>5</td></tr>
<tr><td>Engine</td><td>V9</td><td>Indexes</td><td>0</td></tr>
<tr><td>Created</td><td>Wednesday, April 20, 2011 11:32:11 AM</td><td>Observation Length</td><td>48</td></tr>
<tr><td>Last Modified</td><td>Wednesday, April 20, 2011 11:32:11 AM</td><td>Deleted Observations</td><td>0</td></tr>
<tr><td>Protection</td><td></td><td>Compressed</td><td>NO</td></tr>
<tr><td>Data Set Type</td><td></td><td>Sorted</td><td>NO</td></tr>
<tr><td>Label</td><td></td><td></td><td></td></tr>
<tr><td>Data Representation</td><td>WINDOWS_32</td><td></td><td></td></tr>
<tr><td>Encoding</td><td>wlatin1 Western (Windows)</td><td></td><td></td></tr>
</table>

The %QSCAN Function

If the argument contains a special character, a mnemonic operator, or a macro trigger, you need to use the %QSCAN function. %QSCAN has the same syntax as the %SCAN function, and it works the same as %SCAN except that it also masks mnemonic operators and special characters (including macro triggers) in the function result.

Example

These statements show the results produced by %SCAN and %QSCAN:

```
%let a=one;
%let b=two;
%let c=%nrstr(&a*&b);

%put C: &c;
%put With SCAN: %scan(&c,1,*);
%put With QSCAN: %qscan(&c,1,*);
```

Executing these statements produces the following messages in the SAS log.

Table 9.12 *SAS Log*

```
47    %let a=one;
48    %let b=two;
49    %let c=%nrstr(&a*&b);
50
51    %put C: &c;
C: &a*&b
52    %put With SCAN: %scan(&c,1,*);
With SCAN: one
53    %put With QSCAN: %qscan(&c,1,*);
With QSCAN: &a
```

Using SAS Functions with Macro Variables

The %SYSFUNC Function

You have learned that by using the automatic macro variables SYSDATE9 and SYSTIME you can include the date and time in a title:

```
title1 "Report Produced on &sysdate9";
title2 "at &systime";
```

Report Produced on 20APR2011
at 08:37

SYSDATE9 represents the date on which the SAS session started, and SYSTIME represents the time at which the SAS session started. Suppose you would rather see the date in some other format, or suppose you would rather see the current date or time. You can use the %SYSFUNC function to execute other SAS functions as part of the macro facility.

General form, %SYSFUNC function:

%SYSFUNC *(function (argument(s)) <format>)*

Here is an explanation of the syntax:

function
  is the name of the SAS function to execute.

argument(s)
  is one or more arguments that are used by *function*. Use commas to separate all arguments. An argument can be a macro variable reference or a text expression that produces arguments for a function.

format
  is an optional format to apply to the result of *function*. By default, numeric results are converted to a character string using the BEST12. format, and character results are used as they are, without formatting or translation.

All SAS functions can be used with %SYSFUNC except

ALLCOMB LEXCOMB

ALLPERM LEXCOMBI

DIF LEXPERK

DIM LEXPERM

HBOUND MISSING

INPUT PUT

IORCMSG RESOLVE

LAG SYMGET

LBOUND Variable information functions

Note: Variable information functions include functions such as VNAME and VLABEL. For a complete list of variable information functions, see "Functions and CALL Routines by Category" in *SAS Functions and CALL Routines: Reference.*

Note: You can use the INPUTC or INPUTN function in place of the INPUT function. Similarly, you can use the PUTC or PUTN function in place of the PUT function with %SYSFUNC.

Example

Suppose the following code was submitted on Friday, November 4, 2011:

```
title "%sysfunc(today(),weekdate.) - SALES REPORT";
```

The title on the next report would be Friday, November 4, 2011 - SALES REPORT.

Quoting with %QSYSFUNC

As with macro character functions, if the argument for a %SYSFUNC function contains special characters or mnemonic operators, you must use the quoting version of the function. The %QSYSFUNC function has the same syntax as the %SYSFUNC function. %QSYSFUNC works the same as %SYSFUNC except that it also masks mnemonic operators and special characters in the function result.

Example

Suppose you want to create a report title that includes the current date in WORDDATE. format. You could use this statement:

```
title "Report Produced on %sysfunc(today(),worddate.)";
```

However, that would result in the following title:

```
Report Produced on    November 4, 2011
```

Note: The extra blanks are displayed in the listing output. The blanks are not displayed in an HTML output.

The extra blanks are from the default length of the WORDDATE. format. You need to left-justify the resulting formatted date. You cannot nest functions within %SYSFUNC, but you can use a %SYSFUNC for each function that you need, as shown in this example:

```
title "Report Produced on
          %sysfunc(left(%sysfunc(today(),worddate.)))";
```

However, this statement results in the following error message.

Table 9.13 SAS Log

```
ERROR: The function LEFT referenced by the %SYSFUNC or
       %QSYSFUNC macro function has too many arguments.
```

The LEFT function expects only one argument, but you are passing "November 4, 2011" to it. It interprets the comma as the delimiter between two arguments.

You can mask the comma by using the %QSYSFUNC function instead, as follows:

```
title "Report Produced on
            %sysfunc(left(%qsysfunc(today(),worddate.)))";
```

The modified statement generates the following title:

```
Report Produced on November 4, 2011
```

Combining Macro Variable References with Text

Overview

You can reference macro variables anywhere in your program. Some applications might require placing a macro variable reference adjacent to leading text (text&*variable*) or trailing text (&*variable*text) or referencing adjacent macro variables (&*variable*&*variable*) in order to build a new token. When you combine macro variable references and text, it is important to keep in mind how SAS interprets tokens.

Remember that a token ends when the word scanner detects either the beginning of a new token or a blank after a token.

You can place text immediately before a macro variable reference to build a new token. For example, suppose that data sets are stored in a SAS library, using the naming convention *Yyymon*, where *yy* is a two-digit year such as 02 or 01, and *mon* is a three-letter month such as JUN or AUG. Data set names could include examples such as Y01DEC and Y02MAR. You can write a program that uses a macro variable to build the month portion of the SAS data set name.

```
%let month=jan;
proc chart data=sasuser.y02&month;
   hbar week / sumvar=sale;
run;
proc plot data=sasuser.y02&month;
   plot sale*day;
run;
```

Table 9.14 *Code after Substitution*

```
proc chart data=sasuser.y02jan;
    hbar week / sumvar=sale;
run;
proc plot data=sasuser.y02jan;
    plot sale*day;
run;
```

You can reference macro variables that have no blanks between them to build new tokens.

For example, you can modify the previous program to enable both the month and the year to be substituted:

```
%let year=02;
%let month=jan;
proc chart data=sasuser.y&year&month;
    hbar week / sumvar=sale;
run;
proc plot data=sasuser.y&year&month;
    plot sale*day;
run;
```

Table 9.15 *Code after Substitution*

```
proc chart data=sasuser.y02jan;
    hbar week / sumvar=sale;
run;
proc plot data=sasuser.y02jan;
    plot sale*day;
run;
```

The generated program is identical to the program in the previous example. That is, the compiler sees the same code for both of these examples.

You can place text immediately after a macro variable reference as long as the macro variable name can still be tokenized correctly.

For example, you can modify the previous program to substitute the name of an analysis variable:

```
%let year=02;
%let month=jan;
%let var=sale;
proc chart data=sasuser.y&year&month;
    hbar week / sumvar=&var;
run;
proc plot data=sasuser.y&year&month;
    plot &var*day;
run;
```

Table 9.16 *Code after Substitution*

```
proc chart data=sasuser.y02jan;
    hbar week / sumvar=sale;
run;
proc plot data=sasuser.y02jan;
    plot sale*day
run;
```

The generated program is identical to the program in the previous two examples. That is, although you are changing the code that you submit, you are not changing the code that the compiler sees.

Delimiters in Macro Variable Names

Sometimes you might want to place a macro variable name immediately before text other than a special character. For example, you might want to modify the previous program so that it is easy to switch between using the CHART and PLOT procedures of Base SAS software and the GCHART and GPLOT procedures of SAS/GRAPH software.

```
/* GRAPHICS should be null or G */
%let graphics=g;
%let year=02;
%let month=jan;
%let var=sale;
proc &graphicschart data=sasuser.y&year&month;
    hbar week / sumvar=&var;
run;
proc &graphicsplot data=sasuser.y&year&month;
    plot &var*day;
run;
```

The messages written to the SAS log reveal problems with this program.

Table 9.17 *SAS Log*

```
13      %let graphics=g;
14      %let year=02;
15      %let month=jan;
16      %let var=sale;
17      proc &graphicschart data=sasuser.y&year&month;
            -
            10

WARNING: Apparent symbolic reference GRAPHICSCHART not resolved.

ERROR 10-205: Expecting the name of the procedure to be executed.
```

SAS interprets the macro variable's name to be `graphicschart` instead of `graphics` because there is no delimiter between the macro variable reference and the trailing text.

The word scanner recognizes the end of a macro variable name when it encounters a special character that cannot be part of the name token. In other words, the special character acts as a delimiter. For example, a period (.) is a special character that is treated as part of the macro variable reference and that does not appear when the macro variable is resolved.

To correct the problem in the previous example, you need to add a period after the reference to the macro variable `graphics`.

```
%let graphics=g;
%let year=02;
%let month=jan;
%let var=sale;
 proc &graphics.chart data=sasuser.y&year&month;
   hbar week / sumvar=&var;
run;
proc &graphics.plot data=sasuser.y&year&month;
   plot &var*day;
run;
```

When these SAS statements are executed

- the word scanner treats **&graphics.** as the reference

- the value of the macro variable **graphics** is returned to the input stack

- the word scanner processes **gchart** as one token.

Table 9.18 *Code after Substitution*

```
proc gchart data=sasuser.y02jan;
   hbar week / sumvar=sale;
run;
proc gplot data=sasuser.y02jan;
   plot sale*day;
run;
```

We can extend this example and further modify the previous program to include a macro variable that is used to define the libref:

```
%let lib=sasuser;
%let graphics=g;
%let year=02;
%let month=jan;
%let var=sale;
libname &lib 'SAS-data-library';
proc &graphics.chart data=&lib.y&year&month;
   hbar week / sumvar=&var;
run;
proc &graphics.plot data=&lib.y&year&month;
   plot &var*day;
run;
```

Notice, however, that this code does not perform the desired substitutions.

Table 9.19 *Code after Substitution*

```
libname sasuser 'SAS-data-library';
proc gchart data=sasusery02jan;
   hbar week / sumvar=sale;
run;
proc gplot data=sasusery02jan;
   plot sale*day;
run;
```

The period after &lib is interpreted as a delimiter. You need to use a second period after the delimiter period to supply the necessary token:

```
%let lib=sasuser;
...
libname &lib 'SAS-data-library';
proc &graphics.chart data=&lib..y&year&month;
...
proc &graphics.plot data=&lib..y&hear&month;
```

The first period is treated as a delimiter, and the second period is treated as text.

Table 9.20 *Code after Substitution*

```
proc gchart data=sasuser.y02jan;
...
proc gplot data=sasuser.y02jan;
```

Summary

Text Summary

Basic Concepts

Macro variables can supply a variety of information, from operating system information, to SAS session information, to any text string that you define. Updating multiple references to a variable, data set, or text string is a simple process if you use macro variables in your programs. Macro variables are part of the SAS macro facility, which is a tool for extending and customizing SAS and for reducing the amount of text that you must enter in order to perform common tasks.

Values of macro variables are stored in symbol tables. Values that are stored in the global symbol table are always available. In order to substitute the value of a macro variable in your program, you must reference that macro variable by preceding the macro variable name with an ampersand. You can reference a macro variable anywhere in a SAS program except within data lines.

Using Automatic Macro Variables

SAS provides automatic macro variables that contain information about your computing environment. Automatic macro variables are created when SAS is invoked. Many of these variables have fixed values that are assigned by SAS and which remain constant for the duration of your SAS session. Others have values that are updated automatically based on submitted SAS statements.

Using User-Defined Macro Variables

You can create and define your own macro variables with the %LET statement. The %LET statement enables you to assign a value for your new macro variable and to store that value in the global symbol table. Macro variable values are character strings; except for leading and trailing blanks, values are stored exactly as they appear in the statement.

Processing Macro Variables

When submitted, a SAS program goes to an area of memory called the input stack. From there, the word scanner divides the program into small chunks called tokens and passes them to the appropriate compiler for eventual execution. Certain token sequences are macro triggers, which are sent to the macro processor for resolution. Once a macro variable has been resolved by the macro processor, the stored value is substituted back into the program in the input stack, and word scanning continues.

Displaying Macro Variable Values in the SAS Log

You can use the SYMBOLGEN system option to monitor the value that is substituted for a macro variable reference. You can also use the %PUT statement to write messages, which can include macro variable values, to the SAS log.

Using Macro Functions to Mask Special Characters

The %STR function enables you to quote tokens during compilation in order to mask them from the macro processor. The %NRSTR function enables you to quote tokens that include macro triggers from the macro processor. The %BQUOTE function enables you to quote a character string or resolved value of a text expression during execution of a macro or macro language statement.

Using Macro Functions to Manipulate Character Strings

You can use macro character functions to apply character string manipulations to the values of macro variables. The %UPCASE function enables you to change values from lowercase to uppercase. The %QUPCASE function works the same as %UPCASE except that it also masks special characters and mnemonic operators in the function result. The %SUBSTR function enables you to extract part of a string from a macro variable value. The %QSUBSTR function works the same as %SUBSTR except that it also masks special characters and mnemonic operators in the function result. The %INDEX function enables you to determine the location of the first character of a character string within a source. Using the %SCAN function, you can extract words from the value of a macro variable. The %QSCAN function works the same as %SCAN except that it also masks special characters and mnemonic operators in the function result.

Using SAS Functions with Macro Variables

You can use the %SYSFUNC function to execute other SAS functions. The %QSYSFUNC function works the same as the %SYSFUNC function except that it also masks special characters and mnemonic operators in the function result.

Combining Macro Variable References with Text

You might sometimes need to combine a macro variable reference with other text. You can place text immediately before or immediately after a macro variable reference. You can also combine two macro variable references in order to create a new token. You might need to use a delimiter when you combine macro variable references with text.

Sample Programs

Creating Macro Variables with a %LET Statement

```
options symbolgen;
%let year=2002;
proc print data=sasuser.schedule;
    where year(begin_date)=&year;
    title "Scheduled Classes for &year";
run;
proc means data=sasuser.all sum;
    where year(begin_date)=&year;
    class location;
    var fee;
    title1 "Total Fees for &year Classes";
    title2 "by Training Center";
run;
```

Using Automatic Macro Variables

```
footnote1 "Created &systime &sysday, &sysdate9";
footnote2 "on the &sysscp system using Release &sysver";
title "REVENUES FOR DALLAS TRAINING CENTER";
proc tabulate data=sasuser.all(keep=location course_title fee);
    where upcase(location)="DALLAS";
        class course_title;
        var fee;
        table course_title=" " all="TOTALS",
              fee=" "*(n*f=3. sum*f=dollar10.)
              / rts=30 box="COURSE";
run;
```

Inserting Macro Variables Immediately after Text

```
%let year=02;
%let month=jan;
proc chart data=sasuser.y&year&month;
    hbar week / sumvar=sale;
run;
proc plot data=sasuser.y&year&month;
  plot sale*day;
run;
```

Inserting Macro Variables Immediately before Text

```
%let graphics=g;
%let year=02;
%let month=jan;
%let var=sale;
proc &graphics.chart data=sasuser.y&year&month;
  hbar week / sumvar=&var;
run;
proc &graphics.plot data=sasuser.y&year&month;
  plot &var*day;
```

```
run;
```

Points to Remember

- Macro variables can make your programs more reusable and dynamic.

- When you submit code to SAS, macro variable references are resolved by the macro processor, and their values are substituted into your program.

- You can use the %PUT statement to write any text, including resolved macro variables, to the SAS log.

- If you reference a macro variable within quotation marks, you must use double quotation marks. Macro variable references that are enclosed in single quotation marks cannot be resolved.

- Most macro character functions have corresponding functions (such as %QSUBSTR and %QSCAN) that also mask special characters and mnemonic operators in the function result.

Quiz

Select the best answer for each question. After completing the quiz, check your answers using the answer key in the appendix.

1. Which of the following statements is false?

    a. A macro variable can be defined and referenced anywhere in a SAS program except within data lines.

    b. Macro variables are always user-defined, and their values remain constant until they are changed by the user.

    c. Macro variables are text strings that are independent of SAS data sets.

    d. The values of macro variables can be up to 65,534 characters long.

2. Which of the following TITLE statements correctly references the macro variable **month**?

    a. `title "Total Sales for '&month' ";`

    b. `title "Total Sales for 'month'";`

    c. `title "Total Sales for &month";`

    d. `title Total Sales for "&month";`

3. Which of the following statements generates an error message while trying to display the value of the macro variable **month** in the SAS log?

    a. `options &month;`

    b. `%PUT &month;`

    c. `options symbolgen;`

    d. `%PUT the macro variable MONTH has the value &month.;`

4. Which statement creates a macro variable named **location** that has the value **storage**?

    a. `&let location = storage;`

  b. `let &location = storage;`

  c. `%let location = "storage";`

  d. `%let location = storage;`

5. What value do these statements assign to the macro variable `reptitle`:

```
%let area = "Southeast";
%let reptitle = *  Sales Report for &area Area  *;
```

  a. **Sales Report for Southeast Area**

  b. **Sales Report for "Southeast" Area**

  c. ***Sales Report for "Southeast" Area***

  d. *** Sales Report for "Southeast" Area ***

6. Assuming that you began your SAS session today, which of the following statements correctly sets the macro variable `currdate` to today's date:

  a. `%let currdate = %sysfunc(today(), worddate.);`

  b. `%let currdate = &sysdate9;`

  c. `%let currdate = %sysfunc(date());`

  d. all of the above

7. Macro character functions

  a. can be used to manipulate character strings in macro variable values.

  b. have the same basic syntax as the corresponding DATA step functions and yield similar results.

  c. all of the above

  d. none of the above

8. The four types of tokens that SAS recognizes are

  a. expressions, literals, names, and special characters.

  b. literals, names, numbers, and special characters.

  c. expressions, names, numbers, and special characters.

  d. expressions, literals, numbers, and special characters.

9. What are the resulting values for the macro variables that are defined here?

```
%let month1 = June;
%let month2 = July;
%let period1 = &month1&month2;
%let period2 = May&month1;
%let period3 = &month2.Aug;
```

  a. month1 *June* month2 *July* period1 *June July* period2 *May June* period3 *July Aug*

  b. month1 *June* month2 *July* period1 *JuneJuly* period2 *MayJune* period3 *July.Aug*

  c. month1 *June* month2 *July* period1 *JuneJuly* period2 *MayJune* period3 *JulyAug*

  d. month1 *June* month2 *July* period1 *junejuly* period2 *Mayjune* period3 *julyaug*

10. Which of the following correctly produces a title in which the current date is left-justified in order to remove extra blanks?

a. `title "Report for %sysfunc(left(%sysfunc(today(),worddate.)))";`

b. `title "Report for %sysfunc(left(today(), worddate.))";`

c. `title "Report for %sysfunc(left(%qsysfunc(today(), worddate.)))";`

d. `title "Report for %left(today(), worddate.))";`

## Chapter 10

Processing Macro Variables at Execution Time

Overview

Introduction

Because the macro facility performs its tasks before SAS programs execute, the information that the macro facility supplies does not depend on values that are accessed or computed during the execution of a SAS program. However, sometimes it is necessary to access or create macro variables during the execution of a SAS program. There are several methods that enable the macro facility to create or access macro variables at execution time. In this chapter, you learn to use macro variables during execution of the following:

- a DATA step

- a PROC SQL step

- an SCL program.

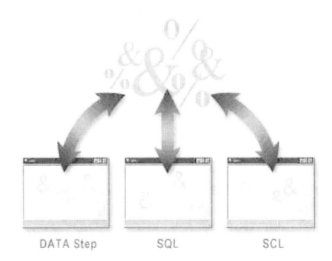

DATA Step   SQL   SCL

Creating a Macro Variable during DATA Step Execution

Overview

In many applications, you need to create macro variables during DATA step execution. You might need to create macro variables and to assign values to them based on the following:

- data values in SAS data sets or in external files

- programming logic

- computed values.

For example, suppose you want to create a report that lists students who are enrolled in a specific course, according to data in the Sasuser.All data set. Suppose you want to include a footnote in your report to indicate whether any student fees are unpaid.

The following program uses SAS programming logic to determine which value is assigned to the macro variable `foot`. Then `foot` is referenced in the FOOTNOTE statement later in the program.

```
options symbolgen pagesize=30;
%let crsnum=3;
data revenue;
   set sasuser.all end=final;
   where course_number=&crsnum;
   total+1;
   if paid='Y' then paidup+1;
   if final then do;
      put total= paidup=; /* Write information
                             to the log. */
      if paidup<total then do;
         %let foot=Some Fees Are Unpaid;
      end;
      else do;
         %let foot=All Students Have Paid;
      end;
   end;
run;

proc print data=revenue;
   var student_name student_company paid;
   title "Payment Status for Course &crsnum";
   footnote "&foot";
run;
```

Running the program produces the following report:

Payment Status for Course 3			
Obs	Student_Name	Student_Company	Paid
1	Bills, Ms. Paulette	Reston Railway	Y
2	Chevarley, Ms. Arlene	Motor Communications	N
3	Clough, Ms. Patti	Reston Railway	N
4	Crace, Mr. Ron	Von Crump Seafood	Y
5	Davis, Mr. Bruce	Semi;Conductor	Y
6	Elsins, Ms. Marisa F.	SSS Inc.	N
7	Gandy, Dr. David	Paralegal Assoc.	Y
8	Gash, Ms. Hedy	QA Information Systems Center	Y
9	Haubold, Ms. Ann	Reston Railway	Y
10	Hudock, Ms. Cathy	So. Cal. Medical Center	Y
11	Kimble, Mr. John	Alforone Chemical	N
12	Kochen, Mr. Dennis	Reston Railway	Y
13	Larocque, Mr. Bret	Physicians IPA	Y
14	Licht, Mr. Bryan	SII	Y
15	McKnight, Ms. Maureen E.	Federated Bank	Y
16	Scannell, Ms. Robin	Amberly Corp.	N
17	Seitz, Mr. Adam	Lomax Services	Y
18	Smith, Ms. Jan	Reston Railway	N
19	Sulzbach, Mr. Bill	Sailbest Ships	Y
20	Williams, Mr. Gene	Snowing Petroleum	Y

All Students Have Paid

Although you can see that several students still have unpaid fees, the footnote indicates that all students have paid. Obviously, the footnote is wrong. That is, the macro variable **foot** resolves to the value **All Students Have Paid** when it should not do so. Look at the following example.

Example

In order to understand the problem with this example, you should consider how macro variable processing works in conjunction with SAS processing. Remember that when both macro language statements and SAS language statements occur in the same step, the macro processor executes macro language statements before any SAS language statements are executed.

Remember, you want to create a report that lists students who are enrolled in a specific course, according to data in the Sasuser.All data set, and you want to include a footnote in your report to indicate whether any student fees are unpaid. The following program uses SAS programming logic to determine which value is assigned to the macro variable `foot`. Then `foot` is referenced in the FOOTNOTE statement later in the program.

```
options symbolgen pagesize=30;
%let crsnum=3;
data revenue;
   set sasuser.all end=final;
   where course_number=&crsnum;
   total+1;
   if paid='Y' then paidup+1;
   if final then do;
      put total= paidup=; /* Write information
                             to the log. */
      if paidup<total then do;
         %let foot=Some Fees Are Unpaid;
      end;
      else do;
         %let foot=All Students Have Paid;
      end;
   end;
run;


proc print data=revenue;
   var student_name student_company paid;
   title "Payment Status for Course &crsnum";
   footnote "&foot";
run;
```

In this example, the first %LET statement inside the DATA step is passed to the macro processor as soon as the word scanner encounters it. The macro processor then creates a macro variable named `foot` in the symbol table and assigns the value **Some Fees Are Unpaid** to the variable.

The word scanner then continues to read the program and passes the second %LET statement in the DATA step to the macro processor as well. This time, the macro processor reassigns the value **All Students Have Paid** to `foot` in the symbol table.

When the RUN statement in the DATA step is encountered, SAS recognizes that the step is complete, and executes it. Remember that at this point the DATA step no longer includes any of the %LET statements (which have already been executed by the macro processor). Because the %LET statements are always processed by the macro processor before the DATA step is executed, the value of `foot` is always whatever the last %LET statement assigns.

Here is a representation of the program that is processed by the DATA step compiler as a result of the above code.

Table 10.1 *Code after Substitution*

```
data revenue;
   set sasuser.all end=final;
   where course_number=3;
   total+1;
   if paid='Y' then paidup+1;
   if final then do;
      put total= paidup=;
      if paidup<total then do;
      end;
      else do;
      end;
   end;
run;
proc print data=revenue;
   var student_name student_company paid;
   title "Payment Status for Course 3";
   footnote "All Students Have Paid";
run;
```

We can solve this problem with the following information.

The SYMPUT Routine

The DATA step provides functions and a CALL routine that enable you to transfer information between an executing DATA step and the macro processor. You can use the SYMPUT routine to create a macro variable and to assign to that variable any value that is available in the DATA step.

General form, SYMPUT routine:

CALL SYMPUT(*macro-variable,text*);

Here is an explanation of the syntax:

macro-variable
    is assigned the character value of *text*.

macro-variable and *text*
    can each be specified as

   • a literal, enclosed in quotation marks

   • a DATA step variable

   • a DATA step expression.

Note: If *macro-variable* already exists, the value of *text* replaces the former value.

When you use the SYMPUT routine to create a macro variable in a DATA step, the macro variable is not actually created and assigned a value until the DATA step is executed. Therefore, you cannot successfully reference a macro variable that is created with the SYMPUT routine by preceding its name with an ampersand until after the step boundary that causes DATA step execution.

In the next few sections that you will see several examples of how the SYMPUT routine can be used in different situations.

Using SYMPUT with a Literal

In the SYMPUT routine, you use a literal string for the following:

- the first argument to specify an exact name for the name of the macro variable

- the second argument to specify the exact character value to assign to the macro variable.

To use a literal with the SYMPUT routine, you enclose the literal string in quotation marks.

CALL SYMPUT(*'macro-variable'*, *'text'*)**;**

Example

Remember the previous example, in which you wanted to conditionally assign a value to the macro variable **foot** based on values that are generated during DATA step execution. You can use the SYMPUT routine with literal strings as both arguments in order to accomplish this.

```
options symbolgen pagesize=30;
%let crsnum=3;
data revenue;
   set sasuser.all end=final;
   where course_number=&crsnum;
   total+1;
   if paid='Y' then paidup+1;
   if final then do;
   if paidup<total then do;
      call symput('foot','Some Fees Are Unpaid');
   end;
   else do;
      call symput('foot','All Students Have Paid');
   end;
end;
run;

proc print data=revenue;
   var student_name student_company paid;
   title "Payment Status for Course &crsnum";
   footnote "&foot";
run;
```

This time, the value assigned to **foot** is either **Some Fees Are Unpaid** or **All Students Have Paid**, depending on the value of the DATA step variable **Paidup**, because the value is assigned during the execution of the DATA step. When you submit this code, you get the following output.

Payment Status for Course 3			
Obs	Student_Name	Student_Company	Paid
1	Bills, Ms. Paulette	Reston Railway	Y
2	Chevarley, Ms. Arlene	Motor Communications	N
3	Clough, Ms. Patti	Reston Railway	N
4	Crace, Mr. Ron	Von Crump Seafood	Y
5	Davis, Mr. Bruce	Semi;Conductor	Y
6	Elsins, Ms. Marisa F.	SSS Inc.	N
7	Gandy, Dr. David	Paralegal Assoc.	Y
8	Gash, Ms. Hedy	QA Information Systems Center	Y
9	Haubold, Ms. Ann	Reston Railway	Y
10	Hudock, Ms. Cathy	So. Cal. Medical Center	Y
11	Kimble, Mr. John	Alforone Chemical	N
12	Kochen, Mr. Dennis	Reston Railway	Y
13	Larocque, Mr. Bret	Physicians IPA	Y
14	Licht, Mr. Bryan	SII	Y
15	McKnight, Ms. Maureen E	Federated Bank	Y
16	Scannell, Ms. Robin	Amberly Corp.	N
17	Seitz, Mr. Adam	Lomax Services	Y
18	Smith, Ms. Jan	Reston Railway	N
19	Sulzbach, Mr. Bill	Sailbest Ships	Y
20	Williams, Mr. Gene	Snowing Petroleum	Y
Some Fees Are Unpaid			

Using SYMPUT with a DATA Step Variable

You can assign the value of a DATA step variable as the value for a macro variable by using the DATA step variable's name as the second argument to the SYMPUT routine.

To use a DATA step variable as the value for a macro variable in the SYMPUT routine, you place the name of the DATA step variable after the name of the macro variable, separated by a comma. You do not enclose the name of the DATA step variable in quotation marks.

CALL SYMPUT(*'macro-variable'*,*DATA-step-variable*);

This form of the SYMPUT routine creates the macro variable named *macro-variable* and assigns to it the current value of *DATA-step-variable*.

When you use a DATA step variable as the second argument,

- a maximum of 32,767 characters can be assigned to the receiving macro variable.

- any leading or trailing blanks that are part of the DATA step variable's value are stored in the macro variable.

- values of numeric variables are automatically converted to character values, using the BEST12. format.

CAUTION:

If you enclose the DATA step variable name in quotation marks, SAS interprets the name as a literal value rather than as a variable name, and the DATA step variable's value is not resolved.

Example

Once again, suppose you want to create a report about students who are enrolled in a particular course. This time, suppose you want to add a title that contains the course title and the course number, and you want to include a footnote that summarizes how many students have paid their fees.

In this example, a DATA step variable named `paidup` records the number of students that have paid, and a DATA step variable named `total` records the total number of students who are registered for the class. Macro variables are created to record the values of `paidup`, the value of `total`, and the value of `Course_title`. These macro variables are referenced later in the program.

```
%let crsnum=3;
data revenue;
    set sasuser.all end=final;
    where course_number=&crsnum;
    total+1;
    if paid='Y' then paidup+1;
    if final then do;
        call symput('numpaid',paidup);
        call symput('numstu',total);
        call symput('crsname',course_title);
    end;
run;
proc print data=revenue noobs;
    var student_name student_company paid;
    title "Fee Status for &crsname (#&crsnum)";
    footnote "Note: &numpaid Paid out of &numstu Students";
run;
```

This time the footnote shows the correct information for how many students have paid.

Fee Status for Local Area Networks (#3)

Student_Name	Student_Company	Paid
Bills, Ms. Paulette	Reston Railway	Y
Chevarley, Ms. Arlene	Motor Communications	N
Clough, Ms. Patti	Reston Railway	N
Crace, Mr. Ron	Von Crump Seafood	Y
Davis, Mr. Bruce	Semi Conductor	Y
Elsins, Ms. Marisa F	SSS Inc.	N
Gandy, Dr. David	Paralegal Assoc.	Y
Gash, Ms. Hedy	QA Information Systems Center	Y
Haubold, Ms. Ann	Reston Railway	Y
Hudock, Ms. Cathy	So. Cal. Medical Center	Y
Kimble, Mr. John	Alforone Chemical	N
Kochen, Mr. Dennis	Reston Railway	Y
Larocque, Mr. Bret	Physicians IPA	Y
Licht, Mr. Bryan	SII	Y
McKnight, Ms. Maureen E	Federated Bank	Y
Scannell, Ms. Robin	Amberly Corp.	N
Seitz, Mr. Adam	Lomax Services	Y
Smith, Ms. Jan	Reston Railway	N
Sulzbach, Mr. Bill	Sailbest Ships	Y
Williams, Mr. Gene	Snowing Petroleum	Y

Note: 14 Paid out of 20 Students

Using CALL SYMPUT with DATA Step Expressions

If you had run the last example using listing output rather than HTML output, you would have seen extra blanks in the title between the course title and the course number, as well as in the footnote.

Table 10.2 *SAS Listing Output*

```
Fee Status for Local Area Networks        (#3)


    Student_Name              Student_Company              Paid

    Bills, Ms. Paulette       Reston Railway                Y
    Chevarley, Ms. Arlene     Motor Communications          N
    Clough, Ms. Patti         Reston Railway                N
    Crace, Mr. Ron            Von Crump Seafood             Y
    Davis, Mr. Bruce          Semi;Conductor                Y
    Elsins, Ms. Marisa F.     SSS Inc.                      N
    Gandy, Dr. David          Paralegal Assoc.              Y
    Gash, Ms. Hedy            QA Information Systems Center  Y
    Haubold, Ms. Ann          Reston Railway                Y
    Hudock, Ms. Cathy         So. Cal. Medical Center       Y
    Kimble, Mr. John          Alforone Chemical             N
    Kochen, Mr. Dennis        Reston Railway                Y
    Larocque, Mr. Bret        Physicians IPA                Y
    Licht, Mr. Bryan          SII                           Y
    McKnight, Ms. Maureen E.  Federated Bank                Y
    Scannell, Ms. Robin       Amberly Corp.                 N
    Seitz, Mr. Adam           Lomax Services                Y
    Smith, Ms. Jan            Reston Railway                N
    Sulzbach, Mr. Bill        Sailbest Ships                Y
    Williams, Mr. Gene        Snowing Petroleum             Y


        Note:         14 Paid out of        20 Students
```

You do not see these blanks if you are using HTML output, but they are still stored in the value of your macro variable.

Remember that when a DATA step variable is used as the second argument in a SYMPUT routine, any leading, or trailing blanks that are part of the DATA step variable's value are stored in the macro variable. Because the value of a macro variable is always a text string, numeric variables are automatically converted using the BEST12. format, and blanks are stored as part of the macro variable's value. In order to avoid including extra blanks, you need to use a DATA step function to remove them.

In these situations that you can use DATA step functions before the SYMPUT routine executes, in order to do the following:

- left-align character strings that have been created by numeric-to-character conversions

- remove extraneous leading and trailing blanks.

Often you want to combine several DATA step functions in order to create a DATA step expression as the second argument of the SYMPUT routine.

CALL SYMPUT(*'macro-variable'*,*expression*);

Note: A DATA step expression can be any combination of DATA step functions, DATA step variables, constants, and logical or arithmetic operators that resolves to a character or numeric constant.

When you use a DATA step expression as the second argument, its current value is evaluated according to the following rules:

- Numeric expressions are automatically converted to character constants using the BEST12. format.

- The resulting value can be up to 32,767 characters long.

- Any leading or trailing blanks that are part of the expression are stored in the macro variable.

Example

In order to remove the extra blanks from the title and footnote of the previous example, you can use DATA step functions. To remove trailing blanks from **crsname**, you can use the TRIM function. To remove leading and trailing blanks from the macro variables **numstu** and **numpaid**, you can use the STRIP function.

```
%let crsnum=3;
data revenue;
   set sasuser.all end=final;
   where course_number=&crsnum;
   total+1;
   if paid='Y' then paidup+1;
   if final then do;

      call symput('numpaid',strip(paidup));
      call symput('numstu',strip(total));
      call symput('crsname',trim(course_title));
   end;
run;

proc print data=revenue noobs;
   var student_name student_company paid;
   title "Fee Status for &crsname (#&crsnum)";
   footnote "Note: &numpaid Paid out of &numstu Students";
run;
```

Table 10.3 *SAS Listing Output*

```
              Fee Status for Local Area Networks (#3)


      NAME                      COMPANY                      PAID

      Bills, Ms. Paulette       Reston Railway                Y
      Chevarley, Ms. Arlene     Motor Communications          N
      Clough, Ms. Patti         Reston Railway                N
      Crace, Mr. Ron            Von Crump Seafood             Y
      Davis, Mr. Bruce          Semi;Conductor                Y
      Elsins, Ms. Marisa F.     SSS Inc.                      N
      Gandy, Dr. David          Paralegal Assoc.              Y
      Gash, Ms. Hedy            QA Information Systems  Center Y
      Haubold, Ms. Ann          Reston Railway                Y
      Hudock, Ms. Cathy         So. Cal. Medical Center       Y
      Kimble, Mr. John          Alforone Chemical             N
      Kochen, Mr. Dennis        Reston Railway                Y
      Larocque, Mr. Bret        Physicians IPA                Y
      Licht, Mr. Bryan          SII                           Y
      McKnight, Ms. Maureen E.  Federated Bank                Y
      Scannell, Ms. Robin       Amberly Corp.                 N
      Seitz, Mr. Adam           Lomax Services                Y
      Smith, Ms. Jan            Reston Railway                N
      Sulzbach, Mr. Bill        Sailbest Ships                Y
      Williams, Mr. Gene        Snowing Petroleum             Y


              Note: 14 Paid out of 20 Students
```

PUT Function

Remember that the values of macro variables are always character strings. You have seen that in the DATA step the SYMPUT routine performs automatic numeric-to-character conversion on any numeric value that you attempt to assign to a macro variable. Messages are written to the SAS log to alert you that automatic conversion has occurred. Remember that the SYMPUT routine automatically uses the BEST12. format for the conversion.

Sometimes you might want to have explicit control over the numeric-to-character conversion. The PUT function returns a character string that is formed by writing a value with a specified format.

You can use the PUT function to do the following:

- perform explicit numeric-to-character conversions

- format the result of a numeric expression.

General form, PUT function:

PUT*(source,format.)*

Here is an explanation of the syntax:

source
> is a constant, a variable, or an expression (numeric or character).

format.
> is any SAS format or user-defined format, which determines

> - the length of the resulting string

> - whether the string is right- or left-aligned.

source and *format.*
> must be the same type (numeric or character).

Example

Suppose you want to create a report that shows the amount of fees that are unpaid for a specific course. In the following example, you use the SYMPUT routine to format the value of the numeric variable **Begin_date** with the MMDDYY10. format and assign that value to the macro variable **date**. Then you also use another call to the SYMPUT routine to format the result of an expression involving **Fee**, **total**, and **paidup** as a dollar amount and assign that value to the macro variable **due**.

```
%let crsnum=3;
data revenue;
   set sasuser.all end=final;
   where course_number=&crsnum;
   total+1;
   if paid='Y' then paidup+1;
   if final then do;
     call symput('crsname',trim(course_title));
     call symput('date',put(begin_date,mmddyy10.));
     call symput('due',strip(put(fee*(total-paidup),dollar8.)));
   end;
run;
```

You can use the macro variables **date** and **due** in a PROC PRINT step to create your report. The values of these macro variables appear in the report with the formatting that you assigned to them when you created them.

```
proc print data=revenue;
   var student_name student_company paid;
   title "Fee Status for &crsname (#&crsnum) Held &date";
   footnote "Note: &due in Unpaid Fees";
run;
```

Fee Status for Local Area Networks (#3) Held 01/08/2001

Obs	Student_Name	Student_Company	Paid
1	Bills, Ms. Paulette	Reston Railway	Y
2	Chevarley, Ms. Arlene	Motor Communications	N
3	Clough, Ms. Patti	Reston Railway	N
4	Crace, Mr. Ron	Von Crump Seafood	Y
5	Davis, Mr. Bruce	Semi Conductor	Y
6	Elsins, Ms. Marisa F.	SSS Inc.	N
7	Gandy, Dr. David	Paralegal Assoc.	Y
8	Gash, Ms. Hedy	QA Information Systems Center	Y
9	Haubold, Ms. Ann	Reston Railway	Y
10	Hudock, Ms. Cathy	So. Cal. Medical Center	Y
11	Kimble, Mr. John	Alforone Chemical	N
12	Kochen, Mr. Dennis	Reston Railway	Y
13	Larocque, Mr. Bret	Physicians IPA	Y
14	Licht, Mr. Bryan	SII	Y
15	McKnight, Ms. Maureen E.	Federated Bank	Y
16	Scannell, Ms. Robin	Amberly Corp.	N
17	Seitz, Mr. Adam	Lomax Services	Y
18	Smith, Ms. Jan	Reston Railway	N
19	Sulzbach, Mr. Bill	Sailbest Ships	Y
20	Williams, Mr. Gene	Snowing Petroleum	Y

Note: $3,900 in Unpaid Fees

The SYMPUTX Routine

The SYMPUTX routine is very similar to the SYMPUT routine. In addition to creating a macro variable and assigning a value to it, the SYMPUTX routine also automatically removes leading and trailing blanks from both arguments.

General form, SYMPUTX routine:

CALL SYMPUTX(*macro-variable,expression*);

Here is an explanation of the syntax:

macro-variable
is assigned the character value of *expression*, and any leading or trailing blanks are removed from both *macro-variable* and *expression*.

macro-variable and *expression*
can each be specified as

- a literal, enclosed in quotation marks

- a DATA step variable

- a DATA step expression.

Note: If *macro-variable* already exists, the value of *expression* replaces the former value.

Example

Remember the example where you created a report about students who are enrolled in a particular course. This time, suppose you want the title to contain the course name and the course number, as well as the date on which the course was held. Also, you want the footnote to list the current amount of unpaid fees for the course.

In this example, three macro variables are created. The macro variable **csrname** records the value of the DATA step variable **Course_title**. The macro variable **date** records the value of the DATA step variable **Begin_date** in MMDDYY10. format. Finally, the macro variable **due** uses the values of the DATA step variables **paidup**, **total**, and **fee** to record the current amount of unpaid fees in DOLLAR8. format. These macro variables are referenced later in the program in the title and footnote statements.

```
%let crsnum=3;
data revenue;
   set sasuser.all end=final;
   where course_number=&crsnum;
   total+1;
   if paid='Y' then paidup+1;
   if final then do;
      call symputx('crsname',course_title);
      call symputx('date',put(begin_date,mmddyy10.));
      call symputx('due',put(fee*(total-paidup),dollar8.));
   end;
run;
proc print data=revenue;
   var student_name student_company paid;
   title "Fee Status for &crsname (#&crsnum) Held &date";
   footnote "Note: &due in Unpaid Fees";
run;
```

Obs	Student_Name	Student_Company	Paid
1	Bills, Ms. Paulette	Reston Railway	Y
2	Chevarley, Ms. Arlene	Motor Communications	N
3	Clough, Ms. Patti	Reston Railway	N
4	Crace, Mr. Ron	Von Crump Seafood	Y
5	Davis, Mr. Bruce	Semi;Conductor	Y
6	Elsins, Ms. Marisa F.	SSS Inc.	N
7	Gandy, Dr. David	Paralegal Assoc.	Y
8	Gash, Ms. Hedy	QA Information Systems Center	Y
9	Haubold, Ms. Ann	Reston Railway	Y
10	Hudock, Ms. Cathy	So. Cal. Medical Center	Y
11	Kimble, Mr. John	Alforone Chemical	N
12	Kochen, Mr. Dennis	Reston Railway	Y
13	Larocque, Mr. Bret	Physicians IPA	Y
14	Licht, Mr. Bryan	SII	Y
15	McKnight, Ms. Maureen E.	Federated Bank	Y
16	Scannell, Ms. Robin	Amberly Corp.	N
17	Seitz, Mr. Adam	Lomax Services	Y
18	Smith, Ms. Jan	Reston Railway	N
19	Sulzbach, Mr. Bill	Sailbest Ships	Y
20	Williams, Mr. Gene	Snowing Petroleum	Y

Fee Status for Local Area Networks (#3) Held 01/08/2001

Note: $3,900 in Unpaid Fees

Creating Multiple Macro Variables during DATA Step Execution

Creating Multiple Macro Variables with CALL SYMPUT

Sometimes you might want to create multiple macro variables within one DATA step. For example, suppose you want to write a program that lists all of the scheduled dates for a particular course, using a macro variable to record the title of the course.

```
%let crsid=C005;
data _null_;
   set sasuser.courses;
   where course_code="&crsid";
   call symput('title',trim(course_title));
```

```
run;

proc print data=sasuser.schedule noobs label;
   where course_code="&crsid";
   var location begin_date teacher;
   title1 "Schedule for &title";
   options nodate nonumber;
run;
```

In this example, the value of the data set variable `Course_title` for the course whose `Course_code` is `C005` is assigned as a value for the macro variable `title`. The value `_null_` on the data statement is used because we do not need a data set to be created in this example.

In order to create a listing for a different course, you would need to change the %LET statement and resubmit the DATA step to assign a new value to `title`. Then you would need to resubmit the PROC PRINT step. Although you would need to resubmit both the DATA step and the PROC PRINT step, these two steps would be identical to the steps that you submitted for the first report. This is an extremely inefficient program.

```
%let crsid=C004;
data _null_;
   set sasuser.courses;
   where course_code="&crsid";
   call symput('title',trim(course_title));
run;

proc print data=sasuser.schedule noobs label;
   where course_code="&crsid";
   var location begin_date teacher;
   title1 "Schedule for &title";
   options nodate nonumber;
run;
```

Instead of executing separate DATA steps to update the same macro variable, you can create related macro variables in one DATA step. To create multiple macro variables, you use the SYMPUT routine with DATA step expressions for both arguments.

General form, SYMPUT routine with DATA step expressions:

CALL SYMPUT(*expression1,expression2*);

Here is an explanation of the syntax:

expression1
> evaluates to a character value that is a valid macro variable name. This value should change each time you want to create another macro variable.

expression2
> is the value that you want to assign to a specific macro variable.

Example

In this example, you use one call to the SYMPUT routine in order to create one macro variable for each value of the DATA step variable `Course_code` and to assign the corresponding value of `Course_title` to each macro variable. That is, for each observation in Sasuser.Courses, the macro processor creates a new macro variable. The new macro variable has the same name as the value of the data set variable

`Course_code` for that observation. The value of the new macro variable is the value of the data set variable `Course_title` for that observation.

```
data _null_;
   set sasuser.courses;
   call symput(course_code, trim(course_title));
run;
%put _user_;
```

The SAS log shows that six observations were read from the data set Sasuser.Courses and that six global macro variables were created and were assigned values.

Table 10.4 *SAS Log*

```
2   data _null_;
3      set sasuser.courses;
4      call symput(course_code, trim(course_title));
5   run;

NOTE: There were 6 observations read from the dataset
      SASUSER.COURSES.
NOTE: DATA statement used:
      real time           0.52 seconds
      cpu time            0.13 seconds

7   %put _user_;
GLOBAL C006 Computer Aided Design
GLOBAL C001 Basic Telecommunications
GLOBAL C002 Structured Query Language
GLOBAL C003 Local Area Networks
GLOBAL C004 Database Design
GLOBAL C005 Artificial Intelligence
```

You can then use these new macro variables to print listings of information for various courses, using only one DATA step, as follows:

```
data _null_;
   set sasuser.courses;
   call symput(course_code,trim(course_title));
run;

%let crsid=C005;
proc print data=sasuser.schedule noobs label;
   where course_code="&crsid";
   var location begin_date teacher;
   title1 "Schedule for &c005";
run;

%let crsid=C002;
proc print data=sasuser.schedule noobs label;
   where course_code="&crsid";
   var location begin_date teacher;
   title1 "Schedule for &c002";
run;
```

This is the output from the first PROC PRINT step.

Schedule for Artificial Intelligence

Location	Begin	Instructor
Dallas	26FEB2001	Hallis, Dr. George
Boston	17SEP2001	Tally, Ms. Julia
Seattle	25FEB2002	Hallis, Dr. George

This is the output from the second PROC PRINT step.

Schedule for Structured Query Language

Location	Begin	Instructor
Dallas	04DEC2000	Wickam, Dr. Alice
Boston	11JUN2001	Wickam, Dr. Alice
Seattle	03DEC2001	Wickam, Dr. Alice

The program in this section is more efficient than the program shown in the previous section since the Sasuser.Courses data set is read only once in the latest example. However, there is still room for improvement.

Referencing Macro Variables Indirectly

Introduction

In the last example, you saw how to use the SYMPUT routine to create a series of macro variables whose names are based on the values of `Course_code`. However, you still needed to modify the TITLE statement in each PROC PRINT step in order to print output for each course.

Suppose you want to write a PROC PRINT step that you can reuse without any modification to print information about each course. You can do this by using an indirect reference in the TITLE statement.

```
data _null_;
   set sasuser.courses;
   call symput(course_code,trim(course_title));
run;

%let crsid=C002;
proc print data=sasuser.schedule noobs label;
   where course_code="&crsid";
   var location begin_date teacher;
   title1 "Schedule for ???";
run;
```

In the example above, the macro variable `C002` (as created by the SYMPUT routine) has a value of `Structured Query Language`. Therefore, the TITLE statement should reference a macro variable that resolves to `Structured Query Language`. Remember that you want this reference to be flexible enough to apply to any of the macro variables that the SYMPUT routine creates, such as `C003` or `C004`, by changing only the %LET statement.

To obtain the value `Structured Query Language`, you need to indirectly reference the macro variable `C002` through a reference to the macro variable `crsid`. If the value of the macro variable `crsid` is *C002*, then you need to proceed in several steps:

1. Resolve the macro variable `crsid` to the value `C002`.

2. Attach an ampersand (`&`) to the front of the resolved value in order to create a new reference (`&C002`).

3. Resolve the resulting macro variable reference to the value `Structured Query Language`.

This sequence seems to imply that you should use the reference `&&crsid` to convert the value of the macro variable `crsid` to the corresponding course description. However, the Forward Re-Scan rule indicates that this is not the correct solution.

The Forward Re-Scan Rule

The Forward Re-Scan rule can be summarized as follows:

- When multiple ampersands or percent signs precede a name token, the macro processor resolves two ampersands (&&) to one ampersand (&), and re-scans the reference.

- To re-scan a reference, the macro processor scans and resolves tokens from left to right from the point where multiple ampersands or percent signs are coded, until no more triggers can be resolved.

According to the Forward Re-Scan rule, you need to use three ampersands in front of a macro variable name when its value matches the name of a second macro variable. This indirect reference resolves to the value of the second macro variable.

Example

Suppose you want to use the macro variable `crsid` to indirectly reference the macro variable `C002`.

Global Symbol Table	
C001	*Basic Telecommunications*
C002	*Structured Query Language*
C003	*Local Area Networks*
C004	*Database Design*
C005	*Artificial Intelligence*
C006	*Computer Aided Design*
CRSID	*C002*

The following table shows several references along with their resolved values.

Reference	Scan	Resolved Value	Re-scan	Resolved Value
&crsid	→	C002	no re-scan	
&&crsid	→	&crsid	→	C002
&&&crsid	→	&C002	→	Structured Query Language

By preceding a macro variable reference with two ampersands, you delay the resolution of the reference until the second scan. The first time the reference is scanned, only the double ampersands are resolved (to one ampersand). In order to create an indirect reference (a reference whose value is a reference to a different macro variable), you must use three ampersands. Therefore, to use an indirect reference that resolves to **Structured Query Language**, the original reference must be **&&&crsid**.

Example

You can use indirect referencing to improve the last example. By using an indirect reference to the macro variable whose name is the same as the current value of the macro variable **crsid**, you can write a PROC PRINT step that you can reuse without modification in order to print a report for each different course.

```
options symbolgen;
data _null_;
   set sasuser.courses;
   call symput(course_code, trim(course_title));
run;


%let crsid=C005;
proc print data=sasuser.schedule noobs label;
   where course_code="&crsid";
   var location begin_date teacher;
   title1 "Schedule for &&&crsid";
run;


%let crsid=C002;
proc print data=sasuser.schedule noobs label;
   where course_code="&crsid";
   var location begin_date teacher;
   title1 "Schedule for &&&crsid";
run;
```

The SAS log shows the steps that lead to the resolution of these macro variables for each PROC PRINT step.

Table 10.5 *SAS Log*

```
43    options symbolgen;
44    data _null_;
45       set sasuser.courses;
46       call symput(course_code, trim(course_title));
47    run;
NOTE: There were 6 observations read from the dataset
      SASUSER.COURSES.
NOTE: DATA statement used:
      real time           0.07 seconds
      cpu time            0.05 seconds

48
49    %let crsid=C005;
50    proc print data=sasuser.schedule noobs label;
51       where course_code="&crsid";
SYMBOLGEN: Macro variable CRSID resolves to C005
52       var location begin_date teacher;
SYMBOLGEN:  && resolves to &.
SYMBOLGEN:  Macro variable CRSID resolves to C005
SYMBOLGEN:  Macro variable C005 resolves to Artificial
            Intelligence
53       title1 "Schedule for &&&crsid";
54    run;

NOTE: There were 3 observations read from the dataset
      SASUSER.SCHEDULE.
      WHERE course_code='C005';
NOTE: PROCEDURE PRINT used:
      real time           0.09 seconds
      cpu time            0.04 seconds

55
56    %let crsid=C002;
57    proc print data=sasuser.schedule noobs label;
58       where course_code="&crsid";

SYMBOLGEN:  Macro variable CRSID resolves to C002
59       var location begin_date teacher;
SYMBOLGEN:  && resolves to &.
SYMBOLGEN:  Macro variable CRSID resolves to C002
SYMBOLGEN:  Macro variable C002 resolves to Structured
            Query Language
60       title1 "Schedule for &&&crsid";
61    run;

NOTE: There were 3 observations read from the dataset
      SASUSER.SCHEDULE.
      WHERE course_code='C002';
NOTE: PROCEDURE PRINT used:
      real time           0.06 seconds
      cpu time            0.04 seconds
```

This is the output from the first PROC PRINT step.

Schedule for Artificial Intelligence

Location	Begin	Instructor
Dallas	26FEB2001	Hallis, Dr. George
Boston	17SEP2001	Tally, Ms. Julia
Seattle	25FEB2002	Hallis, Dr. George

This is the output from the second PROC PRINT step.

Schedule for Structured Query Language

Location	Begin	Instructor
Dallas	04DEC2000	Wickam, Dr. Alice
Boston	11JUN2001	Wickam, Dr. Alice
Seattle	03DEC2001	Wickam, Dr. Alice

Note that the PROC PRINT steps that produced these reports were identical. Only the %LET statement that precedes each PROC PRINT step and the resolved values of the macro variables changed.

Indirect referencing is especially useful when you are working with a series of related macro variables. In Chapter 9, "Introducing Macro Variables," on page 288, you learned how to combine multiple macro variable references in order to build new tokens. You can combine indirect macro variable references with other macro variable references as well. That is, you can use two ampersands in a reference when the value of one macro variable matches part of the name of a second macro variable.

Example

You can create a series of macro variables, `teach1` to `teach`n, each containing the name of the instructor who is assigned to a specific course.

```
options symbolgen;
data _null_;
   set sasuser.schedule;
   call symput('teach'||left(course_number),
             trim(teacher));
run;
```

Note: The concatenation operator | | combines text. In the example above, the literal string `teach` is concatenated to the text that results from left-aligning the resolved value of the variable `Course_number`.

Global Symbol Table	
TEACH1	*Hallis, Dr. George*
TEACH2	*Wickam, Dr. Alice*
TEACH3	*Forest, Mr. Peter*

Then, you can reference one of these variables when a course number is designated. If you designate a course number in a %LET statement, you can use multiple ampersands in order to create a reference to the **teach**n macro variable that corresponds to the current course number.

```
%let crs=3;
proc print data=sasuser.register noobs;
   where course_number=&crs;
   var student_name paid;
   title1 "Roster for Course &crs";
   title2 "Taught by &&teach&crs";
run;
```

The SAS log shows the steps that lead to the resolution of the reference **&&teach&crs**.

Table 10.6   *SAS LOG*

```
65    %let crs=3;
66    proc print data=sasuser.register noobs;
67       where course_number=&crs;
SYMBOLGEN:   Macro variable CRS resolves to 3
68       var student_name paid;
SYMBOLGEN:   Macro variable CRS resolves to 3
69       title1 "Roster for Course &crs";
SYMBOLGEN:   && resolves to &.
SYMBOLGEN:   Macro variable CRS resolves to 3
SYMBOLGEN:   Macro variable TEACH3 resolves to
             Forest, Mr. Peter
70       title2 "Taught by &&teach&crs";
71    run;
```

This is the output from the example.

```
                    Roster for Course 3
                 Taught by Forest, Mr. Peter
```

Student_Name	Paid
Bills, Ms. Paulette	Y
Chevarley, Ms. Arlene	N
Clough, Ms. Patti	N
Crace, Mr. Ron	Y
Davis, Mr. Bruce	Y
Elsins, Ms. Marisa F.	N
Gandy, Dr. David	Y
Gash, Ms. Hedy	Y
Haubold, Ms. Ann	Y
Hudock, Ms. Cathy	Y
Kimble, Mr. John	N
Kochen, Mr. Dennis	Y
Larocque, Mr. Bret	Y
Licht, Mr. Bryan	Y
McKnight, Ms. Maureen E.	Y
Scannell, Ms. Robin	N
Seitz, Mr. Adam	Y
Smith, Ms. Jan	N
Sulzbach, Mr. Bill	Y
Williams, Mr. Gene	Y

Obtaining Macro Variable Values during DATA Step Execution

The SYMGET Function

Earlier you learned how to use the SYMPUT routine to create macro variables in a DATA step. You are also familiar with using a macro variable reference such as **&macvar** to obtain the value of a macro variable before a DATA step executes. Now, suppose you want to obtain the value of a macro variable during DATA step execution. You can obtain a macro variable's value during DATA step execution by using the SYMGET function. The SYMGET function returns the value of an existing macro variable.

General form, SYMGET function:

SYMGET(*macro-variable*)

Here is an explanation of the syntax:

macro-variable
    can be specified as one of the following:

    • a macro variable name, enclosed in quotation marks

    • a DATA step variable name whose value is the name of a macro variable

    • a DATA step character expression whose value is the name of a macro variable.

Example

You can use the SYMGET function to obtain the value of a different macro variable for each iteration of a DATA step. In this example, the data set variable **Teacher** is assigned the value of the macro variable **teach***n* for each observation in the Sasuser.Register data set, where *n* is the value of the data set variable **Course_number** for that observation.

Note: This example assumes that a macro variable named **teach***n* has already been created for each observation in Sasuser.Register.

```
data teachers;
   set sasuser.register;
   length Teacher $ 20;
   teacher=symget('teach'||left(course_number));
run;

proc print data=teachers;
   var student_name course_number teacher;
   title1 "Teacher for Each Registered Student";
run;
```

Global Symbol Table	
TEACH1	*Hallis, Dr. George*
TEACH2	*Wickam, Dr. Alice*
TEACH3	*Forest, Mr. Peter*
CRS	*3*

Part of the SAS output that this program creates is shown below. Notice that the new data set *Teachers* contains a variable named **Teacher** and that the values of this variable are the same as the values of the macro variables **teach1-teach3** in the global symbol table above.

Obs	Student_Name	Course_Number	Teacher
1	Albritton, Mr. Bryan	1	Hallis, Dr. George
2	Amigo, Mr. Bill	1	Hallis, Dr. George
3	Chodnoff, Mr. Norman	1	Hallis, Dr. George
4	Clark, Mr. Rich	1	Hallis, Dr. George
5	Crace, Mr. Ron	1	Hallis, Dr. George
6	Dellmonache, Ms. Susan	1	Hallis, Dr. George
7	Dixon, Mr. Matt	1	Hallis, Dr. George
8	Edwards, Mr. Charles	1	Hallis, Dr. George
9	Edwards, Ms. Sonia	1	Hallis, Dr. George
10	Elsins, Ms. Marisa F.	1	Hallis, Dr. George
11	Griffin, Mr. Lantz	1	Hallis, Dr. George
12	Hall, Ms. Sharon	1	Hallis, Dr. George
13	Haubold, Ms. Ann	1	Hallis, Dr. George

Teacher for Each Registered Student

Creating Macro Variables during PROC SQL Step Execution

The INTO Clause and the NOPRINT Option

You have seen how to create macro variables during DATA step execution. You can also create or update macro variables during the execution of a PROC SQL step. Remember that the SELECT statement in a PROC SQL step retrieves and displays data. The INTO clause in a SELECT statement enables you to create or update macro variables.

When you create or update macro variables during execution of a PROC SQL step, you might not want any output to be displayed. The PRINT | NOPPRINT option specifies whether a SELECT statement's results are displayed in output. PRINT is the default setting.

General form, PROC SQL with the NOPRINT option and the INTO clause:

PROC SQL NOPRINT;

    SELECT *column1<,column2,...>*

        INTO :*macro-variable-1<,:macro-variable-2,...>*

        FROM *table-1 | view-1*

        <WHERE *expression*>

        <other clauses>;

QUIT;

Here is an explanation of the syntax:

column1, column2,...
    specifies one or more columns of the SQL table specified by *table-1 | view-1*.

:macro-variable-1, :macro-variable-2,...
    names the macro variables to create.

expression
    produces a value that is used to subset the data.

other clauses
    are other valid clauses that group, subset, or order the data.

Note: Macro variable names are preceded by a colon.

Note: For more information about PROC SQL, see the SAS documentation.

This form of the INTO clause does not trim leading or trailing blanks. Also, the INTO clause cannot be used when you create a table or a view.

Example

You can create a macro variable named `totalfee` that contains the total of all course fees, and use this macro variable in a later step. You use the NOPRINT option to suppress the output from the PROC SQL step.

```
proc sql noprint;
   select sum(fee) format=dollar10. into :totalfee
      from sasuser.all;
quit;
%let totalfee=&totalfee;

proc means data=sasuser.all sum maxdec=0;
   class course_title;
   var fee;
   title "Grand Total for All Courses Is &totalfee";
run;
```

Note: This form of the INTO clause does not trim leading or trailing blanks, but the %LET statement removes any leading or trailing blanks that are stored in the value of `totalfee`.

The output from this PROC MEANS step shows the sum of all course fees in the DOLLAR10. format.

```
Grand Total for All Courses Is $354,380

The MEANS Procedure
```

Analysis Variable : Fee Course Fee		
Description	N Obs	Sum
Artificial Intelligence	71	28400
Basic Telecommunications	69	54855
Computer Aided Design	66	105600
Database Design	77	28875
Local Area Networks	74	48100
Structured Query Language	77	88550

Creating Variables with the INTO Clause

Earlier you learned how to create a series of related macro variables during execution of the DATA step by using the SYMPUT routine. Sometimes you might want to create a series of related macro variables during execution of a PROC SQL step. You can use the INTO clause to create one new macro variable for each row in the result of the SELECT statement.

General form, SELECT statement with the INTO clause for a range of macro variables:

PROC SQL NOPRINT;

    SELECT *column1*

        INTO :*macro-variable-1* - :*macro-variable-n*

        FROM *table-1 | view-1*

        <WHERE *expression*>

        <*other clauses*>;

QUIT;

Here is an explanation of the syntax:

column1
    specifies the column of the SQL table specified by *table-1 | view-1*.

:*macro-variable-1* - :*macro-variable-n,...*
    names the macro variables to create.

expression
    produces a value that is used to subset the data.

other clauses
    are other valid clauses that group, subset, or order the data.

When storing values into a range of macro variables, or when using the SEPARATED BY option to store multiple values in one macro variable, the INTO clause of PROC SQL trims any leading and trailing blanks. Use the NOTRIM option if you want the blanks to be preserved. This treatment of leading and trailing blanks is in contrast to assigning the value of a DATA step variable for a macro variable in the SYMPUT routine on page 334.

Example

You can create a series of macro variables that contain the course code, location, and starting date of the first three courses that are scheduled in 2002. In this example, the macro variables `crsid1-crsid3` are assigned values of the data set variable `Course_code` from each of the first three rows of the PROC SQL result:

```
proc sql;
   select course_code, location, begin_date format=mmddyy10.
   into :crsid1-:crsid3,
        :place1-:place3,
        :date1-:date3
      from sasuser.schedule
      where year(begin_date)=2002
      order by begin_date;
quit;
```

This is the result of the PROC SQL step.

Course Code	Location	Begin
C003	Dallas	01/07/2002
C004	Boston	01/21/2002
C005	Seattle	02/25/2002
C006	Dallas	03/25/2002

This is a representation of the symbol table after this PROC SQL step has run.

Global Symbol Table	
CRSID1	C003
CRSID2	C004
CRSID3	C005
PLACE1	Dallas
PLACE2	Boston
PLACE3	Seattle
DATE1	01/07/2002
DATE2	01/21/2002
DATE3	02/25/2002

If you do not know how many macro variables are created, you can issue a query to determine how many macro variables are needed and to create a macro variable to store that number. You can then run the query, using the macro variable as the suffix of the final macro variable in each series of macro variables.

Example

Suppose you want to create ranges of macro variables that contain the course code, location, and starting date of all courses that are scheduled in 2002. You do not know the number of courses. If you assign an arbitrarily large number as the suffix of the final macro variable range, only macro variables corresponding to the query result set are created. The macro variable SQLOBS is assigned a value reflecting the number of rows in the result set, matching the number of macro variables created in each range.

```
proc sql noprint;
   select course_code, location,
          begin_date format=mmddyy10.
      into :crsid1-:crsid999,
           :place1-:place999,
           :date1-:date999
      from sasuser.schedule
      where year(begin_date)=2002
      order by begin_date;
   %let numrows=&sqlobs;
   %put There are &numrows courses in 2002;
   %put _user_;
quit;
```

The SAS log shows that **numrows** is assigned a value of **4**. The %PUT statement at the end of the program shows the names and values of all the macro variables that are created in the SELECT statement.

Table 10.7 *SAS Log*

```
114  proc sql noprint;
115    select course_code, location,
116       begin_date format=mmddyy10.
117      into :crsid1-:crsid999,
118        :place1-:place999,
119        :date1-:date999
120      from sasuser.schedule
121      where year(begin_date)=2002
122      order by begin_date;
123    %let numrows=&sqlobs;
124    %put There are &numrows courses in 2002;
There are 4 courses in 2002
125     %put _user_;
GLOBAL SQLOBS 4
GLOBAL CRSID2 C004
GLOBAL SQLOOPS 20
GLOBAL CRSID3 C005
GLOBAL DATE4 03/25/2002
GLOBAL PLACE1 Dallas
GLOBAL CRSID1 C003
GLOBAL PLACE2 Boston
GLOBAL PLACE3 Seattle
GLOBAL SYS_SQL_IP_ALL -1
GLOBAL SYS_SQL_IP_STMT
GLOBAL CRSNUM 3
GLOBAL DATE 01/08/2001
GLOBAL DATE1 01/07/2002
GLOBAL CRSID4 C006
GLOBAL DATE2 01/21/2002
GLOBAL DATE3 02/25/2002
GLOBAL NUMPAID 14
GLOBAL SQLXOBS 0
GLOBAL SQLRC 0
GLOBAL NUMROWS 4
GLOBAL NUMSTU 20
GLOBAL CRSNAME Local Area Networks
GLOBAL DUE $3,900
GLOBAL SQLEXITCODE 0
GLOBAL PLACE4 Dallas
126  quit;
```

Creating a Delimited List of Values

Sometimes, during execution of a PROC SQL step, you might want to create one macro variable that holds all values of a certain data set variable. You can use an alternate form of the INTO clause in order to take all of the values of a column (variable) and concatenate them into the value of one macro variable.

General form, SELECT statement with INTO clause for combining values into one macro variable:

PROC SQL NOPRINT;

      SELECT *column1*

          INTO :*macro-variable-1*

          SEPARATED BY *'delimiter1'*

          FROM *table-1 | view-1*

          <WHERE *expression*>

          <*other clauses*>;

QUIT;

Here is an explanation of the syntax:

column1
    specifies the column of the SQL table specified by *table-1 | view-1*.

:macro-variable-1
    names the macro variable to create.

delimiter1
    is enclosed in quotation marks and specifies the character that is used as a delimiter in the value of the macro variable.

expression
    produces a value that is used to subset the data.

other clauses
    are other valid clauses that group, subset, or order the data.

This form of the INTO clause removes leading and trailing blanks from each value before performing the concatenation of values.

Example

You can use the SQL procedure to create one macro variable named **sites** that contains the names of all training centers that appear in the Sasuser.Schedule data set. The names are separated by blanks.

```
proc sql noprint;
   select distinct location into :sites separated by ' '
      from sasuser.schedule;
quit;
```

Here is a representation of the macro variable **sites** as it is stored in the global symbol table after this PROC SQL step has run.

Global Symbol Table	
Sites	*Boston Dallas Seattle*

Now you can use the new macro variable in a title.

```
proc means data=sasuser.all sum maxdec=0;
   var fee;
   title1 'Total Revenue';
   title2 "from Course Sites: &sites";
run;
```

This is the output from the PROC MEANS step.

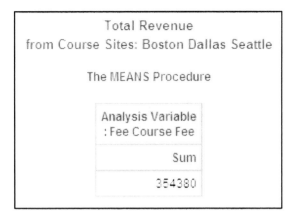

Working with PROC SQL Views

When you submit a PROC SQL step, the PROC SQL program code is placed into the input stack, and word scanning is performed for macro triggers in the same process as in other SAS programs.

In the following code, the macro variable reference **&crsid** is resolved during the creation of the PROC SQL view, resulting in a constant value whenever the view is used. For example, if the value of **crsid** is **C003** when this code is submitted, the view Subcrsid is based on the course code C003.

```
proc sql;
   create view subcrsid as
      select student_name, student_company,paid
         from sasuser.all
         where course_code="&crsid";
quit;
```

A better approach would be to use the SYMGET function to enable the view to look up the macro variable value. In the following example, the view Subcrsid is based on the value of **crsid** when the view is used:

```
proc sql;
   create view subcrsid as
      select student_name,student_company,paid
         from sasuser.all
         where course_code=symget('crsid');
quit;

%let crsid=C003;
proc print data=subcrsid noobs;
   title "Status of Students in Course Code &crsid";
run;

%let crsid=C004;
proc print data=subcrsid noobs;
   title "Status of Students in Course Code &crsid";
```

```
run;
```

PROC SQL does not perform automatic data conversion. You must use the INPUT function to convert the macro variable value to numeric if it is compared to a numeric variable.

The following code performs a query that is based on the numeric equivalent of the current value of the macro variable **crsnum**. The INPUT function is necessary in this WHERE statement because the value of the data set variable **Course_number** is numeric, but **crsnum** has a character value because it is a macro variable.

```
proc sql;
   create view subcnum as
      select student_name, student_company, paid
         from sasuser.all
         where course_number=input(symget('crsnum'),2.);
quit;

%let crsnum=4;
proc print data=subcnum noobs;
   title "Status of Students in Course Number &crsnum";
run;
```

Using Macro Variables in SCL Programs

Overview

SAS Component Language (SCL) programs are placed into the input stack, and word scanning is performed for macro triggers in the same process as in other SAS programs. Macro variable references that are outside of SUBMIT blocks are resolved before execution. Therefore, in the following example, a constant value is compared to the SCL variable **Wage** during SCL execution:

```
MAIN:
   erroroff wage;
   if wage gt &max then erroron wage;
return;
```

Any text within a SUBMIT block is assumed to be SAS code and is therefore ignored by the SCL compiler when the SCL program is compiled. Macro variable references within SUBMIT blocks are not resolved until the SUBMIT block executes and the SAS code within the SUBMIT block is tokenized.

When a SUBMIT block executes, SAS attempts to resolve a macro variable reference (&name) to a corresponding SCL variable. If there is no corresponding SCL variable, the reference is passed to the macro processor for lookup in the global symbol table. You can force a reference (&name) within a SUBMIT block to be passed as a macro variable reference by preceding the name with two ampersands (&&name).

Also, there are several functions and routines that enable SCL programs and the macro facility to exchange information at execution time. We examine these functions and routines.

You have already learned how to use the SYMPUT routine and the SYMGET function in a DATA step. Both the SYMPUT routine and the SYMGET function can be used in SCL programs. The syntax for each is exactly the same as it is in the DATA step.

Also, both the SYMPUT routine and the SYMGET function have numeric equivalents for use in SCL programs.

The SYMPUTN Routine

The SYMPUTN routine enables you to create a macro variable during execution of an SCL program and to assign a numeric value to it.

General form, SYMPUTN routine:

CALL SYMPUTN(*'macro-variable', value* **);**

Here is an explanation of the syntax:

macro-variable
> is the name of a global macro variable enclosed in single quotation marks with no ampersand. Alternatively, it is the name of an SCL variable (*not* enclosed in quotation marks) whose value is the name of a global macro variable.

value
> is the numeric value that is assigned to *macro-variable*, which can be a number of the name of a numeric SCL variable.

Example

Suppose the SCL variable `unitvar` has a value of `unit` and the SCL variable `unitnum` has a numeric value of 200. To create a macro variable whose name is the value of `unitvar` (in this case, `unit`) and assign a value equal to the value of the SCL variable `unitnum` (in this case, 200) you submit the following statement within a SUBMIT block:

```
call symputn(unitvar, unitnum);
```

Similarly, to create a macro variable named `unitvar` and assign a numeric value of 500 to it, you submit the following statement within a SUBMIT block.

```
call symputn('unitvar', 500);
```

The SYMGETN Function

The SYMGETN function enables you to obtain the numeric value of a macro variable during execution of an SCL program.

General form, SYMGETN function:

SCL-variable = **SYMGETN(** *'macro-variable'* **);**

Here is an explanation of the syntax:

SCL-variable
> is the name of a numeric SCL variable to which the value of *macro-variable* is assigned.

macro-variable
> is the name of a global macro variable enclosed in single quotation marks with no ampersand. Alternatively, it is the name of an SCL variable (*not* enclosed in quotation marks) whose value is the name of a global macro variable.

Example

Suppose the SCL variable `unitvar` has a value of `unit`, the macro variable `unit` has a value of 200, and the macro variable `unitvar` has a value of 500. The first statement below creates an SCL variable named `unitnum` and assigns to it a value of 200. The second statement creates an SCL variable named `unit` and assigns it a value of 500.

```
unitnum=symgetn(unitvar);
unit=symgetn('unitvar');
```

Note: For more information about using macro variables in SCL, see the SAS documentation for the macro language.

Summary

Text Summary

Creating a Macro Variable during DATA Step Execution

When you create or update a macro variable with the %LET statement, all macro processing takes place before the execution of the DATA step. The SYMPUT routine enables you to create or update macro variables during DATA step execution. Depending on how the arguments are coded, you can create either a single macro variable or multiple macro variables. You can use the SYMPUT routine with literal strings to create a macro variable and to assign either an exact name or an exact text value to it. You can use the SYMPUT routine with a DATA step variable to assign the value of that DATA step variable to a macro variable.

You can use the SYMPUTX routine to create or update a macro variable during DATA step execution, and to automatically strip leading and trailing blanks from the macro variable name and value. You can also use a DATA step expression as an argument to the SYMPUT routine in order to apply DATA step functions to a value before you assign that value to a macro variable. The PUT function is often useful in conjunction with the SYMPUT and SYMPUTX routines.

Creating Multiple Macro Variables during DATA Step Execution

You can use the SYMPUT or SYMPUTX routine with two DATA step expressions to create a series of related macro variables within one DATA step.

Referencing Macro Variables Indirectly

Sometimes, it is useful to use indirect references to macro variables. For example, you might want to use a macro variable to construct the name of another macro variable. You can reference a macro variable indirectly by preceding the macro variable name with two or more ampersands.

Obtaining Macro Variable Values during DATA Step Execution

The SYMGET function is used by both the DATA step and the SQL procedure to obtain the value of a macro variable during execution. You can use the SYMGET function to assign a macro variable value to a DATA step variable.

Creating Macro Variables during PROC SQL Step Execution
You can access the macro facility in a PROC SQL step by using the INTO clause in the SELECT statement. Various forms of the INTO clause enable you to create a series of macro variables, a varying number of macro variables, or a single macro variable that records a value that is created by concatenating the unique values of an SQL variable. You can use the NOPRINT option to prevent a PROC SQL step from creating output.

Working with PROC SQL Views
When you submit a PROC SQL step, the PROC SQL program code is placed into the input stack, and word scanning is performed for macro triggers in the same process as in other SAS programs.

Using Macro Variables in SCL Programs
SAS Component Language (SCL) also has routines and functions that assign values to macro variables and that obtain values from a macro symbol table. The SYMPUT routine and the SYMGET function can be used in an SCL program in the same way that they can be used in a DATA step program. Also, the SYMPUTN routine can be used to create macro variables and to assign numeric values to those variables during the execution of an SCL program. The SYMGETN function can be used to obtain the numeric value of a macro variable during the execution of an SCL program.

Sample Programs

Using CALL SYMPUT to Create Macro Variables
```
options symbolgen pagesize=30;
%let crsnum=3;
data revenue;
   set sasuser.all end=final;
   where course_number=&crsnum;
   total+1;
   if paid='Y' then paidup+1;
   if final then do;
      if paidup<total then do;
         call symput('foot','Some Fees Are Unpaid');
      end;
      else do;
         call symput('foot','All Students Have Paid');
      end;
   end;
run;
proc print data=revenue;
   var student_name student_company paid;
   title "Payment Status for Course &crsnum";
   footnote "&foot";
run;
```

Referencing Macro Variables Indirectly
```
options symbolgen;
data _null_;
   set sasuser.courses;
   call symput(course_code, trim(course_title));
run;
```

```
%let crsid=C005;
proc print data=sasuser.schedule noobs label;
    where course_code="&crsid";
    var location begin_date teacher;
    title1 "Schedule for &&&crsid";
run;

%let crsid=C002;
proc print data=sasuser.schedule noobs label;
    where course_code="&crsid";
    var location begin_date teacher;
    title1 "Schedule for &&&crsid";
run;
```

Using SYMGET to Obtain Macro Variable Values

```
data teachers;
    set sasuser.register;
    length Teacher $ 20;
    teacher=symget('teach'||left(course_number));
run;

proc print data=teachers;
    var student_name course_number teacher;
title1 "Teacher for Each Registered Student";
run;
```

Creating Macro Variables with the INTO Clause

```
proc sql noprint;
    select course_code, location, begin_date format=mmddyy10.
        into :crsid1-:crsid3,
             :place1-:place3,
             :date1-:date3
        from sasuser.schedule
        where year(begin_date)=2002
        order by begin_date;
quit;
```

Points to Remember

- The SYMPUT routine can be used to create or update macro variables during DATA step execution.

- The values of macro variables are always character values. In the DATA step, SYMPUT performs automatic numeric to character conversion on any numeric value that you attempt to assign to a macro variable.

- The SYMGET function can be used to obtain the value of a macro variable during the execution of a DATA step, a PROC SQL step, or an SCL program.

- The INTO clause can be used in the SELECT statement to create or update macro variables during execution of a PROC SQL step.

- The SYMPUT and SYMPUTN routines can be used to create or update macro variables during the execution of an SCL program.

Quiz

Select the best answer for each question. After completing the quiz, check your answers using the answer key in the appendix.

1. Which of the following is false?

   a. A %LET statement causes the macro processor to create a macro variable before the program is compiled.

   b. To create a macro variable that is based on data calculated by the DATA step, you use the SYMPUT function.

   c. Macro functions are always processed during the execution of the DATA step.

   d. Macro variable references in a DATA step are always resolved before DATA step execution.

2. Which of the following correctly creates a macro variable named **region** and assigns to it a value that is based on the value of the data set variable **Location**?

   a.
```
data new;
    set sasuser.all;
    if location='Boston' then do;
       call symput('region', 'East');
    end;
    else do;
       call symput('region', 'West');
    end;
run;
```

   b.
```
data new;
    set sasuser.all;
    if location='Boston' then do;
       %let region=East;
    end;
    else
       %let region=West;
    end;
run;
```

   c.
```
data new;
    set sasuser.all;
    if location='Boston' then do;
       call symput(region, "East");
    end;
    else
       call symput(region, "West");
    end;
run;
```

   d.
```
data new;
    set sasuser.all;
    if location='Boston' then do;
       symput(region, East);
    end;
```

```
        else
            symput(region, West);
        end;
    run;
```

3. The SYMPUT routine cannot

   a. be used to assign a data set variable as a value to a macro variable.

   b. create a series of macro variables in one DATA step.

   c. automatically convert a numeric value to a character value when used to assign a value to a macro variable in a DATA step.

   d. be used to assign a numeric value to a macro variable in an SCL program.

4. Which of the following programs correctly creates a series of macro variables whose names are values of the data set variable **Course_code**, then indirectly references one of those macro variables in a later step?

   a.
   ```
   data _null_;
       set sasuser.courses;
       call symput(course_code, trim(course_title));
   %let crsid=C005;
   proc print data=sasuser.schedule noobs label;
       where course_code="&crsid";
       var location begin_date teacher;
       title1 "Schedule for &c005";
   run;
   ```

   b.
   ```
   data _null_;
       set sasuser.courses;
       call symput(course_code, trim(course_title));
   run;
   %let crsid=C005;
   proc print data=sasuser.schedule noobs label;
       where course_code="&crsid";
       var location begin_date teacher;
       title1 "Schedule for &&&crsid";
   run;
   ```

   c.
   ```
   data _null_;
       set sasuser.courses;
       call symput('course_code', trim(course_title));
   run;
   %let crsid=C005;
   proc print data=sasuser.schedule noobs label;
       where course_code="&crsid";
       var location begin_date teacher;
       title1 "Schedule for &&&crsid";
   run;
   ```

   d.
   ```
   data _null_;
       set sasuser.courses;
       call symget(course_code, trim(course_title));
   run;

   %let crsid=C005;
   proc print data=sasuser.schedule noobs label;
       where course_code="&crsid";
       var location begin_date teacher;
   ```

```
        title1 "Schedule for &&&crsid";
    run;
```

5. Which of the following statements about the resolution of macro variable references is false?

    a. Two ampersands resolve to one ampersand.

    b. If more than four consecutive ampersands precede a name token, the macro processor generates an error message.

    c. Re-scanning continues until there are no remaining macro triggers that the macro processor can resolve.

    d. The macro processor always re-scans a name token that is preceded by multiple ampersands or by multiple percent signs.

6. In which of the following situations would you use SYMGET rather than a macro variable reference (`&macvar`)?

    a. to create a DATA step variable from a macro variable value during the execution of the DATA step

    b. to include a macro variable reference in a PROC SQL view

    c. to access the value of a macro variable during the execution of an SCL program

    d. all of the above

7. Which of the following correctly creates a macro variable in a PROC SQL step?

    a. `call symput(daily_fee, put(fee/days, dollar8.);`

    b. `%let daily_fee=put(fee/days, dollar8.)`

    c. `select fee/days format=dollar8.`
       `into :daily_fee from sasuser.all;`

    d. `select fee/days format=dollar8.`
       `into daily_fee from sasuser.all;`

8. According to the global symbol table shown here, what is the resolved value for a reference to `&&teach&crs`?

Global Symbol Table	
TEACH1	*Hallis, Dr. George*
TEACH2	*Wickam, Dr. Alice*
TEACH3	*Forest, Mr. Peter*
CRS	*3*

    a. &TEACH3

    b. TEACH3

    c. Forest, Mr. Peter

    d. none of the above

9. Which of the following statements correctly creates a DATA step variable named **Price** and assigns to it the value of the macro variable **daily_fee** during DATA step execution?

    a. `price=&daily_fee;`

    b. `price=symget(daily_fee);`

    c. `price=symget(&daily_fee);`

    d. `price=symget("daily_fee");`

10. Which of the following is false?

    a. The SYMPUT routine can be used to create a macro variable during execution of the DATA step or during execution of an SCL program.

    b. In the DATA step, the SYMPUT routine automatically converts to a character value any numeric value that you attempt to assign as the value of a macro variable.

    c. PROC SQL automatically converts to a numeric value any macro variable value that you attempt to compare to a numeric value.

    d. In an SCL program, the SYMPUTN routine can be used to assign a numeric value to a macro variable.

Chapter 11

Creating and Using Macro Programs

Overview

Introduction

Like macro variables, macro programs (also known as macros) enable you to substitute text into your SAS programs. Macros are different from macro variables because they can use conditional logic to make decisions about the text that you substitute into your programs. Using macros can help make your SAS programs more dynamic and reusable.

For example, suppose you submit a SAS program every day to create registration listings for courses that are to be held later in the current month. Then, suppose that every Friday you also submit a SAS program to create a summary of revenue that has been generated so far in the current month. By using a macro, you can automate the process so that only one SAS program is required. This program submits the daily report and conditionally submits the weekly report if it is Friday. Furthermore, you could create and store a macro that would automate this process, and the only code that you would need to submit each day is this:

```
%reports
```

Basic Concepts

Defining a Macro

In order to create a macro program, you must first define it. You begin a macro definition with a %MACRO statement, and you end the definition with a %MEND statement.

General form, %MACRO statement, and %MEND statement:

%MACRO *macro-name*;

     text

%MEND <*macro-name*>;

Here is an explanation of the syntax:

macro-name
> names the macro. The value of *macro-name* can be any valid SAS name that is not a reserved word in the SAS macro facility.

text
> can be

- constant text, possibly including SAS data set names, SAS variable names, or SAS statements

- macro variables, macro functions, or macro program statements

- any combination of the above.

> *TIP* You might want to include *macro-name* in the %MEND statement in order to make your program more readable. However, the inclusion of *macro-name* in the %MEND statement is entirely optional.

Example

This program creates a macro named **Prtlast** that prints the most recently created data set. (Remember that the automatic macro variable SYSLAST stores the name of the most recently created data set.)

```
%macro prtlast;
   proc print data=&syslast (obs=5);
   title "Listing of &syslast data set";
   run;
%mend;
```

Compiling a Macro

In order to use this macro later in your SAS programs, you must first compile it by submitting the macro definition, as follows:

```
%macro prtlast;
   proc print data=&syslast (obs=5);
```

```
      title "Listing of &syslast data set";
      run;
%mend;
```

When you submit this code, the word scanner divides the macro into tokens and sends the tokens to the macro processor for compilation. The macro processor

- checks all macro language statements for syntax errors (non-macro language statements are not checked until the macro is executed).

- writes error messages to the SAS log and creates a dummy (non-executable) macro if any syntax errors are found in the macro language statements.

- stores all compiled macro language statements and constant text in a SAS catalog entry if no syntax errors are found in the macro language statements. By default, a catalog named Work.Sasmacr is opened, and a catalog entry named Macro-name.Macro is created.

That is, if there are no syntax errors in the macro language statements within the macro, the text between the %MACRO statement and the %MEND statement is stored under the name **Prtlast** for execution at a later time.

Note: You can also store a compiled macro in a permanent SAS catalog. You can learn how to do this in Chapter 12, "Storing Macro Programs," on page 422.

The MCOMPILENOTE= Option

The MCOMPILENOTE= option causes a note to be issued to the SAS log when a macro has completed compilation.

General form, MCOMPILENOTE= option:

OPTIONS MCOMPILENOTE= NONE | NOAUTOCALL | ALL**;**

The option can take one of the three values listed. Here is an explanation of the syntax:

NONE
    is the default value, which specifies that no notes are issued to the log.

NOAUTOCALL
    specifies that a note is issued to the log for completed macro compilations for all macros except autocall macros.

ALL
    specifies that a note is issued to the log for all completed macro compilations.

Note: You can learn more about autocall macros in Chapter 12, "Storing Macro Programs," on page 422.

Example

A macro might actually compile and still contain errors. If there are any errors, an ERROR message is written to the SAS log in addition to the note. Here is an example of the note that is written to the log when a macro compiles without errors:

```
options mcompilenote=all;
%macro mymacro;
%mend mymacro;
```

Table 11.1 *SAS Log*

```
1    options mcompilenote=all;
2    %macro mymacro;
3    %mend mymacro;
NOTE: The macro MYMACRO completed compilation without errors.
```

Calling a Macro

After the macro is successfully compiled, you can use it in your SAS programs for the duration of your SAS session without resubmitting the macro definition. Just as you must reference macro variables in order to access them in your code, you must call a macro program in order to execute it within your SAS program.

A macro call

- is specified by placing a percent sign (%) before the name of the macro

- can be made anywhere in a program except within the data lines of a DATALINES statement (similar to a macro variable reference)

- requires no semicolon because it is not a SAS statement.

To execute the macro **Prtlast** you would call the macro as follows:

```
%prtlast
```

CAUTION:

A semicolon after a macro call might insert an inappropriate semicolon into the resulting program, leading to errors during compilation or execution.

Macros come in three types, depending on how they are called: name style, command style, and statement style. Of the three, name style is the most efficient. This is because calls to name style macros always begin with a percent sign (%), which immediately tells the word scanner to pass the token to the macro processor. With the other two types, the word scanner does not know immediately whether the token should be sent to the macro processor or not. Therefore, time is wasted while the word scanner determines this. All of the macros in this chapter are name style macros.

Example

Suppose a SAS program consists of several program steps that create SAS data sets. Suppose that after each of these program steps that you want to print out the data set that has been created. Remember that the macro **Prtlast** prints the most recently created data set. If **Prtlast** has been compiled, you can call it after each step in order to print each data set.

```
proc sort data=sasuser.courses out=courses;
   by course_code;
run;

%prtlast

proc sort data=sasuser.schedule out=schedule;
   by begin_date;
run;
```

```
%prtlast

proc sort data=sasuser.students out=students;
   by student_name;
run;

%prtlast
```

Note: The example above is simply meant to show you how you can incorporate a macro into your SAS program. Although this is a valid use of the **Prtlast** macro, this might not be the best way to code this example. Since the **Prtlast** macro uses no conditional logic or macro programming statements and it makes no decisions, this example does not illustrate the full power of a macro program. In the rest of this chapter, you see examples of macro programs that are more useful than this one.

Macro Execution

When you call a macro in your SAS program, the word scanner passes the macro call to the macro processor, because the percent sign that precedes the macro name is a macro trigger. When the macro processor receives *%macro-name*, it

1. searches the designated SAS catalog (Work.Sasmacr by default) for an entry named **Macro-name.Macro**

2. executes compiled macro language statements within *Macro-name*

3. sends any remaining text in *Macro-name* to the input stack for word scanning

4. suspends macro execution when the SAS compiler receives a global SAS statement or when it encounters a SAS step boundary

5. resumes execution of macro language statements after the SAS code executes.

Later in this chapter you see detailed examples of macro execution. These examples make more sense once you have learned how to write a more complex macro program than you have seen so far in this chapter.

For now, remember that the macro call is processed by the macro processor before any SAS language statements such as DATA steps are compiled or executed. During macro execution, the macro processor can communicate directly with the following:

*   both global and local symbol tables. For example, the macro processor can store macro variable values with a %LET statement and can resolve macro variable references.

*   the input stack. For example, the macro processor can generate SAS code for tokenization by the word scanner.

Note: You learn more about global and local symbol tables later in this chapter.

Example

This example demonstrates macro execution. Assume that the **Prtlast** macro has been compiled and that it has been stored in the Work.Sasmacr catalog.

1. First, you submit the macro call, as follows:

    ```
    %prtlast
    ```

2. When the word scanner encounters this call, it passes the call to the macro processor. The macro processor searches for the compiled macro in the catalog entry **Work.Sasmacr.Prtlast.Macro**.

Catalog Entry

```
%macro prtlast;
   proc print data=&syslast(obs=5);
   title "Listing of &syslast data set";
   run;
%mend;
```

3. The macro processor begins executing compiled macro language statements. However, in this example, no compiled macro statements are included in the macro.

4. The macro processor places noncompiled items (SAS language statements) on the input stack, and pauses as the word scanner tokenizes the inserted text. In this example, the macro processor places the PROC PRINT step on the input stack.

Input Stack

```
proc print data=&syslast(obs=5);
   title "Listing of &syslast data set";
run;
```

5. The word scanner passes these tokens to the compiler. When the word scanner encounters a macro variable reference such as &syslast, it passes the reference to the macro processor for resolution. The macro processor returns the macro variable value to the input stack and word scanning continues.

6. After all of the statements in the PROC PRINT step have been compiled, the PROC PRINT step is executed, and SAS creates output that includes only the first five observations of the most recently created data set.

7. Once the PROC PRINT step has been executed, the macro processor resumes execution of any remaining macro language statements in the macro (there are none in this example). The macro processor ends execution when it reaches the %MEND statement.

Assume that the most recently created data set is Work.Practice (which is a copy of Sasuser.Courses). Here is the output that is generated by calling the **Prtlast** macro.

		Listing of WORK.PRACTICE data set		
Obs	Course_Code	Course_Title	Days	Fee
1	C001	Basic Telecommunications	3	$795
2	C002	Structured Query Language	4	$1150
3	C003	Local Area Networks	3	$650
4	C004	Database Design	2	$375
5	C005	Artificial Intelligence	2	$400

Here is an example of messages that are written to the SAS log when **%prtlast** is submitted, assuming that the most recently created data set is Work.Practice.

Table 11.2 *SAS Log*

```
37    %prtlast

NOTE: Writing HTML Body file: sashtm3.htm
NOTE: There were 5 observations read from the data set
      WORK.PRACTICE.
NOTE: PROCEDURE PRINT used (Total process time):
      real time           0.04 seconds
      cpu time            0.03 seconds
```

Notice that in this SAS log message, you see a note from PROC PRINT, but not the PROC PRINT code itself since the call to the macro does not display the text that is sent to the compiler.

This example depicts the processing and execution of a simple macro. Later in this chapter you see how more-complex macros that include compiled macro language statements are handled by the macro processor.

Developing and Debugging Macros

Monitoring Execution with System Options

In the last example, you saw that when you call a macro, the text that is sent to the compiler does not appear in the SAS log. But sometimes you might want to see this text. There are SAS system options that can display information about the execution of a macro in the SAS log. This can be especially helpful for debugging purposes.

The MPRINT Option

When the MPRINT option is specified, the text that is sent to the SAS compiler as a result of macro execution is printed in the SAS log.

General form, MPRINT | NOMPRINT option:

OPTIONS MPRINT | NOMPRINT;

Here is an explanation of the syntax:

NOMPRINT
> is the default setting, and specifies that the text that is sent to the compiler when a macro executes is not printed in the SAS log.

MPRINT
> specifies that the text that is sent to the compiler when a macro executes is printed in the SAS log.

You might want to specify the MPRINT system option with the following conditions:

• you have a SAS syntax error or execution error

• you want to see the generated SAS code.

The MPRINT system option is often synchronized with the SOURCE system option to show, or hide, executed SAS code.

Example

Suppose you want to call the **Prtlast** macro and to use the MPRINT system option to show the SAS code that results from the macro execution.

Catalog Entry

```
%macro prtlast;
   proc print data=&syslast (obs=5);
      title "Listing of &syslast data set";
   run;
%mend;
```

The following sample code creates a data set named Sales, specifies the MPRINT option, and references the **Prtlast** macro:

```
data sales;
   price_code=1;
run;
options mprint;
%prtlast
```

The messages that are written to the SAS log show the text that is sent to the compiler. Notice that the macro variable reference (&SYSLAST) is resolved to the value Work.Sales in the MPRINT messages that are written to the SAS log.

Table 11.3 *SAS Log*

```
101  %prtlast
MPRINT(PRTLAST): proc print data=WORK.SALES (obs=5);
MPRINT(PRTLAST): title "Listing of WORK.SALES";
MPRINT(PRTLAST): run;
NOTE: There were 1 observations read from the dataset WORK.SALES.
NOTE: PROCEDURE PRINT used:
      real time           0.04 seconds
      cpu time            0.04 seconds
```

The MLOGIC Option

Another system option that might be useful when you debug your programs is the MLOGIC option. The MLOGIC option prints messages that indicate macro actions that were taken during macro execution.

General form, MLOGIC | NOMLOGIC option:

OPTIONS MLOGIC | NOMLOGIC;

Here is an explanation of the syntax:

NOMLOGIC
   is the default setting, and specifies that messages about macro actions are not printed to the SAS log during macro execution.

MLOGIC
   specifies that messages about macro actions are printed to the log during macro execution.

When the MLOGIC system option is in effect, the information that is displayed in SAS log messages includes

* the beginning of macro execution

* the values of macro parameters at invocation

* the execution of each macro program statement

* whether each %IF condition is true or false

* the end of macro execution.

Example

Suppose you want to repeat the previous example with only the MLOGIC system option in effect. This sample code creates a data set named Sales, sets the MLOGIC system option, and calls the **Prtlast** macro.

```
data sales;
   price_code=1;
run;
options nomprint mlogic;
%prtlast
```

When this code is submitted, the messages that are written to the SAS log show the beginning and the end of macro processing.

Table 11.4 *SAS Log*

```
107    %prtlast
MLOGIC(PRTLAST): Beginning execution.
NOTE: There were 1 observations read from the dataset WORK.SALES.
NOTE: PROCEDURE PRINT used:
      real time           0.02 seconds
      cpu time            0.02 seconds
MLOGIC(PRTLAST): Ending execution.
```

The MLOGIC option, along with the SYMBOLGEN option, is typically turned

* on for development and debugging purposes

* off when the application is in production mode.

Comments in Macro Programs

As with any other programs, your macro programs might benefit from comments. Comments can be especially helpful if you plan to save your macros permanently or to share them with other users. You can place comments within a macro definition by using the macro comment statement.

General form, macro comment statement:

%*comment*;

Here is an explanation of the syntax:

comment
> can be any message. Like other SAS statements, each macro comment statement ends with a semicolon.

Example

The following code uses macro comments to describe the functionality of the macro:

```
%macro printit;
   %* The value of &syslast will be substituted appropriately ;
   %* as long as a data set has been created during this session. ;
   proc print data=&syslast(obs=5);
/* Print only the first 5 observations */
   title "Last Created Data Set Is &syslast";
   run;
%mend;
```

Note: You can also use the comment symbols /* and */ inside a macro. When these symbols appear, the macro processor ignores the text within the comment.

Using Macro Parameters

You have seen the basic form for a macro definition. Your macros often contain macro variables. To make your macros more dynamic, you could use the %LET statement to update the values of the macro variables that are used within the macros. However, parameter lists in your macro definitions enable you to update the macro variables within your macro programs more conveniently. A parameter list is an optional part of the %MACRO statement that names one or more macro variables whose values you specify when you call the macro.

Example

Suppose the compiled macro **Printdsn** contains references to the macro variables **dsn** (which records a data set name) and **vars** (which records a list of data set variables), as follows:

```
%macro printdsn;
   proc print data=&dsn;
      var &vars;
   title "Listing of %upcase(&dsn) data set";
   run;
%mend;
```

You could modify the behavior of **Printdsn** by changing the value of macro variable **dsn** or **vars** with a %LET statement before you call the macro. For example, you could substitute sasuser.courses for **dsn** and course_code course_title days for **vars** at macro execution, as follows:

```
%let dsn=sasuser.courses;
%let vars=course_code course_title days;
%printdsn
```

If the MPRINT system option is turned on when this code is submitted, the following messages are written to the SAS log. Notice that the values that you provided in the %LET statements have been substituted into the macro when it appears in the SAS log.

Table 11.5 *SAS Log*

```
7      options mprint;
8      %let dsn=sasuser.courses;
9      %let vars=course_code course_title days;
10     %printdsn
NOTE: Writing HTML Body file: sashtm.htm
MPRINT(PRINTDSN):  proc print data=sasuser.courses;
MPRINT(PRINTDSN):  var course_code course_title days;
MPRINT(PRINTDSN):  title "Listing of SASUSER.COURSES data set";
MPRINT(PRINTDSN):  run;
NOTE: There were 6 observations read from the data set
      SASUSER.COURSES.
NOTE: PROCEDURE PRINT used (Total process time):
      real time           6.59 seconds
      cpu time            0.28 seconds
```

Then you could submit new %LET statements in order to change the value of **dsn** to sasuser.schedule and to change the value of **vars** to course_code location begin_date when the macro executes, as follows:

```
%let dsn=sasuser.schedule;
%let vars=course_code location begin_date;
%printdsn
```

The messages that are written to the SAS log when this code is submitted show that the new values have been substituted for the macro variable references in the macro.

Table 11.6 *SAS Log*

```
11    %let dsn=sasuser.schedule;
12    %let vars=course_code location begin_date;
13    %printdsn
MPRINT(PRINTDSN):  proc print data=sasuser.schedule;
MPRINT(PRINTDSN):  var course_code location begin_date;
MPRINT(PRINTDSN):  title "Listing of SASUSER.SCHEDULE data set";
MPRINT(PRINTDSN):  run;
NOTE: Writing HTML Body file: sashtm1.htm
NOTE: There were 18 observations read from the data set
      SASUSER.SCHEDULE.
NOTE: PROCEDURE PRINT used (Total process time):
      real time           0.76 seconds
      cpu time            0.08 seconds
```

You can make these macro variables easier to update by using parameters in the macro definition to create the macro variables. Then you can pass values to the macro variables each time you call the macro rather than using separate %LET statements. The next few sections show how to use various types of parameters to create macro variables.

Macros That Include Positional Parameters

When you include positional parameters in a macro definition, a macro variable is automatically created for each parameter when you call the macro. To define macros that include positional parameters, you list the names of macro variables in the %MACRO statement of the macro definition. Positional parameters are so named because the order in which you specify them in a macro definition determines the order in which they are assigned values from the macro call. That is, when you call a macro that includes positional parameters, you specify the values of the macro variables that are defined in the parameters in the same order in which they are defined.

General form, macro definition that includes positional parameters:

%MACRO *macro-name(parameter-1<,...,parameter-n>)*;

   text

%MEND *<macro-name>*;

Here is an explanation of the syntax:

parameter-1<,...,parameter-n>
   specifies one or more positional parameters, separated by commas. You must supply each parameter with a name: you cannot use a text expression to generate it.

To call a macro that includes positional parameters, precede the name of the macro with a percent sign, and enclose the parameter values in parentheses. List the values in the same order in which the parameters are listed in the macro definition, and separate them with commas, as follows:

%macro-name(value-1<,...,value-n>)

The values listed in a macro call

- can be null values, text, macro variable references, or macro calls

- are assigned to the parameter variables using a one-to-one correspondence.

Example

You can use positional parameters to create the macro variables **dsn** and **vars** in the **Printdsn** macro definition, as follows:

```
%macro printdsn(dsn,vars);
   proc print data=&dsn;
      var &vars;
   title "Listing of %upcase(&dsn) data set";
   run;
%mend;
```

In this case, when you call the **Printdsn** macro you assign values to the macro variables that are created in the parameters. In the following example, the value **sasuser.courses** is assigned to the macro variable **dsn**, and the value **course_codecourse_title days** is assigned to the macro variable **vars**. Notice that the value for **dsn** is listed first and the value for **vars** is listed second, since this is the order in which they are listed in the macro definition.

```
%printdsn(sasuser.courses,course_code course_title days)
```

> *Note:* To substitute a null value for one or more positional parameters, use commas as placeholders for the omitted values, as follows:

```
%printdsn(,course_code course_title days)
```

Macros That Include Keyword Parameters

You can also include keyword parameters in a macro definition. Like positional parameters, keyword parameters create macro variables. However, when you use keyword parameters to create macro variables, you specify the name, followed by the equal sign, and the value of each macro variable in the macro definition.

Keyword parameters can be listed in any order. Whatever value you assign to each parameter (or variable) in the %MACRO statement becomes its default value. Null values are allowed.

General form, macro definition that includes keyword parameters:

%MACRO *macro-name(keyword-1=<value-1><,...,keyword-n=<value-n>>)*;

    text

%MEND *<macro-name>*;

Here is an explanation of the syntax:

keyword-1=<value-1><,...,keyword-n=<value-n>>
    names one or more macro parameters followed by equal signs. You can specify default values after the equal signs. If you omit a default value, the keyword parameter has a null value.

When you call a macro whose definition includes keyword parameters, you specify the keyword, followed by the equal sign, and the value for each parameter. The order is not important. If you omit a keyword parameter from the macro call, the keyword variable retains its default value, as follows:

```
%macro-name(keyword-1=value-1<,...,keyword-n=value-n>)
```

Example

You can use keyword parameters to create the macro variables **dsn** and **vars** in the **Printdsn** macro. This example assigns a default value of **sasuser.courses** to the macro variable **dsn** and assigns a default value of **course_codecourse_title days** to the macro variable **vars**:

```
%macro printdsn(dsn=sasuser.courses,
             vars=
course_code course_title days);
   proc print data=&dsn;
      var &vars;
   title "Listing of %upcase(&dsn) data set";
   run;
%mend;
```

To invoke the **Printdsn** macro with a value of **sasuser.schedule** for **dsn** and a value of **teacher course_titlebegin_date** for **vars**, issue the following call:

```
%printdsn(dsn=sasuser.schedule, vars=teacher course_code begin_date)
```

To call the `Printdsn` macro with default values for the parameters
(`sasuser.courses` as the value for `dsn` and `course_codecourse_title days`
as the value for `vars`), you could issue the following call:

```
%printdsn()
```

Note: To call the macro `Printdsn` with default values for the parameters, you could
also issue a macro call that specified these values explicitly, as follows:

```
%printdsn(dsn=sasuser.courses,vars=course_code course_title days)
```

Macros That Include Mixed Parameter Lists

You can also include a parameter list that contains both positional and keyword
parameters in your macro definitions. All positional parameter variables in the
%MACRO statement must be listed before any keyword parameter variable is listed.

General form, macro definition that includes mixed parameters:

%MACRO *macro-name(parameter-1<,...,parameter-n>,*

    keyword-1=<value-1><,...,keyword-n=<value-n>>);

    text

%MEND;

Here is an explanation of the syntax:

parameter-1<,...,parameter-n>
    is listed before *keyword-1=<value-1><,...,keyword-n=<value-n>>.*

Similarly, when you call a macro that includes a mixed parameter list, you must list the
positional values before any keyword values, as follows:

```
%macro-name(value-1<,...,value-n>,
            keyword-1=value-1<,...,keyword-n=value-n>)
```

Example

You can use a combination of positional and keyword parameters to create the macro
variables in the `Printdsn` macro definition. This code uses a positional parameter to
create the macro variable `dsn`, and a keyword parameter to create the macro variable
`vars`:

```
%macro printdsn(dsn, vars=course_title course_code days);
   proc print data=&dsn;
      var &vars;
   title "Listing of %upcase(&dsn) data set";
   run;
%mend;
```

The following call to the `Printdsn` macro assigns the value `sasuser.schedule` to
the macro variable `dsn` and assigns the value `teacher location begin_date` to
the macro variable `vars`. Notice that the value for `dsn` is listed first, since `dsn` is the
positional parameter.

```
%printdsn(sasuser.schedule, vars=teacher location begin_date)
```

Now, suppose you want to execute the `Printdsn` macro, assigning the default value
`course_titlecourse_code days` to the macro variable `vars` and assigning the

value `sasuser.courses` to the macro variable `dsn`. You could issue the following call:

```
%printdsn(sasuser.courses)
```

Because this call omits the keyword parameter (`vars`), the default value for that parameter is used.

Macros That Include the PARMBUFF Option

You can use the PARMBUFF option in a macro definition to create a macro that can accept a varying number of parameters at each invocation. The PARMBUFF option assigns the entire list of parameter values in a macro call, including the parentheses in a name-style invocation, as the value of the automatic macro variable SYSPBUFF.

General form, macro definition with the PARMBUFF option:

%MACRO *macro-name* **/PARMBUFF;**

>   *text*

%MEND;

Here is an explanation of the syntax:

text
> contains a reference to the automatic macro variable **SYSPBUFF**.

Example

The following macro definition creates a macro named `Printz`. `Printz` uses a varying number of parameters and the automatic macro variable SYSPBUFF to display the parameters that are specified in the macro call. The macro also uses a loop to print the data sets that are named as parameters.

```
%macro printz/parmbuff;
   %put Syspbuff contains: &syspbuff;
   %local num;
   %do num=1 %to %sysfunc(countw(&syspbuff));
   %let dsname=%scan(&syspbuff,&num);
      proc print data=sasuser.&dsname;
      run;
   %end;
%mend printz;
```

If you submit a call to the macro that includes two parameters, the `Printz` macro writes the following line to the SAS log and causes two data sets to be printed

```
%printz(courses, schedule)
```

Table 11.7 *SAS Log*

```
Syspbuff contains: (courses,schedule)
```

If you submit a call to the macro that includes one parameter, the `Printz` macro writes the following line to the SAS log and causes one data set to be printed:

```
%printz(courses)
```

Table 11.8   *SAS Log*

```
Syspbuff contains: (courses)
```

Note: If the macro definition includes both a set of parameters and the PARMBUFF option, the macro invocation causes the parameters to receive values and the entire invocation list of values to be assigned to SYSPBUFF.

Understanding Symbol Tables

The Global Symbol Table

You are already somewhat familiar with the global symbol table. Remember that automatic macro variables are stored in the global symbol table. User-defined macro variables that you create with a %LET statement in open code (code that is outside of a macro definition) are also stored in the global symbol table.

Global Symbol Table	
SYSDATE	04APR11
SYSDAY	Monday
SYSVER	9.2
uservar1	value1
uservar2	value2

The global symbol table is created during the initialization of a SAS session and is deleted at the end of the session. Macro variables in the global symbol table

- are available anytime during the session
- can be created by a user
- have values that can be changed during the session (except for some automatic macro variables).

You can create a global macro variable with the following:

- a %LET statement (used outside a macro definition)
- a DATA step that contains a SYMPUT routine
- a DATA step that contains a SYMPUTX routine
- a SELECT statement that contains an INTO clause in PROC SQL
- a %GLOBAL statement.

You should already be familiar with the %LET statement, the SYMPUT routine, and the INTO clause. Let's examine the %GLOBAL statement.

The %GLOBAL Statement

The %GLOBAL statement

- creates one or more macro variables in the global symbol table and assigns null values to them

- can be used either inside or outside a macro definition

- has no effect on variables that are already in the global symbol table.

General form, %GLOBAL statement:

%GLOBAL *macro-variable-1 <...macro-variable-n>*;

Here is an explanation of the syntax:

macro-variable
is either the name of a macro variable or a text expression that generates a macro variable name.

Example

To create a global macro variable inside a macro definition, you can use the %GLOBAL statement. The %GLOBAL statement in the following example creates two global macro variables, **dsn** and **vars**. The %LET statements assign values to the new global macro variables, as follows:

```
%macro printdsn;
   %global dsn vars;
   %let dsn=sasuser.courses;
   %let vars=course_title course_code days;
   proc print data=&dsn;
      var &vars;
   title "Listing of &dsn data set";
   run;
%mend;
```

```
%printdsn
```

Note: You use the %SYMDEL statement to delete a macro variable from the global symbol table during a SAS session. To remove the macro variable **dsn** from the global symbol table, you submit the following statement:

```
%symdel dsn;
```

The Local Symbol Table

A local symbol table is created when a macro that includes a parameter list is called or when a request is made to create a local variable during macro execution. The local symbol table is deleted when the macro finishes execution. That is, the local symbol table exists only while the macro executes.

Local Symbol Table	
parameter1	*value1*
parameter2	*value2*
uservar1	*value1*
uservar2	*value2*

The local symbol table contains macro variables that can be

- created and initialized at macro invocation (that is, by parameters)
- created or updated during macro execution
- referenced anywhere within the macro.

You can create local macro variables with the following:

- parameters in a macro definition
- a %LET statement within a macro definition
- a DATA step that contains a SYMPUT routine within a macro definition
- a DATA step that contains a SYMPUTX routine within a macro definition
- a SELECT statement that contains an INTO clause in PROC SQL within a macro definition
- a %LOCAL statement.

Note: The SYMPUT routine can create a local macro variable if a local symbol table already exists. If no local symbol table exists when the SYMPUT routine executes, it creates a global macro variable.

You have already learned about using parameters in macro definitions. You should also already be familiar with the %LET statement, the SYMPUT routine, and the INTO clause. Let's examine the %LOCAL statement.

The %LOCAL Statement

The %LOCAL statement

- can appear only inside a macro definition
- creates one or more macro variables in the local symbol table and assigns null values to them
- has no effect on variables that are already in the local symbol table.

A local symbol table is not created until a request is made to create a local variable. Macros that do not create local variables do not have a local table. Remember, the SYMPUT routine can create local variables only if the local table already exists.

Since local symbol tables exist separately from the global symbol table, it is possible to have a local macro variable and a global macro variable that have the same name and different values.

Example

In this example, the first %LET statement creates a global macro variable named **dsn** and assigns a value of **sasuser.courses** to it.

The %LOCAL statement within the macro definition creates a local macro variable named **dsn**, and the %LET statement within the macro definition assigns a value of **sasuser.register** to the local variable **dsn**.

The %PUT statement within the macro definition writes the value of the local variable **dsn** to the SAS log, whereas the %PUT statement that follows the macro definition writes the value of the global variable **dsn** to the SAS log:

```
%let dsn=sasuser.courses;

%macro printdsn;
   %local dsn;
   %let dsn=sasuser.register;
   %put The value of DSN inside Printdsn is &dsn;
%mend;

%printdsn
%put The value of DSN outside Printdsn is &dsn;
```

When you submit this code, the following statements are written to the SAS log.

Table 11.9 SAS Log

```
199  %let dsn=sasuser.courses;
200
201  %macro printdsn;
202      %local dsn;
203      %let dsn=sasuser.register;
204      %put The value of DSN inside Printdsn is &dsn;
205  %mend;
206
207  %printdsn
The value of DSN inside Printdsn is sasuser.register
208  %put The value of DSN outside Printdsn is &dsn;
The value of DSN outside Printdsn is sasuser.courses
```

Rules for Creating and Updating Variables

When the macro processor receives a request to create or update a macro variable during macro execution, the macro processor follows certain rules.

Suppose the macro processor receives a %LET statement during a macro call, as follows:

```
%let macvar=value;
```

The macro processor processes the following steps:

1. The macro processor checks to see whether the macro variable **macvar** already exists in the local symbol table. If so, the macro processor updates **macvar** in the

local symbol table with the value *value*. If `macvar` does not exist in the local table, the macro processor goes on to step 2.

2. The macro processor checks to see whether the macro variable `macvar` already exists in the global symbol table. If so, the macro processor updates `macvar` in the global symbol table with the value *value*. If `macvar` does not exist in the global symbol table, the macro processor goes on to step 3.

3. The macro processor creates a macro variable named `macvar` in the local symbol table and assigns a value of *value* to it.

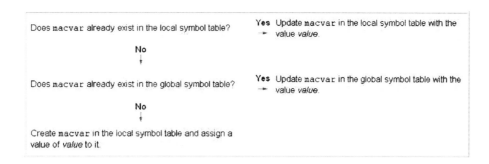

Similarly, suppose the macro processor receives the following reference during a macro call:

`&macvar`

The macro processor takes the following steps:

1. The macro processor checks to see whether the macro variable `macvar` exists in the local symbol table. If so, the macro processor retrieves the value of `macvar` from the local symbol table. If `macvar` does not exist in the local table, the macro processor goes on to step 2.

2. The macro processor checks to see whether the macro variable `macvar` exists in the global symbol table. If so, the macro processor retrieves the value of `macvar` from the global symbol table. If `macvar` does not exist in the global symbol table, the macro processor goes on to step 3.

3. The macro processor returns the tokens to the word scanner. A warning message is written to the SAS log to indicate that the reference was not resolved.

Note: Remember that if the macro processor receives either a %LET statement or a macro variable reference (`&macvar`) in open code, it checks only the global symbol table for existence of the macro variable. If a macro program is not currently executing, a local symbol table does not currently exist.

Multiple Local Symbol Tables

Multiple local symbol tables can exist concurrently during macro execution if you have nested macros. That is, if you define a macro program that calls another macro program, and if both macros create local symbol tables, then two local symbol tables exists while the second macro executes.

Example

Suppose the following two macros, `Outer` and `Inner`, have been compiled. The macro named `Outer` creates a local macro variable named `variX` and assigns a value of `one` to it. Then `Outer` calls another macro program named `Inner`. The macro named *Inner* creates a local macro variable named `variY` and assigns the value of `variX` to it.

```
%macro outer;
   %local variX;
   %let variX=one;
   %inner
%mend outer;

%macro inner;
   %local variY;
   %let variY=&variX;
%mend inner;
```

We examine what happens to the symbol tables when you submit the following code:

```
%let variX=zero;
%outer
```

1. The macro processor receives `%let variX=zero;`. It checks the global symbol table for a macro variable named `variX`. There is none, so the macro processor creates `variX` and assigns a value of *zero* to it.

Global Symbol Table	
variX	zero

2. The macro processor receives `%outer`. The macro processor retrieves the macro `Outer` from `Work.Sasmacr`, and begins executing it.

3. The macro processor encounters `%local variX;`. It creates a local symbol table. The macro processor creates the macro variable `variX` in this local table and assigns a null value to it. This does not affect the macro variable `variX` that is stored in the global symbol table.

Global Symbol Table		Outer Local Symbol Table	
variX	zero	variX	

4. The macro processor encounters `%let variX=one;`. The macro processor checks the local symbol table for `variX` and assigns a value of *one* to it.

Global Symbol Table		Outer Local Symbol Table	
variX	zero	variX	one

5. The macro processor receives `%inner`. It retrieves the macro `Inner` from `Work.Sasmacr`, and begins executing it.

6. The macro processor encounters `%local variY;`. It creates a local symbol table. The macro processor creates a macro variable `variY` in this table and assigns a null value to it. There are now two local symbol tables in existence.

Global Symbol Table		Outer Local Symbol Table		Inner Local Symbol Table	
variX	zero	variX	one	variY	

7. The macro processor encounters `%let variY=&variX;`. It checks the most recently created local table for `variX`. There is no such macro variable in that symbol table, so the macro processor then checks the other local symbol table. It retrieves the value *one* from that symbol table and substitutes the value into the %LET statement. Then the macro processor checks the most recently created local symbol table for a macro variable named `variY`. When it finds this macro variable, it assigns the value *one* to it.

Global Symbol Table		Outer Local Symbol Table		Inner Local Symbol Table	
variX	zero	variX	one	variY	one

8. The `4Inner` macro finishes executing, and the local symbol table that was created within this macro is deleted. There is now only one local symbol table in existence.

Global Symbol Table		Outer Local Symbol Table	
variX	zero	variX	one

9. The `Outer` macro finishes executing, and the local symbol table that was created within this macro is deleted. There are now no local symbol tables in existence. The global symbol table has not been changed since `variX` was created and was assigned a value of *zero*.

Global Symbol Table	
variX	zero

As you can see, each macro program in the example above has its own local symbol table that exists as long as the macro executes. When a macro finishes executing, its local symbol table and all of the local macro variables that are contained in that table are erased. The global symbol table and all of the global macro variables that are contained in it remain.

The MPRINTNEST Option

The MPRINTNEST option allows the macro nesting information to be written to the SAS log in the MPRINT output. This has no effect on the MPRINT output that is sent to an external file.

General form, MPRINTNEST option:

OPTIONS MPRINTNEST | NOMPRINTNEST;

Here is an explanation of the syntax:

MPRINTNEST
  specifies that macro nesting information is written in the MPRINT output in the SAS log.

NOMPRINTNEST
  specifies that macro nesting information is not written in the MPRINT output in the SAS log.

The setting of the MPRINTNEST option does not imply the setting of MPRINT. You must set both MPRINT and MPRINTNEST for output with the nesting information to be written to the SAS log.

Example

Suppose that you have defined three nested macros, as follows:

```
%macro outer;
   data _null_;
      %inner
   run;
%mend outer;

%macro inner;
   put %inrmost;
%mend inner;

%macro inrmost;
   'This is the text of the PUT statement'
%mend inrmost;
```

The SAS log below shows the messages that are written when you set both the MPRINT and MPRINTNEST options and submit a call to the `Outer` macro, as follows:

```
options mprint mprintnest;
%outer
```

Table 11.10 *SAS Log*

```
MPRINT(OUTER):    data _null_;
MPRINT(OUTER.INNER): put
MPRINT(OUTER.INNER.INRMOST): 'This is the text of the PUT statement'
MPRINT(OUTER.INNER): ;
MPRINT(OUTER):    run;

This is the text of the PUT statement
NOTE: DATA statement used (Total process time):
      real time           0.00 seconds
      cpu time            0.00 seconds
```

The MLOGICNEST Option

The MLOGICNEST option allows the macro nesting information to be displayed in the MLOGIC output in the SAS log. The setting of MLOGICNEST does not affect the output of any currently executing macro.

General form, MLOGICNEST option:

OPTIONS MLOGICNEST | NOMLOGICNEST;

Here is an explanation of the syntax:

MLOGICNEST
    specifies that macro nesting information is written in the MLOGIC output in the SAS log.

NOMLOGICNEST
    specifies that macro nesting information is not written in the MLOGIC output in the SAS log.

The setting of MLOGICNEST does not imply the setting of MLOGIC. You must set both MLOGIC and MLOGICNEST for output with nesting information to be written to the SAS log.

Example

Suppose that you have defined three nested macros, as follows:

```
%macro outer;
   %put THIS IS OUTER;
   %inner
%mend outer;

%macro inner;
   %put THIS IS INNER;
   %inrmost
%mend inner;

%macro inrmost;
   %put THIS IS INRMOST;
%mend inrmost;
```

The SAS log below shows the messages that are written when you set both the MLOGIC and MLOGICNEST options and submit a call to the **Outer** macro, as follows:

```
options mlogic mlogicnest;
%outer
```

Table 11.11 *SAS Log*

```
MLOGIC(OUTER):  Beginning execution.
MLOGIC(OUTER):  %PUT THIS IS OUTER
THIS IS OUTER
MLOGIC(OUTER.INNER):  Beginning execution.
MLOGIC(OUTER.INNER):  %PUT THIS IS INNER
THIS IS INNER
MLOGIC(OUTER.INNER.INRMOST):  Beginning execution.
MLOGIC(OUTER.INNER.INRMOST):  %PUT THIS IS INRMOST
THIS IS INRMOST
MLOGIC(OUTER.INNER.INRMOST):  Ending execution.
MLOGIC(OUTER.INNER): Ending execution.
MLOGIC(OUTER): Ending execution.
```

Processing Statements Conditionally

Conditional Execution

You can use macros to control conditional execution of statements. Remember the example from the beginning of this chapter where you wanted to run a daily report to create registration listings for courses to be held later in the month. Remember that you also wanted to run a weekly report each Friday to create a summary of revenue that has been generated so far in the current month. You can accomplish these tasks with one program if you use conditional execution to determine whether the second report should be run.

You can perform conditional execution at the macro level with %IF-%THEN and %ELSE statements.

General form, %IF-%THEN and %ELSE statements:

%IF *expression* **%THEN** *text*;

<**%ELSE** *text*;>

Here is an explanation of the syntax:

expression
    can be any valid macro expression that resolves to an integer.

text
    can be specified as

- constant text

- a text expression

- a macro variable reference, a macro call, or a macro program statement.

If *expression* resolves to zero, then it is false and the %THEN text is not processed (the optional %ELSE text is processed instead). If it resolves to any integer other than zero, then the expression is true and the %THEN text is processed. If it resolves to null or to any noninteger value, an error message is issued.

The %ELSE statement is optional. However, the macro language does not contain a subsetting %IF statement. Thus, you cannot use %IF without %THEN.

%IF-%THEN Compared to IF-THEN

Although they look similar, the %IF-%THEN/%ELSE statement and the IF-THEN/ ELSE statement belong to two different languages. Most of the same rules that apply to the DATA step IF-THEN/ELSE statement also apply to the %IF-%THEN/%ELSE statement. However, there are several important differences between the macro %IF-%THEN statement and the DATA step IF-THEN statement.

%IF-%THEN...	IF-THEN...
is used only in a macro program.	is used only in a DATA step program.
executes during macro execution.	executes during DATA step execution.
uses macro variables in logical expressions and cannot refer to DATA step variables in logical expressions.	uses DATA step variables in logical expressions.
determines what text should be copied to the input stack.	determines what DATA step statement(s) should be executed. When inside a macro definition, it is copied to the input stack as text.

Simple %DO and %END statements often appear in conjunction with %IF-%THEN/ %ELSE statements in order to designate a section of the macro to be processed depending on whether the %IF condition is true or false. Use %DO and %END statements following %THEN or %ELSE in order to conditionally place text that contains multiple statements onto the input stack. Each %DO statement must be paired with an %END statement.

General form, %DO-%END with %IF-%THEN and %ELSE statements:

%IF *expression* **%THEN %DO;**

> *text and/or macro language statements*

%END;

%ELSE %DO;

> *text and/or macro language statements*

%END;

Here is an explanation of the syntax:

text and/or macro language statements
> is either constant text, a text expression, and/or a macro statement.

Note: The statements %IF-%THEN, %ELSE, %DO, and %END are macro language statements that can be used only inside a macro program.

Example

You can control text that is copied to the input stack with the %IF-%THEN while controlling DATA step logic with IF-THEN. In this example, the value of the macro variable **status** determines which variables are included in the new data set. The value

of the data set variable **Location** determines the value of the new data set variable
Totalfee.

```
%macro choice(status);
   data fees;
      set sasuser.all;
      %if &status=PAID %then %do;
         where paid='Y';
         keep student_name course_code begin_date totalfee;
      %end;
      %else %do;
         where paid='N';
         keep student_name course_code
               begin_date totalfee latechg;
         latechg=fee*.10;
      %end;
      /* add local surcharge */
      if location='Boston' then totalfee=fee*1.06;
      else if location='Seattle'  then totalfee=fee*1.025;
      else if location='Dallas'  then totalfee=fee*1.05;
   run;
%mend choice;
```

If the MPRINT and MLOGIC system options are both set, the SAS log displays
messages showing the text that is sent to the compiler. For example, suppose you submit
the following macro call:

```
options mprint mlogic;
%choice(PAID)
```

The following messages are written to the log. Notice that the MLOGIC option shows
the evaluation of the expression in the %IF statement, but it does not show the
evaluation of the expression in the IF statement.

Table 11.12 *SAS Log*

```
160  %choice(PAID)
MLOGIC(CHOICE): Beginning execution.
MLOGIC(CHOICE): Parameter STATUS has value PAID
MPRINT(CHOICE): data fees;
MPRINT(CHOICE): set sasuser.all;
MLOGIC(CHOICE): %IF condition &status=PAID is TRUE
MPRINT(CHOICE): where paid='Y';
MPRINT(CHOICE): keep student_name course_code begin_date totalfee;
MPRINT(CHOICE): if location='Boston' then totalfee=fee*1.06;
MPRINT(CHOICE): else if location='Seattle' then totalfee=fee*1.025;
MPRINT(CHOICE): else if location='Dallas' then totalfee=fee*1.05;
MPRINT(CHOICE): run;
```

Suppose you submit the following macro call:

```
options mprint mlogic;
%choice(OWED)
```

The following messages are sent to the SAS log. Notice that the text that is written to the
input stack is different this time.

Table 11.13 *SAS Log*

```
161  %choice(OWED)
MLOGIC(CHOICE): Beginning execution.
MLOGIC(CHOICE): Parameter STATUS has value OWED
MPRINT(CHOICE): data fees;
MPRINT(CHOICE): set sasuser.all;
MLOGIC(CHOICE): %IF condition &status=PAID is FALSE
MPRINT(CHOICE): where paid='N';
MPRINT(CHOICE): keep student_name course_code begin_date totalfee
                latechg;
MPRINT(CHOICE): latechg=fee*.10;
MPRINT(CHOICE): if location='Boston' then totalfee=fee*1.06;
MPRINT(CHOICE): else if location='Seattle' then totalfee=fee*1.025;
MPRINT(CHOICE): else if location='Dallas' then totalfee=fee*1.05;
MPRINT(CHOICE): run;
```

Earlier you learned the process that occurs when a macro program is compiled. Now that you have seen more-complex macro programs, we can examine this process again.

Remember that during macro compilation, macro statements are checked for syntax errors. If a macro definition contains macro statement syntax errors, error messages are written to the SAS log, and a non-executable (dummy) macro is created.

Example

Suppose you attempt to compile a macro that contains a syntax error. For example, the following program is missing a percent sign in the %IF-%THEN statement:

```
%macro printit;
   %if &syslast ne _NULL_ then %do;
      proc print data=_last_(obs=5);
      title "Last Created Data Set Is &syslast";
      run;
   %end;
%mend;
```

When you submit this macro definition, the macro processor checks the %IF-%THEN statement and the %DO and %END statements for syntax errors. Since there is a syntax error in the %IF-%THEN statement, the following error messages are written to the SAS log.

Table 11.14 *SAS Log*

```
10   %macro printit;
11      %if &syslast ne _NULL_ then %do;
ERROR: Macro keyword DO appears as text. A semicolon or other
       delimiter may be missing.
ERROR: Expected %THEN statement not found. A dummy macro will be
       compiled.
12         proc print data=_last_(obs=5);
13         title "Last Created Data Set Is &syslast";
14         run;
15      %end;
ERROR: There is no matching %DO statement for the %END. This
       statement will be ignored.
16   %mend;
```

Macro Execution with Conditional Processing

Earlier you learned that when the macro processor receives **%macro-name**, it executes compiled macro language statements such as %IF-%THEN. The values of macro variables that are used within the %IF logical expression are resolved during macro execution. The %IF logical expression is automatically evaluated.

Example

Suppose the **Printit** macro has been compiled and has been stored in the Work.Sasmacr catalog.

1. First, you submit a call to the **Printit** macro, as follows:

   ```
   %printit
   ```

2. The macro processor locates the macro in the SAS catalog Work.Sasmacr.

   Catalog Entry *Work.Sasmacr.Printit.Macro*

   ```
   %macro printit;
      %if &syslast ne _NULL_ %then %do;
         proc print data=_last_(obs=5);
         title "Last Created Data Set Is &syslast";
         run;
      %end;
   %mend;
   ```

3. The macro processor begins to execute compiled macro language statements from **Printit** (that is, the %IF-%THEN statement). Because the %IF expression is true, the %DO block is processed.

4. The macro processor places the text that follows the %DO statement (that is, the PROC PRINT step) on the input stack.

   Input Stack

   ```
   proc print data=_last_(obs=5);
      title "Last Created Data Set Is &syslast";
   run;
   ```

5. Word scanning proceeds as usual on the PROC PRINT step. When a macro trigger such as &syslast is encountered, the macro reference is passed to the macro processor for resolution. The macro processor returns resolved values to the input stack.

6. After the word scanner sends all of the tokens from the PROC PRINT step to the compiler, and the RUN statement is encountered, the PROC PRINT step executes.

7. Macro execution pauses while the PROC PRINT step executes, and macro execution stops when the %MEND statement is encountered.

It is possible to conditionally insert individual statements into the input stack, even in the middle of a step.

Example

Suppose you want to generate a report of enrollment at each training center as listed in the data set Sasuser.All. You can specify your macro program so that if a specific course is requested, the macro inserts a WHERE ALSO statement in order to restrict the report to that course. This example also customizes the second title line based on whether a course was selected, as follows:

```
%macro attend(crs,start=01jan2001,stop=31dec2001);
   %let start=%upcase(&start);
   %let stop=%upcase(&stop);
   proc freq data=sasuser.all;
      where begin_date between "&start"d and "&stop"d;
      table location / nocum;
      title "Enrollment from &start to &stop";
      %if &crs= %then %do;
         title2 "for all Courses";
      %end;
      %else %do;
         title2 "for Course &crs only";
         where also course_code="&crs";
      %end;
   run;
%mend;
```

Note: In the program above, the %IF statement **%if &crs=** is true when **crs** has a value of null.

Suppose you submit the following call, which specifies a specific course:

```
%attend(C003)
```

This call results in the following output. Notice that the second title has been written according to the %ELSE %DO statement in the macro.

Enrollment from 01JAN2001 to 31DEC2001 for Course C003 only

The FREQ Procedure

Location		
Location	Frequency	Percent
Boston	20	40.00
Seattle	30	60.00

Table 11.15 *SAS Log*

```
18    %attend(C003)
MPRINT(ATTEND):    proc freq data=sasuser.all;
MPRINT(ATTEND):    where begin_date between "01JAN2001"d and "31DEC2001"d;
MPRINT(ATTEND):    table location / nocum;
MPRINT(ATTEND):    title "Enrollment from 01JAN2001 to 31DEC2001";
MPRINT(ATTEND):    title2 "for Course C003 only";
MPRINT(ATTEND):    where also course_code="C003";
NOTE: WHERE clause has been augmented.
MPRINT(ATTEND):    run;


NOTE: Writing HTML Body file: sashtml.htm
NOTE: There were 2 observations read from the data set SASUSER.SCHEDULE.
      WHERE (Course_Code='C003') and (Begin_Date>='01JAN2001'D and
                                                Begin_Date<='31DEC2001'D);
NOTE: There were 207 observations read from the data set SASUSER.STUDENTS.
NOTE: There were 434 observations read from the data set SASUSER.REGISTER.
NOTE: There were 1 observations read from the data set SASUSER.COURSES.
      WHERE Course_Code='C003';
NOTE: There were 50 observations read from the data set SASUSER.ALL.
      WHERE (begin_date>='01JAN2001'D and begin_date<='31DEC2001'D)
                                                and (course_code='C003');
```

Now suppose you submit the following call, which specifies a start date but does not specify a course:

```
%attend(start=01jul2001)
```

This call results in the following output. Notice that in this output, the second title line is written according to the %IF-%THEN statement in the macro.

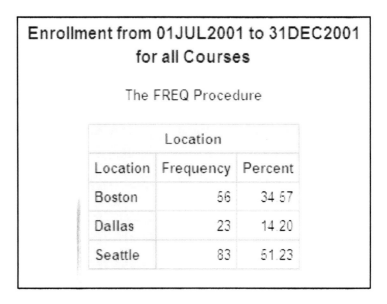

Table 11.16 SAS Log

```
19   %attend(start=01jul2001)
MPRINT(ATTEND):   options mprint;
MPRINT(ATTEND):   proc freq data=sasuser.all;
MPRINT(ATTEND):   where begin_date between "01JUL2001"d and "31DEC2001"d;
MPRINT(ATTEND):   table location / nocum;
MPRINT(ATTEND):   title "Enrollment from 01JUL2001 to 31DEC2001";
MPRINT(ATTEND):   title2 "for all Courses";
MPRINT(ATTEND):   run;

NOTE: There were 6 observations read from the data set SASUSER.SCHEDULE.
      WHERE Course_Code in ('C001', 'C002', 'C003', 'C004', 'C005', 'C006') and
      (Begin_Date>='01JUL2001'D and Begin_Date<='31DEC2001'D);
NOTE: There were 207 observations read from the data set SASUSER.STUDENTS.
NOTE: There were 434 observations read from the data set SASUSER.REGISTER.
NOTE: There were 6 observations read from the data set SASUSER.COURSES.
NOTE: There were 162 observations read from the data set SASUSER.ALL.
      WHERE (begin_date>='01JUL2001'D and begin_date<='31DEC2001'D);
```

Conditional Processing of Parts of Statements

The text that is processed as the result of conditional logic can be a small part of a SAS statement. This makes it possible to conditionally insert text into the middle of a statement.

Example

Suppose you want to print a table of frequency counts from a SAS data set. You can generate either a one-way table or a two-way table, based on the value of a macro parameter. This example creates a one-way table if only the **cols** parameter is specified in the call. It creates a two-way table if the **rows** parameter is also specified.

```
%macro counts (cols=_all_,rows=,dsn=&syslast);
   title "Frequency Counts for %upcase(&dsn) data set";
   proc freq data=&dsn;
      tables
      %if &rows ne %then &rows *;
      &cols;
   run;
%mend counts;
```

Suppose you submit the following call, which specifies both **cols** and **rows**:

```
%counts(dsn=sasuser.all, cols=paid, rows=course_number)
```

Part of the resulting output from this call is shown below. Notice that the macro has created a two-way table.

Frequency Counts for SASUSER.ALL data set

The FREQ Procedure

Frequency Percent Row Pct Col Pct	Table of Course_Number by Paid			
	Course_Number(Course Number)	Paid(Paid Status)		
		N	Y	Total
	1	6	17	23
		1.38	3.92	5.30
		26.09	73.91	
		5.61	5.20	
	2	8	16	24
		1.84	3.69	5.53
		33.33	66.67	
		7.48	4.89	
	3	6	14	20
		1.38	3.23	4.61
		30.00	70.00	
		5.61	4.28	
	4	7	20	27
		1.61	4.61	6.22
		25.93	74.07	
		6.54	6.12	
	5	9	16	25
		2.07	3.69	5.76
		36.00	64.00	
			4.89	

The log shows the generated PROC FREQ code from this macro.

Table 11.17 *SAS Log*

```
28   %counts(dsn=sasuser.all, cols=paid, rows=course_number)
MPRINT(COUNTS):   title "Frequency Counts for SASUSER.ALL data set";
MPRINT(COUNTS):   proc freq data=sasuser.all;
MPRINT(COUNTS):   tables course_number * paid;
MPRINT(COUNTS):   run;

NOTE: There were 18 observations read from the data set SASUSER.SCHEDULE.
      WHERE Course_Code in ('C001', 'C002', 'C003', 'C004', 'C005', 'C006');
NOTE: There were 207 observations read from the data set SASUSER.STUDENTS.
NOTE: There were 434 observations read from the data set SASUSER.REGISTER.
NOTE: There were 6 observations read from the data set SASUSER.COURSES.
NOTE: There were 434 observations read from the data set SASUSER.ALL.
NOTE: PROCEDURE FREQ used (Total process time):
```

Now suppose you submit the following call, which specifies **cols** but does not specify **rows**:

```
%counts(dsn=sasuser.all, cols=paid)
```

The output that results from this call is shown below. Notice that this time the macro has created a one-way table.

Frequency Counts for SASUSER.ALL data set

The FREQ Procedure

Paid Status				
Paid	Frequency	Percent	Cumulative Frequency	Cumulative Percent
N	107	24.65	107	24.65
Y	327	75.35	434	100.00

The log shows the generated TABLES statement.

Table 11.18 *SAS Log*

```
29   %counts(dsn=sasuser.all, cols=paid)
MPRINT(COUNTS):   title "Frequency Counts for SASUSER.ALL data set";
MPRINT(COUNTS):   proc freq data=sasuser.all;
MPRINT(COUNTS):   tables paid;
MPRINT(COUNTS):   run;

NOTE: There were 18 observations read from the data set SASUSER.SCHEDULE.
      WHERE Course_Code in ('C001', 'C002', 'C003', 'C004', 'C005', 'C006');
NOTE: There were 207 observations read from the data set SASUSER.STUDENTS.
NOTE: There were 434 observations read from the data set SASUSER.REGISTER.
NOTE: There were 6 observations read from the data set SASUSER.COURSES.
NOTE: There were 434 observations read from the data set SASUSER.ALL.
NOTE: PROCEDURE FREQ used (Total process time):
```

Case Sensitivity in Macro Comparisons

Remember that comparisons that are made in %IF expressions are case sensitive.

Example

If you construct your %IF statement using incorrect case in any program text, the statement is never true. For example, the %IF statement below is always false because **_null_** is specified in lowercase but is always stored in SAS in uppercase:

```
%macro prtlast;
   %if &syslast=_null_ %then %do;
      %put No data sets created yet.;
   %end;
   %else %do;
      proc print;
         title "Last Created Data Set is &syslast";
      run;
   %end;
%mend;
options mprint mlogic symbolgen;
%prtlast
```

Suppose SYSLAST has a value of _NULL_ when you submit this example. The following messages are written to the SAS log.

Table 11.19 SAS Log

```
29   %prtlast
MLOGIC(PRTLAST): Beginning execution.
SYMBOLGEN: Macro variable SYSLAST resolves to _NULL_
MLOGIC(PRTLAST): %IF condition &syslast = _null_ is FALSE

NOTE: The SAS System stopped processing this step because of errors.
NOTE: PROCEDURE PRINT used:
      real time           1:32.58
      cpu time            0.05 seconds

MPRINT(PRTLAST): proc print;
ERROR: There is not a default input data set (_LAST_ is _NULL_).
SYMBOLGEN: Macro variable SYSLAST resolves to _NULL_
MPRINT(PRTLAST): title "Last Created Data Set is _NULL_";
MPRINT(PRTLAST): run;

NOTE: The SAS System stopped processing this step because of errors.
NOTE: PROCEDURE PRINT used:
      real time           0.01 seconds
      cpu time            0.01 seconds
MLOGIC(PRTLAST): Ending execution.
```

TIP   The %UPCASE function is often useful when you construct %IF statements. For more information about the %UPCASE function, see Chapter 9, "Introducing Macro Variables," on page 288.

Processing Statements Iteratively

Overview

Many macro applications require iterative processing. With the iterative %DO statement that you can repeatedly

- execute macro programming code
- generate SAS code.

General form, iterative %DO statement with %END statement:

%DO *index-variable=start* **%TO** *stop* <**%BY** *increment*>;

> *text*

%END;

Here is an explanation of the syntax:

index-variable

> is either the name of a macro variable or a text expression that generates a macro variable name.

start and *stop*

> specify either integers or macro expressions that generate integers to control how many times the portion of the macro between the iterative %DO and %END statements is processed.

increment

> specifies either an integer (other than 0) or a macro expression that generates an integer to be added to the value of the index variable in each iteration of the loop. By default, *increment* is 1.

text

> can be

> - constant text, possibly including SAS data set names, SAS variable names, or SAS statements
> - macro variables, macro functions, or macro program statements
> - any combination of the above.

%DO and %END statements are valid only inside a macro definition. The *index-variable* is created in the local symbol table if it does not appear in any existing symbol table.

The iterative %DO statement evaluates the value of the index variable at the *beginning* of each loop iteration. The loop stops processing when the index variable has a value that is outside the range of the start and stop values.

Example

You can use a macro loop to create and display a series of macro variables.

This example creates a series of macro variables named **teach1-teachn**, one for each observation in the Sasuser.Schedule data set, and assigns teacher names to them as values. Then the **Putloop** macro uses a %DO statement and a %END statement to create a loop that writes these macro variables and their values to the SAS log, as follows:

```
data _null_;
   set sasuser.schedule end=no_more;
   call symput('teach'||left(_n_),(trim(teacher)));
   if no_more then call symput('count',_n_);
run;

%macro putloop;
   %local i;
   %do i=1 %to &count;
      %put TEACH&i is &&teach&i;
   %end;
%mend putloop;
```

```
%putloop
```

TIP   It is a good idea to specifically declare the index variable of a macro loop as a local variable to avoid the possibility of accidentally changing the value of a macro variable that has the same name in other symbol tables.

When the **Putloop** macro is executed, no code is sent to the compiler, because the %PUT statements are executed by the macro processor. The following messages are written to the SAS log.

Table 11.20   *SAS Log*

```
TEACH1 is Hallis, Dr. George
TEACH2 is Wickam, Dr. Alice
TEACH3 is Forest, Mr. Peter
TEACH4 is Tally, Ms. Julia
TEACH5 is Hallis, Dr. George
TEACH6 is Berthan, Ms. Judy
TEACH7 is Hallis, Dr. George
TEACH8 is Wickam, Dr. Alice
TEACH9 is Forest, Mr. Peter
TEACH10 is Tally, Ms. Julia
TEACH11 is Tally, Ms. Julia
TEACH12 is Berthan, Ms. Judy
TEACH13 is Hallis, Dr. George
TEACH14 is Wickam, Dr. Alice
TEACH15 is Forest, Mr. Peter
TEACH16 is Tally, Ms. Julia
TEACH17 is Hallis, Dr. George
TEACH18 is Berthan, Ms. Judy
```

You can also use a macro loop to generate statements that can be placed inside a SAS program step.

Example

The following macro generates a series of statements within a DATA step. On each iteration, the macro writes a message to the SAS log that puts the current value of the index variable into HEX6. format.

```
%macro hex(start=1,stop=10,incr=1);
   %local i;
   data _null_;
      %do i=&start %to &stop %by &incr;
         value=&i;
         put "Hexadecimal form of &i is " value hex6.;
      %end;
   run;
%mend hex;
```

Note: The HEX6. format converts a number to hexadecimal format.

Suppose you submit the following call:

```
options mprint mlogic;
%hex(start=20,stop=30,incr=2)
```

Some of the messages that are written to the SAS log when Hex executes are shown below. Notice that according to the MLOGIC messages, the loop stops processing when the value of the index variable is 32 (which is beyond the value that is specified for `Stop`).

Table 11.21   *SAS Log*

```
MLOGIC(HEX): %DO loop index variable I is now 30; loop will
                 iterate again.
MPRINT(HEX): value=30;
MPRINT(HEX): put "Hexadecimal form of 30 is " value hex6.;
MLOGIC(HEX): %DO loop index variable I is now 32; loop will
                 not iterate again.
MPRINT(HEX): run;

Hexadecimal form of 20 is 000014
Hexadecimal form of 22 is 000016
Hexadecimal form of 24 is 000018
Hexadecimal form of 26 is 00001A
Hexadecimal form of 28 is 00001C
Hexadecimal form of 30 is 00001E
NOTE: DATA statement used:
      real time           0.06 seconds
      cpu time            0.06 seconds

MLOGIC(HEX): Ending execution.
```

Generating Complete Steps

You can use the iterative %DO statement to build macro loops that create complete SAS steps.

Example

Suppose course offerings for several years are stored in a series of external files that are named by year, such as Raw1999.dat and Raw2000.dat. All the files have the same record layout. Suppose you want to read each file into a separate SAS data set.

The following macro uses a %DO statement to create a loop that creates a data set from each of the specified external files:

```
%macro readraw(first=1999,last=2005);
   %local year;
   %do year=&first %to &last;
      data year&year;
         infile "raw&year..dat";
         input course_code $4.
         location $15.
         begin_date date9.
         teacher $25.;
      run;

      proc print data=year&year;
         title "Scheduled classes for &year";
         format begin_date date9.;
      run;
   %end;
```

```
%mend readraw;
```

Suppose you submit the following call to the **Readraw** macro:

```
%readraw(first=2000,last=2002)
```

The macro creates three data sets named Year2000, Year2001, and Year2002. Remember that in order for this program to run properly, the raw data files must be named appropriately, and they must be stored in the location that the program specifies. The generated DATA step is shown in the log.

Table 11.22 *SAS Log*

```
336   %readraw(first=2000,last=2002)
MLOGIC(READRAW):  Beginning execution.
MLOGIC(READRAW):  Parameter FIRST has value 2000
MLOGIC(READRAW):  Parameter LAST has value 2002
MLOGIC(READRAW):  %LOCAL  YEAR
MLOGIC(READRAW):  %DO loop beginning; index variable YEAR; start value is 2000;
      stop value is 2002; by value is 1.
MPRINT(READRAW):    data year2000;
MPRINT(READRAW):    infile "raw2000.dat";
MPRINT(READRAW):    input course_code $4. location $15. begin_date date9.
                           teacher $25.;
MPRINT(READRAW):    run;
```

Using Arithmetic and Logical Expressions

The %EVAL Function

The %EVAL function evaluates integer arithmetic or logical expressions. Logical expressions and arithmetic expressions are sequences of operators and operands forming sets of instructions that are evaluated to produce a result.

- An arithmetic expression contains an arithmetic operator.

- A logical expression contains a logical operator.

General form, %EVAL function:

%EVAL(*arithmetic or logical expression***)**

The %EVAL function

- translates integer strings and hexadecimal strings to integers

- translates tokens representing arithmetic, comparison, and logical operators to macro-level operators

- performs arithmetic and logical operations.

For arithmetic expressions, if an operation results in a non-integer value, %EVAL truncates the value to an integer. Also, %EVAL returns a null value and issues an error message when non-integer values are used in arithmetic expressions.

%EVAL evaluates logical expressions and returns a value to indicate whether the expression is true or false. A value of **0** indicates that the expression is false, and a value of **1** or any other numeric value indicates that the expression is true.

The %EVAL function *does not* convert the following to numeric values:

- numeric strings that contain a period or E notation

- SAS date and time constants.

Here are some examples.

Examples

The following table shows several examples of arithmetic and logical expressions, as well as the results that %EVAL produces when it evaluates these expressions.

If you submit these statements...	These messages are written to the log...
`%put value=%eval(10 lt 2);`	value=0
`%put value=10+2;` `%put value=%eval(10+2);`	value=10+2 value=12

`%let counter=2;`
`%let counter=%eval(&counter+1);`
`%put counter=&counter;`
	counter=3

`%let numer=2;`
`%let denom=8;`
`%put value=%eval(&numer/&denom);`
	value=0

`%let numer=2;`
`%let demon=8;`
`%put value=%eval(&numer/&denom*&denom);`
`%put value=%eval(&denom*&numer/&denom);`
	value=0
	value=2

`%let real=2.4;`
`%let int=8;`
`%put value=%eval(&real+&int);`
	value=

In the last example above, the decimal value of the **real** variable causes an error message to be written to the SAS log, as shown here.

Table 11.23   *SAS Log*

```
1    %let real=2.4;
2    %let int=8;
3    %put value=%eval(&real+&int);
ERROR: A character operand was found in the %EVAL function
or %IF condition where a numeric operand is required.
The condition was: 2.4+8
value=
```

Because %EVAL does not convert a value that contains a period to a number, the operands are evaluated as character operands.

You have seen that the %EVAL function generates ERROR messages in the log when it encounters an expression that contains non-integer values. In order to avoid these ERROR messages, you can use the %SYSEVALF function. The %SYSEVALF function evaluates arithmetic and logical expressions using floating-point arithmetic.

General form, %SYSEVALF function:

%SYSEVALF(*expression<, conversion-type>***)**

Here is an explanation of the syntax:

expression
  is an arithmetic or logical expression to evaluate.

conversion-type
  converts the value returned by %SYSEVALF to the type of value specified. Conversion-type can be BOOLEAN, CEIL, FLOOR, or INTEGER.

The %SYSEVALF function performs floating-point arithmetic and returns a value that is formatted using the BEST16. format. The result of the evaluation is always text.

Example

The macro in the following example performs all types of conversions for values in the %SYSEVALF function:

```
%macro figureit(a,b);
    %let y=%sysevalf(&a+&b);
    %put The result with SYSEVALF is: &y;
    %put BOOLEAN conversion: %sysevalf(&a +&b, boolean);
    %put CEIL conversion: %sysevalf(&a +&b, ceil);
    %put FLOOR conversion: %sysevalf(&a +&b, floor);
    %put INTEGER conversion: %sysevalf(&a +&b, integer);
    %mend figureit;

%figureit(100,1.59)
```

Executing this program writes the following lines to the SAS log.

Table 11.24 *SAS Log*

```
The result with SYSEVALF is: 101.59
BOOLEAN conversion: 1
CEIL conversion: 102
FLOOR conversion: 101
INTEGER conversion: 101
```

Automatic Evaluation

%SYSEVALF is the only macro function that can evaluate logical expressions that contain floating point, date, time, datetime, or missing values. Specifying a conversion type can prevent problems when %SYSEVALF returns missing or floating-point values to macro expressions or macro variables that are used in other macro expressions that require an integer value.

Keep in mind that any macro language function or statement that requires a numeric or logical expression automatically invokes the %EVAL function. This includes the %SCAN function, the %SUBSTR function, the %IF-%THEN statement, and more.

Summary

Text Summary

Basic Concepts

A macro program is created with a macro definition, which consists of a %MACRO statement and a %MEND statement. The %MACRO statement also provides a name for the macro. Any combination of macro language statements and SAS language statements can be placed in a macro definition. The macro definition must be compiled before it is available for execution. The MCOMPILENOTE= option causes a note to be issued to the SAS log when a macro has completed compilation. To execute a name style macro, you submit a call to the macro by preceding the macro name with a percent sign.

Developing and Debugging Macros

Two system options, MLOGIC, and MPRINT, are useful for macro development and debugging. The MLOGIC option writes messages that trace macro execution to the SAS log. The MPRINT option prints the text that is sent to the compiler after all macro resolution has taken place. The SYMBOLGEN option and macro comments are also useful for macro development and debugging.

Using Macro Parameters

You can use parameter lists in your macro definition in order to make your macros more flexible and easier to adapt. Parameters can be either positional or keyword. You can also use mixed parameter lists that contain both positional and keyword parameters. Parameters define macro variables that can take on different values when you call the macro, including null values. You can use the PARMBUFF option in conjunction with the automatic macro variable SYSPBUFF to define a macro that accepts a varying number of parameters each time you call it.

Understanding Symbol Tables

When a macro executes, it sometimes creates its own temporary symbol table, called a local symbol table. The local symbol table exists in addition to the global symbol table. If a macro creates or resolves macro variables, a local symbol table might be used. In order to fully control macro behavior, you must understand the basic rules that the macro processor uses to determine which symbol table to access under specific circumstances. Statements such as %GLOBAL and %LOCAL enable you to explicitly define where macro variables are stored. The %SYMDEL statement enables you to delete a macro variable from the global symbol table during a SAS session.

You can call a macro within a macro definition. That is, you can nest macros. When a nested macro is called, multiple local symbol tables can exist. The MPRINTNEST and MLOGICNEST options provide nesting information in the messages that are written to the SAS log for the MPRINT and MLOGIC options.

Processing Statements Conditionally

Conditional processing is available with the %IF-%THEN/%ELSE statements. These statements control what action the macro processor takes when an expression evaluates to true or to false. The action could be the execution of other macro programming statements or the placement of text onto the input stack. If the code that is used to describe this action includes multiple statements, you must enclose this code between a %DO statement and a %END statement.

It is possible to conditionally place whole SAS steps, whole SAS statements, or parts of SAS statements onto the input stack.

Processing Statements Iteratively

To perform repetitive actions, you can use %DO loops. You can use iterative processing to generate complete SAS steps, individual statements, or data-dependent steps.

Using Arithmetic and Logical Expressions

You use the %EVAL function to evaluate arithmetic or logical expressions that do not contain any non-integer or missing values. Macro language functions and statements that require a numeric or logical expression automatically use the %EVAL function. You use the %SYSEVALF function to evaluate arithmetic or logical expressions that contain non-integer or missing values.

Sample Programs

Defining a Basic Macro

```
%macro prtlast;
   proc print data=&syslast (obs=5);
   title "Listing of &syslast data set";
   run;
%mend;
```

Defining a Macro with Positional Parameters

```
%macro printdsn(dsn,vars);
   proc print data=&dsn;
      var &vars;
      title "Listing of %upcase(&dsn) data set";
   run;
%mend;
```

Defining a Macro with Keyword Parameters

```
%macro printdsn(dsn=sasuser.courses,
            vars=course_code
            course_title days);
   proc print data=&dsn;
      var &vars;
      title "Listing of %upcase(&dsn) data set";
   run;
%mend;
```

Defining a Macro with Mixed Parameters

```
%macro printdsn(dsn, vars=course_title course_code days);
   proc print data=&dsn;
```

```
            var &vars;
            title "Listing of %upcase(&dsn) data set";
        run;
    %mend;
```

Using the %IF-%THEN Statement

```
%macro choice(status);
    data fees;
        set sasuser.all;
        %if &status=PAID %then %do;
            where paid='Y';
            keep student_name course_code begin_date totalfee;
        %end;
        %else %do;
            where paid='N';
            keep student_name course_code
                begin_date totalfee latechg;
            latechg=fee*1.10;
        %end;
         /* add local surcharge */
        if location='Boston' then totalfee=fee*1.06;
        else if location='Seattle' then totalfee=fee*1.025;
        else if location='Dallas' then totalfee=fee*1.05;
    run;
%mend choice;
```

Using the Iterative %DO Statement

```
%macro hex(start=1,stop=10,incr=1);
    %local i;
    data _null_;
    %do i=&start %to &stop %by &incr;
        value=&i;
        put "Hexadecimal form of &i is " value hex6.;
    %end;
    run;
%mend hex;
options mprint mlogic symbolgen;
%hex(start=20,stop=30,incr=2)
```

Points to Remember

- Macro programs are defined by using a %MACRO statement and a %MEND statement.

- Macros are executed and called by entering a % before the name of the macro.

- The MPRINT, MLOGIC, and SYMBOLGEN system options can be useful for developing and debugging macro programs.

- Parameters can make your macro programs more flexible by creating local macro variables whose values can be updated by the macro call.

- You can use the %IF-%THEN statement to conditionally process whole SAS steps, SAS statements, or parts of statements.

- You can use the iterative %DO statement to create macro loops that can process repetitive tasks.

Quiz

Select the best answer for each question. After completing the quiz, check your answers using the answer key in the appendix.

1. Which of the following is false?

   a. A %MACRO statement must always be paired with a %MEND statement.

   b. A macro definition can include macro variable references, but it cannot include SAS language statements.

   c. Only macro language statements are checked for syntax errors when the macro is compiled.

   d. Compiled macros are stored in a temporary SAS catalog by default.

2. Which of the following examples correctly defines a macro named **Print** that implements parameters named **vars** and **total**?

   a.
   ```
   %macro print(vars, total);
      proc print data=classes;
         var vars;
         sum total;
      run;
   %mend print;
   ```

   b.
   ```
   %macro print('vars', 'total');
      proc print data=classes;
         var &vars;
         sum &total;
      run;
   %mend print;
   ```

   c.
   ```
   %macro print(vars, total);
      proc print data=classes;
         var &vars;
         sum &total;
      run;
   %mend print;
   ```

   d.
   ```
   %macro print(vars, total);
      proc print data=classes;
         var :vars;
         sum :total;
      run;
   %mend print;
   ```

3. Which of the following correctly references the macro named **Printdsn** as shown here:

   ```
   %macro printdsn(dsn,vars);
      %if &vars= %then %do;
         proc print data=&dsn;
         title "Full Listing of %upcase(&dsn) data set";
         run;
      %end;
   ```

```
      %else %do;
         proc print data=&dsn;
            var &vars;
         title "Listing of %upcase(&dsn) data set";
         run;
      %end;
%mend;
```

a. `%printdsn(sasuser.courses, course_title days);`

b. `%printdsn(dsn=sasuser.courses, vars=course_title days)`

c. `%printdsn(sasuser.courses, course_title days)`

d. `%printdsn(sasuser.courses, course_title, days)`

4. If you use a mixed parameter list in your macro program definition, which of the following is false?

   a. You must list positional parameters before any keyword parameters.

   b. Values for both positional and keyword parameters are stored in a local symbol table.

   c. Default values for keyword parameters are the values that are assigned in the macro definition, whereas positional parameters have a default value of null.

   d. You can assign a null value to a keyword parameter in a call to the macro by omitting the parameter from the call.

5. Which of the following is false?

   a. A macro program is compiled when you submit the macro definition.

   b. A macro program is executed when you call it (**%macro-name**).

   c. A macro program is stored in a SAS catalog entry only after it is executed.

   d. A macro program is available for execution throughout the SAS session in which it is compiled.

6. When you use an %IF-%THEN statement in your macro program,

   a. you must place %DO and %END statements around code that describes the conditional action, if that code contains multiple statements.

   b. the %ELSE statement is optional.

   c. you cannot refer to DATA step variables in the logical expression of the %IF statement.

   d. all of the above.

7. Which of the following can be placed onto the input stack?

   a. only whole steps.

   b. only whole steps or whole statements.

   c. only whole statements or pieces of text within a statement.

   d. whole steps, whole statements, or pieces of text within statements.

8. Which of the following creates a macro variable named **class** in a local symbol table?

   a. ```
   data _null_;
      set sasuser.courses;
      %let class=course_title;
   ```
   ```

```
   run;
```

b.
```
   data _null_;
      set sasuser.courses;
      call symput('class', course_title);
   run;
```

c.
```
   %macro sample(dsn);
      %local class;
      %let class=course_title;
      data_null_;
         set &dsn;
      run;
   %mend;
```

d.
```
   %global class;
   %macro sample(dsn);
      %let class=course_title;
      data _null_;
         set &dsn;
      run;
   %mend;
```

9. Which of the following examples correctly defines the macro program *Hex*?

a.
```
   %macro hex(start=1, stop=10, incr=1);
      %local i;
      data _null_;
      %do i=&start to &stop by &incr;
         value=&i;
         put "Hexadecimal form of &i is " value hex6.;
      %end;
      run;
   %mend hex;
```

b.
```
   %macro hex(start=1, stop=10, incr=1);
      %local i;
      data _null_;
      %do i=&start %to &stop %by &incr;
         value=&i;
         put "Hexadecimal form of &i is " value hex6.;
      %end;
      run;
   %mend hex;
```

c.
```
   %macro hex(start=1, stop=10, incr=1);
      %local i;
      data _null_;
      %do i=&start to &stop by &incr;
         value=&i;
         put "Hexadecimal form of &i is " value hex6.;
      run;
   %mend hex;
```

d.
```
   %macro hex(start=1, stop=10, incr=1);
      %local i;
      data _null_;
      %do i=&start to &stop by &incr;
         value=&i;
         put "Hexadecimal form of &i is " value hex6.;
```

```
      %end
        run;
    %mend hex;
```

10. When you submit a call to a compiled macro, what happens?

   a. First, the macro processor checks all macro programming statements in the macro for syntax errors.

   Then the macro processor executes all statements in the macro.

   b. The macro processor executes compiled macro programming statements.

   Then any SAS programming language statements are executed by the macro processor.

   c. First, all compiled macro programming statements are executed by the macro processor.

   After all macro statements have been processed, any SAS language statements are passed back to the input stack in order to be passed to the compiler and then executed.

   d. The macro processor executes compiled macro statements.

   If any SAS language statements are encountered, they are passed back to the input stack.

   The macro processor pauses while those statements are passed to the compiler and then executed.

   Then the macro processor continues to repeat these steps until it reaches the %MEND statement.

Chapter 12
Storing Macro Programs

Overview

Introduction

One of the most useful aspects of macro programming is the ability to reuse your macro programs. In Chapter 11, "Creating and Using Macro Programs," on page 372, you learned that compiled macros are stored in a temporary SAS catalog by default and are available for execution anytime during the current SAS session. You also learned that macros stored in this temporary SAS catalog are deleted at the end of the SAS session.

You might want to store your macros permanently so that you can reuse them in later SAS sessions or share them with others. There are several ways of storing your macro programs permanently and of making them accessible during a SAS session. The methods that you learn in this chapter are

- the %INCLUDE statement

- the autocall macro facility

- permanently stored compiled macros.

Understanding Session-Compiled Macros

In Chapter 11, "Creating and Using Macro Programs," on page 372, you learned that you can submit a macro definition in order to compile a macro. For example, when you submit the macro definition shown here, the macro processor compiles the macro **Prtlast**:

```
%macro prtlast;
   %if &syslast ne _NULL_ %then %do;
      proc print data=&syslast(obs=5);
         title "Listing of &syslast data set";
      run;
   %end;
   %else
      %put No data set has been created yet.;
%mend;
```

By default, the **Prtlast** macro is stored in a temporary SAS catalog as Work.Sasmacr.Prtlast.Macro. Macros that are stored in this temporary SAS catalog are known as session-compiled macros. Once a macro has been compiled, it can be invoked from a SAS program as shown here:

```
proc sort data=sasuser.courses out=bydays;
   by days;
run;
```

```
%prtlast
```

Session-compiled macros are available for execution during the SAS session in which they are compiled. They are deleted at the end of the session. But suppose you want to save your macros so that they are not deleted at the end of the SAS session. The rest of this chapter looks at methods of storing macros permanently.

Storing Macro Definitions in External Files

Overview

One way to store macro programs permanently is to save them to an external file. You can then use the %INCLUDE statement to insert the statements that are stored in the external file into a program. If the external file contains a macro definition, the macro is compiled when the %INCLUDE statement is submitted. Then the macro can be called again later in the same program, or anytime later in the current SAS session.

General form, %INCLUDE statement:

%INCLUDE *file-specification* </SOURCE2>;

Here is an explanation of the syntax:

file-specification
    describes the location of the file that contains the SAS code to be inserted.

SOURCE2
    causes the SAS statements that are inserted into the program to be displayed in the SAS log. If SOURCE2 is not specified in the %INCLUDE statement, then the setting of the *SAS system option* SOURCE2 controls whether the inserted code is displayed.

By storing your macro program externally and using the %INCLUDE statement, you gain several advantages over using session-compiled macros.

- The source code for the macro definition does not need to be part of your program.

- A single copy of a macro definition can be shared by many programs.

- Macro definitions in external files are easily viewed and edited with any text editor.

- No special SAS system options are required in order to access a macro definition that is stored in an external file.

Example

You can compile a macro by using the %INCLUDE statement to insert its definition into a program. Then you can call the macro in order to execute it.

Suppose the following macro definition is stored in the external file C:\sasfiles\prtlast.sas:

```
%macro prtlast;
    %if &syslast ne _NULL_ %then %do;
        proc print data=&syslast (obs=5);
            title "Listing of &syslast data set";
        run;
    %end;
    %else
        %put No data set has been created yet.;
%mend;
```

You could submit the following code to access, compile, and execute the **Prtlast** macro. The PROC SORT step is included in this example in order to create a data set that the **Prtlast** macro can print.

```
%include 'c:\sasfiles\prtlast.sas' /source2;

proc sort data=sasuser.courses out=bydays;
   by days;
run;


%prtlast
```

Note: The location and names of external files are specific to your operating environment.

The following messages are written to the SAS log when this code is submitted. Notice that the macro definition is written to the log because SOURCE2 was specified in the %INCLUDE statement.

Table 12.1 *SAS Log*

```
NOTE: %INCLUDE (level 1) file prtlast.sas is file
            C:\sasfiles\prtlast.sas.
31    +%macro prtlast;
32    +   %if &syslast ne _NULL_ %then %do;
33    +      proc print data=&syslast(obs=5);
34    +      title "Listing of &syslast data set";
35    +      run;
36    +   %end;
37    +   %else
38    +      %put No data set has been created yet.;
39    +%mend;
NOTE: %INCLUDE (level 1) ending.
40
41    proc sort data=sasuser.courses out=bydays;
42       by days;
43    run;

NOTE: There were 6 observations read from the dataset
      SASUSER.COURSES.
NOTE: The data set WORK.BYDAYS has 6 observations and
      4 variables.
NOTE: PROCEDURE SORT used:
      real time          0.04 seconds
      cpu time           0.04 seconds

44
45    %prtlast
NOTE: There were 5 observations read from the dataset
      WORK.BYDAYS.
NOTE: PROCEDURE PRINT used:
      real time          1.07 seconds
      cpu time           0.26 seconds
```

Here is the output that the code generates.

Listing of WORK.BYDAYS data set				
Obs	Course_Code	Course_Title	Days	Fee
1	C004	Database Design	2	$375
2	C005	Artificial Intelligence	2	$400
3	C001	Basic Telecommunications	3	$795
4	C003	Local Area Networks	3	$650
5	C002	Structured Query Language	4	$1150

Storing Macro Definitions in Catalog SOURCE Entries

Overview

Another way of permanently storing macros is to store a macro definition in a SOURCE entry in a SAS catalog. If you decide to store your macro programs in a SAS catalog, you must store each macro program in a separate SOURCE entry. It is a good idea to give each SOURCE entry the same name as the macro program that is stored within it. For example, a macro named **Printit** would be stored in a SOURCE entry that is also named **Printit**.

Note: SAS catalogs are members of SAS libraries that store program source code and other types of content.

To store a macro definition as a SOURCE entry in a SAS catalog, you use the Save As Object window.

Example

To save the **Printit** macro definition to the Sasuser.Mymacs catalog, perform these steps:

1. Select **File ⇨ Save As Object**. In the Save As Object window, select the **Sasuser** library.

2. If the Sasuser.Mymacs catalog does not already exist, you need to create it. You can either select the **Create New Catalog** icon or right-click the Save As Object window and select **New** in order to open the New Catalog window. Enter **Mymacs** as the name for the new catalog and click **OK**.

3. Enter **Printit** in the **Entry Name** field. Make sure that the Entry Type is set to **SOURCE entry (SOURCE)**, and click **Save**.

TIP If you use the Program Editor, you could also use the SAVE command to save your macro definition as a catalog SOURCE entry. To use the SAVE command, you enter save *libref.catalog.entry.source* in the command line where *libref.catalog.entry* is the libref, the catalog name, and the entry name.

The CATALOG Procedure

If you store your macros in a SAS catalog, you might want to view the contents of a particular catalog to see the macros that you have stored there. You can use the Explorer window to view the contents of a SAS catalog by navigating to the catalog and double clicking it. You can also use the CATALOG procedure to list the contents of a SAS catalog. The CONTENTS statement of the CATALOG procedure lists the contents of a catalog in the procedure output.

General form, CATALOG procedure with CONTENTS statement:

PROC CATALOG CATALOG=*libref.catalog***;**

      CONTENTS;

QUIT;

Here is an explanation of the syntax:

libref.catalog
    is a valid two-level catalog name.

Note: CAT= is an alias for CATALOG.

Example

You can use PROC CATALOG to view all of the macros that are stored in the temporary Work.Sasmacr catalog, as follows:

```
proc catalog cat=work.sasmacr;
   contents;
   title "Default Storage of SAS Macros";
quit;
```

This PROC CATALOG step produces results that are similar to the output shown below. The macros that are actually listed are the macros that have been compiled during the current SAS session.

Default Storage of SAS Macros					
Contents of Catalog WORK.SASMACR					
#	Name	Type	Create Date	Modified Date	Description
1	PRTLAST	MACRO	20Apr11:14:22:34	20Apr11:14:22:34	
2	SORTLAST2	MACRO	20Apr11:14:32:22	20Apr11:14:32:22	
3	TRIM	MACRO	20Apr11:15:01:19	20Apr11:15:01:19	

PROC CATALOG can display the names and attributes of compiled macros, but the macro definition itself cannot be viewed.

The CATALOG Access Method

If you store a macro definition in a SOURCE entry of a SAS catalog, you can use the CATALOG access method in a FILENAME statement in conjunction with the %INCLUDE statement to insert the macro definition into a SAS program.

General form, CATALOG access method to reference a single SOURCE entry:

FILENAME *fileref*

      CATALOG *'libref.catalog.entry-name.entry-type'*;

%INCLUDE *fileref*;

Here is an explanation of the syntax:

fileref
    is a valid fileref.

libref.catalog.entry-name.entry-type
    is a four-level SAS catalog entry name.

entry-type
    is SOURCE.

Example

Suppose you have stored the following macro definition as a SOURCE entry in the SAS catalog Sasuser.Mymacs:

```
%macro prtlast;
    %if &syslast ne _NULL_ %then %do;
        proc print data=&syslast(obs=5);
            title "Listing of &syslast data set";
        run;
    %end
    %else
        %put No data set has been created yet.;
%mend;
```

You can use the CATALOG access method along with the %INCLUDE statement to compile the macro **Prtlast**. Then you can reference the macro later in the program.

```
filename prtlast catalog 'sasuser.mymacs.prtlast.source';
%include prtlast;
proc sort data=sasuser.courses out=bydays;
    by days;
run;
%prtlast
```

You can also use the CATALOG access method to reference multiple SOURCE entries as long as the entries are stored in the same SAS catalog.

General form, CATALOG access method to reference multiple SOURCE entries:

FILENAME *fileref* **CATALOG** *'libref.catalog'*;

%INCLUDE *fileref*(*entry-1*);

%INCLUDE *fileref*(*entry-2*);

Here is an explanation of the syntax:

fileref
    is a valid fileref.

libref.catalog
    is a two-level catalog name.

entry-1 and *entry-2*
    are names of SOURCE entries in *library.catalog*.

Example

Suppose you have two macros, named **Prtlast** and **Sortlast**, that are stored in a SAS catalog.

Catalog Entry: **Sasuser.Mymacs.Prtlast.Source**

```
%macro prtlast;
   %if &syslast ne _NULL_ %then %do;
     proc print data=&syslast(obs=5);
     title "Listing of &syslast data set";
     run;
   %end;
   %else
     %put No data set has been created yet.;
%mend;
```

Catalog Entry: **Sasuser.Mymacs.Sortlast.Source**

```
%macro sortlast(sortby);
   %if &syslast ne _NULL_ %then %do;
     proc sort data=&syslast out=sorted;
        by &sortby;
     run;
   %end;
   %else
     %put No data set has been created yet.;
%mend;
```

You can use the CATALOG access method in conjunction with the %INCLUDE statement to compile both macros. Then you can call the macros later in the program. In this example, assume that the macros have the same names as the SOURCE entries in which they are stored:

```
filename prtsort catalog 'sasuser.mymacs';
%include prtsort(prtlast) / source2;
%include prtsort(sortlast) / source2;

data current(keep=student_name course_title begin_date location);
   set sasuser.all;
   if year(begin_date)=2001;
   diff=year(today())-year(begin_date);
```

```
        begin_date=begin_date+(365*diff);
run;

%sortlast(begin_date)
%prtlast
```

This code produces the following output:

\multicolumn{5}{c}{**Listing of WORK.SORTED data set**}

Obs	Student_Name	Location	Begin_Date	Course_Title
1	Bills, Ms. Paulette	Boston	06JAN2011	Local Area Networks
2	Chevarley, Ms. Arlene	Boston	06JAN2011	Local Area Networks
3	Clough, Ms. Patti	Boston	06JAN2011	Local Area Networks
4	Crace, Mr. Ron	Boston	06JAN2011	Local Area Networks
5	Davis, Mr. Bruce	Boston	06JAN2011	Local Area Networks

Using the Autocall Facility

Overview

You can make macros accessible to your SAS session or program by using the autocall facility to search predefined source libraries for macro definitions. These predefined source libraries are known as autocall libraries. You can store your macro definitions permanently in an autocall library, and you can set up multiple autocall libraries.

When you use this approach, you do not need to compile the macro in order to make it available for execution. That is, if the macro definition is stored in an autocall library, then you do not need to submit or include the macro definition before you submit a call to the macro.

Suppose you have stored a file that contains a macro definition in your autocall library. When you submit a call to that macro

- the macro processor searches the autocall library for the macro

- the macro is compiled and stored as it would be if you had submitted it (that is, the compiled macro is stored in the default location of Work.Sasmacr)

- the macro is executed.

Once it has been compiled, the macro can be executed as needed throughout the same SAS session. At the end of the SAS session, the compiled macro is deleted from the Work.Sasmacr catalog, but the source code remains in the autocall library.

Creating an Autocall Library

An autocall library can be either

- a directory that contains source files

- a partitioned data set (PDS)

- a SAS catalog.

The method for creating an autocall library depends on the operating environment that you are using.

To create an autocall library in a directory-based operating system, such as Windows or UNIX, create a directory in which to store macro definitions. Each macro definition in this directory is a separate file that has the extension *.sas* and that has the same name as the macro that it contains.

Example

Suppose you want to save the macro **Prtlast** in an autocall library. In a directory-based operating system, the first step is to create a directory that holds your macro source files. You can use the Save As window to create the directory, and to save the macro definition in that directory. With the **Prtlast** definition in an active code editing window, select **File** ⇨ **Save As**. In the Save As window, navigate to the location where you want to create your autocall library. Select New Folder, enter the directory name, and click OK. Then enter **Prtlast** as the filename, make sure the file type is .sas, and click Save.

> *TIP*   You could also use the FILE command to save your macro definition in an autocall library. To use the FILE command, you enter
> `file '<path>external-file-name'` in the command line.

Default Autocall Library

SAS provides several macros in a default autocall library for you. Some of the macros in the autocall library that SAS provides are listed here.

Macro Syntax	Purpose
%LOWCASE(*argument*)	converts letters in its argument from uppercase to lowercase
%QLOWCASE(*argument*)	converts letters in its argument from uppercase to lowercase, and returns a result that masks special characters and mnemonic operators
%LEFT(*argument*)	removes leading blanks from the argument
%TRIM(*argument*)	removes trailing blanks from the argument
%CMPRES(*argument*)	removes multiple blanks from the argument
%DATATYP(*argument*)	returns the string NUMERIC or CHAR, depending on whether the argument is an integer or a character string

You might be familiar with SAS functions such as TRIM and LEFT. The macros that SAS supplies look like macro functions, but they are in fact macros. One of the useful things about these macros is that in addition to using them in your SAS programs, you can see their source code.

Example

The macro definition for the **Lowcase** macro is shown below. Notice that the comments that are included in this macro provide information about using the macro. All of the macros that SAS provides in the autocall library include explanatory comments so that they can be easy for you to understand and use.

```
%macro lowcase(string);
%****************************************************;
%*                                                 *;
%*  MACRO: LOWCASE                                  *;
%*                                                 *;
%*  USAGE: 1) %lowcase(argument)                    *;
%*                                                 *;
%*  DESCRIPTION:                                    *;
%*     This macro returns the argument passed to    *;
%*     it unchanged except that all upper-case      *;
%*     alphabetic characters are changed to their   *;
%*     lower-case equivalents.                      *;
%*                                                 *;
%*  E.g.:  %let macvar=%lowcase(SAS Institute Inc.); *;
%*  The variable macvar gets the value              *;
%*    "sas institute inc."                          *;
%*  NOTES:                                          *;
%*     Although the argument to the %UPCASE macro    *;
%*     function may contain commas, the argument to  *;
%*     %LOWCASE may not, unless they are quoted.     *;
%*     Because %LOWCASE is a macro, not a function,  *;
%*     it interprets a comma as the end of a parameter. *;
%****************************************************;
%sysfunc(lowcase(%nrbquote(&string)))
%mend;
```

Accessing Autocall Macros

Remember that an autocall library is either a SAS catalog, an external directory, or a partitioned data set. This is true both for the default autocall library that SAS supplies and for autocall libraries that you create.

In order to access a macro definition that is stored in an autocall library, you must use two SAS system options, as follows:

• The MAUTOSOURCE system option must be specified.

• The SASAUTOS= system option must be set to identify the location of the autocall library or libraries.

Both the MAUTOSOURCE and SASAUTOS= system options can be set either at SAS invocation or with an OPTIONS statement during program execution.

The MAUTOSOURCE system option controls whether the autocall facility is available.

General form, MAUTOSOURCE system option:

OPTIONS MAUTOSOURCE | NOMAUTOSOURCE;

Here is an explanation of the syntax:

MAUTOSOURCE
is the default setting, and specifies that the autocall facility is available.

NOMAUTOSOURCE
specifies that the autocall facility is not available.

The SASAUTOS= system option controls where the macro facility looks for autocall macros.

General form, SASAUTOS= system option:

OPTIONS SASAUTOS=_library-1_**;**

OPTIONS SASAUTOS=(_library-1,...,library-n_)**;**

Here is an explanation of the syntax:

the values of _library-1_ through _library-n_
are references to source libraries that contain macro definitions. To specify a source library that you can

- use a fileref to refer to its location

- specify the pathname (enclosed in quotation marks) for the library.

Unless your system administrator has changed the default value for the SASAUTOS= system option, its value is the fileref _Sasautos_, and that fileref points to the location where the default autocall library was created during installation. The Sasautos fileref can refer to multiple locations that are concatenated.

Generally, it is a good idea to concatenate any autocall libraries that you create yourself with the default autocall library in the value of the SASAUTOS= system option. Otherwise, the new autocall library replaces the default or existing libraries in the value of SASAUTOS=, and the autocall facility has access to only the new autocall library.

Example

Suppose you want to access the **Prtlast** macro, which is stored in the autocall library C:\Mysasfiles. You also want to make sure that the default autocall library (which the fileref Sasautos points to) is still available to the autocall facility. You would submit the following code:

```
options mautosource sasautos=('c:\mysasfiles',sasautos);
%prtlast
```

Note: The MAUTOLOCDISPLAY option is a Boolean option that causes a note to be issued to the SAS log indicating where the source code was obtained to compile an autocall macro. The note is similar to the information displayed when using the MLOGIC option. The default setting of this option is NOMAUTOLOCDISPLAY.

When the autocall facility is in effect, if you invoke a macro that has not been previously compiled, the macro facility automatically

1. searches the autocall library (or each autocall library in turn if multiple libraries are identified in the SASAUTOS= system option) for a member that has the same name as the invoked macro

2. brings the source statements into the current SAS session if the member is found

3. issues an error message if the member is not found

4. submits all statements in the member in order to compile the macro

5. stores the compiled macro in the temporary catalog Work.Sasmacr

6. calls the macro.

The autocall facility does not search for a macro in the autocall library if the macro has already been compiled during the current SAS session. In that case, the session-compiled macro is executed.

Using Stored Compiled Macros

The Stored Compiled Macro Facility

Remember that when a macro is compiled, it is stored in the temporary SAS catalog Work.Sasmacr by default. You can also store compiled macros in a permanent SAS catalog. Then you can use the Stored Compiled Macro Facility to access permanent SAS catalogs that contain compiled macros.

There are several advantages to using stored compiled macros:

- SAS does not need to compile a macro definition when a macro call is made.

- Session-compiled macros and the autocall facility are also available in the same session.

- Users cannot modify compiled macros.

Two SAS system options affect stored compiled macros: MSTORED and SASMSTORE=. The MSTORED system option controls whether the Stored Compiled Macro Facility is available.

General form, MSTORED system option:

OPTIONS MSTORED | NOMSTORED;

Here is an explanation of the syntax:

NOMSTORED
: is the default setting, and specifies that the Stored Compiled Macro Facility does not search for compiled macros.

MSTORED
: specifies that the Stored Compiled Macro Facility searches for stored compiled macros in a catalog in the SAS library that is referenced by the SASMSTORE= option.

The SASMSTORE= system option controls where the macro facility looks for stored compiled macros.

General form, SASMSTORE= system option:

OPTIONS SASMSTORE=*libref*;

Here is an explanation of the syntax:

libref
  specifies the libref of a SAS library that contains, or contains, a catalog of stored compiled SAS macros. This libref cannot be Work.

The MSTORED and SASMSTORE= system options can be set either at SAS invocation or with an OPTIONS statement during program execution.

Creating a Stored Compiled Macro

To create a permanently stored compiled macro, you must do the following:

1. assign a libref to the SAS library in which the compiled macro is stored

2. set the system options MSTORED and SASMSTORE=*libref*

3. use the STORE option in the %MACRO statement when you submit the macro definition.

General form, macro definition with STORE option:

%MACRO *macro-name* <*(parameter-list)*> **/STORE**
    <DES=*'description'*>;
    text
%MEND <*macro-name*>;

Here is an explanation of the syntax:

description
  is an optional 156-character description that appears in the catalog directory.

macro-name
  names the macro.

parameter-list
  names one or more local macro variables whose values you specify when you invoke the macro.

text
  can be

  • constant text, possibly including SAS data set names, SAS variable names, or SAS statements

  • macro variables, macro functions, or macro program statements

  • any combination of the above.

There are several restrictions on stored compiled macros.

• Sasmacr is the only catalog in which compiled macros can be stored. You can create a catalog named Sasmacr in any SAS library. You should not rename this catalog or its entries.

• You cannot copy stored compiled macros across operating systems. You must copy the source program and re-create the stored compiled macro.

• The source cannot be re-created from the compiled macro. You should retain the original source program. For convenience, you can store the source program in an autocall library. Alternatively, you can store the source program as a source entry in the same catalog as the compiled macro.

Using the SOURCE Option

An alternative to saving your source program separately from the stored compiled macro is to use the SOURCE option in the %MACRO statement to combine and store the source of the compiled macro with the compiled macro code. The SOURCE option requires that the STORE option and the MSTORED option be set. The %MACRO statement below shows the correct syntax for using the SOURCE option.

```
%macro macro-name<(parameter list)> /STORE SOURCE;
```

The source code that is saved by the SOURCE option begins with the %MACRO keyword and ends with the semicolon following the %MEND statement.

TIP The SOURCE option cannot be used on nested macro definitions.

Example

Suppose you want to store the **Words** macro in compiled form in a SAS library. This example shows the macro definition for **Words**. The macro takes a text string, divides it into words, and creates a series of macro variables to store each word.

Notice that both the STORE option and the SOURCE option are used in the macro definition so that **Words** is permanently stored as a compiled macro and the macro source code is stored with it, as follows:

```
libname macrolib 'c:\storedlib';
options mstored sasmstore=macrolib;

%macro words(text,root=w,delim=%str( ))/store source;
   %local i word;
   %let i=1;
   %let word=%scan(&text,&i,&delim);
   %do %while (&word ne );
      %global &root&i;
      %let &root&i=&word;
      %let i=%eval(&i+1);
      %let word=%scan(&text,&i,&delim);
   %end;
   %global &root.num;
   %let &root.num=%eval(&i-1);
%mend words;
```

If the Sasmacr catalog does not exist in the Macrolib library, it is automatically created. You can list the contents of the Macrolib.Sasmacr catalog to verify that the compiled macro was created, as follows:

```
proc catalog cat=macrolib.sasmacr;
   contents;
   title "Stored Compiled Macros";
quit;
```

Here is the output from the PROC CATALOG step if no other compiled macros are stored in Macrolib.Sasmacr.

Stored Compiled Macros					
Contents of Catalog MACROLIB.SASMACR					
#	Name	Type	Create Date	Modified Date	Description
1	WORDS	MACRO	20Apr11:15:35:55	20Apr11:15:35:55	

Accessing Stored Compiled Macros

In order to access a stored compiled macro, you must do the following:

1. assign a libref to the SAS library that contains a Sasmacr catalog in which the macro was stored

2. set the system options MSTORED and SASMSTORE=*libref*

3. call the macro.

Example

The following program calls the **Words** macro. Assume that the **Words** macro was compiled and stored in an earlier SAS session.

```
libname macrolib 'c:\storedlib';
options mstored sasmstore=macrolib;

%words(This is a test)
%put Number of Words (wnum): &wnum;
%put Word Number 1 (w1): &w1;
%put Word Number 2 (w2): &w2;
%put Word Number 3 (w3): &w3;
%put Word Number 4 (w4): &w4;
```

Here is a portion of the messages that are written to the SAS log when this code is submitted.

Table 12.2 *SAS Log*

```
9     libname macrolib 'c:\storedlib';
NOTE: Libref MACROLIB was successfully assigned as follows:
      Engine:        V9
      Physical Name: c:\storedlib
10      options mstored sasmstore=macrolib;
11
12      %words(This is a test)
13      %put Number of Words (wnum): &wnum;
Number of Words (wnum): 4
14      %put Word Number 1 (w1): &w1;
Word Number 1 (w1): This
15      %put Word Number 2 (w2): &w2;
Word Number 2 (w2): is
16      %put Word Number 3 (w3): &w3;
Word Number 3 (w3): a
17      %put Word Number 4 (w4): &w4;
Word Number 4 (w4): test
```

Accessing Stored Macro Code

If you use the SOURCE option of the %MACRO statement to store your macro source code along with the stored compiled macro, you can use the %COPY statement to access the stored source code.

General form, %COPY statement:

%COPY *macro-name* **/SOURCE** *<other option(s)>*;

Here is an explanation of the syntax:

macro-name
　　is the name of the macro whose source code is accessed.

SOURCE
　　specifies that the source code of the macro is copied to the output destination. If no output destination is specified, the source is written to the SAS log.

other options
　　include the following options:

- LIBRARY= specifies the libref of a SAS library that contains a catalog of stored compiled SAS macros. If no library is specified, the libref specified by the SASMSTORE= option is used. The libref cannot be Work.

- OUTFILE= specifies the output destination of the %COPY statement. The value can be a fileref or an external file.

Example

Suppose you submitted the program below to create a stored compiled macro named **Words**.

```
libname macrolib 'c:\storedlib';
options mstored sasmstore=macrolib;
```

```
%macro words(text,root=w,delim=%str( ))/store source;
   %local i word;
   %let i=1;
   %let word=%scan(&text,&i,&delim);
   %do %while (&word ne );
      %global &root&i;
      %let &root&i=&word;
      %let i=%eval(&i+1);
      %let word=%scan(&text,&i,&delim);
      %end;
   %global &root.num;
   %let &root.num=%eval(&i-1);
%mend words;
```

The %COPY statement writes the source code for the **Words** macro to the SAS log. Here is an example:

```
%copy words/source;
```

The partial SAS log below shows the source code of the **Words** macro.

Table 12.3 *SAS Log*

```
17    %copy words/source;
%macro words(text,root=w,delim=%str( ))/store source;

      %local i word;
      %let i=1;
      %let word=%scan(&text,&i,&delim);
      %do %while (&word ne );
         %global &root&i;
         %let &root&i=&word;
         %let i=%eval(&i+1);
         %let word=%scan(&text,&i,&delim);
      %end;
      %global &root.num;
      %let &root.num=%eval(&i-1);
%mend words;
```

The Stored Compiled Macro Facility can be used in conjunction with the Autocall Facility and with session-compiled macros. When you submit a macro call such as **%words**, the macro processor searches for the macro **Words** as

1. an entry named **Words.Macro** in the temporary Work.Sasmacr catalog.

2. an entry named **Words.Macro** in the Libref.Sasmacr catalog. The MSTORED option must be specified, and the SASMSTORE= option must have a value of *Libref*.

3. an autocall library member named **Words** that contains the macro definition for the macro **Words**. The MAUTOSOURCE option must be specified, and the value of the SASAUTOS= option must point to the autocall library.

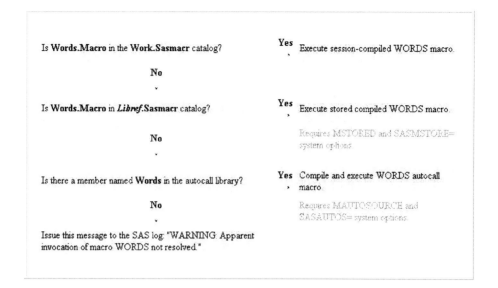

Summary

Text Summary

Understanding Session-Compiled Macros
You can make a macro available to your SAS session by submitting the macro definition before calling the macro. This creates a session-compiled macro. Session-compiled macros are deleted from the temporary SAS catalog Work.Sasmacr at the end of the session.

Storing Macro Definitions in External Files
One way to store your macro definitions permanently is to save them in external files. You can make a macro definition that is stored in an external file accessible to your SAS programs by using the %INCLUDE statement.

Storing Macro Definitions in Catalog SOURCE Entries
You can also store your macro definitions permanently as SOURCE entries in SAS catalogs. You can use the catalog access method to make these macros accessible to your SAS programs. The PROC CATALOG statement enables you to view a list of the contents of a SAS catalog.

Using the Autocall Facility
You can permanently store macro definitions in source libraries called autocall libraries. SAS provides several macro definitions for you in a default autocall library. You can concatenate multiple autocall libraries. To access macros that are stored in an autocall library, you specify the SASAUTOS= and MAUTOSOURCE system options.

Using Stored Compiled Macros
Another efficient way to make macros available to a program is to store them in compiled form in a SAS library. To store a compiled macro permanently, you must set

two system options, MSTORED and SASMSTORE=. Then you submit one or more macro definitions, using the STORE option in the %MACRO statement. The compiled macro is stored as a catalog entry in Libref.Sasmacr. The source program is not stored as part of the compiled macro. You should always maintain the original source program for each macro definition in case you need to redefine the macro. You can use the SOURCE option in the %MACRO statement to store the macro source code with the compiled macro. If you use the SOURCE option in the %MACRO statement, you can use the %COPY statement to access the macro source code later.

Sample Programs

Compiling an Externally Stored Macro Definition with the %INCLUDE Statement

```
%include 'c:\sasfiles\prtlast.sas' / source2;

proc sort data=sasuser.courses out=bydays;
   by days;
run;

%prtlast
```

Listing the Contents of a Catalog

```
proc catalog cat=work.sasmacr;
   contents;
   title "Default Storage of SAS Macros";
quit;
```

Using the Catalog Access Method

```
filename prtlast catalog 'sasuser.mymacs.prtlast.source';
%include prtlast;
proc sort data=sasuser.courses out=bydays;
   by days;
run;
%prtlast
```

Accessing an Autocall Macro

```
options mautosource sasautos=('c:\mysasfiles',sasautos);
%prtlast
```

Creating a Stored Compiled Macro

```
libname macrolib 'c:\storedlib';
options mstored sasmstore=macrolib;

%macro words(text,root=w,delim=%str( ))/store;
   %local i word;
   %let i=1;
   %let word=%scan(&text,&i,&delim);
   %do %while (&word ne );
      %global &root&i;
      %let &root&i=&word;
      %let i=%eval(&i+1);
      %let word=%scan(&text,&i,&delim);
```

```
        %end;
        %global &root.num;
        %let &root.num=%eval(&i-1);
    %mend words;
```

Points to Remember

- You can make macros available to your programs in four ways: as session-compiled macros, with a %INCLUDE statement, through the autocall facility, or as stored compiled macros.

- If you use the autocall facility, you must specify the MAUTOSOURCE and SASAUTOS= system options.

- If you use the stored compiled macro facility, you must specify the MSTORED and SASMSTORE= system options.

- The point at which macro compilation occurs depends on which method you use to access the macro.

Quiz

Select the best answer for each question. After completing the quiz, check your answers using the answer key in the appendix.

1. The %INCLUDE statement

   a. can be used to insert the contents of an external file into a program.

   b. can cause a macro definition that is stored in an external file to be compiled when the contents of that file are inserted into a program and submitted.

   c. can be specified with the SOURCE2 option in order to write the contents of the external file that is inserted into a program to the SAS log.

   d. all of the above

2. If you store a macro definition in a SAS catalog SOURCE entry

   a. the macro definition can be submitted for compilation by using the FILENAME and %INCLUDE statements.

   b. you can use the PROC CATALOG statement to compile the macro.

   c. the SOURCE entry is deleted at the end of the session.

   d. you do not need to compile the macro before you invoke it in a program.

3. Which of the following programs correctly sets the appropriate system options and calls the macro `Prtlast`? Assume that `Prtlast` is stored in an autocall library as a text file and that it has not been compiled during the current SAS session.

   a.
   ```
   libname mylib 'c:\mylib';
   filename macsrc 'mylib.macsrc';
   options mautosource sasautos=(macsrc, sasautos);
   %prtlast
   ```

   b.
   ```
   libname mylib 'c:\mylib';
   filename macsrc catalog 'mylib.macsrc';
   ```

```
%prtlast
```

c. ```
   filename mylib 'c:\mylib';
   options mautosource sasautos=(sasautos,mylib);
   %prtlast
   ```

d. ```
   libname mylib 'c:\mylib';
   options mautosource sasautos=mylib;
   %prtlast
   ```

4. If you use the Stored Compiled Macro Facility,

   a. the macro processor does not compile a macro every time it is used.

   b. the only compiled macros that the Stored Compiled Macro Facility can access are those that are stored in the Sasmacr catalog.

   c. you need to specify the MSTORED and SASMSTORE= system options.

   d. all of the above

5. Which of the following correctly creates a permanently stored compiled macro?

   a. ```
      libname macrolib 'c:\mylib';
      options sasmstore;
      %macro prtlast; / store
         proc print data=&syslast (obs=5);
            title "Listing of &syslast data set";
         run;
      %mend;
      ```

   b. ```
      libname macrolib 'c:\mylib';
      options mstored sasmstore=macrolib;
      %macro prtlast / store;
         proc print data=&syslast (obs=5);
            title "Listing of &syslast data set";
         run;
      %mend;
      ```

   c. ```
      libname macrolib 'c:\mylib';
      options mstored sasmstore=macrolib;
      %macro prtlast;
         proc print data=&syslast (obs=5);
            title "Listing of &syslast data set";
         run;
      %mend;
      ```

   d. ```
      libname macrolib 'c:\mylib';
      %macro prtlast / store;
         proc print data=&syslast (obs=5);
            title "Listing of &syslast data set";
         run;
      %mend;
      ```

6. When you submit the following code, what happens?

   ```
   %macro prtlast;
      proc print data=&syslast (obs=5);
         title "Listing of &syslast data set";
      run;
   %mend;
   ```

   a. A session-compiled macro named **Prtlast** is stored in Work.Sasmacr.

    b. A macro named `Prtlast` is stored in the autocall library.

    c. The `Prtlast` macro is stored as a stored compiled macro.

    d. The `Prtlast` macro is stored as a SOURCE entry in a permanent SAS catalog.

7. Why would you want to store your macros in external files?

    a. You could easily share your macros with others.

    b. You could edit your macros with any text editor.

    c. Your macros would be available for use in later SAS sessions.

    d. all of the above

8. What does the following PROC CATALOG step do?

```
proc catalog cat=mylib.sasmacr;
   contents;
quit;
```

    a. Copy the contents of the Sasmacr catalog to a temporary data set.

    b. List the contents of the Sasmacr catalog as output.

    c. Copy the contents of the output window to the Sasmacr catalog.

    d. none of the above

9. Which of the following is not true about stored compiled macros?

    a. Because these stored macros are compiled, you should save and maintain the source for the macro definitions in a different location.

    b. The Stored Compiled Macro Facility compiles and saves compiled macros in a permanent catalog, in a library that you specify.

    c. You do not need to specify any system options in order to use the Stored Compiled Macro Facility.

    d. You cannot move a stored compiled macro to another operating system.

10. Which of the following is not true?

    a. The autocall macro facility stores compiled SAS macros in a collection of external files called an autocall library.

    b. Autocall libraries can be concatenated together.

    c. One disadvantage of the autocall facility is that the first time you call an autocall macro in a SAS session, the macro processor must use system resources to compile it.

    d. The autocall facility can be used in conjunction with the Stored Compiled Macro Facility.

Part 3

Advanced SAS Programming Techniques

Chapter 13
Creating Indexes

Overview

Introduction

This chapter considers direct access technique. For example, you might want to select a subset based on a value within your data, such as a CustomerID number. You can accomplish this action by creating an index on your CustomerID variable using the INDEX= data set option. A WHERE clause can then use this index. By accessing the desired observations directly, rather than all observations sequentially, your program runs faster.

Using Indexes

Overview

An index can help you quickly locate one or more observations that you want to read. Indexes provide direct access to observations in SAS data sets based on values of one or more key variables. Index applications include the following:

- yield faster access to small subsets of observations for WHERE processing

- perform table lookup operations

- join observations

Without an index, SAS accesses observations sequentially, in the order in which they are stored in a data set. For example, to access the observation in the sample SAS data set shown below that has a value of **Smith** for the variable Name, SAS begins with the first observation and reads through each one until it reaches the observation that satisfies the condition.

SAS Data Set

Anderson	09JAN2000	X	34
Baker	14OCT2001	X	54
Davis	30MAR2000	Y	49
Edwards	28JUN2002	X	52
►Smith	15JAN2000	Y	62
Yates	04AUG2002	X	59

When you index a SAS data set, SAS creates an index file that stores values in ascending value order for a specific variable or variables and includes information about the location of those values in the data file. That is, an index consists of value/identifier pairs that enable you to locate an observation by value. For example, if you create an index on the sample SAS data set that is shown below based on the variable Name, SAS uses the index to find the observation that has a value of **Smith** for Name directly without having to read all the prior observations.

SAS Data Set

Anderson	09JAN2000	X	34
Baker	14OCT2001	X	54
Davis	30MAR2000	Y	49
Edwards	28JUN2002	X	52
► Smith	15JAN2000	Y	62
Yates	04AUG2002	X	59

Types of Indexes

You can create two types of indexes:

- a simple index
- a composite index

A simple index consists of the values of one key variable, which can be character or numeric. When you create a simple index, SAS names the index after the key variable.

A composite index consists of the values of multiple key variables, which can be character, numeric, or a combination. The values of these key variables are concatenated to form a single value. For example, if an index is built on the key variables Lastname and Firstname, a value for the index includes the value for Lastname followed by the value for Firstname. When you create a composite index, you must specify a unique index name that is not the name of any existing variable or index in the data set.

Often, only the first variable of a composite index is used. In the example, you could use the composite index that is specified in the example above (Lastname plus Firstname) for a WHERE expression that uses only Lastname. For example, the expression **where Lastname='Smith'** uses the composite index because Lastname is the first variable in the index. That is, the value for Lastname is the first part of the value that is listed in the index.

Creating Indexes in the DATA Step

Overview

To create an index at the same time that you create a data set, use the INDEX= data set option in the DATA statement.

General form, DATA statement with the INDEX= option:

DATA *SAS-data-file-name* **(INDEX=**

   (*index-specification-1*</UNIQUE><...*index-specification-n*>

   </UNIQUE>**));**

Here is an explanation of the syntax:

SAS-data-file-name
   is a valid SAS data set name.

index-specification
   for a simple index is the name of the key variable.

index-specification
   for a composite index is (*index-name*=(*variable-1...variable-n*)).

UNIQUE
   specifies that values for the key variable must be unique for each observation.

You can create multiple indexes on a single SAS data set. However, keep in mind that creating and storing indexes does use system resources. Therefore, you should create indexes only on variables that are commonly used to select observations.

The UNIQUE option guarantees that values for the key variable or the combination of a composite group of variables remain unique for every observation in the data set. In an existing data set, if the variable or variables on which you attempt to create a unique index have duplicate values, the index is not created. Similarly, if an update tries to add an observation with a duplicate value for the index variable to that data set, the update is rejected.

Examples

The following example creates a simple index on the Simple data set. The index is named Division, and it contains values of the Division variable.

```
data simple (index=(division));
   set sasuser.empdata;
run;
```

The following example creates two simple indexes on the Simple2 data set. The first index is named Division, and it contains values of the Division variable. The second index is called EmpID, and it contains unique values of the EmpID variable.

```
data simple2 (index=(division empid/unique));
   set sasuser.empdata;
run;
```

The following example creates a composite index on the Composite data set. The index is named Empdiv, and it contains concatenated values of the Division variable and the EmpID variable.

```
data composite (index=(Empdiv=(division empid)));
   set sasuser.empdata;
run;
```

When you create or use an index, you might want to verify that it has been created or used correctly. To display information in the SAS log concerning index creation or index usage, set the value of the MSGLEVEL= system option to I.

General form, MSGLEVEL= system option:

OPTIONS MSGLEVEL= N|I;

Here is an explanation of the syntax:

N

    prints notes, warnings, and error messages only. This is the default.

I

    prints additional notes or INFO messages pertaining to index usage, merge processing, and sort utilities along with standard notes, warnings, and error messages.

Example

The following code sets the MSGLEVEL= system option to I and creates the Sasuser.Sale2000 data set with two indexes:

```
options msglevel=i;
data sasuser.sale2000(index=(origin
     flightdate=(flightid date)/unique));
   infile sale2000 dsd;
   input FlightID $ RouteID $ Origin $
         Dest $ Cap1st CapBusiness
         CapEcon CapTotal CapCargo
         Date Psgr1st PsgrBusiness
         PsgrEcon Rev1st RevBusiness
         RevEcon SaleMon $ CargoWgt
         RevCargo;
   format date date9.;
run;
```

Here are the messages that are written to the SAS log when the program above is submitted.

Table 13.1   *SAS Log*

```
NOTE: The infile SALE2000 is:
      File Name=C:\My SAS Files\9.0\sale2000.dat,
      RECFM=V,LRECL=256

NOTE: 153 records were read from the infile SALE2000.
      The minimum record length was 82.
      The maximum record length was 100.
NOTE: The data set SASUSER.SALE2000 has 153 observations
      and 19 variables.
NOTE: Composite index flightdate has been defined.
NOTE: Simple index origin has been defined.
NOTE: DATA statement used (Total process time):
      real time            1.08 seconds
      cpu time             0.04 seconds
```

Determining Whether SAS Used an Index

It is not always possible or more efficient for SAS to use an existing index to access specific observations directly. An index is not used in these circumstances:

- with a subsetting IF statement in a DATA step

- with particular WHERE expressions

- if SAS determines it is more efficient to read the data sequentially

Example

You can use the MSGLEVEL= option to determine whether SAS used an index. The following SAS logs show examples of the INFO messages that indicate whether an index was used.

Table 13.2   *SAS Log*

```
6   options msglevel=i;
7
8   proc print data=sasuser.revenue;
9      where flightid ne 'IA11200';
INFO: Index FlightID not used. Increasing bufno to 3 may help.
```

Table 13.3   *SAS Log*

```
11  options msglevel=i;
12
13  data somflights;
14     set sasuser.revenue;
15     where flightid > 'IA11200';
INFO: Index FlightID selected for WHERE clause optimization.
```

Managing Indexes with PROC DATASETS

Overview

You have seen how to create an index at the same time that you create a data set. You can also create an index on an existing data set or delete an index from a data set. One way to accomplish either of these tasks is to rebuild the data set. However, rebuilding the data set is not the most efficient method for managing indexes.

You can use the DATASETS procedure to manage indexes on an existing data set. This uses fewer resources than rebuilding the data set. You use the MODIFY statement with the INDEX CREATE statement to create indexes on a data set. You use the MODIFY statement with the INDEX DELETE statement to delete indexes from a data set. You can also use the INDEX CREATE statement and the INDEX DELETE statement in the same step.

General form, PROC DATASETS to create and delete an index:

PROC DATASETS LIBRARY= *libref* <NOLIST>;

      MODIFY *SAS-data-set-name*;

      INDEX DELETE *index-name*;

      INDEX CREATE *index-specification*;

QUIT;

Here is an explanation of the syntax:

libref
> points to the SAS library that contains *SAS-data-set-name*.

NOLIST
> option suppresses the printing of the directory of SAS files in the SAS log and as ODS output.

index-name
> is the name of an existing index to be deleted.

index-specification
> for a simple index is the name of the key variable.

index-specification
> for a composite index is *index-name=(variable-1...variable-n)*.

The INDEX CREATE statement in PROC DATASETS cannot be used if the index to be created already exists. In this case, you must delete the existing index of the same name, and then create the new index.

TIP   PROC DATASETS executes statements in order. Therefore, if you delete and create indexes in the same step, you should delete the old indexes first so that the newly created indexes can reuse the space that the deleted indexes had occupied.

Example

The following example creates an index named Origin on the Sasuser.Sale2000 data set. Origin is a simple index that is based on the key variable Origin.

```
proc datasets library=sasuser nolist;
   modify sale2000;
   index create origin;
quit;
```

The following example first deletes the Origin index from the Sasuser.Sale2000 data set, and creates two new indexes on the Sasuser.Sale2000 data set. FlightID is a simple index that is based on the values of the key variable FlightID. Fromto is a composite index that is based on the concatenated values of the key variables Origin and Dest.

```
proc datasets library=sasuser nolist;
   modify sale2000;
   index delete origin;
   index create flightid;
   index create Fromto=(origin dest);
quit;
```

Managing Indexes with PROC SQL

Overview

You can also create or delete indexes from an existing data set within a PROC SQL step. The CREATE INDEX statement enables you to create an index on a data set. The DROP INDEX statement enables you to delete an index from a data set.

General form, PROC SQL to create and delete an index:

PROC SQL;

      CREATE <UNIQUE > **INDEX** *index-name*

             ON *table-name(column-name-1<...,column-name-n>)*;

      DROP INDEX *index-name* **FROM** *table-name*;

QUIT;

Here is an explanation of the syntax:

index-name
    is the same as *column-name-1* if the index is based on the values of one column only.

index-name
    is not the same as any *column-name* if the index is based on multiple columns.

table-name
    is the name of the data set that *index-name* is associated with.

Example

The following example creates a simple index named Origin on the Sasuser.Sale2000 data set. The index is based on the values of the Origin column.

```
proc sql;
   create index origin on sasuser.sale2000(origin);
quit;
```

The following example deletes the Origin index from the Sasuser.Sale2000 data set and creates a new index named Tofrom that is based on the concatenation of the values from the columns Origin and Dest:

```
proc sql;
   drop index origin from sasuser.sale2000;
   create index Tofrom
      on sasuser.sale2000(origin, dest);
quit;
```

Documenting and Maintaining Indexes

Overview

Indexes are stored in the same SAS library as the data set that they index, but in a separate SAS file from the data set. Index files have a member type of INDEX. There is only one index file per data set; all indexes for a data set are stored together in a single file.

The following figure shows the relationship of SAS data set files and SAS index files in a Windows operating environment. Notice that the index files have the same name as the data set with which they are associated, but they have different file extensions. Also, notice that each index file can contain one or more indexes, and that different index files can contain indexes with identical names.

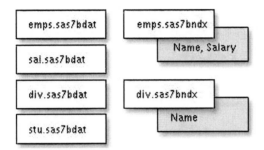

Note: Index files are stored in the same location as the data sets with which they are associated. However, keep the following in mind:

- Index files do not appear in the SAS Explorer window.

- Index files do not appear as separate files in z/OS operating environment file lists.

Sometimes, you might want to view a list of the indexes that exist for a data set. You might also want to see information about the indexes such as whether they are unique, and what key variables they use. Let us consider some ways to document indexes.

Information about indexes is stored in the descriptor portion of the data set. You can use either the CONTENTS procedure or the CONTENTS statement in PROC DATASETS to list information from the descriptor portion of a data set.

Output from the CONTENTS procedure or from the CONTENTS statement in PROC DATASETS contains the following information about the data set:

- general and summary information

- engine/host dependent information

- alphabetic list of variables and attributes

- alphabetic list of integrity constraints

- alphabetic list of indexes and attributes

General form, PROC CONTENTS:

PROC CONTENTS DATA=<*libref.*>*SAS-data-set-name*;
RUN;

Here is an explanation of the syntax:

SAS-data-set-name
    specifies the data set for which the information is listed.

General form, PROC DATASETS with the CONTENTS statement:

PROC DATASETS <LIBRARY=*libref*> <NOLIST>;
        CONTENTS DATA=<*libref.*>*SAS-data-set-name*;
QUIT;

Here is an explanation of the syntax:

SAS-data-set-name
    specifies the data set for which the information is listed.

NOLIST
    suppresses the printing of the directory of SAS files in the SAS log and as ODS output.

Note: If you use the LIBRARY= option, you do not need to specify a libref in the DATA= option. Likewise, if you specify a libref in the DATA= option, you do not need to use the LIBRARY= option.

Example

The following example prints information about the Sasuser.Sale2000 data set. Notice that the library is specified in the LIBRARY= option of the PROC DATASETS statement.

```
proc datasets library=sasuser nolist;
   contents data=sale2000;
quit;
```

The following example also prints information about the Sasuser.Sale2000 data set. Notice that the library is specified in the CONTENTS statement.

```
proc datasets nolist;
   contents data=sasuser.sale2000;
quit;
```

The following example also prints information about the Sasuser.Sale2000 data set:

```
proc contents data=sasuser.sale2000;
run;
```

The PROC DATASETS and PROC CONTENTS output from these programs is identical. The last piece of information that is printed in each set of output is a list of the indexes that have been created for Sasuser.Sale2000, as shown below.

Alphabetic List of Indexes and Attributes				
#	Index	Unique Option	# of Unique Values	Variables
1	Origin		32	
2	flightdate	YES	156	FlightID Date

You can also use either of these methods to list information about an entire SAS library rather than an individual data set. To list the contents of all files in a SAS library with either PROC CONTENTS or with the CONTENTS statement in PROC DATASETS, you specify the keyword _ALL_ in the DATA= option.

Example

The following example prints information about all of the files in the Work data library:

```
proc contents data=work._all_;
run;
```

The following example also prints information about all of the files in the Work data library:

```
proc datasets library=work nolist;
   contents data=_all_;
quit;
```

Remember that indexes are stored in a separate SAS file. When you perform maintenance tasks on a data set, there might be resulting effects on the index file. If you alter the variables or values within a data set, there might be a resulting effect on the value/identifier pairs within a particular index.

The following table describes the effects on an index file or an index file that result from several common maintenance tasks.

Task	Effect
Add an observation or observations to a data set.	Value/identifier pairs are added to the index or indexes.
Delete an observation or observations from a data set.	Value/identifier pairs are deleted from the index or indexes.
Update an observation or observations in a data set.	Value/identifier pairs are updated in the index or indexes.
Delete a data set.	The index file is deleted.
Rebuild a data set with the DATA step.	The index file is deleted.
Sort the data in place with the FORCE option in PROC SORT.	The index file is deleted.

Let us consider some of the other common tasks that you might perform on your data sets, as well as the actions that SAS performs on the index files as a result.

Copying Data Sets

You might want to copy an indexed data set to a new location. You can copy a data set with the COPY statement in a PROC DATASETS step. When you use the COPY statement to copy a data set that has an associated index, a new index file is automatically created for the new data file.

General form, PROC DATASETS with the COPY statement:

PROC DATASETS LIBRARY=*old-libref* <NOLIST>;

        COPY OUT=*new-libref*;

        SELECT *SAS-data-set-name*;

QUIT;

Here is an explanation of the syntax:

old-libref
    names the library from which the data set is copied.

new-libref
    names the library to which the data set is copied.

SAS-data-set-name
    names the data set that is copied.

You can also use the COPY procedure to copy data sets to a new location. Generally, PROC COPY functions the same as the COPY statement in the DATASETS procedure. When you use PROC COPY to copy a data set that has an associated index, a new index file is automatically created for the new data file. If you use the MOVE option in the COPY procedure, the index file is deleted from the original location and rebuilt in the new location.

General form, PROC COPY step:

PROC COPY OUT=*new-libref* **IN=***old-libref*

        <MOVE>;

        SELECT *SAS-data-set-name(s)*;

RUN;

QUIT;

Here is an explanation of the syntax:

old-libref
    names the library from which the data set is copied.

new-libref
    names the library to which the data set is copied.

SAS-data-set-name
    names the data set or data sets that are copied.

Examples

The following programs produce the same result. Both programs copy the Sale2000 data set from the Sasuser library and place it in the Work library. Likewise, both of these programs cause a new index file to be created for Work.Sale2000 that contains all indexes that exist in Sasuser.Sale2000.

```
proc datasets library=sasuser nolist;
   copy out=work;
   select sale2000;
quit;

proc copy out=work in=sasuser;
   select sale2000;
run;
```

Note: If you copy and paste a data set in either SAS Explorer or in SAS Enterprise Guide, a new index file is automatically created for the new data file.

Renaming Data Sets

Another common task is to rename an indexed data set. To preserve the index, you can use the CHANGE statement in PROC DATASETS to rename a data set. The index file is automatically renamed as well.

General form, PROC DATASETS with the CHANGE statement:

PROC DATASETS LIBRARY=*libref*<NOLIST>;

   CHANGE *old-data-set-name* = *new-data-set-name*;

QUIT;

Here is an explanation of the syntax:

libref
 names the SAS library where the data set is stored.

old-data-set-name
 is the current name of the data set.

new-data-set-name
 is the new name of the data set.

Example

The following example copies the Revenue data set from Sasuser into Work, and renames the Work.Revenue data set to Work.Income. The index file that is associated with Work.Revenue is also renamed to Work.Income.

```
proc copy out=work in=sasuser;
   select revenue;
run;

proc datasets library=work nolist;
   change revenue=income;
quit;
```

Renaming Variables

You have seen how to use PROC DATASETS to rename an indexed data set. Similarly, you might want to rename one or more variables within an indexed data set. In order to preserve any indexes that are associated with the data set, you can use the RENAME statement in the DATASETS procedure to rename variables.

General form, PROC DATASETS with the RENAME statement:

PROC DATASETS LIBRARY=*libref* <NOLIST>;

    MODIFY *SAS-data-set-name*;

    RENAME *old-var-name-1 = new-var-name-1*

    <...old-var-name-n = new-var-name-n>;

QUIT;

Here is an explanation of the syntax:

libref
    names the SAS library where the data set is stored.

SAS-data-set-name
    is the name of the data set that contains the variables to be renamed.

old-var-name
    is the original variable name.

new-var-name
    is the new name to be assigned to the variable.

When you use the RENAME statement to change the name of a variable for which there is a simple index, the statement also renames the index. If the variable that you are renaming is used in a composite index, the composite index automatically references the new variable name. However, if you attempt to rename a variable to a name that has already been used for a composite index, you receive an error message.

Example

The following example renames the variable FlightID as FlightNum in the Work.Income data set. If a simple index exists that is named FlightID, the index is renamed FlightNum.

```
proc datasets library=work nolist;
   modify income;
   rename flightid=FlightNum;
quit;
```

Summary

Text Summary

Using Indexes

An index is a SAS file that is associated with a data set and that contains information about the location and the values of key variables in the data set. Indexes enable SAS to directly access specific observations rather than having to read all observations sequentially. An index can be simple or composite.

Creating Indexes in the DATA Step

You can create an index at the same time that you create a data set by using the INDEX= option in the DATA statement. Both simple and composite indexes can be unique, if there are no duplicate values for any key variable in the data set. You can create multiple indexes on one data set. You can use the MSGLEVEL= system option to write informational messages to the SAS log that pertain to indexes. Indexes can improve the efficiency of SAS, but there are certain instances where indexes do not improve efficiency and therefore should not be used.

Managing Indexes with PROC DATASETS and PROC SQL

You can use the INDEX CREATE statement or the INDEX DELETE statement in PROC DATASETS to create or delete an index from an existing data set. Using PROC DATASETS to manage indexes uses less system resources than it would to rebuild the data set and update indexes in the DATA step. If you want to delete an index and create an index in the same PROC DATASETS step, you should delete the old index before you create the new index so that SAS can reuse space from the deleted index. You can also use PROC SQL to create or delete an index from an existing data set.

Documenting and Maintaining Indexes

All indexes that are created for a particular data set are stored in one file in the same SAS library as the data set. You can use PROC CONTENTS to print a list of all indexes that exist for a data set, along with other information about the data set. The CONTENTS statement of the PROC DATASETS step can generate the same list of indexes and other information about a data set.

Many of the maintenance tasks that you perform on your data sets affect the index file that is associated with the data set. When you copy a data set with the COPY statement in PROC DATASETS, the index file is reconstructed for you. When you rename a data set or rename a variable with PROC DATASETS, the index file is automatically updated to reflect this change.

Sample Programs

Creating an Index in the DATA Step

```
options msglevel=i;
data sasuser.sale2000(index=(origin FlightDate=
                      (flightid date)/unique));
   infile 'sale2000.dat';
```

```
        input FlightID $7. RouteID $7. Origin $3.
              Dest $3. Cap1st 8. CapBusiness 8.
              CapEcon 8. CapTotal 8. CapCargo 8.
              Date date9. Psgr1st 8./
              PsgrBusiness 8. PsgrEcon 8.
              Rev1st dollar15.2
              RevBusiness dollar15.2
              RevEcon dollar15.2 SaleMon $7.
              CargoWgt 8./ RevCargo dollar15.2;
   run;
```

Managing Indexes with PROC DATASETS

```
proc datasets library=sasuser nolist;
   modify sale2000;
   index delete origin;
   index create flightid;
   index create Tofrom=(origin dest);
quit;
```

Managing Indexes with PROC SQL

```
proc sql;
   create index Tofrom on
          sasuser.sale2000(origin, dest);
   drop index origin from sasuser.sale2000;
quit;
```

You can also generate reports using the Dictionary.Indexes table

```
proc sql;
   select *
        from dictionary.indexes
          where libname='SASUSER' and
memname='SALE2000';
   quit;
```

Points to Remember

- An index can enable SAS to more efficiently access specific observations of a data set. However, because indexes use system resources, they should be created only on variables that are commonly used to select observations.

- An index is associated with a data set but is stored as a separate file. You can use PROC DATASETS or PROC CONTENTS to generate a report on a data set's indexes. You can also right-click on a data set in SAS Explorer and select **view columns** to view a list of the data set's indexes. You should view this information after you have performed maintenance tasks on your data set to ensure that the index file has been maintained.

Quiz

Select the best answer for each question. After completing the quiz, check your answers using the answer key in the appendix.

1. Which statement is true about an index?

    a. It is an optional file that is associated with a data set.

    b. It provides direct access to specific observations of a data set, based on the value of one or more key variables.

    c. It can be classified as simple or composite, either of which can consist of unique values.

    d. All of the above.

2. Which of the following correctly creates a data set named Flights from the Sasuser.Revenue data set, creates a composite index named Fromto that is based on the values of Origin and Dest, and prints informational messages about the index to the SAS log?

    a.
    ```
    options msglevel=i;
    data flights index=(Fromto=origin dest);
       set sasuser.revenue;
    run;
    ```

    b.
    ```
    options msglevel=n;
    data flights (index=(Fromto=origin dest));
       set sasuser.revenue;
    run;
    ```

    c.
    ```
    options msglevel=i;
    data flights (index=(Fromto=(origin dest)));
       set sasuser.revenue;
    run;
    ```

    d.
    ```
    options msglevel=n;
    data flights (index=Fromto);
       set sasuser.revenue;
    run;
    ```

3. Which of the following is true?

    a. When you add observations to a data set, the index or indexes are automatically updated with additional value/identifier pairs.

    b. When you rename a variable that is used as the key variable in a simple index, you must re-create the index.

    c. When you delete a data set, the index file remains until you delete it as well.

    d. When you copy a data set with the COPY statement, you must also copy the index file in another step.

4. To create an index on an existing data set, you use which of the following?

    a. PROC DATASETS

    b. PROC SQL

    c. the DATA step with the INDEX= option, to rebuild the data set

    d. any of the above

5. Which of the following correctly creates a simple index named Origin on the Revenue data set?

    a.
    ```
    proc sql;
       create index origin on revenue(origin);
    quit;
    ```

b.
```
proc sql;
    modify revenue;
    index=origin;
quit;
```

c.
```
proc sql data=revenue;
    create index origin;
quit;
```

d.
```
proc sql;
    index=origin on revenue;
quit;
```

6. To view a list of the indexes that are associated with a data set, you use which of the following?

   a. PROC COPY or the COPY statement in PROC DATASETS

   b. PROC CONTENTS or the CONTENTS statement in PROC DATASETS

   c. the MSGLEVEL= system option and a PROC PRINT step

   d. any of the above

7. Suppose that the Sasuser.Revenue data set has a simple index named FlightID. Which of the following programs use the index?

   a.
   ```
   proc print data=sasuser.revenue;
       where flightid ne 'IA11200';
   run;
   ```

   b.
   ```
   data someflights;
       set sasuser.revenue;
       where flightid > 'IA11200';
   run;
   ```

   c.
   ```
   data someflights;
       set sasuser.revenue;
       if flightid > 'IA11200';
   run;
   ```

   d.
   ```
   proc print data=sasuser.revenue;
       where origin='RDU' or flightid='IA03400';
   run;
   ```

Chapter 14
Combining Data Vertically

Overview

Introduction

Combining data vertically refers to the process of concatenating or interleaving data. In some cases the data might be in SAS data sets. In other cases the data might be stored in raw data files.

In this chapter you learn how to create a SAS data set by concatenating multiple raw data files using the FILENAME and INFILE statements. You also learn how to concatenate SAS data sets using PROC APPEND.

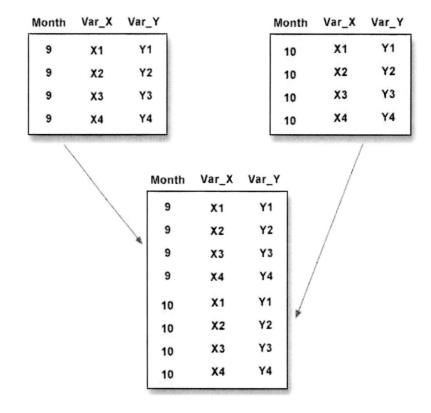

Using a FILENAME Statement

Overview

You already know that you can use a FILENAME statement to associate a fileref with a single raw data file. You can also use a FILENAME statement to concatenate raw data files by assigning a single fileref to the raw data files that you want to combine.

General form, FILENAME statement:

FILENAME *fileref* **(***'external-file1' 'external-file2' ...'external-filen'***);**

Here is an explanation of the syntax:

fileref
is any SAS name that is eight characters or fewer.

external-file
is the physical name of an external file. The physical name is the name that is recognized by the operating environment.

CAUTION:

All of the file specifications must be enclosed in one set of parentheses.

When the fileref is specified in an INFILE statement, each raw data file that has been referenced can be sequentially read into a data set using an INPUT statement.

TIP If you are not familiar with the content and structure of your raw data files, you can use PROC FSLIST to view them.

Example

In the following program, the FILENAME statement creates the fileref Qtr1, which references the raw data files Month1.dat, Month2.dat, and Month3.dat. The files are stored in the C:\Sasuser directory in the Windows operating environment. In the DATA step, the INFILE statement identifies the fileref, and the INPUT statement describes the data, just as if Qtr1 referenced a single raw data file.

```
filename qtr1 ('c:\sasuser\month1.dat''c:\sasuser\month2.dat'
               'c:\sasuser\month3.dat');
data work.firstqtr;
   infile qtr1;
   input Flight $ Origin $ Dest $
         Date : date9. RevCargo : comma15.;
run;
```

Table 14.1 *RAW Data File Month1.dat (first five records)*

```
----+----10---+----20---+----30---+----40
IA10200 SYD HKG 01JAN2000 $191,187.00
IA10201 SYD HKG 01JAN2000 $169,653.00
IA10300 SYD CBR 01JAN2000 $850.00
IA10301 SYD CBR 01JAN2000 $970.00
IA10302 SYD CBR 01JAN2000 $1,030.00
```

Table 14.2 *Raw Data File Month2.dat (first five records)*

```
----+----10---+----20---+----30---+----40
IA10200 SYD HKG 01FEB2000 $177,801.00
IA10201 SYD HKG 01FEB2000 $174,891.00
IA10300 SYD CBR 01FEB2000 $1,070.00
IA10301 SYD CBR 01FEB2000 $1,310.00
IA10302 SYD CBR 01FEB2000 $850.00
```

Table 14.3 *Raw Data File Month3.dat (first five records)*

```
----+----10---+----20---+----30---+----40
IA10200 SYD HKG 01MAR2000 $181,293.00
IA10201 SYD HKG 01MAR2000 $173,727.00
IA10300 SYD CBR 01MAR2000 $1,150.00
IA10301 SYD CBR 01MAR2000 $910.00
IA10302 SYD CBR 01MAR2000 $1,170.00
```

The SAS log indicates that the raw data files referenced by Qtr1 are sequentially read into the SAS data set Work.FirstQtr.

Note: The Read count for the three raw data files is 50 records each. The Write count to the output SAS data set is 150 observations.

Table 14.4 *SAS Log*

```
9    filename qtr1 ('c:\sasuser\month1.dat''c:\sasuser\month2.dat'
10                  'c:\sasuser\month3.dat');

11   data work.firstqtr;
12      infile qtr1;
13      input Flight $ Origin $ Dest $
14      Date : date9. RevCargo : comma15.;
15   run;

NOTE: The infile QTR1 is:
      File Name=c:\sasuser\month1.dat,
      File List=('c:\sasuser\month1.dat' 'c:\sasuser\month2.dat'
               'c:\sasuser\month3.dat'),
      RECFM=V,LRECL=256

NOTE: The infile QTR1 is:
      File Name=c:\sasuser\month2.dat,
      File List=('c:\sasuser\month1.dat' 'c:\sasuser\month2.dat'
               'c:\sasuser\month3.dat'),
      RECFM=V,LRECL=256

NOTE: The infile QTR1 is:
      File Name=c:\sasuser\month3.dat,
      File List=('c:\sasuser\month1.dat' 'c:\sasuser\month2.dat'
               'c:\sasuser\month3.dat'),
      RECFM=V,LRECL=256

NOTE: 50 records were read from the infile QTR1.
      The minimum record length was 33.
      The maximum record length was 37.
NOTE: 50 records were read from the infile QTR1.
      The minimum record length was 33.
      The maximum record length was 37.
NOTE: 50 records were read from the infile QTR1.
      The minimum record length was 33.
      The maximum record length was 37.
NOTE: The data set WORK.FIRSTQTR has 150 observations
      and 5 variables.
NOTE: DATA statement used (Total process time):
      real time           4.02 seconds
      cpu time            0.93 seconds
```

The following PROC PRINT output shows a portion of the observations in the Work.FirstQtr data set.

```
proc print
    data=work.firstqtr (firstobs=45 obs=55);
    format date date9.
           revcargo dollar11.2;
run;
```

Obs	Flight	Origin	Dest	Date	RevCargo
45	IA03505	RDU	BNA	01JAN2000	$2,697.00
46	IA03904	RDU	MCI	01JAN2000	$4,161.00
47	IA04503	LHR	GLA	01JAN2000	$3,498.00
48	IA04703	LHR	FRA	01JAN2000	$3,225.00
49	IA05002	BRU	LHR	01JAN2000	$1,989.00
50	IA05003	BRU	LHR	01JAN2000	$2,379.00
51	IA10200	SYD	HKG	01FEB2000	$177,801.00
52	IA10201	SYD	HKG	01FEB2000	$174,891.00
53	IA10300	SYD	CBR	01FEB2000	$1,070.00
54	IA10301	SYD	CBR	01FEB2000	$1,310.00
55	IA10302	SYD	CBR	01FEB2000	$850.00

Using the FILEVAR= Option

Overview

You can make the process of concatenating raw data files more flexible by using an INFILE statement with the FILEVAR= option. The FILEVAR= option enables you to dynamically change the currently opened input file to a new input file.

General form, INFILE statement with the FILEVAR= option:

INFILE *file-specification* **FILEVAR=** *variable*;

Here is an explanation of the syntax:

FILEVAR= *variable*
  names a variable whose change in value causes the INFILE statement to close the current input file and open a new input file.

variable
  contains a character string that is a physical filename.

When you use an INFILE statement with the FILEVAR= option, the file specification is a placeholder, not an actual filename or fileref that had been assigned previously to a file. SAS uses this placeholder for reporting processing information to the SAS log. The file specification must conform to the same rules as a fileref.

When the INFILE statement executes, it reads from the file that the FILEVAR= variable specifies. Like automatic variables, this variable is not written to the data set.

Example

Suppose you want to create a SAS data set that contains three months of data stored in three raw data files. The three months are the current month, and the previous two months are a rolling quarter.

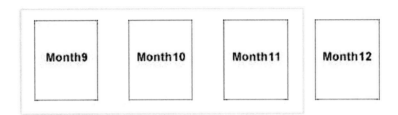

In the following INFILE statement, Temp is an arbitrarily named placeholder, not an actual filename or fileref that had been assigned to a file previously. The FILEVAR= variable Nextfile contains the name of the raw data file to read (for example, Month9.dat, Month10.dat, or Month11.dat). A RUN statement is not included because the program is not complete.

```
data work.quarter;
   infile temp filevar=nextfile;
   input Flight $ Origin $ Dest $
         Date : date9. RevCargo : comma15.;
```

Table 14.5 *Raw Data File Month9.dat (first five records)*

```
----+----10---+----20---+----30---+----40
IA10200 SYD HKG 01SEP2000 $189,441.00
IA10201 SYD HKG 01SEP2000 $175,473.00
IA10300 SYD CBR 01SEP2000 $1,370.00
IA10301 SYD CBR 01SEP2000 $710.00
IA10302 SYD CBR 01SEP2000 $1,210.00
```

Table 14.6 *Raw Data File Month10.dat (first five records)*

```
----+----10---+----20---+----30---+----40
IA10200 SYD HKG 01OCT2000 $182,457.00
IA10201 SYD HKG 01OCT2000 $160,923.00
IA10300 SYD CBR 01OCT2000 $1,030.00
IA10301 SYD CBR 01OCT2000 $870.00
IA10302 SYD CBR 01OCT2000 $770.00
```

Table 14.7 *Raw Data File Month11.dat (first five records)*

```
----+----10---+----20---+----30---+----40
IA10200 SYD HKG 01NOV2000 $176,637.00
IA10201 SYD HKG 01NOV2000 $164,997.00
IA10300 SYD CBR 01NOV2000 $1,230.00
IA10301 SYD CBR 01NOV2000 $1,230.00
IA10302 SYD CBR 01NOV2000 $790.00
```

Note: You can also use multiple INFILE statements or operating system techniques to combine raw data files. This chapter discusses only the FILENAME statement and the INFILE statement with the FILEVAR= option.

Assigning the Names of the Files to Read

The next step is to assign the names of the three files to read to the variable Nextfile:

```
data work.quarter;
   infile temp filevar=nextfile;
   input Flight $ Origin $ Dest $
        Date : date9. RevCargo : comma15.;
```

In this case, use the raw data files Month9.dat, Month10.dat, and Month11.dat. Notice that the titles of the raw data files are very similar. They each start with "Month" and are followed by numerals and the file extension .dat:

- Month9.dat

- Month10.dat

- Month11.dat

You can use an iterative DO loop and the PUT function to automatically change the values that are assigned to Nextfile.

Example

In the following code, the DO statement creates the index variable Month and assigns it the values of 9, 10, and 11. The assignment statement then assigns the name of the raw data file to Nextfile using the current value of Month and the PUT function. The PUT function converts the numeric value of Month to a text value with a length of 2.

Month9.dat, Month10.dat, and Month11.dat are stored in the C:\Sasuser directory in the Windows operating environment. On the right side of the assignment statement, the text string c:\sasuser\month is concatenated with the current value of Month using the double exclamation point (!!) concatenation operator. c:\sasuser\month**Month** is then concatenated with the text string .dat.

```
data work.quarter;
   do Month = 9, 10, 11;
      nextfile="c:\sasuser\month"
                !!put(Month,2.)!!".dat";
      infile temp filevar=nextfile;
      input Flight $ Origin $ Dest $
           Date : date9. RevCargo : comma15.;
   end;
```

The following table shows the value of Nextfile as the value of Month changes.

When Month=	Nextfile=
9	c:\sasuser\Month 9.dat
10	c:\sasuser\Month10.dat
11	c:\sasuser\Month11.dat

> **T I P**   Depending on the characters that are available on your keyboard, the symbol that
> you use as the concatenation operator can be a double vertical bar (‖), a double
> broken vertical bar (¦¦), or a double exclamation point (!!).

Using the COMPRESS Function

Note the space between Month and 9 in c:\sasuser\month 9.dat. You can eliminate the
space by using the COMPRESS function.

When Month=	Nextfile=
9	c:\sasuser\Month 9.dat
10	c:\sasuser\Month10.dat
11	c:\sasuser\Month11.dat

General form, COMPRESS function:

COMPRESS(*source, <characters-to-remove>*);

Here is an explanation of the syntax:

source
   specifies a source string that contains the characters to remove.

characters-to-remove
   specifies the character or characters that SAS removes from the source string.

Note: If a value for *characters-to-remove* is omitted, the COMPRESS function removes
   blank spaces from the source.

Example

In the following code, the COMPRESS function removes blank spaces from the value of
Nextfile:

```
data work.quarter;
   do Month = 9, 10, 11;
      nextfile="c:\sasuser\month"!!put(Month,2.)!!".dat";
      nextfile=compress (nextfile,' ');
      infile temp filevar=nextfile;
      input Flight $ Origin $ Dest $
           Date : date9. RevCargo : comma15.;
      end;
```

The COMPRESS function can be combined with the assignment statement for greater
efficiency:

```
data work.quarter;
   do Month = 9, 10, 11;
      nextfile="c:\sasuser\month"!!compress(put(Month,2.)!!".dat",' ');
      infile temp filevar=nextfile;
      input Flight $ Origin $ Dest $
           Date : date9. RevCargo : comma15.;
```

```
          end;
```

With the addition of the COMPRESS function, when the value of Month equals 9, Nextfile is assigned the correct value, c:\sasuser\month9.dat.

When Month=	Nextfile=
9	c:\sasuser\Month9.dat
10	c:\sasuser\Month10.dat
11	c:\sasuser\Month11.dat

An OUTPUT statement within the DO loop outputs each observation to the SAS data set Work.Quarter. A STOP statement prevents an infinite loop of the DATA step.

```
data work.quarter;
   do Month = 9, 10, 11;
      nextfile="c:\sasuser\month"
                !!compress(put(Month,2.)!!".dat",' ');
      infile temp filevar=nextfile;
      input Flight $ Origin $ Dest $ Date : date9.
            RevCargo : comma15.;
      output;
   end;
   stop;
```

The program is almost complete.

Using the END= Option

When you read past the last row in an input file, the DATA step normally stops processing. In this example, we are reading three raw data files. We must not read past the last record in the first two files, because that would cause the DATA step to prematurely stop processing. You can use the END= option with the INFILE statement to determine when you are reading the last record in the last raw data file.

General form, INFILE statement with the END= option:

INFILE *file-specification* **END**=*variable*;

Here is an explanation of the syntax:

variable
    names a variable that SAS sets to these values:

- 0 (false) when the current input data record *is not* the last record in the input file
- 1 (true) when the current input record *is* the last record in the input file.

Note: Like automatic variables, the END= variable is not written to the SAS data set.

You can test the value of the END= variable to determine whether the DATA step should continue processing.

Example

The END= variable Lastobs is created in the INFILE statement. The DO UNTIL statement conditionally executes until the value of Lastobs equals 1 (true). A RUN statement completes the program.

```
data work.quarter;
   do Month = 9, 10, 11;
   nextfile="c:\sasuser\month"
          !!compress(put(Month,2.)!!".dat",' ');
       do until (lastobs);
       infile temp filevar=nextfile end=lastobs;
       input Flight $ Origin $ Dest $ Date : date9.
           RevCargo : comma15.;
       output;
     end;
   end;
   stop;
run;
```

PROC PRINT output shows a portion of the observations in the SAS data set Work.Quarter. Notice that the variables Nextfile and Lastobs are not written to the data set.

```
proc print
    data=work.quarter
    (firstobs=45 obs=55);
    format date date9.
        revcargo dollar11.2;
run;
```

Obs	Month	Flight	Origin	Dest	Date	RevCargo
45	9	IA04300	LHR	CDG	01SEP2000	$1,750.00
46	9	IA05002	BRU	LHR	01SEP2000	$1,859.00
47	9	IA05005	BRU	LHR	01SEP2000	$2,197.00
48	9	IA05101	LHR	GVA	01SEP2000	$3,741.00
49	9	IA05202	GVA	LHR	01SEP2000	$4,069.00
50	9	IA05204	GVA	LHR	01SEP2000	$3,741.00
51	10	IA10200	SYD	HKG	01OCT2000	$162,457.00
52	10	IA10201	SYD	HKG	01OCT2000	$160,923.00
53	10	IA10300	SYD	CBR	01OCT2000	$1,030.00
54	10	IA10301	SYD	CBR	01OCT2000	$870.00
55	10	IA10302	SYD	CBR	01OCT2000	$770.00

Using Date Functions

You can make your program more flexible by eliminating the need to include explicit month numbers in your SAS statements. To create a program that always reads the current month and the previous two months, you can use date functions to obtain the current month number to begin the rolling quarter.

Example

In the following program, the MONTH and TODAY functions are used to obtain the value of the variable Monthnum. The TODAY function returns the current date from the system clock as a SAS date value. The month number is then extracted from the current date using the MONTH function.

The value of Midmon is calculated by subtracting 1 from the value of Monthnum. The value of Lastmon is then calculated by subtracting 1 from the values of Midmon. The following table shows the values Monthnum, Midmon, and Lastmon if the current date is October 22, 2013.

Variable	Value
monthnum	10
midmon	9
lastmon	8

In the previous example, the DO statement created the index variable Month and assigned it the values of 9, 10, and 11. Here, the DO statement assigns Month the values of Monthnum, Midmon, and Lastmon:

```
data work.quarter (drop=monthnum midmon lastmon);
   monthnum=month(today());
   midmon=monthnum-1;
   lastmon=midmon-1;
   do Month = monthnum, midmon, lastmon;
      nextfile="c:\sasuser\month"
                !!compress(put(Month,2.)!!".dat",' ');
      do until (lastobs);
         infile temp filevar=nextfile end=lastobs;
         input Flight $ Origin $ Dest $ Date : date9.
             RevCargo : comma15.;
         output;
      end;
   end;
   stop;
run;
```

The following PROC PRINT output shows a portion of the observations in Work.Quarter.

```
proc print data=work.quarter
           (firstobs=45 obs=55);
   format date date9.
          revcargo dollar11.2;
run;
```

Obs	Month	Flight	Origin	Dest	Date	RevCargo
45	4	IA02705	RDU	MIA	01APR2000	$3,828.00
46	4	IA02800	MIA	RDU	01APR2000	$5,148.00
47	4	IA02804	MIA	RDU	01APR2000	$5,852.00
48	4	IA02805	MIA	RDU	01APR2000	$4,160.00
49	4	IA03200	ANC	SFO	01APR2000	$45,974.00
50	4	IA03401	ANC	RDU	01APR2000	$95,914.00
51	3	IA10200	SYD	HKG	01MAR2000	$181,293.00
52	3	IA10201	SYD	HKG	01MAR2000	$173,727.00
53	3	IA10300	SYD	CBR	01MAR2000	$1,150.00
54	3	IA10301	SYD	CBR	01MAR2000	$910.00
55	3	IA10302	SYD	CBR	01MAR2000	$1,170.00

Using the INTNX Function

In the previous example the current month was October. What happens if the current month is January or February?

Suppose the current date is February 16, 2013. Using the following program, the values for Midmon (January) and Lastmon (December) would be **1** and **0** respectively. Since there is no "0" month, the program would fail to read the third raw data file.

```
data work.quarter (drop=monthnum midmon lastmon);
   thisday=today();
   monthnum=month(thisday);
   midmon=month(intnx('month',thisday,-1));
   lastmon=month(intnx('month',thisday,-2));
   do Month = monthnum, midmon, lastmon;
      nextfile="c:\sasuser\month"
            !!compress(put(Month,2.)!!".dat",' ');
      do until (lastobs);
         infile temp filevar=nextfile end=lastobs;
         input Flight $ Origin $ Dest $ Date : date9.
            RevCargo : comma15.;
         output;
      end;
   end;
   stop;
run;
```

Variable	Value
monthnum	2
midmon	1
lastmon	0

You can use the INTNX function with the TODAY and MONTH functions to correctly determine the values of Midmon and Lastmon for any given date. Remember that the INTNX function increments a date, time, or datetime value by a given interval or intervals, and returns a date, time, or datetime value.

Example

Suppose the current date is January 30, 2013. In the following program Monthnum is assigned a value of *1* using the TODAY and MONTH functions. The INTNX function is used with the TODAY and MONTH functions to assign a value of **12** to Midmon and a value of **11** to Lastmon.

```
data work.quarter (drop=monthnum midmon lastmon);
   monthnum=month(today());
   midmon=month(intnx('month',today(),-1));
   lastmon=month(intnx('month',today(),-2));
   do Month = monthnum, midmon, lastmon;
      nextfile="c:\sas\month"!!compress(put(Month,2.)!!".dat'
      do until (lastobs);
         infile temp filevar=nextfile end=lastobs;
         input Flight $ Origin $ Dest $ Date : date9.
            RevCargo : comma15.;
         output;
      end;
   end;
   stop;
run;
```

Variable	Value
monthnum	1
midmon	12
lastmon	11

The following PROC PRINT output shows a portion of the observations in
Work.Quarter.

```
proc print data=work.quarter
            (firstobs=45 obs=55);
   format date date9.
          revcargo dollar11.2;
run;
```

Obs	Month	Flight	Origin	Dest	Date	RevCargo
45	4	IA02705	RDU	MIA	01APR2000	$3,828.00
46	4	IA02800	MIA	RDU	01APR2000	$5,146.00
47	4	IA02804	MIA	RDU	01APR2000	$5,852.00
48	4	IA02805	MIA	RDU	01APR2000	$4,180.00
49	4	IA03200	ANC	SFO	01APR2000	$45,974.00
50	4	IA03401	ANC	RDU	01APR2000	$95,914.00
51	3	IA10200	SYD	HKG	01MAR2000	$181,293.00
52	3	IA10201	SYD	HKG	01MAR2000	$173,727.00
53	3	IA10300	SYD	CBR	01MAR2000	$1,150.00
54	3	IA10301	SYD	CBR	01MAR2000	$910.00
55	3	IA10302	SYD	CBR	01MAR2000	$1,170.00

Appending SAS Data Sets

Overview

Now that you have seen several methods for concatenating raw data files, use the
APPEND procedure to concatenate two SAS data sets.

General form, PROC APPEND:

PROC APPEND BASE=_SAS-data-set_ **DATA=**_SAS-data-set_;
RUN;

Here is an explanation of the syntax:

BASE=_SAS-data-set_
   names the data set to which you want to add observations.

DATA=_SAS-data-set_
   names the SAS data set containing observations that you want to append to the end of the
   BASE= data set.

PROC APPEND reads only the data in the DATA= SAS data set, not the BASE= SAS
data set. Therefore, this action is very efficient. PROC APPEND concatenates data sets
even though there might be variables in the BASE= data set that do not exist in the
DATA= data set.

When the BASE= data set contains more variables than the DATA= data set, missing
values for the additional variables are assigned to the observations that are read in from
the DATA= data set, and a warning message is written to the SAS log.

Example

The SAS data sets Work.Cap2001 and Work.Capacity both contain the following variables: Cap1st, CapBusiness, CapEcon, Dest, FlightID, Origin, and RouteID. However, the BASE= data set (Work.Cap2001) contains an additional variable, Date, that is not included in the DATA= data set (Work.Capacity).

When the following program is submitted, the SAS log indicates that the variable **Date** was not found in the DATA= file.

```
proc append base=work.cap2001
            data=work.capacity;
run;
```

Table 14.8 *SAS Log*

```
NOTE: Appending WORK.CAPACITY to WORK.CAP2001.
WARNING: Variable Date was not found on DATA file.
NOTE: There were 50 observations read from the data set WORK.CAPACITY.
NOTE: 50 observations added.
NOTE: The data set WORK.CAP2001 has 100 observations and 8 variables.
NOTE: PROCEDURE APPEND used (Total process time):
```

The PROC PRINT output of the appended version of Work.Cap2001 shows that missing values have been assigned to Date in the observations that were read in from the DATA= data set.

```
proc print data=work.cap2001
           (firstobs=45 obs=55);
run;
```

Obs	FlightID	RouteID	Origin	Dest	Cap1st	CapBusiness	CapEcon	Date
45	IA02503	0000025	RDU	IND	12	0	138	21JAN2001
46	IA02504	0000025	RDU	IND	12	0	138	24JAN2001
47	IA02600	0000026	IND	RDU	12	0	138	02JAN2001
48	IA02605	0000026	IND	RDU	12	0	138	05JAN2001
49	IA02603	0000026	IND	RDU	12	0	138	16JAN2001
50	IA02703	0000027	RDU	MIA	12	0	138	17JAN2001
51	IA00100	0000001	RDU	LHR	14	30	163	.
52	IA00201	0000002	LHR	RDU	14	30	163	.
53	IA00300	0000003	RDU	FRA	14	30	163	.
54	IA00400	0000004	FRA	RDU	14	30	163	.
55	IA00500	0000005	RDU	JFK	16		251	.

Note: You can also use the DATA step SET statement to combine SAS data vertically. If multiple data set names appear in the SET statement, the resulting output data set is a concatenation of all the data sets listed. Unlike the APPEND procedure, the SET statement in the DATA step reads all observations in all input data sets in order to concatenate them. Therefore, the APPEND procedure is more efficient than the SET statement in the DATA step for concatenating data sets because it reads only the data in the DATA= data set.

In the following program, SAS reads all of the observations from Work.Cap2001, and it then reads all of the observations from Work.Capacity.

```
data work.new;
```

```
        set work.cap2001 work.capacity;
run;
```

Note: You can also use the SQL procedure to combine SAS data vertically. For information about using the SQL procedure to combine data vertically, see Chapter 4, "Combining Tables Vertically Using PROC SQL," on page 126.

Using the FORCE Option

In the previous example, the DATA= data set (Work.Capacity) contained fewer variables than the BASE= data set (Work.Cap2001). However, you might need to append data sets when the DATA= data set contains more variables than the BASE= data set.

You must use the FORCE option with the APPEND procedure to concatenate data sets when the DATA= data set contains variables that are not in the BASE= data set.

General form, PROC APPEND with the FORCE option:

PROC APPEND BASE=*SAS-data-set* **DATA=***SAS-data-set* <FORCE>;

CAUTION:
The FORCE option can cause loss of data due to truncation or dropping of variables.

The structure of the BASE= data set is used for the appended data set.

Example

Remember that the SAS data sets Work.Cap2001 and Work.Capacity both contain the following variables: Cap1st, CapBusiness, CapEcon, Dest, FlightID, Origin, and RouteID. In this case, the DATA= data set (Work.Cap2001) contains an additional variable, Date, that is not included in the BASE= data set (Work.Capacity).

When the following program is submitted, the SAS log indicates that the data sets were not appended because the variable Date was not found in the BASE= file.

```
proc append base=work.capacity
            data=work.cap2001;
run;
```

Table 14.9 *SAS Log*

```
NOTE: Appending WORK.CAP2001 to WORK.CAPACITY.
WARNING: Variable Date was not found on BASE file.
ERROR: No appending done because of anomalies listed above.
       Use FORCE option to append these files.
NOTE: 0 observations added.
NOTE: The data set WORK.CAPACITY has 50 observations and 7 variables.
NOTE: Statements not processed because of errors noted above.
NOTE: PROCEDURE APPEND used (Total process time):
      real time           0.02 seconds
      cpu time            0.03 seconds
NOTE: The SAS System stopped processing this step because of errors.
```

When the FORCE option is used with PROC APPEND, the SAS log indicates that observations have been read from the DATA= data set, but that dropping or truncating occurs.

```
proc append base=work.capacity
             data=work.cap2001 force;
run;
```

Table 14.10 *SAS Log*

```
NOTE: Appending WORK.CAP2001 to WORK.CAPACITY.
WARNING: Variable Date was not found on BASE file.
NOTE: FORCE is specified, so dropping/truncating will occur.
NOTE: There were 50 observations read from the data set WORK.CAP2001.
NOTE: 50 observations added.
NOTE: The data set WORK.CAPACITY has 100 observations and 7 variables.
NOTE: PROCEDURE APPEND used (Total process time):
      real time            0.03 seconds
      cpu time             0.03 seconds
```

PROC PRINT output shows that the variable **Date** has been dropped from the appended version of Work.Capacity.

```
proc print
    data=work.capacity
        (firstobs=45 obs=55);
run;
```

Obs	FlightID	RouteID	Origin	Dest	Cap1st	CapBusiness	CapEcon
45	IA04500	0000045	LHR	GLA	14	.	125
46	IA04600	0000046	GLA	LHR	14	.	125
47	IA04700	0000047	LHR	FRA	14	.	125
48	IA04800	0000048	FRA	LHR	14	.	125
49	IA04900	0000049	LHR	BRU	14	.	125
50	IA05000	0000050	BRU	LHR	14	.	125
51	IA00100	0000001	RDU	LHR	14	30	163
52	IA00101	0000001	RDU	LHR	14	30	163
53	IA00201	0000002	LHR	RDU	14	30	163
54	IA00301	0000003	RDU	FRA	14	30	163
55	IA00603	0000006	JFK	RDU	16	34	251

Appending Variables with Different Lengths

If the DATA= data set contains variables with greater lengths than like-named variables in the BASE= data set, the FORCE option must be used with PROC APPEND. Using the FORCE option enables you to append the data sets. However, the DATA= variable values might be truncated.

Example

In the SAS data set Work.Acities, the variable City has a length of 22. In the SAS data set Work.WestAust, City has a length of 50. You can use the CONTENTS procedure to view the attributes of the variables in each data set.

```
proc contents data=work.acities;
run;
```

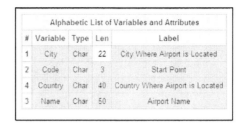

```
proc contents data=work.westaust;
run;
```

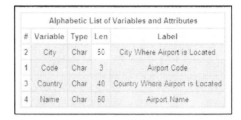

When the following program is submitted, the SAS log indicates that the data sets were not appended because of different lengths for City in the BASE= and DATA= data sets.

```
proc append base=work.acities
            data=work.westaust;
run;
```

Table 14.11   *SAS Log*

```
NOTE: Appending WORK.WESTAUST to WORK.ACITIES.
WARNING: Variable City has different lengths on BASE and
         DATA files (BASE 22 DATA 50).
ERROR: No appending done because of anomalies listed above.
       Use FORCE option to append these files.
NOTE: 0 observations added.
NOTE: The data set WORK.ACITIES has 50 observations and 4 variables.
NOTE: Statements not processed because of errors noted above.
NOTE: PROCEDURE APPEND used (Total process time):
      real time            1.44 seconds
      cpu time             0.06 seconds
NOTE: The SAS System stopped processing this step because of errors.
```

When the FORCE option is used, the SAS log indicates that the data sets are appended, but that dropping or truncating occurs.

```
proc append base=work.acities
            data=work.westaust force;
run;
```

Table 14.12 SAS Log

```
NOTE: Appending WORK.WESTAUST to WORK.ACITIES.
WARNING: Variable City has different lengths on BASE and DATA files
         (BASE 22 DATA 50).
NOTE: FORCE is specified, so dropping/truncating will occur.
NOTE: There were 50 observations read from the data set WORK.WESTAUST.
NOTE: 50 observations added.
NOTE: The data set WORK.ACITIES has 100 observations and 4 variables.
NOTE: PROCEDURE APPEND used (Total process time):
      real time           1.44 seconds
      cpu time            0.06 seconds
```

PROC CONTENTS output for the appended version of Work.Acities shows that the variable City has retained a length of 22 from the BASE= data set. Also notice that the variable Code has retained the label Start Point from the BASE= data set.

```
proc contents
     data=work.acities;
run;
```

			Alphabetic List of Variables and Attributes	
#	Variable	Type	Len	Label
1	City	Char	22	City Where Airport is Located
2	Code	Char	3	Start Point
4	Country	Char	40	Country Where Airport is Located
3	Name	Char	50	Airport Name

PROC PRINT output shows that some of the values of City are truncated in the appended version of Work.Acities.

```
proc print
     data=work.acities
         (firstobs=45 obs=55);
run;
```

Obs	City	Code	Name	Country
45	Portland, ME	PWM	Portland International Jetport	USA
46	Raleigh-Durham, NC	RDU	Raleigh-Durham International Airport	USA
47	Seattle, WA	SEA	Seattle-Tacoma International Airport	USA
48	San Francisco, CA	SFO	San Francisco International Airport	USA
49	Singapore	SIN	Changi International Airport	Singapore
50	Sydney, New South Wale	SYD	Kingsford Smith	Australia
51	Argyle Downs, Western	AGY		Australia
52	Albany, Western Austra	ALH		Australia
53	Big Bell, Western Aust	BBE		Australia
54	Bedford Downs, Western	BDW		Australia
55	Beagle Bay, Western Au	BEE		Australia

Appending Variables with Different Types

If the DATA= data set contains a variable that does not have the same type as the corresponding variable in the BASE= data set, the FORCE option must be used with

PROC APPEND. Using the FORCE option enables you to append the data sets. However, missing values are assigned to the DATA= variable values for the variable whose type did not match.

Example

In the SAS data set Work.Allemps, the variable Phone is a character variable. In the SAS data set Work.Newemps, Phone is a numeric variable. You can use PROC CONTENTS to view the attributes of the variables in each data set.

```
proc contents data=work.allemps;
run;
```

Alphabetic List of Variables and Attributes			
#	Variable	Type	Len
5	Division	Char	30
1	EmplD	Char	6
2	LastName	Char	15
4	Location	Char	13
3	Phone	Num	8

```
proc contents data=work.newemps;
run;
```

Alphabetic List of Variables and Attributes			
#	Variable	Type	Len
5	Division	Char	30
1	EmplD	Char	6
2	LastName	Char	15
4	Location	Char	13
3	Phone	Char	4

When the following program is submitted, the SAS log indicates that there is a type mismatch for the variable Phone and that data sets were not appended.

```
proc append base=work.allemps
            data=work.newemps;
run;
```

Table 14.13 *SAS Log*

```
NOTE: Appending WORK.NEWEMPS to WORK.ALLEMPS.
WARNING: Variable Phone not appended because of type mismatch.
ERROR: No appending done because of anomalies listed above.
      Use FORCE option to append these files.
NOTE: 0 observations added.
NOTE: The data set WORK.ALLEMPS has 550 observations and 5 variables.
NOTE: Statements not processed because of errors noted above.
NOTE: PROCEDURE APPEND used (Total process time):
      real time         0.08 seconds
      cpu time          0.01 seconds
NOTE: The SAS System stopped processing this step because of errors.
```

When the FORCE option is used, the SAS log indicates that the data sets are appended, but that the variable Phone is not appended due to the type mismatch.

```
proc append base=work.allemps
            data=work.newemps force;
run;
```

Table 14.14 *SAS Log*

```
NOTE: Appending WORK.NEWEMPS to WORK.ALLEMPS.
WARNING: Variable Phone not appended because of type mismatch.
NOTE: FORCE is specified, so dropping/truncating will occur.
NOTE: There were 19 observations read from the data set WORK.NEWEMPS.
NOTE: 19 observations added.
NOTE: The data set WORK.ALLEMPS has 569 observations and 5 variables.
NOTE: PROCEDURE APPEND used (Total process time):
      real time           0.05 seconds
      cpu time            0.02 seconds
```

PROC CONTENTS output for the appended version of Work.Allemps shows that the variable Phone has retained the type of character from the BASE= data set.

```
proc contents
     data=work.allemps;
run;
```

Alphabetic List of Variables and Attributes			
#	Variable	Type	Len
5	Division	Char	30
1	EmplD	Char	6
2	LastName	Char	15
4	Location	Char	13
3	Phone	Char	4

PROC PRINT output of the appended version of Work.Allemps shows that the values for Phone are missing in the records that were read in from the DATA= data set.

```
proc print
     data=work.allemps
          (firstobs=45 obs=55);
run;
```

Obs	EmpID	LastName	Phone	Location	Division
45	E00213	DICKEY	1519	CARY	AIRPORT OPERATIONS
46	E00226	BAUCOM	1124	CARY	AIRPORT OPERATIONS
47	E00231	SPENCER	2868	CARY	AIRPORT OPERATIONS
48	E00236	BAILEY	1088	CARY	AIRPORT OPERATIONS
49	E00243	FILIPOWSKI	1635	CARY	AIRPORT OPERATIONS
50	E00249	YUAN	3241	CARY	AIRPORT OPERATIONS
51	E00490	CANCELLO		ROME	FINANCE & IT
52	E00496	PRESTON		LONDON	FINANCE & IT
53	E00499	ZILSTORFF		COPENHAGEN	AIRPORT OPERATIONS
54	E00500	LEY		FRANKFURT	FINANCE & IT
55	E00503	BRAMMER		COPENHAGEN	SALES & MARKETING

Additional Features

In addition to using the methods for appending raw data files that were discussed earlier in this chapter, you can also append raw data files using a SAS data set or an external file that contains the names of the raw data files to be appended.

Storing Raw Data Filenames in a SAS Data Set

In the following program, five raw data files, Route1.dat, Route2.dat, Route3.dat, Route4.dat, and Route5.dat, are concatenated to create the SAS data set Work.NewRoute. The names of the raw data files are stored in the SAS data set Sasuser.Rawdata, which is referenced using a SET statement. The name of the FILEVAR= variable, Readit, is the name of the variable in Sasuser.Rawdata whose value is the name of the file to be read.

```
data work.newroute;
  set sasuser.rawdata;
  infile in filevar = readit end = lastfile;
  do while(lastfile = 0);
    input  @1 RouteID $7. @8 Origin $3. @11 Dest $3.
           @14 Distance 5. @19 Fare1st 4.
           @23 FareBusiness 4. @27 FareEcon 4.
           @31 FareCargo 5.;
    output;
  end;
run;
```

Obs	readit
1	route1.dat
2	route2.dat
3	route3.dat
4	route4.dat
5	route5.dat

Storing Raw Data Filenames in an External File

In the following program, Route1.dat, Route2.dat, Route3.dat, Route4.dat, and Route5.dat are also concatenated to create the SAS data set Work.NewRoute. In this example, the names of the raw data files are stored in the external file Rawdatafiles.dat, which is referenced in the first INFILE statement. The name of the FILEVAR= variable, Readit, is the name of the variable read from Rawdatafiles.dat. The value of Readit is the name of the raw data file to be read.

Table 14.15 *Raw Data File Rawdatafiles.dat*

```
1---+----10---+----20
route1.dat
route2.dat
route3.dat
route4.dat
route5.dat
```

```
data work.newroute;
   infile 'rawdatafiles.dat';
   input readit $10.;
   infile in filevar=readit end=lastfile;
```

```
        do while(lastfile = 0);
           input  @1 RouteID $7. @8 Origin $3. @11 Dest $3.
                  @14 Distance 5. @19 Fare1st 4.
                  @23 FareBusiness 4. @27 FareEcon 4.
                  @31 FareCargo 5.;
           output;
        end;
run;
```

Summary

Text Summary

Using a FILENAME Statement

You can use a FILENAME statement to concatenate raw data files by assigning a single fileref to the raw data files that you want to combine. When the fileref is specified in an INFILE statement, each raw data file that has been referenced can be sequentially read into a data set using an INPUT statement.

Using an INFILE Statement

You can make the process of concatenating raw data files more flexible by using an INFILE statement with the FILEVAR= option. The FILEVAR= option enables you to dynamically change the currently opened input file to a new input file. When the INFILE statement executes, it reads from the file that the FILEVAR= variable specifies.

In some cases, you might need to use the COMPRESS function to eliminate spaces in the filenames that you generate.

When you read the last record in a raw data file, the DATA step normally stops processing. When you are concatenating raw data files, you do not want to read past the last record until you reach the end of the last input file. You can determine whether you are reading the last record in the last raw data file by using the END= option with the INFILE statement. You can then test the value of the END= variable to determine whether the DATA step should continue processing.

If you are working with date-related data, you might be able to make your program more flexible by eliminating the need to include explicit month numbers in your SAS statements. To create a program that always reads the current month and the previous two months, you can use the MONTH and TODAY functions to obtain the month number of today's date to begin the rolling quarter. In some cases, you might need to use the INTNX function with the TODAY and MONTH functions to correctly determine the month numbers.

Appending SAS Data Sets

You can use PROC APPEND to concatenate two SAS data sets. PROC APPEND reads only the data in the DATA= SAS data set, not in the BASE= SAS data set. PROC APPEND concatenates data sets even though there might be variables in the BASE= data set that do not exist in the DATA= data set.

The FORCE option must be used if the DATA= data set contains variables that have the following characteristics:

- They are not in the BASE= data set.

- They are longer than the variables in the BASE= data set.

- They do not have the same type as the variables in the BASE= data set.

The FORCE option can cause loss of data because of truncation or dropping of variables. The following table summarizes the consequences of using the FORCE option.

Characteristics of variables in the DATA= data set	FORCE required?	Consequences of using the FORCE option
They are in the BASE=data set, but the BASE= data set has more variables.	no	Missing values are assigned to the extra BASE= data set variables.
They are not in the BASE= data set.	yes	Extra DATA= data set variables are dropped.
They are longer than the corresponding variables in the BASE= data set.	yes	DATA= data set variable values might be truncated.
They do not have the same type as the corresponding variables in the BASE= data set.	yes	Missing values are assigned to the DATA= data set variables with the data type mismatch.

Additional Features

You can also append raw data files using a SAS data set or an external file that contains the names of the raw data files to be appended.

Sample Programs

Combining Raw Data Files Using a FILENAME Statement

```
filename qtr1 ('c:\data\month1.dat''c:\data\month2.dat'
               'c:\data\month3.dat');
data work.firstqtr;
   infile qtr1;'
   input Flight $ Origin $ Dest $
         Date : date9. RevCargo : comma15.;
run;
```

Combining Raw Data Files Using an INFILE Statement

```
data quarter (drop=monthnum midmon lastmon);
   monthnum=month(today());
   midmon=month(intnx('month',today(),-1));
   lastmon=month(intnx('month',today(),-2));
   do month = monthnum, midmon, lastmon;
      nextfile="c:\sasuser\month"
               !!compress(put(month,2.)!!".dat",' ');
      do until (lastobs);
         infile temp filevar=nextfile end=lastobs;
         input Flight $ Origin $ Dest $ Date : date9.
               RevCargo : comma15.;
         output;
```

```
            end;
        end;
        stop;
    run;
```

Combining SAS Data Sets Using PROC APPEND

```
proc append base=work.acities
            data=work.airports force;
run;
```

Points to Remember

- When you use an INFILE statement with the FILEVAR= option, the file specification is just a placeholder, not an actual filename or fileref that has been previously assigned to a file.

- Like automatic variables, the FILEVAR= variable and the END= variable are not written to the data set.

- Using the FORCE option with PROC APPEND can cause loss of data because of truncation or dropping of variables.

- The structure of the BASE= data set is used for the appended data set.

Quiz

Select the best answer for each question. After completing the quiz, check your answers using the answer key in the appendix.

1. Which of the following statements associates the fileref OnSale with the raw data files London.dat, Paris.dat, and Zurich.dat? The files are stored in the C:\Routes\New directory in the Windows operating environment.

   a. ```
   filename onsale (c:\routes\new\london.dat,
       c:\routes\new\paris.dat,
       c:\routes\new\zurich.dat);
   ```

   b. ```
   filename onsale 'c:\routes\new\london.dat'
       'c:\routes\new\paris.dat'
       'c:\routes\new\zurich.dat';
   ```

   c. ```
   filename onsale ('c:\routes\new\london.dat'
       'c:\routes\new\paris.dat'
       'c:\routes\new\zurich.dat');
   ```

   d. ```
   filename onsale 'c:\routes\new\london.dat
       c:\routes\new\paris.dat
       c:\routes\new\zurich.dat';
   ```

2. Which of the following statements is true?

   a. The FILEVAR= option can be used to dynamically change the currently opened input file to a new physical file.

   b. The FILEVAR= variable is not written to the data set.

   c. The FILEVAR= variable must contain a character string that is a physical filename.

d. all of the above

3. Given the following program, which table correctly shows the corresponding values of the variables Month and Readfile?

```
data work.revenue;
   do month = 8, 9, 10;
      readfile=compress("c:\data\month"
        !!put(month,2.)!!".dat");
      do until (lastobs);
         infile temp filevar=readfile
           end=lastobs;
         input Date : date7. Location $
               Sales : dollar10.;
         output;
      end;
   end;
   stop;
run;
```

a.

When x=	readfile=
8	month8.dat
9	month9.dat
10	month10.dat

b.

When x=	readfile=
8	c:\data\month8.dat
9	c:\data\month9.dat
10	c:\data\month10.dat

c.

When x=	readfile=
8	c:\data\month 8.dat
9	c:\data\month 9.dat
10	c:\data\month10.dat

d.

When x=	readfile=
8	month8
9	month9
10	month10

4. If the current date is March 30, 2003, which table correctly shows the corresponding values of the variables y1, y2, y3, and Nextfile?

```
data work.quarter (drop=monthnum midmon lastmon);
   y3=year(today());
   y2=y3-1;
   y1=y3-2;
   do i = y3, y2, y1;
      nextfile="c:\data\Y"!!put(i,4.)!!".dat";
      do until (lastobs);
         infile temp filevar=nextfile
           end=lastobs;
         input Flight $ Origin $ Dest $
              Date : date9.;
         output;
      end;
   end;
   stop;
run;
```

a.

When i=	Nextfile=
y1	c:\data\Y2001.dat
y2	c:\data\Y2002.dat
y3	c:\data\Y2003.dat

b.

When i=	Nextfile=
y1	Y2001.dat
y2	Y2002.dat
y3	Y2003.dat

c.

When i=	Nextfile=
y1	c:\data\Y2003.dat
y2	c:\data\Y2002.dat
y3	c:\data\Y2001.dat

d.

When i=	Nextfile=
y1	c:\data\Y3.dat
y2	c:\data\Y2.dat
y3	c:\data\Y1.dat

5. What happens when SAS processes the last data record in an input file?

   a. The END= variable is set to *1*.

   b. The END= variable is set to *0*.

   c. The END= variable is set to the number of records in the input file.

   d. The END= variable is written to the SAS data set.

6. Which program appends Work.London to Work.Flights?

   a.
```
proc append base=work.london
             data=work.flights;
run;
```

   b.
```
proc append data=work.london
             base=work.flights;
run;
```

   c.
```
proc append data=work.london work.flights;
run;
```

   d.
```
proc append data=work.flights work.london;
run;
```

7. What happens when the following program is submitted?

```
proc append base=staff.marketing
             data=staff.sales force;
run;
```

Data Set Description for Staff.Marketing		
Variable	**Type**	**Length**
LastName	char	12
FirstName	char	10
EmpID	char	5
Office	char	4
Phone	char	12

Data Set Description for Staff.Sales		
Variable	**Type**	**Length**
LastName	char	20
FirstName	char	10
EmpID	char	5
Office	char	4
Phone	char	12

a. The length of LastName is converted to 20 in Staff.Marketing.

b. LastName is dropped from Staff.Marketing.

c. Missing values are assigned to LastName observations that are read in from Staff.Sales.

d. Some of the values of LastName might be truncated in the observations that are read in from Staff.Sales.

8. Which program appends Work.April to Work.Y2003?

Data Set Description for Work.Y2003		
Variable	**Type**	**Length**
FlightNum	num	8
FirstClass	num	8
BusinessClass	num	8
Coach	num	8

Data Set Description for Work.April		
Variable	**Type**	**Length**
FlightNum	char	4
FirstClass	num	8
BusinessClass	num	8
Coach	num	8

a.
```
proc append base=work.y2003
            data=work.april;
   run;
```

b.
```
proc append base=work.april
            data=work.y2003 force;
   run;
```

c.
```
proc append base=work.y2003
            data=work.april force;
   run;
```

d.
```
proc append base=work.april
            data=work.y2003;
   run;
```

9. What happens when the SAS data set Work.NewHires is appended to the SAS data set Work.Employees using PROC APPEND?

Data Set Description for Work.Employees		
Variable	**Type**	**Length**
Division	num	8
EmpID	num	8
Name	char	20
Room	char	5
Extension	num	8

Data Set Description for Work.NewHires		
Variable	**Type**	**Length**
Division	num	8
EmpID	num	8
Name	char	20
Extension	num	8

a. Missing values are assigned to Room for the observations that are read in from Work.NewHires.

b. Missing values are assigned to Room for all of the observations in Work.Employees.

c. Room is dropped from Work.Employees.

d. The values of Name are truncated in the observations that are read in from Work.NewHires.

10. You do not need to use the FORCE option with PROC APPEND when the following is true:

a. the DATA= data set contains variables that are not in the BASE= data set.

b. the BASE= data set contains variables that are not in the DATA= data set.

c. the variables in the DATA= data set are longer than the corresponding variables in the BASE= data set.

d. the variables in the DATA= data set have a different type than the corresponding variables in the BASE= data set.

Chapter 15
Combining Data Horizontally

Overview

Introduction

Combining data horizontally refers to the process of merging or joining multiple data sets into one data set. This process is referred to as a horizontal combination because, in the final data set, each observation (or horizontal row) will have variables from more than one input data set.

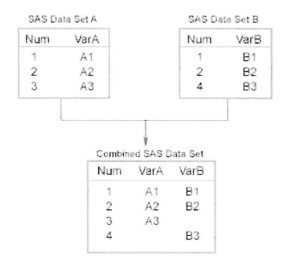

It is useful to combine data horizontally if you have several data sets that contain different but related information. For example, suppose you have one data set that contains employee data with the variables IDNumber, Name, and Address, and another data set that contains employee data with the variables IDNumber and Salary. You can combine the data from these two input data sets horizontally to create an output data set that contains IDNumber, Name, Address, and Salary.

This chapter focuses on several methods of combining data horizontally in the DATA step, and compares a DATA step match-merge with a PROC SQL join. This chapter also covers several techniques for horizontally combining data from an input data set with values that are not stored in a SAS data set.

Reviewing Terminology

Overview

Before you examine the various techniques for combining data horizontally, here is a review of some of the terminology that this chapter uses.

Term	Definition
combining data horizontally	A technique in which data is retrieved from an auxiliary source or sources, based on the values of variables in the primary source.
performing a table lookup	A technique in which data is retrieved from an auxiliary source or sources, based on the values of variables in the primary source.
base table	The primary source in a horizontal combination. In this chapter, the base table is always a SAS data set.
lookup table or tables	Any input data source, except the base table, that is used in a horizontal combination.
lookup values or return value	The data value or values that are retrieved from the lookup table or tables during a horizontal combination.
key variable or variables	One or more variables that reside in both the base table and the lookup table. Usually, key values are unique in the lookup table but are not necessarily unique in the base table.
key value or values	A lookup is successful when the key value in the base table finds a matching key value in the lookup table.

Note: The terms *combining data horizontally* and *performing a table lookup* are synonymous and are used interchangeably throughout this chapter.

Note: This chapter compares PROC SQL techniques with DATA step techniques. In PROC SQL terms, a *SAS data set* is usually referred to as a *table*, a *variable* is usually referred to as a *column*, and an *observation* is usually referred to as a *row*.

The following figure illustrates a base table and a lookup table that are used in a horizontal combination. The key variable is Num. The key values are listed vertically below Num.

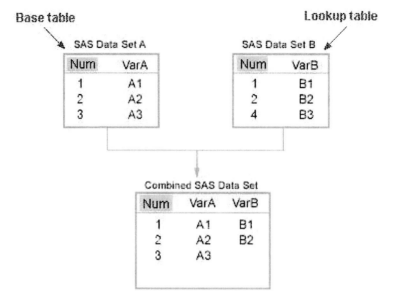

Relationships between Input Data Sources

One important factor to consider when you perform a table lookup is the relationship between the input data sources. In order to combine data horizontally, you must be able to match observations from each input data source. For example, there might be one or more variables that are common to each input data source. The relationship between input data sources describes how the observations in one source relate to the observations in the other source according to these key values.

The following terms describe the possible relationships between base tables and lookup tables:

*   one-to-one match

*   one-to-many match

*   many-to-many match

*   nonmatching data

In a one-to-one match, key values in both the base table and the lookup table are unique. Therefore, for each observation in the base table, no more than one observation in the lookup table has a matching key value.

Base Table		Lookup Table	
Num	**VarA**	**Num**	**VarB**
1	A1	1	B1
2	A2	2	B2
3	A3	3	B3
4	A4	4	B4

In a one-to-many match, key values in the base table are unique, but key values in the lookup table are not unique. That is, for each observation in the base table, there can be one observation or possibly multiple observations in the lookup table that have a matching key value.

Base Table

Num	VarA
1	A1
2	A2

Lookup Table

Num	VarB
1	B1
1	B2
1	B3
2	B4

In a many-to-many match, key values are not unique in the base table or in the lookup table. That is, at least one observation in the base table matches multiple observations in the lookup table, and at least one observation in the lookup table matches multiple observations in the base table.

Many-to-many is a theoretical or mathematical possibility, but it rarely represents a legitimate business application. If a business application appears to be many-to-many, it is usually because a duplicate row was accidentally added to the lookup table.

Base Table

Num	VarA
1	A1
1	A2
3	A3
4	A4
4	A1

Lookup Table

Num	VarB
1	B1
1	B2
1	B3
3	B4
4	B1

Sometimes you will have a one-to-one, a one-to-many, or a many-to-many match that also includes nonmatching data. That is, there are observations in the base table that do not match any observations in the lookup table, or there are observations in the lookup table that do not have matching observations in the base table. If your base table or lookup table or tables include nonmatching data, you will have one of the following:

- *a dense match*, in which every or nearly every observation in one table has a matching observation in the other table. In the following figure, the first observation in the base table is unmatched.

Base Table

Num	VarA
1	A1
2	A2
3	A3
4	A4

Lookup Table

Num	VarB
2	B1
3	B2
4	B3

- *a sparse match*, in which there are many nonmatching observations.

Base Table		Lookup Table	
Num	**VarA**	**Num**	**VarB**
1	A1	2	B1
2	A2	4	B2
3	A3	5	B3
6	A5		

Working with Lookup Values Outside of SAS Data Sets

Overview

Remember that it is not necessary for your lookup table to be a SAS data set. Suppose you want to combine the data from your base table with lookup values that are not stored in a SAS data set. You can use the following techniques to hardcode lookup values into your program:

- the IF-THEN/ELSE statement
- SAS arrays
- user-defined SAS formats
- hash objects.

The IF-THEN/ELSE Statement

You should be familiar with the syntax and use of the IF-THEN/ELSE statement. Overall, this technique is easy to use and easy to understand. Because of its simplicity and because you can use other DATA step syntax with it, the IF-THEN/ELSE statement can be quite versatile as a technique for performing lookup operations. You can use this technique if your lookup values are not stored in a data set, and you can use it to handle any of the possible relationships between your base table and your lookup table. You can use it to retrieve single or multiple values. For example, you can use DO groups to provide multiple values based on a condition.

Keep in mind that this technique requires maintenance. If you expect your lookup values to change, or you have a large number of lookup values, or if you use the lookup values in multiple programs, the resources required for maintaining the IF-THEN/ELSE statements in your programs might make this technique inappropriate. Also, this technique might result in a prohibitively long program or even in a program that will not execute because it times out.

Example: Using the IF-THEN/ELSE Statement to Combine Data

Suppose you have a data set, Mylib.Employees, that contains information about employees. Mylib.Employees contains a variable named IDnum that records each employee's unique identification number. If you want to combine the data from

Mylib.Employees with a list of employees' birthdates that is not stored in a data set, you can use the IF-THEN/ELSE statement to do so.

```
data mylib.employees_new;
   set mylib.employees;
   if IDnum=1001 then Birthdate='01JAN1963'd;
   else if IDnum=1002 then Birthdate='08AUG1946'd;
   else if IDnum=1003 then Birthdate='23MAR1950'd;
   else if IDnum=1004 then Birthdate='17JUN1973'd;
run;
```

SAS Arrays

You should be familiar with the syntax and use of the ARRAY statement. With the ARRAY statement, you can either hardcode your lookup values into the program, or you can read them into the array from a data set. Elements of a SAS array are referenced positionally. That is, you use a numeric value as a pointer to the array element, so you must be able to identify elements of the array either by position or according to another numeric value. You can use multiple values or numeric mathematical expressions to determine the array element to be returned.

This technique is capable of returning only a single value from the lookup operation. The dimensions of the array must be supplied at compile time either by hardcoding or through the use of macro variables.

Example: Using the ARRAY Statement to Combine Data

We will consider our example of combining the data from Mylib.Employees with a list of lookup values. Remember that Mylib.Employees contains data about employees, which includes their identification numbers (IDnum) but does not include their birthdates. You can use the ARRAY statement to hardcode the birthdates into a temporary array named Birthdates, and then use the array to combine the birthdates with the data in Mylib.Employees.

In the following DATA step, the values that are specified as subscripts for the array correspond to values of the variable IDnum in the base table, Mylib.Employees. The assignment statement for the new variable Birthdate retrieves a value from the Birthdates array according to the current value of IDnum.

```
data mylib.employees_new;
   array birthdates{1001:1004} _temporary_ ('01JAN1963'd
         '08AUG1946'd '23MAR1950'd '17JUN1973'd);
   set mylib.employees;
   Birthdate=birthdates{IDnum};
run;
```

User-Defined SAS Formats

You should be familiar with the syntax and use of the FORMAT procedure with the VALUE statement. Formats can be referenced in FORMAT statements, PUT statements, and PUT functions in assignment WHERE or IF statements.

The FORMAT procedure uses a binary search (a rapid search technique) through the lookup table. Another benefit of using this technique is that maintenance is centralized; if a lookup value changes, you have to change it in only one place (in the format), and every program that uses the format will use the new value.

Example: Using the FORMAT Procedure to Combine Data

Once again, suppose the data set Mylib.Employees contains information about employees according to their employee identification numbers (`IDnum`), but does not contain employees' birthdates. You can use a format to combine employees' birthdates with the data that is stored in Mylib.Employees.

The following PROC FORMAT step uses a VALUE statement to hardcode the lookup values in the BIRTHDATE format. The DATA step uses the PUT function to associate the lookup values from the format with the values of IDnum. The INPUT function associates the lookup value with the DATE9. informat, and assigns the formatted values to a new variable named Birthdate.

```
proc format;
   value birthdate 1001 = '01JAN1963'
                   1002 = '08AUG1946'
                   1003 = '23MAR1950'
                   1004 = '17JUN1973';
   run;


   data mylib.employees_new;
   set mylib.employees;
   Birthdate=input(put(IDnum,birthdate.),date9.);
run;
```

Combining Data with the DATA Step Match-Merge

The DATA Step Match-Merge

You should already know how to merge multiple data sets in the DATA step when there is a BY variable that is common to each of the input data sets. When you use the MERGE statement to perform a table lookup operation, your lookup values must be stored in one or more SAS data sets. This technique requires that both the base table and the lookup table or tables be either sorted by or indexed on the BY variable or variables.

You can specify any number of input data sets in the MERGE statement as long as all input data sets have a common BY variable. The MERGE statement can combine data sets of any size. The MERGE statement is capable of returning multiple values. You can use multiple BY variables to perform lookups that are dependent on more than one variable. The MERGE statement returns both matches and nonmatches by default, but you can use DATA step syntax to return only exact matches or to include only specific variables from the lookup table.

CAUTION:

Although you can use the MERGE statement to combine data from sources that have any type of relationship, this technique might not produce the desired results when you are working with a many-to-many match. When the data sets are merged in a DATA step, the observations are matched and combined sequentially. Once an observation is read, it is never reread. That is, the DATA step MERGE statement does not create a Cartesian product. Therefore, the DATA step MERGE statement is probably not an appropriate technique to use for performing lookup operations when you are working with a many-to-many match.

Working with Multiple Lookup Tables

Sometimes you might need to combine data from three or more related SAS data sets in order to create one new data set. For example, the three data sets listed below all contain different data about a fictional airline's flights and airports. Sasuser.Acities contains data about various airports, Sasuser.Revenue contains data about the revenue generated by various flights, and Sasuser.Expenses contains data about the expenses incurred by various flights. The variables in each of these data sets are listed here.

Sasuser.Acities Variables	Sasuser.Revenue Variables	Sasuser.Expenses Variables
City	Date	Date
Code	Dest	FlightID
Country	FlightID	Expenses
Name	Origin	
	RevBusiness	
	RevEcon	
	Rev1st	

Suppose you want to create a new data set, named Sasuser.Alldata, that contains data from each of these three input data sets. As shown below, the Sasuser.Alldata data set contains the new variable Profit, which is calculated from the revenue values that are stored in Sasuser.Revenue and the expense values that are stored in Sasuser.Expenses.

Sasuser.AllData Variables
Date
Dest
FlightID
Origin
Profit
DestAirport
DestCity

You can specify any number of input data sets in the MERGE statement as long as all input data sets have a common BY variable. However, you can see from the data set variable lists above that these three data sets do not have one common variable. We will consider a method for performing a match-merge on these three data sets.

Although the three data sets Sasuser.Acities, *Sasuser.Revenue*, and Sasuser.Expenses do not have a common BY variable, there are several variables that are common to two of the three data sets. As shown below, Date and FlightID are both common to Revenue and Expenses. The variable Code in the Acities data set and the variable Dest in the Revenue data set, while named differently, contain the same data with the same type and length.

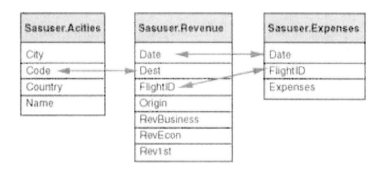

Notice that Code in Acities and Dest in Revenue are listed as corresponding to one another even though they have different names. When you are looking for common variables between data sets, the variable names are not important since they can be changed with the RENAME= option in the MERGE statement. Instead, you should look for variables that record the same information and that have the same type in each input data set. Common variables do not need to have the same length, although you should remember that the length of the variable in the first-listed data set will determine the length of the variable in the output data set.

Note: Any variables that have the same name in multiple data sets in the MERGE statement must also have the same type. If any variables in different input data sets have identical names but do not have identical types, ERROR and WARNING messages are written to the SAS log, and the match-merge fails.

In this case, both Code in Acities and Dest in Revenue record the three-letter abbreviation of an airport.

TIP You can use PROC CONTENTS to view information about variables such as type, length, and description.

Since there are variables that are common to two different pairs of the three data sets shown above, you can combine these data sets into one data set by using the MERGE statement in two subsequent DATA steps. That is, you can perform one match-merge on two of the data sets to create one new data set that combines data from both. Then you can perform another match-merge on the new data set and the remaining original data set. Consider the following example.

Example

In the following program, both Sasuser.Expenses and Sasuser.Revenue are sorted by FlightID and Date and are placed into temporary data sets in preparation for the merge. Then these two sorted data sets are merged in a DATA step that creates a temporary output data set named Revexpns. In order to reduce the total number of variables in the output data set, a new variable named Profit is created, and the variables that are used to create Profit are dropped from Revexpns.

```
proc sort data=sasuser.expenses out=expenses;
   by flightid date;
run;

proc sort data=sasuser.revenue out=revenue;
   by flightid date;
run;

data revexpns (drop=rev1st revbusiness revecon expenses);
   merge expenses(in=e) revenue(in=r);
   by flightid date;
```

```
      if e and r;
      Profit=sum(rev1st, revbusiness, revecon, -expenses);
   run;
```

Note: The use of the temporary IN= variables E and R in the IF statement above ensures that only observations that contain data from each of the two input data sets are included in the output data set.

In the following program, the output data set named Revexpns is sorted by Dest. Sasuser.Actities is sorted by Code and is placed in a temporary data set. Remember that Dest and Code are corresponding variables even though they have different names.

The sorted data sets are then merged in a DATA step. Since two data sets must have at least one variable that matches exactly in order to be merged, the RENAME= option renames Code to Dest in the output data set. The DATA step merges Revexpns and Acities into a new output data set named Alldata.

```
proc sort data=revexpns;
   by dest;
run;

proc sort data=sasuser.acities out=acities;
   by code;
run;

data sasuser.alldata;
   merge revexpns(in=r) acities
         (in=a rename=(code=dest) keep=city name code);
   by dest;
   if r and a;
run;

proc print data=sasuser.alldata(obs=5) noobs;
   title 'Result of Merging Three Data Sets';
   format Date date9.;
run;
```

The PROC PRINT step prints the first five observations in the Sasuser.Alldata data set that is created in this example, as shown here.

Result of Merging Three Data Sets						
FlightID	Date	Origin	Dest	Profit	City	Name
IA03300	06DEC1999	RDU	ANC	34010	Anchorage, AK	Anchorage International Airport
IA03300	18DEC1999	RDU	ANC	73471	Anchorage, AK	Anchorage International Airport
IA03300	30DEC1999	RDU	ANC	77755	Anchorage, AK	Anchorage International Airport
IA03301	13DEC1999	RDU	ANC	110402	Anchorage, AK	Anchorage International Airport
IA03301	25DEC1999	RDU	ANC	111151	Anchorage, AK	Anchorage International Airport

Using PROC SQL to Join Data

The SQL Procedure

Another method that you can use to join data sets that do not have a common variable is the SQL procedure. You should already be familiar with using PROC SQL to create a table from the results of an inner join.

In a PROC SQL step, you can choose from each input data set only the specific variables that you want to include in the new data set. The input data sets do not need to contain a common BY variable, nor do they need to be sorted or indexed. However, if the lookup table has an index, the SQL procedure can take advantage of the index to provide faster retrieval of lookup values.

You can join up to 256 tables by using the SQL procedure, to combine data horizontally from sources that have any type of relationship (one-to-one, one-to-many, many-to-many, or nonmatching).

Note: Although numerous types of joins are possible with PROC SQL, only inner joins are discussed in this chapter. Therefore, in the remainder of this chapter, a PROC SQL join refers to an inner join on multiple tables, whose results are stored in a new table. You can learn more about PROC SQL joins in Chapter 3, "Combining Tables Horizontally Using PROC SQL," on page 82.

One drawback to using the SQL procedure to perform table lookups is that you cannot use DATA step syntax with PROC SQL. Therefore, complex business logic is difficult to incorporate into the join. However, by using PROC SQL you can often accomplish in one step what it takes multiple PROC SORT and DATA steps to accomplish.

Example: Working with Multiple Lookup Tables

The following example joins Sasuser.Revenue, Sasuser.Expenses, and Sasuser.Acities into a new data set named Work.Sqljoin:

```
proc sql;
   create table sqljoin as
      select revenue.flightid, revenue.date format=date9.,
             revenue.origin, revenue.dest,
             sum(revenue.rev1st,
                 revenue.revbusiness,
                 revenue.revecon)
             -expenses.expenses as Profit,
             acities.city,
             acities.name
         from sasuser.expenses, sasuser.revenue,
             sasuser.acities
         where expenses.flightid=revenue.flightid
             and expenses.date=revenue.date
             and acities.code=revenue.dest
         order by revenue.dest,
             revenue.flightid,
             revenue.date;
   quit;
```

```
proc print data=work.sqljoin(obs=5);
   title 'Result of Joining Three Data Sets';
run;
```

The PROC PRINT step produces the first five observations of the Work.Sqljoin data set that is created in the PROC SQL step above, as shown here:

Result of Joining Three Data Sets							
Obs	FlightID	Date	Origin	Dest	Profit	City	Name
1	IA03300	06DEC1999	RDU	ANC	34010	Anchorage, AK	Anchorage International Airport
2	IA03300	18DEC1999	RDU	ANC	73471	Anchorage, AK	Anchorage International Airport
3	IA03300	30DEC1999	RDU	ANC	77755	Anchorage, AK	Anchorage International Airport
4	IA03301	13DEC1999	RDU	ANC	110402	Anchorage, AK	Anchorage International Airport
5	IA03301	25DEC1999	RDU	ANC	111151	Anchorage, AK	Anchorage International Airport

Note: Notice that the Work.Sqljoin data set is identical to the Sasuser.Alldata data set that was previously created in the DATA step merge.

Comparing DATA Step Match-Merges and PROC SQL Joins

Overview

You have seen that it is possible to create identical results with a DATA step match-merge and a PROC SQL inner join. Although the results might be identical, these two processes are very different, and trade-offs are associated with choosing one method over the other. The following tables summarize some of the advantages and disadvantages of each of these two methods.

Table 15.1 *DATA Step Match-Merge*

Advantages	Disadvantages
• There is no limit to the number of input data sets.	• Data sets must be sorted by or indexed on the BY variable or variables before merging.
• Allows for complex business logic to be incorporated into the new data set by using DATA step processing, including arrays and DO loops, in addition to MERGE features.	• The BY variable or variable must be present in all data sets, and the names of the key variable or variables must match exactly.
• Multiple BY variables enable lookups that depend on more than one variable.	• An exact match on the key value or value must be found.

Table 15.2 *PROC SQL Join*

Advantages	Disadvantages
• Data sets do not have to be sorted or indexed, but an index can be used to improve performance.	• The maximum number of tables that can be joined at one time is 256.
• Multiple data sets can be joined in one step without having common variables in all data sets.	• Complex business logic is difficult to incorporate into the join.
• You can create data sets (tables), views, or reports with the combined data.	• PROC SQL might require more resources than the DATA step with the MERGE statement for simple joins.

Although it is possible to produce identical results with a DATA step match-merge and a PROC SQL join, these two processes will not always produce results that are identical by default.

Consider the following simplified examples to see how each method works in various circumstances.

The following two steps show two different ways to produce the same combination of two data sets, Data1 and Data2, that have a common variable, X. If Data1 contains two variables, X and Y, and Data2 contains two variables, X and Z, then both of the following steps produce an output data set named Data3 that contains three variables, X, Y, and Z.

Note: The code shown in the following two steps illustrates a simple comparison of a DATA step match-merge and a PROC SQL join. This comparison will be explored in the next several sections.

```
data data3;
   merge data1 data2;
   by x;
run;

proc sql;
   create table data3 as
      select data1.x, data1.y, data2.z
         from data1, data2
         where data1.x=data2.x;
quit;
```

The contents of Data3 will vary depending on the values that are in each input data set and on the method used for merging. Consider the following examples.

Examples

One-to-one matches produce identical results whether the data sets are merged in a DATA step or joined in a PROC SQL step. Suppose that Data1 and Data2 contain the same number of observations. Also, suppose that in each data set, the values of X are unique, and that each value appears in both data sets.

When these data sets are either merged in a DATA step or joined in a PROC SQL step, Data3 will contain one observation for each unique value of X, and it will have the same number of observations as Data1 and Data2.

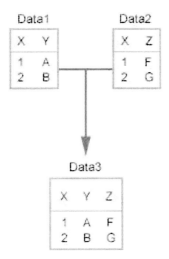

One-to-many matches produce identical results whether the data sets are merged in a DATA step or joined in a PROC SQL step. Suppose that Data1 contains unique values for X, but that Data2 does not contain unique values for X. That is, Data2 contains multiple observations that have the same value of X and therefore contains more observations than Data1.

When these two data sets are either merged in a DATA step or joined in a PROC SQL step, Data3 will contain the same number of observations as Data2. In Data3, one observation from Data1 that has a particular value for X might be matched with multiple observations from Data2 that have the same value for X.

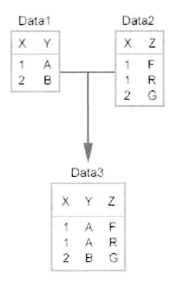

Many-to-many matches produce different results depending on whether the data sets are merged in a DATA step or joined in a PROC SQL step. Suppose the values of X are not unique in both Data1 and Data2.

When the data sets are merged in a DATA step, the observations are matched and combined sequentially.

In the example below, Data3 will contain the same number of observations as the larger of the two input sets. In cases where there is a many-to-many match on the values of the BY variable, a DATA step match-merge probably does not produce the desired output because the output data set will not contain all of the possible combinations of matching observations.

When the data sets are joined in a PROC SQL step, each match appears as a separate observation in the output data set. In the example below, the first observation that has a value of 1 for X in Data1 is matched and combined with each observation from Data2 that has a value of 1 for X. Then, the second observation that has a value of 1 for X in Data1 is matched and combined with each observation from Data2 that has a value of 1 for X, and so on.

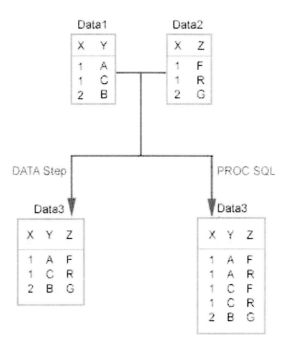

Nonmatching data between the data sets produces different results depending on whether the data sets are merged in a DATA step or combined by using a PROC SQL inner join.

When data sets that contain nonmatching values for the BY variable are merged in a DATA step, the observations in each are processed sequentially. Data3 will contain one observation for each unique value of X that appears in either Data1 or Data2. For nonmatching values of X, the observation in Data3 will have a missing value for the variable that is taken from the other input data set.

In this PROC SQL step, the output data set will contain only those observations that have matching values for the BY variable. In the example below, Data3 does not have any observations with missing values, because any observation from Data1 or from Data2 that contains a nonmatching value for X is not included in Data3.

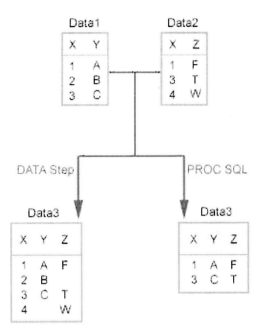

You have seen the results of DATA step match-merges and PROC SQL joins in several simple scenarios. To help you understand the differences more fully, consider how the DATA step processes a match-merge and how PROC SQL processes a join.

DATA Step Match-Merge

When you merge data sets in a DATA step, the observations in each input data set are read sequentially and are matched and combined in the output data set. The example below depicts a DATA step match-merge of two simple input data sets.

Execution of a DATA Step Match-Merge

1. This example shows the execution of the DATA step below. This DATA step creates a new data set by performing a basic match-merge on two input data sets.

   ```
   data work.data3;
      merge data1 data2;
      by x;
   run;
   ```

2. During the compilation phase, SAS reads the descriptor portions of the input data sets and creates the PDV with every variable from every input data set, by default.

3. Execution begins. SAS looks at the first observation in each input data set to determine whether the BY values match. If so, SAS reads the first observation from each data set into the PDV.

4. SAS writes the merged observation to the output data set.

5. If the BY values do not match, SAS reads from the input data set with the lowest BY value. If the BY value matches the BY value from the previous observation, SAS does not reinitialize the PDV but overwrites the values in the PDV. If the BY value does not match the previous BY value, SAS reinitializes the PDV. The PDV and the output data set then contain missing values for variables that are unique to the other data set.

6. SAS continues to match-merge observations until all observations from all input data sets have been read and written to the new data set. In this example, Work.Data3 contains three variables and four observations.

PROC SQL Join

A PROC SQL join uses a different process than a DATA step merge to combine tables

Conceptually, PROC SQL first creates a Cartesian product of all input tables. That is, PROC SQL first matches each row with every other row in the other input tables. Then, PROC SQL eliminates any observations from the result set that do not satisfy the WHERE clause. The PROC SQL query optimizer uses methods to minimize the Cartesian product that must be built.

Execution of a PROC SQL Join

1. This example shows the execution of the PROC SQL step below. This PROC SQL step creates a new table to hold the results of an inner join on two input tables. This discussion provides a conceptual view of how PROC SQL works rather than a literal depiction of the join process. In reality, PROC SQL uses optimization routines that make the process more efficient.

```
proc sql;
   create table work.data3 as
      select *
        from data1, data 2
        where data1.x=data2.x;
quit;
```

2. Conceptually, PROC SQL first creates a Cartesian product of the two input tables, where each row from the first table is combined with each row from the second table. PROC SQL starts by taking the first row from Work.Data1 and combining it with every row of Work.Data2.

3. Next, PROC SQL takes the second row from Work.Data1 and combines it with every row from Work.Data2.

4. PROC SQL continues in this manner until it has combined each row from Work.Data1 with every row from Work.Data2. This is the Cartesian product of the two input tables.

5. Finally, PROC SQL eliminates from the output table those rows that do not satisfy the condition in the WHERE clause. In this example, rows that do not have matching values for X are eliminated so that the two columns for X have identical values for each row.

6. The results are written to the output table. In SAS tables, column names must be unique. Only one column X is in the output table Work.Data4. In this example, Work.Data3 contains three columns and four rows. None of the rows in Work.Data3 contains any missing values.

Earlier in this chapter, you learned that a DATA step match-merge will probably not produce the desired results when the data sources that you want to combine have a many-to-many match. You also learned that PROC SQL and the DATA step match-merge do not, by default, produce the same results when you combine data sources that contain nonmatching data. Now that you have seen how DATA step match-merges and

PROC SQL joins work, consider an example of using each of these techniques to combine data from a many-to-many match that also contains nonmatching data.

Example: Combining Data from a Many-to-Many Match

Suppose you want to combine the data from Sasuser.Flightschedule and Sasuser.Flightattendants. The Sasuser.Flightschedule data set contains data about flights that have been scheduled for a fictional airline. The data set Sasuser.Flightattendants contains information about the flight attendants of a fictional airline. A partial listing of each of these data sets is shown below.

Table 15.3 *SASuser.Flightschedule (Partial Listing)*

Date	Destination	FlightNumber	EmpID
01MAR2000	YYZ	132	1739
01MAR2000	YYZ	132	1478
01MAR2000	YYZ	132	1130
01MAR2000	YYZ	132	1390
01MAR2000	YYZ	132	1983
01MAR2000	YYZ	132	1111
01MAR2000	YYZ	182	1076
01MAR2000	YYZ	182	1118

Table 15.4 *Sasuser.Flightattendants (Partial Listing)*

EmpID	JobCode	LastName	FirstName
1350	FA3	Arthur	Barbara
1574	FA2	Cahill	Marshall
1437	FA3	Carter	Dorothy
1988	FA3	Dean	Sharon
1983	FA2	Dunlap	Donna
1125	FA2	Eaton	Alicia
1475	FA1	Fields	Diana
1422	FA1	Fletcher	Marie

Suppose you want to combine all variables from the Sasuser.Flightschedule data set with the first and last names of each flight attendant who is scheduled to work on each flight. Sasuser.Flightschedule contains data for 45 flights. Three flight attendants are scheduled to work on each flight. Therefore, your output data set should contain 135 observations (three for each flight).

You could use the following PROC SQL step to combine Sasuser.Flightschedule with Sasuser.Flightattendants.

```
proc sql;
   create table flightemps as
      select flightschedule.*, firstname, lastname
         from sasuser.flightschedule, sasuser.flightattendants
            where flightschedule.empid=flightattendants.empid;
quit;
```

The resulting Flightemps data set contains 135 observations.

Now, suppose you use the following DATA step match-merge to combine these two data sets.

```
proc sort data=sasuser.flightattendants out=fa;
   by empid;
run;

proc sort data=sasuser.flightschedule out=fs;
   by empid;
run;

data flightemps2;
   merge fa fs;
   by empid;
run;
```

The resulting Flightemps2 data set contains 272 observations. The DATA step match-merge does not produce the correct results because it combines the data sequentially. In the correct results, there are three observations for each unique flight from Sasuser.Flightschedule, and there are no missing values in any of the observations. By contrast, the results from the DATA step match-merge contain six observations for each unique flight and many observations that have missing values.

In the last example, data was combined from two data sets that have a many-to-many match. The PROC SQL join produced the correct results, but the DATA step match-merge did not. However, you can produce the correct results in a DATA step. First, consider using multiple SET statements to combine data.

Using Multiple SET Statements

You can use multiple SET statements to combine observations from several SAS data sets.

For example, the following DATA step creates a new data set named Combine. Each observation in Combine contains data from one observation in Dataset1 and data from one observation in Dataset2.

```
data combine;
   set dataset1;
   set dataset2;
run;
```

When you use multiple SET statements, the following results occur:

- Processing stops when SAS encounters the end-of-file (EOF) marker on either data set (even if there is more data in the other data set). Therefore, the output data set contains the same number of observations as the smallest input data set.

- The variables in the program data vector (PDV) are not reinitialized when a second SET statement is executed.

- For any variables that are common to both input data sets, the value or values from the data set in the second SET statement will overwrite the value or values from the data set in the first SET statement in the PDV.

Keep in mind that using multiple SET statements to combine data from multiple input sources that do not have a one-to-one match can be complicated. If you are working with data sources that do not have a one-to-one match, or that contain nonmatching data, you will need to add additional DATA step syntax in order to produce the results that you want.

Example: Using Multiple SET Statements with a Many-to-Many Match

Remember that in the previous example you wanted to combine Sasuser.Flightschedule with Sasuser.Flightattendants. Your resulting data set should contain all variables from the Sasuser.Flightschedule data set with the first and last names of each flight attendant who is scheduled to work on each flight. Sasuser.Flightschedule contains data for 45 flights, and three flight attendants are scheduled to be on each flight. Therefore, your output data set should contain 135 observations (three for each flight).

You can use the following DATA step to perform this table lookup operation. In this program, the first SET statement reads an observation from the Sasuser.Flightschedule data set. Then the DO loop executes, and the second SET statement reads each observation in Sasuser.Flightattendants. The EmpID variable in Sasuser.Flightattendants is renamed so that it does not overwrite the value for EmpID that has been read from Sasuser.Flightschedule. Instead, these two values are used for comparison to control which observations from Sasuser.Flightattendants should be included in the output data set for each observation from Sasuser.Flightschedule.

```
data flightemps3(drop=empnum jobcode);
   set sasuser.flightschedule;
   do i=1 to num;
      set sasuser.flightattendants
          (rename=(empid=empnum))
          nobs=num point=i;
      if empid=empnum then output;
   end;
run;
```

The resulting Flightemps3 data set contains 135 observations and no missing values. Keep in mind that although it is possible to use a DATA step to produce the same results that a PROC SQL join creates by default, the PROC SQL step might be much more efficient.

Combining Summary Data and Detail Data

Overview

You have seen how to combine data from multiple data sets. Suppose you want to calculate percentages based on individual values from a data set as compared to a summary statistic of the data. You need to complete these tasks:

- create a summary statistic

- combine the summary data with the detail rows of the original data set

- calculate the percentages

For example, the data set Sasuser.Monthsum has one row for every value of SalesMonth (month and year) from 1997 to 1999. Each row contains information about the revenue generated by an airline.

Table 15.5   SAS Data Set Sasuser.Monthsum (Partial Listing)

Sales Month	RevCargo
JAN1997	$171,520,869.10
JAN1998	$238,786,807.60
JAN1999	$280,350,393.00
FEB1997	$177,671,530.40
FEB1998	$215,959,695.50
FEB1999	$253,999,924.00

Suppose you want to produce a report that shows what percentage of the total cargo revenue for the three-year period was generated in each month of each year. You could summarize the data to get the total revenue for cargo for the three-year period and assign that value to a new variable called Cargosum in a summary data set.

Table 15.6   Summary Data Set

Cargosum
$8,593,432,002.35

Combine the summary data (Cargosum) with the detail data in Sasuser.Monthsum to calculate percentages of the total cargo revenue for each month.

Table 15.7 *Partial Listing of the Combined Data Set*

Sales Month	RevCargo	Month No	Cargosum	PctRev
JAN1997	$171,520,869.10	1	$8,593,432,002.35	\<RevCargo/Cargosum>
JAN1998	$238,786,807.60	1	$8,593,432,002.35	\<RevCargo/Cargosum>
JAN1999	$280,350,393.00	1	$8,593,432,002.35	\<RevCargo/Cargosum>
FEB1997	$177,671,530.40	2	$8,593,432,002.35	\<RevCargo/Cargosum>
FEB1998	$215,959,695.50	2	$8,593,432,002.35	\<RevCargo/Cargosum>
FEB1999	$253,999,924.00	2	$8,593,432,002.35	\<RevCargo/Cargosum>

We will examine this task more closely.

The MEANS Procedure

You should already know how to use the MEANS procedure for producing summary statistics. By default, PROC MEANS generates a report that contains descriptive statistics. The descriptive statistics can be routed to a SAS data set by using an OUTPUT statement. The default report can be suppressed by using the NOPRINT option.

General form, PROC MEANS with OUTPUT statement:

PROC MEANS DATA=*input-SAS-data-set* **NOPRINT;**

   \<VAR *variable(s);*>

   OUTPUT OUT= *output-SAS-data-set*

      *statistic=output-variable(s)***;**

RUN;

Here is an explanation of the syntax:

input-SAS-data-set
   identifies the data set on which the summary statistic is generated.

variable(s)
   is the name or names of the variable or variables that are being analyzed.

output-SAS-data-set
   names the data set where the descriptive statistics will be stored.

statistic
   is one of the summary statistics generated.

output-variable(s)
   names the variable or variables in which to store the value or values of statistic in the output data set.

The output data set that a PROC MEANS step creates contains the requested statistics as values for output-variable(s), as well as two additional variables that are automatically included, as follows:

- _TYPE_ contains information about the class variables

- _FREQ_ contains the number of observations that an output level represents.

Example

The following program creates a summary data set named Sasuser.Summary. Sasuser.Summary contains the sum of the values of Revcargo from Sasuser.Monthsum, stored in the variable Cargosum.

```
proc means data=sasuser.monthsum noprint;
   var revcargo;
   output out=sasuser.summary sum=Cargosum;
run;

proc print data=sasuser.summary;
run;
```

Because of the NOPRINT option, the PROC MEANS step does not produce a report. Printing the Sasuser.Summary data set produces the following report.

Obs	_TYPE_	_FREQ_	Cargosum
1	0	36	$8593432002.35

Once you have created the summary statistic, you need to combine this summary information with the detail rows of the data set so that you can calculate the percentages. Remember that you can use multiple SET statements to combine data horizontally. Consider how this process works by using multiple set statements to combine the detail rows of Sasuser.Monthsum with the summary data that we created in Sasuser.Summary.

Example

This example creates a new data set named Percent1 that combines

- summary data (total revenue for cargo from the three-year period) from Sasuser.Summary

- detail data (month and total cargo for the month) from Sasuser.Monthsum.

Percent1 also contains a new variable named PctRev that records the calculated percentage of the total revenue that each observation represents.

Remember, the automatic variable _N_ tracks of how many times the DATA step iterates. The following DATA step uses _N_ to prevent SAS from reaching end of file on Sasuser.Summary after the first iteration of the step. Since variables read from a SAS data set are not reinitialized, the value of Cargosum is retained in the PDV as each observation is read from Sasuser.Monthsum.

1. This example shows the compilation and execution of the DATA step below. This DATA step creates a new data set that combines summary data from one input data set (Sasuser.Summary) and detail data from a second input data set (Sasuser.Monthsum).

```
data sasuser.percent1(drop=cargosum);
   if _N_=1 then set sasuser.summary(keep=cargosum);
   set sasuser.monthsum(keep=salemon revcargo);
   PctRev=revcargo/cargosum;
run;
```

2. During the compilation phase, SAS reads the descriptor portion of the input data set and creates the PDV. _N_ is a temporary variable that is included in the PDV, although it will not be included in the output data set.

3. Execution begins. On the first iteration of the DATA step, _N_ has a value of 1. The IF statement evaluates as true, so the first SET statement reads the value of Cargosum from Sasuser.Summary into the PDV.

4. The second SET statement reads the first observation in Sasuser.Monthsum into the PDV.

5. SAS calculates the value of PctRev and records it in the PDV.

6. At the bottom of the DATA step, SAS writes the values in the PDV to the output data set. _N_ is not included in the output data set since it is a temporary variable. CargoSum is dropped from the output data set as well.

7. On the second iteration of the DATA step, the value of _N_ is *2*, so the IF statement evaluates to false and the first SET statement does not execute. However, the value of CargoSum is retained in the PDV.

8. The second SET statement reads the second observation from Sasuser.Monthsum into the PDV.

9. The value for PctRev is calculated and recorded in the PDV. SAS writes the values in the PDV to the output data set (except for _N_ and CargoSum).

10. The DATA step continues to execute until all observations have been read from Sasuser.Monthsum.

Another method of combining summary data and detail data is to create the summary statistic in a DATA step and combine it with the detail data in the same step. To do this you must do the following:

- read the data once and calculate the summary statistic

- re-read the data to combine the summary statistic with the detail data to calculate the percentages

The Sum Statement

You can use the sum statement to obtain a summary statistic within a DATA step. The sum statement adds the result of an expression to an accumulator variable.

General form, sum statement:

variable+expression;

Here is an explanation of the syntax:

variable
    specifies the name of the accumulator variable. This variable must be numeric. The variable is automatically set to 0 before the first observation is read. The variable's value is retained from one DATA step iteration to the next.

expression
    is any numeric SAS expression.

CAUTION:

If the expression produces a missing value, the sum statement ignores it. This action is different from the assignment statements that assign a missing value if the expression produces a missing value.

Note: The sum statement and assignment statement are among the few SAS statements that does not begin with a keyword.

The sum statement adds the result of the expression that is on the right side of the plus sign (+) to the numeric variable that is on the left side of the plus sign. At the top of the DATA step, the value of the numeric variable is not set to missing as it usually is when reading raw data. Instead, the variable retains the new value in the program data vector for use in processing the next observation.

Example

The following example uses a sum statement to generate the summary statistic in a DO UNTIL loop. On the first iteration of the DATA step, the DO UNTIL loop reads each observation of Sasuser.Monthsum and keeps a running tally of the total value of RevCargo from each observation. On each subsequent iteration of the DATA step, this tally (stored in the variable TotalRev) is divided into RevCargo to calculate the new variable PctRev.

Note: Remember that the END= a set statement option creates a temporary variable that contains an end-of-file indicator.

1. This example shows the execution of the DATA step below. This DATA step reads the same data set, Sasuser.Monthsum, twice: first, to create a summary statistic; second, to merge the summary statistic back into the detail data to calculate PCTREV and create a new data set, Sasuser.Percent2.

```
data sasuser.percent2(drop=totalrev);
   if _N_=1 then do until (LastObs);
      set sasuser.monthsum(keep=revcargo) end=lastobs;
      TotalRev+revcargo;
   end;
   set sasuser.monthsum(keep=salemon revcargo);
   PctRev=revcargo/totalrev;
run;
```

2. During the compilation phase, SAS reads the descriptor portion of the input data set and creates the PDV. _N_, LastObs, and TotalRev are temporary variables that are included in the PDV but not written to the output data set.

3. Execution begins. The temporary variables are initialized with values. The IF statement resolves to true on the first iteration of the DATA step, so the DO UNTIL loop begins to execute. Remember, in a DO UNTIL loop, the condition is evaluated at the bottom of the loop.

4. The first SET statement reads the first observation from Sasuser.Monthsum and writes the value for RevCargo to the PDV.

5. The value of TotalRev is increased by the value of RevCargo and overwritten in the PDV.

6. At the bottom of the DO loop, SAS evaluates the UNTIL expression. It resolves to false since the value of LastObs is 0, so the loop continues to execute.

7. The first SET statement reads the second observation from Sasuser.Monthsum, overwriting the value for RevCargo in the PDV and adding this value to the accumulator variable TotalRev.

8. The DO UNTIL loop continues to execute until the first SET statement reads the last observation from Sasuser.Monthsum and the value of LastObs is set to **1**. At this point, the value for TotalRev in the PDV is the sum of all values for RevCargo in Sasuser.Monthsum. The loop is satisfied.

9. The second SET statement reads the same data set as the first SET statement. However, this time SaleMon and RevCargo are read into the PDV. TotalRev remains populated in the PDV.

10. PctRev is calculated for observation 1 and recorded in the PDV. Then, SAS writes the values in the PDV to the output data set Sasuser.Percent2, except for the temporary variables and the variable TotalRev.

11. On the second iteration of the DATA step, the value of _N_ increases to **2**, so the IF expression is false. The second SET statement reads from the second observation of Sasuser.Monthsum into the PDV.

12. The value for the accumulator variable TotalRev is retained from the previous iteration and used to calculate a new value for PctRev, which is recorded in the PDV. SAS writes the values in the PDV to the output data set.

13. The DATA step iterates until end-of-file on Sasuser.Monthsum.

Using an Index to Combine Data

Overview

Suppose you want to combine data from two data sets, and one of the data sets is much larger than the other. Also, suppose you want to select only those observations from the larger data set that match an observation from the smaller data set according to the value of one or more common variables.

You should already know how to create an index on a SAS data set. You have learned that PROC SQL can take advantage of an index to improve performance on a join. You can also take advantage of an index in a DATA step to combine data from matching observations in multiple data sets if the index is built on variables that are common to all input data sets.

For example, suppose you want to combine data from the matching observations in Sasuser.Dnunder and Sasuser.Sale2000. Only a portion of the flights that are in Sasuser.Sale2000 (which has 156 observations) are also in Sasuser.Dnunder (which has only 57 observations). Suppose you want to select only the matching observations.

Assume that Sasuser.Sale2000 has a composite index named Flightdate associated with it. The values for Flightdate are unique and are based on the values of the variables FlightID and Date. You can use the FLIGHTDATE index to efficiently select only the matching observations via direct access.

Sasuser.Sale2000 Variables	**Sasuser.Dnunder Variables**	**Sasuser.NewOne Variables**
FlightID	Date	FlightID
RouteID	Expenses	RouteID
Origin	FlightID	Date
Dest	RouteID	Expenses
Cap1st		Rev1st
CapBusiness		RevBusiness
CapEcon		RevEcon
CapTotal		RevCargo
CapCargo		Profit
Date		
Psgr1st		
PsgrBusiness		
PsgrEcon		
Rev1st		
RevBusiness		
RevEcon		
SaleMon		
CargoWgt		
RevCargo		

The next few sections show how to use the Flightdate index to combine matching observations from the Sasuser.Sale2000 data set and the Sasuser.Dnunder data set.

The KEY= Option

You have seen how to use multiple SET statements in a DATA step in order to combine summary data and detail data in a new data set. You can also use multiple SET statements to read only the matching observations.

You specify the KEY= option in the SET statement to use an index to retrieve matching observations from the lookup data set.

General form, SET statement with KEY= option:

SET *SAS-data-set-name* **KEY=** *index-name*;

Here is an explanation of the syntax:

index-name
   is the name of an index that is associated with the *SAS-data-set-name* data set.

To use the SET statement with the KEY= option to perform a lookup operation, your lookup values must be stored in a SAS data set that has an index. This technique is appropriate only when you are working with one-to-one matches, with a lookup table of any size. It is possible to return multiple values with this technique and use other DATA step syntax as well.

When SAS encounters a SET statement with the KEY= option, SAS uses the index to retrieve an observation with a key value that matches the key value from the PDV.

For example, if the Sasuser.Sale2000 data set has an index named Flightdate associated with it, the following SET statement uses the Flightdate index to locate observations in Sale2000 that have specific values for FlightID and Date:

```
set sasuser.sale2000 key=flightdate;
```

When the SET statement in the example above begins to execute, there must already be a value for FlightID and a value for Date in the PDV. SAS then uses the Flightdate index to retrieve an observation from Sasuser.Sale2000. This observation must have values for FlightID and Date that match the values for FlightID and Date that are already in the PDV.

In order to assign a key value in the PDV before the SET statement with the KEY= option executes, you precede that SET statement with another SET statement in the DATA step. Consider this example in context.

Example

Remember that you want to combine Sasuser.Sale2000 and Sasuser.Dnunder, and that Sasuser.Sale2000 has an index named Flightdate that is based on the values of the FlightID and Date variables. You can use two SET statements to combine these two data sets, and use the KEY= option in the second SET statement to take advantage of the index.

In the following example, these results occur:

- the first SET statement reads an observation sequentially from the Sasuser.Dnunder data set. SAS writes the values from this observation to the PDV, and then moves to the second SET statement.

- the second SET statement uses the Flightdate index on Sasuser.Sale2000 to find an observation in Sasuser.Sale2000 that has values for FlightID and Date that match the values of FlightID and Date that were populated by the first SET statement.

- Work.Profit is the output data set.

CAUTION:

If you use the KEY= option to read a SAS data set, you cannot use WHERE processing on that data set in the same DATA step.

1. This example shows the execution of a DATA step that uses two SET statements to combine data from two input data sets (Sasuser.Sale2000 and Sasuser.Dnunder) into one output data set (Work.Profit). The DATA step uses an index on the larger of the two input data sets, Sasuser.Sale2000, to find matching observations.

```
data work.profit;
   set sasuser.dnunder;
   set sasuser.sale2000(keep=routeid flightid date rev1st
                        revbusiness revecon revcargo)
                        key=flightdate;
   Profit=sum(rev1st, revbusiness, revecon, revcargo,
              -expenses);
run;
```

2. SAS reads the descriptor portions of the input data sets and creates the PDV.

3. The first SET statement executes and creates the PDV. SAS reads the first observation in Sasuser.Dnunder into the PDV.

4. When the second SET statement executes, the KEY= option uses the Flightdate index to directly access the observation in Sasuser.Sale2000 that has values for FlightID and Date that match the values already in the PDV. The matching observation is then read into the PDV.

5. SAS calculates the value for Profit and records it in the PDV. Then, SAS writes the current observation from the PDV to the output data set.

6. The DATA step continues to iterate. Only the variable Profit is reinitialized to missing. The first SET statement reads the second observation in Sasuser.Dnunder into the PDV, overwriting the previous values.

7. The second SET statement uses the Flightdate index to find a matching observation in Sasuser.Sale2000. The matching observation is read into the PDV, overwriting the previous values. A new value for Profit is calculated and recorded. The current observation is written to the output data set.

8. The DATA step continues to iterate until end of file on Sasuser.Dnunder.

Remember that when SAS encounters a SET statement with the KEY= option, the value of the key variable on which the KEY= index is built must already exist in the PDV. Therefore, it is very important for the two SET statements to be in the exact order shown.

Example

If you examine the Work.Profit output data set closely, you will notice that the final observation in the output data set contains values for several variables that are identical to values in the previous observation. This action happened when the second SET statement failed to find a matching observation in sasuser.sale2000.

The observation that contains unmatched data is printed to the log. As you can see in the log sample below, the unmatched observation includes an _Error_ variable whose value is **1**, which indicates unmatched data. The _N_ variable indicates the iteration of the DATA step in which the error occurred.

Table 15.8 *SAS Log*

```
FlightID=IA11802 RouteID=0000108 Date=30DEC2000 Expenses=3720
Rev1st=1270 RevBusiness=. RevEcon=5292 RevCargo=1940 Profit=4782

_ERROR_=1 _IORC_=1230015 _N_=57
NOTE: There were 57 observations read from the data set
      SASUSER.DNUNDER.
NOTE: The data set WORK.PROFIT has 57 observations and 9 variables.
NOTE: DATA statement used (Total process time):
      real time          0.38 seconds
      cpu time           0.04 seconds
```

Notice that the observation that is printed in the SAS log above also contains a variable named _IORC_.

The _IORC_ Variable

When you use the KEY= option, SAS creates an automatic variable named _IORC_, which stands for INPUT/OUTPUT Return Code. You can use _IORC_ to determine whether the index search was successful. If the value of _IORC_ is zero, SAS found a matching observation. If the value of _IORC_ is not zero, SAS did not find a matching observation.

To prevent writing the data error to the log (and to your output data set), do the following:

*   check the value of _IORC_ to determine whether a match has been found

- set _ERROR_ to 0 if there is no match

- delete the nonmatching data or write the nonmatching data to an errors data set

Example

The following example uses the Flightdate index to combine data from Sasuser.Sale2000 with data from Sasuser.Dnunder, and writes the combined data to a new data set named Work.Profit3. Unmatched observations are written to Work.Errors. No observations should be written to the SAS log.

```
data work.profit3 work.errors;
   set sasuser.dnunder;
   set sasuser.sale2000(keep=routeid flightid date rev1st
        revbusiness revecon revcargo)key=flightdate;
   if _iorc_=0 then do;
      Profit=sum(rev1st, revbusiness, revecon, revcargo,
              -expenses);
      output work.profit3;
   end;
   else do;
      _error_=0;
      output work.errors;
   end;
run;
```

If you examine the results from the program above, you will notice that there is one fewer observation in the Work.Profit3 output data set than there was in the Work.Profit output data set. The unmatched observation is written to the Work.Errors data set.

Using a Transaction Data Set

Overview

Sometimes, rather than just combining data from two data sets, you might want to update the data in one data set with data that is stored in another data set. That is, you might want to update a master data set by overwriting certain values with values that are stored in a transaction data set.

For example, suppose the data set Mylib.Empmaster contains data that is outdated. The current data is stored in another data set named Mylib.Empchanges. Mylib.Empmaster contains 148 observations, and Mylib.Empchanges contains six observations. The variable EmpID contains unique values in both data sets.

A partial listing of Mylib.Empmaster and the full listing of Mylib.Empchanges is shown below. Notice that there is one observation in each data set with a value of **1065** for EmpID. The values of JobCode and Salary are different in these observations.

Table 15.9 *Mylib.Empmaster (Partial Listing)*

DateOfBirth	DateOfHire	EmpID	Gender	JobCode	Salary
05MAR1957	30MAR1990	1009	M	TA1	$40,432

DateOfBirth	DateOfHire	EmpID	Gender	JobCode	Salary
01JAN1956	20OCT1979	1017	M	TA3	$57,201
23MAY1963	27OCT1982	1036	F	TA3	$55,149
14APR1962	17SEP1990	1037	F	TA1	$39,98
13NOV1967	26NOV1989	1038	F	TA1	$37,146
17JUL1961	27AUG1984	1050	M	ME2	$49,234
29JAN1942	*10JAN1985*	*1065*	*M*	*ME2*	*$49,126*
18OCT1970	06OCT1989	1076	M	PT1	$93,181

Table 15.10 Mylib.Empchanges

DateOfBirth	DateOfHire	EmpID	Gender	JobCode	Salary
30JUN1955	31JAN1982	1639	F	TA3	$59,164
29JAN1942	*10JAN1985*	*1065*	*M*	*ME3*	*$53,326*
03DEC1961	10Oct1985	1561	M	TA3	$51,120
25SEP1965	07OCT1989	1221	F	FA3	$41,854
11AUG1970	01NOV2000	1447	F	FA1	$30,340
13SEP1968	05NOV2000	1998	M	SCP	$32,240

If you could see the full listing of Mylib.Empmaster, you would see that each of the observations in Mylib.Empchanges has a matching observation in Mylib.Empmaster based on the values of EmpID. There are also many observations in Mylib.Empmaster that do not have a matching observation in Mylib.Empchanges. To update Mylib.Empmaster, you want to find all of the matching observations and change their values for JobCode and Salary to the new values from Mylib.Empchanges. You can use the UPDATE statement to make these changes.

Using the UPDATE Statement

You use the UPDATE statement to update a master data set with a transaction data set. The UPDATE statement can perform the following tasks:

- change the values of variables in the master data set
- add observations to the master data set
- add variables to the master data set

General form, UPDATE statement:

DATA *master-data-set*;

       UPDATE *master-data-set transaction-data-set*;

       BY *by-variable(s)*;

RUN;

Here is an explanation of the syntax:

master-data-set
> names the SAS data set used as the master file.

transaction-data-set
> names the SAS data set that contains the changes to be applied to the master data set.

by-variable(s)
> names a variable that appears in both *master-data-set* and in *transaction-data-set*. Each observation in *master-data-set* must have a unique value for *by-variable*, but *transaction-data-set* can contain more than one observation with the same *by-variable* value.

The UPDATE statement replaces values in the master data set with values from the transaction data set for each observation with a matching value of the BY variable. Any observations in either the master data set or the transactional data set that have nonmatching values for the BY variable are included in the output data set. Also, by default, SAS does not replace existing values in the master data set with missing values if those values are coded as periods (for numeric variables) or blanks (for character variables) in the transaction data set.

When you use the UPDATE statement, keep in mind the following restrictions.

- Only two data set names can appear in the UPDATE statement.

- The master data set must be listed first.

- A BY statement that gives the matching variable must be used.

- Both data sets must be sorted by or have indexes based on the BY variable.

- In the master data set, each observation must have a unique value for the BY variable.

Example

Remember that you want to update the master data set Mylib.Empmaster with the transactional data set Mylib.Empchanges. You can use the UPDATE statement to accomplish this task, as shown in the program below. Remember, both data sets must be sorted by or indexed on the BY variable.

```
proc sort data=mylib.empmaster;
   by empid;
run;

proc sort data=mylib.empchanges;
   by empid;
run;

data mylib.empmaster;
   update mylib.empmaster mylib.empchanges;
   by empid;
run;
```

The first eight observations of the updated Mylib.Empmaster data set are shown below. Notice that the observation that has a value of `1065` for EmpID now contains the updated values for JobCode and Salary.

```
proc print data=mylib.empmaster (obs=8) noobs;
run;
```

DateOfBirth	DateOfHire	EmpID	Gender	JobCode	Salary
05MAR1957	30MAR1990	1009	M	TA1	$40,432
01JAN1956	20OCT1979	1017	M	TA3	$57,201
23MAY1963	27OCT1982	1036	F	TA3	$55,149
14APR1962	17SEP1990	1037	F	TA1	$39,981
13NOV1967	26NOV1989	1038	F	TA1	$37,146
17JUL1961	27AUG1984	1050	M	ME2	$49,234
29JAN1942	10JAN1985	1065	M	ME3	$53,326
18OCT1970	06OCT1989	1076	M	PT1	$93,181

Summary

Text Summary

Reviewing Terminology
You can review definitions of terms that are important in this chapter. You can also review diagrams and descriptions of the various relationships between input sources for a table lookup operation.

Working with Lookup Values Outside of SAS Data Sets
You can use the IF-THEN/ELSE statement in the DATA step to combine data from a base table with lookup values that are not stored in a SAS data set. You can also use the FORMAT procedure or the ARRAY statement to combine data from a base table with lookup values that are not stored in a SAS data set.

Combining Data with the DATA Step Match-Merge
You can use the MERGE statement in the DATA step to combine data from multiple data sets as long as the input data sets have a common variable. You can merge more than two data sets that lack a common variable in multiple DATA steps if each input data set contains at least one variable that is also in at least one other input data set.

Using PROC SQL to Join Data

You can also use PROC SQL to join data from multiple tables if there is no single column that is common to all input tables. If you create a new table with the results of an inner join in a PROC SQL step, the results can be very similar to the results of a DATA step match-merge.

Comparing DATA Step Match-Merges and PROC SQL Joins

It is possible to create identical results with a basic DATA step match-merge and a PROC SQL join. However, there are significant differences between these two methods, as well as advantages and disadvantages to each. In some cases, such as when there is a one-to-one or a one-to-many match on values of the BY variables in the input data sets, these two methods produce identical results. In other cases, such as when there is a many-to-many match on values of the BY variables, or if there are nonmatching values of the BY variables, these two methods produce different results. These differences reflect the fact that the processing is different for a DATA step match-merge and a PROC SQL join. Even if you are working with many-to-many matches or nonmatching data, it is possible to use other DATA step techniques such as multiple SET statements to create results that are identical to the results that a PROC SQL step creates.

Combining Summary Data and Detail Data

In order to perform tasks such as calculating percentages based on individual values from a data set based on a summary statistic of the data, you need to combine summary data and detail data. One way to create a summary data set is to use PROC MEANS. Once you have a summary data set, you can use multiple SET statements to combine the summary data with the detail data in the original data set. It is also possible to create summary data with a sum statement and to combine it with detail data in one DATA step.

Using an Index to Combine Data

You can use an index to combine data from matching observations in multiple data sets if the index is built on variables that are common to all input data sets. Especially if one of the input data sets is very large, an index can improve the efficiency of the merge. You use the KEY= option in a SET statement in conjunction with another SET statement to use an index to combine data. You can use the _IORC_ variable to prevent unmatched data from being included in the output data set.

Using a Transaction Data Set

Sometimes, you might want to update the data in one data set with data that is stored in another data set. You use the UPDATE statement to update a master data set with a transaction data set. The UPDATE statement replaces values in the master data set with values from the transaction data set for each observations with a matching value of the BY variable.

Sample Programs

Combining Data with the IF-THEN/ELSE Statement

```
data mylib.employees_new;
   set mylib.employees;
   if IDnum=1001 then Birthdate='01JAN1963'd;
   else if IDnum=1002 then Birthdate='08AUG1946'd;
   else if IDnum=1003 then Birthdate='23MAR1950'd;
   else if IDnum=1004 then Birthdate='17JUN1973'd;
run;
```

Combining Data with the ARRAY Statement

```
data mylib.employees_new;
   array birthdates{1001:1004} _temporary_ ('01JAN1963'd
         '08AUG1946'd '23MAR1950'd '17JUN1973'd);
   set mylib.employees;
   Birthdate=birthdates(IDnum);
run;
```

Combining Data with the FORMAT Procedure

```
proc format;
   value birthdate 1001 = '01JAN1963'
                   1002 = '08AUG1946'
                   1003 = '23MAR1950'
                   1004 = '17JUN1973';
run;

data mylib.employees_new;
   set mylib.employees;
   Birthdate=input(put(IDnum,birthdate.),date9.);
run;
```

Performing a DATA Step Match-Merge

```
proc sort data=sasuser.expenses out=expenses;
   by flightid date;
run;

proc sort data=sasuser.revenue out=revenue;
   by flightid date;
run;

data revexpns (drop=rev1st revbusiness revecon
      expenses);
   merge expenses(in=e) revenue(in=r);
   by flightid date;
   if e and r;
   Profit=sum(rev1st, revbusiness, revecon,
         -expenses);
run;

proc sort data=revexpns;
   by dest;
run;

proc sort data=sasuser.acities out=acities;
   by code;
run;

data sasuser.alldata;
   merge revexpns(in=r) acities
         (in=a rename=(code=dest)
         keep=city name code);
   by dest;
   if r and a;
run;
```

Performing a PROC SQL Join

```
proc sql;
   create table sqljoin as
   select revenue.flightid,
          revenue.date format=date9.,
          revenue.origin, revenue.dest,
          sum(revenue.rev1st,
              revenue.revbusiness,
               revenue.revecon)
          -expenses.expenses as Profit,
          acities.city, acities.name
      from sasuser.expenses, sasuser.revenue,
         sasuser.acities
      where expenses.flightid=revenue.flightid
          and expenses.date=revenue.date
          and acities.code=revenue.dest
      order by revenue.dest, revenue.flightid,
              revenue.date;
quit;
```

Combining Summary Data and Detail Data

```
proc means data=sasuser.monthsum noprint;
   var revcargo;
   output out=sasuser.summary sum=Cargosum;
run;

data sasuser.percent1;
   if _n_=1 then set sasuser.summary
                     (keep=cargosum);
   set sasuser.monthsum
       (keep=salemon revcargo);
   PctRev=revcargo/cargosum;
run;

data sasuser.percent2(drop=totalrev);
   if _n_=1 then do until(lastobs);
      set sasuser.monthsum(keep=revcargo)
          end=lastobs;
      totalrev+revcargo;
   end;
   set sasuser.monthsum (keep=salemon revcargo);
   PctRev=revcargo/totalrev;
run;
```

Using an Index to Combine Data

```
data work.profit work.errors;
   set sasuser.dnunder;
   set sasuser.sale2000(keep=routeid
       flightid date rev1st revbusiness
       revecon revcargo)key=flightdate;
   if _iorc_=0 then do;
      Profit=sum(rev1st, revbusiness, revecon,
             revcargo, -expenses);
      output work.profit;
   end;
```

```
        else do;
          _error_=0;
          output work.errors;
        end;
    run;
```

Using a Transaction Data Set

```
proc sort data=mylib.empmaster;
    by empid;
run;

proc sort data=mylib.empchanges;
    by empid;
run;

data mylib.empmaster;
    update mylib.empmaster mylib.empchanges;
    by empid;
run;
```

Points to Remember

- In a DATA step match-merge, you can use the RENAME= option to give identical names to variables in input data sets if those variables contain the same data and have the same type and length.

- You use the OUTPUT statement and the NOPRINT option with the MEANS procedure to route the statistics to an output data set and suppress the default report.

- The automatic variable _N_ tracks how many times a DATA step has iterated. The _N_ variable is useful when combining data from a summary data set with data from a larger detail data set.

- When you use the UPDATE statement, both data sets must be sorted by or have indexes based on the BY variable.

Quiz

Select the best answer for each question. After completing the quiz, check your answers using the answer key in the appendix.

1. According to the data set descriptions below, which of the variables that are listed qualify as BY variables for a DATA step match-merge?

Variable	Type	Length	Description
Code	char	5	Department code
Totemps	num	3	Total number of employees
Region	char	4	Location of the department
Manager	num	5	Employee ID number

Variable	Type	Length	Description
IDnum	num	5	Employee ID number
Name	char	20	Employee name
Division	char	3	Division abbreviation
Hiredate	num	8	Date of hire
Supervisor	char	20	Name of supervisor

a. Code and IDnum

b. Manager and Supervisor

c. Manager and IDnum

d. There are no variables that are common to both of these data sets.

2. Suppose you want to merge Dataset1, Dataset2, and Dataset3. Also suppose that Dataset1 and Dataset2 have the common variable Startdate, that Dataset2 and Dataset3 have the common variable Instructor, and that these data sets have no other common variables. How can you use a DATA step to merge these three data sets into one new data set?

   a. You use a MERGE statement in one DATA step to merge Dataset1, Dataset2, and Dataset3 by Startdate and Instructor.

   b. You sort Dataset1 and Dataset2 by Startdate and merge them into a temporary data set in a DATA step. Then you sort the temporary data set and Dataset3 by Instructor and merge them into a new data set in a DATA step.

   c. You can merge these data sets only with a PROC SQL step.

   d. You cannot merge these three data sets at all because they do not have a common variable.

3. Which of the following programs correctly creates a table with the results of a PROC SQL inner join matched on the values of empcode?

   a.
   ```
   proc sql;
      select newsals.empcode allemps.lastname
            newsals.salary contrib.amount
         from sasuser.allemps, sasuser.contrib,
            sasuser.newsals
         where empcode=allemps.empid
            and empcode=contrib.empid;
   quit;
   ```

   b.
   ```
   proc sql;
      create table usesql as
         select newsals.empcode allemps.lastname
               newsals.salsry contrib.amount
            from sasuser.allemps, sasuser.contrib,
               sasuser.newsals
   quit;
   ```

   c.
   ```
   proc sql;
      create table usesql as;
         select newsals.empcode, allemps.lastname,
               newsals.salary, contrib.amount;
            from sasuser.allemps, sasuser.contrib,
               sasuser.newsals;
            where empcode=allemps.empid
   ```

```
                    and empcode=contrib.empid;
    quit;

d.  proc sql;
        create table usesql as
            select newsals.empcode, allemps.lastname,
                   newsals.salary, contrib.amount
                from sasuser.allemps, sasuser.contrib,
                       sasuser.newsals
                where empcode=allemps.empid
                       and empcode=contrib.empid;
    quit;
```

4. To process a default DATA step match-merge, SAS first reads the descriptor portion of each input data set to create the PDV and the descriptor portion of the new data set. Which of the following accurately describes the rest of this process?

   a. Next, SAS sequentially match-merges observations reading them into the PDV, and then writes them to the new data set. When the BY value changes in all the input data sets, the PDV is initialized to missing. Missing values for variables, as well as missing values that result from unmatched observations, are written to the new data set.

   b. Next, SAS sequentially match-merges observations reading them into the PDV, and then writes them to the new data set. After each DATA step iteration, the PDV is initialized to missing. Missing values for variables, as well as missing values that result from unmatched observations, are omitted from the new data set.

   c. Next, SAS creates a Cartesian product of all possible combinations of observations, writes them to the PDV, and then to the new data set. Then SAS goes through the new data set and eliminates all observations that do not have matching values of the BY variable.

   d. Next, SAS creates a Cartesian product of all possible combinations of observations, writes them to the PDV, and then to the new data set. The new data set is then ordered by values of the BY variable.

5. Which of the following statements is false about using multiple SET statements in one DATA step?

   a. You can use multiple SET statements to combine observations from several SAS data sets.

   b. Processing stops when SAS encounters the end-of-file (EOF) marker on either data set (even if there is more data in the other data set).

   c. You can use multiple SET statements in one DATA step only if the data sets in each SET statement have a common variable.

   d. The variables in the PDV are not reinitialized when a second SET statement is executed.

6. Select the program that correctly creates a new data set named Sasuser.Summary that contains one observation with summary data that was created from the Salary variable of the Sasuser.Empdata data set.

   a. ```
      proc sum data=sasuser.emdata noprint;
          output out=sasuser.summary sum=Salarysum;
      run;
      ```

   b. ```
      proc means data=sasuser.empdata noprint;
          var salary;
      ```

```
        output out=sasuser.summary sum=Salarysum;
   run;
```

c. ```
   proc sum data=sasuser.empdata noprint;
       var salary;
       output out=sasuser.summary sum=Salarysum;
   run;
   ```

d. ```
   proc means data=sasuser.empdata noprint;
       output=sasuser.summary sum=Salarysum;
   run;
   ```

7. If the value of Cargosum is $1000 at the end of the first iteration of the DATA step shown below, what is the value of Cargosum in the PDV when the DATA step is in its third iteration?

```
data sasuser.percent1;
    if _n_=1 then set sasuser.summary (keep=cargosum);
    set sasuser.monthsum (keep=salemon revcargo);
    PctRev=revcargo/cargosum;
run;
```

a. $1000

b. $3000

c. The value is missing.

d. The value cannot be determined without seeing the data that is in Sasuser.Summary.

8. According to the data set shown, what is the value of Totalrev in the PDV at the end of the fourth iteration of the DATA step?

```
data sasuser.percent2(drop=totalrev);
    if _n_=1 then do until(lastobs);
        set sasuser.monthsum2(keep=revcargo)
            end=lastobs;
        totalrev+revcargo;
    end;
    set sasuser.monthsum2
        (keep=salemon revcargo);
    PctRev=revcargo/totalrev;
run;
```

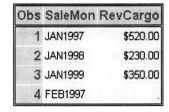

Obs	SaleMon	RevCargo
1	JAN1997	$520.00
2	JAN1998	$230.00
3	JAN1999	$350.00
4	FEB1997	.

a. The value is missing.

b. $350.00

c. $520.00

d. $1100.00

9. Which of the following programs correctly uses an index to combine data from two input data sets?

a. ```
   data work.profit;
       set sasuser.sale2000(keep=routeid flightid date
           rev1st revbusiness revecon revcargo)
           key=flightdate;
       set sasuser.dnunder;
   ```
   ```

```
        Profit=sum(rev1st, revbusiness, revecon, revcargo,
              -expenses);
    run;
```

b.
```
data work.profit;
    set sasuser.dnunder;
    set sasuser.sale2000(keep=routeid flightid date
        rev1st revbusiness revecon revcargo)
        key=flightdate;
    where routeid='0000103';
    Profit=sum(rev1st, revbusiness, revecon, revcargo,
          -expenses);
    run;
```

c.
```
data work.profit;
    set sasuser.dnunder;
    set sasuser.sale2000(keep=routeid flightid date
        rev1st revbusiness revecon revcargo);
        key=flightdate;
    Profit=sum(rev1st, revbusiness, revecon, revcargo,
          -expenses);
    run;
```

d.
```
data work.profit;
    set sasuser.dnunder;
    set sasuser.sale2000(keep=routeid flightid date
        rev1st revbusiness revecon revcargo)
        key=flightdate;
    Profit=sum(rev1st, revbusiness, revecon, revcargo,
          -expenses);
    run;
```

10. Which of the following statements about the _IORC_ variable is false?

   a. It is automatically created when you use either a SET statement with the KEY= option or the MODIFY statement with the KEY= option in a DATA step.

   b. A value of zero for _IORC_ means that the most recent SET statement with the KEY= option (or MODIFY statement with the KEY= option) did not execute successfully.

   c. A value of zero for _IORC_ means that the most recent SET statement with the KEY= option (or MODIFY statement with the KEY= option) executed successfully.

   d. You can use the _IORC_ variable to prevent nonmatching data from being included when you use an index to combine data from multiple data sets.

Chapter 16
Using Lookup Tables to Match Data

Overview

Introduction

Sometimes, you need to combine data from two or more data sets into a single observation in a new data set according to the values of a common variable. When the data sources are two or more data sets that have a common structure, you can use a match-merge to combine the data sets. However, in some cases the data sources do not share a common structure. When data sources do not have a common structure, you can use a lookup table to match them. A lookup table is a table that contains key values.

Key	Var_X
1998	X1
1999	X2
2000	X3
2001	X4
2002	X5

+

Key	Var_Y	Var_Z
1998	Y1	Z1
1999	Y2	Z2
2000	Y3	Z3
2001	Y4	Z4
2002	Y5	Z5

=

Year	Var_X	Var_Y	Var_Z
1998	X1	Y1	Z1
1999	X2	Y2	Z2
2000	X3	Y3	Z3
2001	X4	Y4	Z4
2002	X5	Y5	Z5

The technique that you use to perform a table lookup is dependent on your data. This chapter focuses on using multidimensional arrays to perform table lookups and transposing SAS data sets in preparation for a match-merge.

Using Multidimensional Arrays

Review of the Multidimensional Array Statement

When a lookup operation depends on more than one ordinal numeric key, you can use a multidimensional array. You use an ARRAY statement to create an array. The ARRAY statement defines a set of elements that you process as a group.

General form, multidimensional ARRAY statement:

ARRAY *array-name* {*rows,cols,...*} <*$*> <*length*>

<*array-elements*> <(*initial values*)>;

Here is an explanation of the syntax:

array-name
  names the array.

rows
  specifies the number of array elements in the row dimension.

cols
  specifies the number of array elements in the column dimension.

array-elements
  names the variables that make up the array.

initial values
  specifies initial values for the corresponding elements in the array, separated by commas or spaces.

Note: The keyword *_TEMPORARY_* might be used instead of *array-elements* to avoid creating new data set variables.

When you work with arrays, remember the following:

- the name of the array must be a SAS name that is not the name of a SAS function or variable in the same DATA step

- the variables listed as array elements must all be the same type (either all numeric or all character)

- the initial values that are specified can be numbers or character strings. You must enclose all character strings in quotation marks

Note: If you use the _TEMPORARY_ keyword in an array statement, remember that temporary data elements behave like DATA step variables with the following exceptions:

- They do not have names. Refer to temporary data elements by the array name and dimension.

- They do not appear in the output data set.

- You cannot use the special subscript asterisk (*) to refer to all the elements.

- Temporary data element values are always automatically retained, rather than being reset to missing at the beginning of the next iteration of the DATA step.

Example

Suppose you need to determine the wind chill values for the flights that are represented in the SAS data set Sasuser.Flights. The data set contains three variables: Flight (the flight number), Temp (the average outdoor temperature during the flight), and Wspeed (the average wind speed during the flight).

Figure 16.1 SAS Data Set Sasuser.Flights

Obs	Flight	Temp	Wspeed
1	IA2736	-8	9
2	IA6352	-4	16

Wind chill values are derived from the air temperature and wind speed as shown in the following wind chill lookup table. To determine the wind chill for each flight, you can create a multidimensional array that stores the wind chill values shown in the table. You can then match the values of Temp and Wspeed with the wind chill values that are stored in the array.

Figure 16.2 Temperature (in degrees Fahrenheit)

	-10	-5	0	5	10	15	20	25	30
5	-22	-16	-11	-5	1	7	13	19	25
10	-28	-22	-16	-10	-4	3	9	15	21
15	-32	-26	-19	-13	-7	0	6	13	19
20	-35	-29	-22	-15	-9	-2	4	11	17
25	-37	-31	-24	-17	-11	-4	3	9	16
30	-39	-33	-26	-19	-12	-5	1	8	15
35	-41	-34	-27	-21	-14	-7	0	7	14
40	-43	-36	-29	-22	-15	-8	-1	6	13

Wind Speed (in miles per hour)

In the following program, the ARRAY statement creates the two-dimensional array WC and specifies the dimensions of the array: four rows and two columns. No variables are created from the array because the keyword _TEMPORARY_ is used. The initial values that are specified correspond to the values in the wind chill lookup table. For this example, only the values in the first two columns and four rows in the wind chill lookup table are included in the array.

```
data work.wndchill (drop=column row);
  array WC{4,2} _temporary_
      (-22,-16,-28,-22,-32,-26,-35,-29);
  set sasuser.flights;
  row=round(wspeed,5)/5;
  column=(round(temp,5)/5)+3;
  WindChill=wc{row,column};
run;
```

Figure 16.3 *Temperature (in degrees Fahrenheit)*

	-10	-5	0	5	10	15	20	25	30
5	-22	-16	-11	-5	1	7	13	19	25
10	-28	-22	-16	-10	-4	3	9	15	21
15	-32	-26	-19	-13	-7	0	6	13	19
20	-35	-29	-22	-15	-9	-2	4	11	17
25	-37	-31	-24	-17	-11	-4	3	9	16
30	-39	-33	-26	-19	-12	-5	1	8	15
35	-41	-34	-27	-21	-14	-7	0	7	14
40	-43	-36	-29	-22	-15	-8	-1	6	13

Wind Speed (in miles per hour)

The value of WindChill for each flight is determined by referencing the array based on the values of Wspeed and Temp in the Sasuser.Flights data set. The row number for the array reference is determined by the value of Wspeed. The column number for the array reference is determined by the value of Temp.

Table Representation of the WC Array

```
data work.wndchill (drop = column row);
  array WC{4,2} _temporary_
        (-22,-16,-28,-22,-32,-26,-35,-29);
  set sasuser.flights;
  row = round(wspeed,5)/5;
  column = (round(temp,5)/5)+3;
  WindChill= wc{row,column};
run;
```

-22	-16
-28	-22
-32	-26
-35	-29

The rounding unit for the value of Wspeed is 5 because the values for wind speed in the wind chill table are rounded to every 5 miles-per-hour. Wspeed is then divided by 5 to derive the row number for the array reference.

Like the value for Wspeed, the value of Temp is rounded to the nearest 5, and then divided by 5. The offset of 3 is added to the value because the third column in the wind chill lookup table represents 0 degrees.

```
data work.wndchill (drop = column row);
  array WC{4,2} _temporary_
        (-22,-16,-28,-22,-32,-26,-35,-29);
  set sasuser.flights;
  row = round(wspeed,5)/5;
  column = (round(temp,5)/5)+3;
  WindChill= wc{row,column};
run;
```

PROC PRINT output shows the completed data set.

```
proc print data=work.wndchill;
run;
```

Obs	flight	temp	wspeed	WindChill
1	IA2736	-8	9	-28
2	IA6352	-4	16	-26

Populating an Array from a SAS Data Set

Overview

In the previous section, the wind chill lookup table was loaded into the WC array when the array was created. In many cases, you might prefer to load an array with values that are stored in a SAS data set rather than loading them in an ARRAY statement. Lookup values should be stored in a SAS data set when the following conditions are true:

- there are too many values to initialize easily in the array

- the values change frequently

- the same values are used in many programs

Example

Suppose you want to compare the actual cargo revenue values in the SAS data set Sasuser.Monthsum to the target cargo revenue values in the SAS data set Sasuser.Ctargets.

Sasuser.Monthsum contains the actual cargo and passenger revenue figures for each month from 1997 through 1999.

Table 16.1   *SAS Data Set Sasuser.Monthsum (first five observations of selected variables)*

Obs	SaleMon	RevCargo	MonthNo
1	JAN1997	$171,520,869.10	1
2	JAN1998	$238,786,807.60	1
3	JAN1999	$280,350,393.00	1
4	FEB1997	$177,671,530.40	2
5	FEB1998	$215,959,695.50	2

The SAS data set Sasuser.Ctargets contains the target cargo revenue figures for each month from 1997 through 1999.

Table 16.2 *SAS Data Set Sasuser.Ctargets*

Obs	Year	Jan	Feb	Mar	Apr	May	Jun
1	1997	192284420	86376721	28526103	260386468	109975326	102833104
2	1998	108645734	147656369	202158055	41160707	264294440	267135485
3	1999	85730444	74168740	39955768	312654811	318149340	187270927

Obs	Jul	Aug	Sep	Oct	Nov	Dec
1	196728648	236996122	112413744	125401565	72551855	136042505
2	208694865	83456868	286846554	275721406	230488351	24901752
3	123394421	34273985	151565752	141528519	178043261	181668256

You want to create a new SAS data set, Work.Lookup1, that lists the actual and target values for each month. Work.Lookup1 should have the same structure as Sasuser.Monthsum: an observation for each month and year, as well as a new variable, Ctarget (target cargo revenues). The value of Ctarget is derived from the target values in Sasuser.Ctargets.

Table 16.3 *SAS Data Set Work.Lookup1 (first five observations of selected variables)*

Obs	SaleMon	RevCargo	Ctarget
1	JAN1997	$171,520,869.10	$192,284,420.00
2	JAN1998	$238,786,807.60	$108,645,734.00
3	JAN1999	$280,350,393.00	$85,730,444.00
4	FEB1997	$177,671,530.40	$86,376,721.00
5	FEB1998	$215,959,695.50	$147,656,369.00

Sasuser.Monthsum and Sasuser.Ctargets cannot be merged because they have different structures:

- Sasuser.Monthsum has an observation for each month and year.

- Sasuser.Ctargets has one column for each month and one observation for each year.

However, the data sets have two common factors: month and year. You can use a multidimensional array to match the actual values for each month and year in Sasuser.Monthsum with the target values for each month and year in Sasuser.Ctargets.

Creating an Array

The first step is to create an array to hold the values in the target data set, Sasuser.Ctargets. The array needs two dimensions: one for the year values and one for the month values. In the following program, the first ARRAY statement creates the two-dimensional array, Targets.

Remember that the dimension of an array does not have to range from one to the number of elements. You can specify a range for the values of the dimension when you define the array. In this case, the dimensions of the array are specified as 3 rows (one for each year: 1997, 1998, and 1999) and 12 columns (one for each month).

```
data work.lookup1;
   array Targets{1997:1999,12} _temporary_;
   if _n_=1 then do i= 1 to 3;
             set sasuser.ctargets;
             array mnth{*} Jan--Dec;
             do j=1 to dim(mnth);
                targets{year,j}=mnth{j};
             end;
   end;
   set sasuser.monthsum(keep=salemon revcargo monthno);
   year=input(substr(salemon,4),4.);
   Ctarget=targets{year,monthno};
   format ctarget dollar15.2;
run;
```

The following table represents the Targets array. Notice that the array is not populated. The next step is to load the array elements from Sasuser.Ctargets.

Table 16.4 *Table Representation of Targets Array*

	1	2	3	4	5	6	7	8	9	10	11	12
1997												
1998												
1999												

Note: The row dimension for the Targets array could have been specified using the value 3. Here is an example:

```
array Targets{3,12} _temporary_;
```

However, using the notation 1997:1999 simplifies the program by eliminating the need to map numeric values to the year values.

Loading the Array Elements

The Targets array needs to be loaded with the values in Sasuser.Ctargets. One method for accomplishing this task is to load the array within a DO loop.

Table 16.5 *SAS Data Set Sasuser.Ctargets*

Year	Jan	Feb	Mar	Apr	May	Jun
1997	192284420	86376721	28526103	260386468	109975326	102833104
1998	108645734	147656369	202158055	41160707	264294440	267135485

Year	Jan	Feb	Mar	Apr	May	Jun
1999	85730444	74168740	39955768	312654811	318149340	187270927

	Jul	Aug	Sep	Oct	Nov	Dec
	196728648	236996122	112413744	125401565	72551855	136042505
	208694865	83456868	286846554	275721406	230488351	24901752
	123394421	34273985	151565752	141528519	178043261	181668256

The IF-THEN statement specifies that the Targets array is loaded only once, during the first iteration of the DATA step. The DO loop executes three times, once for each observation in Sasuser.Ctargets.

The ARRAY statement within the DO loop creates the Mnth array, which stores the values from Sasuser.Ctargets. The dimension of the Mnth array is specified using an asterisk, which enables SAS to automatically count the array elements.

Note: If you use an asterisk to specify the dimensions of an array, you must list the array elements. You cannot use an asterisk to specify an array's dimensions if the elements of the array are specified with the _TEMPORARY_ keyword.

The array elements Jan through Dec are listed using a double hyphen (- -). The double hyphen (- -) is used to read the specified values based on their positions in the PDV.

```
data work.lookup1;
  array Targets{1997:1999,12} _temporary_;
  if _n_=1 then do i= 1 to 3;
          set sasuser.ctargets;
          array Mnth{*} Jan--Dec;
          do j=1 to dim(mnth);
              targets{year,j}=mnth{j};
          end;
  end;
  set sasuser.monthsum(keep=salemon revcargo monthno);
  year=input(substr(salemon,4),4.);
  Ctarget=targets{year,monthno};
  format ctarget dollar15.2;
run;
```

The following table shows the values in the Mnth array after the first iteration of the DO loop.

Table 16.6 *Table Representation of Mnth Array (after the first iteration of the DO loop)*

Jan	Feb	Mar...	...Oct	Nov	Dec
192284420	86376721	260386468	125401565	72551855	136042505

Within the nested DO loop, the Targets array reference is matched to the Mnth array reference in order to populate the Targets array. The DIM function returns the number of elements in the Mnth array (in this case 12) and provides an ending point for the nested DO loop.

```
data work.lookup1;
  array Targets{1997:1999,12} _temporary_;
  if _n_=1 then do i= 1 to 3;
            set sasuser.ctargets;
            array Mnth{*} Jan--Dec;
            do j=1 to dim(mnth);
                targets{year,j}=mnth{j};
            end;
  end;
  set sasuser.monthsum(keep=salemon revcargo monthno);
  year=input(substr(salemon,4),4.);
  Ctarget=targets{year,monthno};
  format ctarget dollar15.2;
run;
```

Table 16.7 *Table Representation of Mnth Array (after the second iteration of the DO loop)*

Jan	Feb	Mar...	...Oct	Nov	Dec
108645734	147656369	202158055	275721406	230488351	24901752

Table 16.8 *Table Representation of Mnth Array (after the third iteration of the DO loop)*

Jan	Feb	Mar...	...Oct	Nov	Dec
85730444	74168740	39955768	141528519	178043261	181668256

Table 16.9 *Table Representation of Populated Targets Array*

	1	2	3...	...10	11	12
1997	192284420	86376721	260386468	125401565	72551855	136042505
1998	108645734	147656369	202158055	275721406	230488351	24901752
1999	85730444	74168740	39955768	141528519	178043261	181668256

Note: The dimension of the Mnth array could also be specified using the numeric value 12. However, the asterisk notation enables the program to be more flexible. For example, using the asterisk, the program would not need to be edited if the target data set contained data for only 11 months. Remember that if you use an asterisk to count the array elements, you must list the array elements.

Reading the Actual Values

The last step is to read the actual values stored in Sasuser.Monthsum. Remember that you need to know the month and year values for each observation in order to locate the correct target revenue values.

Table 16.10 *SAS Data Set Sasuser.Monthsum (first five observations of selected variables)*

SaleMon	RevCargo	MonthNo
JAN1997	$171,520,869.10	1
JAN1998	$238,786,807.60	1
JAN1999	$280,350,393.00	1
FEB1997	$177,671,530.40	2
FEB1998	$215,959,695.50	2

The values for month are read from the numeric variable MonthNo. The year values are contained within the character variable SaleMon and can be extracted using the SUBSTR function. In this example, the SUBSTR function extracts four characters from SaleMon, starting at the fourth character. Note that the INPUT function is used to convert the value that is extracted from SaleMon from character to numeric in the assignment statement for Year. A numeric format performs the character to numeric conversion so the value of Year is used as an array reference.

The values of Ctarget are then looked up from the Targets array based on the values of Year and MonthNo.

```
data work.lookup1;
   array Targets{1997:1999,12} _temporary_;
   if _n_=1 then do i= 1 to 3;
              set sasuser.ctargets;
              array Mnth{*} Jan--Dec;
              do j=1 to dim(mnth);
                 targets{year,j}=mnth{j};
              end;
   end;
   set sasuser.monthsum(keep=salemon revcargo monthno);
   year=input(substr(salemon,4),4.);
   Ctarget=targets{year,monthno};
   format ctarget dollar15.2;
run;
```

Table 16.11 *Table Representation of Targets Array*

	1	2	3...	...10	11	12
1997	192284420	86376721	260386468	125401565	72551855	136042505
1998	108645734	147656369	202158055	275721406	230488351	24901752
1999	85730444	74168740	39955768	141528519	178043261	181668256

PROC PRINT output shows the new data set Work.Lookup1, which contains the actual cargo values (RevCargo) and the target cargo values (Ctarget).

Work.Lookup1 (first ten observations)

```
proc print data=work.lookup1 (obs=10);
    var salemon revcargo ctarget;
run;
```

Obs	SaleMon	RevCargo	Ctarget
1	JAN1997	$171,520,869.10	$192,284,420.00
2	JAN1998	$238,786,807.60	$108,645,734.00
3	JAN1999	$280,350,393.00	$85,730,444.00
4	FEB1997	$177,671,530.40	$86,375,721.00
5	FEB1998	$215,959,695.50	$147,658,389.00
6	FEB1999	$253,999,924.00	$74,168,740.00
7	MAR1997	$196,591,378.20	$28,526,103.00
8	MAR1998	$239,056,025.55	$202,158,055.00
9	MAR1999	$281,433,310.00	$39,955,768.00
10	APR1997	$380,804,120.20	$260,386,468.00

Using PROC TRANSPOSE

Overview

In the previous section, we compared actual revenue values to target revenue values using an array as a lookup table. Remember the following:

- Sasuser.Monthsum has an observation for each month and year.

  Table 16.12 *SAS Data Set Sasuser.Monthsum (first five observations of selected variables)*

SaleMon	RevCargo	MonthNo
JAN1997	$171,520,869.10	1
JAN1998	$238,786,807.60	1
JAN1999	$280,350,393.00	1
FEB1997	$177,671,530.40	2
FEB1998	$215,959,695.50	2

- Sasuser.Ctargets has one variable for each month and one observation for each year.

  Table 16.13 *SAS Data Set Sasuser.Ctargets (selected variables)*

Year	Jan	Feb	Mar	Apr	May	Jun
1997	192284420	86376721	28526103	260386468	109975326	102833104

Year	Jan	Feb	Mar	Apr	May	Jun
1998	108645734	147656369	202158055	41160707	264294440	267135485
1999	85730444	74168740	39955768	312654811	318149340	187270927

Using arrays was a good solution because the orientation of the data sets differed. An alternate solution is to transpose Sasuser.Ctargets using PROC TRANSPOSE, and then merge the transposed data set with Sasuser.Monthsum by the values of Year and Month.

General form, PROC TRANSPOSE:

PROC TRANSPOSE <DATA=*input-data-set*>

        <OUT=*output-data-set*>

        <NAME=*prefix text*>

        <PREFIX=*variable-name*>;

    BY <DESCENDING> *variable-1*

        <...<DESCENDING> *variable-n*>

        <NOTSORTED>;

    VAR *variable(s)*;

RUN;

Here is an explanation of the syntax:

DATA=*input-data-set*
  names the SAS data set to transpose.

OUT=*output-data-set*
  names the output data set.

NAME=*variable-name*
  specifies the name for the variable in the output data set that contains the name of the variable that is being transposed to create the current observation.

PREFIX=*variable-name*
  specifies a prefix to use in constructing names for transposed variables in the output data set. For example, if PREFIX=VAR, the names of the variables are VAR1, VAR2, ...,VAR*n*.

BY statement
  is used to transpose each BY group.

VAR *variable(s)*
  names one or more variables to transpose.

Note: If output-data-set does not exist, PROC TRANSPOSE creates it by using the DATA*n* naming convention.

Note: If you omit the VAR statement, the TRANSPOSE procedure transposes all of the numeric variables in the input data set that are not listed in another statement.

Note: You must list character variables in a VAR statement if you want to transpose them.

The TRANSPOSE procedure creates an output data set by restructuring the values in a SAS data set. When the data set is restructured, selected variables are transposed into observations. The TRANSPOSE procedure can often eliminate the need to write a lengthy DATA step to achieve the same result. The output data set can be used in subsequent DATA or PROC steps for analysis, reporting, or further data manipulation.

PROC TRANSPOSE does not print the output data set. Use PROC PRINT, PROC REPORT, or some other SAS reporting tool to print the output data set.

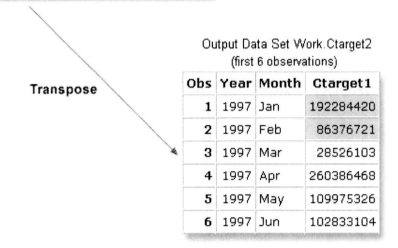

Example

The following program transposes the SAS data set Sasuser.Ctargets. The OUT= option specifies the name of the output data set, Work.Ctarget2. All of the variables in Sasuser.Ctargets are transposed because all of the variables are numeric and a VAR statement is not used in the program.

```
proc transpose data=sasuser.ctargets
     out=work.ctarget2;
run;
```

Table 16.14 *Input Data Set Sasuser.Ctargets (selected variables)*

Year	Jan	Feb	Mar	Apr	May	Jun
1997	192284420	86376721	28526103	260386468	109975326	102833104
1998	108645734	147656369	202158055	41160707	264294440	267135485
1999	85730444	74168740	39955768	312654811	318149340	187270927

Table 16.15 *Output Data Set: Work.Ctarget2*

Obs	_NAME_	COL1	COL2	COL3
1	Year	1997	1998	1999
2	Jan	192284420	108645734	85730444
3	Feb	86376721	147656369	74168740
4	Mar	28526103	202158055	39955768
5	Apr	260386468	41160707	31265481
6	May	109975326	264294440	318149340
7	Jun	102833104	267135485	187270927
8	Jul	196728648	208694865	123394421
9	Aug	236996122	83456868	34273985
10	Sep	112413744	286846554	151565752
11	Oct	125401565	275721406	141528519
12	Nov	72551855	230488351	178043261
13	Dec	136042505	24901752	181668256

Notice that in the output data set, the variables are named _NAME_, COL1, COL2, and COL3.

NAME is the default name of the variable that PROC TRANSPOSE creates to identify the source of the values in each observation in the output data set. This variable is a character variable whose values are the names of the variables that are transposed from the input data set. For example, in Work.Ctarget2 the values in the first observation in the output data set come from the values of the variable Year in the input data set.

The remaining transposed variables are named COL1...COL*n* by default. In Work.Ctarget2, the values of the variables COL1, COL2, and COL3 represent the target cargo revenue for each month in the years 1997, 1998, and 1999.

Adding Descriptive Variable Names

You can use PROC TRANSPOSE options to give the variables in the output data set more descriptive names. The NAME= option specifies a name for the _NAME_ variable.

The PREFIX= option specifies a prefix to use in constructing names for transposed variables in the output data set. For example, if PREFIX=Ctarget, the names of the variables are Ctarget1, Ctarget2, and Ctarget3.

```
proc transpose data=sasuser.ctargets
    out=work.ctarget2
    name=Month
    prefix=Ctarget;
run;
```

Table 16.16 *Output Data Set: Work.Ctarget2*

Obs	Month	Ctarget1	Ctarget2	Ctarget3
1	Year	1997	1998	1999
2	Jan	192284420	108645734	85730444
3	Feb	86376721	147656369	74168740
4	Mar	28526103	202158055	39955768
5	Apr	260386468	41160707	31265481
6	May	109975326	264294440	318149340
7	Jun	102833104	267135485	187270927
8	Jul	196728648	208694865	123394421
9	Aug	236996122	83456868	34273985
10	Sep	112413744	286846554	151565752
11	Oct	125401565	275721406	141528519
12	Nov	72551855	230488351	178043261
13	Dec	136042505	24901752	181668256

Note: The RENAME=data set option can also be used with PROC TRANSPOSE to change variable names.

```
proc transpose data=sasuser.ctargets
    out=work.ctarget2 (rename=(col1=Ctarget1
        col2=Ctarget2 col3=Ctarget3))
    name=Month;
run;
```

The default label for the _NAME_ variable is *NAME OF FORMER VARIABLE.* To see this, print the transposed data set using PROC PRINT with the LABEL option. You can use a LABEL statement to override the default label.

```
proc transpose data=sasuser.ctargets
    out=work.ctarget2
    name=Month
    prefix=Ctarget;
run;
proc print data=work.ctarget2 label;
label Month=MONTH;
run;
```

Merging the Transposed Data Set

Structuring the Data for a Merge

Remember that the transposed data set, Work.Ctarget2, needs to be merged with Sasuser.Monthsum by the values of Year and Month. Neither data set is currently structured correctly for the merge.

Table 16.17 *SAS Data Set: Work.Ctarget2 (first five observations)*

Obs	Month	Ctarget1	Ctarget2	Ctarget3
1	Year	1997	1998	1999
2	Jan	192284420	108645734	85730444
3	Feb	86376721	147656369	74168740
4	Mar	28526103	202158055	39955768
5	Apr	260386468	41160707	31265481

Table 16.18 *SAS Data Set Sasuer.Monthsum (first five observations of selected variables)*

Obs	SaleMon	RevCargo	MonthNo
1	JAN1997	$171,520,869.10	1
2	JAN1998	$238,786,807.60	1
3	JAN1999	$280,350,393.00	1
4	FEB1997	$177,671,530.40	2
5	FEB1998	$215,959,695.50	2

Using a BY Statement with PROC TRANSPOSE

In order to correctly structure Work.Ctarget2 for the merge, a BY statement needs to be used with PROC TRANSPOSE. For each BY group, PROC TRANSPOSE creates one observation for each variable that it transposes. The BY variable itself is not transposed.

The following program transposes Sasuser.Ctargets by the value of Year. The resulting output data set, Work.Ctarget2, now contains 12 observations for each year (1997, 1998, and 1999).

```
proc transpose data=sasuser.ctargets
     out=work.ctarget2
     name=Month
```

```
                              prefix=Ctarget;
                              by year;
              run;
```

Table 16.19 *Input Data Set Sasuser.Ctargets (selected variables)*

Obs	Year	Jan	Feb	Mar	Apr	May	Jun
1	1997	192284420	86376721	28526103	260386468	109975326	102833104
2	1998	108645734	147656369	202158055	41160707	264294440	267135485
3	1999	85730444	74168740	39955768	312654811	318149340	187270927

Table 16.20 *Output Data Set Work.Ctarget2 (first 12 observations)*

Obs	Year	Month	Ctarget1
1	1997	Jan	192284420
2	1997	Feb	86376721
3	1997	Mar	28526103
4	1997	Apr	260386468
5	1997	May	109975326
6	1997	Jun	102833104
7	1997	Jul	196728648
8	1997	Aug	236996122
9	1997	Sep	112413744
10	1997	Oct	125401565
11	1997	Nov	72551855
12	1997	Dec	136042505

CAUTION:
The original SAS data set must be sorted or indexed before using a BY statement with PROC TRANSPOSE unless you use the NOTSORTED option.

Sorting the Work.Ctarget2 Data Set

The last step in preparing Work.Ctarget2 for the merge is to use the SORT procedure to sort the data set by Year and Month as shown in the following program:

```
proc sort data=work.ctarget2;
```

```
  by year month;
run;
```

Notice that in the sorted version of Work.Ctarget2, the values of month are sorted alphabetically within year.

Table 16.21 *SAS Data Set Work.Ctarget2 (sorted, first 12 observations)*

Obs	Year	Month	Ctarget1
1	1997	Apr	260386468
2	1997	Aug	236996122
3	1997	Dec	136042505
4	1997	Feb	86376721
5	1997	Jan	192284420
6	1997	Jul	196728648
7	1997	Jun	102833104
8	1997	Mar	28526103
9	1997	May	109975326
10	1997	Nov	72551855
11	1997	Oct	125401565
12	1997	Sep	112413744

Reorganizing the Sasuser.Monthsum Data Set

The data in Sasuser.Monthsum must also be reorganized for the merge because the month and year values in that data set are combined in the variable SaleMon.

Table 16.22 *SAS Data Set Sasuser.Monthsum (first five observations of selected variables)*

Obs	SaleMon	RevCargo	MonthNo
1	JAN1997	$171,520,869.10	1
2	JAN1998	$238,786,807.60	1
3	JAN1999	$280,350,393.00	1
4	FEB1997	$177,671,530.40	2

Obs	SaleMon	RevCargo	MonthNo
5	FEB1998	$215,959,695.50	2

The following program creates two new variables, Year and Month, to hold the year and month values. The values for Year are created from SaleMon using the INPUT and SUBSTR functions. The values for Month are extracted from SaleMon using the LOWCASE and SUBSTR functions.

```
data work.mnthsum2;
   set sasuser.monthsum(keep=SaleMon RevCargo);
   length Month $ 3;
   Year=input(substr(SaleMon,4),4.);
   Month=propcase(SaleMon);
run;
```

Table 16.23   *SAS Data Set Work.Mnthsum2 (first six observations)*

Obs	SaleMon	RevCargo	Month	Year
1	JAN1997	$171,520,869.10	Jan	1997
2	JAN1998	$238,786,807.60	Jan	1998
3	JAN1999	$280,350,393.00	Jan	1999
4	FEB1997	$177,671,530.40	Feb	1997
5	FEB1998	$215,959,695.50	Feb	1998
6	FEB1999	$253,999,924.00	Feb	1999

Sorting the Work.Mnthsum2 Data Set

As with Work.Ctarget2, the last step in preparing for the merge is to sort the data set by the values of Year and Month as shown in the following program:

```
proc sort data=work.mnthsum2;
   by year month;
run;
```

Notice that in the sorted version of Work.Mnthsum2, the values of month are sorted alphabetically within year.

Table 16.24   *SAS Data Set Work.Mnthsum2 (sorted, first twelve observations)*

Obs	SaleMon	RevCargo	Month	Year
1	APR1997	$380,804,120.20	Apr	1997
2	AUG1997	$196,639,501.10	Aug	1997
3	DEC1997	$196,504,413.00	Dec	1997

Obs	SaleMon	RevCargo	Month	Year
4	FEB1997	$177,671,530.40	Feb	1997
5	JAN1997	$171,520,869.10	Jan	1997
6	JUL1997	$197,163,278.20	Jul	1997
7	JUN1997	$190,560,828.50	Jun	1997
8	MAR1997	$196,591,378.20	Mar	1997
9	MAY1997	$196,261,573.20	May	1997
10	NOV1997	$190,228,066.70	Nov	1997
11	OCT1997	$196,957,153.40	Oct	1997
12	SEP1997	$190,535,012.50	Sep	1997

Completing the Merge

When the data is structured correctly, Work.Mnthsum2 and Work.Ctarget2 can be merged by the values of Year and Month as shown in the following program:

```
data work.merged;
   merge work.mnthsum2 work.ctarget2;
   by year month;
run;
```

Table 16.25 *SAS Data Set Work.Mnthsum2 (first five observations)*

Obs	SaleMon	RevCargo	Month	Year
1	APR1997	$380,804,120.20	Apr	1997
2	AUG1997	$196,639,501.10	Aug	1997
3	DEC1997	$196,504,413.00	Dec	1997
4	FEB1997	$177,671,530.40	Feb	1997
5	JAN1997	$171,520,869.10	Jan	1997

Table 16.26 *SAS Data Set Work.Ctarget2 (first five observations)*

Obs	Year	Month	Ctarget1
1	1997	Apr	260386468
2	1997	Aug	236996122
3	1997	Dec	136042505

Obs	Year	Month	Ctarget1
4	1997	Feb	86376721
5	1997	Jan	192284420

PROC PRINT output shows the resulting data set Work.Merged. The values of RevCargo represent the actual cargo revenue for each month. The values of Ctarget1 represent the target cargo values for each month.

```
proc print
     data=work.merged (obs=10);
   format ctarget1 dollar15.2;
   var month year revcargo ctarget1;
run;
```

SAS Data Set Work.Merged (partial output)

Obs	Month	Year	RevCargo	Ctarget1
1	Apr	1997	$380,804,120.20	$260,386,468.00
2	Aug	1997	$196,639,501.10	$236,996,122.00
3	Dec	1997	$196,504,413.00	$136,042,505.00
4	Feb	1997	$177,671,530.40	$86,376,721.00
5	Jan	1997	$171,520,869.10	$192,284,420.00
6	Jul	1997	$197,163,273.20	$196,728,648.00
7	Jun	1997	$190,560,828.50	$102,833,104.00
8	Mar	1997	$196,591,373.20	$28,526,103.00
9	May	1997	$196,261,573.20	$109,975,326.00
10	Nov	1997	$190,228,066.70	$72,551,855.00

Using Hash Objects as Lookup Tables

Overview

Beginning with SAS 9, the hash object is available for use in a DATA step. The hash object provides an efficient, convenient mechanism for quick data storage and retrieval.

Unlike an array, which uses a series of consecutive integers to address array elements, a hash object can use any combination of numeric and character values as addresses. Also unlike arrays, which return only a single value, hash objects can return multiple values from a given lookup. A hash object can be loaded from hardcoded values or a SAS data set, is sized dynamically, and exists for the duration of the DATA step.

The hash object is a good choice for lookups that use unordered data that can fit into memory because it provides in-memory storage and retrieval and does not require the data to be sorted or indexed.

The Structure of a Hash Object

When a lookup depends on character key values, you can use the hash object. A hash object resembles a table with rows and columns and contains a key component and a data component.

The key component has these characteristics:

- might consist of numeric and character values
- maps key values to data rows
- must be unique
- can be a composite

The data component has these characteristics:

- can contain multiple data values per key value
- can consist of numeric and character values

Example

Suppose you have a data set named Sasuser.Contrib that lists the quarterly contributions to a retirement fund. You can use the hash object to calculate the difference between the actual contribution and the goal amount for each quarter.

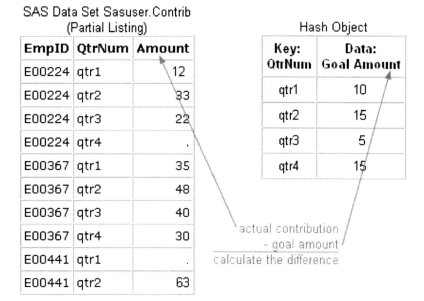

The following program creates a hash object that stores the quarterly goal for employee contributions to the retirement fund. To calculate the difference between actual contribution and the goal amount, the program retrieves the goal amount from the hash object based on the key values.

```
data work.difference (drop= goalamount);
   if _N_ = 1 then do;
      declare hash goal( );
      goal.definekey("QtrNum");
      goal.definedata("GoalAmount");
      goal.definedone( );
      call missing(goalamount);
      goal.add(key:'qtr1', data:10 );
      goal.add(key:'qtr2', data:15 );
      goal.add(key:'qtr3', data: 5 );
      goal.add(key:'qtr4', data:15 );
   end;
   set sasuser.contrib;
   goal.find();
   Diff = amount - goalamount;
run;
```

We will see how the hash object is set up.

DATA Step Component Objects

The hash object is a DATA step component object. *Component objects* are data elements that consist of attributes and methods. *Attributes* are the properties that specify the information that is associated with an object. *Methods* define the operations that an object can perform.

To use a DATA step component object in your SAS program, you must first declare and create (instantiate) the object.

Declaring the Hash Object

You declare a hash object using the DECLARE statement.

General form, DECLARE statement:

DECLARE *object-name* <(<*argument_tag-1: value-1*<, ...*argument_tag-n: value-n*>>)>;

object
> specifies the component object.

object-name
> specifies the name for the component object.

arg_tag
> specifies the information that is used to create an instance of the component object.

value
> specifies the value for an argument tag. Valid values depend on the component object.

Valid values for *object* are as follows:

- *hash* indicates a hash object.

- *hiter* indicates a hash iterator object.

Note: The hash iterator object retrieves data from the hash object in ascending or descending key order.

The following DECLARE statement creates a hash object named Goal.

```
data work.difference (drop= goalamount);
   if _N_ = 1 then do;
      declare hash goal();
```

At this point, you have declared a hash object named Goal.

Note: The DECLARE statement is an executable statement.

Defining Keys and Data

Remember that the hash object uses lookup keys to store and retrieve data. The keys and the data are DATA step variables that you use to initialize the hash object by using object dot notation method calls.

General form, object dot notation method calls:

object.method(<*argument_tag-1: value-1*<, ...*argument_tag-n: value-n*>>);

Here is an explanation of the syntax:

object
> specifies the name for the DATA step component object.

method
> specifies the name of the method to invoke.

argument-tag
> identifies the arguments that are passed to the method.

value
> specifies the argument value.

A key component is defined by passing the key variable name to the DEFINEKEY method. A data component is defined by passing the data variable name to the DEFINEDATA method. When all key and data components are defined, the DEFINEDONE method is called. Keys and data can consist of any number of character or numeric DATA step variables.

The following code initializes the key variable QtrNum and the data variable GoalAmount.

```
data work.difference (drop= goalamount);
   length goalamount 8;
   if _N_ = 1 then do;
      declare hash goal();
      goal.definekey ("QtrNum");
      goal.definedata ("GoalAmount");
      goal.definedone();
```

Using the Call Missing Routine

Since the variable GOALAMOUNT is not in an input data set and does not appear on the left side of an equal sign in an assignment statement, SAS issues a note stating that this variable is not initialized.

To avoid receiving these notes, use the CALL MISSING routine with the key and data variables as parameters. The CALL MISSING routine assigns a missing value to the specified character or numeric variables.

```
data Work.Difference (drop= goalamount);
if _N_ = 1 then do; declare hash goal();
   goal.definekey("QtrNum");
   goal.definedata("GoalAmount");
   goal.definedone();
   call missing(goalamount);
```

Loading Key and Data Values

So far, you have declared and instantiated the hash object, and initialized the hash object's key and data variables. You are now ready to populate the hash object using the ADD method. The following code uses the ADD method to load the key values qtr1, qtr2, qtr3, and qtr4 and the corresponding data values 10, 15, 5, and 15 into the hash object.

```
data work.difference (drop= goalamount);
if _N_ = 1 then do;
   declare hash goal( );
   goal.definekey("QtrNum");
   goal.definedata("GoalAmount");
   goal.definedone( );
   call missing(goalamount);
   goal.add(key:'qtr1', data:10 );
   goal.add(key:'qtr2', data:15 );
   goal.add(key:'qtr3', data: 5 );
   goal.add(key:'qtr4', data:15 );
end;
```

Retrieving Matching Data

Use the FIND method to retrieve matching data from the hash object. The FIND method generates a numeric return code that indicates whether the key is found in the hash object. A return code of zero indicates a successful find. A nonzero value indicates a find

failure. If the key is in the hash object, then the FIND method also sets the data variable
to the value of the data item so that it is available for use after the method call.

```
data work.difference (drop= goalamount);
   if _N_ = 1 then do;
      declare hash goal( );
      goal.definekey("QtrNum");
      goal.definedata("GoalAmount");
      goal.definedone( );
      call missing(goalamount);
      goal.add(key:'qtr1', data:10 );
      goal.add(key:'qtr2', data:15 );
      goal.add(key:'qtr3', data: 5 );
      goal.add(key:'qtr4', data:15 );
   end;
   set sasuser.contrib;
   rc=goal.find();
   Diff = amount - goalamount;
run;
```

Hash Object Processing

We will consider what happens when the program is submitted for execution.

```
data Work.Difference (drop= goalamount);
   if _N_ = 1 then do;
      declare hash goal( );
      goal.definekey("QtrNum");
      goal.definedata("GoalAmount");
      goal.definedone( );
      call missing(goalamount);
      goal.add(key:'qtr1', data:10 );
      goal.add(key:'qtr2', data:15 );
      goal.add(key:'qtr3', data: 5 );
      goal.add(key:'qtr4', data:15 );
   end;
   set sasuser.contrib;
   rc=goal.find();
   Diff = amount - goalamount;
run;
```

The program executes until the SET statement encounters end of file on sasuser.contrib.
PROC PRINT output shows the completed data set.

```
proc print data=work.difference;
run;
```

Obs	QtrNum	EmpID	Amount	Diff
1	qtr1	E00224	12	2
2	qtr2	E00224	33	18
3	qtr3	E00224	22	17
4	qtr4	E00224		
5	qtr1	E00367	35	25
6	qtr2	E00367	48	33
7	qtr3	E00367	40	35
8	qtr4	E00367	30	15
9	qtr1	E00441		
10	qtr2	E00441	63	48

Creating a Hash Object from a SAS Data Set

Suppose you need to create a report that shows revenue, expenses, profits, and airport information. You have two data sets that contain portions of the required data. The SAS data set Sasuser.Revenue contains flight revenue data. The SAS data set Sasuser.Acities contains airport data, including the airport code, location, and name.

Table 16.27 SAS Data Set Sasuser.Revenue (first five observations)

Origin	Dest	FlightID	Date	Rev1st	RevBusiness	RevEcon
ANC	RDU	IA03400	02DEC1999	15829	28420	68688
ANC	RDU	IA03400	14DEC1999	20146	26460	72981
ANC	RDU	IA03400	26DEC1999	20146	23520	59625
ANC	RDU	IA03401	09DEC1999	15829	22540	58671
ANC	RDU	IA03401	21DEC1999	20146	22540	65826

Table 16.28 SAS Data Set Sasuser.Acities (first five observations)

City	Code	Name	Country
Auckland	AKL	International	New Zealand
Amsterdam	AMS	Schiphol	Netherlands
Anchorage, AK	ANC	Anchorage International Airport	USA
Stockholm	ARN	Arlanda	Sweden
Athens (Athinai)	ATH	Hellinikon International Airport	Greece

To create the report, you can use a hash object to retrieve matching airport data from Sasuser.Acities.

In the following code, the DECLARE statement creates the Airports hash object and loads it from Sasuser.Acities.

```
data work.report;
   if _N_=1 then do;
      declare hash airports (dataset: "sasuser.acities");
```

Using a Non-Executing SET Statement

To initialize the attributes of hash variables that originate from an existing SAS data set, you can use a non-executing SET statement.

Because the IF condition is false during execution, the SET statement is compiled but not executed. The PDV is created with the variables Code, City, and Name from Sasuser.Acities.

```
data work.report;
   if _N_=1 then do;
      if 0 then
         set sasuser.acities (keep=Code City Name);
```

When you use this technique, CALL MISSING is not required.

Working with Multiple Data Variables

The hash object that you worked with earlier in this chapter contains one key variable and one data variable. In this example, you need to associate more than one data value with each key.

In the following code, the DECLARE statement creates the Airports hash object and loads it from Sasuser.Acities. The DEFINEKEY method call defines the key to be the value of the variable Code. The DEFINEDATA method call defines the data to be the values of the variables City and Name.

```
data work.report;
     if 0 then
         set sasuser.acities (keep=Code City Name);
   if _N_=1 then do;
   declare hash airports (dataset: "sasuser.acities")
   airports.definekey ("Code");
   airports.definedata ("City", "Name");
   airports.definedone();
end;
```

Table 16.29 Hash Object Airports

Key: Code	Data: City	Data: Name
ANC	Anchorage, AK	Anchorage International Airport
BNA	Nashville, TN	Nashville International Airport
CDG	Paris	Charles de Gaulle

Key: Code	Data: City	Data: Name
LAX	Los Angeles, CA	Los Angeles International Airport
RDU	Raleigh-Durham, NC	Raleigh-Durham International Airport

Note: To define all data set variables as data variables for the hash object, use the ALL: "YES" option. Here is an example:

hashobject.DEFINEDATA (ALL:"YES");

Note: The hash object can store multiple key variables as well as multiple data variables.

Retrieving Multiple Data Values

You can use the FIND method multiple times in order to retrieve multiple data values. In the following program, the FIND method retrieves the values of City and Name from the Airports hash object based on the value of Origin.

```
data work.report;
   if _N_=1 then do;
       if 0 then set sasuser.acities (keep=Code City Name);
      declare hash airports (dataset: "sasuser.acities");
      airports.definekey ("Code");
      airports.definedata ("City", "Name");
      airports.definedone();
   end;
 set sasuser.revenue;
 rc=airports.find(key:origin);
 OriginCity=city;
 OriginAirport=name;
 rc=airports.find(key:dest);
DestCity=city;
DestAirport=name;
run;
```

PROC PRINT output shows the completed data set.

```
proc print data=work.report;
   var origin dest flightid date origincity originairport
      destcity destairport;
run;
```

Figure 16.4 *Partial Output (first five observations of selected variables)*

Obs	Origin	Dest	FlightID	Date	OriginCity	OriginAirport	DestCity	DestAirport
1	ANC	RDU	IA03400	02DEC1999	Anchorage, AK	Anchorage International Airport	Raleigh-Durham, NC	Raleigh-Durham International Airport
2	ANC	RDU	IA03400	14DEC1999	Anchorage, AK	Anchorage International Airport	Raleigh-Durham, NC	Raleigh-Durham International Airport
3	ANC	RDU	IA03400	28DEC1999	Anchorage, AK	Anchorage International Airport	Raleigh-Durham, NC	Raleigh-Durham International Airport
4	ANC	RDU	IA03401	09DEC1999	Anchorage, AK	Anchorage International Airport	Raleigh-Durham, NC	Raleigh-Durham International Airport
5	ANC	RDU	IA03401	21DEC1999	Anchorage, AK	Anchorage International Airport	Raleigh-Durham, NC	Raleigh-Durham International Airport

Using Return Codes with the FIND Method

Remember that method calls generate a numeric return code that indicates whether the method succeeded or failed. A value of **0** indicates that the method succeeded. A nonzero value indicates that the method failed.

To store the value of the return code in a variable, specify the variable name RC at the beginning of the method call. Here is an example:

```
rc=hashobject.find (key:keyvalue);
```

The return code variable can be used in conditional logic to ensure that the FIND method found a KEY value in the hash object that matches the KEY value from the PDV.

Example

Error messages are written to the log when the following program is submitted.

```
data work.report;
   if _N_=1 then do;
         if 0 then set sasuser.acities (keep=Code City Name);
      declare hash airports (dataset: "sasuser.acities");
      airports.definekey ("Code");
      airports.definedata ("City", "Name");
      airports.definedone ();
   end;
set sasuser.revenue;
airports.find(key:origin);
OriginCity=city;
OriginAirport=name;
airports.find(key:dest);
DestCity=city;
DestAirport=name;
```

```
run;
```

Table 16.30 *SAS Log*

```
NOTE: There were 50 observations read from the data set SASUSER.ACITIES.
ERROR: Key not found.
ERROR: Key not found.
ERROR: Key not found.
ERROR: Key not found.
ERROR: Key not found.
ERROR: Key not found.
NOTE: The SAS System stopped processing this step because of errors.
NOTE: There were 142 observations read from the data set SASUSER.REVENUE.
WARNING: The data set WORK.REPORT1 may be incomplete. When this step was
         stopped there were 142 observations and 14 variables.
```

A closer examination of the output shows that the data set Work.Report contains errors. For example, notice that in observations 6 through 8 the value of both OriginCity and DestCity is **Canberra, Australian C** and the values of OriginAirport and DestAirport are missing.

The errors occur because the Airports hash object does not include the key value WLG or a corresponding Name value for the key value CBR.

Figure 16.5 *SAS Data Set Work.Report (observations 6 through 8 of selected variables)*

Obs	Origin	Dest	FlightID	Date	OriginCity	OriginAirport	DestCity	DestAirport
6	CBR	WLG	IA10500	04DEC1999	Canberra, Australian C		Canberra, Australian C	
7	CBR	WLG	IA10500	16DEC1999	Canberra, Australian C		Canberra, Australian C	
8	CBR	WLG	IA10500	28DEC1999	Canberra, Australian C		Canberra, Australian C	

Conditional logic can be added to the program to create blank values if the values loaded from the input data set, Sasuser.Revenue, cannot be found in the Airports hash object:

- If the return code for the FIND method call has a value of **0**, indicating that the method succeeded, the values of City and Name are assigned to the appropriate variables (OriginCity and OriginAirport or DestCity and DestAirport).

- If the return code for the FIND method call has a nonzero value, indicating the method failed, the values of City and Name are assigned blank values.

```
data work.report;
   if _N_=1 then do;
         if 0 then set sasuser.acities(keep=Code City Name);
      declare hash airports (dataset: "sasuser.acities");
      airports.definekey ("Code");
      airports.definedata ("City", "Name");
      airports.definedone ();
   end;
set sasuser.revenue;
rc=airports.find(key:origin);
```

```
if rc=0 then do;
   OriginCity=city;
   OriginAirport=name;
end;
else do;
   OriginCity='';
   OriginAirport='';
end;
rc=airports.find(key:dest);
if rc=0 then do;
   DestCity=city;
   DestAirport=name;
end;
else do;
   DestCity='';
   DestAirport='';
end;
run;
```

PROC PRINT output shows the completed data set. Notice that in observations 6 through 8, the value of DestCity is now blank and no error messages appear in the log.

```
proc print data=work.report;
   var origin dest flightid date origincity originairport
      destcity destairport;
run;
```

Figure 16.6 *SAS Data Set Work.Report (first eight observations of selected variables)*

Obs	Origin	Dest	FlightID	Date	OriginCity	OriginAirport	DestCity	DestAirport
1	ANC	RDU	IA03400	02DEC1999	Anchorage, AK	Anchorage International Airport	Raleigh-Durham, NC	Raleigh-Durham International Airport
2	ANC	RDU	IA03400	14DEC1999	Anchorage, AK	Anchorage International Airport	Raleigh-Durham, NC	Raleigh-Durham International Airport
3	ANC	RDU	IA03400	26DEC1999	Anchorage, AK	Anchorage International Airport	Raleigh-Durham, NC	Raleigh-Durham International Airport
4	ANC	RDU	IA03401	09DEC1999	Anchorage, AK	Anchorage International Airport	Raleigh-Durham, NC	Raleigh-Durham International Airport
5	ANC	RDU	IA03401	21DEC1999	Anchorage, AK	Anchorage International Airport	Raleigh-Durham, NC	Raleigh-Durham International Airport
6	CBR	WLG	IA10500	04DEC1999	Canberra, Australian C			
7	CBR	WLG	IA10500	16DEC1999	Canberra, Australian C			
8	CBR	WLG	IA10500	26DEC1999	Canberra, Australian C			

Table 16.31 SAS Log

```
NOTE: There were 50 observations read from the data set SASUSER.ACITIES.
NOTE: There were 142 observations read from the data set SASUSER.REVENUE.
NOTE: The data set WORK.REPORT2 has 142 observations and 15 variables.
```

Summary

Text Summary

Introduction

Sometimes, you need to combine data from two or more data sets into a single observation in a new data set according to the values of a common variable. When data sources do not have a common structure, you can use a lookup table to match them.

Using Multidimensional Arrays

When a lookup operation depends on more than one ordinal numeric key, you can use a multidimensional array. Use an ARRAY statement to create an array. The ARRAY statement defines a set of elements that you plan to process as a group.

Using Stored Array Values

In many cases, you might prefer to load an array with values that are stored in a SAS data set rather than loading them in an ARRAY statement. Lookup tables should be stored in a SAS data set when the following conditions are true:

- there are too many values to initialize easily in the array

- the values change frequently

- the same values are used in many programs

The first step in loading an array from a data set is to create an array to hold the values from the source data set. The next step is to load the array elements. One method for accomplishing this task is to load the array within a DO loop. The last step is to read the base data set.

Using PROC TRANSPOSE

The TRANSPOSE procedure can be used to prepare data when the orientation of the data sets differs. PROC TRANSPOSE creates an output data set by restructuring the values in a SAS data set, thereby transposing selected variables into observations. The transposed (output) data set can then be merged with another data set in order to match the data.

The output data set contains several default variables.

- _NAME_ is the default name of the variable that PROC TRANSPOSE creates to identify the source of the values in each observation in the output data set. This variable is a character variable whose values are the names of the variables that are transposed from the input data set. To override the default name, use the NAME= option.

- The remaining transposed variables are named COL1...COL*n* by default. To override the default names, use the PREFIX= option.

Merging the Transposed Data Set

You might need to use a BY statement with PROC TRANSPOSE in order to correctly structure the data for a merge. For each BY group, PROC TRANSPOSE creates one observation for each variable that it transposes. The BY variable itself is not transposed. In order to structure the data for a merge, you might also need to sort the output data set. Any other source data sets might need to be reorganized and sorted as well. When the data is structured correctly, the data sets can be merged.

Using Hash Objects as Lookup Tables

Beginning with SAS 9, the hash object is available for use in a DATA step. The hash object provides an efficient, convenient mechanism for quick data storage and retrieval.

A hash object resembles a table with rows and columns; it contains a key component and a data component. Unlike an array, which uses a series of consecutive integers to address array elements, a hash object can use any combination of numeric and character values as addresses.

The hash object is a DATA step component object. Component objects are data elements that consist of attributes and methods. To use a DATA step component object in your SAS program, you must first declare and create (instantiate) the object. After you declare the hash object's key and data components, you can populate the hash object from hardcoded values or a SAS data set.

Use the FIND method call return code that is a numeric value. The value specifies whether the method succeeded or failed. A value of 0 indicates that the method succeeded. A nonzero value indicates that the method failed. The return code variable can be used in conditional logic to ensure that the FIND method found a KEY value in the hash object that matches the KEY value from the PDV.

Sample Programs

Using a Multidimensional Array

```
data work.wndchill (drop = column row);
  array WC{4,2} _temporary_
     (-22,-16,-28,-22,-32,-26,-35,-29);
  set sasuser.flights;
  row = round(wspeed,5)/5;
  column = (round(temp,5)/5)+3;
  WindChill= wc{row,column};
run;
```

Using Stored Array Values

```
data work.lookup1;
  array Targets{1997:1999,12} _temporary_;
  if _n_=1 then do i= 1 to 3;
     set sasuser.ctargets;
     array Mnth{*} Jan--Dec;
     do j=1 to dim(mnth);
        targets{year,j}=mnth{j};
     end;
  end;
```

```
        set sasuser.monthsum(keep=salemon revcargo monthno);
        year=input(substr(salemon,4),4.);
        Ctarget=targets{year,monthno};
        format ctarget dollar15.2;
    run;
```

Using PROC TRANSPOSE and a Merge

```
proc transpose data=sasuser.ctargets
        out=work.ctarget2
        name=Month
        prefix=Ctarget;
    by year;
 run;


proc sort data=work.ctarget2;
    by year month;
run;


data work.mnthsum2;
    set sasuser.monthsum(keep=SaleMon RevCargo);
    length Month $ 8;
    Year=input(substr(SaleMon,4),4.);
    Month=substr(SaleMon,1,1)
            ||lowcase(substr(SaleMon,2,2));
run;


proc sort data=work.mnthsum2;
    by year month;
run;


data work.merged;
    merge work.mnthsum2 work.ctarget2;
    by year month;
run;
```

Loading a Hash Object from Hardcoded Values

```
data work.difference (drop= goalamount);
    if _N_ = 1 then do;
        declare hash goal( );
        goal.definekey("QtrNum");
        goal.definedata("GoalAmount");
        goal.definedone( );
        call missing(goalamount);
        goal.add(key:'qtr1', data:10 );
        goal.add(key:'qtr2', data:15 );
        goal.add(key:'qtr3', data: 5 );
        goal.add(key:'qtr4', data:15 );
    end;
    set sasuser.contrib;
    rc=goal.find();
    Diff = amount - goalamount;
run;
```

Loading a Hash Object from a SAS Data Set

```
data work.report;
   if _N_=1 then do;
           if 0 then set sasuser.acities(keep=Code City Name);
      declare hash airports (dataset: "sasuser.acities");
      airports.definekey ("Code");
      airports.definedata ("City", "Name");
      airports.definedone();
end;
set sasuser.revenue;
rc=airports.find(key:origin);
if rc=0 then do;
   OriginCity=city;
   OriginAirport=name;
end;
else do;
   OriginCity='';
   OriginAirport='';
end;
rc=airports.find(key:dest);
if rc=0 then do;
   DestCity=city;
   DestAirport=name;
end;
else do;
   DestCity='';
   DestAirport='';
end;
run;
```

Points to Remember

- The name of an array must be a SAS name that is not the name of a SAS function or SAS variable in the same DATA step.

- Array elements must be either all numeric or all character.

- The initial values specified for an array can be numeric values or character strings. You must enclose all character strings in quotation marks.

- The input SAS data set must be sorted or indexed before using a BY statement with PROC TRANSPOSE unless you use the NOTSORTED option.

- The hash object is a good choice for lookups using unordered data that can fit into memory because it provides in-memory storage and retrieval and does not require the data to be sorted.

- The hash object is sized dynamically, and exists for the duration of the DATA step.

Quiz

Select the best answer for each question. After completing the quiz, check your answers using the answer key in the appendix.

1. Which SAS statement correctly specifies the array Sales as illustrated in the following table?

   Table Representation of Sales Array

m1	m2	m3	m4
m5	m6	m7	m8
m9	m10	m11	m12

   a. `array Sales{3,4} m1-m12;`

   b. `array Sales{4,3} m1-m12;`

   c. `array {3,4} Sales m1-m12;`

   d. `array {4,12} Sales m1-m12;`

2. Which of the following statements creates temporary array elements?

   a. `array new {*} _temporary_;`

   b. `array new {6} _temporary_;`

   c. `array new {*} _temporary_ Jan Feb Mar Apr May Jun;`

   d. `array _temporary_ new {6} Jan Feb Mar Apr May Jun;`

3. Which DO statement processes all of the elements in the Yearx array?

   `array Yearx{12} Jan--Dec;`

   a. `do i=1 to dim(yearx);`

   b. `do i=1 to 12;`

   c. `do i=Jan to Dec;`

   d. *a* and *b*

4. Given the following program, what is the value of Points in the fifth observation in the data set Work.Results?

   ```
   data work.results;
      array score{2,4} _temporary_
           (40,50,60,70,40,50,60,70);
      set work.contest;
      Points=score{week,finish};
   run;
   ```

   SAS Data Set Work.Contest

Obs	Name	Week	Finish
1	Tuttle	1	1
2	Gomez	1	2
3	Chapman	1	3
4	Venter	1	4
5	Vandeusen	2	1
6	Tuttle	2	2
7	Venter	2	3
8	Gomez	2	4

   a. 40

   b. 50

   c. 60

d. 70

5. Array values should be stored in a SAS data set when which of the following is true?

   a. There are too many values to initialize easily in an array.

   b. The values change frequently.

   c. The same values are used in many programs.

   d. All of the above.

6. Given the following program, which statement is not true?

```
data work.lookup1;
    array Targets{1997:1999,12} _temporary_;
    if _n_=1 then do i= 1 to 3;
                set sasuser.ctargets;
                array Mnth{*} Jan--Dec;
                do j=1 to dim(mnth);
                    targets{year,j}=mnth{j};
                end;
    end;
    set sasuser.monthsum(keep=salemon revcargo monthno);
    year=input(substr(salemon,4),4.);
    Ctarget=targets{year,monthno};
run;
```

   a. The IF-THEN statement specifies that the Targets array is loaded once.

   b. During the first iteration of the DATA step, the outer DO loop executes three times.

   c. After the first iteration of the DO loop, the pointer drops down to the second SET statement.

   d. During the second iteration of the DATA step, the condition _N_=1 is false. So, the DO loop does not execute.

7. Given the following program, which variable names will appear in the data set Work.New?

					SAS Data Set Work.Revenue

```
proc transpose
      data=work.revenue
      out=work.new;
run;
```

Obs	Year	Jan	Feb	Mar	Apr
1	2000	1.003.561	922.080	836.068	973.016
2	2001	1.078.552	1.013.798	1.047.812	1.005.575
3	2002	1.182.442	1.657.323	1.079.866	1.466.640

   a. Year, Jan, Feb, Mar, Apr

   b. Year, 2000, 2001, 2002

   c. _NAME_, Col1, Col2, Col3

   d. _NAME_, Jan, Feb, Mar, Apr

8. Which program creates the output data set Work.Temp2?

SAS Data Set Work.Temp

Obs	Month1	Month2	Month3
1	13604250	24901752	18166825
2	72551855	23048835	17804326
3	12540156	27572140	14152851
4	11241374	28684655	15156575

SAS Data Set Work.Temp2

Obs	Month	Quarter1	Quarter2	Quarter3	Quarter4
1	Month1	13604250	72551855	12540156	11241274
2	Month2	24901752	23048835	27572140	28684655
3	Month3	18166825	17804326	14152851	15156575

a.
```
proc transpose data=work.temp
       out=work.temp2
       prefix=Quarter;
   run;
```

b.
```
proc transpose data=work.temp
       out=work.temp2
       name=Month
       prefix=Quarter;
   run;
```

c.
```
proc transpose data=work.temp
       out=work.temp2
       prefix=Month
       name=Quarter;
   run;
```

d.
```
proc transpose data=work.temp
       out=work.temp2
       prefix=Month
       index=Quarter;
   run;
```

9. Which version of the data set Work.Sales2 is created by the following program?

SAS Data Set Work.Sales

```
proc transpose data=work.sales
     out=work.sales2
     name=Week;
     by employee;
run;
```

Obs	Employee	Week1	Week2
1	Almers	3393.50	2192.25
2	Bonaventure	5093.75	2247.50
3	Johnson	1813.30	2082.75
4	LaMance	1572.50	2960.00

a.

Obs	Week	COL1	COL2	COL3	COL4
1	Week1	3393.50	5093.75	1813.30	1572.5
2	Week2	2192.25	2247.50	2028.75	2960.0

b.

Obs	Employee	Week	COL1
1	Almers	Week1	3393.50
2	Almers	Week2	2192.25
3	Bonnaventure	Week1	5093.75
4	Bonnaventure	Week2	2247.50
5	Johnson	Week1	1813.30
6	Johnson	Week2	2028.75
7	LaMance	Week1	1572.50
8	LaMance	Week2	2960.00

c.

Obs	Week	Almers	Bonnaventure	Johnson	LaMance
1	Week1	3393.50	5093.75	1813.30	1572.5
2	Week2	2192.25	2247.50	2028.75	2960.0

d.

Obs	Employee	_NAME_	Week
1	Almers	Week1	3393.50
2	Bonnaventure	Week1	5093.75
3	Johnson	Week1	1813.30
4	LaMance	Week1	1572.50
5	Almers	Week2	2192.25
6	Bonnaventure	Week2	2247.50
7	Johnson	Week2	2028.75
8	LaMance	Week2	2960.00

10. Which program creates the data set Work.Fishsize?

SAS Data Set Work.Fishdata

Obs	Location	Date	Length1	Weight1	Length2	Weight2
1	Cole Pond	02JUN95	31	0.25	32	0.30
2	Cole Pond	04AUG95	29	0.23	30	0.25
3	Eagle Lake	02JUN95	32	0.35	32	0.25
4	Eagle Lake	04AUG95	33	0.30	33	0.28

SAS Data Set Work.Fishsize

Obs	Location	Date	_NAME_	Measurement1
1	Cole Pond	02JUN95	Length1	31.00
2	Cole Pond	02JUN95	Weight1	0.25
3	Cole Pond	02JUN95	Length2	32.00
4	Cole Pond	02JUN95	Weight2	0.30
5	Cole Pond	04AUG95	Length1	29.00
6	Cole Pond	04AUG95	Weight1	0.23
7	Cole Pond	04AUG95	Length2	30.00
8	Cole Pond	04AUG95	Weight2	0.25
9	Eagle Lake	02JUN95	Length1	32.00
10	Eagle Lake	02JUN95	Weight1	0.35
11	Eagle Lake	02JUN95	Length2	32.00
12	Eagle Lake	02JUN95	Weight2	0.25
13	Eagle Lake	04AUG95	Length1	33.00
14	Eagle Lake	04AUG95	Weight1	0.30
15	Eagle Lake	04AUG95	Length2	33.00
16	Eagle Lake	04AUG95	Weight2	0.28

a.
```
proc transpose data=work.fishdata
     out=work.fishsize
     prefix=Measurement;
run;
```

b.
```
proc transpose data=work.fishdata
     out=work.fishsize
     prefix=Measurement;
     by location;
run;
```

c.
```
proc transpose data=work.fishdata
     out=work.fishsize
     prefix=Measurement;
     by date;
run;
```

d.
```
proc transpose data=work.fishdata
     out=work.fishsize
     prefix=Measurement;
     by location date;
run;
```

Chapter 17
Formatting Data

Overview

Introduction

Custom formats are used to display variable values in certain ways, such as formatting a product number so that it is displayed as descriptive text. You should already be familiar with using the FORMAT procedure to create and store formats.

In this chapter you learn to document formats, use formats located in any catalog, create formats with overlapping ranges, and use the PICTURE statement to create a format for inserting message characters into numbers. You also learn an easy way to update formats by creating a SAS data set from a format, updating the data set, and then re-creating the format from the updated SAS data set.

Creating Custom Formats Using the VALUE Statement

Review of Creating Non-Overlapping Formats

You can use the VALUE statement in the FORMAT procedure to create a custom format for displaying data in a particular way. For example, suppose you have airline data and you want to create several custom formats that you can use for your report-writing tasks. You need formats that enable you to do the following:

- group airline routes into zones

- label airport codes as International or Domestic

- group cargo revenue figures into ranges.

The following PROC FORMAT step creates these three formats:

```
proc format;
   value $routes
         'Route1' = 'Zone 1'
         'Route2' - 'Route4' = 'Zone 2'
         'Route5' - 'Route7' = 'Zone 3'
         ' ' = 'Missing'
         other = 'Unknown';
   value $dest
         'AKL','AMS','ARN','ATH','BKK','BRU',
         'CBR','CCU','CDG','CPH','CPT','DEL',
         'DXB','FBU','FCO','FRA','GLA','GVA',
         'HEL','HKG','HND','JED','JNB','JRS',
         'LHR','LIS','MAD','NBO','PEK','PRG',
```

```
            'SIN','SYD','VIE','WLG' = 'International'
            'ANC','BHM','BNA','BOS','DFW','HNL',
            'IAD','IND','JFK','LAX','MCI','MIA',
            'MSY','ORD','PWM','RDU','SEA','SFO' = 'Domestic';
      value revfmt
            . = 'Missing'
            low - 10000 = 'Up to $10,000'
            10000 <- 20000 = '$10,000+ to $20,000'
            20000 <- 30000 = '$20,000+ to $30,000'
            30000 <- 40000 = '$30,000+ to $40,000'
            40000 <- 50000 = '$40,000+ to $50,000'
            50000 <- 60000 = '$50,000+ to $60,000'
            60000 <- HIGH  = 'More than $60,000';
run;
```

The PROC FORMAT step creates three formats: $ROUTES. and $DEST., which are character formats, and REVFMT., which is numeric.

$ROUTES. groups airline routes into zones. In $ROUTES., the following is true:

- both single values and ranges are assigned labels

- missing values are designated by a space in quotation marks and are assigned the label "Missing"

- the keyword OTHER is used to assign the label "Unknown" to any values that are not addressed in the range

$DEST. labels airport codes as either International or Domestic. In $DEST., the following is true:

- unique character values are enclosed in quotation marks and separated by commas

- both missing values and values that are not included in the range are not handled in this format

REVFMT. groups cargo revenue figures into ranges. In REVFMT., the following is true:

- the less than operator (<) is used to show a non-inclusive range (`10000<-20000` indicates that the first value is not included in the range)

- the keyword LOW is used to specify the lower limit of a variable's value range, but it does not include missing values

- missing values are designated with a period (.) and assigned the label Missing

- the keyword HIGH is used to specify the upper limit of a variable's value range

Creating a Format with Overlapping Ranges

There are times when you need to create a format that groups the same values into different ranges. To create overlapping ranges, use the MULTILABEL option in the VALUE statement in PROC FORMAT.

General form, VALUE statement with the MULTILABEL option:

VALUE *format-name* **(MULTILABEL);**

Here is an explanation of the syntax:

format-name
  is the name of the character or numeric format that is being created.

Example

Suppose you want to create a format that groups dates into overlapping categories. In the table below, notice that each month appears in two groups.

Value	Label
Jan - Mar	1st Quarter
Apr - Jun	2nd Quarter
Jul - Sep	3rd Quarter
Oct - Dec	4th Quarter
Jan - Jun	First Half of Year
Jul- Dec	Second Half of Year

In the PROC FORMAT step below, the MULTILABEL option has been added to indicate that the DATES. format has values with overlapping ranges:

```
proc format;
   value dates (multilabel)
        '01jan2000'd - '31mar2000'd = '1st Quarter'
        '01apr2000'd - '30jun2000'd = '2nd Quarter'
        '01jul2000'd - '30sep2000'd = '3rd Quarter'
        '01oct2000'd - '31dec2000'd = '4th Quarter'
        '01jan2000'd - '30jun2000'd = 'First Half of Year'
        '01jul2000'd - '31dec2000'd = 'Second Half of Year';
run;
```

Multilabel formatting allows an observation to be included in multiple rows or categories. To use the multilabel formats, you can specify the MLF option on class variables in procedures that support it:

- PROC TABULATE

- PROC MEANS

- PROC SUMMARY

The MLF option activates multilabel format processing when a multilabel format is assigned to a class variable. For example, these statements are true of the following TABULATE procedure code:

- The FORMAT= option specifies DOLLAR15.2 as the format for the value in each table cell

- The CLASS statement identifies Date as the class variable and uses the MLF option to activate multilabel format processing.

- The row dimension of the TABLE statement creates a row for each formatted value of Date.

- The FORMAT statement references the new format DATES. for the class variable Date.

```
proc tabulate data = sasuser.sale2000 format = dollar15.2;
   class Date / mlf;
   var RevCargo;
   table Date, RevCargo*(mean median);
   format Date dates.;
run;
```

	RevCargo	
	Mean	Median
Date		
1st Quarter	$24,839.08	$4,939.00
2nd Quarter	$14,949.77	$4,579.50
3rd Quarter	$19,836.00	$3,591.00
4th Quarter	$20,403.13	$1,940.00
First Half of Year	$19,894.42	$4,823.00
Second Half of Year	$20,261.35	$2,100.00

TIP For more information about using the MULTILABEL option, see the SAS documentation for the FORMAT procedure.

Creating Custom Formats Using the PICTURE Statement

Overview

You have learned that the VALUE statement can associate a text label with a discrete numeric or character value. Suppose you want to insert text characters into a numeric value. For example, you might have stored phone numbers as numeric values like 1111231234 that you want to display as **(111) 123-1234**. You can use the PICTURE statement to create a template for printing numbers.

General form, PROC FORMAT with the PICTURE statement:

PROC FORMAT;

    PICTURE *format-name*

                value-or-range='picture';

RUN;

Here is an explanation of the syntax:

format-name
    is the name of the format that you are creating.

value-or-range
    is the individual value or range of values that you want to label.

picture
    specifies a template for formatting values of numeric variables. The template is a sequence of characters enclosed in quotation marks. The maximum length for a picture is 40 characters.

Ways to Specify Pictures

Pictures are specified with three types of characters:

- digit selectors

- message characters

- directives.

Consider using digit selectors and message characters first. You learn about directives in a later topic.

Digit selectors are numerals (0 through 9) that define positions for numbers. If you use nonzero digit selectors, zeros are added to the formatted value as needed. If you use zeros as digit selectors, no zeros are added to the formatted value.

In the picture definitions below, you can see the difference between using nonzero digit selectors (99) and zero digit selectors (00) on the formatted values.

Picture Definition	Data Values	Formatted Values
`picture month 1-12='99';`	1	01
	12	12
`picture month 1-12='00';`	1	1
	12	12

Message characters are nonnumeric characters that are printed as specified in the picture. They are inserted into the picture after the numeric digits are formatted. Digit selectors must come before message characters in the picture definition. The prefix option can be used to append text in front of any digits. In the picture definition below, the text string JAN consists of message characters.

Picture Definition	Data Value	Formatted Value
`picture month 1='99 JAN';`	1	01 JAN

Example

The following PICTURE statement contains both digit selectors and message characters. Because the RAINAMT. format has nonzero digit selectors, values are printed with leading zeros. The keyword OTHER is used to print values and message characters for any values that do not fall into a specified range.

```
proc format;
   picture rainamt
           0-2='9.99 slight'
           2<-4='9.99 moderate'
           4<-<10='9.99 heavy'
           other='999 check value';
run;
data rain;
   input Amount;
   datalines;
   4
   3.9
   20
   .5
   6
   ;
proc print data=rain;
   format amount rainamt.;
run;
```

The following output shows the values with the RAINAMT. format applied.

Obs	Amount
1	4.00 moderate
2	3.90 moderate
3	020 check value
4	0.50 slight
5	6.00 heavy

The final way to specify a picture is with a directive. Directives are special characters that you can use in the picture to format date, time, or datetime values. If you use a directive, you must specify the DATATYPE= option in the PICTURE statement. This option specifies that the picture applies to a SAS date, SAS time, or SAS datetime value.

General form, PICTURE statement with the DATATYPE= option:

PICTURE *format-name*

  value-or-range, 'picture' (**DATATYPE=***SAS-date-value-type***);**

Here is an explanation of the syntax:

format-name
 is the name of the format that you are creating.

value-or-range
 is the individual value or range of values that you want to label.

picture
 specifies a template with directives for formatting numeric values.

SAS-date-value-type
 is either *DATE, TIME*, or *DATETIME*.

Guidelines for Specifying Directives

The percent sign (%) followed by a letter indicates a directive. Directives that you can use to create a picture format are listed in the table below.

Directive	Result
%a	abbreviated weekday name
%A	full weekday name
%b	abbreviated month name
%B	full month name
%d	day of the month as a number 1-31, with no leading zero
%H	24-hour clock as a number 0-23, with no leading zero
%I	12-hour clock as a number 1-12, with no leading zero
%j	day of the year as a number 1-366, with no leading zero
%m	month as a number 1-12, with no leading zero
%M	minute as a decimal number 0-59, with no leading zero
%p	AM or PM
%S	second as a number 0-59, with no leading zero
%U	week number of the year (Sunday is the first day of the week) as a number 0-53, with no leading zero
%w	weekday as a number (1=Sunday, to 7)

Directive	Result
%y	year without century as a number 0-99, with no leading zero
%Y	year with century as a number

Although directives generally return numbers with no leading zeros, you can add 0 in the directive so that if a one-digit numeric value is returned, it is preceded by a 0.

As shown below, when you create a picture with directives, the number of characters inside quotation marks is the maximum length of the formatted value. You must add trailing blanks to the directive if your values contain more characters than the picture. The formatted value is truncated if you do not.

Formatted Result	Picture Definition
d d - m m m y y y y 1 2 3 4 5 6 7 8 9 10	' % 0 d - % b % Y ' 1 2 3 4 5 6 7 8 9 10

Example

Suppose you want to display values for employee hire dates in the format *dd-mmmyyyy* (such as `25-JAN2000`). This format requires spaces for 10 characters.

The following code creates this format. There are a few things that you should notice about the picture definition:

- The keywords LOW and HIGH are used to include all values.

- The 0 in the %d directive indicates that if the day of the month is one digit, it should be preceded by a 0.

- Because there are only eight characters inside the single quotation marks, you must add two blank spaces to set the length to 10.

```
proc format;
   picture mydate
          low-high='%0d-%b%Y  ' (datatype=date);
run;

proc print data=sasuser.empdata
     (keep=division hireDate lastName obs=5);
   format hiredate mydate.;
run;
```

The output below shows the values for HireDate formatted with the MYDATE. picture format.

The SAS System

Obs	Division	HireDate	LastName
1	FLIGHT OPERATIONS	11-MAR1992	MILLS
2	FINANCE & IT	19-DEC1983	BOWER
3	HUMAN RESOURCES & FACILITIES	12-MAR1985	READING
4	HUMAN RESOURCES & FACILITIES	16-OCT1989	JUDD
5	AIRPORT OPERATIONS	19-DEC1981	WONSILD

TIP For more information about using the PICTURE statement, see the documentation for the FORMAT procedure.

Managing Custom Formats

Using FMTLIB with PROC FORMAT to Document Formats

When you have created a large number of permanent formats, it can be easy to forget the exact spelling of a specific format name or its range of values. Remember that adding the keyword FMTLIB to the PROC FORMAT statement displays a list of all the formats in the specified catalog, along with descriptions of their values.

```
libname myfmts 'c:\sas\newfmt';
proc format lib=myfmts fmtlib;
run;
```

You can also use the SELECT and EXCLUDE statements to process specific formats rather than an entire catalog.

General form, PROC FORMAT with FMTLIB and the SELECT and EXCLUDE statements:

PROC FORMAT LIB=*library* **FMTLIB;**

    SELECT *format-name***;**

    EXCLUDE *format-name***;**

RUN;

Here is an explanation of the syntax:

library
    is the name of the library where the formats are stored. If you do not specify the LIB= option, formats in the Work library are listed.

format-name
    is the name of the format that you want to select or exclude.

Example

The following code displays only the documentation for the $ROUTES. format. Notice that you do not use a period at the end of the format name when you specify the format in the SELECT statement.

```
libname myfmts 'c:\sas\newfmt';
proc format lib=myfmts fmtlib;
   select $routes;
run;
```

Table 17.1 *SAS Output*

FORMAT NAME : $ROUTES LENGTH: 7 NUMBER OF VALUES: 5 MIN LENGTH: 1 MAX LENGTH: 40 DEFAULT LENGTH: 7 FUZZ: 0		
START	END	LABEL (VER. V7|V8 29AUG2002:11:13:14)
		Missing
Route1	Route1	Zone 1
Route2	Route4	Zone 2
Route5	Route7	Zone 3
OTHER	**OTHER**	Unknown

TIP   If you specify more than one format on the SELECT or EXCLUDE statement, separate each format name with a space as follows:

```
select $routes newdate;
```

Using PROC CATALOG to Manage Formats

Because formats are saved as catalog entries, you can use the CATALOG procedure to manage your formats. Using PROC CATALOG enables you to do the following:

- create a listing of the contents of a catalog
- copy a catalog or selected entries within a catalog
- delete or rename entries within a catalog

General form, PROC CATALOG step:

PROC CATALOG CATALOG=*libref.catalog***;**

      CONTENTS *<OUT=SAS-data-set>***;**

      COPY OUT=*libref.catalog* *<options>***;**

      SELECT *entry-name.entry-type(s)***;**

      EXCLUDE *entry-name.entry-type(s)***;**

      DELETE *entry-name.entry-type(s)***;**

RUN;

QUIT;

Here is an explanation of the syntax:

libref.catalog
> with the CATALOG= argument is the SAS catalog to be processed.

SAS-data-set
> is the name of the data set that will contain the list of the catalog contents.

libref.catalog
> with the OUT= argument is the SAS catalog to which the catalog entries will be copied.

entry-name.entry-type(s)
> are the full names of catalog entries (in the form *name.type*) that you want to process.

Example

The first PROC CATALOG step below copies the $ROUTES. format from the Library.Formats catalog to the Work.Formats catalog. Notice that in the SELECT statement, you specify the $ROUTES. character format using the full catalog entry name, ROUTES.FORMATC.

```
proc catalog catalog=myfmts.formats;
   copy out=work.formats;
   select routes.formatc;
run;
proc catalog cat=work.formats;
   contents;
run;
quit;
```

The second PROC CATALOG step displays the contents of the Work.Formats catalog. A note is written to the log when the format is copied from one catalog to another.

Contents of Catalog WORK.FORMATS					
#	Name	Type	Create Date	Modified Date	Description
1	DATES	FORMAT	25Apr11:09:29:20	25Apr11:09:29:20	
2	MYDATE	FORMAT	25Apr11:09:55:18	25Apr11:09:55:18	
3	RAINAMT	FORMAT	25Apr11:09:53:47	25Apr11:09:53:47	

TIP For more information about PROC CATALOG, including other statements and options that you can use, see the SAS documentation.

Using Custom Formats

Overview

After you have created a custom format, you can use SAS statements to permanently assign the format to a variable in a DATA step, or you can temporarily specify a format in a PROC step to determine how the data values appear in output. You should already be familiar with referencing a format in a FORMAT statement.

Another way to assign, change, or remove the format that is associated with a variable in an existing SAS data set is to use the DATASETS procedure to modify the descriptor portion of a data set.

General form, DATASETS procedure with the MODIFY and FORMAT statements:

PROC DATASETS LIB=*SAS-library* <NOLIST>;

      MODIFY *SAS-data-set*;

      FORMAT *variable(s) format*;

QUIT;

Here is an explanation of the syntax:

SAS-library
    is the name of the SAS library that contains the data that you want to modify.

NOLIST
    suppresses the directory listing.

SAS-data-set
    is the name of the SAS data set you want to modify.

variable
    is the name of one or more variables whose format you want to assign, change, or remove.

format
    is the name of a format to apply to the variable or variables that are listed before it. If you do not specify a format, any format that is associated with the variable is removed.

Note: The DATASETS procedure is interactive and remains in memory until you issue the QUIT statement.

Example

In the following code, two variables in the SAS data set Flights are changed. The format $DEST. is associated with the variable Dest and the format is removed from the variable Baggage.

```
proc datasets lib=Mylib;
   modify flights;
   format dest $dest.;
   format baggage;
quit;
```

Using a Permanent Storage Location for Formats

When you permanently associate a format with a variable in a data set, it is important to ensure that the format that you are referencing is stored in a permanent location. Remember that the storage location for the format is determined when the format is created in the FORMAT procedure.

When you create formats that you want to use in subsequent SAS sessions, it is useful to take these steps:

1. Assign the Library libref to a SAS library in the SAS session in which you are running the PROC FORMAT step.

2. Specify LIB=LIBRARY in the PROC FORMAT step that creates the format.

3. Include a LIBNAME statement in the program that references the format to assign the Library libref to the library that contains the permanent format catalog.

You can store formats in any catalog that you choose. However, you must identify the format catalogs to SAS before you can access them. You learn about this in a later topic.

When a format is referenced, SAS automatically looks through the following libraries in this order:

1. Work.Formats

2. Library.Formats

The Library libref is recommended for formats because it is automatically searched when a format is referenced. If you store formats in libraries or catalogs other than those in the default search path, you must use the FMTSEARCH= system option to tell SAS where to find your formats.

General form, FMTSEARCH= system option:

OPTIONS FMTSEARCH= *(catalog-1 catalog-2...catalog-n)*;

Here is an explanation of the syntax:

catalog
    is the name of one or more catalogs to search. The value of *catalog* can be either *libref* or *libref.catalog*. If only the libref is given, SAS assumes that Formats is the catalog name.

The Work.Formats catalog is always searched first, and the Library.Formats catalog is searched next, unless one or both catalogs appear in the FMTSEARCH= list.

Example

Suppose you have formats that are stored in the Rpt library and in the Prod.Newfmt catalog. The following OPTIONS statement tells SAS where to find your formats:

```
options fmtsearch=(rpt prod.newfmt);
```

Because no catalog is specified with the Rpt libref, the default catalog name Formats is assumed. This OPTIONS statement creates the following search order:

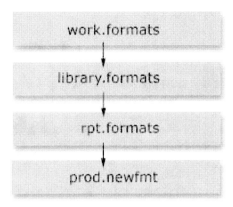

Because the Work and Library librefs were not specified in the FMTSEARCH= option, they are searched in default order.

Avoiding Format Errors

Consider what happens if you forget to specify a catalog in the FMTSEARCH= option, misspell a format name, or make some other mistake that causes SAS to fail to locate the format that you have specified.

By default, the FMTERR system option is in effect. If you use a format that SAS cannot load, SAS issues an error message and stops processing the step. To prevent this, you must change the system option FMTERR to NOFMTERR. When NOFMTERR is in effect, SAS substitutes a default format for the missing format and continues processing.

General form, FMTERR system option:

OPTIONS FMTERR | NOFMTERR;

Here is explanation of the syntax:

FMTERR
   specifies that when SAS cannot find a specified variable format, it generates an error message and stops processing. Substitution of a default format does not occur.

NOFMTERR
   replaces missing formats with the *w.* or $w. default format and continues processing.

Example

Suppose the FMTERR system option is in effect. In a previous example, we created the $ROUTES. format to group airline routes into zones. In the following code, the $ROUTES. format is misspelled:

```
proc print data=sasuser.cargorev(obs=10);
   format route $route.;
run;
```

Because FMTERR is in effect, the format cannot be located and SAS stops processing the step. An error message is written to the log.

Table 17.2 *SAS Log*

```
30    proc print data=sasuser.cargorev(obs=10);
31       format route $route.;
ERROR: The format $ROUTE was not found or could not be loaded.
32    run;


NOTE: The SAS System stopped processing this step because of errors.
```

If the NOFMTERR system option is specified, substitution of a default format occurs, and SAS continues to process the step.

```
options nofmterr;
proc print data=sasuser.cargorev(obs=10);
   format Route $route.;
run;
```

SAS substitutes the $w. format for the $ROUTE. format that it could not locate. No message is written to the log and processing continues. You can see from the output that the format that you intended to use has not been applied.

Obs	Month	Date	RevCargo	Route
1	1	14610	2260	Route2
2	1	14610	220293	Route3
3	1	14610	4655	Route1
4	1	14610	4004	Route1
5	1	14611	8911	Route1
6	1	14611	102900	Route3
7	1	14612	1963	Route3
8	1	14612	3321	Route5
9	1	14612	2562	Route3
10	1	14612	9447	Route1

Creating Formats from SAS Data Sets

Overview

You have seen that you can create a format by specifying values and labels in a PROC FORMAT step. You can also create a format from a SAS data set that contains value information (called a control data set). To do this, you use the CNTLIN= option to read the data and create the format.

General form, CNTLIN= option in PROC FORMAT:

PROC FORMAT LIBRARY=*libref.catalog*

                     CNTLIN=*SAS-data-set***;**

Here is an explanation of the syntax:

libref.catalog
> is the name of the catalog in which you want to store the format.

SAS-data-set
> is the name of the SAS data set that you want to use to create the format.

Example

Suppose you have a SAS data set named Routes that has variables that are required to create a format. You specify the data set in the CNTLIN= option as follows:

```
proc format lib=myfmts cntlin=routes;
run;
```

As you can see, the code for creating a format from a SAS data set is simple. However, the control data set must contain certain variables before it can be used to create a format. Therefore, most data sets must be restructured before they can be used.

Rules for Control Data Sets

When you create a format using programming statements, you specify the name of the format, the range or value, and the label for each range or value as shown in the VALUE statement below:

```
value rainfall 0='none';
```

The control data set you use to create a format must contain variables that supply this same information. That is, the data set that is specified in the CNTLIN= option must meet the following requirements:

- It must contain the variables FmtName, Start, and Label, which contain the format name, value or beginning value in the range, and label.

- It must contain the variable End if a range is specified. If there is no End variable, SAS assumes that the ending value of the format range is equal to the value of Start.

- It must contain the variable Type for character formats, unless the value for FmtName begins with a $.

- It must be grouped by FmtName if multiple formats are specified.

Example

Overview
Suppose you want to create a format that labels a three-letter airport code with the name of the city where the airport is located. You have a data set, Sasuser.Acities, that contains airport codes and airport cities. However, the data does not have the required variables for the CNTLIN= option.

Table 17.3 *SAS Data Set Sasuser.Acities (Partial Listing)*

City Where Airport Is Located	Start Point	Airport Name	Country Where Airport Is Located
Auckland	AKL	International	New Zealand
Amsterdam	AMS	Schiphol	Netherlands
Anchorage, AK	ANC	Anchorage International Airport	USA
Stockholm	ARN	Arlanda	Sweden
Athens (Athinai)	ATH	Hellinikon International Airport	Greece
Birmingham, AL	BHM	Birmingham International Airport	USA
Bangkok	BKK	Don Muang International Airport	Thailand

To create a format from this data set, you need to do these things:

1. List data set variables.

2. Restructure the data.

Step 1: List Data Set Variables

Remember that you need to have the variables FmtName, Start, and Label. You can submit a PROC CONTENTS step to get a listing of the variables in the Sasuser.Acities data set.

Partial Output

```
proc contents data=sasuser.acities;
run;
```

Alphabetic List of Variables and Attributes				
#	Variable	Type	Len	Label
1	City	Char	22	City Where Airport is Located
2	Code	Char	3	Start Point
4	Country	Char	40	Country Where Airport is Located
3	Name	Char	50	Airport Name

TIP You can also get a list of variable names by using PROC DATASETS with a CONTENTS statement or by viewing the properties of the SAS data set in the SAS Explorer window.

Step 2: Restructure the Data

Once you have looked at the data and know the variable names, you are ready to write a DATA step to manipulate the data. The variable Code is the three-letter airport code and the variable City is the city where the airport is located. You can rename the variable Code to Start and the variable City to Label, but you also need to create the variable FmtName.

The code below is an efficient way to prepare your data. The DATA step uses the following statements:

- the KEEP statement to write only the specified variables to the output data set

- the RETAIN statement to create the variable FmtName and set the value to '$airport'

- the RENAME data set option to rename the variable Code to Start (you do not need a variable named End because you are labeling discrete values rather than ranges) and to rename the variable City to Label

```
data sasuser.aports;
   keep Start Label FmtName;
   retain FmtName '$airport';
   set sasuser.acities (rename=(Code=Start
       City= Label));
run;

proc print data=sasuser.aports(obs=10) noobs;
run;
```

Below is the listing of the first ten observations in the new data set Sasuser.Aports.

FmtName	Label	Start
$airport	Auckland	AKL
$airport	Amsterdam	AMS
$airport	Anchorage, AK	ANC
$airport	Stockholm	ARN
$airport	Athens (Athinai)	ATH
$airport	Birmingham, AL	BHM
$airport	Bangkok	BKK
$airport	Nashville, TN	BNA
$airport	Boston, MA	BOS
$airport	Brussels (Bruxelles)	BRU

This data set is now in the proper format to be used to create a format with the CNTLIN= option.

Once you have the data in the proper format, you can use the CNTLIN= option to create the format. The first PROC FORMAT step creates a format from the data set Sasuser.Aports. The second PROC FORMAT step documents the new format.

```
proc format library=sasuser cntlin=sasuser.aports;
run;

proc format library=sasuser fmtlib;
   select $airport;
run;
```

The first few lines of the output are shown below.

Table 17.4 *Partial SAS Output*

FORMAT NAME : $AIRPORT LENGTH: 22 NUMBER OF VALUES: 52 MIN LENGTH: 1 MAX LENGTH: 40 DEFAULT LENGTH: 22 FUZZ: 0		
START	END	LABEL (VER. V7|V8 21OCT2002:14:13:14)
AKL	AKL	Auckland
AMS	AMS	Amsterdam
ANC	ANC	Anchorage, AK
ARN	ARN	Stockholm
ATH	ATH	Athens (Athinai)
BHM	BHM	Birmingham, AL
BKK	BKK	Bangkok

Apply the Format

Consider the format that is applied to the data set Sasuser.Cargo99. The following PROC PRINT code assigns the $AIRPORT. format to both the Dest and Origin variables:

```
options fmtsearch=(sasuser);
proc print data=sasuser.cargo99 (obs=5);
   var origin dest cargorev;
   format origin dest $airport.;
run;
```

Obs	Origin	Dest	CargoRev
1	RDU	LHR	$111,720.00
2	RDU	LHR	$109,270.00
3	RDU	LHR	$109,270.00
4	RDU	LHR	$116,130.00
5	RDU	LHR	$108,290.00

TIP For more information about using the CNTLIN= option, see the SAS documentation for the FORMAT procedure.

Creating SAS Data Sets from Custom Formats

Overview

You know how to create a format from a SAS data set, but what if you want to create a SAS data set from a format? To do this, you use the CNTLOUT= option.

General form, CNTLOUT= option in PROC FORMAT:

PROC FORMAT LIBRARY=_libref.catalog_ **CNTLOUT=**_SAS-data-set_;

      SELECT _format-name format-name..._;

      EXCLUDE _format-name format-name..._;

RUN;

Here is an explanation of the syntax:

libref.catalog
    is the name of the catalog in which the format is located.

SAS-data-set
    is the name of the SAS data set that you want to create.

format-name
    is the name of the format that you want to select or exclude.

The output control data set will contain variables that completely describe all aspects of each format, including optional settings. The output data set contains one observation per range per format in the specified catalog. You can use either the SELECT or EXCLUDE statement to include specific formats in the data set.

Creating a SAS data set from a format is very useful when you need to modify a format but no longer have the SAS data set you used to create the format. When you need to update a format, you take the following actions:

1. Create a SAS data set from the values in a format using CNTLOUT=.

2. Edit the data set using any number of methods.

3. Create a format from the updated SAS data set using CNTLIN=.

Example

Overview
In the last example, you created the $AIRPORT. format. Suppose you want to add the following airport codes to the format:

Value	Label
YYC	Calgary, AB
YYZ	Toronto, ON
YQB	Quebec, QC
YUL	Montreal, QC

Step 1: Create a SAS Data Set from the Format
First, you write the $AIRPORT. format as a SAS data set. In the code below, the output data set is named Sasuser.Fmtdata. The SELECT statement is used so that the resulting data set has only the data for the $AIRPORT. format. Without the SELECT statement, the data would have observations for all the formats in the Sasuser.Formats catalog.

```
proc format lib=sasuser cntlout=sasuser.fmtdata;
   select $airport;
run;
```

When you use the CNTLOUT= option, SAS creates an output data set that has many variables for storing information about the format. The output data set Sasuser.Fmtdata has 50 rows and 21 columns. In the PRINT procedure below, the VAR statement specifies that only a few of the variables are printed:

```
proc print data=sasuser.fmtdata (obs=5) noobs;
   var fmtname start end label min max
       default length fuzz;
run;
```

FMTNAME	START	END	LABEL	MIN	MAX	DEFAULT	LENGTH	FUZZ
AIRPORT	AKL	AKL	Auckland	1	40	22	22	0
AIRPORT	AMS	AMS	Amsterdam	1	40	22	22	0
AIRPORT	ANC	ANC	Anchorage, AK	1	40	22	22	0
AIRPORT	ARN	ARN	Stockholm	1	40	22	22	0
AIRPORT	ATH	ATH	Athens (Athinai)	1	40	22	22	0

As you can see, the data set contains End and other variables that were not in the original data. When you use the CNTLIN= option, if there is no End variable in the data set, SAS assumes that the Start and End variables have the same value. When you write the format as a data set using the CNTLOUT= option, both variables are in the data set.

Step 2: Edit the Data Set

The next step in updating the format is to edit the data set. You could use PROC SQL or a DATA step to add observations to the data set, or you could add observations using the VIEWTABLE window. Whatever method you choose, you must add values for the FmtName, Start, End, and Label variables. If Start and End are both present, you must enter values for both variables. Otherwise, SAS will return an error. You do not have to add values for the other variables in the data set.

Step 3: Create a Format from the SAS Data Set

Once the data set is edited and saved, you can create a format from the data set using the CNTLIN= option. The following code creates the $AIRPORT. format and then uses FMTLIB to document it:

```
proc format library=sasuser cntlin=sasuser.fmtdata;
run;

proc format lib=sasuser fmtlib;
   select $airport;
run;
```

The partial output shown below includes the new airports in the format.

Table 17.5 *Partial SAS Output*

FORMAT NAME : $AIRPORT LENGTH: 22 NUMBER OF VALUES: 56 MIN LENGTH: 1
MAX LENGTH: 40 DEFAULT LENGTH: 22 FUZZ: 0

START	END	LABEL (CONT'D)

FORMAT NAME : $AIRPORT LENGTH: 22 NUMBER OF VALUES: 56 MIN LENGTH: 1
MAX LENGTH: 40 DEFAULT LENGTH: 22 FUZZ: 0

SYD	END	Sydney, New South Wales
VIE	VIE	Wien (Vienna)
WLG	WLG	Wellington
YQB	YQB	Quebec, QC
YUL	YUL	Montreal, QC
YYC	YYC	Calgary, AB
YYZ	YYZ	Toronto, ON

TIP For more information about using the CNTLOUT= option, see the SAS documentation for the FORMAT procedure.

Summary

Text Summary

Creating Custom Formats Using the VALUE Statement

Character and numeric formats are created by using VALUE statements in a FORMAT procedure. When you specify a libref in the LIBRARY= option, the format is stored in the specified library. If no catalog name is specified, the format is saved in the Formats catalog by default.

Creating Formats with Overlapping Ranges

Use the MULTILABEL option to create a format that has overlapping ranges. When a format has overlapping ranges, the values in the format might have more than one label. This format can be used in procedures that support the MLF option.

Creating Custom Formats Using the PICTURE Statement

The PICTURE statement is used to create a template for formatting values of numeric variables. Pictures are specified using digit selectors, message characters, and directives.

Documenting Formats

Use the FMTLIB keyword in the PROC FORMAT statement to get documentation about the formats in the specified catalog. The output displays the format name, start and end values, and the label. You can also use the SELECT and EXCLUDE statements to process specific formats rather than an entire catalog.

Managing Formats

Because formats are saved as catalog entries, you use PROC CATALOG to copy, rename, delete, or create a listing of the entries in a catalog.

Using Custom Formats

Once you have created a format, you can reference it as you would reference a SAS format. If you have stored the format in a location other than Work.Formats, you must use the FMTSEARCH= system option to add the location to the search path so that SAS can locate the format. It can be useful to change the default FMTERR system option to NOFMTERR. Changing the default system option enables SAS to substitute the *w.* or $*w.* format and continue processing if SAS does not find a format you reference.

You can permanently associate a format with a variable by modifying the data set using PROC DATASETS.

Creating Formats from SAS Data Sets

Use the CNTLIN= option to specify a SAS data set that you want to use to create a format. The SAS data set must contain the variables FmtName, Start, and Label. If the values have ranges, there must also be an End variable.

Creating SAS Data Sets from Formats

Use the CNTLOUT= option to create a SAS data set from a format. This is useful for maintaining formats because you can easily update a SAS data set.

Sample Programs

Creating a Multilabel Format

```
proc format;
    value dates (multilabel)
            '01jan2000'd - '31mar2000'd = '1st Quarter'
            '01apr2000'd - '30jun2000'd = '2nd Quarter'
            '01jul2000'd - '30sep2000'd = '3rd Quarter'
            '01oct2000'd - '31dec2000'd = '4th Quarter'
            '01jan2000'd - '30jun2000'd = 'First Half of Year'
            '01jul2000'd - '31dec2000'd = 'Second Half of Year';
    run;
```

Creating a Picture Format

```
proc format;
    picture rainamt
            0-2='9.99 slight'
            2<-4='9.99 moderate'
            4<-<10='9.99 heavy'
            other='999 check value';
    run;
```

Creating a Picture Format Using Directives

```
proc format;
    picture mydate
            low-high='%0d-%b%Y  ' (datatype=date);
    run;
```

Restructuring a SAS Data Set and Creating a Format from the Data

```
data sasuser.aports;
   keep Start Label FmtName;
   retain FmtName '$airport';
   set sasuser.acities (rename=(Code=Start
       City= Label));
run;


proc format library=sasuser cntlin=sasuser.aports;
run;
```

Creating a SAS Data Set from a Format

```
proc format lib=sasuser cntlout=sasuser.fmtdata;
   select $airport;
run;
```

Points to Remember

- By default, SAS searches for formats in the Work.Formats and Library.Formats catalogs. If you store formats in other catalogs, you must use the FMTSEARCH= system option to tell SAS where to look for your formats.

- You can use the CNTLIN= option to create a format from a SAS data set, but the data set must contain the following variables:

  - FmtName, Start, and Label

  - Type for character formats, unless the value for FmtName begins with a $

  - End if a range is specified

Quiz

Select the best answer for each question. After completing the quiz, check your answers using the answer key in the appendix.

1. Which SAS system option is used to identify format catalogs to SAS?

    a. FMTERR

    b. FMTLIB

    c. NOFMTERR

    d. FMTSEARCH=

2. Given the following PROC FORMAT step, how is the value 70 displayed when the AGEGRP. format is applied?

```
proc format;
   picture agegrp
           1-<13='00 Youth'
           13-<20='00 Teen'
           20-<70='00 Adult'
           70-high='000 Senior';
run;
```

   a. 000 Senior

   b. 70 Adult

   c. 70 Senior

   d. 070 Senior

3. When the NOFMTERR system option is in effect, what happens when SAS encounters a format that it cannot locate?

   a. Creates the format in the default Work.Formats directory and continues processing.

   b. Substitutes the $w. or w. format and continues processing.

   c. Stops processing and writes an error message to the log.

   d. Skips processing at that step and continues with the next step and writes a note to the log.

4. Which of the following variables must be in the data set that is specified in the CNTLIN= option?

   a. End

   b. FmtName

   c. Value

   d. Description

5. Given the following code, what option is missing?

```
proc format;
   value times (?)
         '00:00't-'04:59't = 'Red Eye'
         '05:00't-'11:59't = 'Morning'
         '12:00't-'17:59't = 'Afternoon'
         '18:00't-'23:59't = 'Evening'
         '00:00't-'11:59't = 'AM'
         '12:00't-'23:59't = 'PM';
run;
```

   a. MULTILABEL

   b. MULTIRANGE

   c. MLF

   d. MULTIFORMAT

6. Which PROC FORMAT option is used to create a SAS data set from a format?

   a. CNTLIN=

   b. LIB=

   c. CNTLOUT=

   d. FMTLIB

7. Given the following OPTIONS statement, in what order will SAS search to find a user-defined format?

```
options fmtsearch=(work abc.newfmt sasuser);
```

   a. **Work.Formats ⇨ Abc.Newfmt ⇨ Sasuser.Formats ⇨ Library.Formats**

    b. **Work.Formats** ⇨ **Library.Formats** ⇨ **Abc.Newfmt** ⇨ **Sasuser.Formats**

    c. **Work.Formats** ⇨ **Abc.Newfmt** ⇨ **Sasuser.Format**

    d. the default search order

8. What option is used with PROC FORMAT to document the formats in a particular format catalog?

    a. FMTSEARCH

    b. FMTERR

    c. CATALOG

    d. FMTLIB

9. Which set of statements would you add to the PROC CATALOG code to copy the LEVELS. and $PICKS. formats from the Sasuser.Formats catalog to the Work.Formats catalog?

```
proc catalog cat=sasuser.formats;
    ?
    ?
run;
```

    a.
```
copy out=sasuser.formats;
select levels.format $picks.format;
```

    b.
```
copy out=work.formats;
select levels $picks;
```

    c.
```
copy out=work.formats;
select levels.format picks.formatc;
```

    d.
```
copy out=work.formats;
select levels.format $picks.format;
```

10. Given the following PROC FORMAT step, how is the value 6.1 displayed when the SKICOND format is applied?

```
proc format;
    value skicond
          0-3='Poor'
          3<-6='Fair'
          6<-9='Good'
          9<-high='Excellent';
run;
```

    a. 6.1

    b. Fair

    c. Good

    d. .

Chapter 18
Modifying SAS Data Sets and Tracking Changes

Overview

Introduction

There are times when you want to modify the observations in a SAS data set without replacing the data set. You can do this in a DATA step with the MODIFY statement. Using the MODIFY statement, you can replace, delete, or append observations in an existing data set without creating an additional copy of the data. In this chapter, you learn to modify all the observations in a data set, match observations using a BY statement, and locate observations using an index.

When you modify data, it is often essential to safeguard your data and track the changes that are made. In this chapter you learn how to create integrity constraints to protect your data. You also learn two different methods of tracking changes, audit trails and generation data sets. You use audit trails to track changes that are made to a data set in place, and you use generation data sets to track changes that are made when the data set is rebuilt.

Using the MODIFY Statement

When you submit a DATA step with a MERGE, UPDATE, or SET statement, and if the output data set already exists, SAS creates a second copy of the output data set. Once execution is complete, SAS deletes the original copy of the data set. As a result, the original data set is replaced by the new data set with the same name. The new data set can contain a different set of variables than the original data set. The attributes of the variables in the new data set can be different from those of the original data set.

```
data a;
    set a;
    <additional
     SAS
     statements>
run;
```

In contrast, when you submit a DATA step with a MODIFY statement, the input and output data sets must be the same. SAS does not create a second copy of the data, but updates the data set in place. New variables can be added to the program data vector (PDV), but they are not written to the data set. Therefore, the set of variables in the data set does not change when the data is modified.

```
data a;
    modify a;
    <additional
     SAS
     statements>
run;
```

When you use the MODIFY statement, there is an implied REPLACE statement at the bottom of the DATA step instead of an OUTPUT statement. Using the MODIFY statement, you can update the following:

- every observation in a data set

- observations using a transaction data set and a BY statement

- observations located using an index

CAUTION:

If the system terminates abnormally while a DATA step that is using the MODIFY statement is processing, you can lose data and possibly damage your master data set. You can recover from the failure by doing the following:

- restoring the master data set from a backup and restarting the step, or

- keeping an audit trail file and using it to determine which master observations have been updated.

First we consider using the MODIFY statement to modify all the observations in the data set.

Modifying All Observations in a SAS Data Set

Overview

When every observation in a SAS data set requires the same modification, you can use the MODIFY statement and specify the modification using an assignment statement.

General form, MODIFY statement with an assignment statement:

DATA *SAS-data-set*;

    MODIFY *SAS-data-set*;

    existing-variable = expression;

RUN;

Here is an explanation of the syntax:

SAS-data-set
    is the name of the SAS data set that you want to modify.

existing-variable
    is the name of the variable whose values you want to update.

expression
    is a function or other expression that you want to apply to the variable.

Example

Suppose an airline has decided to give passengers more leg room. The airline must decrease the number of seats in the business and economy classes. The SAS data set Capacity has the variables CapEcon and CapBusiness that hold values for the number of seats in the economy and business classes.

In the program below, the assignment statement for CapEcon reduces the number of seats in the economy class to 95% of the original number, and the assignment statement for CapBusiness reduces the number of seats in the business class to 90% of the original number. The INT function is used in both assignment statements to return the integer portion of the result.

Note: If you choose to run this example, you must copy the data set Capacity from the Sasuser library to the Work library.

```
proc print data=capacity (obs=4);
run;

data capacity;
   modify capacity;
   CapEcon = int(CapEcon * .95);
   CapBusiness = int(CapBusiness * .90);
run;

proc print data=capacity (obs=4);
run;
```

The following output shows the data before the MODIFY statement.

Obs	FlightID	RouteID	Origin	Dest	Cap1st	CapBusiness	CapEcon
1	IA00100	0000001	RDU	LHR	14	30	163
2	IA00201	0000002	LHR	RDU	14	30	163
3	IA00300	0000003	RDU	FRA	14	30	163
4	IA00400	0000004	FRA	RDU	14	30	163

The following output shows the data after the MODIFY statement. You can see that the values in CapBusiness and CapEcon have been reduced.

Obs	FlightID	RouteID	Origin	Dest	Cap1st	CapBusiness	CapEcon
1	IA00100	0000001	RDU	LHR	14	27	154
2	IA00201	0000002	LHR	RDU	14	27	154
3	IA00300	0000003	RDU	FRA	14	27	154
4	IA00400	0000004	FRA	RDU	14	27	154

Modifying Observations Using a Transaction Data Set

Overview

You can use a MODIFY statement to update all observations in a data set, but there are times when you want to update only selected observations. You can modify a master SAS data set with values in a transaction data set by using the MODIFY statement with a BY statement to apply updates by matching observations.

General form, MODIFY statement with a BY statement:

DATA *SAS-data-set*;

> **MODIFY** *SAS-data-set transaction-data-set*;

> **BY** *key-variable*;

RUN;

Here is an explanation of the syntax:

SAS-data-set
> is the name of the SAS data set that you want to modify (also called the master data set).

transaction-data-set
> is the name of the SAS data set with updated values.

key-variable
> is the name of the variable whose values are matched in the master and transaction data sets.

Note: In the MODIFY statement, you must list the master data set followed by the transaction data set.

The BY statement matches observations from the transaction data set with observations in the master data set. When the MODIFY statement reads an observation from the transaction data set, it uses dynamic WHERE processing (SAS internally generates a WHERE statement) to locate the matching observation in the master data set. The matching observation in the master data set can be replaced, deleted, or appended. By default, the observation is replaced.

Note: Because the MODIFY statement uses WHERE processing to locate matching observations, neither data set requires sorting. However, having the master data set sorted or indexed and the transaction data set sorted reduces processing overhead, especially for large files.

Example

Suppose you have a master data set, Capacity, which has route numbers for an airline. Some of the route numbers have changed, and the changes are stored in a transaction data set, Newrtnum. The master data set is updated by matching values of the variable FlightID.

```
proc print data=capacity(obs=5);
run;

data capacity;
   modify capacity sasuser.newrtnum;
   by flightid;
run;

proc print data=capacity(obs=5);
run;
```

The following PROC PRINT output displays the first five rows of the data set Capacity before updates were applied.

Obs	FlightID	RouteID	Origin	Dest	Cap1st	CapBusiness	CapEcon
1	IA00100	0000001	RDU	LHR	14	30	163
2	IA00201	0000002	LHR	RDU	14	30	163
3	IA00300	0000003	RDU	FRA	14	30	163
4	IA00400	0000004	FRA	RDU	14	30	163
5	IA00500	0000005	RDU	JFK	16	.	251

For each matching observation, the values for RouteID are updated.

Obs	FlightID	RouteID	Origin	Dest	Cap1st	CapBusiness	CapEcon
1	IA00100	0000101	RDU	LHR	14	30	163
2	IA00201	0000002	LHR	RDU	14	30	163
3	IA00300	0000003	RDU	FRA	14	30	163
4	IA00400	0000400	FRA	RDU	14	30	163
5	IA00500	0000035	RDU	JFK	16	.	251

Handling Duplicate Values

When you use the MODIFY and BY statements to update a data set, WHERE processing starts at the top of the master data set, finds the first match, and updates it. Consider what happens if there are duplicate values in the master or transaction data sets. Suppose you have the following code to make updates to the master data set M using the transaction data set T:

```
data m;
    modify m t;
    by a;
run;
```

If duplicate values of the BY variable exist in the master data set, only the first observation in the group of duplicate values is updated.

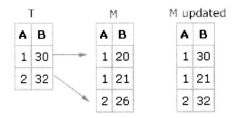

If duplicate values of the BY variable exist in the etransaction data set, the transactions overwrite each other so that only the last transaction in the group is the result in the master data set.

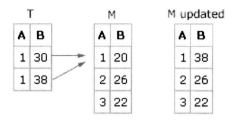

Alternatively, you can write code to accumulate the numeric value of each transaction.

Handling Missing Values

If there are missing values in the transaction data set, SAS does not replace the data in the master data set with missing values unless they are special missing values.

Note: A special missing value is a type of numeric missing value that enables you to represent different categories of missing data by using the letters A-Z or an underscore. You designate special missing values using the MISSING statement in the DATA step. For more information, see the SAS documentation.

You can specify how missing values in the transaction data set are handled by using the UPDATEMODE= option in the MODIFY statement.

General form, MODIFY statement with the UPDATEMODE= option:

MODIFY *master-data-set transaction-data-set*
          UPDATEMODE=MISSINGCHECK | NOMISSINGCHECK;

Here is an explanation of the syntax:

master-data-set
    is the name of the SAS data set that you want to modify.

transaction-data-set
    is the name of the SAS data set in which the updated values are stored.

MISSINGCHECK
    prevents missing values in the transaction data set from replacing values in the master data set unless they are special missing values. MISSINGCHECK is the default.

NOMISSINGCHECK
    allows missing values in the transaction data set to replace the values in the master data set. Special missing values in the transaction data set still replace values in the master data set.

Modifying Observations Located by an Index

Overview

You have learned that you can use a BY statement to access values that you want to update in a master data set by matching. When you have an indexed master data set, you can use the index to directly access the observations that you want to update. To do this, you use the following statements:

- a MODIFY statement with the KEY= option to name an index to locate the observations for updating

- a SET statement or INPUT statement to read a transaction data set with a like-named variable or variables whose values are supplied to the index

---

General form, MODIFY statement with the KEY= option:

MODIFY *SAS-data-set* **KEY=***index-name***;**

Here is an explanation of the syntax:

SAS-data-set
    is the master data set, or the data set that you want to update.

index-name
    is the name of the simple or composite index that you are using to locate observations.

Updating with an index is different from updating using a BY statement. When you use the MODIFY statement with the KEY= option to name an index, the following must occur:

- You must explicitly specify the update that you want to occur.

- Each observation in the transaction data set must have a matching observation in the master data set. If you have multiple observations in the transaction data set for one master observation, only the first observation in the transaction data set is applied. The other observations generate run-time errors and terminate the DATA step (unless you use the UNIQUE option, which is discussed later in this chapter).

Example

Suppose that airline cargo weights for 1999 are stored in the master data set Cargo99, which has a composite index named FlghtDte on the variables FlightID and Date. Some of the data is incorrect and the data set needs to be updated. The correct cargo data is stored in the transaction data set Newcgnum.

In the program below, the KEY= option specifies the FlghtDte index. When a matching observation is found in Cargo99, three variables (CapCargo, CargoWgt, and CargoRev) are updated.

Note: If you choose to run this example, you must copy the data set Cargo99 from the Sasuser library to the Work library.

```
proc print data=cargo99(obs=5);
run;

data cargo99;
   set sasuser.newcgnum (rename =
      (capcargo = newCapCargo
      cargowgt = newCargoWgt
      cargorev = newCargoRev));
   modify cargo99 key=flghtdte;
   capcargo = newcapcargo;
   cargowgt = newcargowgt;
   cargorev = newcargorev;
run;

proc print data=cargo99(obs=5);
run;
```

The output below shows the first five observations of the SAS data set Cargo99 before it was modified by Newcgnum.

Obs	FlightID	RouteID	Origin	Dest	CapCargo	Date	CargoWgt	CargoRev
1	IA00100	0000001	RDU	LHR	82400	01JAN1999	45600	$111,720.00
2	IA00100	0000001	RDU	LHR	82400	01AUG1999	44600	$109,270.00
3	IA00100	0000001	RDU	LHR	82400	20AUG1999	44600	$109,270.00
4	IA00100	0000001	RDU	LHR	82400	02SEP1999	47400	$116,130.00
5	IA00100	0000001	RDU	LHR	82400	29DEC1999	44200	$108,290.00

The output below shows the first five observations of the SAS data set Cargo99 after it was modified by Newcgnum. Notice that the three variables in the first observation were updated by the values in Newcgnum.

Obs	FlightID	RouteID	Origin	Dest	CapCargo	Date	CargoWgt	CargoRev
1	IA00100	0000001	RDU	LHR	35055	01JAN1999	.	$121,879.90
2	IA00100	0000001	RDU	LHR	82400	01AUG1999	44600	$109,270.00
3	IA00100	0000001	RDU	LHR	82400	20AUG1999	44600	$109,270.00
4	IA00100	0000001	RDU	LHR	82400	02SEP1999	47400	$116,130.00
5	IA00100	0000001	RDU	LHR	82400	29DEC1999	44200	$108,290.00

Handling Duplicate Values

When you use an index to locate observations to update, duplicate values of the indexed variable in the transaction data set might cause problems. We consider what happens with various scenarios when you use the following code to update the master data set M with values from the transaction data set T. The index on the M data set is built on the variable A:

```
data m;
   set t (rename=(b=newb));
   modify m key=a;
   b=newb;
run;
```

If there are duplications in the master data set, only the first occurrence is updated.

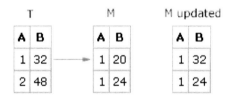

TIP   If you want all duplicates in the master data set to be updated with the transaction value, use a DO loop to execute a SET statement with the KEY= option multiple times.

If there are nonconsecutive duplications in the transaction data set, SAS updates the first match in the master data set. The last duplicate transaction value is the result in the master data set after the update.

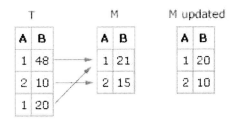

If there are consecutive duplications in the transaction data set (that is, some that do not have a match in the master data set), then SAS performs a one-to-one update until it finds a non-match. At that time, the DATA step terminates with an error.

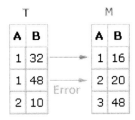

Adding the UNIQUE option to the MODIFY statement enables you to avoid the error in the DATA step. The UNIQUE option causes the DATA step to return to the top of the index each time it looks for a match. The UNIQUE option can be used only with the KEY= option.

General form, MODIFY statement with the UNIQUE option:

MODIFY *SAS-data-set* **KEY=***index-name* **/UNIQUE;**

Here is an explanation of the syntax:

SAS-data-set
   is the name of the SAS data set that you want to modify (the master data set).

index-name
   is the name of the simple or composite index that you are using to locate observations.

You can specify the UNIQUE option in order to do one of the following:

- apply multiple transactions to one master observation

- identify that each observation in the master data set contains a unique value of the index variable.

When you use the UNIQUE option and there are consecutive duplications in the transaction data set, SAS updates the first observation in the master data set. This is similar to what happens when you have nonconsecutive duplications in the transaction data set. If the values in the transaction data set should be added to the value in the master data set, you can write a statement to accumulate the values from all the duplicates.

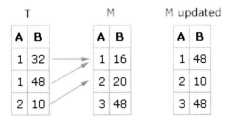

Controlling the Update Process

Overview

When the DATA step contains a MODIFY statement, SAS writes the current observation to its original place in the SAS data set. This action occurs by default through an implied REPLACE statement at the bottom of the DATA step.

However, you can override this default behavior by explicitly adding the OUTPUT, REPLACE, or REMOVE statement.

General form for OUTPUT, REPLACE, and REMOVE statements:

OUTPUT;

REPLACE;

REMOVE;

Here is an explanation of the syntax:

OUTPUT
adds the current observation to the end of the data set.

REPLACE
writes the current observation to the same location in the data set.

REMOVE
removes the current observation from the data set.

Using OUTPUT, REPLACE, or REMOVE statements in a DATA step with a MODIFY statement can change the default replacement of observations. You can use these three statements together as long as the sequence is logical.

CAUTION:
If you use an OUTPUT statement in conjunction with a REPLACE or REMOVE statement, make sure that the OUTPUT statement is executed after any REPLACE or REMOVE statements to ensure the integrity of the index position.

Example

If the SAS data set Transaction has a variable named Code that has values of **yes**, **no**, and **new**, you can submit the following program in order to do one of the following:

- delete rows where the value of Code is **no**

- update rows where the value of Code is **yes**

- append rows where the value of Code is **new**.

```
data master;
   set transaction;
   modify master key = id;
   a = b;
   if code = 'no' then remove;
   else if code = 'yes' then replace;
   else if code = 'new' then output;
```

```
run;
```

Note: You cannot run this example because Transaction and Master are fictitious data sets.

Monitoring I/O Error Conditions

When you use the MODIFY statement with a BY statement or KEY= option to update a data set, error checking is important for several reasons. The most important reason is that these tools use nonsequential access methods, so there is no guarantee that an observation is located so that it satisfies the request. Error checking enables you to perform updates or not, depending on the outcome of the I/O condition.

The automatic variable _IORC_ (Input Output Return Code) is created when you use the MODIFY statement with the BY statement or KEY= option. The value of _IORC_ is a numeric return code that indicates the status of the most recently executed I/O operation. Checking the value of this variable enables you to detect abnormal I/O conditions and direct execution in particular ways rather than having the application terminate abnormally.

Using _IORC_ with %SYSRC

Because the values of the _IORC_ automatic variable are internal and subject to change, %SYSRC, an autocall macro, was created to enable you to test for specific I/O conditions while protecting your code from future changes in _IORC_ values.

General form, _IORC_ with the %SYSRC autocall macro:

IF _IORC_=%SYSRC (*mnemonic*) **THEN** *executable_statement*;

Here is an explanation of the syntax:

mnemonic
    is a code for a specific I/O condition.

Note: %SYSRC is in the autocall library. You must have the MACRO system option in effect to use this macro.

When you use %SYSRC, you can check the value of _IORC_ by specifying one of the mnemonics listed below.

Mnemonic	Meaning
_DSENMR	The observation in the transaction data set does not exist in the master data set (used only with the MODIFY and BY statements).
_DSEMTR	Multiple transaction data set observations do not exist in the master data set (used only with the MODIFY and BY statements).
_DSENOM	No matching observation (used with the KEY= option).
_SOK	The observation was located.

Example

Suppose you are using the MODIFY statement with the KEY= option to update a SAS data set. In the program below, when _IORC_ has the value _SOK, the observation is updated. When _IORC_ has the value _DSENOM, no matching observation is found, so the observation is appended to the data set by the OUTPUT statement and _ERROR_ is reset to 0 in the do group.

```
data master;
   set transaction;
   modify master key = id;
   if _IORC_=%sysrc(_sok) then
      do;
         a = b;
         replace;
      end;
   else
      if _IORC_=%sysrc(_dsenom) then
         do;
            output;
            _ERROR_ = 0;
         end;
run;
```

TIP   For more information about the _IORC_ automatic variable and %SYSRC, see information about error-checking tools in the SAS documentation.

Understanding Integrity Constraints

Overview

Now that you know how to modify data in place, you might be wondering how you can protect or ensure the integrity of your data when it is modified. Integrity constraints are rules that you can specify in order to restrict the data values that can be stored for a variable in a data set. SAS enforces integrity constraints when values that are associated with a variable are added, updated, or deleted using techniques that modify data in place, such as the following:

- a DATA step with the MODIFY statement

- an interactive data editing window

- PROC SQL with the INSERT INTO, SET, or UPDATE statements

- PROC APPEND

When you add an integrity constraint to the table that contains data, SAS checks all data values to determine whether they satisfy the constraint before the constraint is added.

Type	Action
CHECK	ensures that a specific set or range of values are the only values in a column. It can also check the validity of a value in one column based on a value in another column within the same row.

Type	Action
NOT NULL	guarantees that a column has nonmissing values in each row.
UNIQUE	enforces uniqueness for the values of a column.
PRIMARY KEY	uniquely defines a row within a table, which can be a single column or a set of columns. A table can have only one primary key. The PRIMARY KEY constraint includes the attributes of the NOT NULL and UNIQUE constraints.
FOREIGN KEY	specifies variables whose values are linked to the values of the primary key variables in another data set. This parent/child relationship limits modifications that are made to both tables.

Note: When you place integrity constraints on a SAS data set, you specify the type of constraint that you want to create. Each constraint has a different action.

You can use integrity constraints in two ways, general and referential. General constraints operate within a data set, and referential constraints operate between data sets.

General Integrity Constraints

General integrity constraints enable you to restrict the values of variables within a single data set. The following integrity constraints can be used as general integrity constraints:

- CHECK
- NOT NULL
- UNIQUE
- PRIMARY KEY.

Note: A PRIMARY KEY constraint is a general integrity constraint as long as it does not have any FOREIGN KEY constraints referencing it. When PRIMARY KEY is used as a general constraint, it is simply a shortcut for assigning the NOT NULL and UNIQUE constraints.

Referential Integrity Constraints

Referential constraints enable you to link the data values of a column in one data set to the data values of columns in another data set. You create a referential integrity constraint when a FOREIGN KEY integrity constraint in one data set references a PRIMARY KEY integrity constraint in another data set. To create a referential integrity constraint, you must do the following:

1. Define a PRIMARY KEY constraint on the first data set.

2. Define a FOREIGN KEY constraint on other data sets.

Placing Integrity Constraints on a Data Set

Overview

Integrity constraints can be created using either the DATASETS procedure or the SQL procedure.

Although you can use either procedure to create integrity constraints on existing data sets, you must use PROC SQL if you want to create integrity constraints at the same time that you create the data set. In this chapter you learn to use PROC DATASETS to place integrity constraints on an existing data set.

General form, DATASETS procedure with the IC CREATE statement:

PROC DATASETS LIB=*libref*<NOLIST>;

      MODIFY *SAS-data-set*;

      IC CREATE *constraint-name=constraint*

          <MESSAGE=*'Error Message'*>;

QUIT;

Here is an explanation of the syntax:

libref
    is the library in which the data set is stored. If you do not specify the LIB= option, the procedure uses the Work library.

NOLIST
    suppresses the directory listing.

SAS-data-set
    is the name of the data set to which you want to apply the integrity constraint.

constraint-name
    is any name that you want to give the integrity constraint.

constraint
    is the type of constraint that you are creating, specified in the following format:

    • NOT NULL *(variable)*

    • UNIQUE *(variables)*

    • CHECK *(where-expression)*

    • PRIMARY KEY *(variables)*

    • FOREIGN KEY *(variables)* REFERENCES *table-name*.

Error Message
    is an optional message written to the log when the constraint is violated.

Note: You can use IC or INTEGRITY CONSTRAINT interchangeably.

To learn how to create integrity constraints using the SQL procedure, see Chapter 5, "Creating and Managing Tables Using PROC SQL," on page 167.

Example

Suppose you have a data set that contains route information and passenger capacity for each class in an airline. You need to create integrity constraints to ensure that, when the data set is updated, the following conditions are true:

- The route ID number is both unique and required (PRIMARY KEY).

- The capacity for business class passengers must either be missing or be greater than the capacity for first class passengers (CHECK).

In the code below, the IC CREATE statement is used to create two general integrity constraints on variables in the data set Capinfo:

- The PRIMARY KEY constraint is placed on the RouteID variable. This constraint ensures that when values of RouteID are updated, they must be unique and nonmissing.

  Note: The same effect could be achieved by applying both the UNIQUE and NOT NULL constraints, but the PRIMARY KEY constraint is used as a shortcut.

- The CHECK constraint uses the WHERE expression to ensure that the only values of CapBusiness that are allowed are those greater than Cap1st or missing.

Note: If you choose to run this example, you must copy the data set Capinfo from the Sasuser library to the Work library.

```
proc datasets nolist;
   modify capinfo;
   ic create PKIDInfo=primary key(routeid)
      message='You must supply a Route ID Number';
   ic create Class1=check(where=(cap1st<capbusiness or capbusiness=.))
      message='Cap1st must be less than CapBusiness';
quit;
```

Notice that the NOLIST option is used to prevent a listing of the Work library that PROC DATASETS produces by default. When the constraint is created, a message is written to the SAS log.

Table 18.1 *SAS Log*

```
45 modify capinfo;
46 ic create PKIDInfo = primary key (routeid)
47 message = 'You must supply a Route ID Number';
NOTE: Integrity constraint PKIDInfo defined.
48 ic create Class1 = check (where = (cap1st < capbusiness
49 or capbusiness = .)) message = 'Cap1st must be less
50 than CapBusiness';
NOTE: Integrity constraint Class1 defined.
51 run;
```

Note: For the UNIQUE and PRIMARY KEY constraints, SAS builds indexes on the columns that are involved if an appropriate index does not already exist. Any index that is created by an integrity constraint can be used for other purposes, such as WHERE processing or the KEY= option in a SET statement.

TIP For more information about creating integrity constraints, see the SAS documentation for the DATASETS procedure.

How Constraints Are Enforced

Once integrity constraints are in place, SAS enforces them whenever you modify the data set in place. Techniques for modifying data in place include using the following elements:

- a DATA step with the MODIFY statement

- interactive data editing windows

- PROC SQL with the INSERT INTO, SET, or UPDATE statements

- PROC APPEND

Example

The code in the previous example placed a check constraint on Cap1st and CapBusiness to ensure that values for the capacity in business class were either greater than first class or missing. Suppose you ran the following program to triple the capacity in first class. This would probably violate the check constraint for some observations.

```
data capinfo;
   modify capinfo;
   cap1st=cap1st*3;
run;
```

The observations that failed to pass the integrity constraint are written to the SAS log. As you can see, all these observations would have had values of Cap1st greater than those of CapBusiness.

Table 18.2 *SAS Log*

```
FlightID=IA00100 RouteID=0000001 Origin=RDU Dest=LHR Cap1st=42
CapBusiness=30 CapEcon=163
_ERROR_=1 _IORC_=660130 _N_=1
FlightID=IA00201 RouteID=0000002 Origin=LHR Dest=RDU Cap1st=42
CapBusiness=30 CapEcon=163
_ERROR_=1 _IORC_=660130 _N_=2
FlightID=IA00300 RouteID=0000003 Origin=RDU Dest=FRA Cap1st=42
CapBusiness=30 CapEcon=163
_ERROR_=1 _IORC_=660130 _N_=3
FlightID=IA00400 RouteID=0000004 Origin=FRA Dest=RDU Cap1st=42
CapBusiness=30 CapEcon=163
_ERROR_=1 _IORC_=660130 _N_=4
FlightID=IA02900 RouteID=0000029 Origin=SFO Dest=HNL Cap1st=42
CapBusiness=30 CapEcon=163
_ERROR_=1 _IORC_=660130 _N_=29
FlightID=IA03000 RouteID=0000030 Origin=HNL Dest=SFO Cap1st=42
CapBusiness=30 CapEcon=163
_ERROR_=1 _IORC_=660130 _N_=30
FlightID=IA03300 RouteID=0000033 Origin=RDU Dest=ANC Cap1st=42
CapBusiness=30 CapEcon=163
_ERROR_=1 _IORC_=660130 _N_=33
FlightID=IA03400 RouteID=0000034 Origin=ANC Dest=RDU Cap1st=42
CapBusiness=30 CapEcon=163
_ERROR_=1 _IORC_=660130 _N_=34
NOTE: There were 50 observations read from the data set WORK.CAPINFO.
NOTE:  The data set WORK.CAPINFO has been updated. There were 42
       observations rewritten, 0 observations added and 0
       observations deleted.
NOTE: There were 8 rejected updates, 0 rejected adds, and 0 rejected
       deletes.
```

If you used the VIEWTABLE window or another interactive window to make this update, SAS displays the error message that is defined for the integrity constraint.

Note: Rejected observations can be collected in a special file using the audit trail functionality that you learn about later in this chapter.

Copying a Data Set and Preserving Integrity Constraints

The APPEND, COPY, CPORT, CIMPORT, and SORT procedures preserve integrity constraints when their operation results in a copy of the original data file. Integrity constraints are also preserved if you copy a data set using the SAS Explorer window.

> *TIP* For more information about preserving integrity constraints, see the SAS documentation.

Documenting Integrity Constraints

Overview

To view the descriptor portion of your data, including the integrity constraints that you have placed on a data set, you can use the CONTENTS statement in the DATASETS procedure.

General form, DATASETS procedure with the CONTENTS statement:

PROC DATASETS LIB=*libref* <NOLIST>;

      CONTENTS DATA=*SAS-data-set*;

QUIT;

Here is an explanation of the syntax:

libref
    is the library in which the data set is stored.

NOLIST
    suppresses the directory listing.

SAS-data-set
    is the name of the data set that you want information about.

Note: The CONTENTS statement in the DATASETS procedure results in the same information as the CONTENTS procedure.

Example

The following code displays information about the Capinfo data set, including the integrity constraints that were added to this data set in the last example. Notice that the NOLIST option is used here to suppress the listing of all data sets in the Work library. With this option, only the information for the Capinfo data set is listed.

```
proc datasets nolist;
   contents data=capinfo;
quit;
```

Only the integrity constraints portion of the output is shown below.

	Alphabetic List of Integrity Constraints			
#	Integrity Constraint	Type	Variables	Where Clause	User Message
1	Class1	Check		(Cap1st<CapBusiness) or (CapBusiness=.)	First Class Capacity must be less than Business Capacity
2	PKIDInfo	Primary Key	RouteID		You must supply a Route ID Number

Removing Integrity Constraints

Overview

To remove an integrity constraint from a data set, use the DATASETS procedure with the IC DELETE statement.

General form, DATASETS procedure with the IC DELETE statement:

PROC DATASETS LIB=*libref* <NOLIST>;

    MODIFY *SAS-data-set*;

    IC DELETE *constraint-name*;

QUIT;

Here is an explanation of the syntax:

libref
    is the name of the library in which the data set is stored. If you do not specify the LIB= option, the procedure uses the Work library.

NOLIST
    suppresses the directory listing.

SAS-data-set
    is the name of the data set that has the integrity constraint.

constraint-name
    is the name of the integrity constraint that you want to delete.

Example

The code below removes the integrity constraints on the Capinfo data set:

```
proc datasets;
    modify capinfo;
    ic delete pkidinfo;
    ic delete class1;
 quit;
```

A message is written to the SAS log when the integrity constraint is deleted.

Table 18.3 *SAS Log*

```
53      modify capinfo;
54       ic delete pkidinfo;
NOTE: Integrity constraint PKIDInfo deleted.
55       ic delete class1;
NOTE: All integrity constraints defined on WORK.CAPINFO.DATA
      have been deleted.
56    run;NOTE: Integrity constraint PKIDInfo deleted.
```

Understanding Audit Trails

As you modify a data set, you might want to track the changes that you make by using an audit trail. An audit trail is an optional SAS file that logs modifications to a SAS table. Audit trails are used to track changes that are made to the data set in place. Specifically, audit trails track changes that are made with the following:

- the VIEWTABLE window

- the data grid

- the MODIFY statement in the DATA step

- the UPDATE, INSERT, or DELETE statement in PROC SQL

For each addition, deletion, and update to the data, the audit trail automatically stores a copy of the variables in the observation that was updated, and also stores information such as who made the modification, what was modified, and when the modification was made. The audit trail can also store additional information in user-defined variables.

The following PROC CONTENTS output lists the variables in an audit trail file for a data set that has two variables, A and B. You learn more about these variables later in this chapter.

#	Variable	Type	Len	Pos	Format	Label
1	A	Num	8	0		
2	B	Num	8	8		
3	Who	Char	20	16		Name
4	Why	Char	20	36		Reason
5	_ATDATETIME_	Num	8	56	DATETIME19.	
10	_ATMESSAGE_	Char	8	114		
6	_ATOBSNO_	Num	8	64		
9	_ATOPCODE_	Char	2	112		
7	_ATRETURNCODE_	Num	8	72		
8	_ATUSERID_	Char	32	80		

CAUTION:

Any procedure or action that replaces the data set (such as the DATA step, CREATE TABLE in PROC SQL, or SORT without the OUT= option) deletes the audit trail. Audit trails should not be deleted with system tools such as Windows Explorer.

A SAS table can have only one audit trail file. The following statements are true about the audit trail file:

- It is a read-only file.

- It is created by PROC DATASETS.

- It must be in the same library as the data file that is associated with it.

- It has the same name as the data set it is monitoring, but with a member type of AUDIT.

Initiating and Reading Audit Trails

Overview

You initiate an audit trail using the DATASETS procedure with the AUDIT and INITIATE statements.

General form, DATASETS procedure to initiate an audit trail:

PROC DATASETS LIB=*libref* <NOLIST>**;**

    AUDIT *SAS-data-set* <*SAS-password*>**;**

    INITIATE;

QUIT;

Here is an explanation of the syntax:

AUDIT
    initiates and controls event logging to an audit file.

libref
    is the name of the library where the data set to be audited resides.

NOLIST
    suppresses the directory listing.

SAS-data-set
    is the name of the SAS data set that you want to audit.

SAS-password
    is the SAS data set password, if one exists.

INITIATE
    begins the audit trail on the data set specified in the AUDIT statement.

Example

The following code initiates an audit trail on the data set Capinfo.

Note: If you choose to run this example, you must copy the data set Capinfo from the Sasuser library to the Work library.

```
proc datasets nolist;
   audit capinfo;
   initiate;
quit;
```

Table 18.4 *SAS Log*

```
60   audit capinfo;
61   initiate;
WARNING: The audited data file WORK.CAPINFO.DATA is not
         password protected.
         Apply an ALTER password to prevent accidental
         deletion or replacement of it and any associated
         audit files.
62   quit;
NOTE: The data set WORK.CAPINFO.AUDIT has 0 observations
      and 13 variables.
```

Note: The audit trail file uses the SAS password that is assigned to the parent data set. Therefore, it is recommended that you alter the password for the parent data set. Use the ALTER= data set option to assign an alter-password to a SAS data set or to access a Read-, Write-, or Alter- protected SAS data set. If another password is used or no password is used, then the audit file is still created, but is not protected.

TIP For more information about audit trails, see the SAS documentation for the DATASETS procedure.

Reading Audit Trail Files

When the audit trail is initiated, it has no observations until the first modification is made to the audited data set. When the audit trail file contains data, you can read it with any component of SAS that reads a data set. To refer to the audit trail file, use the TYPE= data set option.

General form, TYPE= data set option to specify an audit file:

(TYPE=AUDIT)

Examples

The following PROC CONTENTS code displays the contents of the audit trial file:

```
proc contents data=mylib.sales (type=audit);
run;
```

The following PROC PRINT code lists the data in the audit trail file for the data set Capinfo:

```
proc print data=capinfo (type=audit);
run;
```

Controlling Data in the Audit Trail

Overview

Now that you have seen how to initiate audit trails and read an audit trail file, consider the information the audit trail file contains. The audit trail file can contain three types of variables:

- data set variables that store copies of the columns in the audited SAS data set

- audit trail variables that automatically store information about data modifications

- user variables that store user-entered information

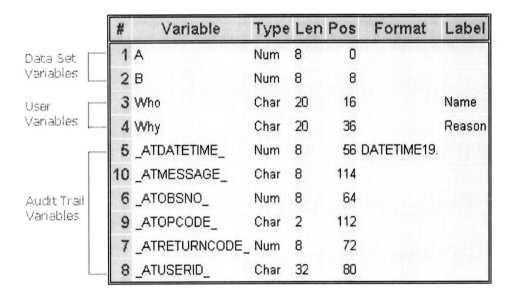

	#	Variable	Type	Len	Pos	Format	Label
Data Set Variables	1	A	Num	8	0		
	2	B	Num	8	8		
User Variables	3	Who	Char	20	16		Name
	4	Why	Char	20	36		Reason
Audit Trail Variables	5	_ATDATETIME_	Num	8	56	DATETIME19.	
	10	_ATMESSAGE_	Char	8	114		
	6	_ATOBSNO_	Num	8	64		
	9	_ATOPCODE_	Char	2	112		
	7	_ATRETURNCODE_	Num	8	72		
	8	_ATUSERID_	Char	32	80		

You can use additional statements in the PROC DATASETS step to control which variables appear in the audit trail. We consider each of the three types of variables that can be found in an audit trail.

Data Set Variables

As you might expect, the audit trail file has the same set of variables that are in the audited data set. If the data set contains the variables A and B, the variables A and B are also in the audit trail file.

Next consider the audit trail variables that automatically store information about changes that you make to the data.

Audit Trail Variables

Audit trail variables automatically store information about data modifications. Audit trail variable names begin with AT followed by a specific string, such as DATETIME.

Audit Trail Variable	Information Stored
ATDATETIME	date and time of a modification
ATUSERID	login user ID associated with a modification
ATOBSNO	observation number affected by the modification unless REUSE=YES
ATRETURNCODE	event return code
ATMESSAGE	SAS log message at the time of the modification
ATOPCODE	code describing the type of operation

Values of the _ATOPCODE_ Variable

The _ATOPCODE_ variable contains a code that describes the type of operation that wrote the observation to the audit file. For example, if you modified all observations in an audited data set, the audit file would contain twice as many observations as the original data set. The audit file would contain one observation that matched the original observation with an _ATOPCODE_ value of DR, and one updated observation with an _ATOPCODE_ value of DW.

Here are the possible values of the _ATOPCODE_ variable.

ATOPCODE	Event
DA	added data record image
DD	deleted data record image
DR	before-update record image
DW	after-update record image
EA	observation add failed
ED	observation delete failed
EU	observation update failed

You can define what information is stored in the audit file by using the LOG statement when you initiate the audit trail.

Using the LOG Statement to Control the Data in the Audit Trail

When you initiate an audit trail, options in the LOG statement determine the type of entries that are stored in the audit trail, along with their corresponding _ATOPCODE_ values. The ERROR_IMAGE option controls E operation codes. The BEFORE_IMAGE option controls the DR operation code, and the DATA_IMAGE option controls all other

D operation codes. If you omit the LOG statement when you initiate the audit trail, the default behavior is to log all images.

General form, LOG statement:

LOG <*audit-settings*>;

Here is an explanation of the syntax:

audit-settings
    are any of the following:

- BEFORE_IMAGE=*YES|NO* controls storage of before-update record images (the 'DR' operation).

- DATA_IMAGE=*YES|NO* controls storage of after-update record images (for example, other operations starting with 'D').

- ERROR_IMAGE=*YES|NO* controls storage of unsuccessful update record images (for example, operations starting with 'E').

Example

The following code initiates an audit trail on the data set Capinfo but stores only error record images. This means that the audit file contains only records where an error occurred. The _ATOPCODE_ values can be only EA, ED, and EU.

Note: If you choose to run this example, you must copy the data set Capinfo from the Sasuser library to the Work library.

```
proc datasets nolist;
    audit capinfo;
    initiate;
    log data_image=NO before_image=NO;
quit;
```

User Variables

User variables allow the person editing the file to enter information about changes that they are making to the data. Although the data values are stored in the audit file, you can update them in the data set like any other variable.

User variables are created by using the USER_VAR statement in the audit trail specification.

General form, USER_VAR statement:

USER_VAR *variable-name* <$><*length*><LABEL=*'variable-label'*>;

Here is an explanation of the syntax:

variable-name
> is the name of the user variable that you are creating.

$
> indicates the variable is a character variable.

length
> specifies the length of the variable (the default is 8).

variable-label
> specifies a label for the variable enclosed in quotation marks.

Note: You can create more than one user variable in a single USER_VAR statement.

User variables are unique in SAS in that they are stored in one file (the audit file) and opened for update in another file (the data set). When the data set is opened for update, the user variables are displayed, and you can edit them as if they are part of the data set.

Example

Suppose you must monitor the updates for the data set Capinfo. The following code initiates an audit trail for the data set Capinfo and creates two user variables, who and why, to store who made changes to the data set and why the changes were made.

Note: If you choose to run this example, you must copy the data set Capinfo from the Sasuser library to the Work library.

```
proc datasets nolist;
   audit capinfo;
   initiate;
   user_var who $20 label = 'Who made the change'
            why $20 label = 'Why the change was made';
quit;
```

Once these user variables are set up, they are retrieved from the audit trail and displayed when the data set is opened for update. You can enter data values for the user variables as you would for any data variable. The data values are saved to the audit trail as each observation is saved. The user variables are not available when the data is opened for browsing or printing. To rename a user variable or modify its attributes, you modify the data set, not the audit file.

Controlling the Audit Trail

Overview

Once you activate an audit trail, you can suspend and resume logging, and terminate (delete) the audit trail by resubmitting a PROC DATASETS step with additional statements. You use the DATASETS procedure to suspend and then resume the audit trail. You also use this procedure to delete or terminate an audit trail.

General form, DATASETS procedure to suspend, resume, or terminate an audit trail:

PROC DATASETS LIB=_libref_<NOLIST>;

    AUDIT _SAS-data-set_ <_SAS-password_>;

    SUSPEND | RESUME | TERMINATE;

QUIT;

Here is an explanation of the syntax:

libref
    is the name of the library where the table to be audited resides.

NOLIST
    suppresses the directory listing.

SAS-data-set
    is the name of the SAS data set that you want to audit.

SAS-password
    is the SAS data file password, if one exists.

SUSPEND
    suspends event logging to the audit file, but does not delete the audit file.

RESUME
    resumes event logging to the audit file, if it was suspended.

TERMINATE
    terminates event logging and deletes the audit file.

TIP Because each update to the data file is also written to the audit file, the audit trail can negatively affect system performance. You might want to consider suspending the audit trail for large, regularly scheduled batch updates.

Example

The following code terminates the audit trail on the data set Capinfo.

Note: If you choose to run this example, you must copy the data set Capinfo from the Sasuser library to the Work library.

```
proc datasets nolist;
   audit capinfo;
   terminate;
quit;
```

A message is written to the log when the audit trail is terminated.

Table 18.5 *SAS Log*

```
65   audit capinfo;
66   terminate;
NOTE: Deleting WORK.CAPINFO (memtype=AUDIT).
67 quit;
```

Understanding Generation Data Sets

You have learned that you can keep an audit trail to track observation updates made to an individual data set in place. However, if you replace the data set, the audit trail is lost. Generation data sets enable you to maintain multiple versions or generations of a SAS data set. A new generation is created each time the file is replaced.

By default, generation data sets are not in effect. As the SAS data set A is replaced, there are two copies of A in the SAS library. When the DATA step completes execution, SAS removes the original copy of the data set A from the library.

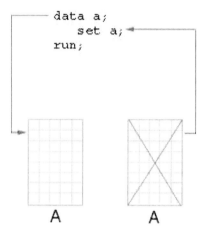

When generation data sets are in effect and the SAS data set A is replaced, there are two copies of A in the SAS library. When the DATA step completes execution, SAS keeps the original copy of the SAS data set A in the library and renames it.

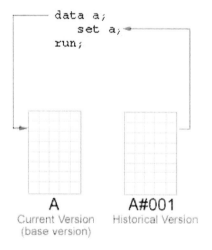

Each generation of a generation data set is stored as part of a generation group. Each generation data set in a generation group has the same root member name, but each has a different version number. The most recent version is called the base version. When generations are in effect, SAS filenames are limited to 28 characters. The last four characters are reserved for the version numbers.

Note: Generation data sets are not supported on VMS.

Initiating Generation Data Sets

Overview

To initiate generation data sets and to specify the maximum number of versions to maintain, you use the output data set option GENMAX= when creating or replacing a data set. If the data set already exists, you can use the GENMAX= option with the DATASETS procedure and the MODIFY statement.

General form, DATASETS procedure, and MODIFY statement with the GENMAX= option:

PROC DATASETS LIB=*libref* <NOLIST>**;**

> **MODIFY** *SAS-data-set* (**GENMAX=***n*)**;**

QUIT;

Here is an explanation of the syntax:

libref
> is the library that contains the data that you want to modify.

NOLIST
> suppresses the directory listing.

SAS-data-set
> is the name of the SAS data set that you want to modify.

n

> is the number of historical versions that you want to keep, including the base version:

> - *n=0*, no historical versions are kept (this is the default).

> - *n>0*, the specified number of versions of the file that are are kept. The number includes the base version.

Example

The following DATASETS procedure modifies the data set Cargorev and requests that up to four versions be kept (one base version and three historical versions).

Note: If you choose to run this example, you must copy the data set Cargorev from the Sasuser library to the Work library.

```
proc datasets nolist;
   modify cargorev (genmax=4);
quit;
```

No message is written to the log when you specify the GENMAX= option.

Creating Generation Data Sets

Remember, new versions of a generation data set are created only when a data set is replaced, not when it is modified in place. To create new generations, use one of the following approaches:

- a DATA step with a SET statement

- a DATA step with a MERGE statement
- PROC SORT without the OUT= option
- PROC SQL with a CREATE TABLE statement

Processing Generation Data Sets

Overview

Once you have a generation group that contains more than one generation data set, you might want to select a particular data set to process. To select a particular generation, you use the GENNUM= data set option.

General form, GENNUM= data set option:

GENNUM=n

Here is an explanation of the syntax:

n

specifies a particular historical version of a data set:

- $n>0$ is an absolute reference to a historical version by its generation number.
- $n<0$ is a relative reference to a historical version.
- $n=0$ is the current version.

Examples

To print the current version of the data, you do not need to use the GENNUM= option. Simply use code such as the following:

```
proc print data=year;
run;
```

To print the youngest historical version, you have several choices. You can specify either the absolute or relative reference in the GENNUM= option, as shown:

```
proc print data=year(gennum=4);  /*absolute reference*/
run;

proc print data=year(gennum=-1);  /*relative reference*/
run;
```

You can also view information about a specific generation using the GENNUM= option with PROC CONTENTS, as shown:

```
proc contents data=year(gennum=-1);  /*relative reference*/
run;
```

Now that you have seen a few examples of using the GENNUM= option, consider how generation numbers change.

How Generation Numbers Change

When you use the GENNUM= option, you can refer to either the absolute or relative generation number. It is helpful to understand how generation numbers change so that you can identify the generation that you want to process.

First, consider how SAS names generation data sets. The first time a data set with generations in effect is replaced, SAS keeps the replaced data set, and appends a four-character version number to its member name. The name includes the pound symbol (#) and a three-digit number. That is, for a data set named A, the replaced data set becomes A#001. When the data set is replaced for the second time, the replaced data set becomes A#002. That is, A#002 is the version that is chronologically closest to the base version. The table below shows the result after three replacements.

Data Set Name	Explanation
A	base (current) version
A#003	most recent (youngest) historical version
A#002	second most recent historical version
A#001	oldest historical version

The limit for version numbers that SAS can append is #999. After 1000 replacements, SAS rolls over the youngest version number to #000.

Now we consider how absolute and relative generation numbers (specified on the GENNUM= option) change. Each time SAS creates a new generation, the absolute generation number increases sequentially. As older generations are deleted, their absolute generation numbers are retired.

In contrast, the relative generation number always refers to generations in relation to the base generation. The base or current generation is always 0 and -1 is the youngest historical version.

The following table shows data set names and their absolute and relative GENNUM= numbers.

Table 18.6 *Data Set Names with GENNUM= Numbers*

Iteration	SAS Code	Data Set Names	GENNUM=Absolute Reference	GENNUM=Relative Reference	Explanation
1	`data Year (genmax= 3);`	Year	1	0	The data set Year is created, and three generations are requested.
2	`data Year;`	Year Year#001	2 1	0 -1	Year is replaced. Year from iteration 1 is renamed Year#001.

Iteration	SAS Code	Data Set Names	GENNUM=Absolute Reference	GENNUM=Relative Reference	Explanation
3	`data Year;`	Year	3	0	Year is replaced. Year from iteration 2 is renamed Year#002.
		Year#002	2	-1	
		Year#001	1	-2	
4	`data Year;`	Year	4	0	Year is replaced. Year from iteration 3 is renamed Year#003. Year#002 from iteration 1, which is the oldest, is deleted.
		Year#003	3	-1	
		Year#002	2	-2	
5	`data Year (genmax= 2);`	Year	5	0	Year is replaced, and the number of generations is changed to 2. Year from iteration 4 is renamed Year#004. The two oldest versions are deleted.
		Year#004	4	-1	

You have learned that you use PROC DATASETS to initiate generation data sets on an existing SAS data set. Once you have created generation data sets, you can use PROC DATASETS to perform management tasks such as the following:

- deleting all or some of the generations

- renaming an entire generation group or any member of the group to a new base name.

General form, PROC DATASETS with the CHANGE and DELETE statements:

PROC DATASETS LIB=*libref* <NOLIST>;

      CHANGE *SAS-data-set*<(GENNUM=*n*)>=*new-data-set-name*;

      DELETE *SAS-data-set*<(GENNUM=*n* | HIST | ALL)>;

QUIT;

Here is an explanation of the syntax:

libref
    is the library that contains the data that you want to modify.

NOLIST
    suppresses the directory listing.

SAS-data-set
    is the name of the SAS data set you want to change or delete.

new-data-set-name
    is the new name for the SAS data set in the *CHANGE* statement.

n
    is the absolute or relative reference to a generation number.

HIST
    refers to all generations except the base version.

ALL
    refers to the base version and all generations.

Examples

The following code uses the CHANGE statement to rename the data set SalesData to Sales. If generations have been created, the base name of all generations is renamed.

```
proc datasets library=quarter1 nolist;
   change salesData=sales;
quit;
```

The following code uses the GENNUM= option to rename only the second historical data set:

```
proc datasets library=quarter1 nolist;
   change sales(gennum=2)=newsales;
quit;
```

The following code deletes one historical version. This action might leave a hole in the generation group.

```
proc datasets library=quarter1 nolist;
   delete newsales(gennum=-1);
quit;
```

When you use the GENNUM= option with the DELETE statement, you can use the HIST and ALL keywords. The following code uses the HIST keyword to delete all of the historical versions:

```
proc datasets library=quarter1 nolist;
   delete newsales(gennum=HIST);
quit;
```

The following code uses the ALL keyword in the GENNUM= option to delete all of the SAS data sets in a generation group:

```
proc datasets library=quarter1 nolist;
   delete newsales(gennum=ALL);
quit;
```

TIP   For more information about using the DATASETS procedure to process data, see the SAS documentation.

Summary

Text Summary

Using the MODIFY Statement

When you use the MODIFY statement to modify a SAS data set, SAS does not create a second copy of the data as it does when you use the SET, MERGE, or UPDATE statements. The descriptor portion of the SAS data set stays the same. Updated observations are written back to the same location as the original observation.

Modifying All Observations in a SAS Data Set

You can use the MODIFY statement with an assignment statement to modify all the observations in a SAS data set.

Modifying Observations Using a Transaction Data Set

To modify a master data set using a transaction data set, you use the MODIFY statement with a BY statement to specify the matching variable or variables. When you use the MODIFY or BY statements, SAS uses a dynamic WHERE clause to locate observations in the master data set. You can specify how missing values in the transaction data set are handled by using the UPDATEMODE= option in the MODIFY statement.

Modifying Observations Located by an Index

You can use the MODIFY statement with the KEY= option to name a simple or composite index for the SAS data set that is being modified. The KEY= argument retrieves observations from the master data set based on index values that are supplied by like-named variables in a transaction data set. If you have contiguous duplications in the transaction data set (that is, some that have no match in the master data set), you can use the UNIQUE option to cause a KEY= search to always begin at the top of the index file for each duplicate transaction.

Controlling the Update Process

When the DATA step contains a MODIFY statement, SAS writes the current observation back to its original place in the SAS data set. This action by default occurs as the last action in the step as if a REPLACE statement were the last statement in the step. However, you can override this default behavior by explicitly adding the OUTPUT, REPLACE, or REMOVE statement.

You can use the automatic variable _IORC_ with the %SYSRC autocall macro to test for specific I/O error conditions that are created when you use the BY statement or the KEY= option in the MODIFY statement. The automatic variable _IORC_ contains a return code for each I/O operation that the MODIFY statement attempts to perform. The best way to test for values of _IORC_ is to use the mnemonic codes that are provided by the SYSRC autocall macro.

Placing Integrity Constraints on a Data Set

Integrity constraints are rules that you can specify in order to restrict the data values that can be stored for a variable in a SAS data file. SAS enforces integrity constraints when values that are associated with a variable are added, updated, or deleted. You can place integrity constraints on an existing data set using the IC CREATE statement in the DATASETS procedure.

Documenting and Removing Integrity Constraints

You can view information about the integrity constraints on a data set using the CONTENTS statement in the DATASETS procedure. If you want to remove integrity constraints from a file, you use the IC DELETE statement.

Initiating and Terminating Audit Trails

An audit trail is an optional SAS file that logs modifications to a SAS table. You initiate an audit trail using the DATASETS procedure with the AUDIT and INITIATE statements. You also suspend, resume, and terminate audit trails using the DATASETS procedure. Once there is data in the audit trail file, you can read it with the TYPE= data set option.

Controlling Data in the Audit Trail

The audit trail file can contain three types of variables:

- data set variables that store copies of the columns in the audited SAS data file

- audit trail variables that automatically store information about data modifications

- user variables that store user-entered information

You can use the LOG statement to control which types of records are written to an audit trail file.

Initiating Generation Data Sets

Each generation of a generation data set is stored as part of a generation group. A new generation is created each time the data set is replaced. Each generation in a generation group has the same root member name, but each has a different version number. You initiate generation data sets by using the GENMAX= option to specify the number of generation data sets to keep.

Processing Generation Data Sets

To select a particular generation to process, you use the GENNUM= data set option. GENNUM= is an input data set option that identifies which generation to open. The GENNUM can be a relative or absolute reference to a generation within a generation group. You can rename or delete generations using the CHANGE and DELETE statements in a PROC DATASETS step.

Sample Programs

Modifying a Data Set Using the MODIFY Statement with a BY Statement or the KEY= Option

```
data capacity;
    modify capacity sasuser.newrtnum;
    by flightid;
run;

data cargo99;
    set sasuser.newcgnum (rename =
        (capcargo = newCapCargo
         cargowgt = newCargoWgt
         cargorev = newCargoRev));
    modify cargo99 key=flghtdte;
    capcargo = newcapcargo;
    cargowgt = newcargowgt;
    cargorev = newcargorev;
run;
```

Placing Integrity Constraints on Data

```
proc datasets nolist;
    modify capinfo;
    ic create PKIDInfo=primary key(routeid)
        message='You must supply a Route ID Number';
    ic create Class1=check(where=(cap1st<capbusiness
                                  or capbusiness=.))
        message='Cap1st must be less than CapBusiness';
quit;
```

Initiating an Audit Trail

```
proc datasets nolist;
```

```
    audit capinfo;
    initiate;
quit;
```

Initiating Generation Data Sets

```
proc datasets nolist;
    modify cargorev (genmax=4);
quit;
```

Points to Remember

- The MODIFY statement in a DATA step is used to make updates to a SAS data set in place. The descriptor portion of the SAS data set cannot be changed.

- Integrity constraints are enforced only when modifications are made to the data. If the data set is replaced, integrity constraints are lost.

- Audit trail files track changes made to data sets in place with the following:

  - the MODIFY statement in the DATA step

  - the UPDATE, INSERT, or DELETE statement in PROC SQL

- Generation data sets are used to track changes that are made when a data set is replaced by the following:

  - using the SET, MERGE, or UPDATE statements in the DATA step

  - sorting data in place with PROC SORT

  - using the CREATE TABLE statement in PROC SQL

Quiz

Select the best answer for each question. After completing the quiz, check your answers using the answer key in the appendix.

1. Which type of integrity constraint would you place on the variable StoreID to ensure that there are no missing values and that there are no duplicate values?

   a. UNIQUE

   b. CHECK

   c. PRIMARY KEY

   d. NOT NULL

2. Which code creates an audit trail on the SAS data set Reports.Quarter1?

   a.
   ```
   proc datasets nolist;
       audit quarter1;
       initiate;
   quit;
   ```

   b.
   ```
   proc datasets lib=reports nolist;
       audit initiate reports.quarter1;
   quit;
   ```

c. ```
proc datasets lib=reports nolist;
    initiate audit quarter1;
quit;
```

d. ```
proc datasets lib=reports nolist;
    audit quarter1;
    initiate;
quit;
```

3. Which DATA step uses the transaction data set Records.Overnight to update the master data set Records.Snowfall by accumAmt?

a. ```
data records.snowfall;
    modify records.snowfall records.overnight
    key=accumAmt;
run;
```

b. ```
data records.snowfall;
    modify records.overnight records.snowfall;
    by accumAmt;
run;
```

c. ```
data records.snowfall;
    modify records.snowfall records.overnight;
    by accumAmt;
run;
```

d. ```
data records.snowfall;
    modify records.snowfall records.overnight;
    update accumAmt;
run;
```

4. The automatic variable _IORC_ is created when you use the MODIFY statement with a BY statement or the KEY= option. How can you use the value of _IORC_?

a. to determine whether the index specified on the KEY= option is a valid index

b. to determine the number of observations that were updated in the master data set

c. to determine the status of the I/O operation

d. to determine the number of observations that could not be updated in the master data set

5. Which PROC DATASETS step creates an integrity constraint named val_age on the data set Survey to ensure that values of the variable Age are greater than or equal to 18?

a. ```
proc datasets nolist;
    modify age;
    ic create val_age=check(where=(age>=18));
quit;
```

b. ```
proc datasets nolist;
    modify Survey;
    ic create val_age=check(age>=18);
quit;
```

c. ```
proc datasets nolist;
    modify survey;
    integrity constraint
            val_age=check(where=(age>=18));
```
```

```
   quit;
```

d. ```
proc datasets nolist;
   modify survey;
   ic create val_age=check(where=(age>=18));
quit;
```

6. Which statement about using the MODIFY statement in a DATA step is true?

   a. MODIFY creates a second copy of the data while variables in the data are being matched with a WHERE clause and then deletes the second copy.

   b. You cannot modify the descriptor portion of the data set using the MODIFY statement.

   c. You can use the MODIFY statement to change the name of a variable.

   d. If the system terminates abnormally while a DATA step that is using the WHERE statement is processing, SAS automatically saves a copy of the unaltered data set.

7. Which of the following statements about audit trails is true?

   a. They create historical versions of data so that a copy of the data set is saved each time the data is replaced.

   b. They record information about changes to observations in a data set each time the data set is replaced.

   c. They record information about changes to observations in a data set each time the data is modified in place.

   d. The audit trail file has the same name as the SAS data file that it is monitoring, but has #AUDIT at the end of the data set name.

8. Which code initiates generation data sets on the existing SAS data set Sasuser.Amounts and specifies that five historical versions are saved in addition to the base version?

   a. ```
proc datasets lib=sasuser nolist;
   modify Amounts (genmax=6);
quit;
```

   b. ```
proc datasets lib=sasuser nolist;
   modify Amounts (genmax=5);
quit;
```

   c. ```
proc datasets lib=sasuser nolist;
   modify Amounts (gennum=6);
quit;
```

   d. ```
proc datasets lib=sasuser nolist;
   modify Amounts (gennum=5);
quit;
```

9. Which statement about using the KEY= option in the MODIFY statement is true?

   a. SAS locates the variables to update using the index specified in the KEY= option and then automatically overlays nonmissing transaction values as it does when you use the MODIFY or BY statements.

   b. When you use the KEY= option, you must explicitly state the update that you want to make. SAS does not automatically overlay nonmissing transaction values.

   c. The KEY= option is used to specify a variable to match for updating observations.
```

d. The index named in the KEY= option must be a simple index.

10. Which code deletes all generations of the data set Sasuser.Amounts including the base data set?

a.
```
proc datasets lib=sasuser nolist;
    delete amounts (gennum=ALL);
quit;
```

b.
```
proc datasets lib=sasuser nolist;
    delete amounts (gennum=HIST);
quit;
```

c.
```
proc datasets lib=sasuser nolist;
    delete amounts (gennum=0);
quit;
```

d.
```
proc datasets lib=sasuser nolist;
    delete amounts;
quit;
```

Part 4

Optimizing SAS Programs

Chapter 19
Introduction to Efficient SAS Programming

Overview

Introduction

As an experienced programmer, you want your SAS programs to obtain the desired results while minimizing the use of resources such as CPU time, real time, memory, and I/O. It is particularly important to optimize your SAS programs if you write or maintain production programs and work with large data sets. However, before you can select the most efficient programming technique to perform a particular task, you must carefully consider the technical environment and the resource constraints at your site. There is no single set of programming techniques that is most efficient in all situations. Instead, trade-offs in resource usage are associated with each technique.

In this chapter you learn about analyzing the requirements for efficiency at your site and about running benchmarks to select the most efficient SAS programming techniques.

Note: This chapter has no quiz.

Overview of Computing Resources

The following resources are used to run a SAS program:

Resource	Description
CPU time	the amount of time that the central processing unit (CPU) uses to perform requested tasks such as calculations, reading and writing data, conditional logic, and iterative logic.
real time	the clock time (elapsed time) it takes to execute a job or step. Real time is heavily dependent on the capacity of the system and on the load (the number of users who are sharing the system's resources).
	Because you cannot always control the capacity demand and the load demand on your system, real time is sometimes a less useful measure of program efficiency than CPU time. However, excessive use of real time often motivates programmers to improve a program's efficiency. Some procedures enable you to use threaded processing to reduce real time. Threaded processing can increase CPU time. Therefore, it is recommended that you track both CPU time and real time.
memory	the size of the work area in volatile memory that is required for holding executable program modules, data, and buffers.
data storage space	the amount of space on a disk or tape that is required for storing data. Data storage space is measured in a variety of units, some of which are used only in certain operating environments, as described below: • All operating environments use bytes, kilobytes, megabytes, gigabytes, and terabytes. • z/OS also uses blocks, tracks, and cylinders.
I/O	a measurement of the Read and Write operations that are performed as data and programs are copied from a storage device to memory (input) or from memory to a storage or display device (output).

Assessing Efficiency Needs at Your Site

The first step in making an effective decision about how to optimize your SAS programs is to assess your site's technical environment, your program or programs, and your data.

Assessing Your Technical Environment

To determine which resources are scarce or costly at your site, work with your IT department to analyze the following characteristics of your technical environment:

Category	Characteristics
hardware	• amount of available memory
	• number of CPUs
	• number and type of peripheral devices
	• communications hardware
	• network bandwidth
	• storage capacity
	• I/O bandwidth
	• capacity to upgrade
operating environment	• resource allocation
	• scheduling algorithms
	• I/O methods
system load	• number of users or jobs sharing system resources
	• network traffic (expected)
	• predicted increase in load in the future
SAS environment	• which SAS software products are installed
	• number of CPUs and amount of memory that is allocated for SAS programming
	• which methods are available for running SAS programs at your site

In most cases, one or two resources are the most limited or most expensive for your programs. You can usually decrease the amount of critical resources that are used if you are willing to sacrifice some efficiency of the resources that are less critical at your site.

Assessing Your Programs

Developing an efficient program requires time and thought. To determine whether the additional amount of resources that are saved is worth the time and effort spent to achieve the savings, consider the following characteristics of each of your programs:

Characteristics	Guidelines for Optimizing
size of the program	As the program increases in size, the potential for savings increases. Focus on improving the efficiency of *large programs*.

Characteristics	Guidelines for Optimizing
number of times the program runs	The difference in resources used by an inefficient program and an efficient program that is run once or a few times is relatively small, whereas the cumulative difference for a program that is run frequently is large. Focus on improving the efficiency of programs that are *run many times*.

Assessing Your Data

The effectiveness of any efficiency technique depends greatly on your data. When you know the characteristics of your data, you can select the techniques that take advantage of those characteristics. Consider the following characteristics of your data:

Characteristic	Guidelines for Optimizing
volume of data	As the volume of data increases, the potential for savings also increases. Focus on improving the efficiency of programs that use large data sets or many data sets.
type of data	Specific efficiency techniques might work better with some types of data (for example, data that has missing values) than with others.

Understanding Efficiency Trade-offs

As you optimize SAS programs, it is important to understand that there are trade-offs. Decreasing the use of one resource frequently increases the use of another. The following table shows examples of some common efficiency trade-offs.

Decreased Use of This Resource	Result: Possible Increased Use of This Resource
disk space	CPU time
I/O (by reading or writing more data at one time)	memory
real time (by enabling threading in SAS 9)	CPU time

As these trade-offs illustrate, there is no single best way to optimize a SAS program. It depends on your situation. However, this chapter and the following chapters provide information that can help you determine which programming techniques are most efficient in your environment.

- Chapter 20, "Controlling Memory Usage," on page 659
- Chapter 21, "Controlling Data Storage Space," on page 676
- Chapter 22, "Using Best Practices," on page 708
- Chapter 23, "Querying Data Efficiently," on page 747

Using SAS System Options to Track Resources

You can specify one or more of the SAS system options STIMER, MEMRPT, FULLSTIMER, and STATS to track and report on resource use. The availability, usage, and functionality of these options vary by operating environment, as described below:

Option	z/OS	UNIX and Windows
STIMER	Specifies that the CPU time is to be tracked throughout the SAS session. Can be set at invocation only. Is the default setting.	Specifies that CPU time and real-time statistics are to be tracked and written to the SAS log throughout the SAS session. Can be set either at invocation or by using an OPTIONS statement. Is the default setting.
MEMRPT	Specifies that memory usage statistics are to be tracked throughout the SAS session. Can be set either at invocation or by using an OPTIONS statement. Is the default setting.	Not available as a separate option; this functionality is part of the FULLSTIMER option.
FULLSTIMER	Specifies that all available resource usage statistics are to be tracked and written to the SAS log throughout the SAS session. Can be set either at invocation or by using an OPTIONS statement. In the z/OS operating environment, FULLSTIMER is an alias for the FULLSTATS option. This option is ignored unless STIMER or MEMRPT is in effect.	Specifies that all available resource usage statistics are to be tracked and written to the SAS log throughout the SAS session. Can be set either at invocation or by using an OPTIONS statement. In Windows operating environments, some statistics are not calculated accurately unless FULLSTIMER is specified at invocation.

Option	z/OS	UNIX and Windows
STATS	Tells SAS to write statistics that are tracked by any combination of the preceding options to the SAS log. Can be set either at invocation or by using an OPTIONS statement. Is the default setting.	Not available as a separate option.

SAS system options are initialized with default settings when SAS is invoked. However, the default settings for some SAS system options vary both by operating environment and by site. For details, see the SAS documentation for your operating environment.

You can turn off any of these system options by using the options below:

- NOSTIMER

- NOMEMRPT

- NOFULLSTIMER

- NOSTATS

Note: In the z/OS operating environment, NOFULLSTIMER is an alias for the NOFULLSTATS option.

Note: Guidelines for interpreting the statistics that are generated by the FULLSTIMER SAS system option are also available at support.sas.com.

Note: You can also use SAS Application Response Measurement (ARM) macros to monitor the performance of your applications. ARM macros are not covered in this course. To learn more about ARM macros, see the SAS documentation and detailed information about ARM macros at support.sas.com.

Using Benchmarks to Compare Techniques

To decide which SAS programming technique is most efficient for a particular task, you can benchmark (measure and compare) the resource usage for each technique that you are comparing. You should benchmark with the actual data to determine the most efficient technique.

Guidelines for Benchmarking

Your benchmarking is most likely to yield useful results if you follow these guidelines:

- Before you test the programming techniques, turn on the SAS system options that report resource usage.

  As explained earlier, to track and report on resource usage, you can use some or all of the system options STIMER, MEMRPT, FULLSTIMER, and STATS. The availability, usage, and functionality of these options vary by operating environment. You can also specify MSGLEVEL=I to display additional notes in the SAS log. Use the FULLSTIMER option to log a complete list of the resources that are used.

  Note: To turn on the FULLSTIMER option, use the following statement:

  ```
  options fullstimer;
  ```

- Execute the code for each programming technique in a separate SAS session.

  The first time that program code (including the DATA step, functions, formats, and SAS procedures) is referenced, the operating system might have to load the code into memory or assign virtual address space to it. The first time data is read, it is often loaded into a cache from which it can be retrieved more quickly the next time it is read. The resource usage that is required for performing these actions is overhead. Using separate SAS sessions for each technique change can minimize the effect of the overhead on your resource statistics.

- In each programming technique that you are testing, include only the SAS code that is essential for performing the task.

  If you include too many elements in the code for each technique, you do not know what caused the results. If the program that you are benchmarking is not large, you can optimize it by changing individual programming techniques, one at a time, and running the entire program after each change to measure the effect on resource usage. However, a more complex program might be easier to optimize by identifying the steps that use the most resources and extracting those steps into separate programs. You can measure the effects of different programming techniques by repeatedly changing, running, and measuring the separate programs. When isolating parts of your program, be careful to measure their resource usage under the conditions in which they are used in the complete program.

- If your system is doing other work at the same time that you are running your benchmarking tests, be sure to run the code for each programming technique several times.

  Running the code several times reduces any variability in resource consumption that is associated with other work that the system is doing. How you handle multiple measurements depends on the resource, as indicated below:

  - Use the minimum real time and CPU time measurements, because these represent most closely the amount of time your programming technique actually requires. The larger time values (especially in the case of real time) are the result of interference from other work that the computer was doing while your program ran.

  - The amount of memory should not vary from trial to trial. If memory does vary, it is possible that your program sometimes shares a resource with another program. In this situation, you must determine whether the higher or lower memory consumption is more likely to be the case when your program is used in production.

  - I/O can be an especially elusive resource to measure. With modern file systems and storage systems, the effect of your program on the I/O activity of the computer sometimes must be observed by operating system tools, file system tools, or storage system tools because it cannot be captured by your SAS session. Data is often aggressively cached by modern file systems and storage systems, and file caches are greatly affected by other activity in the file system. Be realistic when you measure I/O—it is possible to achieve good performance on a system that is not doing other work, but performance is likely to worsen when the application is deployed in a more realistic environment.

- Run your benchmarking tests under the conditions in which your final program will run.

  Results might vary under different conditions, so it is important to control the conditions under which your benchmarks are tested. For example, if batch execution and large data sets are used in your environment, you should incorporate these conditions into your benchmarking environment.

• After testing is finished, consider turning off the options that report resource usage.

The options that report resource usage are themselves consumers of resources. If it is a higher priority in your environment to minimize resource usage than to periodically check an application's resource usage, then it is most efficient to turn off these options.

Note: To turn off the FULLSTIMER option, use the following statement:

```
options nofullstimer;
```

Summary

Overview of Computing Resources

Resources that are required for running a SAS program include the following: CPU time, real time, memory, data storage space, and I/O.

Understanding Efficiency Trade-offs

It is important to understand the trade-offs that are involved in optimizing your SAS programs. Decreasing the use of one resource frequently increases the use of another. There is no single best way to optimize a SAS program; it depends on your situation.

Using SAS System Options to Track Resources

You can specify one or more of the SAS system options STIMER, MEMRPT, FULLSTIMER, and STATS to track and report on resource use. (In the z/OS environment, FULLSTIMER is an alias for FULLSTATS.) The availability, usage, and functionality of these options varies by operating environment.

Using Benchmarks to Compare Techniques

To determine which SAS programming technique is most efficient for a particular task, you can benchmark (measure and compare) the resource usage of each technique.

Chapter 20
Controlling Memory Usage

Overview

Introduction

As you have learned, there is no single set of programming techniques that is most
efficient or appropriate in all situations. However, if reducing execution time is an
important consideration in your computing environment, one way of achieving that goal
is to reduce the number of times SAS has to read from or write to the storage medium.

In this chapter you learn to use options and a statement to control the size and number of
data buffers, which in turn can affect your programs' execution times by reducing the
number of I/O operations that SAS must perform.

Controlling Page Size and the Number of Buffers

Measuring I/O

Improvement in I/O can come at the cost of increased memory consumption. In order to understand the relationship between I/O and memory, it is helpful to know when data is copied to a buffer and where I/O is measured. When you create a SAS data set using a DATA step, the following actions occur:

1. SAS copies a page of data from the input data set to a buffer in memory.

2. One observation at a time is loaded from the buffer into the program data vector.

3. Each observation is written from the PDV to an output buffer.

4. The contents of the output buffer are written to the disk when the buffer is full.

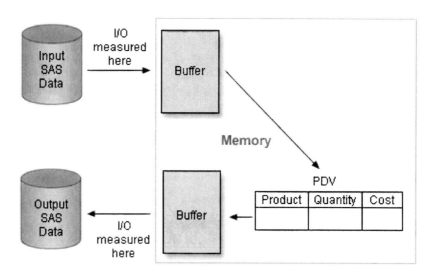

The process for reading external files is similar. However, each record is first read from the system buffer into the single-record input buffer before it is parsed and read into the program data vector.

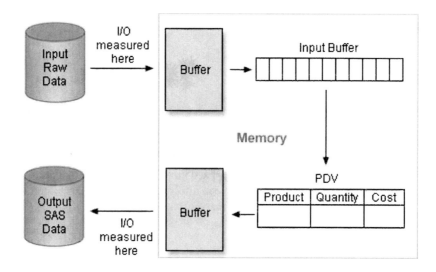

In both cases, I/O is measured when input data is copied to the buffer in memory and when it is copied from the output buffer to the output data set.

Page Size

Think of a buffer as a container in memory that holds exactly one page of data. A page is described as follows:

- It is the unit of data transfer between the storage device and memory.

- It is fixed in size when the data set is created, either to a default value or to a user-specified value.

A larger page size can reduce execution time by reducing the number of times SAS has to read from or write to the storage medium. However, the improvement in execution time comes at the cost of increased memory consumption.

Reporting Page Size

You can use the CONTENTS procedure or the CONTENTS statement in the DATASETS procedure to report the page size and the number of pages.

Partial PROC CONTENTS Output

```
proc contents
     data=company.order_fact;
run;
```

Engine/Host Dependent Information	
Data Set Page Size	8192
Number of Data Set Pages	1231
First Data Page	1
Max Obs per Page	92
Obs in First Data Page	64
Number of Data Set Repairs	0
Filename	C:\company\order_fact.sas7bdat
Release Created	9.0101M3
Host Created	XP_PRO

The total number of bytes that a data file occupies equals the page size multiplied by the number of pages. For example, the page size for Company.Order_fact is 8192 and the number of pages is 9423. Therefore, the data file occupies 77,193,216 bytes.

Note: Information that is available from PROC CONTENTS depends on the operating environment.

Note: In uncompressed data files, there is a 40-byte overhead (in a 64-bit operating environment) or a 24-byte overhead (in a 32-bit operating environment) per page plus a 1-bit per observation overhead (rounded up to the nearest byte), used to denote an observation's status as deleted or not deleted. You can learn about the structure of uncompressed and compressed data files in Chapter 21, "Controlling Data Storage Space," on page 676.

Using the BUFSIZE= Option

To select a default page size, SAS uses an algorithm that is based on observation length, engine, and operating environment. The default page size is optimal for most SAS activities, especially on computers that support multiple SAS jobs concurrently. However, in some cases, choosing a page size or buffer size that is larger than the default can speed up execution time by reducing the number of times that SAS must read from or write to the storage medium.

You can use the BUFSIZE= system option or data set option to control the page size of an output SAS data set. The new buffer size is a permanent attribute of the data set. After it is specified, it is used whenever the data set is processed.

General form, BUFSIZE= option:

BUFSIZE= MIN | MAX | *n*;

Here is an explanation of the syntax:

MIN

    sets the page size to the smallest possible number in your operating environment.

MAX

    sets the page size to the maximum possible number in your operating environment.

n

    specifies the page size in bytes. For example, a value of 8 specifies a page size of 8 bytes, and a value of 4K specifies a page size of 4096 bytes. The default is 0, which causes SAS to use the optimal page size for the operating environment.

CAUTION:

    MIN might cause unexpected results and should be avoided. Use BUFSIZE=0 to reset the buffer page size to the default value in your operating environment.

Note: The syntax that is shown here applies to the OPTIONS statement. On the command line or in a configuration file, the syntax is specific to your operating environment. For details, see the SAS documentation for your operating environment.

Only certain page size or buffer size values are valid for each operating environment. If you request an invalid value for your operating environment, SAS automatically rounds up to the next valid page size or buffer size. BUFSIZE=0 is interpreted as a request for the default page size or buffer size.

In the following program, the BUFSIZE= system option specifies a page size of 30720 bytes.

```
options bufsize=30720;
filename orders 'c:\orders.dat';
data company.orders_fact;
   infile orders;
   <more SAS code>
run;
```

Before you change the default page size, it is important to consider the access pattern for the data as well as the I/O transfer rate of the underlying hardware. In some cases, increasing the page size might degrade performance, particularly when the data is processed using direct (random) access.

Note: The default value for BUFSIZE= is determined by your operating environment and is set to optimize sequential access. To improve performance for direct access, you should change the value for BUFSIZE=. For the default setting and possible settings for direct access, see the BUFSIZE= system option in the SAS documentation for your operating environment.

Note: You can override the BUFSIZE= system option by using the BUFSIZE= data set option.

CAUTION:

If you use the COPY procedure to copy a data set to a library that is accessed via a different engine, the original page size or buffer size is not necessarily retained.

Using the BUFNO= Option

You can use the BUFNO= system or data set option to control the number of buffers that are available for reading or writing a SAS data set. By increasing the number of buffers, you can control how many pages of data are loaded into memory with each I/O transfer.

Note: Increasing the number of buffers might not affect performance under the Windows and UNIX operating environments, especially when you work with large data sets. By default, the Windows and UNIX operating environments read one buffer at a time. Under the windowing environment, you can override this default by turning on the SGIO system option when you invoke SAS. For details about the SGIO system option, see the SAS documentation for the Windows operating environment.

The following techniques might help minimize I/O consumption:

• When you work with a small data set, allocate as many buffers as there are pages in the data set so that the entire data set can be loaded into memory. This technique is most effective if you read the same observations several times during processing.

• Under the z/OS operating environment, increase the number of buffers that are allocated, rather than the size of each buffer, as the size of the data set increases.

General form, BUFNO= option:

BUFNO= MIN | MAX |*n*;

Here is an explanation of the syntax:

MIN
    causes SAS to use the minimum optimal value for the operating environment. This is the default.

MAX
    sets the number of buffers to the maximum possible number in your operating environment, up to the largest four-byte, signed integer, which is 2^{31}-1, or approximately 2 billion.

n
    specifies the number of buffers to be allocated.

Note: The recommended maximum for this option is 10.

Note: The syntax that is shown here applies to the OPTIONS statement. On the command line or in a configuration file, the syntax is specific to your operating environment. For details, see the SAS documentation for your operating environment.

In the following program, the BUFNO= system option specifies that 4 buffers are available.

```
options bufno=4;
filename orders 'c:\orders.dat';
data company.orders_fact;
   infile orders;
```

```
    <more SAS code>
run;
proc print data=company.orders_fact;
run;
```

The buffer number is not a permanent attribute of the data set and is valid only for the current step or SAS session.

Figure 20.1 *Current SAS Session*

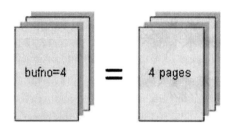

Note: You can override the BUFNO= system option by using the BUFNO= data set option.

Note: In SAS 9 and later, the BUFNO= option has no effect on thread-enabled procedures under the z/OS operating environment.

The product of BUFNO= and BUFSIZE=, rather than the specific value of either option, determines how much data can be transferred in one I/O operation. Increasing the value of either option increases the amount of data that can be transferred in one I/O operation.

BUFSIZE	BUFNO	Bytes Transferred in One I/O Operation
6144	2	12,288
6144	10	61,440
30,720	2	61,440
30,720	10	307,200

The number of buffers and the buffer size have a minimal effect on CPU usage.

Comparative Example: Using the BUFSIZE= Option and the BUFNO= Option

Settings for the Examples

Suppose you want to compare the resource usage when a data set is read using different buffer sizes and a varying number of buffers. The following sample programs compare settings for the BUFNO= option and the BUFSIZE= option.

You can use these samples as models for creating benchmark programs in your own environment. Your results might vary depending on the structure of your data, your operating environment, and the resources that are available at your site.

Note: 6144 bytes is the default page size under the z/OS operating environment.

Programming Techniques

❶ `BUFSIZE=6144, BUFNO=2`

This program reads the data set Retail.Order_fact and creates the data set Work.Orders. The BUFSIZE= option specifies that Work.Orders is created with a buffer size of 6144 bytes. The BUFNO= option specifies that 2 pages of data are loaded into memory with each I/O transfer.

```
data work.orders (bufsize=6144 bufno=2);
   set retail.order_fact;
run;
```

❷ `BUFSIZE=6144, BUFNO=5`

This program reads the data set Retail.Order_fact and creates the data set Work.Orders. The BUFSIZE= option specifies that Work.Orders is created with a buffer size of 6144 bytes. The BUFNO= option specifies that 5 pages of data are loaded into memory with each I/O transfer.

```
data work.orders (bufsize=6144 bufno=5);
   set retail.order_fact;
run;
```

❸ `BUFSIZE=6144, BUFNO=10`

This program reads the data set Retail.Order_fact and creates the data set Work.Orders. The BUFSIZE= option specifies that Work.Orders is created with a buffer size of 6144 bytes. The BUFNO= option specifies that 10 pages of data are loaded into memory with each I/O transfer.

```
data work.orders (bufsize=6144 bufno=10);
   set retail.order_fact;
run;
```

❹ `BUFSIZE=12288, BUFNO=2`

This program reads the data set Retail.Order_fact and creates the data set Work.Orders. The BUFSIZE= option specifies that Work.Orders is created with a buffer size of 12288 bytes. The BUFNO= option specifies that 2 pages of data are loaded into memory with each I/O transfer.

```
data work.orders (bufsize=12288 bufno=2);
   set retail.order_fact;
run;
```

❺ `BUFSIZE=12288, BUFNO=5`

This program reads the data set Retail.Order_fact and creates the data set Work.Orders. The BUFSIZE= option specifies that Work.Orders is created with a buffer size of 12288 bytes. The BUFNO= option specifies that 5 pages of data are loaded into memory with each I/O transfer.

```
data work.orders (bufsize=12288 bufno=5);
   set retail.order_fact;
run;
```

❻ `BUFSIZE=12288, BUFNO=10`

This program reads the data set Retail.Order_fact and creates the data set Work.Orders. The BUFSIZE= option specifies that Work.Orders is created with a buffer size of 12288 bytes. The BUFNO= option specifies that 10 pages of data are loaded into memory with each I/O transfer.

```
data work.orders (bufsize=12288 bufno=10);
   set retail.order_fact;
run;
```

Using the SASFILE Statement

Overview

Another way of improving performance is to use the SASFILE statement to hold a SAS data file in memory so that the data is available to multiple program steps. Keeping the data file open reduces I/O processing and open/close operations, including the allocation and freeing of memory for buffers.

General form, SASFILE statement:

SASFILE *SAS-data-file* <*(password-option(s))*> **OPEN | LOAD | CLOSE;**

Here is an explanation of the syntax:

SAS-data-file
   is a valid SAS data file (a SAS data set with the member type DATA).

password-option(s)
   specifies one or more password options.

OPEN
   opens the file and allocates the buffers, but defers reading the data into memory until a procedure or statement is executed.

LOAD
   opens the file, allocates the buffers, and reads the data into memory.

CLOSE
   closes the file and frees the buffers.

The SASFILE statement opens a SAS data file and allocates enough buffers to hold the entire file in memory. Once the data file is read, the data is held in memory, and it is available to subsequent DATA and PROC steps or applications until either of the following occurs:

- a SASFILE CLOSE statement frees the buffers and closes the file

- the SAS session ends, which automatically frees the buffers and closes the file

In the following program, the first SASFILE statement opens the SAS data file Company.Sales, allocates the buffers, and reads the data into memory.

```
sasfile company.sales load;
proc print data=company.sales;
   var Customer_Age_Group;
run;
proc tabulate data=company.sales;
   class Customer_Age_Group;
   var Customer_BirthDate;
   table Customer_Age_Group,Customer_BirthDate*(mean median);
run;
sasfile company.sales close;
```

Note: The SASFILE statement can also be used to reduce CPU time and I/O in SAS programs that repeatedly read one or more SAS data views. Use a DATA step to create a SAS data file in the Work library that contains the view's result set. Then use the SASFILE statement to load that data file into memory.

Note: Although a file that is opened with the SASFILE statement can be used for subsequent input or update processing, it cannot be used for subsequent utility or output processing. For example, you cannot replace the file or rename its variables.

Guidelines for Using the SASFILE Statement

When the SASFILE statement executes, SAS allocates the number of buffers based on the number of pages for the data file and index file. If the file in memory increases in size during processing because of changes or additions to the data, the number of buffers also increases.

It is important to note that I/O processing is reduced only if there is sufficient real memory. If there is not sufficient real memory, the operating environment might use the following:

- virtual memory

- the default number of buffers

If SAS uses virtual memory, there might be a degradation in performance.

If you need to repeatedly process part of a SAS data file and the entire file does not fit into memory, use a DATA step with the SASFILE statement to create a subset of the file that does fit into memory. Then process that subset repeatedly. This action saves CPU time in the processing steps because those steps read a smaller file, in addition to the benefit of the file being resident in memory.

Note: When using a SASFILE statement, monitor the paging activity (the I/O activity that is done by the virtual memory management subsystem of your operating environment) while your program runs. If the paging activity increases substantially, consider keeping less data in memory.

Comparative Example: Using the SASFILE Statement

Using Different Data File Sizes

Suppose you want to create multiple reports from SAS data files that vary in size. Using small, medium, and large data files, you can compare the resource usage when the PRINT, TABULATE, MEANS, and FREQ procedures are used with and without the SASFILE statement to create reports.

Name of Data File	Number of Rows	Page Size	Number of Pages	Number of Bytes
Retail.Small	45,876	24,576	540	13,279,232
Retail.Medium	458,765	24,576	5,398	132,669,440
Retail.Large	4,587,654	24,576	53,973	1,326,448,640

The following sample programs compare six techniques for using data file sizes. You can use these samples as models for creating benchmark programs in your own environment. Your results might vary depending on the structure of your data, your operating environment, and the resources that are available at your site.

Programming Techniques

 Small Data File without the SASFILE Statement

This program creates reports using the PRINT, TABULATE, MEANS, and FREQ procedures. The SAS data file *Retail.Small* is opened and closed with each procedure.

```
proc print data=retail.small;
   where cs=100;
   var Customer_Age_Group;
run;
proc tabulate data=retail.small;
   class Customer_Age_Group;
   var Customer_BirthDate;
   table Customer_Age_Group,Customer_BirthDate*(mean median);
run;
proc means data=retail.small;
   var Customer_Age;
   class Customer_Group;
   output out=summary sum=;
run;
proc freq data=retail.small;
   tables Customer_Country;
run;
```

❷ Medium Data File without the SASFILE Statement

This program creates reports using the PRINT, TABULATE, MEANS, and FREQ procedures. The SAS data file Retail.Medium is opened and closed with each procedure.

```
proc print data=retail.medium;
   where cm=100;
   var Customer_Age_Group;
run;
proc tabulate data=retail.medium;
   class Customer_Age_Group;
   var Customer_BirthDate;
   table Customer_Age_Group,Customer_BirthDate*(mean median);
run;
proc means data=retail.medium;
   var Customer_Age;
   class Customer_Group;
   output out=summary sum=;
run;
proc freq data=retail.medium;
   tables Customer_Country;
run;
```

❸ Large Data File without the SASFILE Statement

This program creates reports using the PRINT, TABULATE, MEANS, and FREQ procedures. The SAS data file Retail.Large is opened and closed with each procedure.

```
proc print data=retail.large;
   where cl=100;
   var Customer_Age_Group;
run;
proc tabulate data=retail.large;
   class Customer_Age_Group;
   var Customer_BirthDate;
   table Customer_Age_Group,Customer_BirthDate*(mean median);
run;
proc means data=retail.large;
   var Customer_Age;
   class Customer_Group;
   output out=summary sum=;
run;
proc freq data=retail.large;
   tables Customer_Country;
run;
```

❹ Small Data File with the SASFILE Statement

In this program, the SASFILE LOAD statement opens the SAS data file Retail.Small and loads the entire file into memory. The data is then available to the PRINT, TABULATE, MEANS, and FREQ procedures. The SASFILE CLOSE statement closes Retail.Small and frees the buffers.

```
sasfile retail.small load;
proc print data=retail.small;
   where cs=100;
   var Customer_Age_Group;
run;
proc tabulate data=retail.small;
   class Customer_Age_Group;
   var Customer_BirthDate;
   table Customer_Age_Group,Customer_BirthDate*(mean median);
run;
proc means data=retail.small;
   var Customer_Age;
   class Customer_Group;
   output out=summary sum=;
run;
proc freq data=retail.small;
   tables Customer_Country;
run;
sasfile retail.small close;
```

❺ Medium Data File with the SASFILE Statement

In this program, the SASFILE LOAD statement opens the SAS data file Retail.Medium and loads the entire file into memory. The data is then available to the PRINT, TABULATE, MEANS, and FREQ procedures. The SASFILE CLOSE statement closes Retail.Medium and frees the buffers.

```
sasfile retail.medium load;
proc print data=retail.medium;
   where cm=100;
   var Customer_Age_Group;
run;
proc tabulate data=retail.medium;
   class Customer_Age_Group;
   var Customer_BirthDate;
   table Customer_Age_Group,Customer_BirthDate*(mean median);
run;
proc means data=retail.medium;
   var Customer_Age;
   class Customer_Group;
   output out=summary sum=;
run;
proc freq data=retail.medium;
   tables Customer_Country;
run;
sasfile retail.medium close;
```

❻ Large Data File with the SASFILE Statement

In this program, the SASFILE LOAD statement opens the SAS data file Retail.Large and loads the entire file into memory. The data is then available to the PRINT, TABULATE, MEANS, and FREQ procedures. The SASFILE CLOSE statement closes Retail.Large and frees the buffers.

```
sasfile retail.large load;
proc print data=retail.large;
   where cl=100;
   var Customer_Age_Group;
run;
proc tabulate data=retail.large;
   class Customer_Age_Group;
   var Customer_BirthDate;
   table Customer_Age_Group,Customer_BirthDate*(mean median);
run;
proc means data=retail.large;
   var Customer_Age;
   class Customer_Group;
   output out=summary sum=;
run;
proc freq data=retail.large;
   tables Customer_Country;
run;
sasfile retail.large close;
```

General Recommendations

- If you need to repeatedly process a SAS data file that fits entirely in memory, use the SASFILE statement to reduce I/O and some CPU usage.

- If you use the SASFILE statement and the SAS data file does not fit entirely in memory, the code executes, but there might be a degradation in performance.

- If you need to repeatedly process part of a SAS data file and the entire file does not fit into memory, use a DATA step with the SASFILE statement to create a subset of the file that does fit into memory. Then process that subset repeatedly. This action saves CPU time in the processing steps because those steps read a smaller file, in addition to the benefit of the file being resident in memory.

Additional Features

Using the IBUFSIZE= System Option

Beginning with SAS 9, you can use the IBUFSIZE= system option to specify the page size for an index file. Typically, you do not need to specify an index page size. However, you might need to use the IBUFSIZE= option if you have the following:

- your application is experiencing a lot of I/O in the index file
- the length of an index value is very large

The main resource that is saved when reducing levels in the index is I/O. If your application is experiencing a lot of I/O in the index file, increasing the page size might help. However, you must re-create the index file after increasing the page size. The number of pages that are required for the index varies with the page size, the length of the index value, and the values themselves.

General form, IBUFSIZE= system option:

IBUFSIZE= MAX | *n*;

Here is an explanation of the syntax:

MAX
> sets the page size for an index file to the maximum possible number. For IBUFSIZE=, the maximum value is 32,767 bytes.

n
> specifies the page size in bytes.

CAUTION:
   The MIN setting should be avoided.

When an index is used to process a request, such as for WHERE processing, SAS searches the index file in order to rapidly locate the requested record or records. The page size affects the number of levels in the index. The more pages there are, the more levels in the index. The more levels, the longer the index search takes. Increasing the page size allows more index values to be stored on each page, thus reducing the number of pages (and the number of levels).

Use IBUFSIZE=0 to reset the index page size to the default value in your operating environment.

Note: For details about using the IBUFSIZE= system option, see the SAS documentation.

Summary

Controlling Page Size and the Number of Buffers

When you read a SAS data set or an external file, I/O is measured when input data is copied to the buffer in memory and when it is copied from the output buffer to the output data set.

A page is the unit of data transfer between the storage device and memory.

Increasing the page size can speed up execution time by reducing the number of times SAS has to read from or write to the storage medium. You can use the CONTENTS procedure to report the page size and the number of pages.

You can use the BUFSIZE= system option or data set option to control the page size of an output SAS data set. The new buffer size is permanent. After it is specified, it is used whenever the data set is processed.

You can use the BUFNO= system or data set option to control how many buffers are available for reading or writing a SAS data set. By increasing the number of buffers, you can control how many pages of data are loaded into memory with each I/O transfer.

The product of BUFNO= and BUFSIZE=, rather than the specific value of either option, determines how much data can be transferred in one I/O operation. Increasing either option increases the amount of data that can be transferred in one I/O operation. However, the improvement in I/O comes at the cost of increased memory consumption.

Using the SASFILE Statement

Another way to improve performance is to use the SASFILE statement to hold a SAS data file in memory so that the data is available to multiple program steps. Keeping the data set open reduces I/O processing and open/close operations, including the allocation and freeing of memory for buffers.

When the SASFILE statement executes, SAS allocates the number of buffers based on the number of pages for the data file and index file. If the file in memory increases in size during processing because of changes or additions to the data, the number of buffers also increases.

I/O processing is reduced only if there is sufficient real memory. If SAS uses virtual memory, there can be a degradation in performance.

Additional Features

The IBUFSIZE= system option specifies the page size for an index file. Typically, you do not need to specify an index page size. However, you might need to use the IBUFSIZE= option if the following apply:

- your application is experiencing a lot of I/O in the index file

- the length of an index value is very large

The main resource that is saved when reducing levels in the index is I/O. If your application is experiencing a lot of I/O in the index file, increasing the page size might help. However, you must re-create the index file after increasing the page size. The number of pages that are required for the index varies with the page size, the length of the index value, and the values themselves.

Quiz

Select the best answer for each question. After completing the quiz, check your answers using the answer key in the appendix.

1. Which of the following statements is true regarding the BUFNO= option?

   a. The BUFNO= option specifies the size of each buffer that is used for reading or writing a SAS data set.

   b. The BUFNO= option can improve execution time by limiting the number of input/output operations that are required.

   c. Using the BUFNO= option results in permanent changes to the data set.

   d. Using the BUFNO= option to increase the number of buffers results in decreased memory consumption.

2. Which of the following statements is not true regarding a page?

   a. A page is the unit of data transfer between the storage device and memory.

   b. A page includes the number of bytes that are used by the descriptor portion, the data values, and the overhead.

   c. The size of a page is analogous to buffer size.

   d. The size of a page can be changed at any time.

3. The total number of bytes occupied by a data set equals which of the following?

   a. the page size multiplied by the number of pages.

   b. the page size multiplied by the number of observations.

   c. the sum of the page size and the number of pages.

   d. the number of pages multiplied by the number of variables.

4. Which statement opens the file Work.Quarter1, allocates enough buffers to hold the entire file in memory, and reads the data into memory?

   a. `sasfile work.quarter1 open;`

   b. `sasfile work.quarter1 load;`

   c. `sasfile work.quarter1 bufno=max;`

   d. `sasfile work.quarter1 bufsize=max;`

5. Which of the following statements is true regarding a file that is opened with the SASFILE statement?

   a. The file is available to subsequent DATA and PROC steps or applications until a SASFILE CLOSE statement is executed or until the program ends.

   b. The file is available to subsequent DATA and PROC steps or applications until a SASFILE END statement is executed.

   c. The file is available for subsequent utility or output processing until the program ends.

d. If the file increases in size during processing, the number of buffers remains the same.

Chapter 21
Controlling Data Storage Space

Overview

Introduction

In many computing environments, data storage space is a limited resource. Therefore, it might be more important for you to conserve data storage space than to conserve other resources.

When you store your data in a SAS data file, you use the sum of the data storage space that is required for the following:

- the descriptor portion

- the observations (data portion)

- any storage overhead

- any associated indexes.

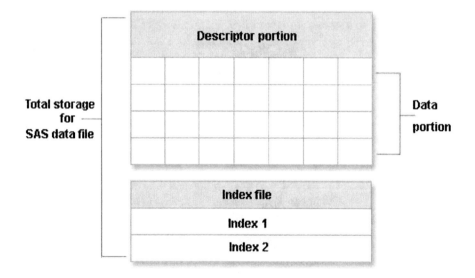

In this chapter you learn to use a variety of techniques for minimizing the amount of space that your SAS data files occupy.

Reducing Data Storage Space for Character Variables

One way to reduce data storage space, which also reduces I/O, is to reduce the length of character variables, potentially eliminating wasted space. Before discussing how to reduce the length of a character variable, consider how SAS assigns lengths to character variables.

Reducing the Length of Character Data with the LENGTH Statement

You can use a LENGTH statement to control the length of character variables.

General form, LENGTH statement for character variables:

LENGTH *variable(s)* **$** *length*;

Here is an explanation of the syntax:

variable(s)
    specifies the name of one or more SAS variables, separated by spaces.

length
    is an integer from 1 to 32,767 that specifies the length of the variable(s).

Note: Make sure the LENGTH statement appears before any other reference to the variable in the DATA step. If the variable has been created by another statement, then a later use of the LENGTH statement does not change its length.

Reducing Data Storage Space for Numeric Variables

Another way to reduce data storage space is to reduce the length of numeric variables. In addition to conserving data storage space, reduced-length numeric variables use less I/O, both when data is written and when it is read. For a file that is read frequently, this savings can be significant. However, in order to safely reduce the length of numeric variables, you need to understand how SAS stores numeric data.

How SAS Stores Numeric Variables

To store numbers of large magnitude and to perform computations that require many digits of precision to the right of the decimal point, SAS stores all numeric values using double-precision floating-point representation. SAS numeric variables have a maximum length of 8 bytes and a minimum length of 2 or 3 bytes, depending on your operating environment. The default length is 8 bytes. Multiple digits are stored per byte.

Floating-point representation is an implementation of scientific notation. For example, the number 234 might be written as .234*10**3 with a base of 10. In this example, .234 is referred to as the mantissa, 10 is the base, and 3 is the exponent. The figures below show how SAS stores a numeric value in 8 bytes. Mainframe environments use base 16.

The first bit stores the sign, the next seven bits store the exponent, and the remaining 56 bits store the mantissa.

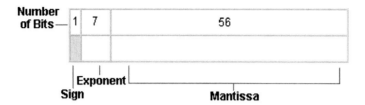

Non-mainframe environments use base 2. The first bit stores the sign, the next 11 bits store the exponent, and the remaining 52 bits store the mantissa.

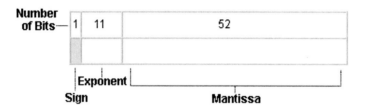

Note: The minimum length for a numeric variable is 2 bytes in mainframe environments and 3 bytes in non-mainframe environments.

Now that you have seen how SAS stores numeric variables, consider how you can assign a length to your numeric variables that is less than the default length of 8 bytes.

Assigning Lengths to Numeric Variables

You can use a LENGTH statement to assign a length from 2 to 8 bytes to numeric variables. Remember, the minimum length of numeric variables depends on the operating environment. Also, keep in mind that the LENGTH statement affects the length of a numeric variable only in the output data set. Numeric variables always have a length of 8 bytes in the program data vector and during processing.

General form, LENGTH statement for numeric variables:

LENGTH *variable(s) length* <DEFAULT=*n*>;

Here is an explanation of the syntax:

variable(s)
  specifies the name of one or more numeric SAS variables, separated by spaces.

length
  is an integer that specifies the length of the variable(s).

DEFAULT=*n*
  this optional argument changes the default number of bytes that SAS uses to store any newly created numeric variables. If you use the DEFAULT= argument, you do not need to list any variables.

DEFAULT= applies only to numeric variables that are created after the LENGTH statement. List specific variables, and their lengths, along with the DEFAULT= argument, if you want the listed variables to receive a specified length. Then the non-listed variables receive the DEFAULT= length.

CAUTION:

Numeric values lose precision if truncated. You learn more about the loss of precision with reduced-length numeric variables in the next section of this chapter.

Example

The following program assigns a length of 4 to the new variable Sale_Percent in the data set ReducedSales. The LENGTH statement in this DATA step does not apply to the variables that are read from the Sales data set; those variables maintain whatever length they had in Sales when they are read into ReducedSales.

```
data reducedsales;
   length default=4;
   set sales;
   Sale_Percent=15;
run;
```

Maintaining Precision in Reduced-Length Numeric Variables

There is a limit to the values that you can precisely store in a reduced-length numeric variable. You have learned that reducing the number of bytes that are used for storing a numeric variable does not affect how the numbers are stored in the program data vector. Instead, specifying a value of less than 8 in the LENGTH statement causes the number to be truncated to the specified length when the value is written to the SAS data set.

You should never use the LENGTH statement to reduce the length of your numeric variables if the values are not integers. Fractional numbers lose precision if truncated. Even if the values are integers, you should keep in mind that reducing the length of a numeric variable limits the integer values that can accurately be stored as a value.

The following table lists the possible storage length for integer values on UNIX or Windows operating environments.

Table 21.1 *UNIX or Windows*

Length (bytes)	Largest Integer Represented Exactly
3	8,192
4	2,097,152
5	536,870,912
6	137,438,953,472
7	35,184,372,088,832
8	9,007,199,254,740,992

The following table lists the possible storage length for integer values on the z/OS operating environment.

Table 21.2 *z/OS*

Length (bytes)	Largest Integer Represented Exactly
2	256
3	65,536
4	16,777,216
5	4,294,967,296
6	1,099,511,627,776
7	281,474,946,710,656
8	72,057,594,037,927,936

Suppose you store an integer that is equal to or less than the number listed above as the largest integer that can be represented exactly in a reduced-length variable. In such a case, SAS truncates bytes that contain only zeros. If the integer that is stored in a reduced-length variable is larger than the recommended limit, SAS truncates bytes that contain numbers other than zero, and the integer value is changed. Similarly, you should not reduce the stored size of non-integer data because it can result in a loss of precision due to the truncation of nonzero bytes.

If you decide to reduce the length of your numeric variables, you might want to verify that you have not lost any precision in your values. Here is one way to do this action.

Using PROC COMPARE

You can use PROC COMPARE to gauge the precision of the values that are stored in a shortened numeric variable. You do this by comparing the original variable with the shortened variable. The COMPARE procedure compares the contents of two SAS data sets, selected variables in different data sets, or variables within the same data set.

General form, PROC COMPARE step to compare two data sets:

PROC COMPARE BASE=*SAS-data-set-one*

                    COMPARE=*SAS-data-set-two*;

RUN;

Here is an explanation of the syntax:

SAS-data-set-one and *SAS-data-set-two*
    specifies the two SAS data sets that you want to compare.

PROC COMPARE is a good technique to use for gauging the loss of precision in shortened numeric variables because it shows you whether there are differences in the stored numeric values even if these differences do not appear once the numeric variables have been formatted. PROC COMPARE looks at the two data sets and compares the following:

• data set attributes

- variable attributes for matching variables
- observations
- values in matching variables

Output from the COMPARE procedure includes the following information:

- a data set summary
- a variables summary
- a listing of common variables that have different attributes
- an observation summary
- a values comparison summary
- a listing of variables that have unequal values
- a detailed list of value comparison results for variables

Example

The data set Company.Discount contains data about sale dates and discounts for certain retail products. There are 35 observations in Company.Discount, which is described below.

Variable	Type	Length	Description
Product_ID	num	8	product ID number
Start_Date	num	4	start date of sale
End_Date	num	5	end date of sale
Unit_Sales_Price	num	8	discounted sales price per unit
Discount	num	8	discount as percent of normal sales price

Suppose you shorten the length of the numeric variable Discount. The DATA step below creates a new data set named Company.Discount_Short, whose only difference from Company.Discount is that the length of the variable Discount is 4 instead of 8.

```
data company.discount_short;
   length Discount 4;
   set Company.Discount;
run;
```

You can use PROC COMPARE to evaluate whether shortening the length of Discount affects the precision of its values by comparing Company.Discount to Company.Discount_Short.

```
proc compare base=company.discount
             compare=company.discount_short;
run;
```

If you were to print these two data sets (Company.Discount and Company.Discount_Short), the values might appear to be identical. However, there are differences in the values as they are stored, but those differences are not apparent in the formatted output.

In the partial output below, you can see that shortening the length of Discount results in a loss of precision in its values; the values for Discount in Company.Discount_Short differ by a maximum of 1.9073E-07. The value comparison results show that although the values for Discount in the first five observations appear as 70% in both data sets, the precise (unformatted) values differ by $-1.907E-7$.

Figure 21.1 *Partial PROC COMPARE Output*

```
                      Variables Summary

      Number of Variables in Common: 5.
      Number of Variables with Differing Attributes: 1.


      Listing of Common Variables with Differing Attributes

      Variable  Dataset                    Type  Length  Format

      Discount  COMPANY.DISCOUNT            Num        8  PERCENT.
                COMPANY.DISCOUNT_SHORT      Num        4  PERCENT.
```

```
                   Values Comparison Summary

      Number of Variables Compared with All Observations Equal: 4.
      Number of Variables Compared with Some Observations Unequal: 1.
      Total Number of Values which Compare Unequal: 35.
      Maximum Difference: 1.9073E-07.
```

```
              Value Comparison Results for Variables

              ||  Discount as Percent of Normal Retail Sal
              ||  .. es Price
              ||      Base    Compare
              ||  Discount   Discount     Diff.      % Diff
      Obs     ||

        1     ||      70%        70%    -1.907E-7   -0.000027
        2     ||      70%        70%    -1.907E-7   -0.000027
        3     ||      70%        70%    -1.907E-7   -0.000027
        4     ||      70%        70%    -1.907E-7   -0.000027
        5     ||      70%        70%    -1.907E-7   -0.000027
```

Comparative Example: Creating a SAS Data Set That Contains Reduced-Length Numeric Variables

Default versus Reduced-Length Numeric Variables

Suppose you want to create a SAS data set to store retail data about a group of orders. Suppose that the data that you want to include in your data set is all numeric data and that it is currently stored in a raw data file.

The following sample programs compare two techniques. You can use these samples as models for creating benchmark programs in your own environment. Your results might vary depending on the structure of your data, your operating environment, and the resources that are available at your site.

Note: Throughout this book, the keyword _NULL_ is often used in place of the data set name in sample programs. Using _NULL_ suppresses the creation of an output data set. Using _NULL_ when benchmarking enables you to determine what resources are used to read a SAS data set.

Programming Techniques

 Default-Length Numeric Variables

This program reads the external data file that is referenced by the fileref Flat1 and creates a new data set called Retail.Longnums that contains 12 numeric variables. Each of the variables in Retail.Longnums has the default storage length of 8 bytes. The second DATA step in this program reads the numeric variables from Retail.Longnums.

```
data retail.longnums;
   infile flat1;
   input   Customer_ID          12.
           Employee_ID          12.
           Street_ID            12.
           Order_Date           date9.
           Delivery_Date        date9.
           Order_ID             12.
           Order_Type           comma16.
           Product_ID           12.
           Quantity             4.
           Total_Retail_Price   dollar13.2
           CostPrice_Per_Unit   dollar13.2
           Discount             5.          ;
run;

data _null_;
   set retail.longnums;
run;
```

❷ Reduced-Length Numeric Variables

This program reads the external data file that is referenced by the fileref Flat1 and creates a new SAS data set called Retail.Shortnums that contains 12 numeric variables. A LENGTH statement is used to reduce the storage length of most of the numeric variables in Retail.Shortnums, as follows:

- Total_Retail_Price and CostPrice_Per_Unit have a storage length of 8 bytes.

- Product_ID has a storage length of 7 bytes.

- Street_ID and Order_ID have a storage length of 6 bytes.

- Employee_ID has a storage length of 5 bytes.

- Customer_ID, Order_Date, Delivery_Date, and Discount have a storage length of 4 bytes.

- Order_Type and Quantity have a storage length of 3 bytes.

The second DATA step reads the reduced-length numeric variables from Retail.Shortnums.

```
data retail.shortnums;
   infile flat1;
          length Quantity  Order_Type    3
          Customer_ID  Order_Date
          Delivery_Date  Discount        4
          Employee_ID                    5
          Street_ID  Order_ID            6
          Product_ID                     7
          Total_Retail_Price
          CostPrice_Per_Unit             8;
   input  Customer_ID         12.
          Employee_ID         12.
          Street_ID           12.
          Order_Date          date9.
          Delivery_Date       date9.
          Order_ID            12.
          Order_Type          comma16.
          Product_ID          12.
          Quantity            4.
          Total_Retail_Price  dollar13.2
          CostPrice_Per_Unit  dollar13.2
          Discount            5.        ;
run;

data _null_;
   set retail.shortnums;
run;
```

Note: Remember that when you reduce the storage length of numeric variables, you risk losing precision in their values. You can use PROC COMPARE to verify the precision of shortened numeric variables.

```
proc compare base=retail.longnums;
             compare=retail.shortnums;
   run;
```

Compressing Data Files

Overview

By default, a SAS data file is uncompressed. You can compress your data files in order to conserve disk space, although some files are not good candidates for compression. The file structure of a compressed data file is different from the structure of an uncompressed file. You use the COMPRESS= data set option or system option to compress a data file. You use the POINTOBS= data set option to enable SAS to access observations in compressed files directly rather than sequentially. You use the REUSE= data set option or system option to specify that SAS should reuse space in a compressed file when observations are added or updated.

Review of Uncompressed Data File Structure

By default, a SAS data file is not compressed. In uncompressed data files, the following statements are true:

- Each data value of a particular variable occupies the same number of bytes as any other data value of that variable.

- Each observation occupies the same number of bytes as any other observation.

- Character values are padded with blanks.

- Numeric values are padded with binary zeros.

- There is a 1-bit per observation overhead (rounded up to the nearest byte) at the end of each page; this bit denotes an observation's status as deleted or not deleted.

- New observations are added at the end of the file. If a new observation does not fit on the current last page of the file, a whole new data set page is added.

- The descriptor portion of the data file is stored at the end of the first page of the file.

The figure below depicts the structure of an uncompressed data file.

Note: In a 64–bit operating environment, each page has a 40–byte overhead. In a 32–bit operating environment, each page has a 24–byte overhead.

In comparison, look at the characteristics of a compressed data file.

Compressed Data File Structure

In compressed data files, the following statements are true:

- An observation is treated as a single string of bytes by ignoring variable types and boundaries.

- Consecutive repeating characters and numbers are collapsed into fewer bytes.

- There is a 24-byte overhead at the beginning of each page in a 32–bit operating environment or 40–byte overhead in a 64–bit operating environment.

- There is a 12-byte- or 24-byte-per-observation overhead following the page overhead. This space is used for deletion status, compressed length, pointers, and flags.

Each observation in a compressed data file can have a different length, which means that some pages in the data file can store more observations than others can. When an updated observation is larger than its original size, it is stored on the same data file page and uses available space. If not enough space is available on the original page, the observation is stored on the next page that has enough space, and a pointer is stored on the original page.

The figure below depicts the structure of a compressed data file.

Deciding Whether to Compress a Data File

Not all data files are good candidates for compression. Remember that in order for SAS to read a compressed file, each observation must be uncompressed. This requires more CPU resources than reading an uncompressed file. However, compression can be beneficial when the data file has one or more of the following properties:

- It is large.

- It contains many long character values.

- It contains many values that have repeated characters or binary zeros.

- It contains many missing values.

- It contains repeated values in variables that are physically stored next to one another.

In character data, the most frequently encountered repeated value is the blank. Long text fields, such as comments and addresses, often contain repeated blanks. Likewise, binary zeros are used to pad numeric values that can be stored in fewer bytes. This happens most often when you assign a small or medium-sized integer to an 8-byte numeric variable.

Note: If saving disk space is crucial, consider storing missing data as a small integer, such as 0 or 9, rather than as a SAS missing value. Small integers can be compressed more than SAS missing values can.

A data file is not a good candidate for compression if it has any of the following characteristics:

- few repeated characters

- small physical size

- few missing values

- short text strings

The following topic explores how to compress a data file.

The COMPRESS= System Option and the COMPRESS= Data Set Option

To compress a data file, you use either the COMPRESS= data set option or the COMPRESS= system option. You use the COMPRESS= system option to compress all data files that you create during a SAS session. Similarly, you use the COMPRESS= data set option to compress an individual data file.

General form, COMPRESS= system option:

OPTIONS COMPRESS= NO | YES | CHAR | BINARY;

Here is an explanation of the syntax:

NO
  is the default setting, which does not compress the data set.

CHAR or YES
  uses the Run Length Encoding (RLE) compression algorithm, which compresses repeating consecutive bytes such as trailing blanks or repeated zeros.

BINARY
  uses Ross Data Compression (RDC), which combines run-length encoding and sliding-window compression.

Note: If you set the COMPRESS= system option to a value other than NO, SAS compresses every data set that is created during the current SAS session, including temporary data sets in the Work library. Although this might conserve data storage space, it uses greater amounts of other resources.

General form, COMPRESS= data set option:

DATA *SAS-data-set* **(COMPRESS= NO | YES | CHAR | BINARY);**

Here is an explanation of the syntax:

SAS-data-set
   specifies the data set that you want to compress.

NO
   is the default setting, which does not compress the data set.

CHAR or YES
   uses the Run Length Encoding (RLE) compression algorithm, which compresses repeating consecutive bytes such as trailing blanks or repeated zeros.

BINARY
   uses Ross Data Compression (RDC), which combines run-length encoding and sliding-window compression.

Note: The COMPRESS= data set option overrides the COMPRESS= system option.

The YES or CHAR setting for the COMPRESS= option uses the RLE compression algorithm. RLE compresses observations by reducing repeated consecutive characters (including blanks) to two-byte or three-byte representations. Therefore, RLE is most often useful for character data that contains repeated blanks. The YES or CHAR setting is also good for compressing numeric data in which most of the values are zero.

The BINARY setting for the COMPRESS= option uses RDC, which combines run-length encoding and sliding-window compression. This method is highly effective for compressing medium to large blocks of binary data (numeric variables).

A file that has been compressed using the BINARY setting of the COMPRESS= option takes significantly more CPU time to uncompress than a file that was compressed with the YES or CHAR setting. BINARY is more efficient with observations that are several hundred bytes or more in length. BINARY can also be very effective with character data that contains patterns rather than simple repetitions.

When you create a compressed data file, SAS compares the size of the compressed file to the size of the uncompressed file of the same page size. Then SAS writes a note to the log indicating the size reduction percent that is obtained by compressing the file.

When you use either of the COMPRESS= options, SAS calculates the size of the overhead that is introduced by compression as well as the maximum size of an observation in the data set that you are attempting to compress. If the maximum size of the observation is smaller than the overhead that is introduced by compression, SAS disables compression, creates an uncompressed data set, and issues a warning message stating that the file was not compressed.

Once a file is compressed, the setting is a permanent attribute of the file. In order to change the setting to uncompressed, you must re-create the file.

Note: Compression of observations is not supported by all SAS engines. See the SAS documentation for the COMPRESS= data set option for more information.

Example

The data set Company.Customer contains demographic information about a retail company's customers. The data set includes character variables such as Customer_Name, Customer_FirstName, Customer_LastName, and Customer_Address. These character variables have the potential to contain many repeated blanks in their values. The following program creates a compressed data set named

Company.Customers_Compressed from Company.Customer even if the COMPRESS=
system option is set to NO.

```
data company.customer_compressed (compress=char);
   set company.customer;
run;
```

SAS writes a note to the SAS log about the compression of the new data set, as shown
below.

Table 21.3 *SAS Log*

```
NOTE: There were 89954 observations read from the data
      set COMPANY.CUSTOMER.
NOTE: The data set COMPANY.CUSTOMER_COMPRESSED has 89954
      observations and 11 variables.
NOTE: Compressing data set COMPANY.CUSTOMER_COMPRESSED
      decreased size by 32.81 percent.
      Compressed is 991 pages; un-compressed would require
      1475 pages.
NOTE: DATA statement used (Total process time):
      real time           3.90 seconds
      cpu time            0.96 seconds
```

In general, you use a compressed data set in your programs in the same way that you
would use an uncompressed data set. However, there are two options that relate
specifically to compressed data sets.

Accessing Observations Directly in a Compressed Data Set

By default, the DATA step processes observations in a SAS data set sequentially.
However, sometimes you might want to access observations directly rather than
sequentially because doing so can conserve resources such as CPU time, I/O, and real
time. You can use the POINT= option in the MODIFY or SET statements to access
observations directly rather than sequentially. You can review information about the
POINT= option in Chapter 13, "Creating Indexes," on page 448. You can also use the
FSEDIT procedure to access observations directly.

Allowing direct access to observations in a compressed data set increases the CPU time
that is required for creating or updating the data set. You can set an option that does not
allow direct access for compressed data sets. If it is not important for you to be able to
point directly to an observation by number within a compressed data set, it is a good idea
to disallow direct access in order to improve the efficiency of creating and updating the
data set. The following topic explains how to disallow direct access to observations in a
compressed data set.

The POINTOBS= Data Set Option

When you work with compressed data sets, you use the POINTOBS= data set option to
control whether observations can be processed with direct access (by observation
number) rather than with sequential access only.

General form, POINTOBS= data set option:

DATA *SAS-data-set* **(COMPRESS=YES | CHAR | BINARY POINTOBS= YES | NO);**

Here is an explanation of the syntax:

SAS-data-set
  specifies the data set that you want to compress.

YES
  is the default setting, which allows random access to the data set.

NO
  does not allow random access to the data set.

Note: In order for you to use the POINTOBS= data set option, the COMPRESS= option must have a value of YES, CHAR, or BINARY for the SAS-data set that is specified.

Allowing random access to a data set does not affect the efficiency of retrieving information from a data set, but it does increase the CPU usage by approximately 10% when you create or update a compressed data set. That is, allowing random access reduces the efficiency of writing to a compressed data set but does not affect the efficiency of reading from a compressed data set. Therefore, if you do not need to access data by observation number, specify POINTOBS=NO. Thus, you can improve performance by approximately 10% when creating a compressed data set and when updating or adding observations to it.

Example

The following program creates a data set named Company.Customer_Compressed from the Company.Customer data set and ensures that random access to the compressed data set is not allowed.

```
data company.customer_compressed (compress=yes pointobs=no);
   set company.customer;
run;
```

The following topic explains how to further reduce the data storage space that is required for your compressed data sets.

The REUSE= System Option and the REUSE= Data Set Option

SAS appends new observations to the end of all data sets by default. If you delete an observation within the data set, empty disk space remains in its place. However, in compressed data sets only, it is possible to track and reuse free space when you add or update observations. By reusing space within a data set, you can conserve data storage space.

The REUSE= system option and the REUSE= data set option specify whether SAS reuses space when observations are added to a compressed data set. If you set the REUSE= data set option to YES in a DATA statement, SAS tracks and reuses space in the compressed data set that is created in that DATA step. If you set the REUSE= system option to YES, SAS tracks and reuses free space in all compressed data sets that are created for the remainder of the current SAS session.

General form, REUSE= system option:

OPTIONS REUSE= NO | YES;

Here is an explanation of the syntax:

NO
> is the default setting, which specifies that SAS does not track unused space in the compressed data set.

YES
> specifies that SAS tracks free space and reuses it whenever observations are added to an existing compressed data set.

General form, REUSE= data set option:

DATA *SAS-data-set* **(COMPRESS=YES REUSE=NO | YES);**

Here is an explanation of the syntax:

SAS-data-set
> specifies the data set that you want to compress.

NO
> is the default setting, which specifies that SAS does not track unused space in the compressed data set.

YES
> specifies that SAS tracks free space and reuses it whenever observations are added to an existing compressed data set.

Note: The REUSE= data set option overrides the REUSE= system option.

If the REUSE= option is set to YES, observations that are added to the SAS data set are inserted wherever enough free space exists, instead of at the end of the SAS data set.

Specifying NO for the REUSE= option results in less efficient usage of space if you delete or update many observations in a SAS data set because there is unused space within the data set. With the REUSE= option set to NO, the APPEND procedure, the FSEDIT procedure, and other procedures that add observations to the SAS data set add observations to the end of the data set, as they do for uncompressed data sets.

You cannot change the REUSE= attribute of a compressed data set after it is created. This means that space is tracked and reused in the compressed SAS data set according to the value of the REUSE= option that was specified when the SAS data set was created, not when you add and delete observations. Also, you should be aware that even with the REUSE= option set to YES, the APPEND procedure adds observations to the end of the data set.

Note: Specifying YES as the value for the REUSE= option causes the POINTOBS= option to have a value of NO even if you specify YES as the value for POINTOBS=. The insertion of a new observation into unused space (rather than at the end of the data set) and the use of direct access are not compatible.

Example

The following program creates a compressed data set named Company.Customer_Compressed from the Company.Customer data set. Because the REUSE= option is set to YES, SAS tracks and reuses any empty space within the compressed data set.

```
data company.customer_compressed (compress=yes reuse=yes);
   set company.customer;
run;
```

How SAS Compresses Data

Look at how SAS compresses data. A fictional data set named Roster is described in the table below.

Variable	Type	Length
LastName	Character	20
FirstName	Character	15

In uncompressed form, each observation in Roster uses a total of 35 bytes to store these two variables: 20 bytes for the first variable, LastName, and 15 bytes for the second variable, FirstName. The image below illustrates the storage of the first observation in the uncompressed version of Roster.

Suppose that you use the CHAR setting for the COMPRESS= option to compress Roster. In compressed form, the repeated blanks are removed from each value. The first observation from Roster uses a total of only 13 bytes: 7 for the first variable, LastName, and 6 for the second variable, FirstName. The image below illustrates the storage of the first observation in the compressed version of Roster.

The @ indicates the number of uncompressed characters that follow. The # indicates the number of blanks that are repeated at this point in the observation. Only a SAS engine can access these bytes. You cannot print or manipulate them.

Ross Data Compression (COMPRESS=BINARY) uses both run-length encoding and sliding window compression. Suppose a SAS data set has these variables:

Name	Type	Length
Answer1	Num	8
Answer2	Num	8
...		
Answer200	Num	8

In uncompressed form, the SAS data file resembles this:

1	2	3	4	5	6	7	8	9
@	+/1	1	#	@	+/1	2	#	%

The @ symbol indicates how many uncompressed characters follow. In the file, +/1 is the sign and exponent. The # indicates the number of binary zeros that were removed. The % represents how many times these values are repeated.

Note: Remember that in a compressed data set, observations might not all have the same length because the length of an observation depends on the length of each value in the observation.

Comparative Example: Creating and Reading Compressed Data Files

Overview

Suppose you want to create two SAS data sets from data that is stored in two raw data files. The raw data file that is referenced by the fileref Flat1 contains numeric data about customer orders for a retail company; you want to create a SAS data set named Retail.Orders from this raw data file. The raw data file that is referenced by the fileref Flat2 contains character data about customers for a retail company; you want to create a SAS data set named Retail.Customers from this raw data file.

In both cases, you can use the DATA step to create either an uncompressed data file or a compressed data file. Furthermore, you can use either binary or character compression in either case.

The following sample programs compare six techniques. You can use these samples as models for creating benchmark programs in your own environment. Your results might vary depending on the structure of your data, your operating environment, and the resources that are available at your site.

Programming Techniques

 Numeric Data, No Compression

The following program creates the SAS data set Retail.Orders, which contains numeric data and is uncompressed. The second DATA step reads the uncompressed data file.

```
data retail.orders(compress=no);
   infile flat1;
   input   Customer_ID          12.
           Employee_ID          12.
           Street_ID            12.
           Order_Date           date9.
           Delivery_Date        date9.
           Order_ID             12.
           Order_Type           comma16.
           Product_ID           12.
           Quantity             4.
           Total_Retail_Price   dollar13.
           CostPrice_Per_Unit   dollar13.
           Discount             5.           ;
run;


data _null_;
   set retail.orders;
run;
```

❷ Numeric Data, BINARY Compression

The following program creates the SAS data set Retail.Orders_binary, which contains numeric data and uses BINARY compression. The second DATA step reads the compressed data file.

```
data retail.orders_binary(compress=binary);
   infile flat1;
   input  Customer_ID          12.
          Employee_ID          12.
          Street_ID            12.
          Order_Date           date9.
          Delivery_Date        date9.
          Order_ID             12.
          Order_Type           comma16.
          Product_ID           12.
          Quantity             4.
          Total_Retail_Price   dollar13.
          CostPrice_Per_Unit   dollar13.
          Discount             5.        ;
run;

data _null_;
   set retail.orders_binary;
run;
```

❸ Numeric Data, CHAR Compression

The following program creates the SAS data set Retail.Orders_char, which contains numeric data and uses CHAR compression. The second DATA step reads the compressed data file.

```
data retail.orders_char(compress=char);
   infile flat1;
   input  Customer_ID          12.
          Employee_ID          12.
          Street_ID            12.
          Order_Date           date9.
          Delivery_Date        date9.
          Order_ID             12.
          Order_Type           comma16.
          Product_ID           12.
          Quantity             4.
          Total_Retail_Price   dollar13.
          CostPrice_Per_Unit   dollar13.
          Discount             5.        ;
run;

data _null_;
   set retail.orders_char;
run;
```

❹ Character Data, No Compression

The following program creates the SAS data set Retail.Customers, which contains character data and is uncompressed. The second DATA step reads the uncompressed data file.

```
data retail.customers(compress=no);
   infile flat2;
   input  Customer_Country      $40.
          Customer_Gender       $1.
          Customer_Name         $40.
          Customer_FirstName    $20.
          Customer_LastName     $30.
          Customer_Age_Group    $12.
          Customer_Type         $40.
          Customer_Group        $40.
          Customer_Address      $45.
          Street_Number         $8.              ;
run;

data _null_;
   set retail.cutomers;
run;
```

❺ Character Data, BINARY Compression

The following program creates the SAS data set Retail.Customers_binary, which contains character data and uses BINARY compression. The second DATA step reads the compressed data file.

```
data retail.customers_binary(compress=binary);
   infile flat2;
   input  Customer_Country      $40.
          Customer_Gender       $1.
          Customer_Name         $40.
          Customer_FirstName    $20.
          Customer_LastName     $30.
          Customer_Age_Group    $12.
          Customer_Type         $40.
          Customer_Group        $40.
          Customer_Address      $45.
          Street_Number         $8.              ;
run;

data _null_;
   set retail.customers_binary;
run;
```

❻ Character Data, CHAR Compression

The following program creates the SAS data set Retail.Customers_char, which contains character data and uses CHAR compression. The second DATA step reads the compressed data file.

```
data retail.customers_char(compress=char);
   infile flat2;
   input  Customer_Country    $40.
          Customer_Gender     $1.
          Customer_Name       $40.
          Customer_FirstName  $20.
          Customer_LastName   $30.
          Customer_Age_Group  $12.
          Customer_Type       $40.
          Customer_Group      $40.
          Customer_Address    $45.
          Street_Number       $8.            ;
run;

data _null_;
   set retail.customers_char;
run;
```

General Recommendations

- Save data storage space by compressing data, but remember that compressed data causes an increase in CPU usage because the data must be uncompressed for processing.

- Use binary compression only if the observation length is several hundred bytes or more.

Using SAS DATA Step Views to Conserve Data Storage Space

Overview

Another way to save disk space is to leave your data in its original location and use a SAS data view to access it. First we examine a SAS data view and how it compares to a SAS data file.

A SAS data file and a SAS data view are both types of SAS data sets. A SAS data file contains both descriptor information and the data. By contrast, a SAS data view, contains only descriptor information and instructions on how to retrieve data stored elsewhere.

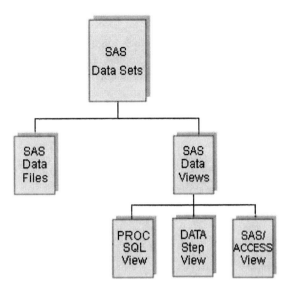

The main difference between SAS data files and SAS data views is where the data is stored. A SAS data file contains data, and a SAS data view does not contain data. Data views can be particularly useful if you are working with data that changes often.

Suppose you have a flat file that you read into a SAS data file. If the data in the flat file changes, you need to update the data file to reflect those changes. However, suppose you use a SAS data view instead of a SAS data file to access the flat file. You do not need to update the SAS data view when the data in your flat file changes, because each time you reference the view that it accesses the most recent data in your flat file.

In most cases, you can use a SAS data view as if it were a SAS data file, although there are a few things to keep in mind when you are working with data views.

Note: There are multiple types of SAS data views. This chapter discusses only DATA step views. To learn more about PROC SQL views, see Chapter 7, "Creating and Managing Views Using PROC SQL," on page 248. For more information about SAS data views and SAS data files, see the SAS documentation.

Now look at DATA step views.

DATA Step Views

A DATA step view contains a partially compiled DATA step that can read data from a variety of sources, such as these:

- raw data files

- SAS data files

- PROC SQL views

- SAS/ACCESS views

- DB2, ORACLE, or other DBMS data

A DATA step view can be created only in a DATA step. A DATA step view cannot contain global statements, host-specific data set options, or most host-specific FILE and INFILE statement options. Also, a DATA step view cannot be indexed or compressed.

You can use DATA step views to do the following:

- always access the most current data in changing files

- avoid storing a copy of a large data file

- combine data from multiple sources

The compiled DATA step does not use much room for storage, so you can create DATA step views to conserve disk space. On the other hand, use of DATA step views can increase CPU usage because SAS must execute the stored DATA step each time you use the view.

To create a DATA step view, specify the VIEW= option after the final DATA set name in the DATA statement.

General form, DATA step to create a DATA step view:

DATA *SAS-data-view* <*SAS-data-file-1 ... SAS data-file-n*> /

        VIEW=*SAS-data-view***;**

    <*SAS statements*>

RUN;

Here is an explanation of the syntax:

SAS-data-view
    names the data view to be created.

SAS-data-file-1 ... SAS-data-file-n
    is an optional list that names any data files to be created.

SAS statements
    includes other DATA step statements to create the data view and any data files that are listed in the DATA statement.

The VIEW= option tells SAS to compile, but not to execute, the source program and to store the compiled code in the DATA step view that is named in the option.

Note: If you specify additional data files in the DATA statement, SAS creates these data files when the view is processed in a subsequent DATA or PROC step. Therefore, you need to reference the data view before you attempt to reference the data files in later steps.

Example

The following program creates a DATA step view named *Company.Newdata* that reads from the file that is referenced by the fileref in the INFILE statement.

```
data company.newdata / view=company.newdata;
   infile <fileref>;
   <DATA step statements>
run;
```

The DESCRIBE Statement

DATA step views retain source statements. You can retrieve these statements by using the DESCRIBE statement. The following example uses the DESCRIBE statement in a DATA step to write a copy of the source code for the data view *Company.Newdata* to the SAS log:

```
data view=company.newdata;
   describe;
run;
```

Creating and Referencing a SAS DATA Step View

In order to use DATA step views successfully, you need to understand what happens when you create and reference one.

When you create a DATA step view, the following actions occur:

- The DATA step is partially compiled.

- The intermediate code is stored in the specified SAS library with a member type of VIEW.

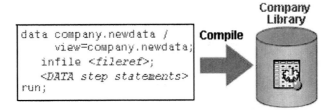

```
data company.newdata /
      view=company.newdata;
  infile <fileref>;
  <DATA step statements>
run;
```
Compile → Company Library

You reference a DATA step view in the same way that you reference a data file. When you reference the view in a subsequent DATA or PROC step, the following actions occur:

- The compiler resolves the intermediate code and generates executable code for the host environment.

- The generated code is executed as the DATA or PROC step requests observations.

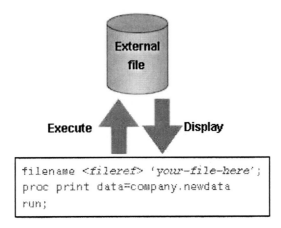

External file

Execute **Display**

```
filename <fileref> 'your-file-here';
proc print data=company.newdata
run;
```

You can use a DATA step view as you would use any other SAS data set, with the exception that you cannot write to the view except under very specific circumstances. Also, you should keep in mind that a SAS data view reads from its source files each time it is used. Therefore, if the data changes, the results change. Likewise, if the structure of the data that a view accesses changes, you probably need to alter the view in order to account for this change.

Note: The OBSBUF= data set option enables you to specify how many observations to read at one time from the source data for the DATA step view. The default size of the view buffer is 32K, which means that the number of observations that can be read into the view buffer at one time depends on the observation length. If the observation length is larger than 32K, then only one observation can be read into the buffer at a time.

Remember that although data views conserve data storage space, processing them can require more resources than processing a data file. Look at a few situations where using a data view can adversely affect processing efficiency.

Referencing a Data View Multiple Times in One Program

SAS executes a view each time it is referenced, even within one program. Therefore, if data is used many times in one program, it is more efficient to create and reference a temporary SAS data file than to create and reference a view.

Example

Instead of referencing a data view in each step in the program, you could add a DATA step to the beginning of the program to create a temporary data file and read the data view into it. Then you could reference the temporary data set in each of the subsequent steps. By referencing the temporary data file rather than the data view in each of the PROC steps, SAS executes the data view only once instead of multiple times.

There are other reasons why extracting data to a temporary data file is a good idea. Suppose you submit this code and it takes a long time to run. If a flat file that is referenced by a view changes while your code is running, you have inconsistent results unless you create a SAS data file before submitting the PROC PRINT, PROC FREQ, and PROC MEANS steps, and reference the data file in your program.

Making Multiple Passes through Data in a Data View

Expect a degradation in performance when you use a SAS data view with a procedure that requires multiple passes through the data. When multiple passes are requested, the view must build a cache (spill file) that contains all generated observations. Then SAS reads the data in the spill file on each of the multiple passes through the data in order to ensure that subsequent passes read the same data that was read by previous passes.

For example, the UNIFORM option of the PRINT statement makes all the columns consistent from page to page by determining the longest value of each variable. In order to do this, SAS must make two passes through the data: one pass to find the longest value of each variable, and a second pass to print the data. If you use the UNIFORM option to print a data view, SAS creates a spill file as it generates observations from the view. Then SAS makes two passes through the observations in the spill file.

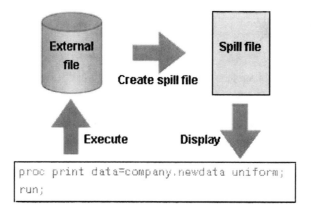

Note: Some statistical procedures pass through the data more than once.

Creating Data Views on Unstable Data

Avoid creating views on files whose structures often change. If the view describes the structure of a raw data file, you need to change the view each time the file changes.

For example, suppose you create a view that combines the data file Company.Roster with the data file Company.Demog. Roster contains the variables LastName and FirstName, and Company.Demog contains the variables LastName, Address, and Age, as shown below.

Company.Roster

Variable	Type	Length
LastName	Character	20
FirstName	Character	15

Company.Demog

Variable	Type	Length
LastName	Character	20
Address	Character	45
Age	Numeric	3

Suppose that both Company.Roster and Company.Demog are sorted by LastName. You could use a MERGE statement to combine these two data files into a view named Company.Roster_View, as shown below.

```
data company.roster_view/view=company.roster_view;
   merge company.roster company.demog;
   by lastname;
run;
```

Now suppose Company.Roster changes so that LastName is named Surname. Your data view must also be updated.

Company.Roster

Variable	Type	Length
Surname	Character	20
FirstName	Character	15

Company.Demog

Variable	Type	Length
LastName	Character	20
Address	Character	45
Age	Numeric	3

```
data roster_view/view=roster_view;
   merge company.roster company.demog(rename=(LastName=Surname));
   by lastname;
run;
```

If Company.Roster changed again so that Surname and FirstName were combined into one variable called FullName, the code for your data view would need additional changes. Although this is a simple example, you can see that a data view that is based on unstable data requires additional maintenance work.

Comparative Example: Creating and Reading a SAS Data View

Overview

Suppose you have two SAS data sets, Retail.Custview and Retail.Custdata, that have been created from the same raw data file. Retail.Custview is a DATA step view, and Retail.Custdata is a data file. You can use these two data sets to compare the disk space that is required for each as well as the resources that are used to read from each view or file.

The following sample programs compare two techniques. You can use these samples as models for creating benchmark programs in your own environment. Your results might vary depending on the structure of your data, your operating environment, and the resources that are available at your site.

Programming Techniques

 Data View

This program reads data from a raw data file, creates a SAS DATA step view named Retail.Custview, and then reads from the new DATA step view. The first DATA step creates the data view Retail.Custview. The second DATA step reads from the DATA step view.

```
data retail.custview / view = retail.custview;
   infile flat1;
   input @1   Customer_ID          12.
         @13  Country              $2.
         @15  Gender               $1.
         @16  Personal_ID          $15.
         @31  Customer_Name        $40.
         @71  Customer_FirstName   $20.
         @91  Customer_LastName    $30.
         @121 Birth_Date           date9.
         @130 Customer_Address     $45.
         @175 Street_ID            12.
         @199 Street_Number        $8.
         @207 Customer_Type_ID     8.;
 run;


data _null_;
   set retail.custview;
run;
```

❷ Data File

This program reads data from a raw data file, creates a SAS data file named Retail.Custdata, and reads from the new SAS data file. The first DATA step creates the data file Retail.Custdata. The second DATA step reads from the data file.

```
data retail.custdata;
   infile flat1;
   input @1   Customer_ID          12.
         @13  Country              $2.
         @15  Gender               $1.
         @16  Personal_ID          $15.
         @31  Customer_Name        $40.
         @71  Customer_FirstName   $20.
         @91  Customer_LastName    $30.
         @121 Birth_Date           date9.
         @130 Customer_Address     $45.
         @175 Street_ID            12.
         @199 Street_Number        $8.
         @207 Customer_Type_ID     8.;
run;


data _null_;
   set retail.custdata;
run;
```

General Recommendations

- Create a SAS DATA step view to avoid storing a SAS copy of a raw data file.

- Use a SAS DATA step view if the content, but not the structure, of the flat file is dynamic.

- Create a DATA step view to combine multiple SAS data sets with a merge or concatenation.

- Create a DATA step view to access frequently used subsets.

Summary

Reducing Data Storage Space for Character Variables

SAS stores character data as one character per byte. You can use the LENGTH statement to increase or reduce the length of a character variable. You can also use other coding techniques to reduce the space that is needed for storing your character data.

Reducing Data Storage Space for Numeric Variables

SAS stores numeric data in floating-point representation. The default length for a numeric variable is 8 bytes. You can use a LENGTH statement to reduce the length of a numeric variable. Reading reduced-length numeric variables requires less I/O but more CPU resources than reading full-length numeric variables. You can use PROC COMPARE to see the precision loss, if any, in the values of reduced-length numeric variables.

Compressing Data Files

By default, a SAS data file is uncompressed. You can compress your data files in order to conserve disk space, although some files are not good candidates for compression. Use the COMPRESS= data set option or system option to compress a data file. Use the POINTOBS=YES data set option to enable SAS to access observations in compressed files directly rather than sequentially. Use the REUSE=YES data set option or system option to specify that SAS should reuse space in a compressed file when observations are added or updated.

Using SAS DATA Step Views to Conserve Data Storage Space

You can leave your data in its original storage location and use SAS data views to access the data in order to reduce the amount of space needed for storing data on disk. A DATA step view is a specific type of data view that is created in a DATA step with the VIEW= option. Use the DESCRIBE statement to write the source code for a data view to the SAS log. Some of the advantages of using DATA step views rather than data files are that they always access the most recent data in dynamic files and that they require less disk space. However, there can be an effect on performance when you use a DATA step view.

Quiz

Select the best answer for each question. After completing the quiz, check your answers using the answer key in the appendix.

1. Which of the following statements about uncompressed SAS data files is true?

    a. The descriptor portion is stored on whatever page has enough room for it.

    b. New observations are always added in the first sufficient available space.

    c. Deleted observation space is tracked.

    d. New observations are always added at the end of the data set.

2. Which of the following statements about compressed SAS data files is true?

    a. The descriptor portion is stored on whatever data set page has enough room for it.

    b. Deleted observation space can be reused.

    c. Compressed SAS data files have a smaller overhead than uncompressed SAS data files.

    d. In a compressed SAS data set, each observation must be the same size.

3. Which of the following programs correctly creates reduced-length numeric variables?

    a.
    ```
    data temp;
        infile file1;
        input x 4.
              y 3.
              z 2.;
        run;
    ```

    b.
    ```
    data temp;
        format x 4.
               y 3.
               z 2.;
        infile file1;
        input x 4.
              y 3.
              z 2.;
    run;
    ```

    c.
    ```
    data temp;
        length x 4
               y 3
               z 2;
        infile file1;
        input x 4.
              y 3.
              z 2.;
        run;
    ```

    d.
    ```
    data temp;
        informat x 4.
                 y 3.
    ```

```
              z 2.;
       infile file1;
       input x 4.
              y 3.
              z 2.;
     run;
```

4. Which of the following statements about SAS data views is true?

   a. SAS data views use less disk space but more CPU resources than SAS data files.

   b. SAS data views can be created only in permanent SAS libraries.

   c. SAS data views use less CPU resources but more disk space than SAS data files.

   d. SAS data views can be created only in temporary SAS libraries.

5. Which of the following programs should you use to detect any loss of precision between the default-length numeric variables in *Company.Regular* and the reduced-length numeric variables in the data set *Company.Reduced*?

   a.
   ```
   proc contents data=company.regular;
       compare data=company.reduced;
   run;
   ```

   b.
   ```
   proc compare base=company.regular
       compare=company.reduced;
   run;
   ```

   c.
   ```
   proc print data=company.regular;
   run;

   proc print data=company.reduced;
   run;
   ```

   d.
   ```
   proc datasets library=company;
       contents data=regular compare=reduced;
   run;
   ```

Chapter 22
Using Best Practices

Overview

Introduction

This chapter demonstrates using SAS best programming practices to optimize performance. As you compare the techniques that are described in this chapter, remember that differences in the use of resources are affected by the operating environment you work in and by the characteristics of your data.

Each topic includes examples that can improve program efficiency. Write programs to generate your own benchmarks, and adopt the programming techniques that produce the most savings for you.

Note: This chapter does not cover the SAS Scalable Performance Data Engine (SAS SPD Engine), which is a SAS 9.1 technology for threaded processing. For details about using the SAS SPD Engine to improve performance, see the SAS documentation.

Executing Only Necessary Statements

Overview

When you execute the minimum number of statements in the most efficient order, you minimize the hardware resources that SAS uses. The resources that are affected include disk usage, memory usage, and CPU usage.

Here are two techniques to keep in mind:

- Subset your data as soon as is logically possible.

- Process your data conditionally by using the most appropriate technique.

Positioning of the Subsetting IF Statement

To subset your data based on a newly derived or computed variable, use the subsetting IF statement in a DATA step in order to process only those observations that meet a specified condition.

The subsetting IF statement causes the DATA step to continue processing only those observations that meet the condition of the expression that is specified in the subsetting IF statement. The resulting SAS data set or data sets contain a subset of the original external file or SAS data set.

Position the subsetting IF statement in the program so that it checks the subsetting condition as soon as it is logically possible. As a result, unnecessary statements do not execute. When the subsetting condition is false, no further statements are processed for that observation.

Also, remember to subset data before performing calculations and to minimize the use of function calls or arithmetic operators. Unnecessary processing of unwanted observations results in higher expenditure of hardware resources.

Comparative Example: Creating a Subset of Data

Overview

Suppose you want to create a subset of data, calculate six new variables, and conditionally output data by reading from the SAS data set Retail.Order_fact. The output data set should contain new variables for the following:

- the month of the order

- the elapsed time between the order date and the delivery date

- the profit, based on the retail price, discount, and unit price

- total profit

- total discount

- total wait time

The subset of data that includes only orders for the month of December is approximately 10% of the data.

You can accomplish this task by using a subsetting IF statement. Placement of this statement in the DATA step can affect the efficiency of the DATA step in terms of CPU time and real time.

The following sample programs compare two techniques. You can use these samples as models for creating benchmark programs in your own environment. Your results might vary depending on the structure of your data, your operating environment, and the resources that are available at your site.

Programming Techniques

❶ A Subsetting IF Statement at the Bottom

This program calculates six new variables before the subsetting IF statement selects only observations whose values for Month are 12.

```
data profit;
   retain TotalProfit TotalDiscount TotalWait Count 0;
   set retail.order_fact;
   MonthOfOrder=month(order_date);
   WaitTime=sum(delivery_date,-order_date);
   if discount gt . then
      CalcProfit=sum((total_retail_price*discount),-costprice_per_unit)
               *quantity;
   else CalcProfit=sum(total_retail_price,-costprice_per_unit)
               *quantity;
   TotalProfit=sum(totalprofit,calcprofit);
   TotalDiscount=sum(totaldiscount,discount);
   TotalWait=sum(totalwait,waittime);
   Count+1;
   if monthoforder=12;
run;
```

❷ A Subsetting IF Statement near the Top

In this program, the subsetting IF statement is positioned immediately after the value for MonthofOrder has been calculated. If the value is not 12, then no further statements are processed for that observation. In this program, calculations are performed on a smaller number of observations, which results in greater program efficiency.

```
data profit;
   retain TotalProfit TotalDiscount TotalWait Count 0;
   set retail.order_fact;
   MonthOfOrder=month(order_date);
   if monthoforder=12;
   WaitTime=sum(delivery_date,-order_date);
   if discount gt . then
      CalcProfit=sum((total_retail_price*discount),-costprice_per_unit)
               *quantity;
   else CalcProfit=sum(total_retail_price,-costprice_per_unit)
               *quantity;
   TotalProfit=sum(totalprofit,calcprofit);
   TotalDiscount=sum(totaldiscount,discount);
   TotalWait=sum(totalwait,waittime);
   Count+1;
run;
```

General Recommendations

Position the subsetting IF statement in a DATA step as soon as is logically possible in order to save the most resources.

Using Conditional Logic Efficiently

You can use conditional logic to change how SAS processes selected observations. Two techniques—IF-THEN/ELSE statements and SELECT statements—can be used interchangeably and perform comparably. Based on the characteristics of your data and depending on your environment, one of these techniques might give you better performance. Choose a technique that conserves your programming time and makes the program easiest to read.

Note: The number of conditions that are tested and the type of variable or variables that are tested affect CPU resources.

For best practices, follow these guidelines for writing efficient IF/THEN or SELECT statement logic:

- When using IF/THEN statements for mutually exclusive conditions, use the ELSE IF statement rather than an IF statement for all conditions except the first.

- Check the most frequently occurring condition first, and continue checking conditions in descending order of frequency.

- When you execute multiple statements based on a condition, put the statements in a DO group.

Before writing conditional logic, determine the distribution of your data values. You can use the following procedures:

- FREQ procedure to examine the distribution of the data values

- GCHART or GPLOT procedure to display the distribution graphically

- UNIVARIATE procedure to examine distribution statistics and to display the information graphically

Comparative Example: Creating Variables Conditionally Using DO Groups

Overview

Suppose you want to calculate an adjusted profit based on the values of the variable Order_Type in the data set Retail.Order_fact. For retail sales, which are represented by the value 1, the adjusted profit should be calculated as 105% of profit. For catalog sales, which are represented by the value 2, the adjusted profit should be calculated as 103% of profit. For Internet sales, which are represented by the value 3, the adjusted profit should be equal to profit.

The following table shows that the values for the variable Order_Type are not uniformly distributed.

Order Type		
Order_Type	Frequency	Percent
1	3579850	75.23
2	635645	13.36
3	542850	11.41

The following table shows that the values for the variable Discount also are not uniformly distributed.

Discount		
Discount	Frequency	Percent
.	4712585	99.04
30%	19740	0.41
40%	15170	0.32
50%	9805	0.21
60%	1045	0.02

The following sample programs compare two techniques. You can use these samples as models for creating benchmark programs in your own environment. Your results might vary depending on the structure of your data, your operating environment, and the resources that are available at your site.

Programming Techniques

❶ IF-THEN/ELSE Statements

This program uses IF-THEN/ELSE statements with DO groups to conditionally execute multiple statements that calculate an adjusted profit. Conditions are checked in descending order of frequency.

```
data retail.order_info_1;
   set retail.order_fact;
   if order_type=1 then
      do;                     /* Retail Sale */
         Float=delivery_date-order_date;
         RevenueQuarter=qtr(order_date);
         AveragePrice=total_retail_price/quantity;
         if discount=. then NetPrice=total_retail_price;
         else NetPrice=total_retail_price-discount;
         Profit=netPrice-(quantity*costprice_per_unit)*1.05;
      end;
   else if order_type=2 then
      do;                     /* Catalog Sale */
         Float=delivery_date-order_date;
         RevenueQuarter=qtr(order_date);
         AveragePrice=total_retail_price/quantity;
         if discount=. then NetPrice=total_retail_price;
         else NetPrice=total_retail_price-discount;
         Profit=netprice-(quantity*costprice_per_unit)*1.03;
      end;
   else
      do;                     /* Internet Sale */
         Float=delivery_date-order_Date;
         RevenueQuarter=qtr(order_date);
         AveragePrice=total_retail_price/quantity;
         if discount=. then NetPrice=total_retail_price;
         else NetPrice=total_retail_price-discount;
         Profit=netprice-(quantity*costprice_per_unit);
      end;
run;
```

❷ SELECT Statements

This program uses SELECT and WHEN statements with DO groups to conditionally execute multiple statements that calculate an adjusted profit. Conditions are checked in descending order of frequency.

```
data retail.order_info_2;
   set retail.order_fact;
   select(order_type);
      when (1)
         do;                                    /* Retail Sale */
            Float=delivery_date-order_date;
            RevenueQuarter=qtr(order_date);
            AveragePrice=total_retail_price/quantity;
            if discount=. then NetPrice=total_retail_price;
            else NetPrice=total_retail_price-discount;
            Profit=netprice-(quantity*costprice_per_unit)*1.05;
         end;
      when (2)
         do;                                    /* Catalog Sale */
            Float=delivery_date-order_date;
            RevenueQuarter=qtr(order_date);
            AveragePrice=total_retail_price/quantity;
            if discount=. then NetPrice=total_retail_price;
            else NetPrice=total_retail_price-discount;
            Profit=netprice-(quantity*costprice_per_unit)*1.03;
         end;
      otherwise
         do;                                    /* Internet Sale */
            Float=delivery_date-order_date;
            RevenueQuarter=qtr(order_date);
            AveragePrice=total_retail_price/quantity;
            if discount=. then NetPrice=total_retail_price;
            else NetPrice=total_retail_price-discount;
            Profit=netprice-(quantity*costprice_per_unit);
         end;
   end;
run;
```

General Recommendations

- Check the most frequently occurring condition first, and continue checking conditions in descending order of frequency, regardless of whether you use IF-THEN/ELSE or SELECT and WHEN statements.

- When you execute multiple statements based on a condition, put the statements in a DO group.

Comparative Example: Creating Variables Conditionally When Calling Functions

Overview

Suppose you want to create a report that includes a new variable that is based on the value of an existing variable in the SAS data set Retail.Order_fact. Values for the new Month variable are extracted from the existing variable Order_Date by using the MONTH function.

The following table shows that the values for Month are fairly evenly distributed.

Month of Order		
Month	**Frequency**	**Percent**
Jan	386535	8.12
Feb	319895	6.72
Mar	350255	7.36
Apr	421265	8.85
May	443535	9.32
Jun	429760	9.03
Jul	438085	9.21
Aug	443075	9.31
Sep	299260	6.29
Oct	373400	7.85
Nov	393750	8.27
Dec	459530	9.66

The following sample programs compare several techniques. You can use these samples as models for creating benchmark programs in your own environment. Your results might vary depending on the structure of your data, your operating environment, and the resources that are available at your site.

Programming Techniques

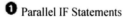 Parallel IF Statements

This program calls the MONTH function 12 times. With these non-exclusive cases, each IF statement executes for each observation that is read from Retail.Order_Fact. This is the least efficient approach.

```
data retail.orders;
   set retail.order_fact;
   if month(order_date)=1 then Month='Jan';
   if month(order_date)=2 then Month='Feb';
   if month(order_date)=3 then Month='Mar';
   if month(order_date)=6 then Month='Jun';
   if month(order_date)=7 then Month='Jul';
   if month(order_date)=8 then Month='Aug';
   if month(order_date)=9 then Month='Sep';
   if month(order_date)=10 then Month='Oct';
   if month(order_date)=11 then Month='Nov';
   if month(order_date)=12 then Month='Dec';
run;
```

❷ ELSE IF Statements, Many Function References

This program uses ELSE IF statements that call the function MONTH. Once the true condition is found, subsequent ELSE IF statements are not executed. This is more efficient than using parallel IF statements, but the MONTH function is executed many times.

```
data retail.orders;
   set retail.order_fact;
   if month(order_date)=1 then Month='Jan';
   else if month(order_date)=2 then Month='Feb';
   else if month(order_date)=3 then Month='Mar';
   else if month(order_date)=4 then Month='Apr';
   else if month(order_date)=5 then Month='May';
   else if month(order_date)=6 then Month='Jun';
   else if month(order_date)=7 then Month='Jul';
   else if month(order_date)=10 then Month='Oct';
   else if month(order_date)=11 then Month='Nov';
   else if month(order_date)=12 then Month='Dec';
run;
```

❸ ELSE IF Statements, One Function Reference

This program uses the MONTH function to find the value of Order_Date, but only once. The MONTH function is called immediately after reading the data set and before any IF-THEN/ELSE statements execute. This is efficient.

```
data retail.orders(drop=mon);
   set retail.order_fact;
   mon=month(order_date);
   if mon=1 then Month='Jan';
   else if mon=2 then Month='Feb';
   else if mon=3 then Month='Mar';
   else if mon=4 then Month='Apr';
   else if mon=5 then Month='May';
   else if mon=6 then Month='Jun';
   else if mon=7 then Month='Jul';
   else if mon=8 then Month='Aug';
   else if mon=9 then Month='Sep';
   else if mon=10 then Month='Oct';
   else if mon=11 then Month='Nov';
   else if mon=12 then Month='Dec';
run;
```

❹ SELECT Group

In this program, the SELECT statement calls the MONTH function only once, before WHEN statements execute and assign values for Month. This is efficient.

```
data retail.orders;
   set retail.order_fact;
   select(month(order_date));
      when (1) Month='Jan';
      when (2) Month='Feb';
      when (3) Month='Mar';
      when (4) Month='Apr';
      when (5) Month='May';
      when (6) Month='Jun';
      when (7) Month='Jul';
      when (8) Month='Aug';
      when (11) Month='Nov';
      when (12) Month='Dec';
      otherwise;
   end;
run;
```

General Recommendations

- Avoid using parallel IF statements, which use the most resources and are the least efficient way to conditionally execute statements.

- Use IF-THEN/ELSE statements and SELECT blocks to be more efficient.

- To significantly reduce the amount of resources used, write programs that call a function only once instead of repetitively using the same function in many statements. SAS functions are convenient, but they can be expensive in terms of CPU resources.

Using DO Groups Efficiently

You can conditionally execute only necessary statements by placing them in DO groups that are associated with IF-THEN/ELSE statements or with SELECT/WHEN statements. Groups of statements execute only when a particular condition is true.

When using a DO group with IF-THEN/ELSE statements, add DO after the THEN clause, and add an END statement after all of the statements that you want executed as a group.

```
data orders;
   set company.orders;
   if order_type = 1 then
      do;
      <multiple executable statements here>
      end;
   else if order_type = 2 then
      do;
      <multiple executable statements here>
       end;
   else if order_type = 3 then
      do;
      <multiple executable statements here>
      end;
```

```
run;
```

Note: Use an IF-THEN DO group when you create multiple variables based on a
condition.

When using a DO group with SELECT/WHEN statements, add DO after the WHEN
condition, and add an END statement after all of the statements that you want executed
as a group. Use an OTHERWISE statement to specify the statements that you want
executed if no WHEN condition is met.

```
data orders;
   set company.orders;
   select (order_type);
      when (1)
         do;
         <multiple executable statements here>
         end;
      when (2)
         do;
         <multiple executable statements here>
         end;
      when (3)
         do;
         <multiple executable statements here>
         end;
      otherwise;
   end;
run;
```

Remember that IF-THEN/ELSE and SELECT/WHEN logic require no intervening
statements between the IF and the ELSE conditions or between the SELECT and the
WHEN conditions.

Comparative Example: Creating Data in DO Groups

Overview

Suppose you want to identify which customer groups are Club Members, Club Gold
Members, or Internet/Catalog members, based on data from the data set
Retail.Customer_hybrid. You also want to identify the nature of customer activity as
inactive, **low activity**, **medium activity**, or **high activity**.

The following table shows the distribution of values for Customer_Type_ID.

Customer Type ID		
Customer_Type_ID	Frequency	Percent
1010	568446	12.39
1020	579156	12.62
1030	571608	12.46
1040	574209	12.52
2010	566457	12.35
2020	571914	12.47
2030	579054	12.62
3010	576810	12.57

The following sample programs compare several techniques. You can use these samples as models for creating benchmark programs in your own environment. Your results might vary depending on the structure of your data, your operating environment, and the resources that are available at your site.

Programming Techniques

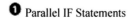 Parallel IF Statements

This program creates a permanent SAS data set named Retail.Customers by reading the Retail.Customer_hybrid data set. Serial IF statements are used to populate the variables Customer_Group and Customer_Activity.

```
data retail.customers;
   length Customer_Group $ 26 Customer_Activity $ 15;
   set retail.customer_hybrid;
   if substr(put(customer_type_ID,4.),1,2)='10' then
      customer_group='Orion Club members';
   if substr(put(customer_type_ID,4.),1,2)='20' then
      customer_group='Orion Club Gold members';
   if substr(put(customer_type_ID,4.),1,2)='30' then
      customer_group='Internet/Catalog Customers';
   if substr(put(customer_type_ID,4.),1,2) in ('10', '20') and
      substr(put(customer_type_ID,4.),3,2)='10' then
         customer_activity='inactive';
   if substr(put(customer_type_ID,4.),1,2) in ('10', '20') and
      substr(put(customer_type_ID,4.),3,2)='20' then
         customer_activity='low activity';
   if substr(put(customer_type_ID,4.),1,2) in ('10', '20') and
      substr(put(customer_type_ID,4.),3,2)='30' then
         customer_activity='medium activity';
   if substr(put(customer_type_ID,4.),1,2) in ('10', '20') and
      substr(put(customer_type_ID,4.),3,2)='40' then
         customer_activity='high activity';
run;
```

❷ SELECT, IF/SELECT Statements

This program creates a permanent SAS data set named Retail.Customers by reading the Retail.Customer_hybrid data set. SELECT/WHEN logic and SELECT/WHEN statements in an IF/THEN DO group populate the variables Customer_Group and Customer_Activity. If the value of the first two digits of Customer_Type_ID is **10**, **20**, or **30**, then Customer_Group is populated. If the value of the first two digits of Customer_Type_ID is **10** or **20**, then Customer_Activity is populated by reading the last two digits of Customer_Type_ID.

```
data retail.customers;
   length Customer_Group $ 26 Customer_Activity $ 15;
   set retail.customer_hybrid;
      select(substr(put(customer_type_ID,4.),1,2));
         when ('10') customer_group='Orion Club members';
         when ('20') customer_group='Orion Club Gold members';
         when ('30') customer_group='Internet/Catalog Customers';
         otherwise;
      end;
   if substr(put(customer_type_ID,4.),1,2) in ('10', '20') then
      do;
         select(substr(put(customer_type_ID,4.),3,2));
            when ('10') customer_activity='inactive';
            when ('20') customer_activity='low activity';
            when ('30') customer_activity='medium activity';
            when ('40') customer_activity='high activity';
            otherwise;
         end;
      end;
run;
```

❸ Nested SELECT Statements

This program creates a permanent SAS data set named Retail.Customers by reading the Retail.Customer_hybrid data set. Nested SELECT statements are used to populate the variables Customer_Group and Customer_Activity.

```
data retail.customers;
   length Customer_Group $ 26 Customer_Activity $ 15;
   set retail.customer_hybrid;
   select(substr(put(customer_type_ID,4.),1,2));
      when ('10')
         do;
            customer_group='Orion Club members';
            select(substr(put(customer_type_ID,4.),3,2));
               when ('10') customer_activity='inactive';
               when ('20') customer_activity='low activity';
               when ('30') customer_activity='medium activity';
               when ('40') customer_activity='high activity';
               otherwise;
            end;
         end;
      when ('20')
         do;
            customer_group='Orion Club Gold members';
            select(substr(put(customer_type_ID,4.),3,2));
               when ('10') customer_activity='inactive';
               when ('20') customer_activity='low activity';
               when ('30') customer_activity='medium activity';
               when ('40') customer_activity='high activity';
               otherwise;
            end;
         end;
      when ('30') customer_group='Internet/Catalog Customers';
      otherwise;
   end;
run;
```

❹ IF-THEN/ELSE IF Statements with a Link

This program creates a permanent SAS data set named Retail.Customers by reading the Retail.Customer_hybrid data set. IF-THEN/ELSE IF statements are used with a link to populate the variables Customer_Group and Customer_Activity.

```
data retail.customers;
   length Customer_Group $ 26 Customer_Activity $ 15;
   set retail.customer_hybrid;
   if substr(put(customer_type_ID,4.),1,2)='10' then
      do;
         customer_group='Orion Club members';
         link activity;
      end;
   else if substr(put(customer_type_ID,4.),1,2)='20' then
      do;
         customer_group='Orion Club Gold members';
         link activity;
      end;
   else if substr(put(customer_type_ID,4.),1,2)='30' then
      customer_group='Internet/Catalog Customers';
   return;
   activity:
   if substr(put(customer_type_ID,4.),3,2)='10' then
      customer_activity='inactive';
   else if substr(put(customer_type_ID,4.),3,2)='20' then
      customer_activity='low activity';
   else if substr(put(customer_type_ID,4.),3,2)='30' then
      customer_activity='medium activity';
   else if substr(put(customer_type_ID,4.),3,2)='40' then
      customer_activity='high activity';
   return;
run;
```

General Recommendations

- Avoid parallel IF statements because they use extra resources.

Eliminating Unnecessary Passes through the Data

Best practices specify that you should eliminate unnecessary passes through the data. To minimize I/O operations and CPU time, avoid reading or writing data more than necessary.

Comparative Example: Creating Multiple Subsets of a SAS Data Set

Overview

Suppose you want to create five subsets of data from the data set *Retail.Customer*. You need a subset for each of five countries.

The following sample programs compare two techniques. You can use these samples as models for creating benchmark programs in your own environment. Your results might vary depending on the structure of your data, your operating environment, and the resources that are available at your site.

Programming Techniques

 Multiple DATA Steps

This program includes multiple DATA steps and subsequently reads data five times from the same Retail.Customer data set. Individual subsetting IF statements appear in five separate DATA steps.

```
data retail.UnitedStates;
   set retail.customer;
   if country='US';
run;

data retail.France;
   set retail.customer;
   if country='FR';
run;

data retail.Italy;
   set retail.customer;
   if country='IT';
run;

data retail.Germany;
   set retail.customer;
   if country='DE';
run;

data retail.Spain;
   set retail.customer;
   if country='ES';
run;
```

❷ A Single DATA Step

This program uses only one DATA step to create five output data sets. The data set Retail.Customer is read only once. Also, IF-THEN/ELSE statements are used to conditionally output data to specific data sets.

```
data retail.UnitedStates
     retail.France
     retail.Italy
     retail.Germany
     retail.Spain;
   set retail.customer;
   if country='US' then output retail.UnitedStates;
   else if country='FR' then output retail.France;
   else if country='IT' then output retail.Italy;
   else if country='DE' then output retail.Germany;
   else if country='ES' then output retail.Spain;
run;
```

General Recommendations

When creating multiple subsets from a SAS data set, use a single DATA step with IF-THEN/ELSE IF logic to output to appropriate data sets.

Using the SORT Procedure with a WHERE Statement to Create Sorted Subsets

It is good programming practice to take advantage of the SORT procedure's ability to sort and subset in the same PROC step. This is more efficient than using two separate steps to accomplish this—a DATA step to subset followed by a procedure step that sorts.

Comparative Example: Creating a Sorted Subset of a SAS Data Set

Overview

Suppose you want to create a sorted subset of a SAS data set named Retail.Customer. You want only data for customers in the United States, France, Italy, Germany, and Spain.

The following sample programs compare two techniques. You can use these samples as models for creating benchmark programs in your own environment. Your results might vary depending on the structure of your data, your operating environment, and the resources that are available at your site.

Programming Techniques

❶ A DATA Step and PROC SORT

This program has two steps. The first step creates a SAS data set by subsetting observations based on the value of the variable Country. The second step sorts the data according to the values for each country. Passing through all the data once and the subset again increases I/O and CPU operations.

```
data retail.CountrySubset;
   set retail.customer;
   where country in('US','FR','IT','DE','ES');
run;


proc sort data=retail.CountrySubset;
   by country;
run;
```

❷ PROC SORT with a WHERE Statement

In one step, this program sorts data and selects only those observations that meet the conditions of the WHERE statement. Processing only one data set once saves CPU and I/O resources.

Note that if this program did not create a second data set named Retail.CountrySubset, it would write over the data set named Retail.Customer with only part of the data.

```
proc sort data=retail.customer out=retail.CountrySubset;
   by country;
   where country in('US','FR','IT','DE','ES');
run;
```

General Recommendations

- When you need to process a subset of data with a procedure, use a WHERE statement in the procedure instead of creating a subset of data and reading that data with the procedure.

• Write one program step that both sorts and subsets. This approach can take less programmer time and debugging time than writing separate program steps that subset and sort.

Using the DATASETS Procedure to Modify Variable Attributes

Use PROC DATASETS instead of a DATA step to modify data attributes. The DATASETS procedure uses fewer resources than the DATA step because it processes only the descriptor portion of the data set, not the data portion. PROC DATASETS retains the sort flag, as well as indexes.

Note: You cannot use the DATASETS procedure to modify the type, length, or position of variables because these attributes directly affect the data portion of the data set. To perform these operations, use the DATA step.

Comparative Example: Changing the Variable Attributes of a SAS Data Set

Overview

Suppose you want to change the variable attributes in Retail.NewCustomer to make them consistent with those in the Retail.Customer data set. The data set Retail.NewCustomer contains 89954 observations and 12 variables.

The following table shows the variable names and formats in each SAS data set.

SAS Data Set	Variable Name	Variable Format
Retail.Customer	Country	$COUNTRY.
Retail.Customer	Birth_Date	DATE9.
Retail.NewCustomer	Country_ID	$COUNTRY.
Retail.NewCustomer	Birth_Date	MMDDYYP10

The following sample programs compare two techniques. You can use these samples as models for creating benchmark programs in your own environment. Your results might vary depending on the structure of your data, your operating environment, and the resources that are available at your site.

Programming Techniques

 A DATA Step

This program uses a DATA step with a RENAME statement and a FORMAT statement to modify attributes for the variables Country_ID and Birth_Date.

```
data retail.newcustomer;
   set retail.newcustomer;
   rename Country_ID=country;
   format birth_date date9.;
run;
```

❷ PROC DATASETS

This program uses PROC DATASETS to modify the names and formats of the variables
Country_ID and Birth_Date.

```
proc datasets lib=retail nolist;
   modify newcustomer;
   rename Country_ID=country;
   format birth_date date9.;
quit;
```

General Recommendations

- To save significant resources, use the DATASETS procedure with the NOLIST option instead of a DATA step to change the attributes of a SAS data set.

Reading and Writing Only Essential Data

Overview

Best practices specify that you should write programs that read and write only essential data. If you process fewer observations and variables, you conserve resources. This topic covers many different techniques that can improve performance.

Selecting Observations Using Subsetting IF versus WHERE Statement

You can use WHERE statements or subsetting IF statements to subset data. Although both statements test a condition to determine whether SAS should select an observation, the WHERE statement is more efficient.

The following graphic illustrates differences between these statements.

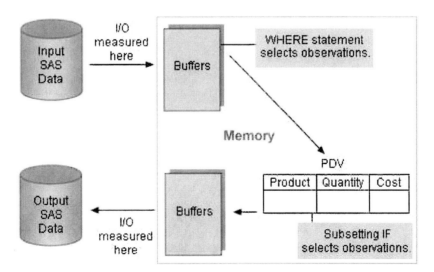

I/O operations are measured as data moves between the disk that contains input SAS data and the input buffer in memory, and when data moves from the output buffer to the disk that contains output data sets. Input data is not affected by the WHERE statement or subsetting IF statement. However, output data is affected by both.

CPU time is measured when data must be processed in the program data vector. CPU time can be saved if fewer observations are processed.

A WHERE statement and a subsetting IF statement make different use of the program data vector. The WHERE statement selects observations before they are loaded into the program data vector, which results in a savings in CPU operations. The subsetting IF statement loads each observation sequentially into the program data vector. If the subsetting condition is true, the observation is processed and is written to the output page buffer.

WHERE statements work on existing variables in existing SAS data sets. Subsetting IF statements can work on any variable in the program data vector, including new or existing variables.

Comparative Example: Creating a Subset of a SAS Data Set

Overview

Suppose you want to create a subset of the data set Retail.Customer. You want to include data for only the United Kingdom. The subset contains approximately 6% of the Retail.Customer data.

The following sample programs compare two techniques. You can use these samples as models for creating benchmark programs in your own environment. Your results might vary depending on the structure of your data, your operating environment, and the resources that are available at your site.

Programming Techniques

 Subsetting IF Statement

This program uses the IF statement to select observations if the value for Country is **GB**.

```
data retail.UnitedKingdom;
   set retail.customer;
   if country='GB';
run;
```

 WHERE Statement

This program uses the WHERE statement to select observations when the value for Country is **GB**. This can be more efficient than using a subsetting IF statement.

```
data retail.UnitedKingdom;
   set retail.customer;
   where country='GB';
run;
```

General Recommendations

- To save CPU resources when the subset is small, use a WHERE statement instead of a subsetting IF statement to subset a SAS data set.

Other Differences between the IF and WHERE Statements

Review the following table to note other differences between the IF and WHERE statements.

Action	The Subsetting IF Statement	The WHERE Statement
Selecting Data	Can select records from external files, observations from SAS data sets, observations created with an INPUT statement, or observations based on the value of a computed or derived variable.	Can select only observations from SAS data sets.
Conditional Execution	Is an executable statement	Is not an executable statement
Grouping Data Using a BY Statement	Has no effect on FIRST. or LAST. flags.	Affects FIRST. or LAST. flags, which are set after processing the WHERE expression.
Merging Data	Selects observations after combining current observations.	Applies the selection criteria to each input data set before combining observations.

Note: If you use the WHERE= data set option and the WHERE statement in the same DATA step, SAS ignores the WHERE statement for input data sets. The WHERE= data set option and the WHERE statement call the same SAS routine.

Using the WHERE Statement with the OBS= and FIRSTOBS= Options

Another way to read and write only essential data is to process a segment of subsetted data. You accomplish this specialized task by using a WHERE expression in conjunction with the OBS= and FIRSTOBS= data set options.

In the following example, the WHERE expression selects observations before the OBS= and FIRSTOBS= options are applied. The values specified for OBS= and FIRSTOBS= are the logical observation numbers in the subset, not the physical observation numbers in the data set.

```
options fmtsearch=(formats);

proc print
     data=company.organization_dim(firstobs=5 obs=8);
     var employee_id employee_gender salary;
     where salary>40000;
run;
```

Obs	Employee_ID	Employee_Gender	Salary
101	120201	Male	$43,280
157	120257	Female	$156,245
158	120258	Male	$83,305
159	120259	Male	$433,800

FIRSTOBS = 5 is the fifth observation in the subset, whereas it was observation 101 in the data set Company.Organization.

OBS = 8 is the eighth observation in the subset, whereas it was observation 159 in the data set Company.Company.Organization..

Selecting Observations When Reading Data from External Files

Positioning a subsetting IF statement in a DATA step so that it reads only the variables that are needed to select the subset—before reading all the data—can reduce the overhead required for processing data.

The following graphic illustrates how data is read from an external file, loaded into the input buffer, and read into the program data vector.

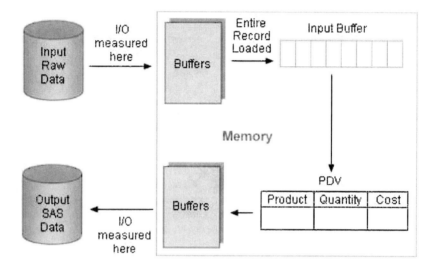

Remember that I/O operations are measured as data moves between disks and buffers—for both input and output data. Each record is loaded into the input buffer before moving to the program data vector for processing, so I/O is not affected by the placement of a subsetting IF statement in the DATA step.

You can reduce the CPU resources that are required for processing data by limiting what is read into the program data vector. Position a subsetting IF statement after an INPUT statement that reads only the data that is required in order to check for specific conditions. Subsequent statements do not execute for unwanted observations.

Note: Converting raw character fields to SAS character variables requires less CPU time than converting raw numeric fields to the real binary encoding of SAS numeric variables.

Comparative Example: Creating a Subset of Data by Reading Data from an External File

Overview

Suppose you want to create a SAS data set by reading a subset of data from an external file that is referenced by the fileref Customerdata. You want the subset to contain only customers in the United Kingdom.

The subset is approximately 6% of the countries in the external file, which contains 89,954 records and 12 fields.

The following sample programs compare two techniques. You can use these samples as models for creating benchmark programs in your own environment. Your results might vary depending on the structure of your data, your operating environment, and the resources that are available at your site.

Programming Techniques

 Reading All Variables and Subsetting

In this program, the INPUT statement reads all variables before the subsetting IF statement checks the value of Country. Then, if the value for Country is **GB**, the observation is written to the output data set Retail.UnitedKingdom.

```
data retail.UnitedKingdom;
   infile customerdata;
   input @1   Customer_ID          12.
         @13  Country              $2.
         @15  Gender               $1.
         @16  Personal_ID          $15.
         @31  Customer_Name        $40.
         @71  Customer_FirstName   $20.
         @91  Customer_LastName    $30.
         @121 Birth_Date           date9.
         @130 Customer_Address     $45.
         @175 Street_ID            12.
         @199 Street_Number        $8.
         @207 Customer_Type_ID     8.;
   if country='GB';
run;
```

❷ Reading Selected Variables and Subsetting

In this program, the first INPUT statement reads only Country and holds the record in the input buffer using the single trailing @ sign. Then the program uses a subsetting IF statement to check the value of Country. If the value for Country is not **GB**, other variables are not read in or written to the output data set Retail.UnitedKingdom. If the value for Country is **GB**, values for other variables are input and written to the output data set Retail.UnitedKingdom.

```
data retail.UnitedKingdom;
   infile customerdata;
   input @13 Country $2. @;
   if country='GB';
   input @1   Customer_ID          12.
         @15  Gender               $1.
         @16  Personal_ID          $15.
         @31  Customer_Name        $40.
         @71  Customer_FirstName   $20.
         @91  Customer_LastName    $30.
         @121 Birth_Date           date9.
         @130 Customer_Address     $45.
         @175 Street_ID            12.
         @199 Street_Number        $8.
         @207 Customer_Type_ID     8.;
run;
```

General Recommendations

- Position a subsetting IF statement in a DATA step so that only variables that are necessary to select the record are read before subsetting. This can result in significant savings in CPU time. There is no difference in I/O or memory usage between the two techniques.

- When selecting records from an external file, read the field or fields on which the selection is being made before reading all the fields into the program data vector.

- Use the single trailing @ sign to hold the input buffer so that you can continue to read the record when the variable or variables satisfy the IF condition.

- Reset the pointer so that you can begin reading the record in the first position by using @1 Customer_ID.

In addition to subsetting observations, you can subset variables by using statements or options that efficiently read and write only essential data.

Subsetting Variables with the KEEP and DROP Statements and Options

To subset variables, you can use either of the following:

- the DROP and KEEP statements

- the DROP= and KEEP= data set options

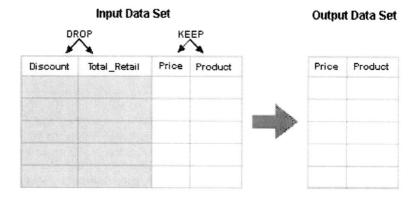

Use of the KEEP= data set option and the DROP= data set option can affect resource usage, depending on whether they are used in a SET or MERGE statement or in a DATA statement.

The following figure shows how options in these statements process data.

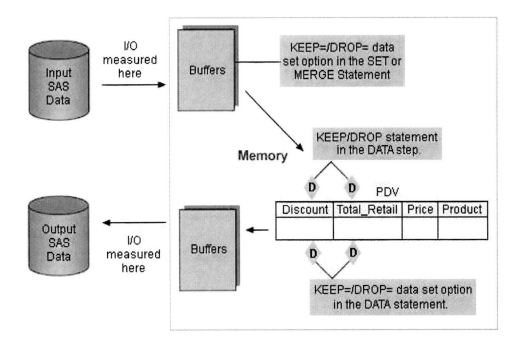

When used in the SET or MERGE statement, the KEEP= and DROP= data set options affect which variables are read into the program data vector. Reading only the variables that need to be processed in the DATA step can sometimes improve efficiency.

When used in the DATA statement, these same options put drop flags on variables to be excluded and affect which variables are written to the output data set.

The DROP and KEEP statements work just like the KEEP= or DROP= options in the DATA statement.

The following table describes differences in how the KEEP statement and the KEEP= data set option write variables to SAS data sets.

DROP or KEEP Statement	DROP= or KEEP= Output Data Set Option	DROP= or KEEP= Input Data Set Option
Writes only the selected variables to all output data sets.	Can write different variables to different output data sets.	Reads only the selected variables into the PDV.
Available only in the DATA step.	Available in the DATA step or most PROC steps.	Available in the DATA step or most PROC steps.

Comparative Example: Creating a Report That Contains Average and Median Statistics

Overview

Suppose you want to create a report that contains the average and median values for the variable Profit, based on the data set Retail.Order_fact. Depending on the number of variables eliminated, it might be more efficient to use the KEEP= option in a SET statement to limit which variables are read.

The following sample programs compare two techniques for reading and writing variables to a data set. You can use these samples as models for creating benchmark programs in your own environment. Your results might vary depending on the structure of your data, your operating environment, and the resources that are available at your site.

Programming Techniques

 Without the KEEP= option

This program reads all variables from the data set Retail.Order_fact and does not restrict which variables are written to the output data set Retail.Profit. PROC MEANS reads all the variables from the data set.

```
data retail.profit;
   set retail.order_fact;
   if discount=. then
      Profit=(total_retail_price-costPrice_Per_Unit)*quantity;
   else Profit=((total_retail_price*discount)-costprice_per_unit)*quantity;
run;
proc means data=retail.profit mean median maxdec=2;
   title 'Order Information';
   class employee_id;
   var profit;
run;
```

❷ KEEP= in the DATA Statement

This program uses the KEEP= data set option in the DATA statement to write two variables to the output data set Retail.Profit. PROC MEANS reads only two variables from the data set.

```
data retail.profit(keep=employee_id profit);
   set retail.order_fact;
   if discount=. then
      Profit=(total_retail_price-costprice_per_unit)*quantity;
   else Profit=((total_retail_price*discount)-costprice_per_unit)*quantity;
run;
proc means data=retail.profit mean median maxdec=2;
   title 'Order Information';
   class employee_id;
   var profit;
run;
```

❸ KEEP= in the DATA and SET Statements

This program uses the KEEP= option in the SET statement to read six variables from Retail.Order_fact, and it uses the KEEP= data set option in the DATA statement to write two variables to the output data set Retail.Profits. PROC MEANS reads only two variables from the data set.

```
data retail.profits(keep=employee_id profit);
   set retail.order_fact(keep=employee_id total_retail_price discount
                              costprice_per_unit quantity);
      if discount=. then
         Profit=(total_retail_price-costprice_per_unit)*quantity;
      else Profit=((total_retail_price*discount)-costprice_per_unit)*quantity;
run;
proc means data=retail.profit mean median maxdec=2;
   title 'Order Information';
   class employee_id;
   var profit;
run;
```

❹ KEEP= in the SET and MEANS Statements

This program uses the KEEP= option in the SET statement to read selected variables from Retail.Order_fact, and it uses the KEEP= data set option in the MEANS statement to process only the variables that are needed for the statistical report. You might do this if you need additional variables in Retail.Profits for further processing, but only two variables for processing by PROC MEANS.

```
data retail.profit;
  set retail.order_fact(keep=employee_id total_retail_price discount
                             costprice_per_unit quantity);
  if discount=. then
     Profit=(total_retail_price-costprice_per_unit)*quantity;
  else Profit=((total_retail_price*discount)-costprice_per_unit)*quantity;
run;
proc means data=retail.profit(keep=employee_id profit) mean median maxdec=2;
   title 'Order Information';
   class employee_id;
   var profit;
run;
```

General Recommendations

- To reduce both CPU time and I/O operations, avoid reading and writing variables that are not needed.

Comparative Example: Creating a SAS Data Set That Contains Only Certain Variables

Overview

Suppose you want to read data from an external file that is referenced by the fileref Rawdata and create a SAS data set that contains only the variables Customer_ID, Country, Gender, and Customer_Name.

The following sample programs compare two techniques. You can use these samples as models for creating benchmark programs in your own environment. Your results might vary depending on the structure of your data, your operating environment, and the resources that are available at your site.

Programming Techniques

 Reading All Fields

In this program, the KEEP= data set option writes only the variables that are needed to the output data set, whereas the INPUT statement reads all fields from the external file.

```
data retail.customers(keep=Customer_ID Country Gender Customer_Name);
   infile rawdata;
   input @1    Customer_ID         12.
         @13   Country             $2.
         @15   Gender              $1.
         @16   Personal_ID         $15.
         @31   Customer_Name       $40.
         @71   Customer_FirstName  $20.
         @91   Customer_LastName   $30.
         @121  Birth_Date          date9.
         @130  Customer_Address    $45.
         @175  Street_ID           12.
         @199  Street_Number       $8.
         @207  Customer_Type_ID    8.;
run;
```

❷ Reading Selected Fields

In this program, the INPUT statement reads selected fields from the external file, and by default, these are written to the output data set. This program is an example of efficient processing.

```
data retail.customers;
   infile rawdata;
   input @1    Customer_ID    12.
         @13   Country        $2.
         @15   Gender         $1.
         @31   Customer_Name  $40.;
run;
```

General Recommendations

- Read only the fields you need from an external data file to save CPU and real-time resources.

- To save CPU resources, avoid converting numeric data that you do not need in further processing.

Note: Remember that numeric data is moved into the program data vector after being converted to real binary, floating point numbers; multiple digits are stored in one byte. Character data is moved into the program data vector with no conversion; one character is stored in one byte.

Storing Data in SAS Data Sets

Overview

In many cases, it is best practice for you to store data in SAS data sets. You can optimize performance if you know when you should create a SAS data set and when you should read data directly from an external file.

Before viewing the comparative example that illustrates different techniques for reading from a SAS data set versus from an external file, consider the following advantages of storing data in SAS data sets.

When you use SAS to repeatedly analyze or manipulate any particular group of data, it is more efficient to create a SAS data set than to read the raw data each time. Although SAS data sets can be larger than external files and can require more disk space, reading from SAS data sets saves CPU time that is associated with reading a raw data file.

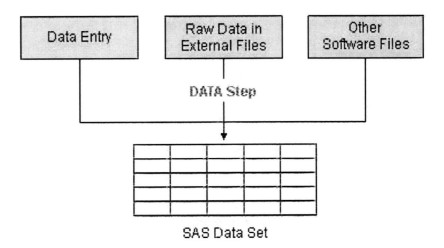

Here are other reasons for storing data in SAS data sets, rather than external files:

- When the data is already in a SAS data set, you can use a SAS procedure on the data without further conversion.

- SAS data sets are self-documenting.

The descriptor portion of a SAS data set documents data set properties, including the following:

- data set labels

- variable labels

- variable formats

- informats

- variable names

Note: Create a temporary SAS data set if the data set is used for intermediate tasks such as merging and if it is needed in that SAS session only. Create a temporary SAS data set when the external file on which the data set is based might change between SAS sessions.

Comparative Example: Reading a SAS Data Set Versus an External File

Overview

Suppose you want to create a SAS data set that contains a large number of variables. One way to accomplish this task is to read an external file that is referenced by the fileref Rawdata. Another way to accomplish this is to read the same data from an existing SAS data set named Retail.Customer.

The following sample programs compare two techniques. You can use these samples as models for creating benchmark programs in your own environment. Your results might vary depending on the structure of your data, your operating environment, and the resources that are available at your site.

Programming Techniques

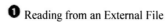 Reading from an External File

In this program, the INPUT statement reads fields of data from an external file that is referenced by the fileref Rawdata and creates 12 variables. For benchmarking purposes, the DATA statement specifies the _NULL_ argument so that you can measure resources used to read data isolated from resources used to write data.

```
data _null_;
   infile rawdata;
   input @1    Customer_ID          12.
         @13   Country              $2.
         @15   Gender               $1.
         @16   Personal_ID          $15.
         @31   Customer_Name        $40.
         @71   Customer_FirstName   $20.
         @91   Customer_LastName    $30.
         @121  Birth_Date           date9.
         @130  Customer_Address     $45.
         @175  Street_ID            12.
         @199  Street_Number        $8.
         @207  Customer_Type_ID     8.;
run;
```

❷ Reading from a SAS Data Set

In this program, the SET statement reads data directly from an existing SAS data set. As in the previous program, the DATA statement uses _NULL_ instead of naming a data set.

```
data _null_;
   set retail.customer;
run;
```

General Recommendations

- To save CPU resources, read a SAS data set instead of an external file.

- To reduce I/O operations, read a SAS data set instead of an external file. Savings in I/O operations are largely dependent on the block size of the external file and the page size of the SAS data set.

Avoiding Unnecessary Procedure Invocation

Overview

Best practices specify that you avoid unnecessary procedure invocation. One way to do this is to take advantage of procedures that accomplish multiple tasks with one invocation.

Several procedures enable you to perform multiple tasks or create multiple reports by invoking the procedure only once. These include the following:

- the SQL procedure
- the DATASETS procedure
- the FREQ procedure
- the TABULATE procedure.

Note: BY-group processing can also minimize unnecessary invocations of procedures.

To illustrate this principle, examine features of the DATASETS procedure.

Executing the DATASETS Procedure

The DATASETS procedure can use RUN-group processing to process multiple sets of statements. RUN-group processing enables you to submit groups of statements without ending the procedure.

When the DATASETS procedure executes, the following actions occur:

- SAS reads the program statements that are associated with one task until it reaches a RUN statement or an implied RUN statement.
- SAS executes all of the preceding statements immediately, and then continues reading until it reaches another RUN statement or an implied RUN statement.

To execute the last task, you must use a RUN statement or a QUIT statement.

```
proc datasets lib=company;
   modify orders;
      rename quantity=Units_Ordered;
      format costprice_per_unit dollar13.2;
      label delivery_date='Date of Delivery';
   run;
   modify customers;
      format customer_birthdate mmddyy10.
   run;
quit;
```

You can terminate the PROC DATASETS execution by submitting a DATA statement, a PROC statement, or a QUIT statement.

RUN-Group Processing

RUN-group processing avoids unnecessary procedure invocation. The procedures that support RUN-group processing include the following:

- CHART, GCHART

- PLOT, GPLOT

- GIS, GMAP

- GLM

- REG

- DATASETS

Using Different Types of RUN Groups with PROC DATASETS

The DATASETS procedure supports four types of RUN groups. Each RUN group is defined by the statements that compose it and cause it to execute.

Some statements in PROC DATASETS act as implied RUN statements because they cause the RUN group that precedes them to execute.

The following statements compose a RUN group and what causes each RUN group to execute:

- The PROC DATASETS statement always executes immediately. No other statement is necessary to cause the PROC DATASETS statement to execute. Therefore, the PROC DATASETS statement alone is a RUN group.

- The MODIFY statement and any of its subordinate statements form a RUN group. These RUN groups always execute immediately. No other statement is necessary to cause a MODIFY RUN group to execute.

- The APPEND, CONTENTS, and COPY statements (including EXCLUDE and SELECT, if present) form their own separate RUN groups. Every APPEND statement forms a single-statement RUN group, every CONTENTS statement forms a single-statement RUN group, and every COPY step forms a RUN group. Any other statement in the procedure, except those that are subordinate to either the COPY or MODIFY statement, causes the RUN group to execute.

Also, one or more of the following statements form a RUN group:

- AGE

- EXCHANGE

- CHANGE

- REPAIR

If any of these statements appear in sequence in the PROC step, the sequence forms a RUN group. For example, if a REPAIR statement appears immediately after a SAVE statement, the REPAIR statement does not force the SAVE statement to execute; it becomes part of the same RUN group. To execute the RUN group, submit one of the following statements:

- PROC DATASETS

- MODIFY

- APPEND

- QUIT

- CONTENTS

- RUN

- COPY

- another DATA or PROC step

Comparative Example: Modifying the Descriptor Portion of SAS Data Sets

Overview

Suppose you want to use the DATASETS procedure to modify the data sets NewCustomer, NewOrders, and NewItems.

The following sample programs compare two techniques. You can use these samples as models for creating benchmark programs in your own environment. Your results might vary depending on the structure of your data, your operating environment, and the resources that are available at your site.

Programming Techniques

 Multiple DATASETS Procedures

This program invokes PROC DATASETS three times to modify the descriptor portion of the data set NewCustomer, two times to modify the descriptor portion of the data set NewOrders, and once to change the name of the data set NewItems.

```
proc datasets lib=company nolist;
   modify newcustomer;
   rename Country_ID=Country
          Name=Customer_Name;
quit;

proc datasets lib=company nolist;
   modify newcustomer;
   format birth_date date9.;
quit;

proc datasets lib=company nolist;
   modify newcustomer;
   label birth_date='Date of Birth';
quit;

proc datasets lib=company nolist;
   modify neworders;
   rename order=Order_ID
          employee=Employee_ID
          customer=Customer_ID;
quit;

proc datasets lib=company nolist;
   modify neworders;
   format order_date date9.;
quit;

proc datasets lib=company nolist;
   change newitems=NewOrder_Items;
quit;
```

❷ Single DATASETS Procedure

This program invokes PROC DATASETS once to modify the descriptor portion of the data sets NewCustomer and NewOrders, and to change the name of the data set NewItems. This technique is more efficient.

```
proc datasets lib=company nolist;
   modify newcustomer;
   rename country_ID=Country
          name=Customer_Name;
   format birth_date date9.;
   label  birth_date='Date of Birth';
   modify neworders;
   rename order=Order_ID
          employee=Employee_ID
          customer=Customer_ID;
   format order_date date9.;
   change newitems=NewOrder_Items;
quit;
```

General Recommendations

- Invoke the DATASETS procedure once and process all the changes for a library in one step to save CPU and I/O resources—at the cost of memory resources.

- Use the NOLIST option on the PROC DATASETS statement. The NOLIST option suppresses printing of the library members in the log. Using NOLIST can save I/O.

Note: Because the specified library could change between invocations of the DATASETS procedure, the procedure is reloaded into memory for each invocation.

Summary

Executing Only Necessary Statements

You minimize the CPU time that SAS uses when you execute the minimum number of statements in the most efficient order.

For a more efficient program, place the subsetting IF statement as soon as logically possible in a DATA step when creating a subset of data.

Review guidelines for using conditional logic efficiently with IF-THEN/ELSE statements or SELECT statements. Remember to minimize the number of statements that use SAS functions or arithmetic operators.

Conditionally execute only necessary statements by placing statements in groups that are associated with IF-THEN/ELSE statements or SELECT/WHEN statements. Groups of statements execute only when a particular condition is true. Review the criteria for using DO groups efficiently.

Eliminating Unnecessary Passes through the Data

You should avoid reading or writing data more than necessary in order to minimize I/O operations.

There are a variety of techniques that you can use. For example, use a single DATA step to create multiple output data sets from one pass of the input data, rather than using multiple DATA steps to process the input data each time you create an output data set. Create sorted subsets by subsetting data with the SORT procedure rather than subsetting data in a DATA step and then sorting. Change variable attributes by using PROC DATASETS rather than a DATA step.

Reading and Writing Only Essential Data

If you process fewer observations and variables, SAS performs fewer I/O operations. To limit the number of observations that are processed, you can use the subsetting IF statement and the WHERE statement. Best programming practices can be applied if you understand other differences between subsetting IF and WHERE statements. You can also improve performance by applying OBS= and FIRSTOBS= processing with a WHERE statement.

To select observations when reading data from external files, position a subsetting IF statement in a DATA step so that it reads only the variables that are needed to select the subset before reading all the data. This can reduce the overhead required to process data.

To limit the number of variables that are processed, you can use either of the following:

- the DROP and KEEP statements
- the DROP= and KEEP= data set options.

In the SET statement, the DROP= or KEEP= data set option controls which variables are read and subsequently processed. In the DATA statement, the DROP= or KEEP= data set option controls which variables are written to an output data set after processing. Using the SET statement with these options is the most efficient and best practice.

Storing SAS Data in SAS Data Sets

When you use SAS to repeatedly analyze or manipulate any particular group of data, create a SAS data set instead of reading the raw data each time.

Reading data from an external file rather than reading from a SAS data set greatly increases CPU usage.

Avoiding Unnecessary Procedure Invocation

Invoke procedures once rather than multiple times. Several procedures enable you to create multiple reports by invoking the procedure only once.

Using a single DATASETS procedure instead of multiple DATASETS procedures to modify the descriptor portion of a data set results in a noticeable savings in both CPU and I/O operations. Also, you can take advantage of RUN-group processing to submit groups of statements without ending the procedure.

Quiz

Select the best answer for each question. After completing the quiz, check your answers using the answer key in the appendix.

1. Placing the subsetting IF statement at the top rather than near the bottom of a DATA step results in a savings in CPU usage. What happens if the subset is large rather than small?

   a. The savings in CPU usage increases as the subset grows larger because the I/O increases.

   b. The savings in CPU usage decreases as the subset grows larger. However, placing the subsetting IF statement at the top of a DATA step always uses fewer resources than placing it at the bottom.

   c. The savings in CPU usage remains constant as the subset grows larger. However, placing the subsetting IF statement near the bottom of a data set is preferable.

   d. The savings in CPU usage decreases as the subset grows larger. However, placing the subsetting IF statement near the bottom of a data set increases the I/O.

2. Which of the following statements is true about techniques that are used for modifying data and attributes?

   a. You can use PROC DATASETS to modify both data values and variable attributes.

   b. You can use PROC DATASETS to modify only data values.

   c. You can use the DATA step to modify both data values and variable attributes.

   d. You can use the DATA step to modify only variable attributes.

3. For selecting observations, is a subsetting IF statement or a WHERE statement more efficient? Why?

   a. A subsetting IF statement is more efficient because it loads all observations sequentially into the program data vector.

   b. A subsetting IF statement is more efficient because it examines what is in the input buffer and selects observations before they are loaded into the program data vector, which results in a savings in CPU operations.

   c. A WHERE statement is more efficient because it loads all observations sequentially into the program data vector.

   d. A WHERE statement is more efficient because it examines what is in the input page buffer and selects observations before they are loaded into the program data vector, which results in a savings in CPU operations.

4. When is it more advantageous to create a temporary SAS data set rather than a permanent SAS data set?

   a. When the external file on which the data set is based might change between SAS sessions.

   b. When the external file on which the data set is based does not change between SAS sessions.

   c. When the data set is needed for more than one SAS session.

    d. When you are converting raw numeric values to SAS data values.

5. When you compare the technique of using multiple DATASETS procedures to using a single DATASETS procedure to modify the descriptor portion of a data set, which is true?

    a. A one-step DATASETS procedure results in an increase in I/O operations.

    b. Multiple DATASETS procedures result in a decrease in I/O operations.

    c. A one-step DATASETS procedure results in a decrease in CPU usage.

    d. Multiple DATASETS procedures result in a decrease in CPU usage.

Chapter 23
Querying Data Efficiently

Overview

Introduction

SAS provides a variety of techniques for querying data. In this chapter, you learn to select the most efficient query techniques from those listed below, based on comparisons of resource usage.

Task	Techniques
selecting a subset	• WHERE statement that references an indexed data set
creating a detail report	• PRINT procedure • SQL procedure
creating a summary report with one or more class variables	• MEANS procedure (or SUMMARY procedure) • TABULATE procedure • REPORT procedure • SQL procedure • DATA step

Note: This chapter does not cover the SAS Scalable Performance Data Engine (SAS SPD Engine). For details about using the SAS SPD Engine to improve performance, see the SAS documentation.

Using an Index for Efficient WHERE Processing

Overview

When processing a WHERE expression, SAS determines which of the following access methods is likely to be most efficient:

Sequential access

SAS examines all observations sequentially in their physical order.

SAS Data Set

Anderson	09JAN2000	X	
Baker	14OCT2001	X	
Davis	30MAR2000	Y	
Edwards	28JUN2002	X	
Smith	15JAN2000	Y	
Yates	04AUG2002	X	

Direct access

SAS Data Set

Anderson	09JAN2000	X	
Baker	14OCT2001	X	
Davis	30MAR2000	Y	
Edwards	28JUN2002	X	
➤ Smith	15JAN2000	Y	
Yates	04AUG2002	X	

SAS uses an index to access specific observations directly. Using an index to process a WHERE expression is referred to as optimizing the WHERE expression.

Using an index to process a WHERE expression improves performance in some situations but not in others. For example, it is more efficient to use an index to select a small subset than a large subset. In addition, an index conserves some resources at the expense of others.

After SAS decides whether to create an index, you also play a role in determining which access method SAS can use. When your program contains a WHERE expression, you should review your program to see if you agree that direct access is likely to be more efficient. If it is, you can make sure that an index is available by creating a new index or by maintaining an existing index.

To help you make a more effective decision about whether to create an index, this topic and the next few topics provide you with a closer look at the following:

- steps that SAS performs for sequential access and direct access

- benefits and costs of index usage

- steps that SAS performs to determine which access method is most efficient

- factors affecting resource usage for indexed access

- guidelines for deciding whether to create, use, and maintain an index

Note: You should already know how to create and maintain indexes by using the INDEX= data set option in the DATA statement, the DATASETS procedure, and the SQL procedure. To review these SAS elements, see Chapter 6, "Creating and Managing Indexes Using PROC SQL," on page 226 and Chapter 13, "Creating Indexes," on page 448.

Note: SAS can also use an index to process a BY statement. BY processing enables you to process observations in a specific order according to the values of one or more variables that are specified in a BY statement. Indexing a data file enables you to use a BY statement without sorting the data file. When you specify a BY statement, SAS checks the value of the Sorted indicator. If the Sorted indicator is set to NO, then SAS looks for an appropriate index. If an appropriate index exists, the software automatically retrieves the observations from the data file in indexed order. Using an index to process a BY statement might not always be more efficient than simply sorting the data file. Therefore, using an index for a BY statement is generally for convenience, not for performance.

Accessing Data Sequentially

When accessing observations sequentially, SAS must examine all observations in their physical order within the data file.

Example

Suppose you want to create a new data set, Company.D02jul2000, that contains a subset of observations from the data set Company.Dates. The following DATA step uses a WHERE statement to select all observations in which Date_ID is **02JUL2000**:

```
data company.d02jul2000;
   set company.dates;
   where date_id='02JUL2000'd;
run;
```

The data set Company.Dates does not contain an index that is defined on the variable Date_ID, so SAS must use sequential access to process the WHERE statement.

Note: If the data set company.dates has been sorted by date_id, SAS searches the data sequentially until the WHERE criterion (**date_id='02JUL2000'd**) has been satisfied.

Accessing Data Directly

When using an index for WHERE processing, SAS accesses each desired observation without reading every observation in the data set.

Example

Suppose you have defined an index on the variable Date_ID in the Company.Dates data set. This time, when you submit the following DATA step, SAS uses the index to process the WHERE statement:

```
data company.d02jul2000;
   set company.dates;
   where date_id='02JUL2000'd;
run;
```

The process of retrieving data via an index (direct access) is more complicated than sequential access, so direct access requires more CPU time per observation retrieved than sequential access. However, for a small subset, using an index can decrease the number of pages that SAS loads into input buffers, which reduces the number of I/O operations.

Note: When the values in the data set are sorted in the order in which they occur in the index, the qualified observations are adjacent to each other. In this situation, SAS loads fewer pages into the input buffer than if the data is randomly distributed throughout the data set. Therefore, fewer I/O operations are required when the data set is sorted.

Benefits and Costs of Using an Index

As the preceding examples show, both benefits and costs are associated with using an index. Weighing these benefits and costs is an important part of deciding whether using an index is efficient.

The main benefits of using an index include the following:

- provides fast access to a small subset of observations

- returns values in sorted order

- can enforce uniqueness

The main costs of using an index include the following:

- requires extra CPU cycles and I/O operations for creating and maintaining an index

- requires increased CPU time and I/O activity for reading the data

- requires extra disk space for storing the index file

- requires extra memory for loading index pages and extra code for using the index

Note: SAS requires additional buffers when an index file is used. When a data file is opened, SAS opens the index file, but not the indexes. Buffers are not required unless SAS uses an index, but SAS allocates the buffers to prepare for using the index. The number of levels of an index determines the number of buffers that are allocated. The maximum number of buffers is three for data files that are open for input. The maximum number is four for data that is open for update. These buffers can be used for other processing if they are not used for indexes.

How SAS Selects an Access Method

When SAS processes a WHERE expression, it first determines whether to use direct access or sequential access by performing the following steps:

1. identifies available indexes

2. identifies conditions that can be optimized

3. estimates the number of observations that qualify

4. compares probable resource usage for both methods

Identifying Available Indexes

Overview

The first step for SAS is to determine whether there are any existing indexes that might be used to process the WHERE expression. Specifically, SAS checks the variable in each condition in the WHERE expression to determine whether the variable is a key variable in an index.

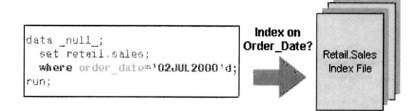

SAS can use either a simple index or a composite index to optimize a WHERE expression. To be considered for use in optimizing a single WHERE condition, one of the following requirements must be met:

- the variable in the WHERE condition is the key variable in a simple index

- the variable in the WHERE condition is the first key variable in a composite index

SAS identifies all indexes that are defined on any variable in the WHERE expression. However, no matter how many indexes are available, SAS can use only one index to process a WHERE expression. So, if multiple indexes are available, SAS must choose between them.

When SAS looks for available indexes, there are three possible outcomes:

Index	Outcome
There is no index defined on any variables in the WHERE expression.	SAS does not continue with the decision process. SAS must use sequential access to process the WHERE expression.
There is one available index that is defined on one or more variables in the WHERE expression.	SAS continues with the decision process and determines whether using the available index is more efficient than using sequential access.
There are multiple available indexes. Each is defined on one or more of the variables in the WHERE expression.	SAS continues with the decision process. SAS must choose between the available indexes in the next few steps. SAS tries to select the index that satisfies the most conditions and that selects the smallest subset of observations.

Note: If a program specifies both a WHERE expression and a BY statement, SAS looks for one index that satisfies conditions for both. If such an index is not found, the BY statement takes precedence so that SAS can ensure that the data is returned in sorted order. With a BY statement, SAS cannot use an index to optimize a WHERE expression if the optimization invalidates the BY order.

Example: Identifying One Available Index

Suppose you submit a program that contains the following WHERE statement, and suppose that the data set has one index, as shown below:

WHERE Statement	Available Index
`where delivery_date='02jul2000'd`	simple index defined on Delivery_Date

This WHERE expression has one condition, and the variable in that condition (Delivery_Date) is the key variable in the simple index. If all other requirements for optimization are met in later steps, then SAS can use this index to optimize the WHERE expression.

Likewise, if the only available index is a composite index in which Delivery_Date is the first key variable, then SAS can use the index if all other requirements for optimization are met.

Even if a WHERE statement has multiple conditions, SAS can use either a simple index or a composite index to optimize just one of the conditions. For example, suppose your program contains a WHERE statement that has two conditions, and suppose that the data set has one index, as shown below:

WHERE Statement	Available Index
where order_date='01jan2000'd and delivery_date='02jul2000'd;	simple index defined on Delivery_Date

Assuming that all other requirements for optimization are met, SAS can use this index to optimize the second condition in this WHERE expression.

Example: Identifying Multiple Available Indexes

Suppose your program contains a WHERE statement with two conditions, and suppose that each condition references a key variable in a different index, as shown below:

WHERE Statement	Available Index
where order_date='01jan2000'd and delivery_date='02jul2000'd;	• simple index defined on Order_Date • simple index defined on Delivery_Date.

Although two indexes are available, SAS can use only one index to optimize a WHERE statement. In a later step of the process, SAS tries to select the index that satisfies the most conditions and that selects the smallest subset of observations.

Compound Optimization

SAS usually uses an index to process just one condition, no matter how many conditions and variables a WHERE expression contains. However, in a process called compound optimization, SAS can use a composite index to optimize multiple conditions on multiple variables, which are joined with a logical operator such as AND. Constructing your WHERE expression to take advantage of multiple key variables in a single index can greatly improve performance.

In order for compound optimization to occur, at least the first two key variables in the composite index must be used in the WHERE conditions. Later in this chapter, you learn about other requirements that must be met in order for compound optimization to occur.

Note: The WHERE expression can also contain non-indexed variables, and the key variables and non-indexed variables can appear in any order in the expression.

Example: Composite Index That Can Be Used to Optimize Multiple Conditions

Suppose your program contains a WHERE statement that has two conditions, and suppose that each condition references one of the first two key variables in a composite index:

WHERE Statement	Available Index
`where order_date='01jan2000'd and` `delivery_date='02jul2000'd';`	composite index defined on the following variables: • Order_Date (first key variable) • Delivery_Date (second key variable) • Product_ID (third key variable)

Because the two variables that are referenced in the WHERE expression are the first two key variables in the composite index, SAS can use the composite index for compound optimization if the WHERE conditions meet all other requirements for optimization.

Example: Composite Index That Can Be Used to Optimize One Condition

The following WHERE statement also contains two conditions, and each condition references one of the variables in the composite index:

WHERE Statement	Available Index
`where order_date='01jan2000'd and` `product_id='220101400106';`	composite index defined on the following variables: • Order_Date (first key variable) • Delivery_Date (second key variable) • Product_ID (third key variable)

As in the previous WHERE statement, Order_Date is the first key variable in the index. However, in this situation, the composite index can be used to optimize only the first condition. The second condition references the third key variable, Product_ID, but the WHERE expression does not reference the second key variable, Delivery_Date. Without a reference to both the first and second key variables, compound optimization cannot occur.

Example: Composite Index That Cannot Be Used for Optimizing

Now suppose your program contains a WHERE statement that references only the second and third key variables in the composite index, as shown below:

WHERE Statement	Available Index
`where delivery_date='02jul2000'd' and` `product_id='220101400106';`	composite index defined on the following variables: • Order_Date (first key variable) • Delivery_Date (second key variable) • Product_ID (third key variable)

In this situation, SAS cannot use the index for optimization at all because the WHERE statement does not reference the first key variable.

Identifying Conditions That Can Be Optimized

In addition to containing key variables, WHERE conditions must meet other requirements in order to be candidates for optimization. SAS considers using an index only for WHERE conditions that contain certain operators and functions. Therefore, the next step for SAS is to consider the operators and functions in the conditions that contain key variables.

Requirements for Optimizing a Single WHERE Condition

SAS considers using an index for a WHERE condition that contains any of the following operators and functions:

Note: For all of the following examples, assume that the data set has simple indexes on the variables Quarter, Date_ID, and Region.

Operator	Example
comparison operators	`where quarter = '1998Q1';`
	`where date_id < '03JUL2000'd;`
	`where quarter in ('1998Q2','1998Q3');`
comparison operators with NOT	`where quarter ne '1999Q1';`
	`where quarter not in ('1999Q1','1999Q4');`
comparison operators with the colon modifier	`where quarter =: '1998';`
You can add a colon modifier (:) to any comparison operator to compare only a specified prefix of a character string.	
The colon modifier cannot be used with PROC SQL; use the LIKE operator instead.	
CONTAINS operator	`where quarter contains 'Q4';`
fully bounded range conditions that specify both an upper and lower limit, which includes the BETWEEN-AND operator	`where '01Jan1999'd < date_id` `    < '31Dec1999'd;`
	`where date_id between '01Jan1999'd` `                  and '31Dec1999'd`
pattern-matching operator LIKE	`where quarter like '%Q%';`
IS NULL or IS MISSING operator	`where quarter is null;`
	`where quarter is missing;`

Function	Example
TRIM function	`where trim(region) = 'Queensland';`

Function	Example
SUBSTR function in the form of **WHERE** SUBSTR (*variable,position,length*)=*'string'*; with these conditions: • *position* = 1 • *length* is less than or equal to the length of *variable* • *length* is equal to the length of the string	`where substr(quarter,1,4) = '1998';`

CAUTION:

Most but not all of the requirements listed above also apply to compound optimization. Requirements for compound optimization are covered later in this chapter.

WHERE Conditions That Cannot Be Optimized

SAS does not use an index to process a WHERE condition that contains any of the elements listed below.

Note: For all of the following examples, assume that the data set has simple indexes on the variables Date_ID, Quarter, and Quantity.

Element in WHERE Condition	Example
any function other than TRIM or SUBSTR	`where weekday(date_id)=2;`
a SUBSTR function that searches a string beginning at any position after the first	`where substr(quarter,6,1)='1';`
the sounds-like operator (=*)	`where quarter=*'1900Q0';`
arithmetic operators	`where quantity=quantity+1;`
a variable-to-variable condition	`where quantity gt threshold;`

Requirements for Compound Optimization

Most of the same operators that are acceptable for optimizing a single condition are also acceptable for compound optimization. However, compound optimization has special requirements for the operators that appear in the WHERE expression:

• The WHERE conditions must be connected by using either the AND operator or, if all conditions refer to the same variable, the OR operator.

• At least one of the WHERE conditions that contain a key variable must contain the EQ or IN operator.

Example: Compound Optimization

Suppose your program contains the following WHERE statement, which selects all people whose name is John Smith. The WHERE statement contains two conditions. Each condition references a different variable:

```
where lastname eq 'Smith' and
      frstname eq 'John';
```

Suppose Lastname is the first key variable and Frstname is the second key variable in a compound index. This WHERE statement meets all requirements for compound optimization:

- The WHERE expression references at least the first two key variables in one composite index.

- The two WHERE conditions are connected by the AND operator.

- At least one of the conditions contains the EQ operator.

If the two conditions in the WHERE statement are reversed, as shown below, the statement still meets all requirements for compound optimization. The order in which the key variables appear does not matter.

```
where frstname eq 'John' and
      lastname eq 'Smith';
```

Now suppose that the conditions in the WHERE statement are joined by the operator OR instead of AND:

```
where frstname eq 'John' or
      lastname eq 'Smith';
```

These conditions cannot be optimized because they are joined by OR but they do not reference the same variable.

Estimating the Number of Observations

Overview

It is more efficient to use indexed access for a small subset and to use sequential access for a large subset. Therefore, after identifying any available indexes and evaluating the conditions in the WHERE expression, SAS estimates the number of observations that will be qualified by the index. Whether SAS uses an index depends on the percentage of observations that are qualified (the size of the subset relative to the size of the data set), as shown below:

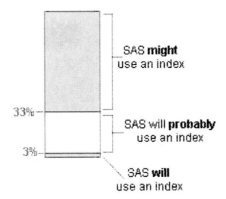

- If the subset is less than 3% of the data set, direct access is almost certainly more efficient than sequential access, and SAS will use an index. In this situation, SAS does not go on to compare probable resource usage.

- If the subset is between 3% and 33% of the data set, direct access is likely to be more efficient than sequential access, and SAS probably uses an index.

- If the subset is greater than 33% of the data set, it is less likely that direct access is more efficient than sequential access, and SAS might or might not use an index.

When multiple indexes exist, SAS selects the one that produces the fewest qualified observations (the smallest subset). SAS does this even when each index returns a subset that is less than 3% of the data set.

Printing Centile Information

To help SAS estimate the number of observations that would be selected by a WHERE expression, each index stores 21 statistics called cumulative percentiles, or centiles. Centiles provide information about the distribution of values for the indexed variable.

Understanding the distribution of values in a data set can help you improve the efficiency of WHERE processing in your programs. You can print centile information for an indexed data file by specifying the CENTILES option in either of these places:

- the CONTENTS procedure

- the CONTENTS statement in the DATASETS procedure

PROC CONTENTS *<options>*;	**PROC DATASETS** *<options>*;
RUN;	**CONTENTS** *<options>*;
	QUIT;

Example

The following SAS program prints centile information for the data set Company.Organization:

```
proc contents data=company.organization centiles;
run;
```

Partial output from this program is shown below. As indicated on the left, an index is defined on the variable Employee_ID. The 21 centile values are listed on the right.

Figure 23.1 *Partial PROC CONTENTS Output*

Alphabetic List of Indexes and Attributes							
#	Index	Unique Option	Owned by IC	Update Centiles	Current Update Percent	# of Unique Values	Variables
1	Employee_ID	YES	YES	5	0	1049	
							120101
							120152
							120205
							120257
							120310
							120362
							120415
							120467
							120520
							120572
							120625
							120677
							120729
							120782
							120834
							120887
							120939
							120992
							121044
							121097
							99999999

The 21 centile values consist of the following:

Position in List	Value Shown in Output Above	Description
1 (first)	120101	the minimum value of the indexed variable (0% of values are lower than this value)
2-20	120152 - 121097	each value is greater than or equal to all other values in one of the 19 percentiles that range from the bottom 5% to the bottom 95% of values, in increments of 5%

Position in List	Value Shown in Output Above	Description
21 (last)	99999999	the maximum value of the indexed variable (100% of values are lower than or equal to this value)

Note: For information about updating and refreshing centiles for a data file, see the SAS documentation.

Comparing Probable Resource Usage

Overview

After SAS estimates the number of qualified observations and selects the index that qualifies the fewest observations, SAS must then determine whether it is faster (more efficient) to satisfy the WHERE expression by using the index or by reading all of the observations sequentially. Specifically, SAS predicts how many I/O operations are required in order to satisfy the WHERE expression for each of the access methods. Then it compares the two resource costs.

Note: Remember, if SAS estimates that a subset contains fewer than 3% of the observations in the data set, SAS does not need to estimate resource usage. In this situation, SAS uses the index to process the WHERE statement.

How SAS Compares Resource Usage

To compare resource usage, SAS performs the following steps:

1. SAS predicts how many I/O operations are required if it uses the index to satisfy the WHERE expression. To do so, SAS positions the index at the first entry that contains a qualified value. In a buffer management simulation that takes into account the current number of available buffers, the RIDs (record identifiers) on that index page are processed, indicating how many I/Os are required in order to read the observations in the data file.

2. SAS calculates the I/O cost of a sequential pass of the entire data file.

3. SAS compares the two resource costs and determines which access method has a lower cost.

Note: If comparing resource costs results in a tie, SAS chooses the index.

Factors That Affect I/O

Several factors affect the number of I/O operations that are required for WHERE processing, including the following:

- subset size relative to data set size

- number of pages in the data file

- order of the data

- cost to uncompress a compressed file for a sequential read

These factors are discussed in more detail below.

Subset Size Relative to Data Set Size

As explained earlier in this chapter, SAS is more likely to use an index to access a small subset of observations. The process of retrieving data with an index is inherently more complicated than sequentially processing the data.

For small subsets, however, the benefit of reading only a few observations outweighs the cost of the complex processing. The smaller the subset, the larger the performance gains. Remember that SAS uses an index if the subset is less than 3% of the data set, and SAS probably uses an index if the subset is between 3% and 33% of the data set.

Number of Pages in the Data File

For a small data file, sequential processing is often just as efficient as index processing. If the data file's page count is less than three pages, then sequential access is faster even if the subset is less than 3% of the entire data set.

Note: The amount of data that can be transferred to one buffer in a single I/O operation is referred to as page size. To see how many pages are in a data file, use either the CONTENTS procedure or the CONTENTS statement in the DATASETS procedure. For more information about reporting the page size for a data file, see Chapter 20, "Controlling Memory Usage," on page 659.

Order of the Data

The order of the data (sort order) affects the number of I/O operations as described below:

Order of the Data	Effect on I/O Operations
observations are randomly distributed throughout the data file	Qualified observations are located on a larger number of data file pages. An I/O operation is required each time that SAS loads a page. Therefore, the more random the data in the data file, the more I/O operations are needed to use the index.
observations are sorted on the indexed variable or variables	The data is ordered more like the index (in ascending value order), so qualified observations are located on fewer data file pages. Therefore, the less random the data in the data file, the fewer I/O operations are needed to use the index.

Note: In general, sorting the data set by the key variable before indexing results in greater efficiency. The more ordered the data file is with respect to the key variable, the more efficient the use of the index. If the data file has more than one index, then sorting the data by the most frequently used key variable is most efficient. Sorting the data set results in more efficient WHERE processing even when SAS does not use an index.

Cost to Uncompress a Compressed File for a Sequential Read

When SAS reads a compressed data file, SAS automatically uncompresses the observations as they are read into the program data vector. This requires additional CPU resources, but fewer I/O operations are required because there are fewer data set pages. When performing a sequential read of a compressed data file, SAS must uncompress all observations in the file. However, when using direct access, SAS must uncompress only the qualified observations. Therefore, the resource cost of uncompressing observations is greater for a sequential read than for direct access.

Note: Compressing a file is a process that reduces the number of bytes that are required for representing each observation. By default, a SAS data file is not compressed. For more information about compressing files, see Chapter 21, "Controlling Data Storage Space," on page 676.

Other Factors That Affect Resource Usage

Data type and length are two other factors that can affect index efficiency.

Numeric key variables typically result in more CPU usage than character key variables, because numeric variables must be converted to formats that can be sequenced when values are read into the index or retrieved from the index. Character values are already in a format that can be sequenced.

Deciding Whether to Create an Index

In previous sections, you learned how SAS determines whether sequential access or direct access is likely to be most efficient for WHERE processing. You also learned about a variety of factors that you can assess to determine which access method is most efficient. After you have made your determination, you can use the following guidelines to decide whether it is efficient to create an index.

Guidelines for Deciding Whether to Create an Index

- Minimize the number of indexes to reduce disk storage and update costs. Create indexes only on variables that are often used in queries or (when data cannot be sorted) in BY-group processing.

- Create an index when you intend to retrieve a small subset of observations from a large data file.

- Do not create an index if the data file's page count is less than three pages. It is faster to access the data sequentially.

- Create indexes on variables that are discriminating. Discriminating variables have many different values that precisely identify observations. A WHERE expression that subsets based on a discriminating variable results in a smaller subset than a WHERE expression that references a non-discriminating variable. A non-discriminating variable is one that has only two values (for example, gender does not make a good variable on which to create an index).

- To minimize I/O operations, sort the data by the key variable before creating the index. Then, to improve performance, maintain the data file in sorted order by the key variable.

Note: If you choose not to use an index and the data set is large, it is still more efficient to sort the data set on the variable or variables that are specified in the WHERE statement.

- Consider how often your applications use an index. An index must be used often in order to compensate for the resources that are used in creating and maintaining it.

- Consider the cost of an index for a data file that is frequently changed.

- When you create an index to process a WHERE expression, do not try to create one index to satisfy all queries.

Consider three sample queries to see how you can apply the guidelines that are listed in the previous section. These queries illustrate the effect of one factor—the size of the subset relative to the size of the data set—on the choice of an access method. For each query, you learn the following:

- which access method SAS is likely to select

- whether you could improve performance by creating an index

Example: Selecting Subsets of Various Sizes from Data Sets of Various Sizes

Suppose you are working with the following two data sets. Each contains information about a company's orders:

Data Set Name	Pages	Observations
Company.Orders_large	285,500	19,033,380
Company.Orders_small	2	140

You want to create queries to generate three subset detail reports, one for each of the following types of subsets:

- small subset from a large data set

- large subset from a large data set

- small subset from a small data set

In all three queries, the WHERE expression specifies the variable Order_Date. You know that this variable is used frequently in queries, and that it is a discriminating variable. According to the guidelines in the previous section, these are both criteria for creating an index on the variable. However, there is currently no index defined on this variable in either data set.

Query 1: Small Subset from a Large Data Set

The first report shows all orders in Company.Orders_large that were made on January 10, 1998. Your query is shown below, along with the subset size that you have estimated:

Query	Subset Size
```data _null_; set company.orders_large; where order_date='10JAN1998'd; run;```	2232 observations (out of 19,033,380)< .02% of the data set

Because the subset is less than 3% of the entire data set, using an index on Order_Date should be more efficient than using sequential access. SAS uses an index for WHERE processing, if an index is available. To improve performance, you should create an index on Order_Date before running this program.

Query 2: Large Subset from a Large Data Set

The second report shows all orders in Company.Orders_large that were made before January 1, 2000. Your query and the estimated subset size are shown below:

Query	Subset Size
```data _null_; set company.orders_large; where order_date<'01JAN2000'd; run;```	12,752,365 observations (out of 19,033,380) =approximately 67% of the data set

Because the subset is more than 33% of the entire data set, using the index is probably less efficient than using sequential access. SAS probably will not use the index for WHERE processing.

Query 3: Small Subset from a Small Data Set

The third report shows all orders in the smaller data set Company.Orders_small that were made on June 30, 1998. Your query and the estimated subset size are shown below:

Query	Subset Size
```data _null_; set company.orders_small; where order_date'30JUN1998'd; run;```	*2* observations (out of 140) =< *2 %* of the data set

Because the subset is less than 3% of the entire data set, SAS will use the index for WHERE processing. However, the data file's page count is less than three pages, so it is more efficient to use sequential access. In this situation, it is best not to create an index.

Using the IDXWHERE= and IDXNAME= Data Set Options

In most situations, it is best to let SAS determine whether to use an index for WHERE processing. However, sometimes you might want to control whether SAS uses an existing index. For example, if you know that your query selects a large subset and that indexed access therefore is not efficient, you can tell SAS to ignore any index and to satisfy the conditions of the WHERE expression with a sequential search of the data set.

Alternatively, if your query selects a small subset and there are multiple available indexes, you can make sure that SAS uses a particular index to process your WHERE statement. Finally, you might want to force SAS to use (or not use) an index when you are benchmarking.

The data set options IDXWHERE= and IDXNAME= control index usage.

Option	Action
IDXWHERE=	specifies whether SAS should use an index to process the WHERE expression, no matter which access method SAS estimates is faster.
	You cannot use IDXWHERE= to override the use of an index for processing a BY statement.
IDXNAME=	causes SAS to use a specific index.

Note: You can use either IDXWHERE= or IDXNAME=, but not both at the same time.

For more information about the IDXWHERE= and IDXNAME= data set options, see Chapter 6, "Creating and Managing Indexes Using PROC SQL," on page 226.

Specifying MSGLEVEL=I to Determine Whether SAS Used an Index

To determine whether SAS used an index to process a WHERE expression, specify I as the value of the MSGLEVEL= system option. MSGLEVEL=I causes SAS to display information about index usage in the SAS log.

Note: To make the most efficient use of resources, use MSGLEVEL=I only for debugging and for verifying index usage.

Note: For more information about the MSGLEVEL= system option, see Chapter 13, "Creating Indexes," on page 448 or Chapter 6, "Creating and Managing Indexes Using PROC SQL," on page 226.

Example: Using IDXWHERE=NO to Prevent Index Usage

Suppose you write the following query, which lists all employees who work in the Sales department.

```
proc print data=company.organization;
   where department='Sales';
run;
```

Now suppose an index is defined on the variable Department in the data set Company.Organization. You know that Department has the value Sales in 65% of the observations, so it is not efficient for SAS to use an index for WHERE processing. To ensure that SAS does not use an index, specify IDXWHERE=NO after the data set name. At the beginning of the program, you can also add an OPTIONS statement that specifies MSGLEVEL=I to display a message about index usage in the SAS log. The revised program is shown below:

```
options msglevel=i;
proc print data=company.organization (idxwhere=no);
   where department='Sales';
run;
```

When you run this program, the SAS log indicates that the index was not used for processing.

Table 23.1 *SAS Log*

```
INFO: Data set option (IDXWHERE=NO) forced a sequential pass of the data
rather than use of an index for where-clause processing.
```

Comparing Procedures That Produce Detail Reports

Overview

When you want to produce a detail report, you can choose between the PRINT procedure and the SQL procedure:

Procedure	Description
PROC PRINT	• can calculate column sums
PROC SQL	• can manipulate data and create a SAS data set in the same step that creates the report
	• can calculate column and row statistics

To perform a particular task, a single-purpose tool like PROC PRINT generally uses fewer computer resources than a multi-purpose tool like PROC SQL.

To illustrate the differences in resource usage between PROC PRINT and PROC SQL, consider some sample queries.

Example: Using PROC PRINT and PROC SQL to Create Detail Reports

Suppose you are working with the data set Company.Products and you want to generate four types of detail reports:

- simple detail report
- subset detail report
- sorted detail report
- sorted subset detail report

For the first three reports, the PROC PRINT program is likely to use fewer resources than the PROC SQL program. For the last report, the resource usage for the two programs is likely to be about the same.

Report 1: Simple Detail Report

The simple detail report lists the product ID, product name, and supplier name for all products. The PROC PRINT program and PROC SQL program for producing this report are shown below:

PROC PRINT	PROC SQL

```
proc print data=company.products;
   var product_id product_name
      supplier_name;
run;
```

```
proc sql;
   select product_id product_name
            supplier_name
         from company.products;
quit;
```

In this situation, the PROC PRINT program is likely to use fewer CPU and memory resources than the PROC SQL program. The I/O resource usage should be approximately the same.

Report 2: Subset Detail Report

The subset detail report lists the product ID, product name, and supplier name for all products that come from Sweden (SE). The PROC PRINT program and PROC SQL program for producing this report are shown below:

PROC PRINT	PROC SQL

```
proc print data=company.products;
   var product_id product_name
      supplier_name;
   where supplier_country='SE';
run;
```

```
proc sql;
   select product_id product_name
            supplier_name
         from company.products
         where supplier_country='SE';
quit;
```

Both steps use WHERE processing to subset the data. In this situation, the PROC PRINT program is likely to use fewer CPU and memory resources than the PROC SQL program. The I/O resource usage should be approximately the same.

Report 3: Sorted Detail Report

The sorted detail report lists the product ID, product name, and supplier name for all products, with observations that are sorted by the supplier country. The PROC PRINT program and PROC SQL program for producing this report are shown below:

PROC PRINT	PROC SQL
| ```
proc sort data=company.products
     out=product;
   by supplier_country;
run;

proc print data=product;
   var product_id product_name
      supplier_name;
run;
``` | ```
proc sql;
   select product_id product_name
             supplier_name
      from company.products
      order by supplier_country;
quit;
``` |

To sort the data, a PROC SORT step has been added to the PROC PRINT program, and an ORDER BY clause has been added to the PROC SQL program. In this situation, the PROC PRINT program is likely to use fewer CPU and memory resources than the PROC SQL program. The I/O resource usage should be approximately the same.

Report 4: Sorted Subset Detail Report

The sorted subset detail report lists the product ID, product name, and supplier name for all products that come from Sweden (SE), with observations that are sorted by the supplier name. The PROC PRINT program and PROC SQL program for producing this report are shown below:

PROC PRINT	PROC SQL
| ```
proc sort data=company.products
     (keep=Product_ID Product_Name
     Supplier_Name Supplier_Country)
     out=product;
     where supplier_country='SE';
   by supplier_name;
run;

proc print data=product;
   var product_id product_name
      supplier_name;
run;
``` | ```
proc sql;
   select product_id product_name
             supplier_name
      from company.products
      where supplier_country='SE'
      order by supplier_name;
quit;
``` |

To sort the data, a PROC SORT step has been added to the PROC PRINT program. The PROC SORT step uses the KEEP= option to subset the observations, which improves efficiency. The PROC SQL step uses an ORDER BY clause for sorting and a WHERE clause for subsetting. In this situation, the CPU and memory usage for the PROC PRINT program and the PROC SQL program are about the same.

Comparing Tools for Summarizing Data

Overview

SAS provides a variety of tools for summarizing data. These summarization tools generate similar but not identical output, and they vary in efficiency.

Note: Throughout this section, all references to the MEANS procedure apply also to the SUMMARY procedure.

Tool	Description
MEANS procedure or SUMMARY procedure	• computes descriptive statistics for numeric variables • can produce a printed report and create an output data set
TABULATE procedure	• produces descriptive statistics in a tabular format • can produce 1-, 2-, or 3-dimensional tables with descriptive statistics • can also create an output data set
REPORT procedure	• combines features of the PRINT, MEANS, and TABULATE procedures with features of the DATA step in a single report-writing tool that can produce a variety of reports • can also create an output data set
SQL procedure	• computes descriptive statistics for one or more SAS data sets or DBMS tables • can produce a printed report or create a SAS data set
DATA step	• can produce a printed report • can also create an output data set

Note: You can also use the FREQ and UNIVARIATE procedures to generate summary data reports, but these procedures are not covered in this chapter. For more information about any of these summarization tools, see the SAS documentation for PROC FREQ and PROC UNIVARIATE in the *Base SAS Procedures Guide*.

Any of these tools can summarize the entire data set or by any combination of one or more class variables.

To group data, PROC MEANS, PROC SUMMARY, and PROC TABULATE use a CLASS statement. PROC SQL uses a GROUP BY clause. Every tool except PROC SQL accepts a BY statement.

Comparing Resource Usage across Summarization Tools

When summarizing data for one or more class variables, the tools in each of the following groups are similar in resource usage:

• PROC MEANS (or PROC SUMMARY), PROC REPORT, and PROC TABULATE

• PROC SQL and the DATA step with PROC SORT

However, the relative efficiency of the two groups of tools can vary based on the number of values of the CLASS variables. You need to test the techniques with your data.

Comparative Example: Displaying Summary Statistics for One Class Variable

Overview

Suppose you want to summarize the data set Retail.Orders by calculating the average quantity of products sold for each value of the class variable Order_Type. You can use several techniques to produce the summary report.

The following programs compare five techniques. You can use these samples as models for creating benchmark programs in your own environment. Your results might vary depending on the structure of your data, your operating environment, and the resources that are available at your site.

Programming Techniques

❶ PROC MEANS

This PROC MEANS step creates a report that displays the mean of the analysis variable Quantity for each value of the class variable Order_Type.

```
proc means data=retail.orders
    (keep=order_type quantity)
    mean maxdec=2;
  class order_type;
  var quantity;
run;
```

❷ PROC REPORT

This PROC REPORT step creates a report that displays the mean of the analysis variable Quantity for each value of the class variable Order_Type.

```
proc report data=retail.orders
    (keep=order_type quantity);
  column order_type quantity;
  define order_type / group width=13
        'Order Type';
  define quantity / mean format=5.2
        'Average Quantity'
        width=8;
run;
```

❸ PROC SORT and a DATA Step

This program uses a PROC SORT step and a DATA step to create a report. The PROC SORT step sorts the data by the values of the variable Order_Type, keeps only the necessary variables, and generates the temporary output data set Orders. The DATA step calculates the mean of the analysis variable Quantity for each value of the BY variable Order_Type and displays these values in a report.

```
proc sort data=retail.orders
     (keep=order_type quantity)
     out=orders;
   by order_type;
run;

data _null_;
   set orders;
   by order_type;
   format average_order 5.2;
   if first.order_type then do;
      num=0;
      sum=0;
   end;
   num+1;
   sum+quantity;
   if last.order_type then do;
      average_order=sum / num;
      file print;
      put @5 'Order Type' @20 'Average Order';
      put;
      put @13 Order_type 1. @27 Average_order 5.2;
   end;
run;
```

❹ PROC SQL

This PROC SQL step creates a report that displays the mean of the analysis variable Quantity for each value of the group variable Order_Type.

```
proc sql;
   select order_type,
     avg(quantity) label='Average Order'
                   format=5.2
     from retail.orders
     group by order_type;
quit;
```

❺ PROC TABULATE

This PROC TABULATE step creates a report that displays the mean of the analysis variable Quantity for each value of the class variable Order_Type.

```
proc tabulate data=retail.orders
     (keep=order_type quantity)
     format=comma8.2;
   class order_type;
   var quantity;
   table order_type, quantity*mean;
run;
```

General Recommendations

- When summarizing data for one class variable, test your data to determine which summarization tools are most efficient.

Using PROC MEANS to Display Summary Statistics for Combinations of Class Variables

To produce summary statistics for combinations of class variables, you can use PROC MEANS in the following ways. These techniques differ in resource usage.

Combinations of Class Variables	Technique	Example

all possible combinations:
 	
a
 	
b
 	
c
 	
a * *b*
 	
a * *c*
 	
b * *c*
 	
a * *b* * *c*
	basic PROC MEANS step	```proc means data=lib.dataset mean;```
		``` class a b c;```
		``` var salary;```
		``` output out=summary1```
		``` mean=average;```
		```run;```

specific combinations:
 	
a * *b* and *a* * *c*
	TYPES statement in PROC MEANS	```proc means data=lib.dataset mean;```
		``` class a b c;```
		``` var salary;```
		``` types a*b a*c;```
		``` output out=summary2```
		``` mean=average;```
		```run;```

specific combinations:
 	
a * *b* and *a* * *c*
	NWAY option in multiple PROC MEANS steps	```proc means data=lib.dataset nway;```
		``` class a b;```
		``` var salary;```
		``` output out=summary3a```
		``` mean=average;```
		```run;```
		
		```proc means data=lib.dataset nway;```
		``` class a c;```
		``` var salary;```
		``` output out=summary3b```
		``` mean=average;```
		```run;```

specific combinations:
 	
a * *b* and *a* * *c*
	WHERE= option in the OUTPUT statement in PROC MEANS	```proc means data=lib.dataset;```
		``` class a b c;```
		``` var salary;```
		``` output out=summary4```
		``` (where=(_type_ in (5,3)))```
		``` n=employees```
		``` mean=average;```
		```run;```

Comparing Resource Usage across Three Techniques for Using PROC MEANS

The three techniques for summarizing data for specific combinations of class variables (all but the basic PROC MEANS step) differ in resource usage as follows:

- The TYPES statement in a PROC MEANS step uses the fewest resources.

- A program that contains the NWAY option in multiple PROC MEANS steps uses the most resources because SAS must read the data set separately for each PROC MEANS step. The NWAY option in a single PROC MEANS step is efficient.

- The WHERE= data set option *in a PROC MEANS step* uses more resources than the TYPES statement in PROC MEANS because SAS must calculate all possible combinations of class variables before subsetting. However, the WHERE= data set option in PROC MEANS uses fewer resources than the NWAY option in multiple PROC MEANS steps.

We learn how to use a basic PROC MEANS step and the three other techniques that are listed above.

Using a Basic PROC MEANS Step to Combine All Class Variables

PROC MEANS (or PROC SUMMARY) creates the following:

- An output report that groups data and displays summary statistics for the combination of all class variables. This is the default action.

- If an OUTPUT statement appears, PROC MEANS creates an output data set with summary statistics for all possible combinations of the *n* class variables (from 1-way to *n*-way), as well as for the entire data set

Example: Displaying Summary Statistics for All Combinations of the Class Variables

Suppose you want to calculate average employee salaries and group results for the combination of the three class variables Employee_Country, Department, and Employee_Gender.

The following PROC MEANS program creates both a report data set and a SAS data set:

```
proc means data=company.organization_dim mean;
   class employee_country department
         employee_gender;
   var salary;
   output out=summary mean=average;
run;
```

The report displays summary statistics for every combination of the three class variables. A partial report is shown below:

Analysis Variable : Salary				
Employee_Country	Department	Employee_Gender	N Obs	Mean
Australia	Administration	Female	8	30334.38
		Male	5	27644.00
	Engineering	Female	1	27645.00
		Male	3	30005.00
	Sales	Female	36	27191.53
		Male	42	27607.98
	Sales Management	Male	3	119756.67
	Stock & Shipping	Female	3	30975.00
		Male	7	35755.00
Belgium	Administration	Female	6	28007.50
		Male	5	31235.00

The output data set contains summary statistics for the following:

- all possible combinations (1-way, 2-way, and 3-way) of the three class variables:
  - Employee_Gender
  - Department
  - Employee_Country
  - Department and Employee_Gender
  - Employee_Country and Employee_Gender
  - Employee_Country and Department
  - Employee_Country and Department and Employee_Gender
- the entire data set

A partial view of the output data set is shown below:

Obs	Employee_Country	Department	Employee_Gender	_TYPE_	_FREQ_	average
1				0	1046	$33,807
2			Female	1	473	$32,611
3			Male	1	575	$34,791
4		Accounts		2	17	$40,026
5		Accounts Management		2	9	$44,131
6		Administration		2	121	$30,367
7		Concession Management		2	11	$33,839
8		Engineering		2	31	$29,815
9		Executives		2	4	$288,333
10		Group Financials		2	3	$44,022

Understanding Types

Each combination of class variables that is used to calculate and group statistics for PROC MEANS is called a type.

For example, the following basic PROC MEANS step specifies the three class variables a, b, and c:

```
proc means data=lib.dataset mean;
   class a b c;
   var salary;
   output out=summary1
         mean=average;
run;
```

This PROC MEANS step generates seven possible types (combinations of the three variables):

Variable Combined	Dimension
a	1-way
b	1-way
c	1-way
b * c	2-way
a * b	2-way
a * c	2-way
a * b * c	3-way

The _TYPE_ variable has a unique value for each combination of class variables, based on their order in the CLASS statement. For example, for each of the seven types (seven possible combinations of three class variables) shown above, SAS assigns a value to _TYPE_ as follows:

TYPE Value	Description of Combination	Variables Combined	Dimension
1	rightmost variable only	c	1-way
2	middle variable only	b	1-way
3	rightmost variable and middle variable	b * c	2-way
4	leftmost variable	a	1-way

TYPE Value	Description of Combination	Variables Combined	Dimension
5	leftmost variable and rightmost variable	a * c	2-way
6	leftmost variable and middle variable	a * b	2-way
7	rightmost variable and middle variable and leftmost variable	a * b * c	3-way

As the number of class variables increases, so does the number of types. However, the highest _TYPE_ (7, in this example) always indicates the combination of all class variables.

SAS includes the _TYPE_ variable in the output data set generated by PROC MEANS. Observations are generated in order of increasing values of the _TYPE_ variable:

Obs	Employee_Country	Department	Employee_Gender	_TYPE_	_FREQ_	average
1				0	1048	$33,807
2			Female	1	473	$32,611
3			Male	1	575	$34,791
4		Accounts		2	17	$40,026
5		Accounts Management		2	9	$44,131
6		Administration		2	121	$30,367
7		Concession Management		2	11	$33,839
8		Engineering		2	31	$29,815
9		Executives		2	4	$288,333
10		Group Financials		2	3	$44,022

The first observation in the output data set has a _TYPE_ value of 0, which indicates that the statistics are generated for the entire data set.

By default, the output data set generated by PROC MEANS contains a separate observation for each unique combination of class variable values within each type. Each unique combination of values within a type is called a level of that type. In the output data set linked above, there are 17 levels for type 2. Therefore, 17 observations have a _TYPE_ value of 2.

The report generated by PROC MEANS contains only the combinations of all class variables, _TYPE_=7. _TYPE_ is not displayed in the report.

Using the TYPES Statement in PROC MEANS to Combine Class Variables

The TYPES statement specifies the desired combinations of class variables. The CLASS statement is required with the TYPES statement.

General form, TYPES statement:

TYPES *request(s)*;

Here is an explanation of the syntax:

request(s)
 specifies the desired combination or combinations of class variables. A request includes one of the following:

- one class variable name

- several class variable names separated by asterisks

- ( ) to request overall results (_TYPE_=0)

To request combinations of class variables more concisely, you can use a grouping syntax by placing parentheses around several variables and joining other variables or variable combinations. The following examples of TYPES statements illustrate the use of grouping syntax:

Example with Grouping Syntax	Equivalent Example without Grouping Syntax
types a*(b c);	types a*b a*c;
types (a b)*(c d);	types a*c a*d b*c b*d;
types (a b c)*d;	types a*d b*d c*d;
types () a*(b c);	types a*b*c a*b a*c;

Example: Using the TYPES Statement in PROC MEANS

Suppose you want to calculate average employee salaries, as in the previous example. This time, you want the two combinations of class variables shown below:

- Employee_Country and Department

- Employee_Country and Employee_Gender

To do this, you can add a TYPES statement to the PROC MEANS step:

```
proc means data=company.organization_dim mean;
   class employee_country department
         employee_gender;
   var salary;
   types employee_country*department
         employee_country*employee_gender;
   output out=summary mean=average;
```

```
run;
```

This PROC MEANS step generates both a report data set and an output data set. The report, shown below, has a separate table for each of the two combinations specified in the TYPES statement:

Analysis Variable : Salary Annual Salary			
Employee Country	Employee Gender	N Obs	Mean
Australia	Female	48	27961.25
	Male	60	33288.75
Belgium	Female	27	32342.22
	Male	33	29754.39
Germany	Female	45	34080.00
	Male	53	27361.70
Denmark	Female	23	27856.52
	Male	28	34893.75
Spain	Female	29	33353.10
	Male	37	29323.11
France	Female	44	28831.70
	Male	54	34143.24
United Kingdom	Female	50	28239.70
	Male	59	32507.88
Italy	Female	34	29634.85
	Male	43	30980.23
Netherlands	Female	30	30834.83
	Male	35	31160.00
United States	Female	143	38152.45
	Male	173	42395.00

Analysis Variable : Salary Annual Salary			
Employee Country	Department	N Obs	Mean
Australia	Administration	13	29299.62
	Engineering	4	29415.00
	Sales	78	27415.77
	Sales Management	3	119756.67
	Stock & Shipping	10	34321.00
Belgium	Administration	11	29474.55

The output data set includes only the combinations that are specified in the TYPES statement. A partial view of the output data set is shown below:

Obs	Employee_Country	Department	Employee_Gender	_TYPE_	_FREQ_	average
1	AU		F	5	48	$27,961
2	AU		M	5	60	$33,289
3	BE		F	5	27	$32,342
4	BE		M	5	33	$29,754
5	DE		F	5	45	$34,060
6	DE		M	5	53	$27,362
7	DK		F	5	23	$27,857
8	DK		M	5	28	$34,694
9	ES		F	5	29	$33,353
10	ES		M	5	37	$29,323

Using the NWAY Option in PROC MEANS to Combine Class Variables

Another way to specify a combination of class variables is to use the NWAY option in PROC MEANS:

General form, NWAY option in the PROC MEANS statement:

PROC MEANS NWAY;

Here is an explanation of the syntax:

NWAY
   specifies that the output data set contains statistics for the combination of all specified class variables (only observations with the highest _TYPE_ value).

The NWAY option generates summary statistics for every combination of all class variables. Therefore, to generate statistics for different combinations of class variables, you can specify a separate PROC MEANS step with the NWAY option for each combination.

Example: Using the NWAY Option in Multiple PROC MEANS Steps

Suppose you want to calculate average employee salaries and to group results for the following combinations of class variables:

- Employee_Country and Department

- Employee_Country and Employee_Gender

You can use two PROC MEANS steps, each containing the NWAY option, as shown below. The first PROC MEANS step generates statistics for the first combination of class variables, and the second PROC MEANS step generates statistics for the second combination of class variables.

```
proc means data=company.organization_dim nway;
   class employee_country department;
   var salary;
   output out=summary1
         n=employees
         mean=average;
run;


proc means data=company.organization_dim nway;
```

```
    class employee_country  employee_gender;
    var salary;
    output out=summary2
           n=employees
           mean=average;
run;
```

When processing this program, SAS must read the data set once for each PROC MEANS step. This processing is not efficient.

This program generates two reports and two output data sets. The report, shown in part below, has a separate table for each PROC MEANS step:

Analysis Variable : Salary Annual Salary							
Employee Country	Department	N Obs	N	Mean	Std Dev	Minimum	Maximum
Australia	Administration	13	13	29289.62	5325.55	26495.00	46230.00
	Engineering	4	4	29415.00	1886.72	27645.00	31670.00
	Sales	78	78	27415.77	2120.28	24015.00	38605.00
	Sales Management	3	3	119756.67	38831.75	87975.00	163040.00
	Stock & Shipping	10	10	34321.00	11702.39	26160.00	60980.00
Belgium	Administration	11	11	29474.55	5054.34	25045.00	43280.00
	Engineering	2	2	28532.50	1799.59	27260.00	29805.00
	Sales	45	45	27428.89	1489.26	25240.00	32470.00
	Sales Management	2	2	119775.00	51576.37	83305.00	156245.00
Germany	Administration	13	13	30708.85	7043.34	25705.00	46100.00
					3805.44	27250.00	36240.00

Analysis Variable : Salary Annual Salary							
Employee Country	Employee Gender	N Obs	N	Mean	Std Dev	Minimum	Maximum
Australia	Female	48	48	27961.25	3460.40	24015.00	46230.00
	Male	60	60	33288.75	21946.98	24100.00	163040.00
Belgium	Female	27	27	32342.22	24827.44	25240.00	156245.00
	Male	33	33	29754.39	10099.16	25045.00	83305.00
Germany	Female	45	45	34060.00	22157.71	24030.00	151940.00
	Male	53	53	27361.70	1922.61	24050.00	38240.00
Denmark	Female	23	23	27856.52	1626.54	25495.00	31495.00
	Male	28	28	34693.75	25677.45	25165.00	151285.00
Spain	Female	29	29	33353.10	25481.59	22705.00	163315.00
	Male	37	37	29323.11	9620.27	21580.00	82880.00

A partial view of each output data set is shown below:

Figure 23.2   *SAS Data Set Work.Summary1*

Obs	Employee_Country	Department	_TYPE_	_FREQ_	employees	average
1	Australia	Administration	3	13	13	$29,300
2	Australia	Engineering	3	4	4	$29,415
3	Australia	Sales	3	78	78	$27,416
4	Australia	Sales Management	3	3	3	$119,757
5	Australia	Stock & Shipping	3	10	10	$34,321
6	Belgium	Administration	3	11	11	$29,475
7	Belgium	Engineering	3	2	2	$28,533
8	Belgium	Sales	3	45	45	$27,429
9	Belgium	Sales Management	3	2	2	$119,775
10	Germany	Administration	3	13	13	$30,709

Figure 23.3   *SAS Data Set Work.Summary2*

Obs	Employee_Country	Employee_Gender	_TYPE_	_FREQ_	employees	average
1	Australia	Female	3	48	48	$27,961
2	Australia	Male	3	60	60	$33,289
3	Belgium	Female	3	27	27	$32,342
4	Belgium	Male	3	33	33	$29,754
5	Germany	Female	3	45	45	$34,060
6	Germany	Male	3	53	53	$27,362
7	Denmark	Female	3	23	23	$27,857
8	Denmark	Male	3	28	28	$34,694
9	Spain	Female	3	29	29	$33,353
10	Spain	Male	3	37	37	$29,323

Using the WHERE= Output Data Set Option in PROC MEANS to Select Desired Types

Yet another way to select desired types is to use the WHERE= output data set option in the OUTPUT statement:

General form, WHERE= output data set option in a basic OUTPUT statement:

OUTPUT <OUT=*SAS-data-set*> **(WHERE=**

(*where-expression-1* <*logical-operator where-expression-n*>**));**

Here is an explanation of the syntax:

SAS-data-set
   specifies the output data set as a 1-level or 2-level name.

where-expression
   is an arithmetic or logical expression that consists of a sequence of operators, operands, and SAS functions. The expression must be enclosed in parentheses.

logical-operator
   can be AND, AND NOT, OR, or OR NOT.

When you use the WHERE= output data set option in the OUTPUT statement, SAS must calculate all possible combinations of class variables. Subsetting does not occur until the results are written to the output data set.

Example: Using the WHERE= Output Data Set Option in PROC MEANS

Suppose you want to calculate average employee salaries and select results for two 2-way combinations of the three class variables Employee_Country, Department, and Employee_Gender. All possible combinations of these variables are listed below:

TYPE Value	Variables Combined	Dimension
1	Employee_Gender	1-way
2	Department	1-way
3	Department * Employee_Gender	2-way
4	Employee_Country	1-way
5	Employee_Country * Employee_Gender	2-way
6	Employee_Country * Department	2-way
7	Employee_Country * Department * Employee_Gender	3-way

To specify the types by _TYPE_ value, you can use the WHERE= output data set option in the OUTPUT statement as shown below:

```
proc means data=company.organization_dim;
   class employee_country department
         employee_gender;
   var salary;
   output out=summary
          (where=(_type_ in (5,6)))
          n=employees
          mean=average;
run;
```

A partial view of the report is shown below. The PROC MEANS report represents the highest type, the NWAY combination, type 7, which was not requested.

Analysis Variable : Salary Annual Salary								
Employee Country	Department	Employee Gender	N Obs	N	Mean	Std Dev	Minimum	Maximum
Australia	Administration	Female	8	8	30334.33	6673.40	26495.00	48230.00
		Male	5	5	27644.00	1210.34	26500.00	29250.00
	Engineering	Female	1	1	27645.00	.	27645.00	27645.00
		Male	3	3	30005.00	1803.05	28090.00	31670.00
	Sales	Female	36	36	27191.53	1631.47	24015.00	30690.00
		Male	42	42	27607.98	2344.85	24100.00	38605.00
	Sales Management	Male	3	3	119756.67	38831.75	87975.00	163040.00
	Stock & Shipping	Female	3	3	30975.00	4441.63	27385.00	35935.00
		Male	7	7	35755.00	13315.33	26180.00	60930.00
Belgium	Administration	Female	8	8	28007.50	1797.21	26155.00	30865.00
		Male			31235.00		26045.00	43230.00

A partial view of the output data set Work.Summary is shown below. The output data set includes types 5 and 6, as requested.

Obs	Employee_Country	Department	Employee_Gender	_TYPE_	_FREQ_	employees	average
1	Australia		Female	5	48	48	$27,961
2	Australia		Male	5	60	60	$33,289
3	Belgium		Female	5	27	27	$32,342
4	Belgium		Male	5	33	33	$29,754
5	Germany		Female	5	45	45	$34,060
6	Germany		Male	5	53	53	$27,362
7	Denmark		Female	5	23	23	$27,857
8	Denmark		Male	5	28	28	$34,694
9	Spain		Female	5	29	29	$33,353
10	Spain		Male	5	37	37	$29,323

Next, compare the resources used by these summarization techniques:

- the TYPES statement in PROC MEANS
- the NWAY option in multiple PROC MEANS steps
- the WHERE= output data set option in PROC MEANS

Comparative Example: Displaying Summary Statistics for Combinations of Class Variables

Overview

Suppose you want to summarize the data set Retail.Organization by calculating average employee salaries for two 3-way combinations of four class variables:

- Employee_Country, Department, and Employee_Gender
- Department, Section, and Employee_Gender

You can use several techniques to produce a report and one or more output data sets.

The following programs compare three techniques. You can use these samples as models for creating benchmark programs in your own environment. Your results might vary depending on the structure of your data, your operating environment, and the resources that are available at your site.

Programming Techniques

❶ TYPES Statement in PROC MEANS

This program calculates the average employee salary for two 3-way combinations of the class variables Employee_Country, Department, Employee_Gender, and Section. The TYPES statement requests the two combinations. The program generates a report data set and an output data set named Summary.

```
proc means data=retail.organization mean;
   class employee_country department
        employee_gender section;
   var salary;
   types employee_country*department*employee_gender
        department*section*employee_gender;
   output out=summary
        n=employees
        mean=average;
run;
```

❷ NWAY Option in Two PROC MEANS Steps

Each of the two PROC MEANS steps in this program calculates the average employee salary for a combination of three of the four class variables Employee_Country, Department, Employee_Gender, and Section. In each step, the NWAY option specifies that all three variables that are specified in the CLASS statement should be combined. The program generates two reports and two output data sets named Summary1 and Summary2.

```
proc means data=retail.organization nway;
   class employee_country department
        employee_gender;
   var salary;
   output out=summary1
        n=employees
        mean=average;
run;

proc means data=retail.organization nway;
   class department section
        employee_gender;
   var salary;
   output out=summary2
        n=employees
        mean=average;
run;
```

❸ WHERE= Option in PROC MEANS

This program calculates the average employee salary for two 3-way combinations of the class variables Employee_Country, Department, Employee_Gender, and Section. The WHERE= data set option in the OUTPUT statement specifies the two combinations by their _TYPE_ values. The program generates a report and an output data set named Summary3.

```
proc means data=retail.organization;
   class employee_country department
        employee_gender section;
   var salary;
   output out=summary3 (where=(_type_ in (7,14)))
        n=employees
        mean=average;
run;
```

General Recommendations

- To summarize data for particular combinations of class variables, use the TYPES statement in PROC MEANS.

Additional Features

The WAYS statement in PROC MEANS provides yet another way to display summary statistics for combinations of class variables. In the WAYS statement, you specify one or more integers that define the number of class variables to combine in order to form all the unique combinations of class variables.

For example, the following program uses the WAYS statement to create summary statistics for the following combinations of the three class variables Employee_Country, Department, and Employee_Gender:

- each individual variable (all 1-way combinations)

- all 2-way combinations (Employee_Country and Department, Employee_Country and Employee_Gender, and Employee_Gender and Department)

```
proc means data=company.organization mean;
   class employee_country department
         employee_gender;
   var salary;
   ways 1 2;
   output out=summary
          mean=average;
run;
```

The WAYS statement can be used instead of or in addition to the TYPES statement.

Note: For more information about the WAYS statement, see the SAS documentation.

Summary

Using an Index for Efficient WHERE Processing

When processing a WHERE expression, SAS determines whether it is more efficient to access observations sequentially, by examining all observations, or directly, by using an index to access specific observations. Using an index to process a WHERE expression might improve performance and is referred to as optimizing the WHERE expression. By deciding whether to create an index, you play a role in determining which access method SAS can use.

In order to decide whether to use an index, you must evaluate the benefits and costs of using an index.

SAS performs a series of steps to determine whether to process a WHERE expression by using an index or by reading all observations sequentially.

Identifying Available Indexes

First, SAS determines whether there are any existing indexes that might be used to process the WHERE expression. Specifically, SAS checks the variable in each condition in the WHERE expression to determine whether the variable is either a key variable in a simple index or the first key variable in a composite index. No matter how many indexes are available, SAS can use only one index to process a WHERE expression. Therefore, if multiple indexes are available, SAS must choose between them.

It is most common for SAS to use an index to process just one condition in a WHERE expression. However, in a process called compound optimization, SAS can use a composite index to optimize multiple conditions on multiple variables, which are joined with a logical operator such as AND.

Identifying Conditions That Can Be Optimized

Second, SAS looks for operators and functions that can be optimized in the WHERE conditions that contain key variables. There are also certain operators and functions that cannot be optimized. For compound optimization, WHERE conditions must meet slightly different criteria in order to be candidates for optimization.

Estimating the Number of Observations

Third, SAS estimates how many observations are qualified by the index. When multiple indexes exist, SAS selects the one that seems to produce the fewest qualified observations (the smallest subset). Whether SAS uses an index depends on the percentage of observations that are qualified (the size of the subset relative to the size of the data set). It is more efficient to use direct access for a small subset and sequential access for a large subset. If SAS estimates that the number of qualified observations is less than 3% of the data file, SAS automatically uses the index and does not compare probable resource usage.

To help SAS estimate how many observations would be selected by a WHERE expression, each index stores 21 statistics called cumulative percentiles, or centiles. Centiles provide information about the distribution of values for the indexed variable.

Comparing Probable Resource Usage

Fourth, SAS decides whether it is more efficient to satisfy the WHERE expression by using the index or by reading all observations sequentially. To make the decision, SAS predicts how many I/O operations are required to satisfy the WHERE expression for each access method, and then compares the two resource costs.

Several factors affect the number of I/O operations that are required for WHERE processing, including the following:

- subset size relative to data set size

- number of pages in the data file

- order of the data

- cost to uncompress a compressed file for a sequential read

Data type and length are two other factors that affect index efficiency.

Deciding Whether to Create an Index

When you use a WHERE expression to select a subset, you can use specific guidelines to decide whether it is efficient to create an index. Depending on factors such as the size of the subset relative to the size of the data set, you might or might not choose to create an index.

In most situations, it is best to let SAS determine whether to use an index for WHERE processing. However, sometimes you might want to control whether SAS uses an existing index. You can use either of the data set options IDXWHERE= or IDXNAME=, but not both at the same time, to control index usage. You can specify MSGLEVEL=I to tell SAS to display information about index usage in the SAS log.

Comparing Procedures That Produce Detail Reports

When you produce a detail report, you can choose between the PRINT procedure and the SQL procedure. To perform a particular task, a single-purpose tool like PROC PRINT generally uses fewer computer resources than a multi-purpose tool like PROC SQL.

For detail reports, a PROC PRINT step often, but not always, uses fewer resources than a PROC SQL step:

- PROC PRINT is usually more efficient than PROC SQL for generating a simple detail report, a subset detail report, and a sorted detail report.

- PROC PRINT and PROC SQL are likely to use similar resources for generating a sorted subset detail report.

Comparing Tools for Summarizing Data

SAS provides a variety of tools for summarizing data, including the MEANS procedure (or SUMMARY procedure), the TABULATE procedure, the REPORT procedure, the SQL procedure, and the DATA step.

If you summarize data for one class variable, the tools in each of the following groups are similar in resource usage:

- PROC MEANS (or PROC SUMMARY), PROC REPORT, and PROC TABULATE

- PROC SQL and the DATA step

However, the relative efficiency of the two groups of tools varies according to the shape of the data.

You can use PROC MEANS in a variety of ways to produce summary statistics for combinations of class variables. Each combination of class variables is called a type.

To summarize data for all combinations of all class variables, you can use a basic PROC MEANS step (or PROC SUMMARY step). To produce summary statistics for specific combinations of class variables, you can use PROC MEANS in the following ways :

- the TYPES statement in a PROC MEANS step

- the NWAY option in multiple PROC MEANS steps

- the WHERE= output data set option in a PROC MEANS step

These three techniques vary in efficiency; the TYPES statement in PROC MEANS is the most efficient.

You can also use the WAYS statement in PROC MEANS to produce summary statistics for specific combinations of class variables.

Quiz

Select the best answer for each question. After completing the quiz, check your answers using the answer key in the appendix.

1. Why can using an index reduce the number of I/O operations that are required for accessing a small subset?

    a. Using an index requires larger I/O memory buffers, which can hold more pages.

    b. The index does not have to be loaded into a memory buffer.

    c. The number of observations that SAS has to load into the program data vector (PDV) is decreased.

    d. The number of pages that SAS has to load into I/O buffers is decreased.

2. You want to select a subset of observations in the data set Company.Products, and you have defined a simple index on the variable Rating. SAS cannot use the index to process which of the following WHERE statements?

    a. `where rating is missing;`

    b. `where rating=int(rating);`

    c. `where rating between 3.5 and 7.5;`

    d. `where rating=5.5;`

3. In which of the following situations is sequential access likely to be more efficient than direct access for WHERE processing?

    a. The subset contains more than 75% of the observations in the data set.

    b. The WHERE expression specifies both key variables in a single composite index.

    c. The data is sorted on the key variable.

    d. The data set is very large.

4. You want to summarize data and group it by one variable. Which of the following tools could not be used?

    a. The DATA step with BY-group processing.

    b. The DATA step without BY-group processing.

    c. PROC SQL with a GROUP BY clause.

    d. PROC MEANS with a CLASS statement.

5. Which of the following techniques does not summarize data for specific combinations of class variables?

    a. the NWAY option in multiple PROC MEANS steps.

    b. the TYPES statement in a PROC MEANS step.

    c. the WHERE= output data set option in a PROC MEANS step.

    d. a basic PROC MEANS step.

Chapter 24
Creating Functions with PROC FCMP

Overview

Introduction

The SAS Function Compiler (FCMP) procedure enables you to create, test, and store user-defined functions, CALL routines, and subroutines for use in other SAS procedures and the DATA step.

Using PROC FCMP

Overview

The FCMP procedure uses the SAS language compiler to create user-defined functions. The compiler subsystem generates machine language code for the computer on which SAS is running.

You can use the functions and subroutines that you create in PROC FCMP with the DATA step, the WHERE statement, the Output Delivery System (ODS), and with the following procedures:

PROC CALIS	PROC OPTLSO
PROC GA	PROC QUANTREG
PROC GENMOD	PROC REPORT COMPUTE blocks
PROC GLIMMIX	SAS Risk Dimensions procedures
PROC MCMC	PROC SEVERITY
PROC MODEL	PROC SIMILARITY
PROC NLIN	PROC SQL (functions with array arguments are not supported)
PROC NLMIXED	PROC SURVEYPHREG
PROC NLP	PROC VARMAX

Writing a PROC FCMP Step

The following syntax is for PROC FCMP:

General form for a basic PROC FCMP step to create and save a function.

PROC FCMP OUTLIB= *libref.data-set.package*;

    Function *function-name(argument-1<$>,...,argument-n<$><length>*;

    programming statements;

    Return *(expression)*;

    ENDSUB;

QUIT;

Here is an explanation of the syntax:

PROC FCMP
    creates, tests, and stores SAS functions for use by other SAS procedures and the DATA step.

ENDSUB
    ends the function's declaration.

FUNCTION
    begins the definition of the function. The FUNCTION definition ends with the ENDSUB statement.

programming statements
    are a series of DATA step statements that describe the function's actions.

OUTLIB
    specifies the package where routines are stored.

RETURN
    specifies the value that is returned by the function.

About PROC FCMP

PROC FCMP can create independent and reusable functions, CALL routines, and subroutines using DATA step syntax that is stored in a data set. The following example shows how to create and save functions with PROC FCMP. This example creates a function called ReverseName. The function rearranges the order of customer names from last name, first name to first name, last name (for example, Lu, Patrick becomes Patrick Lu).

```
proc fcmp outlib=orion.functions.dev;
   function ReverseName(name $) $40;
      return(catx('',scan(name,2,','),scan(name,1,',')));
   endsub;
quit;
```

PROC FCMP Statement

The PROC FCMP statement begins the FCMP step. The OUTLIB= option specifies the three-level name of an output package where the compiled functions are stored. Function and subroutine names must be unique within a package.

```
proc fcmp outlib=orion.functions.dev;
```

The OUTLIB= option is required.

FUNCTION Statement

The definition of a function begins with the FUNCTION statement and ends with an ENDSUB statement.

The following code creates a function called ReverseName.

```
function ReverseName(name $) $40;
```

RETURN Statement

The RETURN statement specifies the value that is returned by the function.

```
return(catx('',scan(name,2,','),scan(name,1,',')));
```

Using the Newly Defined Function

You must specify the CMPLIB= system option in order to use the new function in a DATA step or supported PROC step. The CMPLIB= system option specifies one or more data sets that store user-defined functions. In this example, function ReverseName is saved to orion.functions.

```
options cmplib=orion.functions;
```

The function ReverseName is called in the following code.

```
options cmplib=orion.functions;
data work.emplist;
```

```
      set orion.employeeaddresses;
      NewName=ReverseName(EmployeeName);
run;
```

Using PROC FCMP to Create a Subroutine

The SUBROUTINE statement names the block of code that is processed and specifies the parameters. The OUTARGS statement specifies the parameters that the subroutine updates. The ENDSUB statement ends the definition of the subroutine. In the following example, the subroutine CALC_YEARS is defined to calculate years to maturity from SAS date variables:

```
subroutine calc_years(maturity, current_date, years);
   outargs years;
   years=(maturity - current_date) / 365.25;
endsub;
```

The following code is an example of calling the CALC_YEARS subroutine:

```
data _null_;
  myCD='23jul2017'd;
  now=today();
  how_many_years=.;
  call calc_years(myCD,now,how_many_years);
  put how_many_years=;
run;
```

The following table lists the differences between functions and subroutines:

Descriptions	Function	Subroutine
Accepts arguments	yes	yes
Modifies arguments	no	yes
Returns a value	yes	no
Is an expression	yes	no
Is a statement	no	yes
Can be part of a statement	yes	no
Begins with CALL	no	yes

For more information about PROC FCMP, see "PROC FCMP" in the *Base SAS Procedures Guide.*

Quiz

Select the best answer for each question. After completing the quiz, check your answers using the answer key in the appendix.

1. Which of the following characteristics do not apply to subroutines?

    a. Parameters are passed by value.

    b. The ENDSUB statement ends the definition of the subroutine.

    c. can modify parameters

    d. Do not return a value.

2. You can create one function and one CALL routine in a single FCMP procedure step.

    a. True

    b. False

3. The OUTLIB= option is a required option in the PROC FCMP function.

    a. True

    b. False

4. The OUTARGS statement is used with the FUNCTION and SUBROUTINE statements.

    a. True

    b. False

Part 5

Quiz Answer Keys

Appendix 1
Quiz Answer Keys

Chapter 1: Performing Queries Using PROC SQL

1. Correct answer: a

   The SELECT clause in the program is written incorrectly. Columns that are listed in the clause must be separated by commas, not just blanks.

2. Correct answer: a

   There are two statements, the PROC SQL statement and the SELECT statement. The SELECT statement contains three clauses.

3. Correct answer: b

   The SELECT clause lists the columns from both tables to be queried. You must use a prefix with the Address column because it appears in both tables. The prefix specifies the table from which you want the column to be read.

4. Correct answer: b

   The ORDER BY clause specifies how the rows are to be sorted. You follow the keywords ORDER BY by one or more column names or numbers, separated by commas.

5. Correct answer: c

   In the FROM clause, you list the names of the tables to be queried, separated by commas.

6. Correct answer: b

   To create a new column and assign a column alias to the column, you specify the following in the SELECT clause, in the order shown here: an expression, (optionally) the keyword AS, and a column alias. The case that you use when you create the column name is the one that will be displayed in the output.

7. Correct answer: c

   The GROUP BY clause is used in queries that include one or more summary functions. If you specify a GROUP BY clause in a query that does not contain a summary function, your clause is changed to an ORDER BY clause.

8. Correct answer: c

   The CREATE TABLE statement enables you to store your results in a SAS table instead of displaying the query results as a report.

9. Correct answer: d

   If you are joining two tables that contain a same-named column, then you must use a prefix to specify the table(s) from which you want the column to be read. Remember that if you join tables that don't contain columns that have matching data values, you can produce a huge amount of output. Be sure to specify a WHERE clause to select only the rows that you want.

10. Correct answer: b

    The table names that are specified in the FROM clause must be separated by commas. Note that you can specify columns in the WHERE clause that are not specified in the SELECT clause.

Chapter 2: Performing Advanced Queries Using PROC SQL

1. Correct answer: d

   To remove duplicate values from PROC SQL output, you specify the DISTINCT keyword before the column name in the SELECT clause.

2. Correct answer: d

   To list rows that have no data (that is, missing data), you can use either of these other conditional operators: IS MISSING or IS NULL. The NOT EXISTS operator is used specifically with a subquery, and resolves to true if the subquery returns no values to the outer query.

3. Correct answer: b

   When a WHERE clause references a new column that was defined in the SELECT clause, the WHERE clause must specify the keyword CALCULATED before the column name.

4. Correct answer: c

   To determine how PROC SQL calculates and displays output from summary functions, consider the key factors. This PROC SQL query has a GROUP BY clause, and it does not specify any columns that are outside of summary functions. Therefore, PROC SQL calculates and displays the summary function for each group. There are 7 unique values of FlightNumber, but the HAVING clause specifies only the flights that have an average number of boarded passengers greater than 150. Because 4 of the 7 flight numbers meet this condition, the output will contain 4 rows.

5. Correct answer: b

   Your PROC SQL query needs to use data from both tables. The outer query reads the name and number of books checked out from Library.Circulation. The multiple-value noncorrelated subquery selects the names of volunteers from Library.Volunteers and passes these names back to the outer query. The outer query then selects data for only the volunteers whose names match names returned by the subquery. The subquery is indented under the outer query's WHERE clause, is enclosed in parentheses, and does not require a semicolon inside the closing parenthesis.

6. Correct answer: c

   A noncorrelated subquery is a nested query that executes independently of the outer query. The outer query passes no values to the subquery.

7. Correct answer: a

   The syntax in this PROC SQL query is valid, so the first statement is false. The query contains a correlated subquery, so the second statement is true. The VALIDATE keyword is used after the PROC SQL statement, so the third statement is true. And the last statement correctly indicates that the VALIDATE keyword causes the SAS log to display a special message if the query syntax is valid, or standard error messages if the syntax is not valid.

8. Correct answer: c

In this PROC SQL query, the outer query uses the operator NOT EXISTS with a correlated subquery. The outer query selects all rows from Charity.Donors whose names do not appear in Charity.Current. In other words, this PROC SQL query output lists all donors who did not make a contribution in the current year.

9. Correct answer: c

The third statement about data remerging is correct.

10. Correct answer: c

PROC SQL can execute this query, but the query will not produce the results that you want. If you omit the GROUP BY clause in a query that contains a HAVING clause, then the HAVING clause and any summary functions treat the entire table as one group. Without a GROUP BY clause, the HAVING clause in this example calculates the average circulation for the table as a whole (all books in the library), not for each group (each category of books). The output contains either all the rows in the table (if the average circulation for the entire table is less than 2500) or none of the rows in the table (if the average circulation for the entire table is greater than 2500).

Chapter 3: Combining Tables Horizontally Using PROC SQL

1. Correct answer: a

A Cartesian product is returned when join conditions are *not* specified in a PROC SQL join. In a Cartesian product, each row from the first table is combined with every row from the second table.

2. Correct answer: b

This PROC SQL query is an inner join. It combines the rows from the first table that match rows from the second table, based on the matching criteria specified in the WHERE clause. Columns are not overlaid, so all columns from the referenced tables (including any columns with duplicate names) are displayed. Any unmatched rows from either table are not displayed.

3. Correct answer: d

This PROC SQL query is a right outer join, which retrieves all rows that match across tables, based on the join conditions in the ON clause, plus nonmatching rows from the right (second) table.

4. Correct answer: d

There are two valid formats for writing a PROC SQL inner join. The PROC SQL query shown at the top of this question uses the first inner join format, which does not use a keyword to indicate the type of join. The alternate format is similar to an outer join and uses the keyword INNER JOIN.

5. Correct answer: a

This PROC SQL query is a left outer join, which retrieves all rows that match across tables (based on the join conditions in the ON clause), plus nonmatching rows from the left (first) table. No columns are overlaid, so all columns from both tables are displayed.

6. Correct answer: c

   Inner joins combine the rows from the first table that match rows from the second table, based on one or more join conditions in the WHERE clause. The columns being matched must have the same data type, but they are not required to have the same name. For joins, the tables being joined can have different numbers of columns, and the rows do not need to be sorted.

7. Correct answer: a

   Unlike a table, an in-line view exists only during query execution. Because it is temporary, an in-line view can be referenced only in the query in which it is defined.

8. Correct answer: c

   In order to generate the same output as the DATA step and PRINT steps, the PROC SQL full outer join must use the COALESCE function with the duplicate columns specified as arguments.

9. Correct answer: c

   A maximum of 256 tables can be combined in a single inner join. If the join involves views (either in-line views or PROC SQL views), it is the number of tables that underlie the views, not the number of views, that counts towards the limit of 256.

10. Correct answer: d

    The use of summary functions does not require the use of table aliases. All of the other statements about table aliases that are shown here are true.

Chapter 4: Combining Tables Vertically Using PROC SQL

1. Correct answer: c

   In set operations that use the operator EXCEPT, INTERSECT, or UNION, and no keyword, columns are overlaid based on their position in the SELECT clause. It does not matter whether the overlaid columns have the same name. When columns are overlaid, the column name is taken from the first table that is specified in the SELECT clause.

2. Correct answer: d

   By default, when processing a set operation that contains the EXCEPT, INTERSECT, and UNION set operators, PROC SQL makes an extra pass through the data to eliminate duplicate rows. The keyword ALL is used to suppress that additional pass through the tables, allowing duplicate rows to appear in the result set. Because the OUTER UNION set operator displays all rows, the keyword ALL is invalid and cannot be used with OUTER UNION.

3. Correct answer: d

   The output contains all rows that are unique in the combined set of rows from both tables, and the columns have been overlaid by position. This output is generated by a set operation that uses the set operator UNION without keywords.

4. Correct answer: a

   The PROC SQL set operation that uses the set operator OUTER UNION without a keyword is the only code shown that does not overlay any columns in output.

5. Correct answer: a

   The keyword CORRESPONDING (CORR) can be used alone or together with the keyword ALL.

6. Correct answer: b

   This PROC SQL output includes all rows from the table Pets that do not appear in the table Dogs. No duplicates are displayed. A PROC SQL set operation that contains the set operator EXCEPT without keywords produces these results.

7. Correct answer: b

   The set operator EXCEPT returns all the rows in the first table that do not appear in the second table. The keyword ALL suppresses the extra pass that PROC SQL makes through the data to eliminate duplicate rows. The EXCEPT operator when used alone will also produce the output specified in the question.

8. Correct answer: c

   The set operator UNION returns all rows that are unique in the combined set of rows from both tables.

9. Correct answer: c

   The set operator INTERSECT returns all rows that are common to both tables. Specifying the keyword ALL suppresses PROC SQL's additional pass through the data to eliminate duplicate rows.

10. Correct answer: a

    The DATA step returns all rows from the first table along with all rows from the second table, maintaining the order specified in the BY statement. Same-named columns are overlaid by default. The set operator OUTER UNION returns all rows from both tables. The CORR keyword causes same-named columns to be overlaid. The ORDER BY clause causes the result rows to be ordered by values of the specified column (LName).

Chapter 5: Creating and Managing Tables Using PROC SQL

1. Correct answer: b

   The CREATE TABLE statement that includes a LIKE clause copies the column names and attributes from an existing table into a new table. No rows of data are inserted.

2. Correct answer: a

The CREATE TABLE statement that includes the AS keyword and query clauses creates a table and loads the results of the query into the new table. The WHERE clause selects only the rows for the level-1 flight attendants.

3. Correct answer: c

   UNDO POLICY=REQUIRED is the default setting for PROC SQL. This setting undoes all inserts or updates if 1 or more rows violate the integrity constraint criteria, and restores the table to its original state before the inserts or updates.

4. Correct answer: b

   The NOT NULL integrity constraint specifies that data is required and cannot have a null (missing) value.

5. Correct answer: d

   The DELETE statement deletes rows that are specified in the WHERE clause from the table. If no WHERE clause is specified, all rows are deleted. The DROP TABLE statement drops (deletes) an entire table; the syntax shown in option c is not valid.

6. Correct answer: b

   The UPDATE statement that includes a SET clause is used to modify rows in a table. WHEN-THEN clauses in the CASE expression enable you to update a column value based on specified criteria.

7. Correct answer: a

   The INSERT statement is used to insert new rows into a new or existing table. There is no LOAD statement in PROC SQL, VALUES is a clause, and the CREATE TABLE statement is used to create a table.

8. Correct answer: d

   The ALTER TABLE statement is used to modify attributes of existing columns (include the MODIFY clause), add new column definitions (include the ADD clause), or delete existing columns (include the DROP clause).

9. Correct answer: c

   The DESCRIBE TABLE statement lists the column attributes for a specified table.

10. Correct answer: a

   The CREATE TABLE statement can include column specifications to create an empty table. The entire group of column specifications must be enclosed in a single set of parentheses. You must list each column's name, data type, and (for character columns) length. The length is specified as an integer in parentheses. Multiple column specifications must be separated by commas.

Chapter 6: Creating and Managing Indexes Using PROC SQL

1. Correct answer: d

   The index that is specified is based on one column, so it is a simple index. In the CREATE INDEX statement, you specify the index name after the keywords CREATE INDEX. You do not include a keyword to specify that this is a simple index. The name of the key column is specified in parentheses after the table name. The name of a simple index must be the same as the name of the key column.

2. Correct answer: b

   To create a unique index, the UNIQUE keyword is added to the CREATE INDEX statement, between the keywords CREATE and INDEX.

3. Correct answer: d

   A composite index is based on two or more columns. In the CREATE INDEX statement, you specify the index name after the keywords CREATE INDEX. You do not include a keyword to specify that this is a composite index. The names of the key columns are specified in parentheses after the table name. The name of a composite index cannot be the same as the name of any columns in the table.

4. Correct answer: a

   Specifying the option MSGLEVEL=I causes informational messages about index usage to be written to the SAS log.

5. Correct answer: c

   The DROP INDEX statement drops one or more specified indexes from a table. You specify the name of each index to be dropped after the keywords DROP INDEX. The table name is specified after the keyword FROM. The type of index and the names of the indexed columns are not specified in the statement.

6. Correct answer: b

   The DESCRIBE TABLE statement lists all indexes for one or more tables that you specify, along with other information about the table(s).

7. Correct answer: a

   The IDXWHERE=YES data set option tells SAS to use the best available index, even if the index does not optimize performance.

8. Correct answer: c

   Indexes can be created on either character or numeric columns.

9. Correct answer: d

   Using an index will optimize specific classes of PROC SQL queries. A query in which the key column is specified only in a SELECT clause is not one of these queries.

10. Correct answer: c

    The IDXNAME= data set option directs PROC SQL to use an index that you specify. The specified index must exist and must be suitable by having at least its first or only column match the condition in the WHERE expression.

Chapter 7: Creating and Managing Views Using PROC SQL

1. Correct answer: a

   A PROC SQL view accesses the most current underlying data and can be joined with tables or other views. In addition, a PROC SQL view can

- be used in SAS programs in place of an actual SAS data file
- be derived from one or more tables, PROC SQL views, or DATA step views.

2. Correct answer: d

PROC SQL views are useful because they

- often save space (a view is usually quite small compared with the data that it accesses)
- prevent users from continually submitting queries to omit unwanted columns or rows
- hide complex joins or queries from users.

In addition, PROC SQL views

- ensure that input data sets are always current, because data is derived from tables at execution time
- can be used to shield sensitive or confidential columns from users while enabling the same users to view other columns in the same table.

3. Correct answer: c

You use the CREATE VIEW statement to create a view. The keywords CREATE VIEW are followed by the name of the view and the keyword AS.

4. Correct answer: b

The DESCRIBE VIEW statement displays the view definition in the SAS log.

5. Correct answer: a

A view can be used in a PROC SQL step just as you would use an actual SAS table.

6. Correct answer: d

The USING clause enables you to embed a LIBNAME statement in your view definition. The USING clause must be the last clause in the CREATE VIEW statement.

7. Correct answer: d

PROC SQL views can access data from a SAS data file, a DATA step view, a PROC SQL view, or a relational database table.

8. Correct answer: d

When you are working with PROC SQL views, it is best to

- avoid using an ORDER BY clause in a view. If you specify an ORDER BY clause, the data must be sorted each time the view is referenced.
- avoid creating views that are based on tables whose structure might change. A view is no longer valid when it references a nonexistent column.
- specify a one-level name in the FROM clause if the view resides in the same SAS data library as the contributing table(s). Using a one-level name in the FROM clause prevents you from having to change the view if you assign a different libref to the SAS data library that contains the view and its contributing table or tables.

9. Correct answer: c

You can update a PROC SQL view provided that the view does not join or link to another table, the view does not have a subquery, or you try to update a derived column. You can update a view that contains a WHERE clause. The WHERE clause can be in the UPDATE clause or in the view. You cannot update a view that contains any other clause such as an ORDER BY or a HAVING clause.

10. Correct answer: b

The DROP VIEW statement drops a view from the specified library.

Chapter 8: Managing Processing Using PROC SQL

1. Correct answer: a

PROC SQL options are specified in the PROC SQL statement. After you specify an option, it remains in effect until you change it or you re-invoke PROC SQL.

2. Correct answer: b

The INOBS= option restricts the number of rows that PROC SQL takes as input from any single source. The INOBS= option is similar to the SAS system option OBS= and is useful for debugging queries on large tables. The OUTOBS= option restricts the number of rows that PROC SQL displays or writes to a table.

3. Correct answer: c

After you specify an option, it remains in effect until you change it or you re-invoke PROC SQL. You can use the RESET statement to add, drop, or change PROC SQL options without re-invoking the SQL procedure. In the correct answer, the RESET statement adds the NUMBER option and the OUTOBS= option. The resulting output lists the first 10 rows in the table Sasuser.Flightattendants where the value of Jobcode equals FA2 and includes a column named Row.

4. Correct answer: d

The DOUBLE | NODOUBLE option specifies whether PROC SQL output is double-spaced in listing output. The FLOW | NOFLOW | FLOW=n | FLOW=n m option controls the appearance of wide character columns in listing output. Neither option affects the appearance of HTML output.

5. Correct answer: d

The STIMER | NOSTIMER option in PROC SQL specifies whether PROC SQL writes timing information for each statement to the SAS log, instead of as a cumulative value for the entire procedure. NOSTIMER is the default. In order to use the STIMER option in PROC SQL, the SAS system option STIMER (the default) must also be in effect. If you use the system option alone, you will receive timing information for the entire procedure, not on a statement-by-statement basis.

6. Correct answer: d

A Dictionary table is a special, read-only SAS data view that contains information about SAS data libraries, SAS data sets, SAS macros, and external files that are in use or available in the current SAS session. A Dictionary table also contains the settings for SAS system options that are currently in effect.

7. Correct answer: d

Dictionary tables are created each time they are referenced in a SAS program, updated automatically, and limited to read-only access. Accessing a Dictionary table causes SAS to determine the current state of the SAS session and return the information that you want.

8. Correct answer: d

   Dictionary tables can be accessed by running a PROC SQL query against the table, using the Dictionary libref. Though SAS librefs are usually limited to eight characters, Dictionary is an automatically assigned, reserved word. You can also access a Dictionary table by referring to the PROC SQL view of the table that is stored in the Sashelp library.

9. Correct answer: b

   To see how a Dictionary table is defined, submit a DESCRIBE TABLE statement. The DESCRIBE TABLE statement writes a CREATE TABLE statement to the SAS log for the table specified in the DESCRIBE TABLE statement.

10. Correct answer: a

    To display information about the files in a specific library, specify the column names in a SELECT statement and the Dictionary table name in the FROM clause. The library name in the WHERE clause must be specified in uppercase letters because that is how it is stored in SAS and it must be enclosed in quotation marks.

Chapter 9: Introducing Macro Variables

1. Correct answer: b

   Macro variables are always text strings that are independent of SAS data sets. The value of a macro variable can be up to 65,534 characters long, and the name of a macro variable can be up to 32 characters long. A macro variable can be defined or referenced anywhere in a SAS program except within data lines. There are two types of macro variables: automatic and user-defined.

2. Correct answer: c

   To reference a macro variable, you precede the name with an ampersand. You do not need to enclose the macro variable reference in quotation marks.

3. Correct answer: a

   There are two ways to display the value of a macro variable in the SAS log: you can turn on the SYMBOLGEN system option to list the values of all macro variables that are used, or you can use the %PUT statement to write specific text, including macro variable values, to the log.

4. Correct answer: d

   You use the %LET statement to define a macro variable. You do not need to enclose the value in quotation marks. If you do include quotation marks in the assigned value for a macro variable, the quotation marks will be stored as part of the value.

5. Correct answer: d

   Macro variables are stored as character strings. Quotation marks and most special characters are stored exactly as they are assigned, but leading blanks are stripped from assigned values. You can also include references to other macro variables within %LET statements.

6. Correct answer: d

SYSDATE9 is an automatic macro variable that stores the date that your SAS session began in ddmmmyyyy format. You can use the %SYSFUNC function along with any DATA step function, so both the TODAY() function and the DATE() function will result in the current date.

7. Correct answer: c

Macro character functions such as %UPCASE and %SUBSTR enable you to perform character manipulations on your macro variable values.

8. Correct answer: b

The word scanner recognizes four types of tokens. Expressions are not a type of token.

9. Correct answer: c

You can combine macro variable references with text to create new text strings. If you precede a macro variable with text, the ampersand at the beginning of the macro variable name signals the end of the text and the beginning of a macro variable name. If you want text to follow the macro variable value, you must signal the end of the macro variable name with a period.

10. Correct answer: c

You use the %QSYSFUNC function in this case, in order to mask the comma that results from the worddate. format. You must mask this comma since the LEFT() function expects only one argument.

Chapter 10: Processing Macro Variables at Execution Time

1. Correct answer: c

Most macro functions are handled by the macro processor before any SAS language statements in the DATA step are executed. For example, the %LET statement and any macro variable references (&macvar) are passed to the macro processor before the program is compiled. In order to create or update macro variables during DATA step execution, you use the SYMPUT routine.

2. Correct answer: a

To create a macro variable and assign to it a value that is based on the value of a DATA step variable, you use the SYMPUT routine. In the SYMPUT routine, to assign a literal string as a macro variable name, you enclose the literal in quotation marks. To assign a literal string as a value of the macro variable, you enclose the literal in quotation marks.

3. Correct answer: d

The SYMPUT routine enables you to assign a data set variable as the value of a macro variable. You can also use the SYMPUT routine to create a series of related macro variables. Because all macro variable values are character strings, SYMPUT automatically converts any numeric value that you attempt to assign as a value for a macro variable. In an SCL program, you must use SYMPUTN rather than SYMPUT if you are attempting to assign a numeric value to a macro variable.

4. Correct answer: b

You can use multiple ampersands to create an indirect reference when the value of one macro variable is the name of another. If you enclose the DATA step variable name in quotation marks in the SYMPUT routine, the new macro variable will have the same name as the DATA step variable rather than having the DATA step variable's value as a name. Use the SYMGET function to obtain the value of a macro variable during the execution of a DATA step.

5. Correct answer: b

   If more than four consecutive ampersands precede a name token, rescanning continues from left to right until no more triggers can be resolved. The Forward Re-scan rule describes how the macro processor resolves macro variable references that start with multiple ampersands or with multiple percent signs.

6. Correct answer: d

   A macro variable reference (&macvar) is resolved before any SAS language statements are sent to the compiler. The SYMGET function enables you to obtain the value of a macro variable during the execution of a DATA step or a PROC SQL step. The SYMGET function can also be used to obtain the value of a macro variable during the execution of an SCL program.

7. Correct answer: c

   To create a macro variable during the execution of a PROC SQL step, use the INTO clause of the SELECT statement. In the INTO clause, you precede the name of the macro variable with a colon.

8. Correct answer: c

   You can use multiple ampersands to delay the resolution of a macro variable reference. You can also combine macro variable references in order to create new tokens. In this example, the reference &&teach&crs resolves to &teach3 on the first scan. On the next scan, &teach3 resolves to Forest, Mr. Peter.

9. Correct answer: d

   You can use the SYMGET function in an assignment statement to obtain the current value of a macro variable and to assign that value to a DATA step variable. The SYMGET function enables you to obtain the value of a macro variable during execution of a DATA step, a PROC SQL step, or an SCL program.

10. Correct answer: c

    The SYMPUT routine can be used in either the DATA step or in an SCL program. In the DATA step, the SYMPUT routine will perform automatic conversion on numeric values that you attempt to assign as values for macro variables, using the BEST12. format. In an SCL program, you should use the SYMPUTN routine if you want to assign a numeric value as a value for a macro variable. In a PROC SQL step, you need to use the INPUT function in order to convert macro variable values to numeric before you compare them to other numeric values.

Chapter 11: Creating and Using Macro Programs

1. Correct answer: b

   A macro definition must begin with a %MACRO statement and must end with a %MEND statement. The macro definition can include macro language statements as well as SAS language statements. When the macro is compiled, macro language statements are checked for syntax errors. The compiled macro is stored in a temporary SAS catalog by default.

2. Correct answer: c

   To include positional parameters in a macro definition, you list the parameters in parentheses and separate them with commas. When the macro is executed, macro variables will be created in the local symbol table and will have the same names as the parameters. You can then use these macro variables within the macro.

3. Correct answer: c

   To call a macro that includes positional parameters, you precede the macro name with a percent sign. You list the values for the macro variables that are defined by the parameters in parentheses. List values in the same order in which the parameters are listed, and separate them with commas. Remember that a macro call is not a SAS language statement and does not require a semicolon.

4. Correct answer: d

   In a mixed parameter list, positional parameters must be listed before any keyword parameters. Both positional and keyword parameters create macro variables in the local symbol table. To assign a null value to a keyword parameter, you list the parameter without a value in the macro call.

5. Correct answer: c

   When you submit a macro definition, the macro is compiled and is stored in a SAS catalog. Then when you call the macro, the macro is executed. The macro is available for execution anytime throughout the current SAS session.

6. Correct answer: d

   You can use %IF-%THEN statements to conditionally process code. Within a %IF-%THEN statement, you must use %DO and %END statements to enclose multiple statements. %IF-%THEN statements are similar to IF THEN statements in the DATA step, but they are part of the macro language.

7. Correct answer: d

   By using %IF-%THEN statements, you can place whole steps, individual statements, or parts of statements onto the input stack.

8. Correct answer: c

   There are several ways to create macro variables in the local symbol table. Macro variables that are created by parameters in a macro definition or by a %LOCAL statement are always created in the local table. Macro variables that are created by a %LET statement or by the SYMPUT routine inside a macro definition might be created in the local table as well.

9. Correct answer: b

   To define macros with %DO loops you use a %DO statement and a %END statement. Be sure to precede all keywords in the statements with percent signs since the %DO and %END statements are macro language statements. Also, be sure to end these statements with semicolons.

10. Correct answer: d

    When you submit a call to a compiled macro, the macro is executed. Specifically, the macro processor executes compiled macro language statements first. When any SAS language statements are encountered, the macro processor places these statements onto the input stack and pauses while they are passed to the compiler and then executed. Then the macro processor continues to repeat these steps until the %MEND statement is reached.

Chapter 12: Storing Macro Programs

1. Correct answer: d

   The %INCLUDE statement can be used to insert the contents of an external file into a SAS program. If a macro definition is stored in an external file, the %INCLUDE statement causes the macro definition to be compiled when it is inserted into the SAS program. The contents of the macro definition will be written to the SAS log only if the SOURCE2 option is specified.

2. Correct answer: a

   When a macro definition is stored as a catalog SOURCE entry, you must compile it before you can call it from a SAS program. You compile a macro that is stored as a catalog SOURCE entry by using the CATALOG access method. This creates a session-compiled macro that will be deleted at the end of the SAS session. The PROC CATALOG statement enables you to view a list of the contents of a SAS catalog.

3. Correct answer: c

   To call a macro that is stored in an autocall library, you must specify both the MAUTOSOURCE system options and the SASAUTOS= system option. The SASAUTOS= system option can be set to include multiple pathnames or filerefs. Once these two system options are set, you can call the macro by preceding the macro name with a percent sign.

4. Correct answer: d

   The Stored Compiled Macro Facility enables you to store compiled macros permanently so that you can reuse them in later SAS sessions without compiling them again. Compiled macros must be stored in a catalog named *Sasmacr*, and both the MSTORED system option and the SASMSTORE= system option must be specified.

5. Correct answer: b

   In order to create a permanently stored compiled macro, you must specify the MSTORED system option. The SASMSTORE= system option must be specified to point to the library in which you want your macros to be stored. You must also use the STORE option in the %MACRO statement.

6. Correct answer: a

   When you submit a macro definition, SAS creates a session-compiled macro and stores it in the temporary SAS catalog Work.Sasmacr. This macro will be deleted at the end of the SAS session.

7. Correct answer: d

   If you store your macro definitions in external files, you can easily share these files with others. Also, you can edit a macro definition that is stored in an external file with any text editor, and you can reuse the macro in other SAS sessions.

8. Correct answer: b

The PROC CATALOG step enables you to view a list of the contents of a SAS catalog. This might be especially useful if you store your macro definitions as SOURCE entries in permanent SAS catalogs. You might also use the PROC CATALOG step to see a list of the session-compiled macros that are stored in Work.Sasmacr.

9. Correct answer: c

In order to use the Stored Compiled Macro Facility, you need to specify the MSTORED and SASMSTORE= system options. The Stored Compiled Macro Facility saves the compiled macro in a permanent SAS catalog, but it does not save the macro definition. You cannot move a compiled macro across operating systems. Since you cannot re-create the macro definition from a compiled macro, it is a good idea to save your source program permanently as well.

10. Correct answer: a

The autocall macro facility stores macro definitions — not compiled macros — permanently. The first time an autocall macro is called during a SAS session, the macro is compiled and a session-compiled macro is created in Work.Sasmacr. You can have multiple autocall libraries that are concatenated, and you can use the autocall facility in conjunction with the Stored Compiled Macro Facility.

Chapter 13: Creating Indexes

1. Correct answer: d

An index is a separate file from a data set that contains information about observations within the data set. Specifically, an index contains value/identifier pairs that indicate the location of observations within the data set and the value of one or more key variables in that observation.

2. Correct answer: c

To create an index at the same time that you create a data set, you use the INDEX= option in the DATA statement. You must assign a unique name to a composite index, while a simple index is automatically assigned the name of the key variable as its name. You can set the value of the MSGLEVEL= system option to I in order to see messages about indexes in the SAS log.

3. Correct answer: a

For many maintenance tasks that you perform on a data set, SAS automatically performs corresponding tasks to the index file. For example, if you delete a data set, the index file is deleted as well. If you rename a data set with the CHANGE statement in the DATASETS procedure, SAS automatically renames the index file. If you copy a data set to a new location with the COPY statement in the DATASETS procedure, SAS automatically reconstructs the index file in the new location.

4. Correct answer: d

You can use the DATASETS procedure or the SQL procedure to create or delete an index from an existing data set. You can also rebuild the index with a DATA step and use the INDEX= option to create an index on the rebuilt data set. However, rebuilding a data set uses more system resources than adding an index to an existing data set with either the DATASETS or the SQL procedure.

5. Correct answer: a

You use the CREATE INDEX statement of the SQL procedure to create an index on an existing data set. In the SQL procedure, you must name the index in the CREATE INDEX statement; for a simple index, the index name must match the name of the key variable.

6. Correct answer: b

You can use either the CONTENTS procedure or the CONTENTS statement in the DATASETS procedure to generate a list of information about a data set, including a list of existing indexes. All indexes for a data set are stored in a single file that is separate from but has the same name as the data set.

7. Correct answer: b

An index can improve the efficiency with which SAS is able to access certain observations in a data set. However, an index is not always useful. SAS will not use an index to process subsetting IF statements, or other statements that SAS determines might be more efficiently processed without an index.

Chapter 14: Combining Data Vertically

1. Correct answer: c

When a FILENAME statement is used to assign a fileref to multiple raw data files, the list of files must be enclosed in a single set of parentheses. Each filename specified must be enclosed in quotation marks.

2. Correct answer: d

The FILEVAR= option enables you to dynamically change the currently opened input file to a new input file. The FILEVAR= variable must contain a character string that is a physical filename. Like automatic variables, the FILEVAR= variable is not written to the data set.

3. Correct answer: b

The DO statement creates the index variable x and assigns it the values of 8, 9, and 10. The assignment statement assigns the name of a raw data file to Readfile using the current value of x and the PUT function, which concatenates the values of x with the text strings c:\data\month and .dat. The COMPRESS function removes blank spaces from the values of Readfile.

4. Correct answer: a

The TODAY function returns the current date from the system clock as a SAS date value. The year number is then extracted from the current date using the YEAR function. The value of the current year, 2003, is assigned to y3. The year values 2002 and 2001 are assigned to y2 and y1, respectively. The PUT function concatenates the text string c:\data\Y with the year values and the text string .dat.

5. Correct answer: a

The END= option names a variable whose value is controlled by SAS. The value of the variable is 1 when you read the last record in an input file. Otherwise it is 0. You can test the value of the END= variable to determine if the DATA step should continue processing. Like automatic variables, the END= variable is not written to the SAS data set.

6. Correct answer: b

PROC APPEND uses the BASE= and DATA= arguments. BASE=*SAS-data-set* names the data set to which you want to add observations. DATA=*SAS-data-set* names the SAS data set containing observations that you want to append to the end of the BASE= data set.

7. Correct answer: d

   If a DATA= data set contains variables that are longer than the corresponding variables in the BASE= data set, the FORCE option must be used with PROC APPEND. Using the FORCE option enables you to append the data sets. However, some of the variable values may be truncated in the observations that are read in from the DATA= data set.

8. Correct answer: c

   You must use the FORCE option with PROC APPEND when the DATA= data set contains a variable that does not have the same type as the corresponding variable in the BASE= data set.

9. Correct answer: a

   When the BASE= data set contains more variables than the DATA= data set, missing values for the additional variables are assigned to the observations that are read in from the DATA= data set.

10. Correct answer: b

    The FORCE option does *not* need to be used if the BASE= data set contains variables that are not in the DATA= data set. The FORCE option must be used if

    • the DATA= data set contains variables that are not in the BASE= data set

    • the variables in the DATA= data set are longer than the corresponding variables in the BASE= data set

    • the variables in the DATA= data set have a different type than the corresponding variables in the BASE= data set.

Chapter 15: Combining Data Horizontally

1. Correct answer: c

   Remember that common variables might not have the same names. Manager and IDnum are the only two variables listed that match according to type and description. You can use the RENAME= option to rename one of these variables so that they can be used as BY variables in the MERGE statement of the DATA step.

2. Correct answer: b

   In order to merge multiple data sets in a DATA step, the data sets must have a common variable. However, if there are variables that are common to at least two of the input data sets, and if each input data set contains at least one of these variables, then you can use subsequent DATA steps to merge the data sets. You can also use a PROC SQL step to merge data sets that do not have common variables.

3. Correct answer: d

You can use PROC SQL to join data from data sets that do not have a single common variable among them. If you create a new table with the result of an inner join in a PROC SQL step, the resulting data set can be similar or identical to the result of a DATA step match-merge.

4. Correct answer: a

In a DATA step match-merge, SAS reads observations from the input data sets sequentially and match-merges them with observations from other input data sets. Combined observations are created when SAS reads observations from all input data sets into the PDV. These observations, as well as any observations that contain missing or nonmatched values, are then written to the new data set. A PROC SQL join creates a Cartesian product of matches and then eliminates nonmatching data.

5. Correct answer: c

You can use multiple SET statements in one DATA step to combine observations from several data sets. The data sets do not need to have a common variable.

6. Correct answer: b

You can use the MEANS procedure to create a new data set that contains a summary statistic. The NOPRINT option suppresses the default report. The OUTPUT statement routes the results from the MEANS procedure to a new data set. The VAR statement specifies one or more numeric variables from the input data set.

7. Correct answer: a

The _N_ variable records how many times the DATA step has iterated. In the example, _N_ is used to ensure that the first SET statement executes only one time so the one observation is read from Sasuser.Summary, but the end of file marker is not read. Since the values in the PDV are not reinitialized after each DATA step iteration, the value of CARGOSUM is retained throughout DATA step execution. Therefore, if the value of Cargosum is $1000 in the first iteration, it will be $1000 in each subsequent iteration as well.

8. Correct answer: d

Totalrev is the accumulator variable of the sum statement, which is automatically initialized with a value of 0. If the expression in a sum statement produces a missing value, SAS replaces the missing value with a value of 0. As the DATA step iterates, the sum statement retains the accumulator variable so that it will accumulate a total.

9. Correct answer: d

You use the KEY= option in a SET statement to cause SAS to use an index to combine data from multiple data sets. When the SET statement with the KEY= option executes, the program data vector must already contain a value for the indexed variable. You cannot use WHERE processing on a data set that has been read with the KEY= option within the same DATA step.

10. Correct answer: b

When you use the KEY= option, SAS creates an automatic variable named _IORC_, which stands for INPUT/OUTPUT Return Code. If the value of _IORC_ is zero, the index search was successful. The _IORC_ variable is also created automatically when you use a MODIFY statement in a DATA step.

Chapter 16: Using Lookup Tables to Match Data

1. Correct answer: a

   An array is specified using the keyword ARRAY followed by the name of the array and the dimensions of the array. In a two-dimensional array, the two dimensions can be thought of as a table of rows and columns. The first dimension in the ARRAY statement specifies the number of rows. The second dimension specifies the number of columns.

2. Correct answer: b

   To create temporary array elements, specify the keyword _TEMPORARY_ after the array name and dimension. Remember that if you use an asterisk to count the array elements, you must list the array elements. You cannot use the asterisk and the _TEMPORARY_ keyword together in an ARRAY statement.

3. Correct answer: d

   To process all of the elements in an array, you can use either the DIM function with the array name as the argument or specify the array dimension.

4. Correct answer: a

   The ARRAY statement creates the two-dimensional array Score and specifies the dimensions of the array: two rows and four columns. The value of Points for each observation is determined by referencing the array based on the values of Week and Finish in the Work.Contest data set. The row number for the array reference is determined by the value of Week. The column number for the array reference is determined by the value of Finish.

5. Correct answer: d

   Lookup tables should be stored in a SAS data set when there are too many values to initialize easily in an array, the values change frequently, or the same values are used in many programs.

6. Correct answer: c

   The IF-THEN statement specifies that the Targets array is loaded only once, during the first iteration of the DATA step. During the first iteration of the DATA step, the condition _N_=1 is true, so the outer DO loop executes three times; once for each observation in Sasuser.Ctargets. After the third iteration of the DO loop, the pointer drops down to the second SET statement and the values from the first observation in Sasuser.Monthum are read into the program data vector. During the second iteration of the DATA step, the condition _N_=1 is false. So, the DO loop doesn't execute again.

7. Correct answer: c

   The TRANSPOSE procedure creates an output data set by restructuring the values in an input SAS data set. When the data set is restructured, selected variables are transposed into observations. The procedure creates several variable names by default. _NAME_ is the default name of the variable that PROC TRANSPOSE creates to identify the source of the values in each observation in the output data set. The remaining transposed variables are named COL1...COLn by default.

8. Correct answer: b

   You can use several options with PROC TRANSPOSE to give the variables in the output data set descriptive names. The NAME= option specifies a name for the _NAME_ variable. The PREFIX= option specifies a prefix to use in constructing names for the other variables in the output data set.

9. Correct answer: b

   A BY statement can be used with PROC TRANSPOSE. For each BY group, PROC TRANSPOSE creates one observation for each variable that it transposes. The BY variable itself is not transposed. The original data set must be sorted or indexed prior to using a BY statement with PROC TRANSPOSE.

10. Correct answer: d

    The observations in Work.Fishsize are grouped by Location and Date. For each BY group, PROC TRANSPOSE creates four observations, one for each variable (Length1, Weight1, Length2, and Weight2) that it is transposing.

Chapter 17: Formatting Data

1. Correct answer: d

   By default, SAS searches for custom formats in the Work and Library libraries. The FMTSEARCH= system option specifies other catalogs to search when a format is referenced.

2. Correct answer: c

   A non-inclusive range is used such that the age at the high end of the range is not included. To create the picture format, three zeros are used to create a position for a three-digit numeric value. Because zero is used as a digit selector rather than a nonzero value, leading zeros are not included in the formatted value.

3. Correct answer: b

   By default, FMTERR is in effect so SAS stops processing if it cannot find a format that is referenced. When NOFMTERR is in effect, SAS substitutes the $w. or w. format and continues processing.

4. Correct answer: b

   A data set that is used to create a format with the CNTLIN= option must have the variables FmtName, Start, and Label. If a range is specified, it must also include the variable End.

5. Correct answer: a

   The format created by this value statement has overlapping ranges, so the MULTILABEL option must be used. A multilabel format can be used by any procedure that supports the MLF option.

6. Correct answer: c

   The CNTLOUT= option is used to create a SAS data set from a format.

7. Correct answer: b

SAS will search in the order specified on the FMTSEARCH= option. By default, SAS searches in the Work and Library libraries first unless they are specified on the option. Because Library is not specified here, it is searched after Work.

8. Correct answer: d

The FMTLIB keyword is used to document the formats in a catalog. You can use the SELECT and EXCLUDE statements to process specific formats rather than the entire catalog.

9. Correct answer: c

In the COPY statement, OUT= specifies the catalog to which you want to copy the format catalog entry. In the SELECT statement, you specify the catalog entries by their entire name. Remember that numeric formats are stored with the extension .FORMAT and character formats are stored with the extension .FORMATC.

10. Correct answer: c

The value 6.1 falls in the range 6<-9, which is labeled 'Good.' The non-inclusive range does not include the value 6, but it does include values above 6.

Chapter 18: Modifying SAS Data Sets and Tracking Changes

1. Correct answer: c

The PRIMARY KEY integrity constraint includes both the NOT NULL and UNIQUE constraints.

2. Correct answer: d

To initiate an audit on an existing SAS data set with the DATASETS procedure, you specify the data set in the AUDIT statement, and then you specify the INITIATE statement. You specify the library with the LIB= option.

3. Correct answer: c

In the MODIFY statement, you specify the master data set followed by the transaction data set. Then you specify the key variable in the BY statement.

4. Correct answer: c

The value of _IORC_ is a numeric return code that indicates the status of the most recently executed I/O operation. Checking the value of this variable allows you to detect abnormal I/O conditions and direct execution in particular ways.

5. Correct answer: d

In the MODIFY statement, you list the SAS data set that you want to modify. Then you use the IC CREATE statement to create the integrity constraint. This integrity constraint is a CHECK constraint with a WHERE clause to specify the condition that the variable values must meet.

6. Correct answer: b

The MODIFY statement in a DATA step can be used only to modify the values in a data set. It cannot be used to modify the descriptor portion of the data set.

7. Correct answer: c

Audit trails are used to track changes that are made to a data set in place.

8. Correct answer: a

You use the DATASETS procedure and the MODIFY statement to specify a number of generation data sets for a data set. The GENMAX= option is used to specify the number of versions to save. The number you specify includes the base version.

9. Correct answer: b

When you use the KEY= option, you must specify the update that you want to make to the data set.

10. Correct answer: a

The keyword ALL is used to indicate that you want to delete all generations of the specified data set, including the base version. The keyword HIST deletes the generation data sets, but saves the base version.

Chapter 19: Introduction to Efficient SAS Programming

This chapter has no quiz.

Chapter 20: Controlling Memory Usage

1. Correct answer: b

You can use the BUFNO= system option or data set option to control how many buffers are available for reading or writing a SAS data set. Using BUFNO= can improve execution time by limiting the number of input/output operations that are required for a particular SAS data set. However, the improvement in I/O comes at the cost of increased memory consumption. The number of buffers is not a permanent attribute of the data set and is valid only for the current step or SAS session.

2. Correct answer: d

A page is fixed in size when the data set is created, either to a default value or a specified value. You can use the BUFSIZE= option to control the page size of an output SAS data set. The new buffer size is permanent. After it is specified, it is used whenever the data set is processed.

3. Correct answer: a

The total number of bytes occupied by a data set equals the page size multiplied by the number of pages. You can use the CONTENTS procedure to report the page size and the number of pages.

4. Correct answer: b

The SASFILE LOAD statement opens the file, allocates the buffers, and reads the data into memory.

5. Correct answer: a

When a SAS data file is opened using the SASFILE statement, the data is held in memory, and is available to subsequent DATA and PROC steps or applications, until either a SASFILE CLOSE statement is executed or the SAS session ends. Though a file that is opened with the SASFILE statement can be used for subsequent input or update processing, it cannot be used for subsequent utility or output processing. If the file in-memory increases in size during processing, the number of buffers also increases.

Chapter 21: Controlling Data Storage Space

1. Correct answer: d

    The descriptor portion of an uncompressed data file is always stored at the end of the first data set page. New observations are always added to the end of the data set, and deleted observation space is neither tracked nor reused.

2. Correct answer: b

    The descriptor portion of a compressed data file is always stored at the end of the first data set page. If you specify REUSE=YES, SAS tracks and reuses deleted observation space within a compressed data file. Therefore, every observation in a compressed data file can be a different size. Compressed data files do have a larger overhead than uncompressed data files.

3. Correct answer: c

    Use the LENGTH statement to assign a reduced length to a numeric variable. If you do not use the LENGTH statement to define a reduced length for numeric variables, their default length is 8 bytes. The FORMAT statement associates a format with a variable, and the INFORMAT statement associates an informat with a variable.

4. Correct answer: a

    SAS data views use significantly less disk space than SAS data files. However, SAS data views might need more CPU resources than SAS data files. You can create a SAS data view in either the temporary SAS library or in a permanent SAS library.

5. Correct answer: b

    Use the COMPARE procedure to detect any differences in the values of two data sets. The COMPARE statement is not valid syntax in either the CONTENTS procedure or the DATASETS procedure. Printing both data sets might not reveal differences in the precise values of the shortened variables, depending on the formats that are used.

Chapter 22: Using Best Practices

1. Correct answer: b

    As SAS processes a larger subset of the data, more CPU resources are required. However, positioning of the subsetting IF statement in a DATA step can affect performance and efficiency.

2. Correct answer: c

   The DATA step is the only technique that can be used to modify both data values and variable attributes. The DATASETS procedure enables you to modify only variable attributes.

3. Correct answer: d

   For selecting observations, a WHERE statement is more efficient than a subsetting IF statement because it examines what is in the input page buffer and selects observations before they are loaded into the program data vector, which results in a savings in CPU operations.

4. Correct answer: a

   It is more advantageous to create a temporary SAS data set rather than a permanent SAS data set when the external file on which the data set is based is frequently updated between SAS sessions.

5. Correct answer: c

   A one-step DATASETS procedure results in a savings of CPU usage and I/O operations. PROC DATASETS supports RUN-group processing, which enables you to process multiple SAS data sets from the same library with one invocation of the procedure.

Chapter 23: Querying Data Efficiently

1. Correct answer: d

   When using an index to select a subset, SAS loads only the pages that contain at least one qualified observation into input buffers. When accessing observations sequentially, SAS must load all pages into input buffers. Loading more pages requires more I/O operations.

2. Correct answer: b

   SAS does not use an index for a WHERE condition that contains a function other than TRIM or SUBSTR.

3. Correct answer: a

   The size of the subset relative to the size of the data set is an important factor in determining which access method is most efficient. If a subset is large (more than 33% of the data set), it is likely to be more efficient to use sequential access than direct access. Direct access is usually more efficient when you select a small subset (less than 33% of the data set), especially if the data set is large (has a high page count). However, if the data set is very small (less than three pages), using an index is not efficient. The number of key variables specified in a WHERE expression does not determine which access method is most efficient. If the two key variables that are specified are the first two variables in the same index, the WHERE expression is a candidate for compound optimization. Sorting the data also does not determine which access method is most efficient. However, sorting the data before subsetting improves the efficiency of WHERE processing regardless of the access method.

4. Correct answer: b

5. Correct answer: d

Chapter 24: Creating Functions with PROC FCMP

1. Correct answer: a

2. Correct answer: False

3. Correct answer: True

4. Correct answer: False

Index

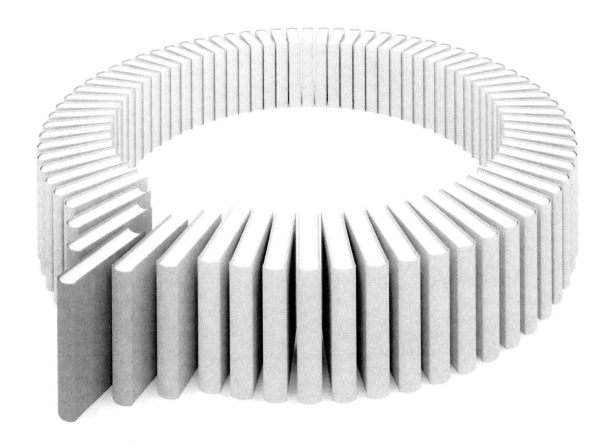

Gain Greater Insight into Your SAS® Software with SAS Books.

Discover all that you need on your journey to knowledge and empowerment.

support.sas.com/bookstore
for additional books and resources.

CPSIA information can be obtained at www.ICGtesting.com
Printed in the USA
LVOW09s0313090316

478367LV00006B/42/P

9 781629 593548